Ceramics Masterclass

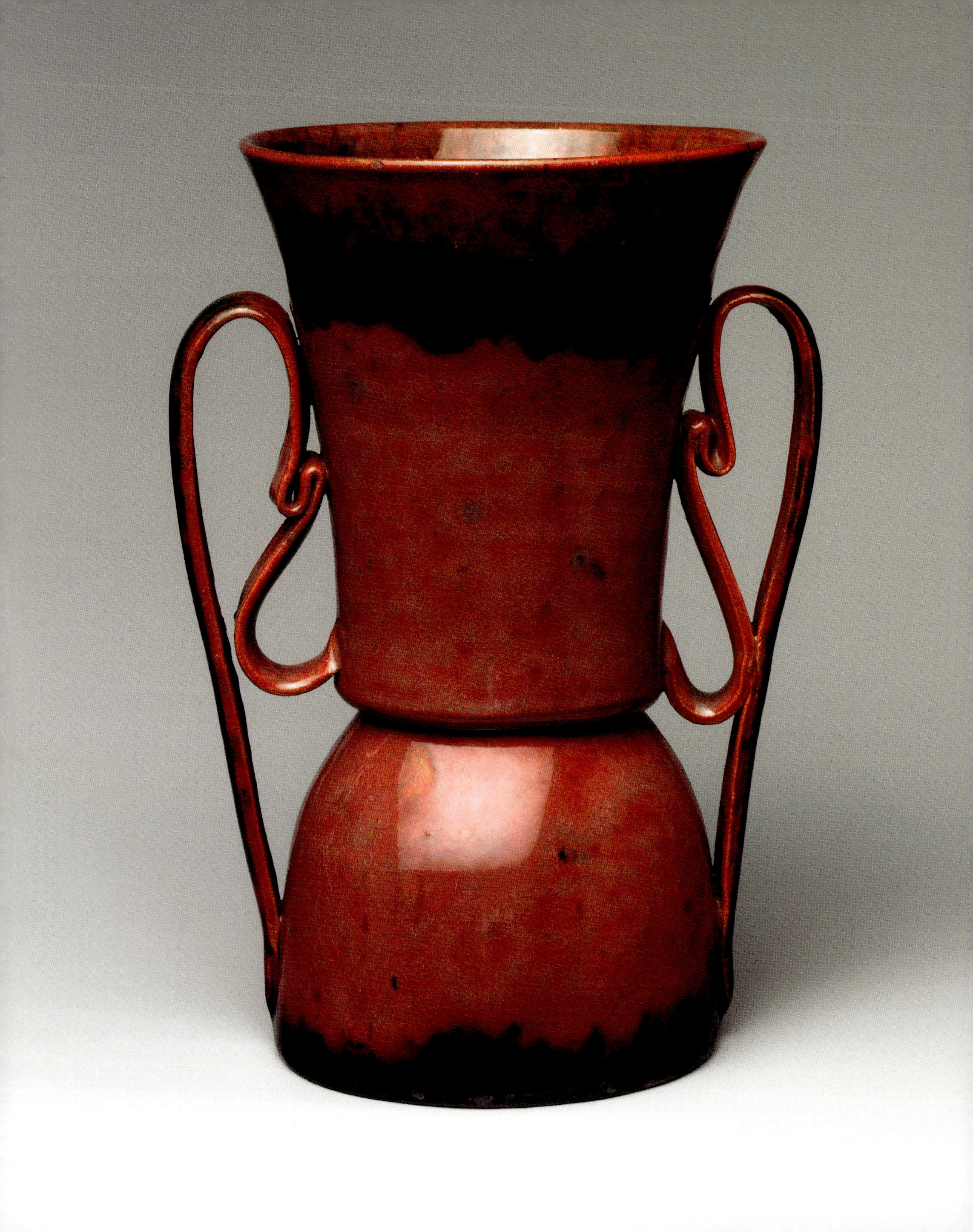

Ceramics Masterclass

CREATIVE TECHNIQUES OF 100 GREAT ARTISTS

Louisa Taylor

T&H

Previous page
Vase 1890–1905
George Ohr; Artokoloro/Alamy Stock Photo

Pages 272–73
Linear Vases 2016
© Louisa Taylor. Photo: Matthew Booth.

On the cover

Front
Watershed 2012
Alison Britton

Back, Above
Blue Wall Sculpture 2018
Wouter Dam

Centre
Vase *c.* 2015
Hideaki Miyamura

Below
Push 2018
Anne Marie Laureys

For Tillie and Zach

First published in the United Kingdom in 2020 by
Thames & Hudson Ltd, 6–24 Britannia Street,
London WC1X 9JD

This paperback edition first published in 2026

This book was produced by
White Lion Publishing, an imprint of The Quarto Group
1 Triptych Place
London SE1 9SH

Commissioning Editor	Alice Graham
Project Editor	Laura Bulbeck
Editor	Lindsay Kaubi
Designer	Josse Pickard
Proofreader	Sarah Hoggett
Indexer	Helen Snaith
Production Controller	Rohana Yusof
Publisher	Philip Cooper

EU Authorized Representative: Interart S.A.R.L.
19 rue Charles Auray, 93500 Pantin, Paris, France
productsafety@thameshudson.co.uk
www.interart.fr

A CIP catalogue record for this book is available from the British Library

ISBN: 978-0-500-29939-5
01

Printed in China

MIX
Paper | Supporting responsible forestry
FSC® C016973

Contents

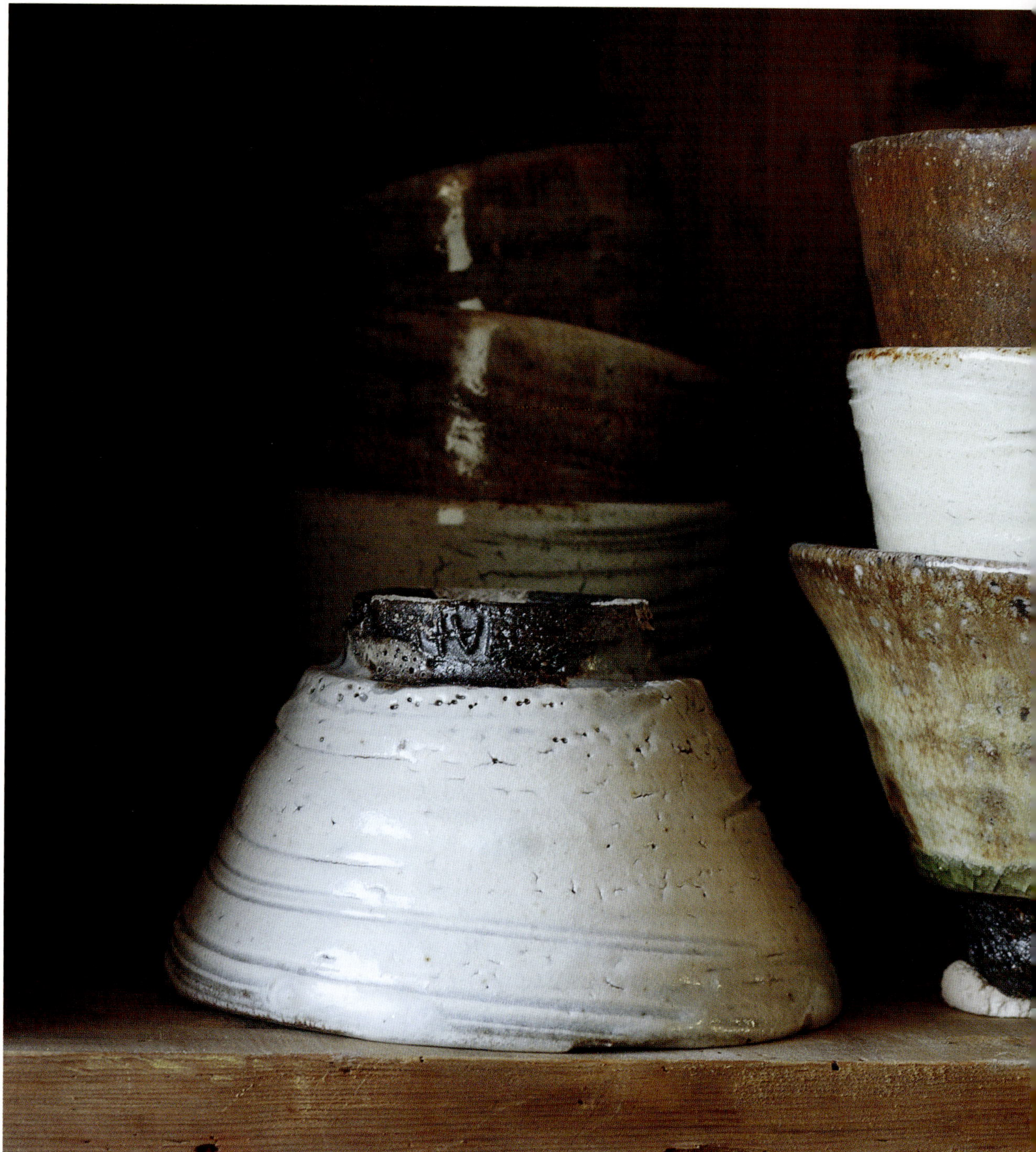

Bowls and glaze samples by Anne Mette Hjortshøj
A beautiful selection of wood-fired bowls, exploring an array of slips, brush marks and textural surfaces accentuated by this unique firing process.

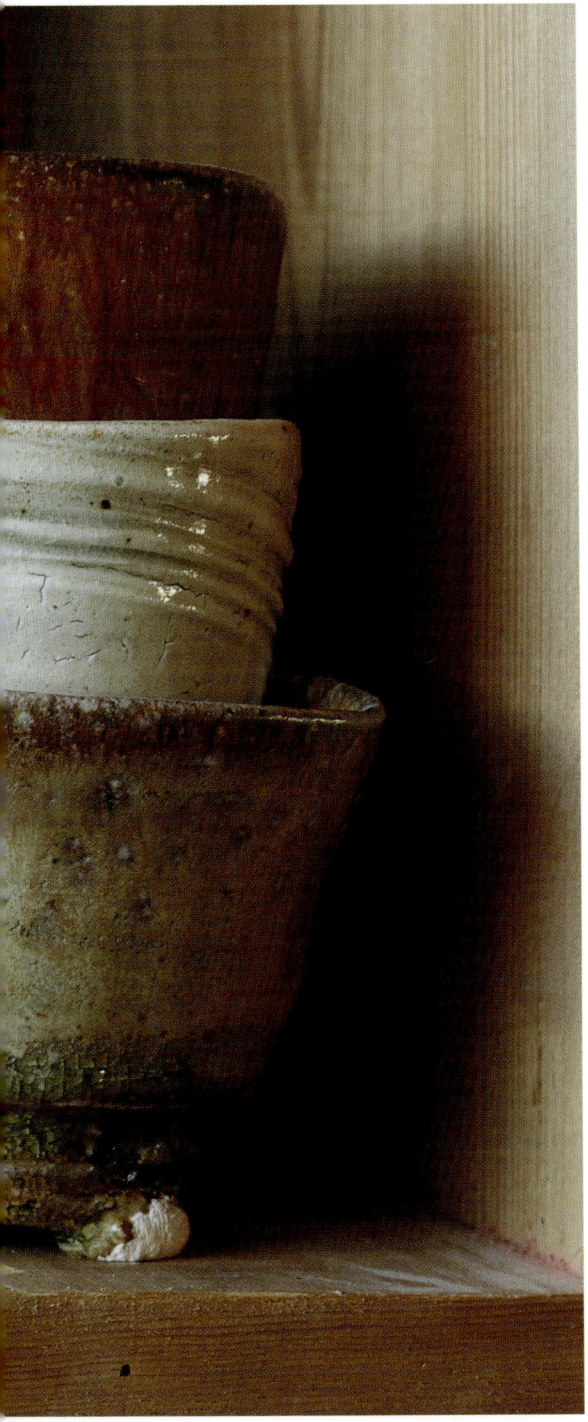

For thousands of years, clay has been deeply entwined with our human existence. Shards of pottery excavated from archaeological sites all over the world offer a glimpse into ancient civilizations and document the progression of humankind. When viewing these primal works, one can't help but be humbled by the sight of a thumbprint or personal mark recorded in the clay, as if the creator is saying, 'I was here!' Fast forward to the 21st century and the same material is still just as integral to our daily lives, from cups and the plates we dine on to the ceramic technology that enables our modern gadgets and devices to operate.

In terms of being taken seriously as a material for artistic expression, well, it has been something of a bumpy ride for clay. Its rich associations with craft traditions have been hard to shake in the fine art world. But why should this matter? This is a question that many contemporary artists now address vigorously through their work. The divide that was so prevalent in the 20th century is gradually diminishing and boundaries that once held the medium back are becoming increasingly blurred.

The chapters in this book loosely define the genres of work within the discipline of ceramics – but this by no means constitutes a definitive list. In fact, artists in the broad sense of the term – potters, ceramicists, sculptors, makers, designer-makers, visual artists – could span any number of these headings, and genre is very much open to interpretation. The main idea is to examine the use of ceramics as a form of artistic expression and the exciting territories it continues to reach.

A brief history of ceramics

With more than 10,000 years of ceramic history to explore, the intention is to delve into the timeline of ceramics – more specifically, studio practice and ceramics as a form of expression – and take a look at the defining points in the history of this art form. It is thought that the practice of transforming soft malleable clay into a durable material first occurred more than 25,000 years ago but the actual making of pottery came much later, with the settlements of new communities. Some of the earliest examples are of Jōmon pottery from the Jōmon culture in Japan (*c.* 14,500–300 BC) and this is echoed in other locations throughout the world, including Africa, the Middle East, Egypt, South America, Asia and Europe.

Pottery making techniques used today evolved from these historical traditions – predominantly coil-building and pinching skills – that were employed to make utilitarian wares for the cooking and storage of food. It is not known exactly when the potter's wheel first came into use; however, in ancient Egyptian mythology, the god Khnum was depicted as forming the first humans on a potter's wheel. Evidence and scientific research suggest it may have originated in Mesopotamia (historical region of west Asia) around 6000 to 2400 BC.

Our innate desire to decorate and adorn is what makes us uniquely human. The decoration of primitive pottery may have occurred for many reasons – perhaps to show an alliance to a tribe or clan, to convey a narrative to others or simply to express artistic identity. Examples of pottery such as that from the Neolithic period (*c.* 6400–3500 BC) were intricately marked using tools and hand painted with slips made from iron-rich ochres. The first glazes were developed around 4000 BC in Egypt (or Mesopotamia) in the form of Egyptian paste, or faience. Sourced from natron, a naturally occurring rock, it produced an opulent turquoise blue colour and it was used for decorative bead and jewelry making. From 1600 BC developments were made with low-fired glazes and oxides of metal that were used to decorate tiles, figurines and vessels. Islamic art of the Middle East, famous for beautiful calligraphic and floral motifs on tin glaze, filtered through to Europe after the Moors invaded Spain *c.* AD 711.

The Chinese potters of the Han dynasty (206 BC to AD 220) can largely be credited with experimenting with feldspathic glazes on stoneware and for advancing kiln technology. Famous celadons of the Song dynasty (AD 960–1270), which emulate sacred jade, are largely considered to be the finest examples of pottery in the world. The purity of form and colour has influenced a number of modern-day artists, including Bernard Leach (see p.136), Gwyn Hanssen Pigott (see p.70) and Edmund de Waal (see p.250), to name a few. In Japan, the emergence of Zen Buddhism around 1200 led to the development of the tea ceremony ritual and specific ceramic forms including *chawan* (tea bowls), caddies and jars. The Japanese raku technique, which involves removing red-hot pottery from a kiln to induce cracks and pits, was first instigated *c.* 1598.

Between the 12th and 17th centuries, European pottery became more decorative. From the realistic works of French potter Bernard Palissy (see p.86) to the lively slip-decorated chargers of Thomas Toft (see p.88), clay was beginning to find its creative voice. By the 18th and 19th centuries, when new shipping routes operated by the East India Company traded in tea, silk and precious porcelain, the influence of China and the East began to be felt in Europe. This ignited a ferocious race to discover the secrets of Chinese porcelain, and subsequently important industrial ceramic production was established in Germany, France and the UK.

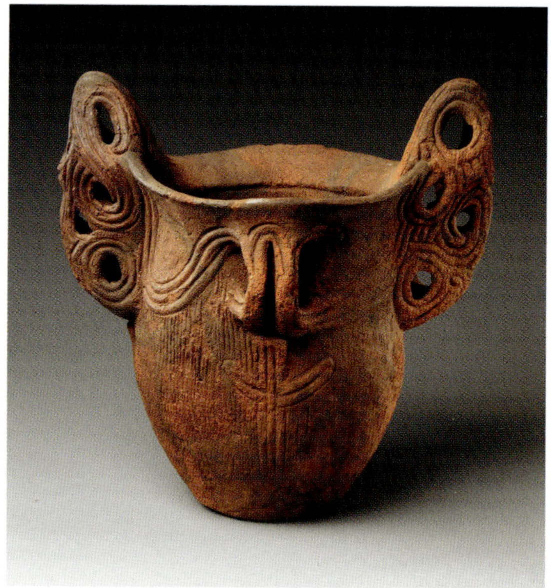

(Above) Jōmon period deep vessel with handles *c.* 3500–2500 BC
Earthenware with carved and incized decoration
Height: 33 cm (13 in.)

Jōmon pottery is considered to be the oldest pottery in the world. It originated in Japan (*c.* 14,500–*c.* 300 BC), and is characterized by an orange-red earthenware body. The term Jōmon translates as 'rope-patterned', and describes the decorative patterns that adorn the surface.

(Right) Song Dynasty vase in the shape of Neolithic jade cong 12–13th century
Porcelain with raised decoration under celadon glaze
26.4 × 10.2 × 10.2 cm (10 ⅖ × 4 × 4 in.)

A defining feature of Song Dynasty pottery is its beautiful celadon glaze, developed to emulate precious jade. The shape of this vase reflects earlier bronze and jade artefacts that characterized Chinese culture of the period.

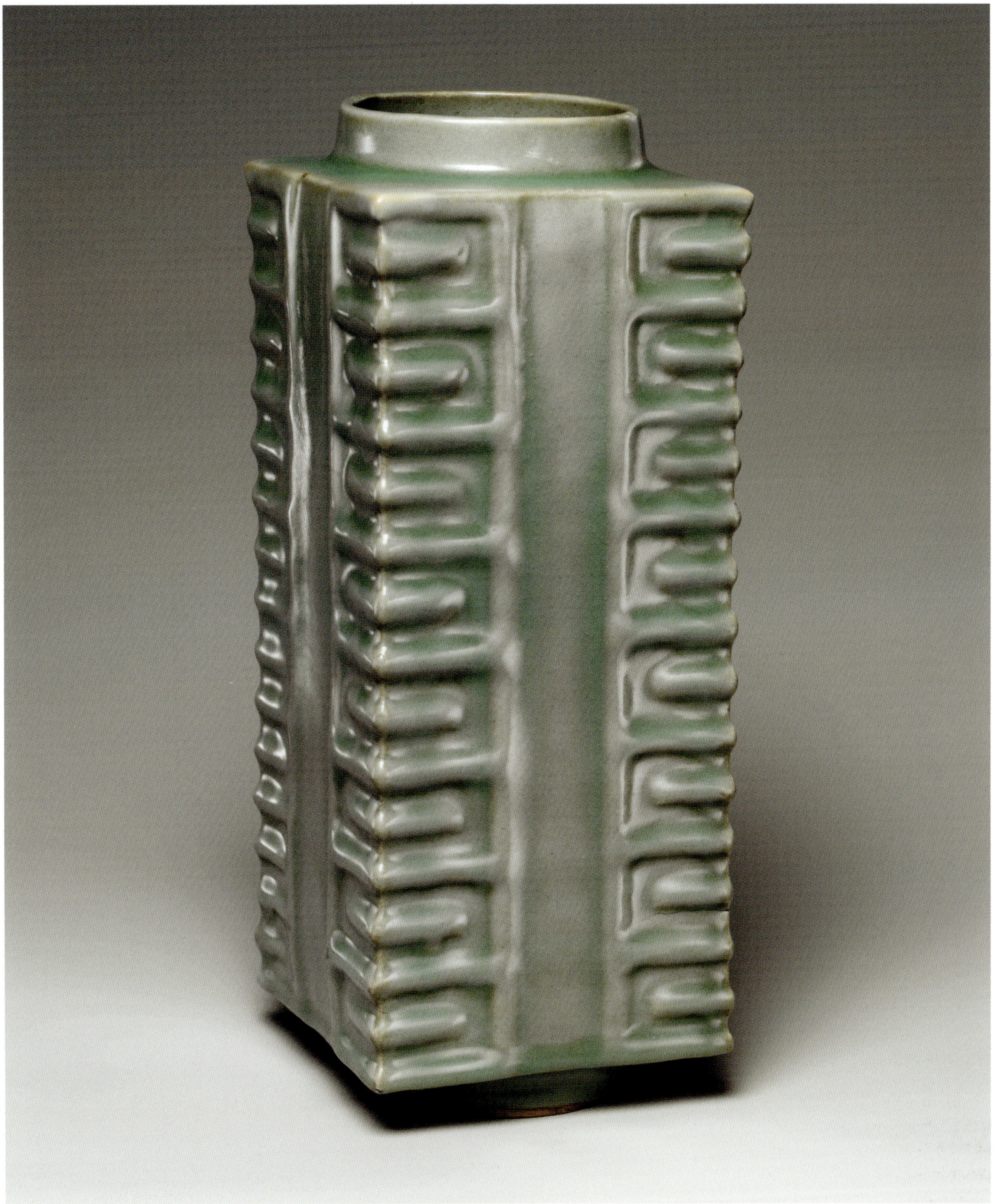

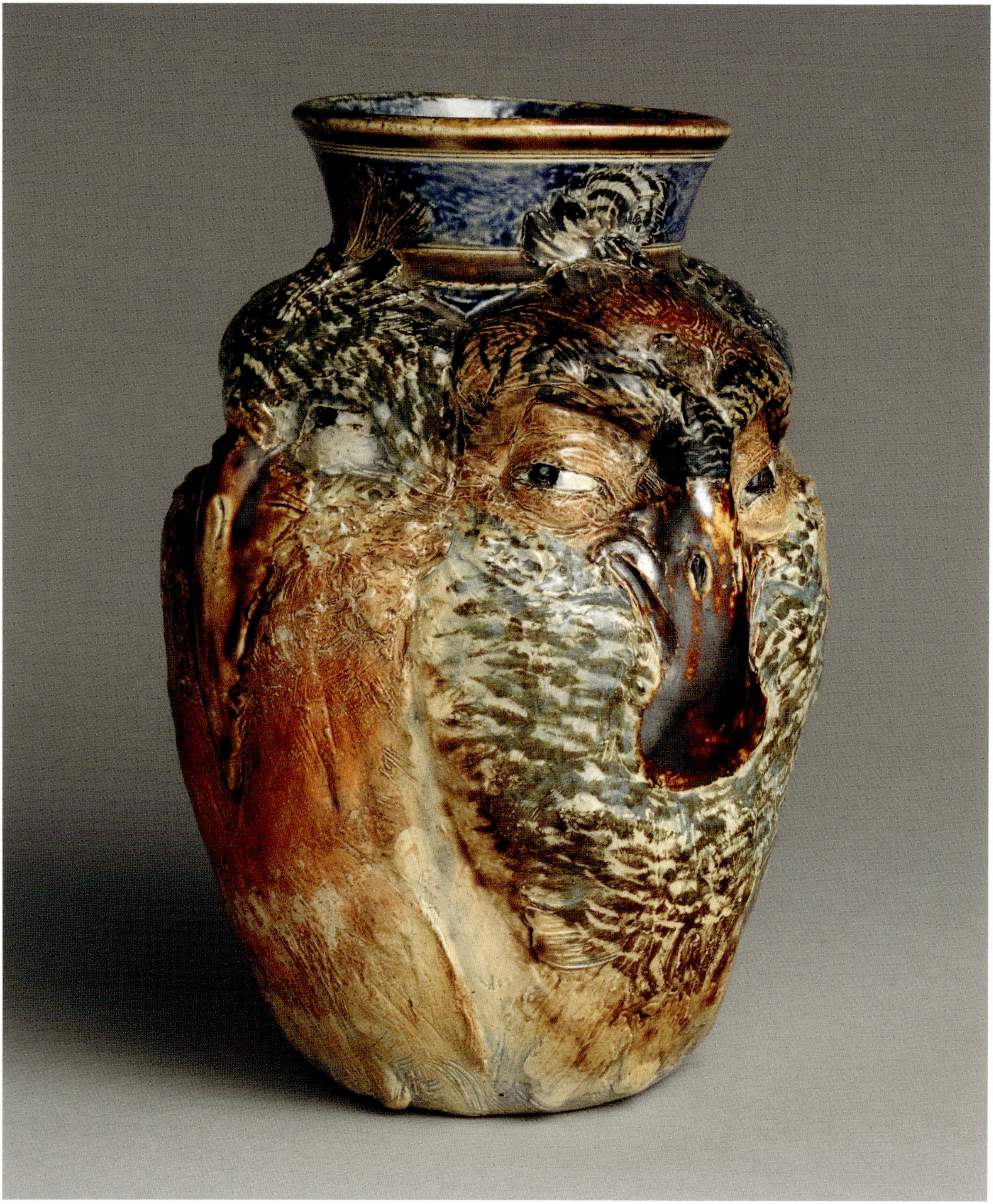

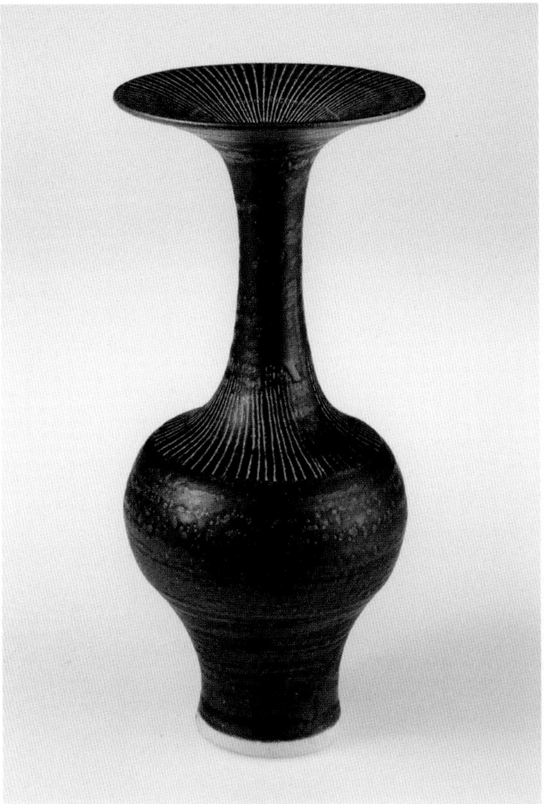

(Above) Bottle by Lucie Rie (1902–95) 1975
Porcelain, brown glaze and sgraffito
22.2 × 11 × 11 cm (8 ¾ × 4 ⅓ × 4 ⅓ in.)

This elegant bottle form remains as modern and contemporary as the day it was made. Rie decorated this bottle in brown-black glaze, then applied delicate sgraffito lines to highlight the curves and profile of this beautiful piece.

(Left) Jar with four birds by the Martin Brothers 1892
Stoneware
21.1 × 15.2 × 15.6 cm (8 ⅓ × 6 × 6 ⅛ in.)

Victorian potters the Martin Brothers were renowned for their eccentric style. This unusual jar is hand decorated with four characterful bird motifs that appear to grimace and gurn around the pot.

In Britain, the first part of the 20th century, from 1900 to 1950, saw a shift away from the highly decorative, low-fired industrial ceramics of the Victorian period towards high-fired individual works. By this time, the influence of the Arts and Crafts movement and the ideas of William Morris (1834–96) – who encouraged the rejection of mass industrialization – had swept across Europe and North America. This was exemplified by the Martin Brothers' (see p.170) grotesque Wally Birds, widely considered to be the starting point of the 'artist-potter' concept.

A significant turning point for studio ceramics came in 1920 when Bernard Leach established the Leach Pottery in St Ives, Cornwall, with help from his friend, the Japanese potter Shōji Hamada (see p.140). Leach's passion for clay stemmed from his travels to Japan in 1909. He had intended to teach etching and printmaking but instead became fascinated by pottery and trained under Japanese masters. With him, he brought a traditionalist attitude to pottery – a belief expressed in Leach's classic work *A Potter's Book* (1940), which placed importance on form, function and truth to materials. This was in contrast to Leach's contemporary, William Staite Murray (see p.52), who recognized clay as a fine-art medium and did not see a distinction between his pots and the art establishment.

The onset of World War II all but halted the progression of studio ceramics. However, it also led to the resettlement in the UK of three refugees from Europe: Lucie Rie (see p.54), Hans Coper (see p.58) and Ruth Duckworth (see p.66). The three brought with them sensibilities schooled in European modernism, paving the way for a fresh perspective on the discipline. Post-World War II, prominent artist Pablo Picasso (see p.172) engaged with clay. His eagerness to experiment and explore the material began to push clay from its humble functional status into the fine-art arena.

By the mid-1950s, the rise of abstract expressionism in America had gained fresh impetus and it was inspiring a new generation of makers who sought freedom from the traditional restraints of functional pottery. Peter Voulkos (see p.68) was at the forefront of this change and was perhaps the first to bridge the gap between painting, sculpture and ceramics. His influence instigated the California Clay movement and, alongside him, Ron Nagle (see p.208), Ken Price (see p.210) and others brought significant change, which continues to resonate strongly today. The American

Funk movement was a spin-off led by Robert Arneson (see p.176), who grounded his ideas in abstract expressionism but with more provocative intent, often concerning the figure.

Clay was now a key subject in art schools and with this development new talent emerged. At the Royal College of Art in London during the 1970s, an influential group of female artists, including Elizabeth Fritsch (see p.60) and Alison Britton (see p.72), challenged and deconstructed notions of ceramics and particularly functional pottery through their radical work – a movement that came to be known as 'The New Ceramics'. The rise of the female-led voice continued with the colourful works of American potter Betty Woodman (see p.252), who was associated with the pattern and decoration movement of the mid-1970s to 1980s in the USA. The period from 1980 to the end of the century saw a diverse range of styles emerge, from brightly coloured textile-like assemblages to sleek functional wares that were in tune with the minimalism of the early 1990s.

A ground-breaking shift occurred in 2003 when Grayson Perry (see p.94) won the prestigious Turner Prize with his collection of illustrated pottery vases. This event changed the landscape for ceramics, enabling new audiences to engage with the subject. All this came at a time when ceramics was culled from many schools and art colleges, leading to concerns of a de-skilled generation. However, what is clear is that today clay is experiencing a rethink. New technologies, experimentation and drive to explore process are propelling the material to a place of immense innovation. Boundaries between what we view as 'craft' and 'high art' have become less defined through the conceptual works of artists such as Edmund de Waal, Richard Slee (see p.216) and Nicole Cherubini (see p.254). Even the rules of what we define as ceramics have become broader, from the ephemeral works of Phoebe Cummings (see p.256), to the research-led installations of Clare Twomey (see p.246). As this book demonstrates, artists continually seek to disrupt and innovate.

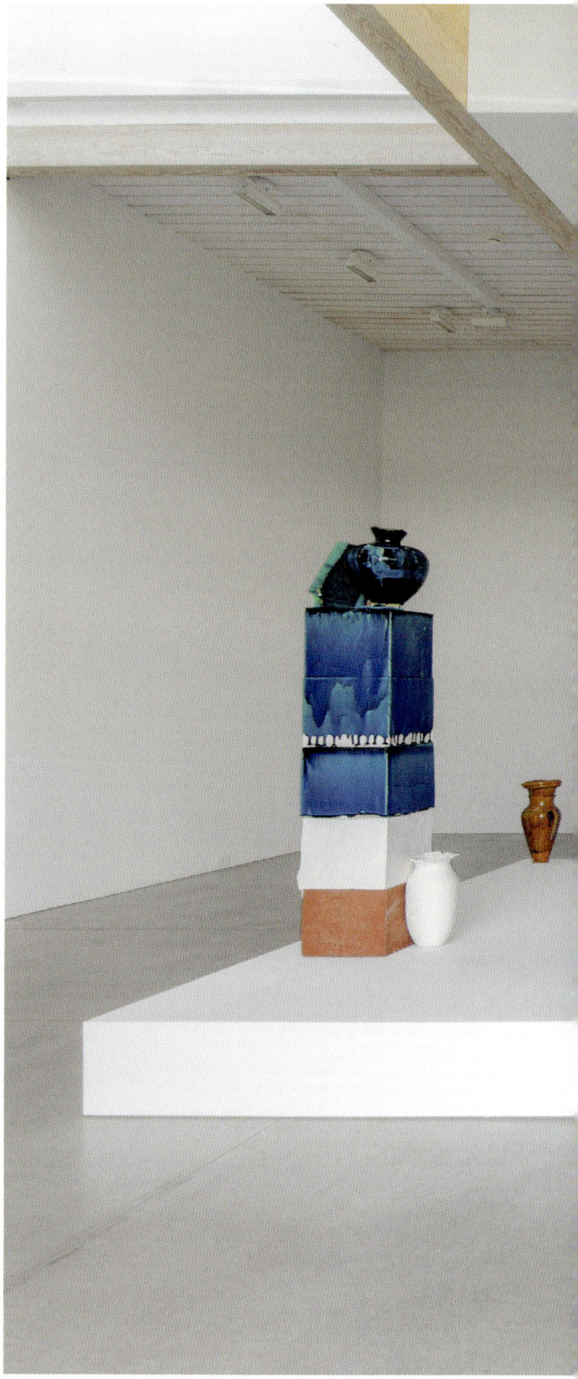

About this book

In recent years, ceramics has been, to some extent, experiencing, a revival. The demand for all things clay has never been higher, with evening classes and courses booked up with long waiting lists and popular social media platforms flooded with images of

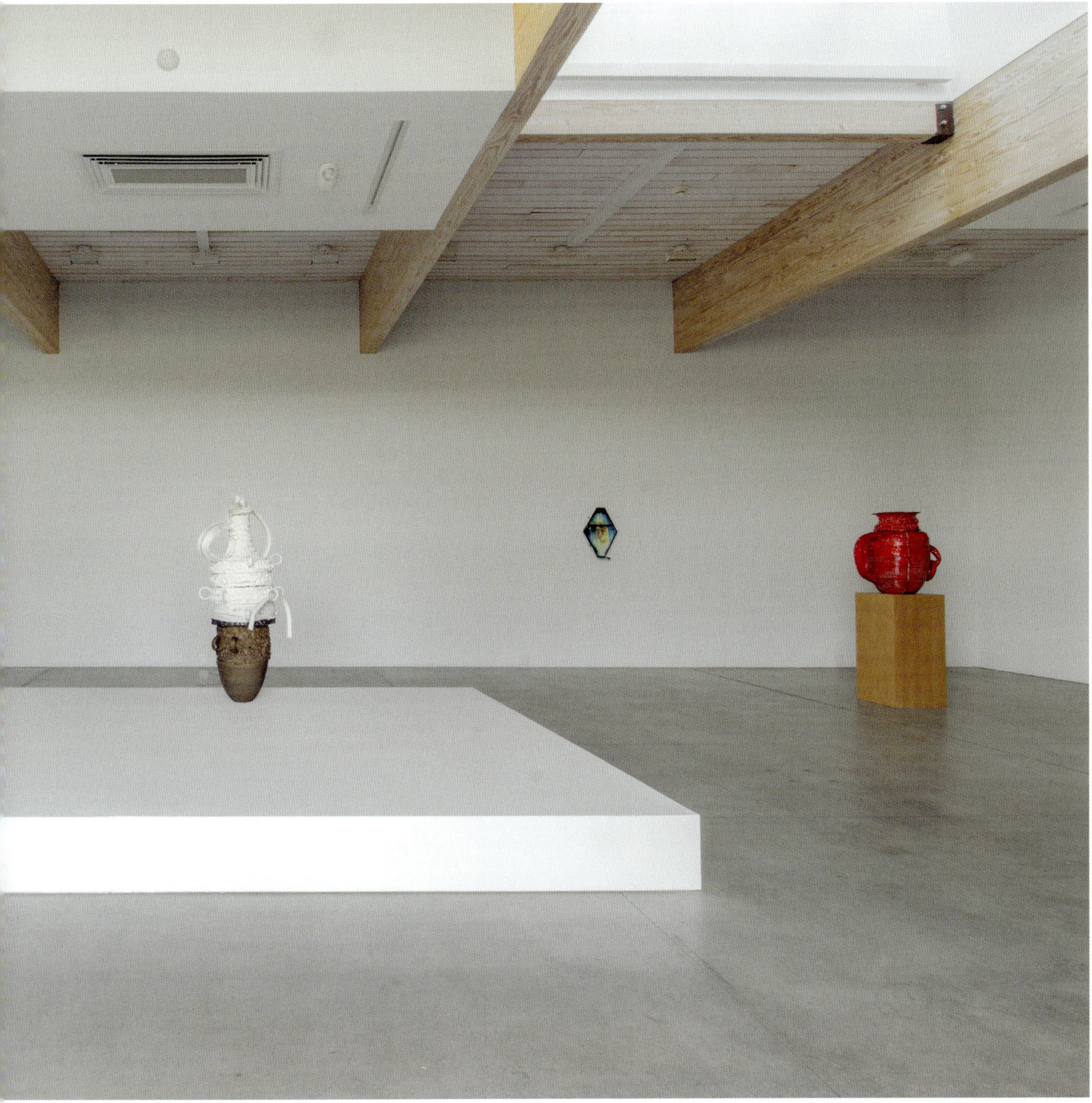

Nicole Cherubini installation, Art OMI, Ghent, New York, 2016
A view of Cherubini's installation of related works that explore the conventions of high art through the use of clay. The artist has carefully curated the exhibition space to instigate dialogue and prompt further discussion.

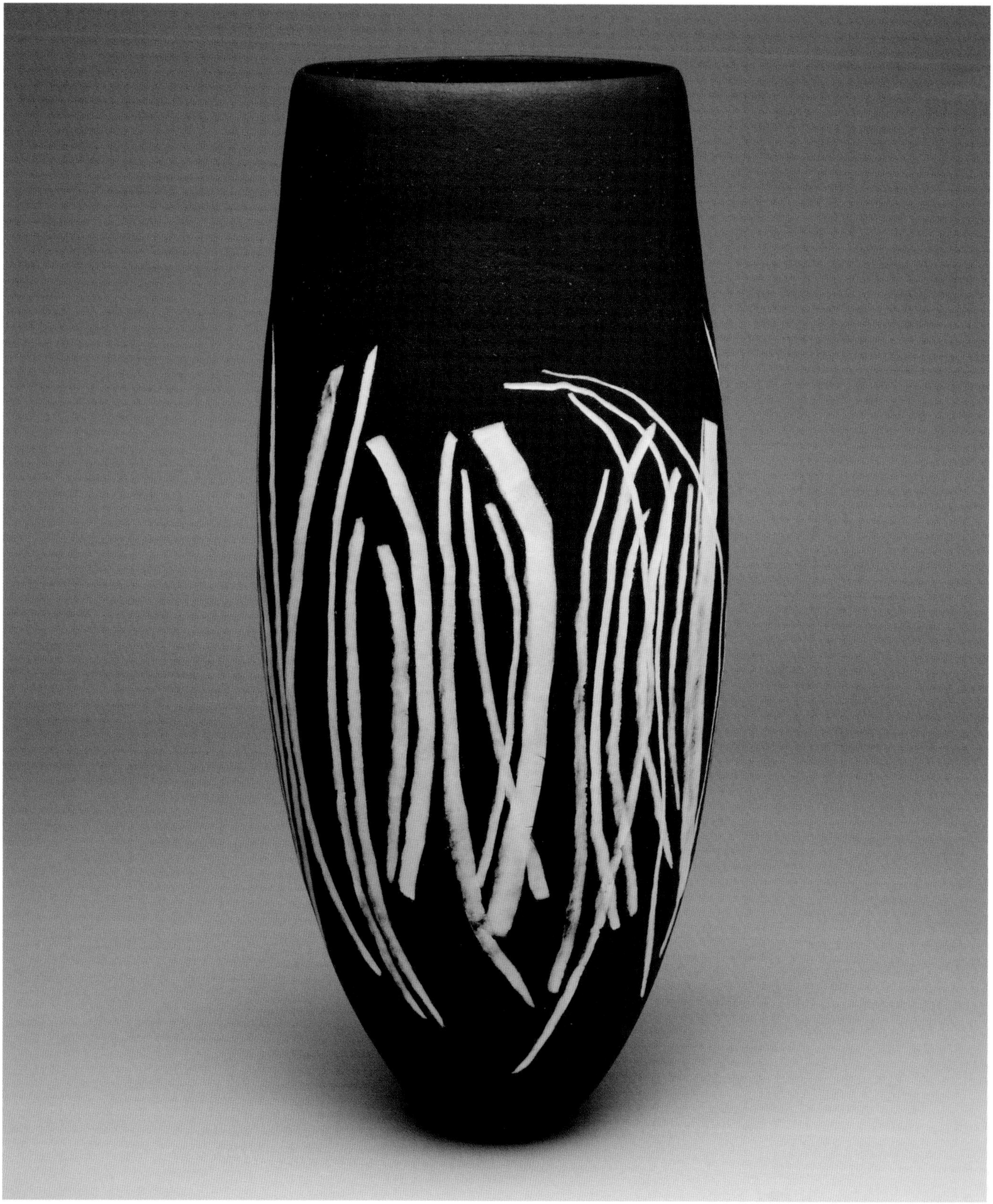

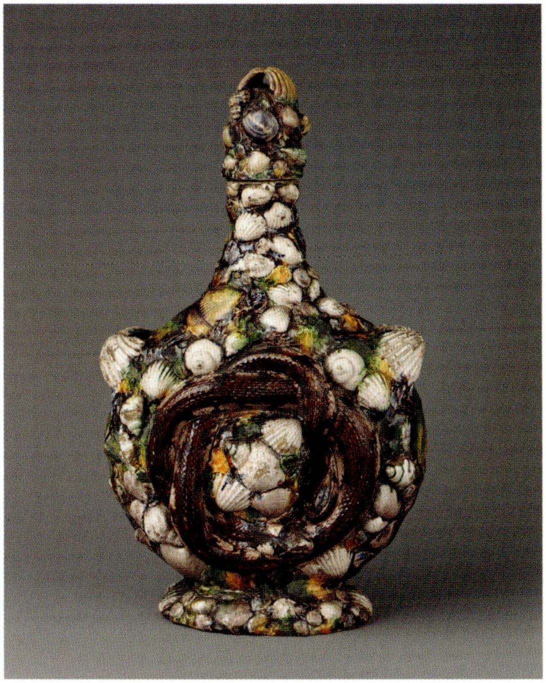

(Above) Pilgrim flask by Bernard Palissy (1510–90) *c.* 1556–67
Earthenware with colourless and transparent or opaque pigmented green, purple, blue, yellow, red-brown and black lead glazes
Height: 31 cm (12 ⅕ in.)

Bernard Palissy is widely regarded as the most innovative and original ceramicist of the French Renaissance. Renowned for his naturalistic works, Palissy richly decorated the pilgrim flask with shells, foliage and snakes taken from moulded casts of real-life specimens.

(Left) *Standing Form, Dancing Lines* by Gabriele Koch (born 1948) 2019
Stoneware clay, smoke fired
Height: 48 cm (19 in.)

Gabriele Koch draws influence from geological landscapes, and layering of sediment rock formations. She hand built this form using stoneware clay with integrated strips of porcelain. The piece was burnished by hand to achieve a tactile surface. It was bisque fired to 1000°C (1832°F) and developed its final colour and distinctive patterning by a carefully orchestrated smoke firing.

unique ceramic creations made by budding potters. This effect can be felt in the art world, too, with a new appreciation for the material, with artists such as Grayson Perry pushing clay into fine art application. Auction prices for the crafted works of Lucie Rie and Hans Coper continue to fetch hefty figures and set new records for studio ceramics.

So, what compels an artist to explore clay in the first instance? Perhaps, one of the main reasons why clay appeals is because it provides great freedom and an opportunity to explore three dimensions. For some, the acquisition of technical knowledge and mastery of skill is a massive draw. It is incredibly satisfying to see your skill level develop from making wobbly, uneven pots to something very accomplished. There is also an element of magic and wonderment that comes from putting a piece in a kiln and watching it transform into something beyond your expectations.

The focus of this book is to examine and study the broad spectrum of the discipline, offering a snapshot of some of the key works that define it. The book aims to celebrate the sheer innovation and breadth of the material, from the very functional to the highly conceptual, demonstrating the individual pursuit of the artist and their relationship to ceramics.

Throughout, you will see how the history of ceramics – its core DNA – (and art in general), intersects with contemporary studio practice. Certainly, the influence of 16th-century potter Bernard Palissy resides strongly in a number of artists who make naturalistic forms, such as Malene Hartmann Rasmussen (see p.106) and Michelle Erickson (see p.212). Likewise, the lively pottery of Pablo Picasso was said to capture the imagination of Peter Voulkos, a pivotal figure in the rise of the Californian Clay movement during the mid-20th century.

The intention of the book is not to be a 'how to' as such, nor prescriptive in its advice. Instead, it acts as a fantastic resource to further your imagination and build confidence with the material. Careful analysis of each featured work and the creative tips panels offer instructive and practical guidance to implement into your own creations. The holistic approach of this book should serve to inspire and inform both beginners and more experienced artists. Ultimately, this will enable you to develop a more constructive understanding, and appreciation that might change the direction of your work. With so much scope for experimentation and discovery, the aim is for you to feel enthused and excited about the potential of clay, igniting curiosity and new-found passion to instigate your own creative journey.

Creative tips and techniques

Each entry in this book is accompanied by a series of technical and creative tips that relate to the techniques used by the featured artists and shown in their work. Although all artists employ different methods to achieve their desired effects, it is possible to identify some recurrent themes and examine methods that artists use repeatedly. Understanding these techniques and how they work with each other is one of the first steps any aspiring artist should take when learning to make ceramics.

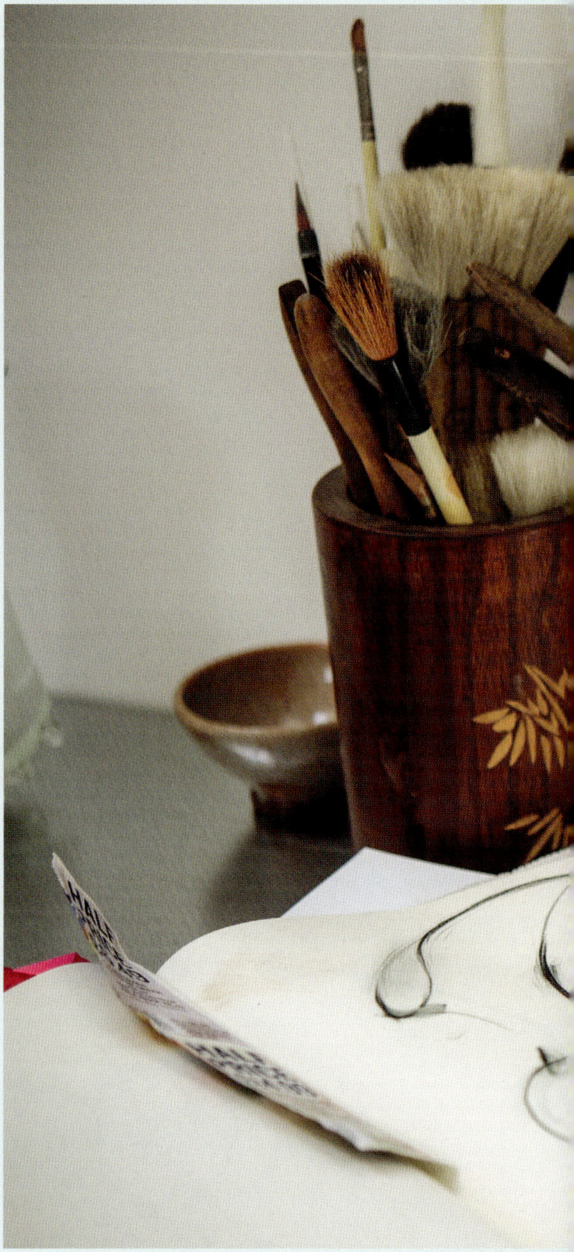

Subject matter

One of the most difficult challenges to overcome before you even get started is knowing what you want to make. This can sometimes be difficult to articulate and you may draw a blank. To overcome this creative block, ask yourself – what inspires me? Sources of inspiration can be found all around, from the natural world, architecture, literature, mythology, art from different cultures, to costume, fashion design and more. You might work from photographs you have taken or you could explore a personal narrative from memories. Perhaps your ideas are purely fantastical – an exploration of a vivid imagination. Think about the specific qualities clay can bring to your work that other materials cannot. Keep a sketchbook, write down things that interest you, visit museums and exhibitions. The more aware you are of your motivations, the easier it will be to translate your ideas into clay.

As you will see throughout this book, the work of the featured artists all has a strong grounding in their ideas. Some have very precise strategic aims, others work intuitively and are led by the material and its processes. Subject matter can come from direct sources; for example, Annie Turner (see p.230) uses photography to document her local landscape and interprets the colours and shapes into a sculptural response. Some contemporary artists may have a strong message that they want to convey through the material, such as Jessica Stoller (see p.240) who explores themes surrounding idealized femininity. Ceramics is a subject drenched in history and embedded with values that continue to drive artists to establish new, exciting territory.

Material

Clay is an intriguing material and compels many artists to explore its diverse properties. It can be shaped and sculpted into just about any conceivable form, and this versatility is very appealing. Understanding the nuances of clay, such as its stages of drying and knowing when to proceed or not, is just as important as the ideas that inform its conception. The type of clay an artist has used to make their work is often significant, too. Perhaps it shares a connection to the landscape in some way, or has associations with past techniques and traditions.

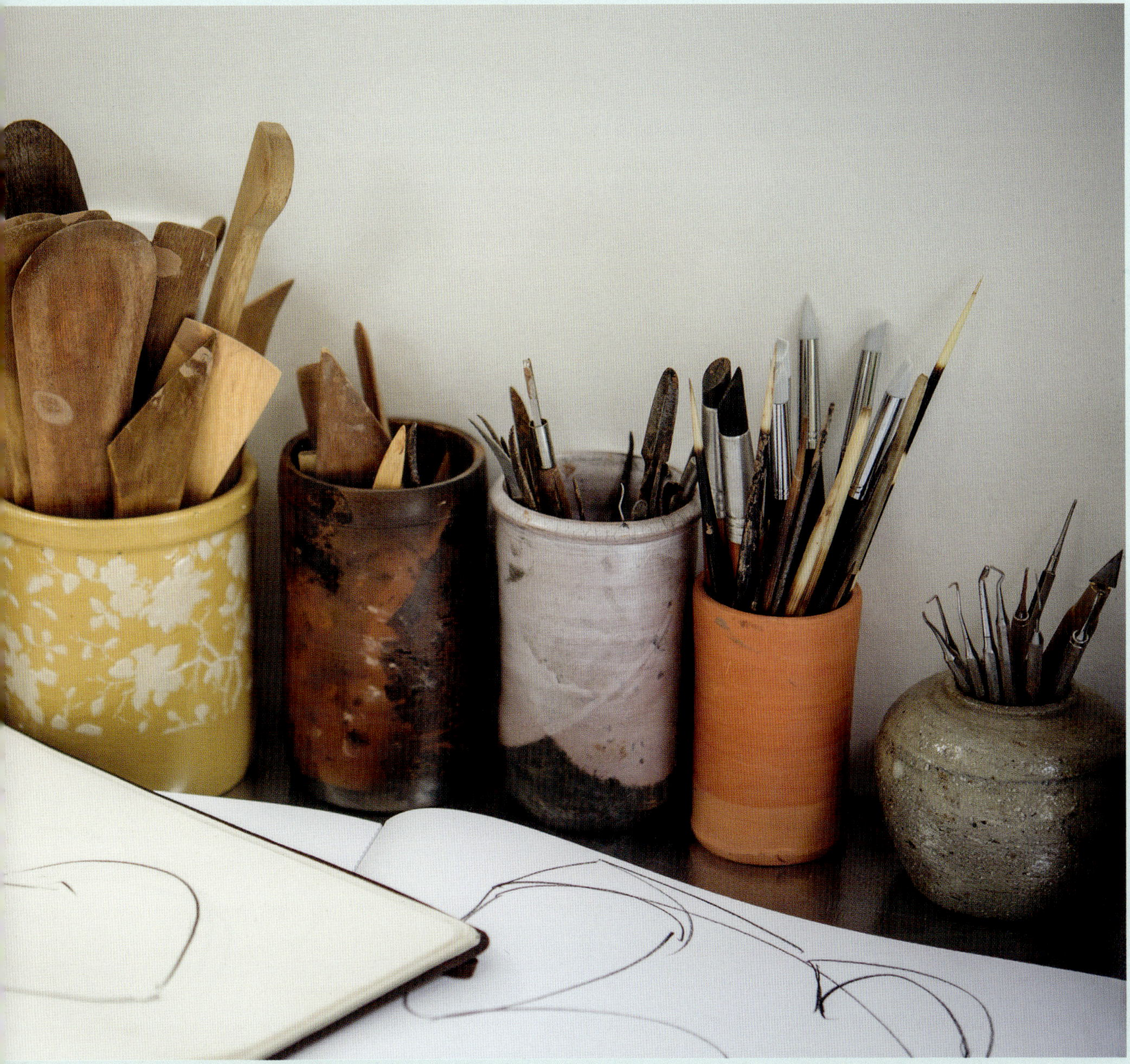

Magdalene Odundo sketchbooks and tools
Magdalene Odundo explores new forms by sketching out her ideas prior to making. Her drawings consist of just a few simple outlines, but are confident and expressive. On view is a selection of the tools and brushes she uses to construct her sensuous hand-built forms.

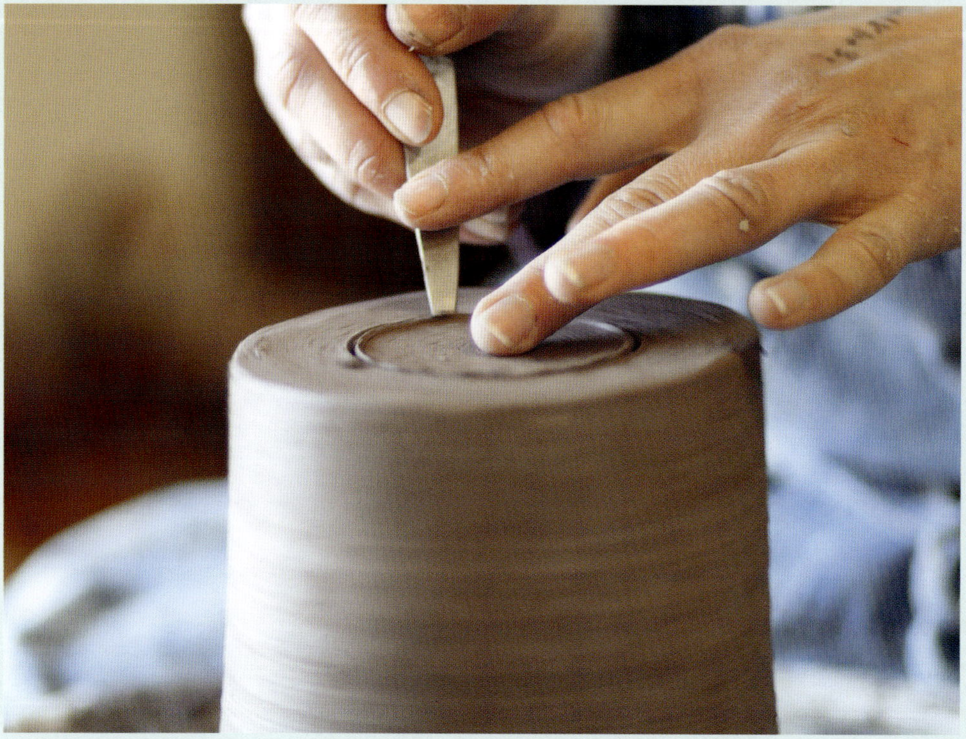

(Left) Cutting a lid on a thrown vessel
Anne Mette Hjortshøj makes a lid for a teapot by cutting a round section away from the main body. She then proceeds to make a gallery ledge for the lid to locate securely.

(Right) Throwing a bottle form
To make a bottle form on the pottery wheel, the clay is collared in with the finger tips to narrow the neck of the vessel. The inside wall is then brought upwards to elongate the neck. The technique is repeated until the desired shape is reached.

(Far right) Glaze test reference board
Ceramic glazes require the application of heat in order to transform into the final colour. A glaze reference board is a useful way to document and record all your successful test results.

Aside from clay, there is the thrill of glazing and surface development – and the materiality that defines these properties. Some artists in this book, such as Gitte Jungersen (see p.222), have developed their own materials – and push the boundaries of what we define as ceramic.

Process

A process is a series of steps or actions taken in order to achieve a particular end result. Commonly with ceramics, it involves the acquisition of the skills needed to achieve a certain aesthetic. At a basic level, clay can be manipulated and shaped by hand. Hand-building methods include coiling, slab building and pinching. Though apparently simple techniques, a strong quality of form in a coil-built pot requires adept hand skills and haptic knowledge gained from many hours spent working with the material. More technical – and requiring more equipment – are processes such as throwing, mould making, slip casting, jigger and jollying, although it is important to remember that just because it is difficult to learn to throw or make a complex mould does not mean that the results are better. The strength in a piece comes from the maker's approach and how they convey their ideas through the material.

There are numerous ways to achieve the same outcome in ceramics and artists are always seeking new methods to streamline their processes. You can be quite free with how you choose to make your work – if a technique works for you, then go for it! Consider how that process relates to that work and if it adds anything or takes it away. For example, a delicate pinch pot beaker has a very different sensibility to one that has been thrown.

If you plan to make a series, consider how the process will impact on the collection of works. Casting will produce identical pieces, but building by hand will inevitably introduce differences. Some artists rely on the interaction between the kiln and their work to produce certain outcomes, particularly if they wood fire their pots, which gives the work a unique character.

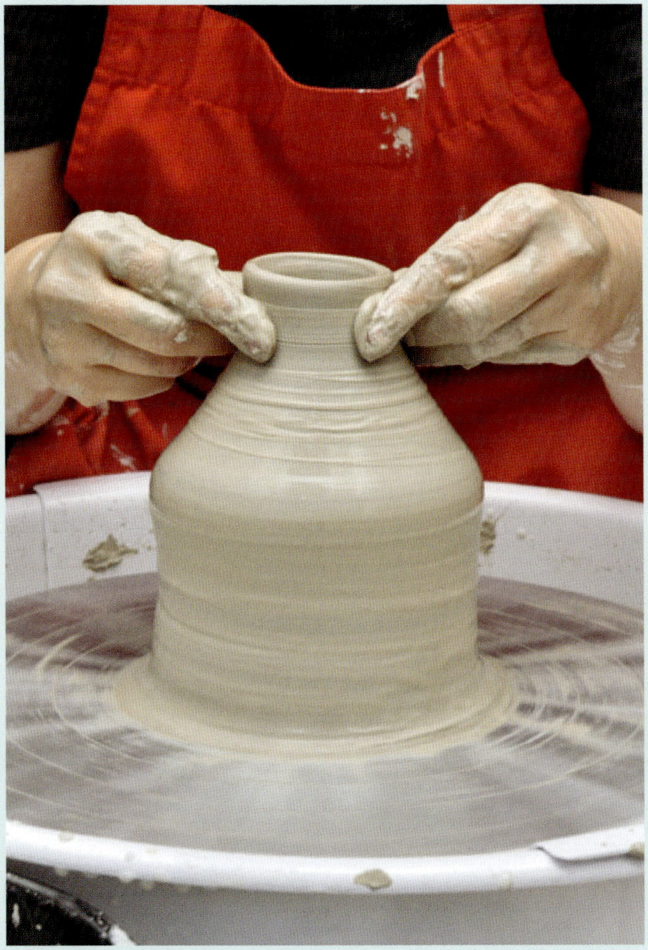

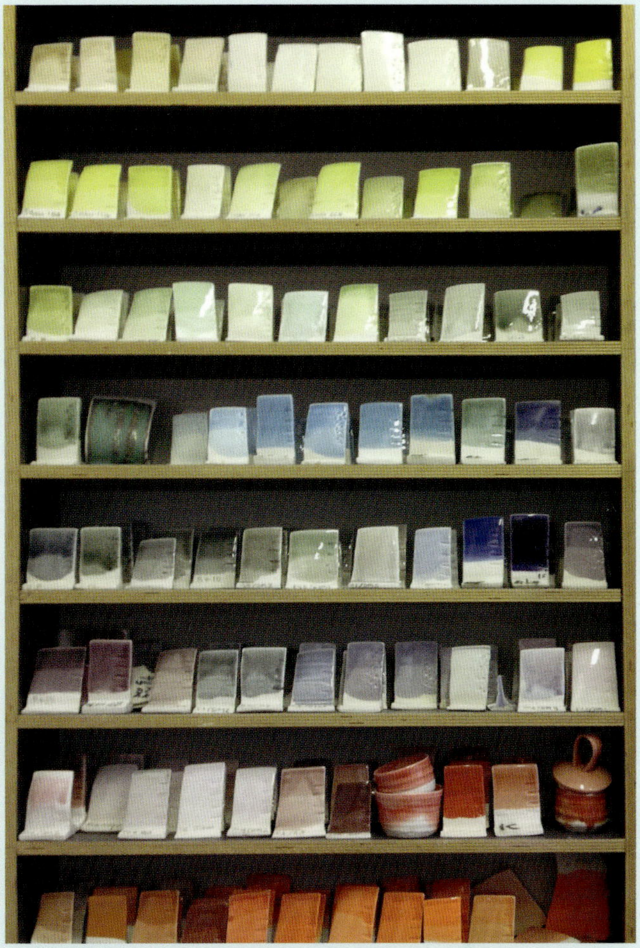

Surface

The ceramic surface is one of the most exciting and dynamic areas of ceramic practice, providing an opportunity to explore texture, glaze, pattern and tone. Indeed, clay artists have a lot of fun creating works that mimic real objects, something that the material is perfect for. In this book you will see the many inspiring ways artists bring visual interest into their work, from slip decoration, resist techniques, feature glazes, innovative glaze application, enamels and transfers to lacquer and oil paints.

Committing to a surface application is where a lot of makers lack confidence, because the process can feel very final. The success of the piece often depends on how well the glaze comes out. A good pot with a bad glaze can be very disappointing. Equally, a good glaze does not make a bad pot better: it is still a bad pot. Therefore, it is important that the surface and form are considered in equal measure. Before you commit to your making, it can be useful to think ahead and decide on the final look. This will help you decide the suitability of your clay body choice and the temperature you aim to fire to. Be methodical with your approach, as this will really help to build up your confidence and encourage you to take bigger steps. With experience, you can expand your scientific knowledge and become more accomplished with your surface application.

Composition

As with the disciplines of painting and drawing, the ceramic artist has to consider the two-dimensional plane and how their surface decoration will work within that space. For ceramics, however, this expands further into the three-dimensional realm, since the artist also has to think about how the piece occupies physical space. This includes looking at the interplay of light and shadow; the reflectivity of surfaces; the texture, height and width of each object; and the positioning of handles, spouts and lids, etc. And if the object is part of a series, what is the relationship between the pieces when they're shown together?

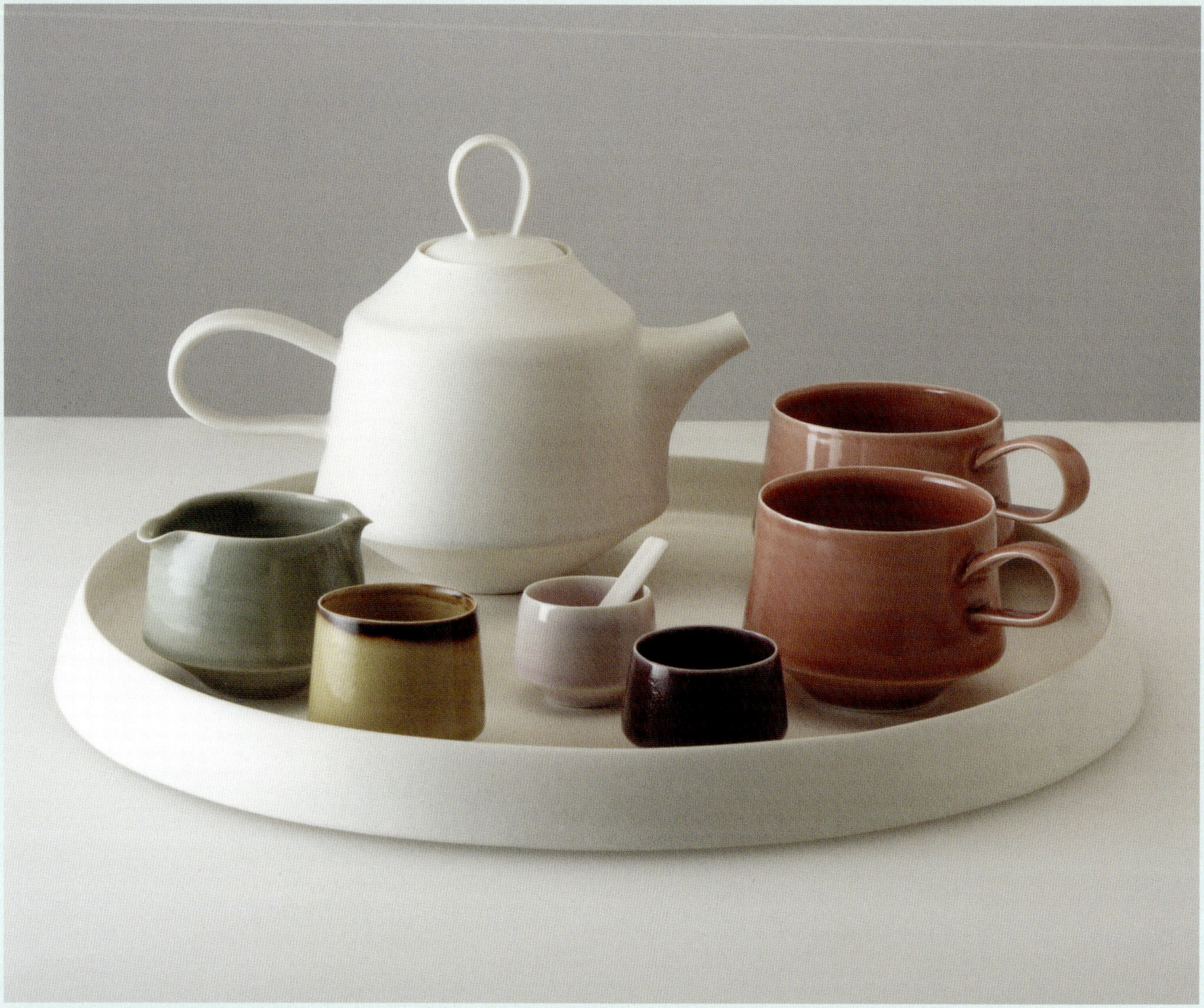

(Above) Hartley tea set by Louisa Taylor 2011
Thrown and assembled porcelain
22 × 38 cm (8 ⅔ × 15 in.)

The composition of this tea set has been carefully planned to carry the viewer's eye up and around the collection of individual pieces. Starting from the cups, to the lid of the teapot and down to the smaller vessels, the intention is to create a satisfying flow.

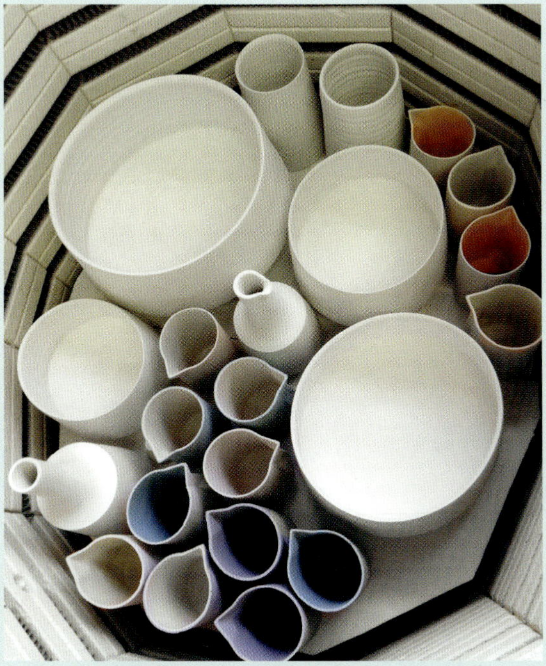

(Above) **Bisque firing**
Emptying the kiln after a low bisque firing, 1000°C (1832°F). In principle, clay items can be stacked and touching for a bisque firing, but there must be adequate space between each one for a glaze firing, otherwise they could stick together.

You will see examples of artists who group objects together to convey a wider context. The success of their displays is not achieved by simply arranging a few things on a plinth. A great deal of thought and planning goes into the execution of the display, taking into account the height, proportion, and overall scale. A strong composition leads the viewer's eye across the plane and invites closer inspection. It should have a good sense of balance and feel comfortable to the eye. Many artists follow a pyramid formation, leading to a skyline with a mixture of high and low forms. Other visual tricks include repeating colours and including a variety of textures to break up the surfaces. An element of styling also comes into it, the intention being to create a viewpoint that evokes a sense of drama.

Form

Within composition, there is also strength of form. A form can be defined as a physical presence, shape and structure. It can express mass and volume or the shape as a whole and is a term commonly used to describe a three-dimensional object. There are many different aspects of form besides its physical profile, including medium, texture, colour and even culture; for example, a Chinese vessel will follow different principles of form compared to a European one.

Technical

The technical heading will focus on very specific and specialized techniques implemented by the talented artists featured in this book and what we can learn from them – for example, Kim Simonsson (see p.192) – who developed an inventive flocking technique to mimic the appearance of moss, the highly experimental solid glaze panels of Gitte Jungersen, or Rafa Pérez (see p.214) who combines organic material and combinations of opposing clay bodies to create his expanded forms.

Ceramics is a very technical subject and the failure rate can be high. The information will provide advice and useful tips regarding drying times, glaze compositions and kiln firing temperatures that will all impact your work in some way. Occasionally, with even the best planning, organization and care, the outcome is completely out of your control, which can either be very thrilling or very stressful! However, with this uncertainty comes potential for discovery. An accidental kiln over-fire could cause an exciting effect in your glaze. Perhaps your overlapped glazes have created a fantastic new colour, or the freshly thrown pot you accidently knocked with your hand now has a sense of spontaneity and excitement. So much relies on the success of specific processes – but like any discipline, these rules are made to be broken, too, so don't be too precious or afraid to move out of your comfort zone. In the pages of this book there are many useful insights and suggestions on how to improve your technique and ideas to try out. Just enjoy experimenting and playing!

Basic materials

This section provides a brief overview of the types of materials specific to ceramic production, from the various clays available to the raw materials used for decoration.

What is clay?

Clay is a naturally occurring material found in abundance throughout the world. It is a mixture of soil, rock and organic matter formed over thousands of years. The geological composition of an area has a direct impact on the structure and characteristics of the clay, resulting in a material unique to that region. For example, in China, huge deposits of kaolin (china clay) – prized for its white colour and strength – were discovered in the 7th century and led to the development of porcelain.

There are a number of ways to source clay. You could dig it up directly from the ground and process it yourself or make clay to a recipe; however, the most common method is to purchase clay from a pottery supplier. Each method has its pros and cons. Processing your own clay is very time consuming and physical, but it is low cost and brings unique character to your work. Commercial clays are the preferred choice for most ceramicists simply because of ease and the choice and breadth offered. The cost is higher but these clays have been formulated by the manufacturer to achieve desirable qualities and to be suitable for specific processes. Most clays in their raw state can be recycled and reused continuously.

Types of clay

Before choosing your clay, think about what you want to achieve as the end result and work backwards. For example, if you intend to make functional thrown pots that are fired to stoneware temperature with a rich glaze, choose a hardy clay body – either a smooth or a semi-grogged stoneware that can withstand the knocks of daily use. If you want to make bright, decorative sculptural work not intended for function, consider using a white earthenware body that will enhance your glazes. The choice can be overwhelming, but many pottery suppliers will send clay samples for you to test before you invest in a batch. Below is a brief overview of the most common types of clay.

1. Red earthenware: Firing temperature 960-1180°C (1760–2156°F), shrinkage 8–12%

A traditional clay body, red/brown in its raw state, changing to rich orange when fired. The colour is the result of high iron content (5–6%), which has a low melting point. Therefore, this clay has to be fired in the earthenware temperature range. Above 1200°C (2192°F) the clay is at risk of bubbling and blistering. Red earthenware is particularly good for slip decoration, where a strong contrast between the clay body and decoration is desirable. The clay is very plastic, smooth and malleable, ideal for throwing and modelling. Typical uses: chimney pots, garden pots, roof tiles and domestic ware. Note that the redness of the clay body will pollute coloured glazes, so apply a coat of either white slip or glaze first, followed by your surface decoration.

2. Smooth white body: Firing temperature 960–1300°C (1760–2372°F), shrinkage 8–12%

A smooth white body is suited to throwing, modelling and press-moulding. The malleable nature of the clay allows for crisp detailing and precision cuts. Its plasticity lessens its suitability for large-scale hand building and slab work, because it does not have a lot of integral strength. Available as earthenware or stoneware – the white colour acts as a neutral base, perfect for carrying colourful glazes.

3. Fine-grogged body: Firing temperature 960–1300°C (1760–2372°F), shrinkage 8–12%

A good all-rounder, suitable for a variety of different processes and techniques, from throwing to hand building. The addition of fine grog to the clay body adds strength and makes it ideal for slab building and complex structures. The body colour is a light buff when fired, which can dirty bright glazes, but this is not an issue if you intend to cover the clay with a thick glaze or use it for reduction/wood firing. This clay body is very strong and suitable for beginners who are learning to throw.

4. Coarse-grogged body: Firing temperature 960–1300°C (1760–2372°F), shrinkage 5–10%

Very gritty clays are incredibly strong and can withstand tough extremes. They're ideal for a range of purposes, from large-scale sculptural work to hand-built forms. They are a good choice if your work is intended for the outside. Coarse-grogged clay can span a variety of firing temperatures, but for best results use stoneware temperature. The integral strength of the clay is perfect for the demands of the raku technique, because it is able to withstand thermal shock (extreme hot to cold). The large particle size of the grog within the clay improves the drying and shrinkage of the clay but can be very abrasive on your hands when throwing with it.

5. Porcelain: Firing temperature 1220–1350°C (2228–2462°F), shrinkage 15–20%

Porcelain is a very elegant clay body, renowned for its translucent properties. It is extremely plastic and notoriously difficult to use, requiring an advanced skill set. The benefit of using porcelain is that it can be worked incredibly thin, and offers a beautiful purity of colour. It is a high-temperature clay body, best suited for throwing, small-scale hand building and modelling. Note that porcelain has a high shrinkage rate of up to 20%, which you need to take into account, especially when producing batch work.

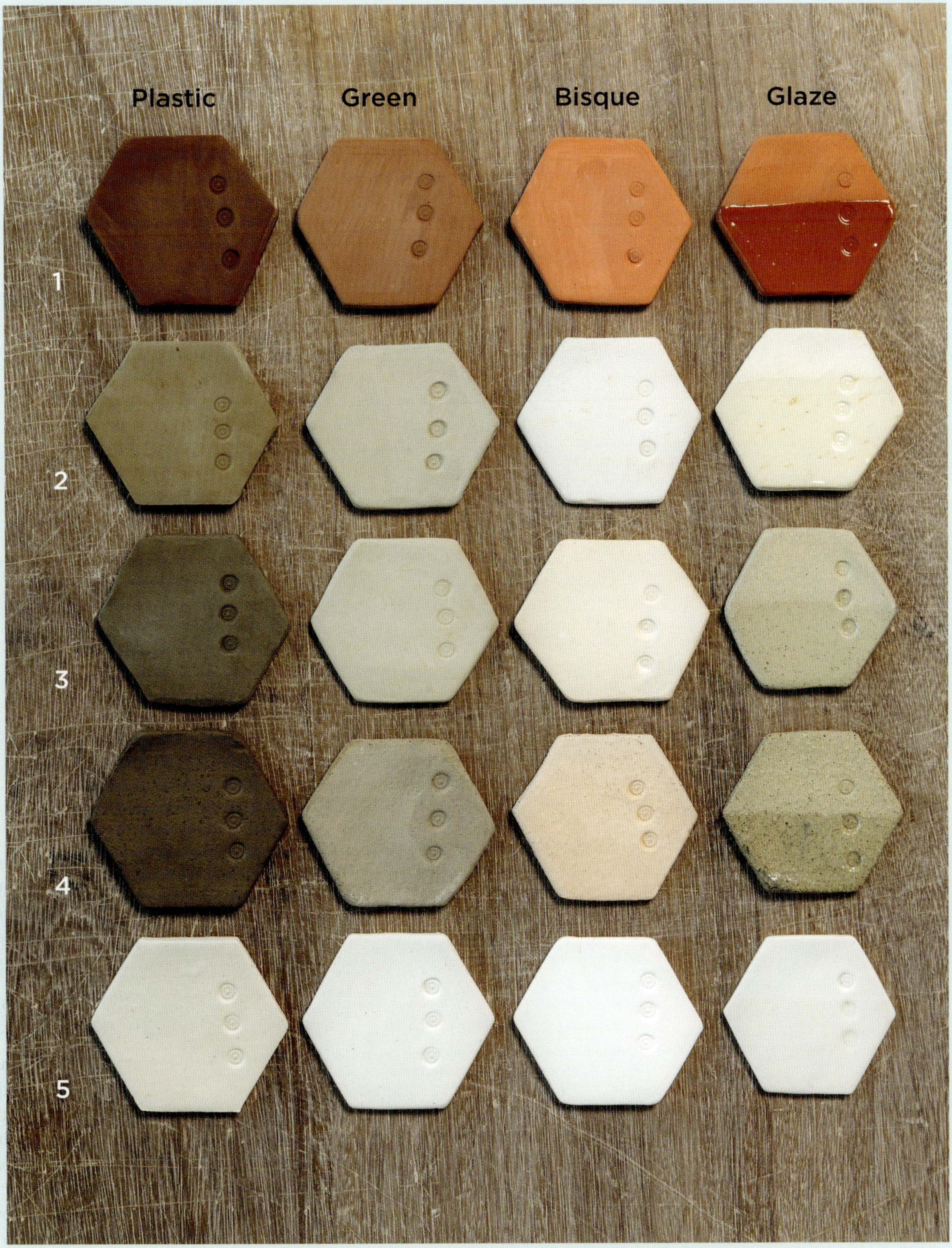
Plastic
Green
Bisque
Glaze
1
2
3
4
5

Stages of clay

Clay is unlike any other creative material. It starts out soft and malleable, able to be shaped into any form imaginable, and through a series of processes and the application of heat, it transforms into a permanent state. If we were to examine clay under a microscope, we would see a structure consisting of tiny platelets. Water is held between these platelets and this is essentially what gives clay its integral structure. If clay particles are very fine – for example, porcelain – the clay will be responsive and 'plastic', but this can make some clays difficult to work with. If the particles are large – a coarse-grogged body – the clay is less plastic and flexible but very strong for hand building.

Throughout this book, you will see artists exploiting the various stages of clay, constantly questioning and analysing its unique properties. Below is an outline of the three main stages of clay and the differences between them.

Plastic

The clay is at its most workable, malleable state. Plastic stage offers the point of flexibility needed to form and manipulate clay into its initial shape, particularly using coil building, modelling or press moulding. Clay can be joined easily by smearing and smudging together, but plastic clay lacks strength and is susceptible to sagging under its own weight.

Leather-hard

If clay is left exposed to air it will eventually become firm and less malleable. Leather-hard clay can be compared to the texture and feeling of cheese (or leather, as the name suggests). At this point, the clay still has some flexibility but too much bending will cause it to crack. The leather-hard stage is ideal for slab building, where you need strength and rigidity. This is also the ideal stage to refine and shape your work, because the clay will come away cleanly without smearing.

Green

When clay has reached green state, it is completely dry and ready to be fired – characterized by a chalky, pale colour. You cannot join clay once it has reached green state. Green clay should feel warm to the touch, not cold – which could imply the piece is too damp to fire. Greenware is very brittle and can break with the slightest touch, so careful handling is crucial. You can lightly sponge irregularities, but do not use excessive water or you could risk dissolving the clay.

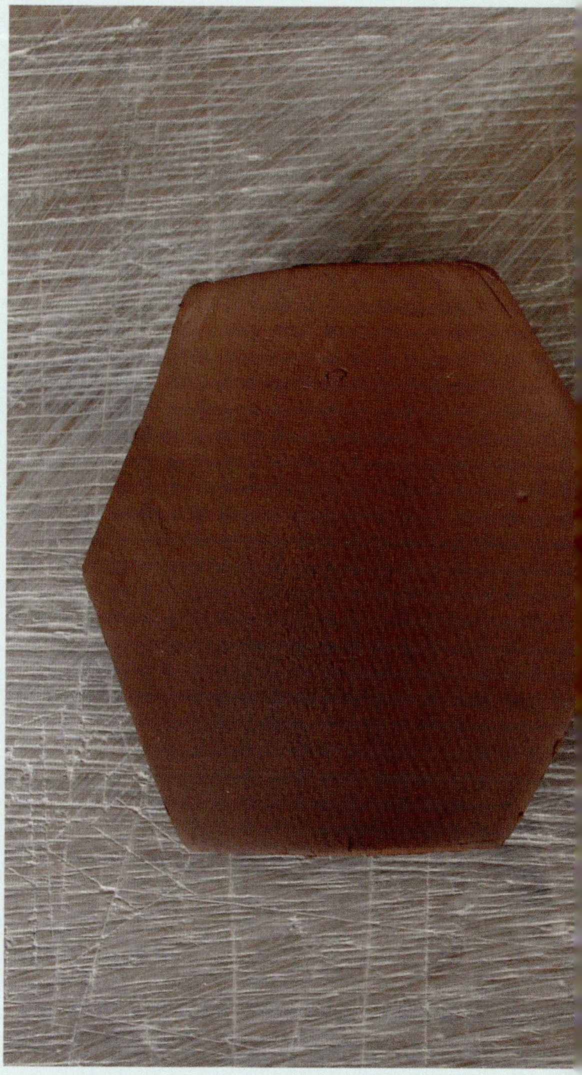

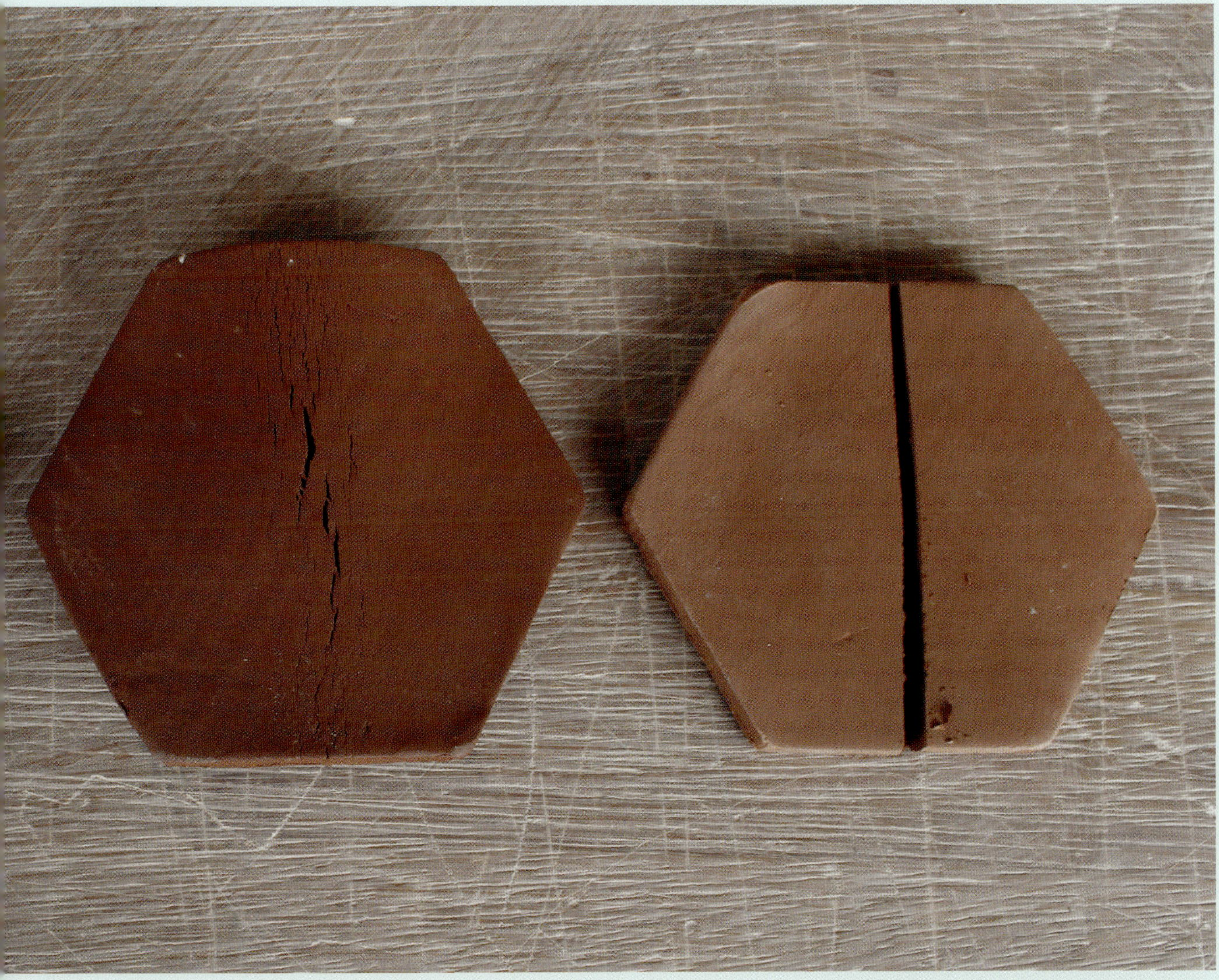

Left to right: Plastic; leather-hard; green
Being aware of the key stages of clay will enable you to get the best from the material in relation to your specific making process.

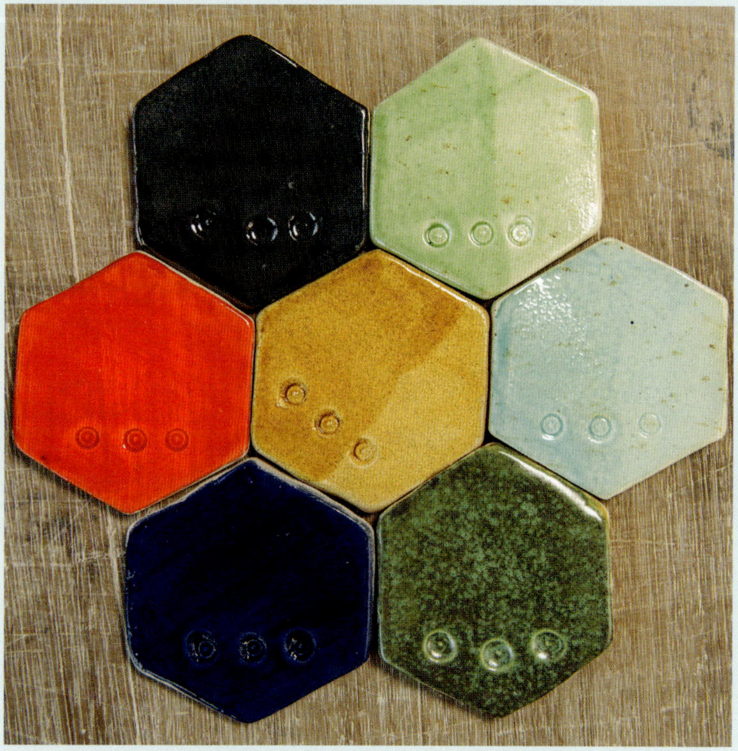

(Left) Earthenware glaze samples
Earthenware or low-temperature range (cone 05-02) is ideal for achieving bright and vibrant colourful glazes such as these examples.

(Right) Melted flux material
Left to right: Cornish stone (Cornwall stone); potash feldspar (custer); soda feldspar (Kona F-4). Fired to 1280°C (2336°F), the material has melted to a thick blob. This indicates how it will behave in a recipe; the Cornish stone is creamy white, potash feldspar is smooth and soda feldspar has a softer melt.

Raw glaze materials

Creating your own glazes from ceramic materials is very appealing and rewarding, but can feel a little daunting when starting out. You don't need to have huge scientific knowledge to achieve spectacular results. An enquiring mind and enthusiasm will stand you in good stead and you can learn a lot just from the process of testing and refining. Below is an overview of the basic materials used for the production of ceramics. It is important to bear in mind that many of the materials are from natural sources and vary from country to country. Some ceramic materials are labelled differently but are chemically similar. These equivalents have been included within parentheses. See also Glaze recipes on page 274, and if glazing is an area that interests you, seek further reading for extra guidance.

Flint and Quartz (silica)

Silica is present in all clays and provides the glass component in glazes. Flint and quartz are two pure forms of silica and they derive from silicate rocks that are commercially mined. There is not a huge difference between them, one is not necessarily better than the other, it simply comes down to preference. In general, flint melts at a quicker rate than quartz, which is good for glazes, but it is not as pure in colour as quartz. Silica has an incredibly high melting point (1700°C/3092°F) and requires a flux to lower that temperature.

Feldspars

Feldspars are naturally occurring minerals that are mined from the earth. The role of feldspar within a glaze is to act as a flux to lower the melting point of silica. Feldspars are generally suited for the stoneware temperature range: 1200–1300°C (2192–2372°F). Glazes can be made from feldspar alone, but they are quite dense and milky and craze easily. Some of the artists featured in this book, such as Takuro Kuwata (see p.124) and Brian Rochefort (see p.128), exploit the gloopy properties of feldspar for visual effect. Common feldspar types include custer feldspar (potash feldspar), Kona F-4 feldspar, soda feldspar, Cornwall stone and nepheline syenite.

Clay-based

Clay-based materials are sources of alumina and their purpose in a glaze is to aid stability and adhesion to the

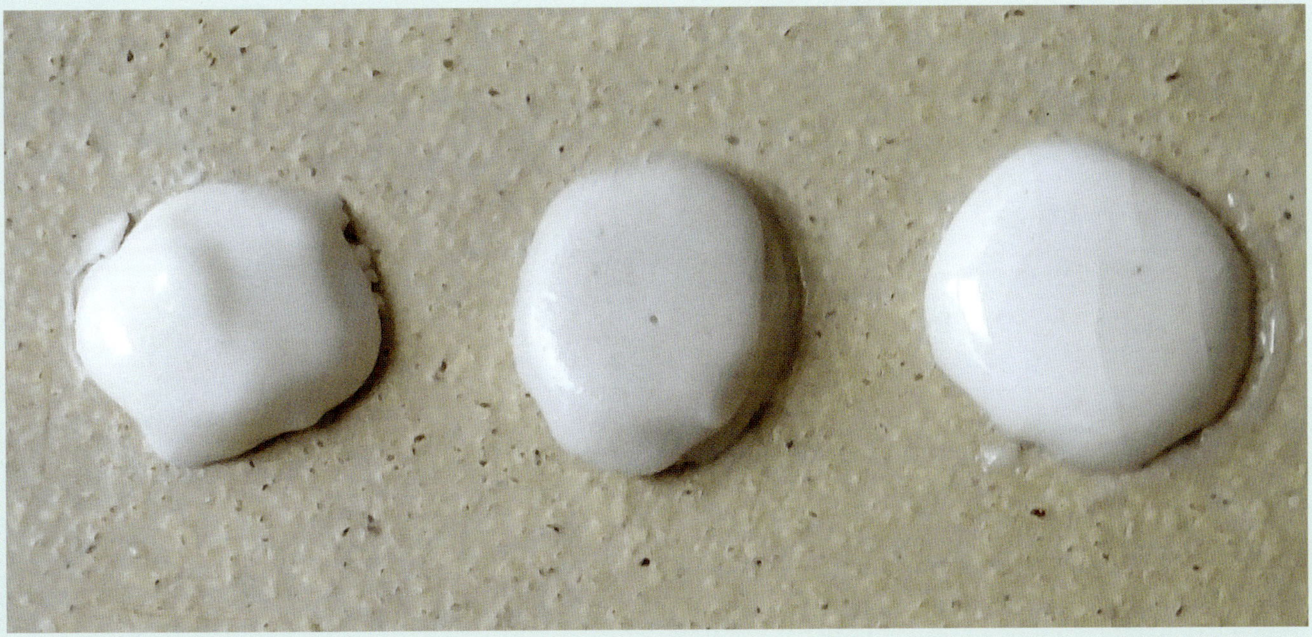

ceramic surface. A high amount of alumina in a glaze can produce a matt finish and create dry textures. You can also use clay materials as a base to make decorative slips and engobes. Clay-based materials include China clay (EPK, kaolin), Kentucky ball clay (TVWD/HVAR ball clay), Albany slip clay and red clay powder.

Modifiers

Modifiers are glaze materials that are added to a base glaze to promote specific surface qualities, such as colour, gloss, matt, dryness, tonality, opacity and crystal development. They can aid the melting of the feldspar material and provide stability in the glaze recipe. Often a glaze is referred to by the unique characteristics of the modifier, for example, 'a barium glaze'. Examples of modifiers: Dolomite, Gerstley Borate (colemanite), Borax, Barium Carbonate, talc and whiting.

Ash

Ash from organic sources, such as wood, is naturally high in silica, the glass forming element of a glaze. You can make a very simple glaze with just 50% ash and 50% red clay powder. You can use ash from a fire, log burner or pit, but make sure that no other fuel source, such as coal, is present that could contaminate the ash. The ash must be thoroughly washed, dried and sieved to remove sulphates before it is added to the remaining ingredients. Different tree species can affect the way the ash behaves in the glaze and produce unique qualities.

Frits

A frit is formed when a toxic or unstable material is melted together with silica and then ground to a powder, which renders it both safer and more suitable to use. Although frits will form a glass by themselves, they are normally used as bases to which other ingredients are added. Frits are used as a safer substitute for lead or boron, which are powerful fluxes required for earthenware temperatures. The main frits are lead bisilicate, lead sesquisilicate, Ferro 3110 alkaline leadless frit, Ferro 3124 high alkaline frit (T Frit – high alkaline frit; B Frit – calcium borate frit; E Frit – borax frit; and F Frit – low expansion frit).

Colour tone

You can introduce colour into your clay body, slip decoration or glaze using two main sources:

Metal oxide compounds

Oxides of metal are naturally occurring pigments from the earth and are the simplest ways to add colour to your ceramic creations. Oxides produce rich, earthy colours by themselves, but can offer great breadth and variety when added to a glaze. Oxides are sensitive to the type of glaze and firing. For example, if copper oxide is added to an alkaline base recipe, it will turn rich turquoise – but when added to an acidic base, it will produce vibrant green. Oxidized and reduction atmospheres will impact the oxide, too (see Firing, p.46). Carbonates produce the same colour but are weaker than an oxide. One of the difficulties when using oxides is that they look very different in their raw state compared to when they are fired and this can make it hard to predict the outcome. Some oxides – such as cobalt and manganese dioxide – in larger amounts can have a fluxing effect and destabilize your glaze recipe. The benefit of oxides is that they can be applied as a wash to enhance texture and bleed through glaze. Oxides are equally good without glaze and can produce dark metallic tones. Below is a chart to advise on suggested amounts and the colours you can achieve.

Oxide	Amount %	Colour
Copper	1–3%	Light to dark green. Turquoise in an alkaline glaze base. Blood red in reduction firing.
Cobalt	0.2–1%	Light to dark blue. Cobalt is a very powerful oxide and can dominate.
Iron oxide	2–4%	Light tan to dark brown.
Manganese dioxide	2–6%	Light brown to dark grey-brown. Manganese can create plum purple in an alkaline base.
Chrome oxide	1–2%	Grass green colour. Bright yellow in an alkaline base.
Rutile	2–8%	Light fawn to dark fawn. Can produce iridescence in Chun-type glazes.
Nickel oxide	1–3%	Grey brown. Neon pink in combination with a barium glaze.
Vanadium pent oxide	1–8%	Grey-yellow mottled textured surfaces.

Commercial stains

Commercial stains are produced by the ceramics industry from metal oxides in various combinations. The advantage of a stain over an oxide is that the colour in its raw state is close to the colour achieved when fired. Stains are excellent for bright colours, including reds, oranges, yellows, pinks and light blues. The colour is consistent and predictable; however, it can look tonally flat compared to an oxide. Another disadvantage is the higher cost of the product. You also need a greater quantity to colour your glaze or clay body – typically 4 to 10%. Stains are at full strength at 12%. You need to use the correct type of stain to best suit your work:

Underglaze: For decoration onto bisqueware. Mix the powder with a little water and apply as if using paint. A clear glaze is applied over the top to enhance the colours.

Body stain: Use to colour your clay body (preferably white clay). A recommended amount is 8 to 10% stain per 100 g (3.5 oz) of clay. This is useful if you plan to use the *neriage/ nerikomi* technique or create agateware.

Glaze stain: Use to colour your glaze. Stains can be used at earthenware and stoneware temperatures (oxidized and reduction), although some colours (for example, pink) can burn out at higher temperatures. You can mix glaze stains with oxides to broaden your palette and bring greater tonality to your glaze. If you add 6% stain to a white opaque glaze, you can achieve sugary pastel colours.

(Top) Bowl decorated with copper oxide
To achieve this effect, the pot was coated with a wash of copper oxide and water at the bisque stage. The wash was then lightly cleaned away with a damp sponge, leaving the residue behind in the linear texture. A smooth dolomite stoneware glaze was applied on top and the piece was fired to 1280°C (2336°F). The oxide has bled through the glaze, creating delicate green and metallic shades.

(Bottom) Glaze stains sample tile
This tile illustrates three different glaze stains. From left to right: sun yellow, bramley green and azure blue. The stain was mixed with water and applied to an unglazed bisque surface. A shiny transparent glaze was applied on top and fired to 1280°C (2336°F).

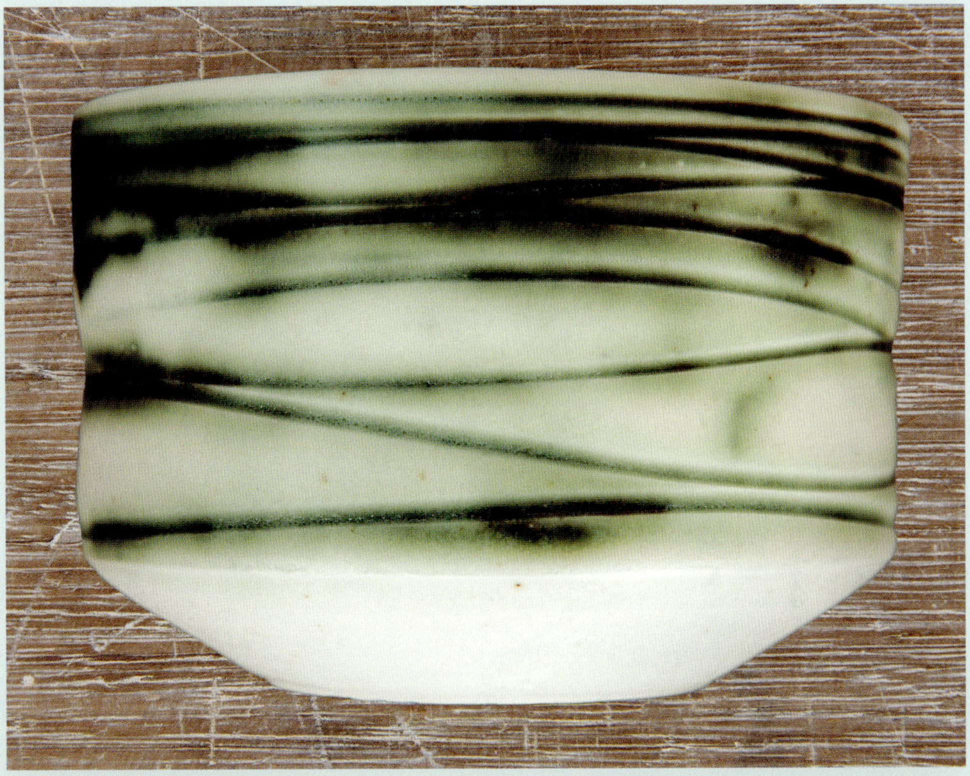

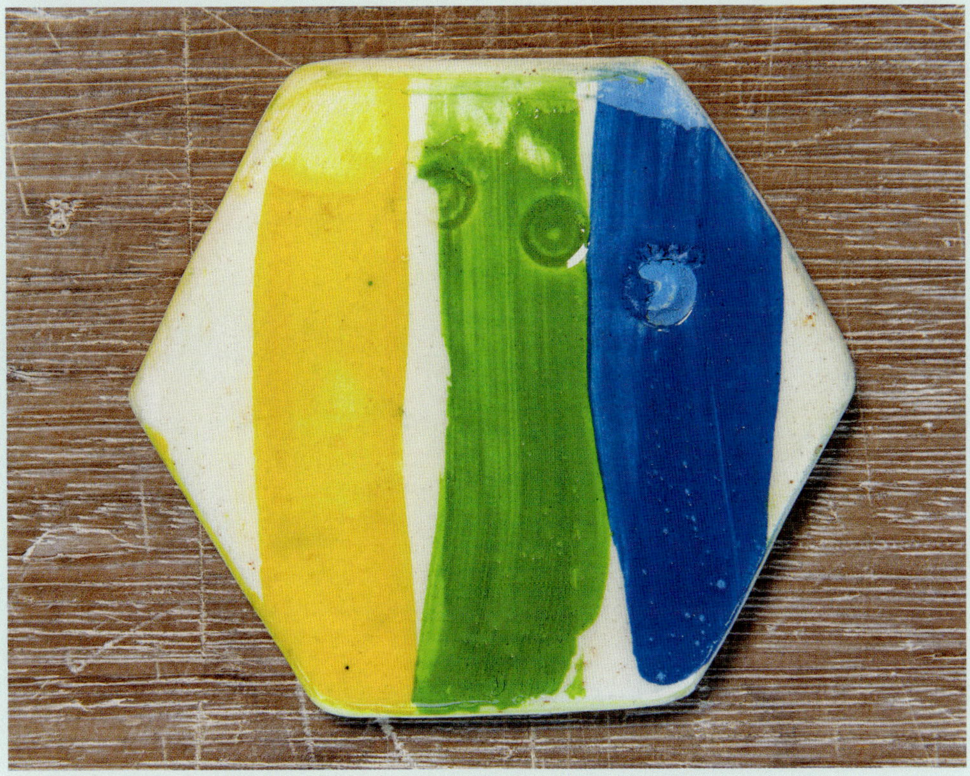

Basic tools

On the following pages are a range of basic tools used for working with clay. You don't need to spend a fortune on a huge array of tools; in fact, you can achieve a lot with just your hands. However, it is good to invest in the core essentials, starting with a pottery knife, cutting wire, sponge, some wooden modelling tools and a wooden or metal rib/kidney. You could be resourceful and make your own tools from old credit cards, shaped pieces of wood and bent strips of metal.

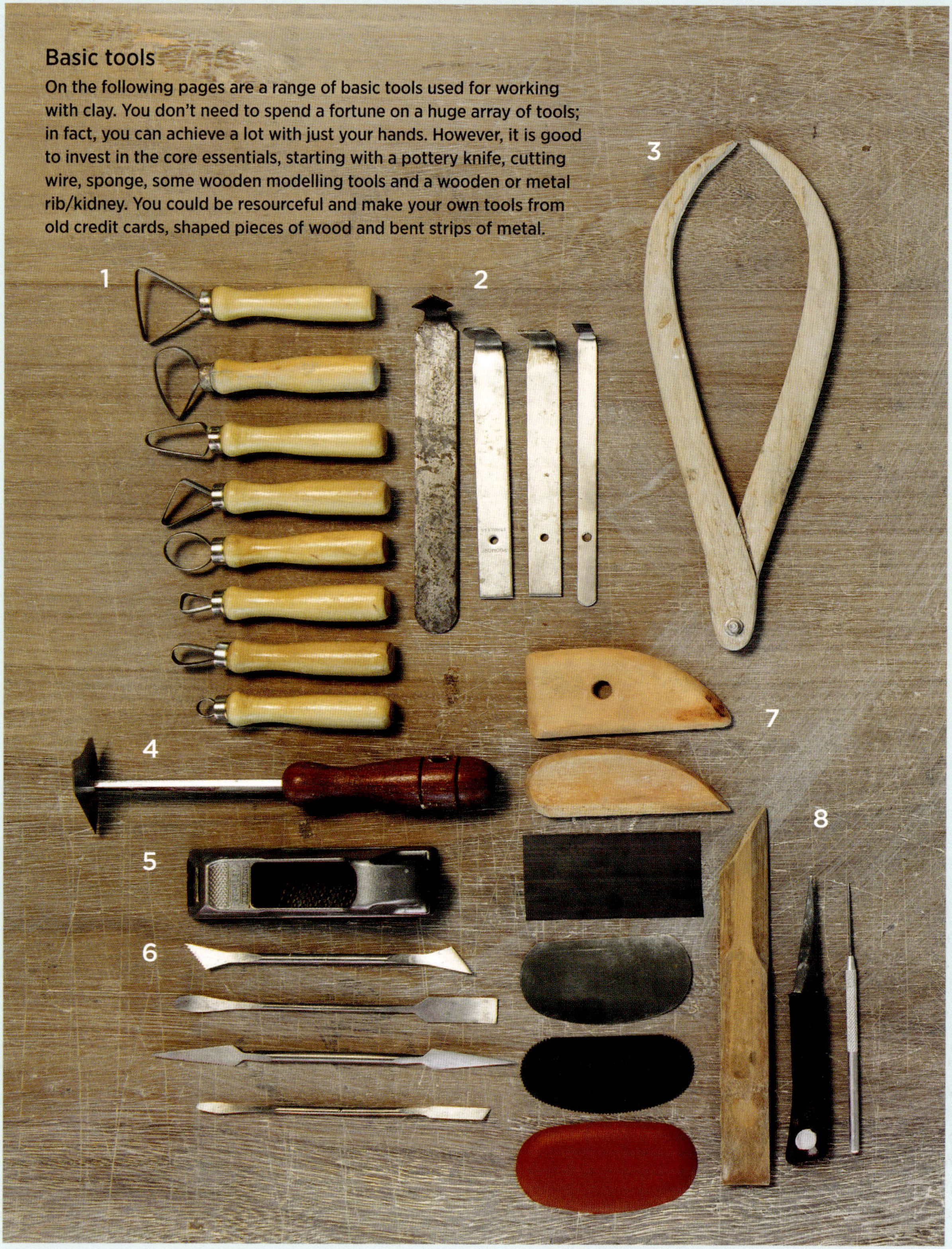

1 Wire loop/strip tools

A collection of wire loop/strip tools is very useful for trimming (turning) wheel-thrown pottery to define the profile and add decorative details to the surface. The design of the tool allows the clay to flow freely through the centre without getting clogged up. Each tool offers a slightly different profile; some will create crisp edges of varying widths, while others produce curves and ridges. You can also use these tools for gouging clay out of hand-built forms to make them lighter. You can even make coils to build with by running a round looped tool through a block of clay. Small looped tools can be used in conjunction with sgraffito techniques for cleanly scraping away a slipped surface to reveal the colour beneath.

2 Steel trimming tools

These steel tools are similar to wire loop tools but have a sharp bladed edge for precision cutting. Intended for throwing and trimming on the pottery wheel, they are available in different shapes with tips that range from long and rectangular to triangular with an angled point. The sharpness of the tool is ideal for creating a strong profile and clean cuts. As with all bladed tools, they will become blunt eventually, but they can be sharpened with a handheld grindstone or bench grinding wheel. You can make your own versions of these tools from strips of metal that have been cut and shaped into a profile of your choice.

3 Callipers

A simple set of callipers can be used to take measurements as you work; for example, when making a lid to fit a gallery on a functional pot. If you regularly throw but struggle to maintain an even size within your batch, set the callipers to your specified height or width and refer to them regularly to ensure consistency between each piece. Wooden or plastic callipers are more suitable for clay than those made from metal, which can rust and seize up. Another method for taking measurements is to use an old credit card or piece of plastic and scratch/mark it with a series of lines that relate to the outside and inside widths of the piece you are making. This is a good technique for repetitive work when recreating pieces from a series.

4 Large trimming/sculpting tool

This large handheld tool is a bigger version of the steel trimming tool. It can be used for refining leather-hard forms on the pottery wheel, but it is ideal for shaping plaster forms on a lathe or whirler machine. This tool is available to buy in many different profiles, but the tool featured here is a good all-rounder because it has a curve, point and flat side enabling you to create a variety of different shapes.

5 Surform file

A surform file is typically used for woodwork, but the coarse-rasped blade lends itself well to shaping clay and plaster work. You will need separate tools for each material, though, because plaster will contaminate clay. A surform can remove a lot of material very quickly when pushed across a surface and it is excellent for refining leather-hard coil pots and sculptural forms. To ensure successful use, the clay must be the right consistency. If it is too soft, the clay will clog the file; too dry and it could blunt the blade and create harmful dust.

6 Steel modelling tools

A good set of steel modelling tools is essential if you intend to work in plaster. The double-ended design can accommodate a variety of tasks required for precision modelling, such as a serrated edge for sculpting an initial shape and a flat blade to refine the profile. Curves, points and fine chisels can be used to carve intricate details and patterns into your model.

7 Wooden ribs and metal kidney shapers

Wooden ribs are used to aid the potter when throwing a curved open profile, straight sides or to remove excess clay. Traditional ribs are made from bamboo, which has a natural curve and is easy to grip, but there are many different shapes and styles available to purchase – you can also make your own. A metal kidney is one of the most useful tools to own and is excellent for scraping and refining surfaces. Similarly, a serrated kidney will help blend coils as you work and remove lumps and bumps. To finish, a rubber kidney will compress the clay surface, resulting in a smooth, waxy sheen.

8 Cutting tools: bamboo knife, pottery knife and needle

These cutting tools are essential for working with clay at any stage. A bamboo knife is suited to wheel work when cutting away excess clay or shaping a form. The ultimate tool is a metal knife, which is incredibly versatile for just about all jobs, from slicing to trimming and scoring clay. A pottery needle is also multipurpose – it is predominantly used to check the thickness of the base of a pot when throwing, but can also be used for cross-hatching and scoring when joining clay, or to gauge glaze thickness. It is also handy to have a few scalpels in your toolkit. The fine blade is very good for removing seams from slip-cast forms and for precision cuts.

9 Sponges

You can never have enough sponges to hand when working with clay. They are essential for tidying surfaces up and for strengthening the overall profile. Shown here are rectangular fettling sponges (black with a wooden handle) for smoothing slip-cast forms and general clay work. The long dowel with a cylindrical sponge attached – aptly named 'sponge on a stick' – is intended for throwing and enables the user to soak up excess water left in the base of a piece. The conical sponge is used for defining holes and softening edges. A small round sponge fits comfortably in the palm and is ideal for throwing. You can also use the texture of a sponge in conjunction with decorative features such stencilling. The soft fibres of a natural sponge will give you a better finish, avoiding the scratchy marks created by a synthetic sponge.

10 Brushes

Brushes for decorating clay surfaces differ from those used for painting on a canvas. This is because normal paintbrushes can be too scratchy or not able to carry enough of the ceramic pigment. Hake brushes are a traditional Asian-style brush with very soft, dense bristles encased in a wooden handle. They are typically used for slip decoration but are just as good for decorating with glaze. The thick bristles hold the slip or glaze and produce a luscious coating of pigment without leaving any unsightly marks. They are available in many different widths. It is also useful to have a few regular bristle brushes for fine, detailed work or for applying wax or latex resists.

11 Small handheld extruder and dies

A small extruder is a handy tool for creating texture and surface interest. Place a coil of soft clay into the extruder barrel and push the plunger down to squeeze the clay through the die. On a bigger scale, you can buy a wall or table-mounted extruder to create a variety of interesting shapes of any design. You can use an extruder to prepare lengths of coils for hand building, to make 'feature' handles and also to create hollow tube shapes.

12 Wooden modelling tools

It is a shrewd investment to have a good selection of modelling tools in your kit. They are incredibly versatile and can be used for a multitude of tasks. The double-ended examples shown here are excellent for creating marks and textures, blending coils and for detailed modelling. Small handheld tools with metal blades and ribbon (loop) nibs will enable you to make precision cuts. A rubber-tipped tool is perfect for sealing joins and adhering sprig decoration to a clay surface.

13 Slip trailer tool with interchangeable nozzles

A slip trailer is typically used for slip decoration but also lends itself well to applying glaze. It consists of a rubber bulb into which you insert a nozzle of variable size. The bulb is squeezed to push out the air and the vacuum draws up the liquid. Slip trailers are great for expressive mark making, writing and creating decorative patterns. If you enjoy slip decorating, it is useful to have a few available so that you can fill them with different colours to save swapping over each time.

14 Clay cutting wire

A cutting wire is a very simple but effective tool for cutting clay from the block or for slicing bases of thrown forms away from the wheel/bat. Wires are available in various widths, lengths and thicknesses to accommodate different tasks. For example, a thick wire will withstand heavy-duty use and is suitable for preparing clay. If you're using a smooth, delicate clay such as porcelain, invest in a very fine wire to avoid tearing the clay. Some wires can be used for decorative purposes: a twisted wire or coiled wire will create scallop marks when pulled through clay. Hang your wires up after use to avoid tangles or kinks.

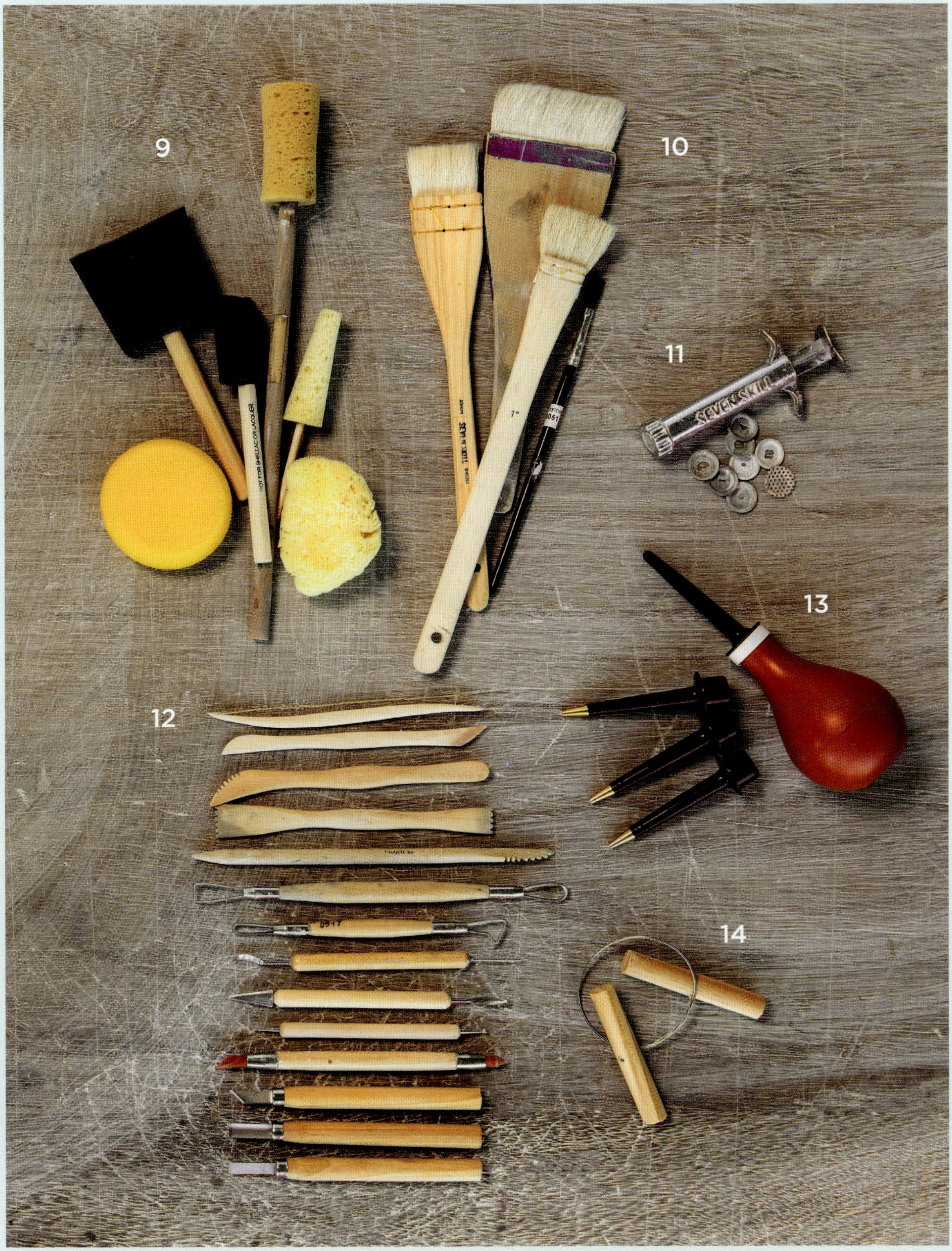
9
10
11
12
13
14

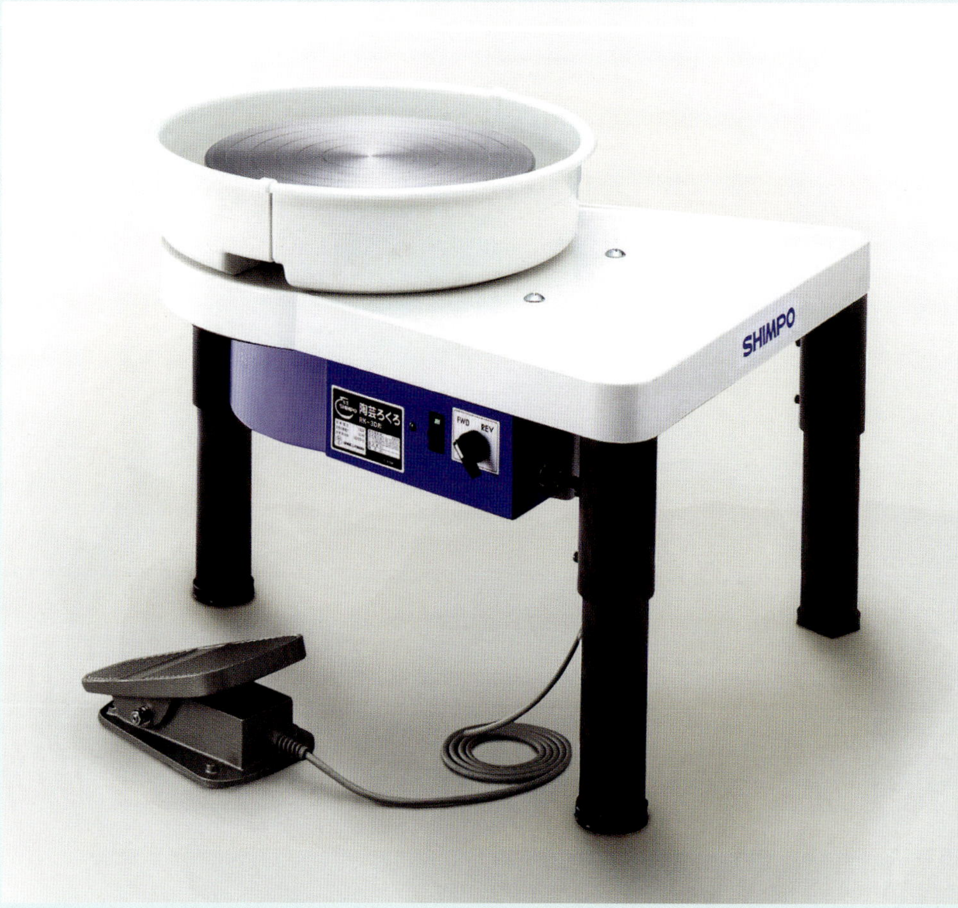

(Left) Electric pottery wheel
This is a typical example of an electric pottery wheel, with an adjustable foot pedal and removable splash container. There are many different types to choose from to suit smaller spaces such as this one, right though to wheels with a built-in saddle seat that resemble a piece of furniture.

(Right) Noborigama multi-chamber wood kiln, mid firing
This kiln, belonging to Anne Mette Hjortshøj can achieve temperatures exceeding 1300°C (2372°F). The principle of this type of firing is to achieve a reduction atmosphere (no oxygen present).

(Far Right) Banding wheel
A wooden modelling tool is used to sculpt and emphasize the features of the artwork. The piece is placed on a banding wheel which enables the artist to easily rotate and change the angle they are working on.

General equipment

It is very easy to get carried away with buying equipment for a new studio but you can get started with a few key items as listed here, and build up your tool collection as and when you need them.

Pottery wheel

There are two main types of pottery wheel: electric and momentum. Which you use comes down to your own personal preference. An electric wheel is easy to use and is powered by a foot pedal that accelerates the speed. A momentum wheel (or kick wheel) requires more energy from the user because it is driven either by a fly-wheel pushed by the user's foot or via a foot-treadle, which is rocked back and forth. The direction the wheel spins in is important, too. In the West, the wheel typically spins anticlockwise, which favours the right-handed user. In the East, the wheel spins clockwise, requiring the user to work to the left. Most pottery wheels will have a function to accommodate both directions.

Kiln

A kiln is an essential piece of equipment for ceramic practice. The most common type is an electric kiln that has coiled elements embedded into the chamber walls. As electrical current is passed through the coils a radiant heat is produced, which fires the ware. Oxygen is present in the kiln throughout the firing. Electric kilns are straightforward to programme using a controller, which sets the firing schedule over a series of ramp segments. Alternatively, you may prefer a kiln that is fuelled by gas or solid fuels, including wood or coal. This is known as a reduction firing (no oxygen is present in the chamber). Kiln designs vary to suit an individual's needs. The two main designs are front loading: accessed from a door at the front, which is easier to load and unload; or a top loader: this is accessed from the top. Top loader kilns are generally cheaper to buy, but can be more awkward to load large works. For more information, see the text on Firing (p.46).

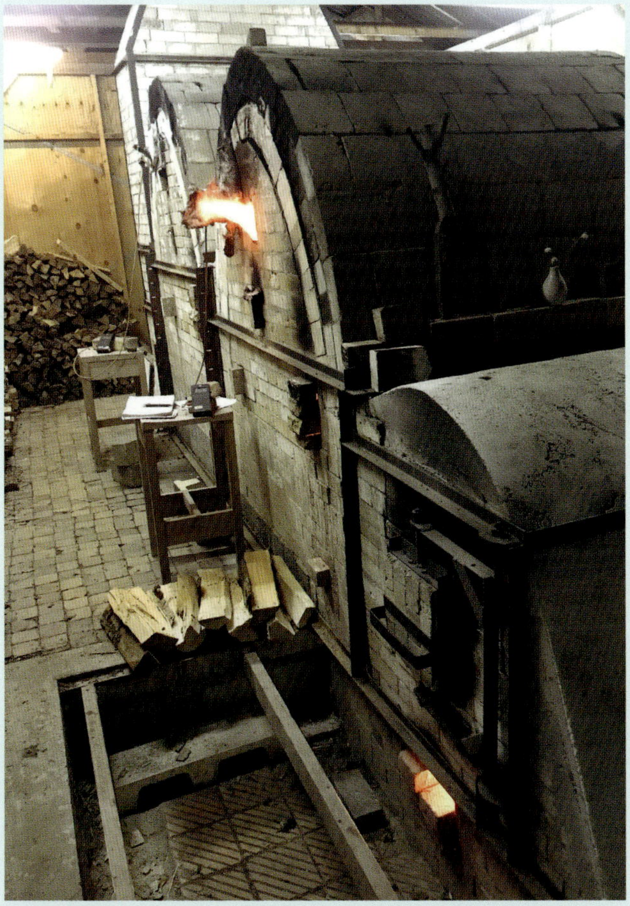

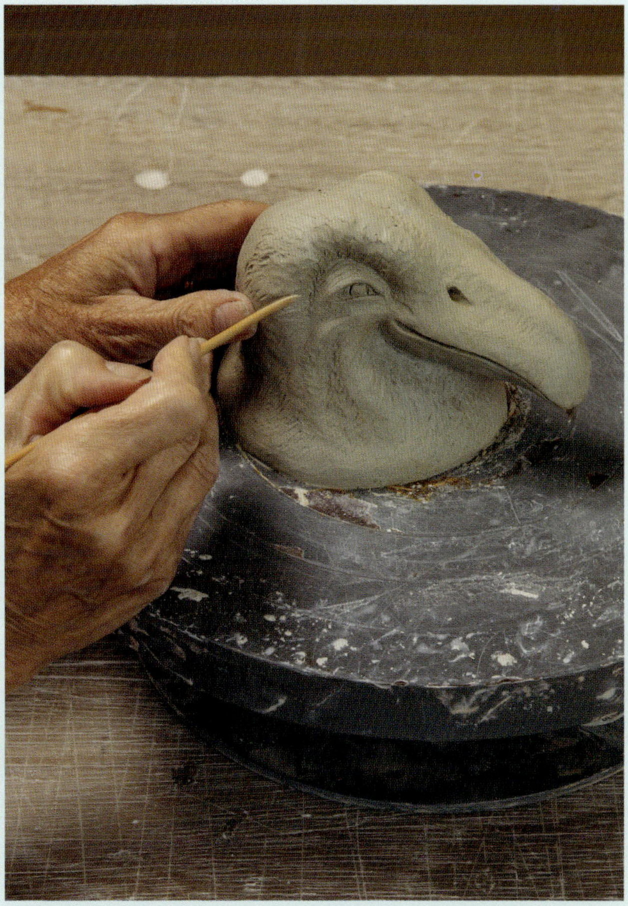

Studio tools

Banding wheel
Wooden paddles for shaping forms
Wooden boards to store and transport work
Wooden bats to fit on the pottery wheel
Plaster work: compass, plastic cottling, soft soap (barrier)
Rubber bands
Large weighing scales
Plastic wrap and newspaper to cover work
Fabric squares for rolling clay on
Rolling pin and wooden slats to gauge thickness
Towels, large sponge, buckets for cleaning
Apron or overalls – preferably wipe-clean rather than cloth, which can trap dust

Glazing and finishing tools

Dust mask, preferably with filter
Digital scales for weighing materials
Sieves for processing glaze material
Glaze tongs to grip work as it is submerged into glaze liquid
Plastic bowls for mixing
Measuring jugs
Wooden slats to stir glaze and support the sieve when mixing a glaze
Protective gloves – latex/non-latex for mixing and preparing glaze
Lidded containers to store glaze materials
Diamond pad and wet-and-dry sandpaper for removing flaws and polishing surfaces smooth

Firing tools

Heat-resistant gloves for handling hot items from the kiln
Kiln and kiln furniture, including shelves and props
Bat wash to extend the life of your kiln shelves

Basic techniques

At the heart of all ceramics techniques are skill and application. There are numerous ways to achieve an outcome using clay, and techniques like coil building are relatively straightforward to implement with minimum experience; other techniques such as throwing, however, require an investment of time and perseverance. Ultimately, the joy comes from just exploring the material and making discoveries along the way. Here is an overview of the main construction techniques used in the production of ceramics.

Preparation

Good preparation of clay prior to working helps to reduce the risk of technical issues, such as the warping and distortion that may arise through an inconsistent mix – especially if clay has been stored for a long time. This is particularly important for throwing clay, where a smooth, homogenous consistency will aid the technique. The two most common techniques are wedging (cut and slice) and kneading (ox-head or spiral method). If you are only able to master one, then ox-head kneading is the most accessible. It is much like kneading bread dough; clay is rotated through the hands and pushed back at regular intervals. Each time, this creates a layer that squeezes out trapped air and blends the material together. The kneaded block should resemble its namesake, an ox-head shape.

Joining

If you take two bits of soft clay and simply press them together, they may initially stick but will eventually fall apart as the clay dries out. This is because the clay surface has nothing to grip onto as it shrinks. Therefore, it is very important to join clay with a physical bond. This technique is called cross-hatching and involves using a pointed tool, such as a pottery needle or knife, to score the areas to be joined with vigorous marks, followed by a coating of slip, which acts as the glue to stick it all together. You should use this technique for joining leather-hard clay and in-between coils and other hand-built forms. Don't be too dainty with your scoring – scratch substantial angles and undercuts into your surface, as this will lead to a more secure bond and reduce the risk of cracking.

Cracks

Technical flaws and cracks go hand in hand with ceramics and can strike at any point in the making process. The unforgiving nature of the material can lead to huge disappointment, especially when lots of time and effort have been invested in a piece. However, common, and sometimes avoidable, mistakes in the making and drying stages are often the reason: poor preparation, clay being too dry when joined, over-handling of a piece or drying too quickly can all cause cracking. Cracks that

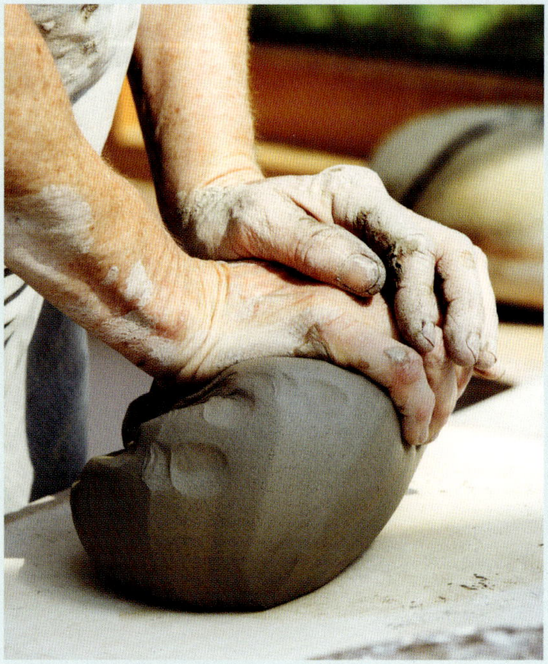

(Above) Kneading clay
Clay should be thoroughly kneaded and prepared prior to use, especially for throwing.

(Right) Joining clay
To minimize the risk of cracking, cross-hatch the areas to be joined with a series of scratched lines, followed by an application of slurry (a mix of clay body and water).

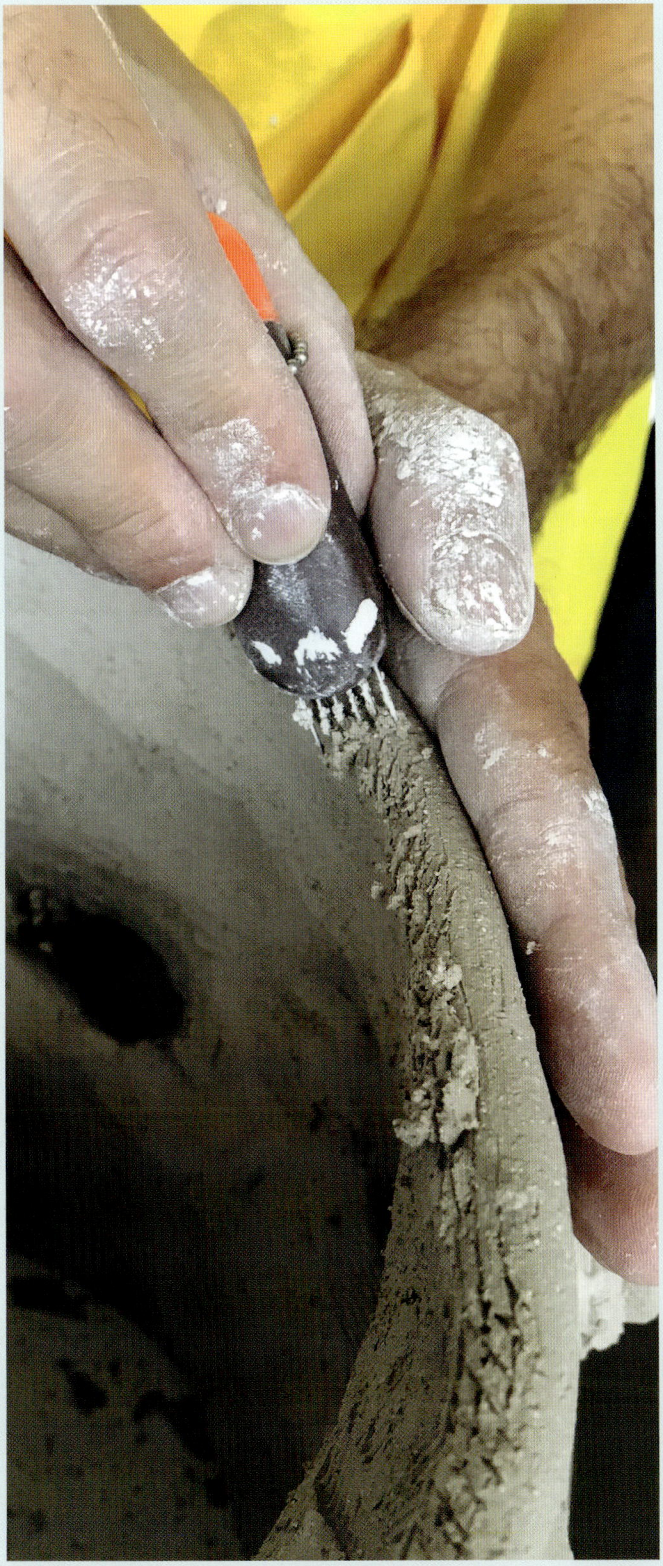

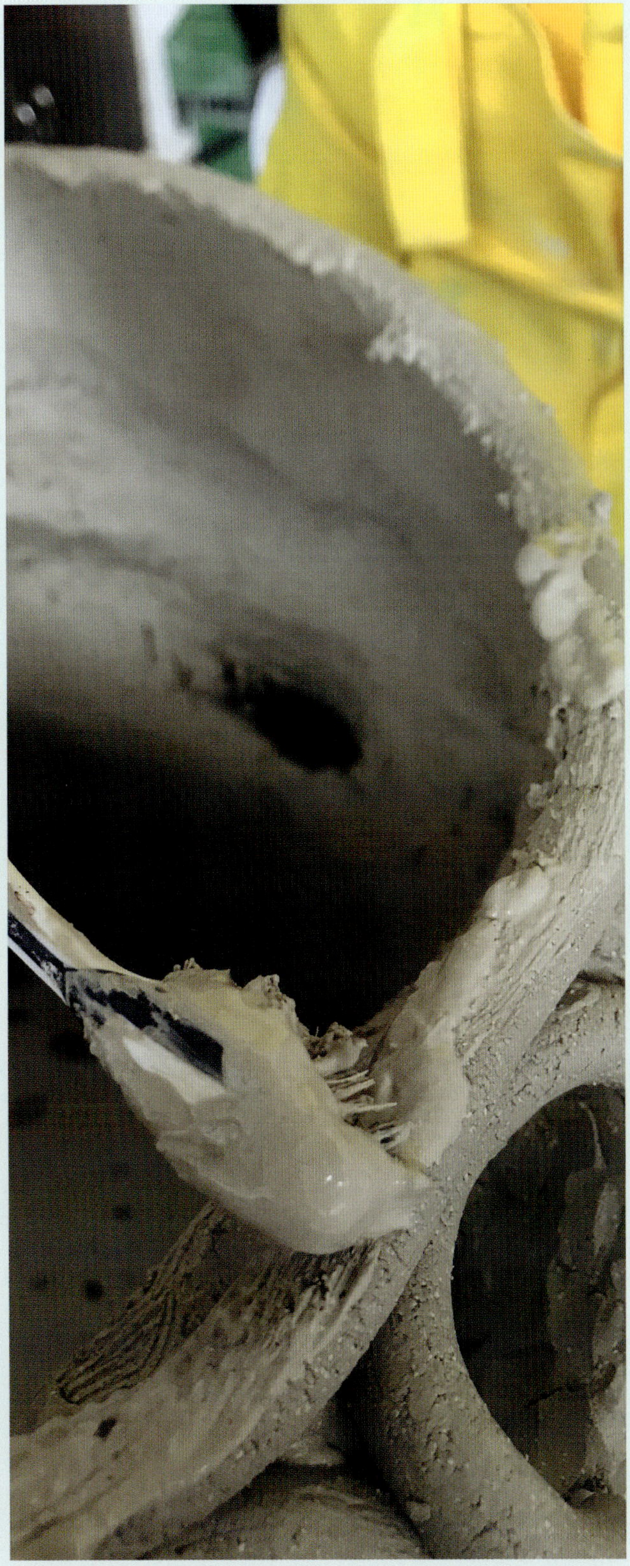

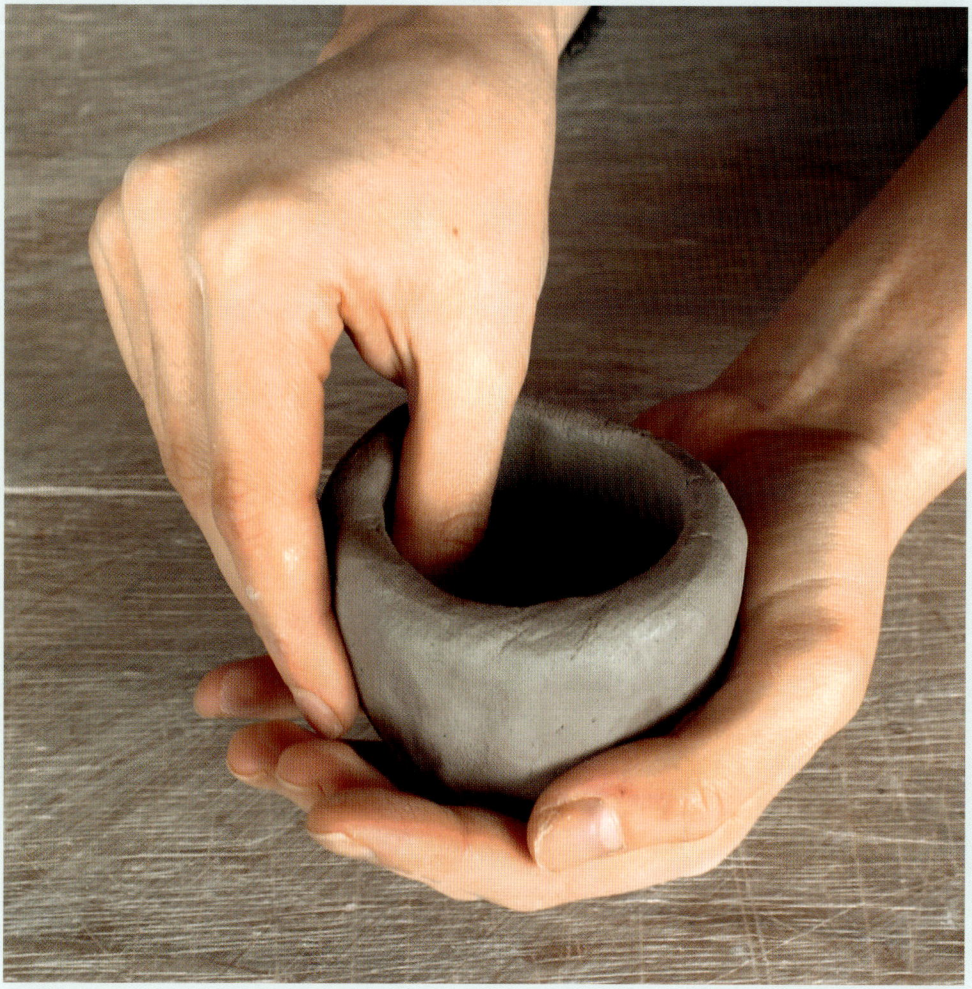

(Left) Pinching technique
You can form a very simple pot in clay just with the pinching motion of your thumb and fingers.

(Right) Coil building
A long coil is attached to the vessel and smoothed into position before adding the next one.

occur during firing can be caused by poor compatibility between clay body and glaze, inconsistent firing schedules or simply by opening the kiln while it is too hot. Through experience and perseverance you can overcome many of these issues. Good preparation will build up your resilience to the unpredictability of clay, and anticipating the high failure rate by preparing spares and allowing for extra time will stand you in good stead.

Forming processes

Manipulating clay by simply squeezing and shaping it between your hands feels very intuitive and has been the predominant method of ceramic fabrication for thousands of years. Hand building is very accessible for beginners or those with less experience, as you can achieve a lot with just a few basic techniques.

Pinching

If you have memories of using clay at school, it is most likely you made a pinch pot. Pinching is a very versatile technique, involving just the movement of fingers against the wall of a clay vessel. It is often used in conjunction with coiling and slab-work to thin out areas or soften edges. To begin, start with a rounded ball of clay placed in the palm of your hand. Take the thumb on your other hand and insert it into the centre of the ball with your fingers on the outside wall. Apply a little pressure between your fingertips and thumb and gently rotate the pot as you raise the walls. The difficultly lies in controlling the shape and retaining a strong profile. You may need to allow the pot to firm to leather-hard stage before you refine it further. Building on these skills, you can use the pinching technique to sculpt and add tactility to thrown and press-moulded forms.

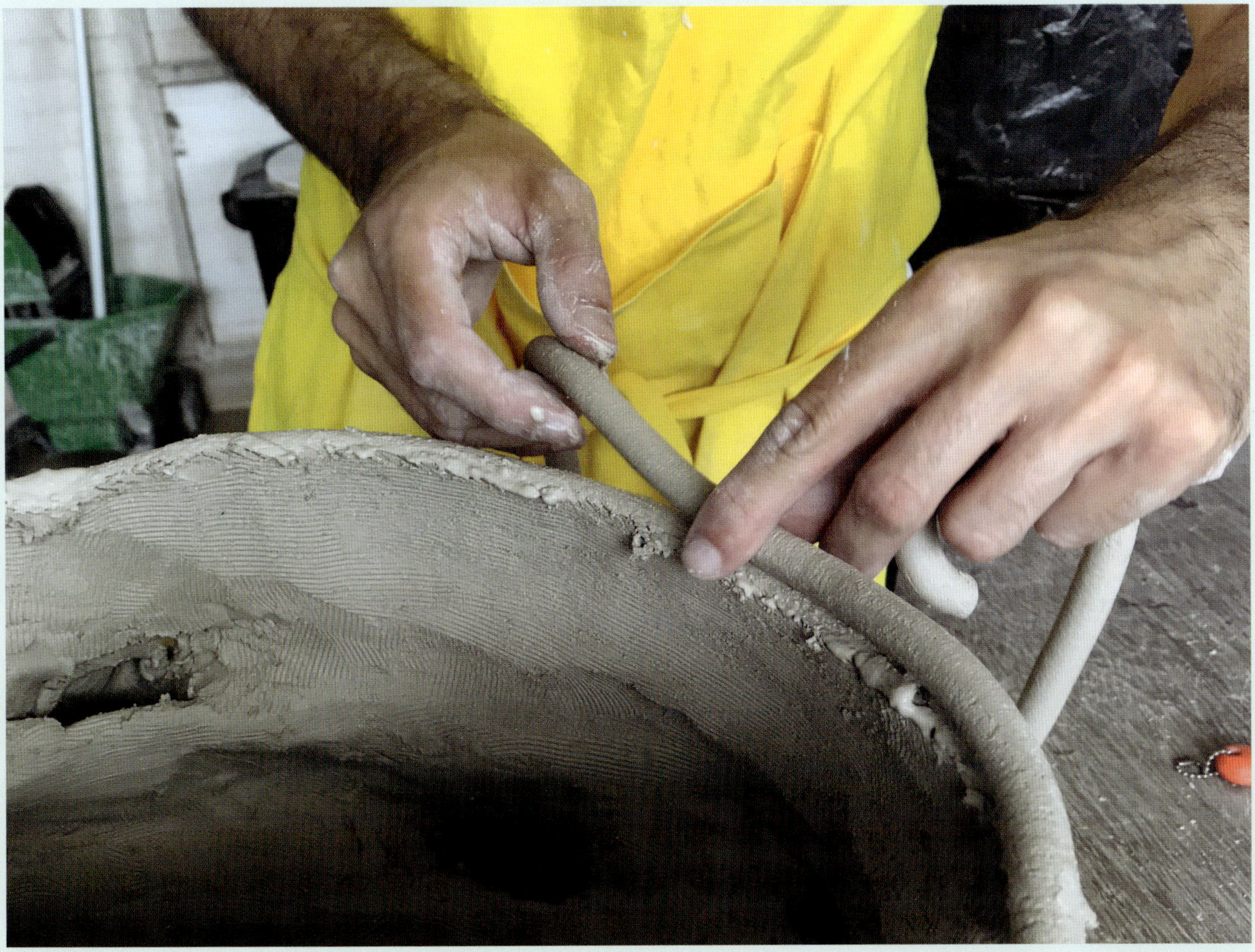

Coil building

Coiling is an organic process, allowing the maker more time to respond to their piece as it gradually takes shape. First you need to roll out (either by hand or using an extruder) long sausages of clay of even size and consistency. It is sensible to prepare a large batch of coils in advance and wrap them in plastic so that you do not have to interrupt your making. To start forming your piece, first roll out its base to the size and shape of your pot. Cross-hatch and apply slip before joining your first coil. Hold the coil high in one hand and with the other strike your thumb downward to smear the clay. Continue to add more coils, pausing at intervals of five to six coils to blend everything together. You can do this with a wooden tool or a serrated metal kidney. Coil pots can sag under their own weight, so you may need to firm the clay with a heat-gun or blowtorch before proceeding to add more coils. You can shape your pot by tapping it lightly with a wooden paddle or by cutting out triangular darts of clay and stitching them back together. To finish, you can refine the form with a surform tool to remove lumps, followed by scraping and smoothing with metal and rubber kidney tools.

Slab building

The benefit of constructing with slabs is that it enables you to build a form relatively quickly and on a large scale. Ideally the clay should be at leather-hard stage in order to have some rigidity when it is handled and manoeuvred into position. You can prepare a slab in a similar way to rolling pastry. Roll your clay on top of a fabric sheet to prevent it from sticking to the bench. You can set the thickness of your slab by rolling on top of wooden slats cut to a depth of your choice. Roll the clay in different directions, turning the slab over and around to ensure an even consistency and to prevent warping. When joining slabs together, cross-hatch and coat with slip thoroughly – otherwise your piece could crack down the seams. You can also prepare slabs by drawing a bow-harp through a block of clay or by flattening clay through a slab roller – a type of press that is useful for preparing large sheets of clay.

Hand moulding

Clay can be shaped into a multitude of forms by either pressing small wads or a sheet of clay into an internal profile or by laying it over a former (hump mould). Moulds are typically made from plaster, which is used for its absorbent properties. This method is a quick way to create a recognizable shape – for example, a shallow dish – with relative ease. You can also exploit the transferable qualities of clay by rolling it out onto textured panels or you could make your own moulds from found items. Another advantage to moulding is that it allows the maker to produce batches of identical objects or limited runs.

Slip casting

Slip casting derives from an industrial ceramic process in which liquid clay (held in suspension) is poured into a plaster mould to create an accurate cast. The quality of the resulting cast is incredibly crisp and precise compared to a press-moulded cast. Usually, the model is sculpted from plaster, clay, wood or foam. In modern practice, many artists design their models using CAD software and have them 3D printed. This opens up potential for highly complex and intricate designs that would be very challenging to sculpt by hand. Depending on the size and shape of the model, the mould is prepared in a series of segments to aid the release of the cast item. To take a cast, slip is poured into the mould and left for a duration of time – approximately five to twenty minutes – after which it is emptied and the cast left to firm before being removed from the mould.

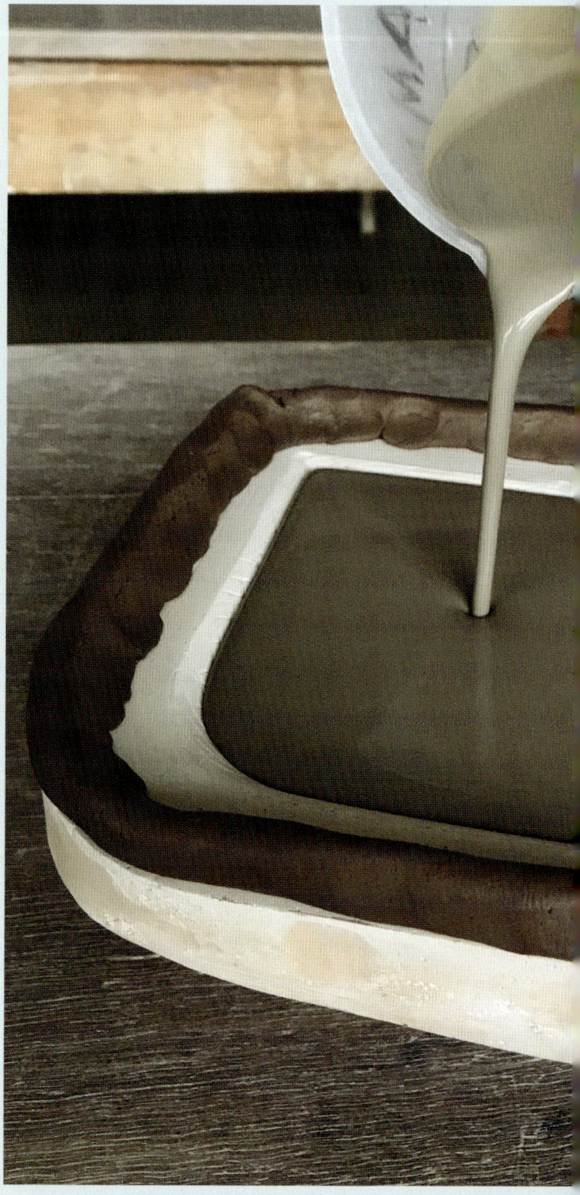

Throwing

Throwing on the pottery wheel is a wonderfully rewarding skill to learn. It is very challenging and can be likened to learning a musical instrument or new language. The general understanding is that it takes around 10,000 hours to become accomplished. Therefore, it is important to allow yourself time to learn and not set unrealistic expectations. Ultimately, the key to success is lots of practice and repetition. Throwing is built on the principle of centrifugal force – the outward force on a mass when rotated. The skill lies in the potter being in control of the clay and preventing it from collapsing. There are three key stages of throwing:

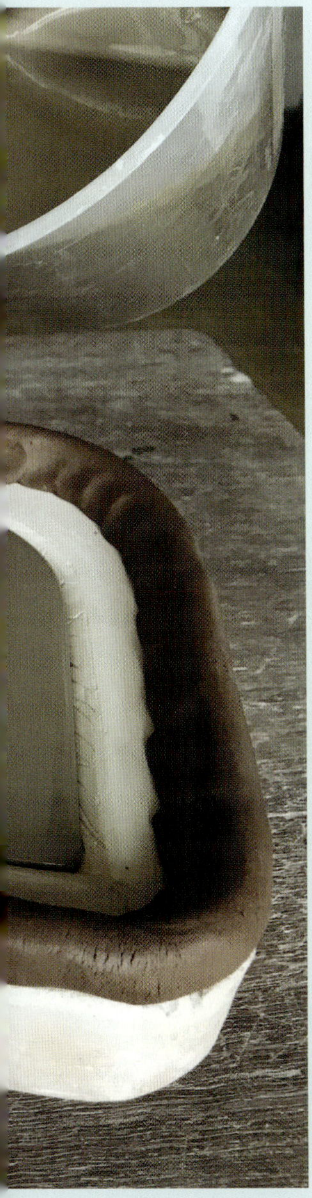

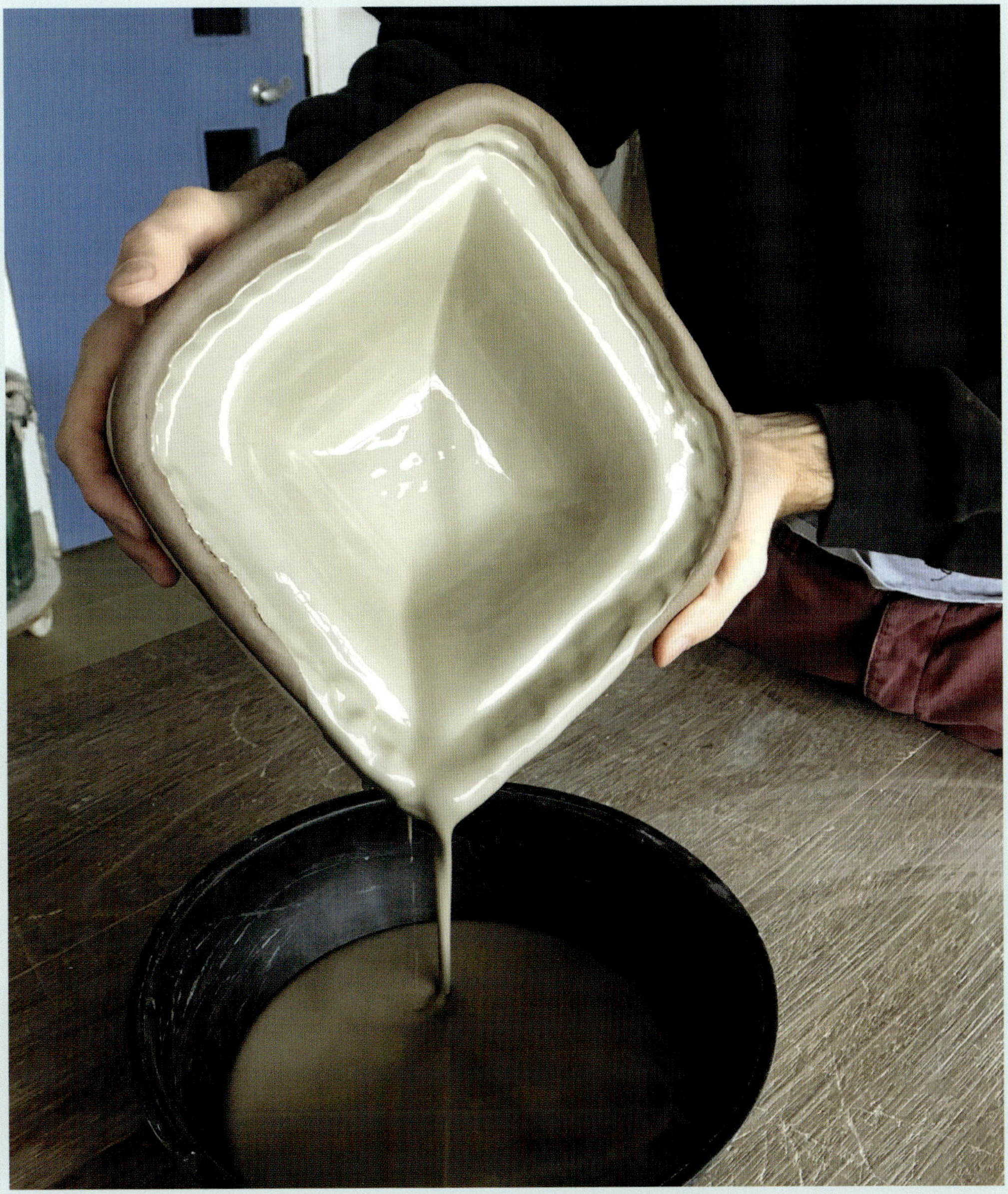

Slip casting
An example of a simple drop-out mould for slip casting. A clay coil is attached to the mould to form a reservoir. Casting slip is poured into the mould and left for approximately 10 minutes before being poured out. From here you can move onto making more complex, multi-part moulds.

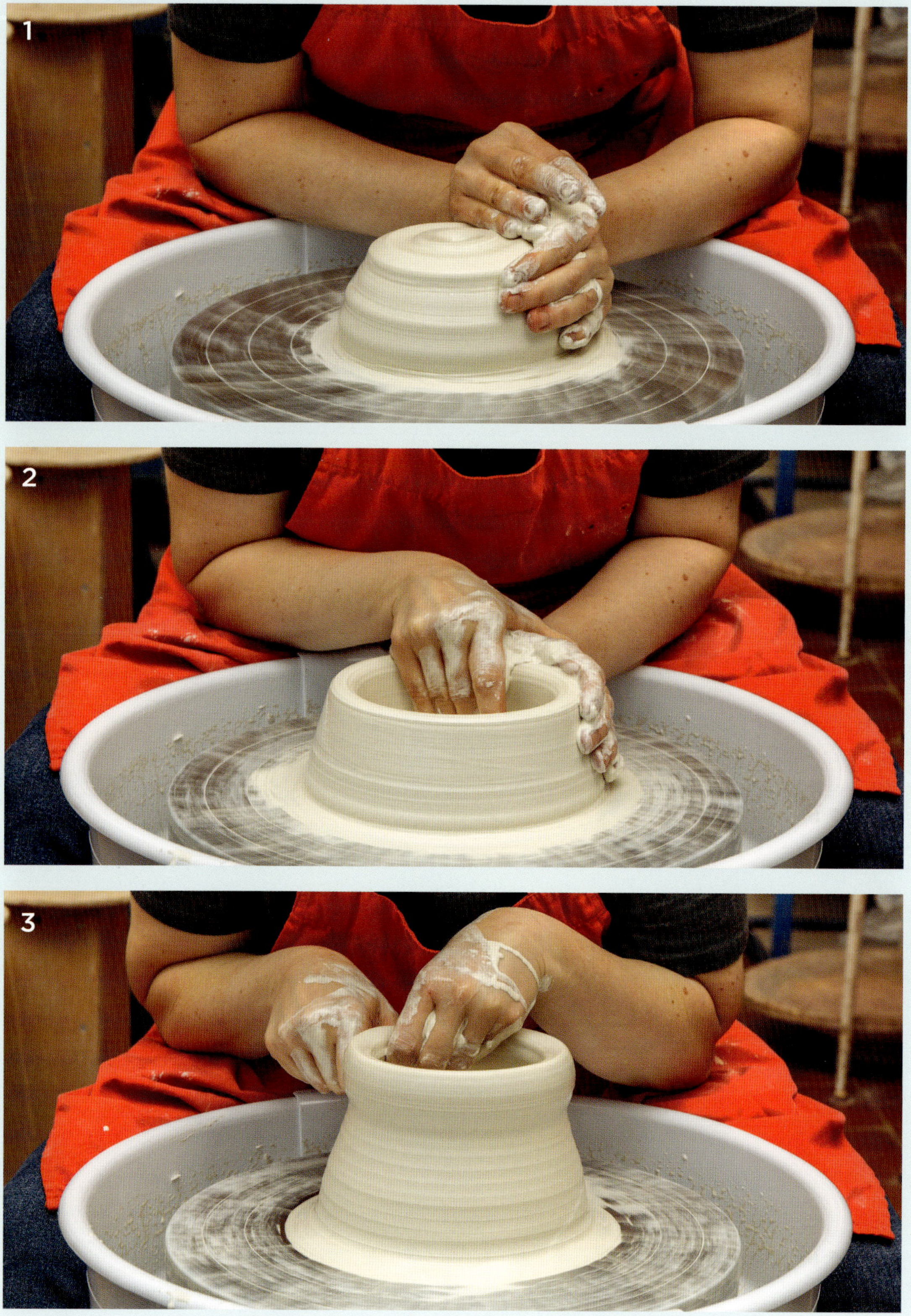
1
2
3

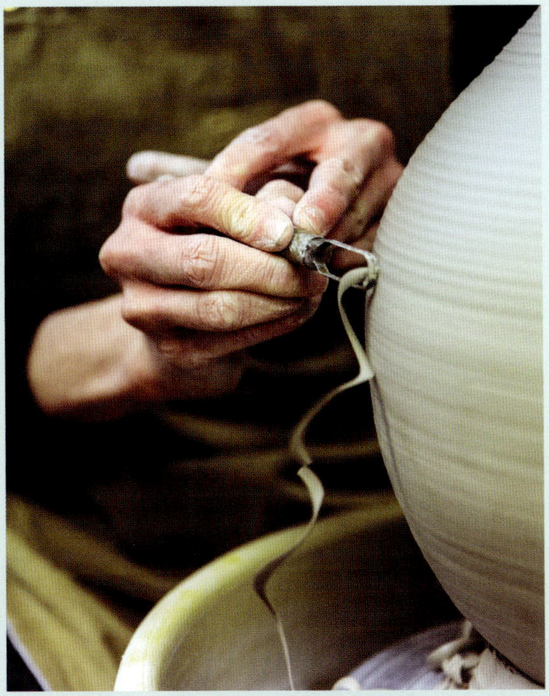

(Above) **Trimming/turning**
The purpose of trimming/turning is to refine the profile of a form and/or add finishing details such as a foot ring on a bowl or a knob on a lid.

1. Centring: Pressure is applied through the hands to transform an uneven ball of clay into a smooth dome that runs true. This stage can be very difficult and is often where beginners struggle. The wheel should be spinning fast to exploit the centrifugal force bearing down on the clay.

2. Making the base: Once the clay is centred, a hole can be created in the middle of the ball and opened up to form the base. This stage requires a medium speed.

3. Pulling up the walls: This is the magical part of the process when the pot walls are formed. The clay is swelled outwards from inside to create a ridge and the clay is drawn upwards with the knuckle, expanding the height of the vessel. A slow speed maintains control of the pot, allowing the profile to be shaped and refined. Once finished, the pot is sliced at the base with a wire and lifted off the wheel. Clay has a memory and even though it distorts as the piece is moved, it will spring straight back into shape when placed on a board.

Water should be used throughout the throwing process to lubricate the clay. The key to success with throwing is to accomplish a cylinder form. Challenge yourself to make 100 identical pots. You can learn a lot just by cutting up the pot to check the wall thickness is consistent. From here, you can move on to a bowl, bottles and enclosed forms.

Trimming/turning

To finish a thrown form, you can shape and trim away excess clay once it has reached the leather-hard stage. Unlike throwing, you do not need to use water for this process. Place the pot upside down on the wheelhead, and re-centre it before you begin, otherwise you will end up with uneven wall thickness. This can be tricky but comes with practice. Most pottery wheels have concentric circles carved into the metal wheelhead. You can use these as a guide to line up your pot. Another method is to rotate the wheel at a medium speed and, with a sharp tap of the hand, the pull of centrifugal force will bring your pot back on centre. Place three straps of clay at the rim to secure your pot to the wheelhead. With a steady hand and sharp tool, trim clay away in long ribbons. This process can radically change your work from rough to sleek finished piece; however, there is always a risk that your lovingly crafted piece can be turned into a flowerpot by accidently trimming away too much clay from the base.

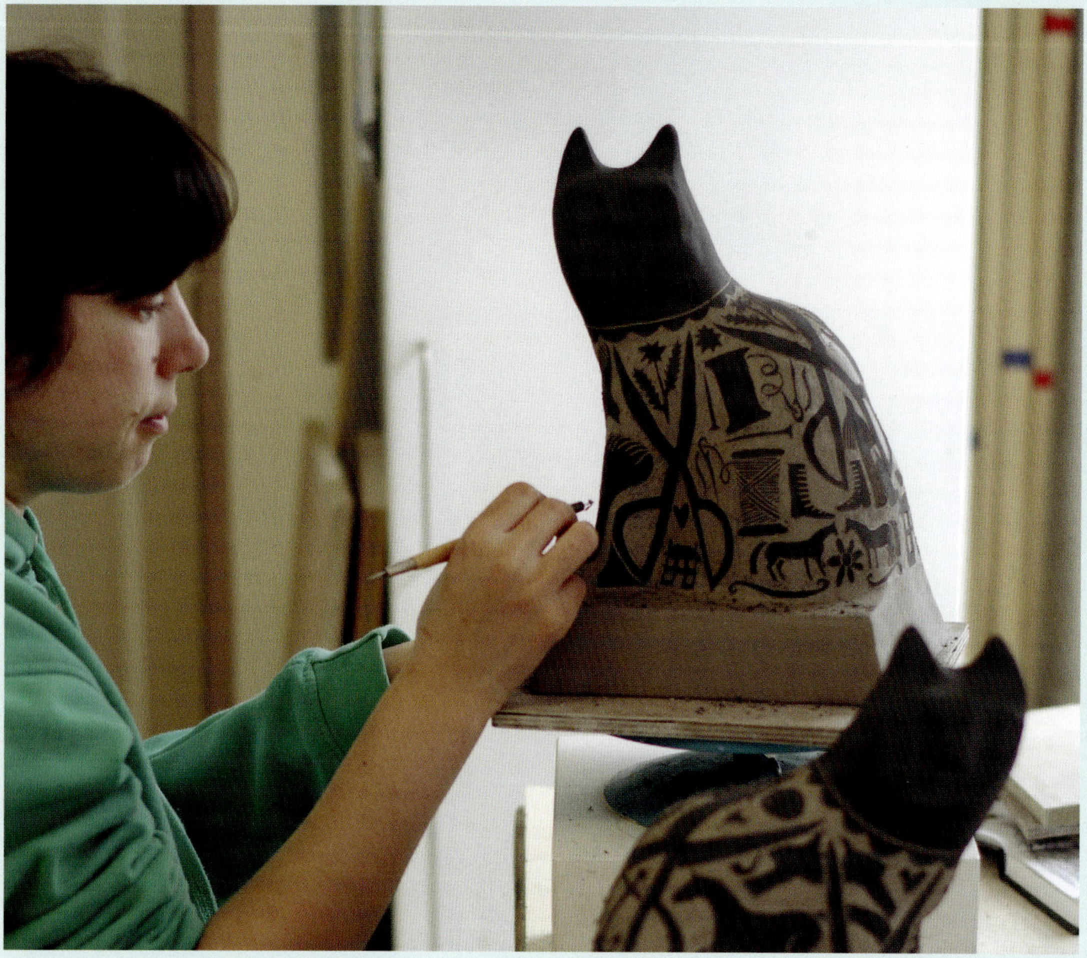

Decoration

Unlike painting in the conventional sense, ceramic decorative processes have to be subjected to a firing process. With this comes great excitement, entwined with feelings of nervousness – as one is never fully in control of the final outcome. Below, the main methods of decorating your work are described.

Slip decoration

Slip is liquid clay made from water and dry clay powder, coloured with oxide or commercial stain – it is not the same as casting slip. Slip decoration is one of the oldest ceramic techniques and it dates back centuries. The beauty of this technique comes from its simplicity. Slip is applied to leather-hard clay and the artist is free to treat the clay as a canvas. Traditional techniques include marbling, feathering, stencilling, slip trailing, painting, sgraffito and many more. Once the piece has been bisque fired, the slip decoration is coated in a transparent or honey glaze to accentuate the rich colours.

Glaze

A glaze is a layer of glass fused to the ceramic surface. Its purpose is to offer a practical coating that is impenetrable to water, as well as for aesthetic value. As you will see throughout this book, many of the featured artists push the definition of glaze to the extreme and create works of extraordinary intrigue and beauty. One of the most difficult challenges with glazing is that it looks very different in its raw state to the way it looks when it has been fired. This is partly why ceramics can be very addictive – swaying from moments of huge euphoria to utter dismay. For this reason, it is very important to test your glazes before decorating your work in order to avoid disappointment.

(Left) Sgraffito technique
Artist Vicky Lindo decorates her cat forms by scratching through a layer of coloured slip to reveal an attractive contrast between the pattern and clay body.

(Right) Ceramic transfer sheets
A selection of ready-made ceramic transfer sheets purchased from a pottery supplier. You can also design your own and get them made digitally or screen-printed by a specialist company.

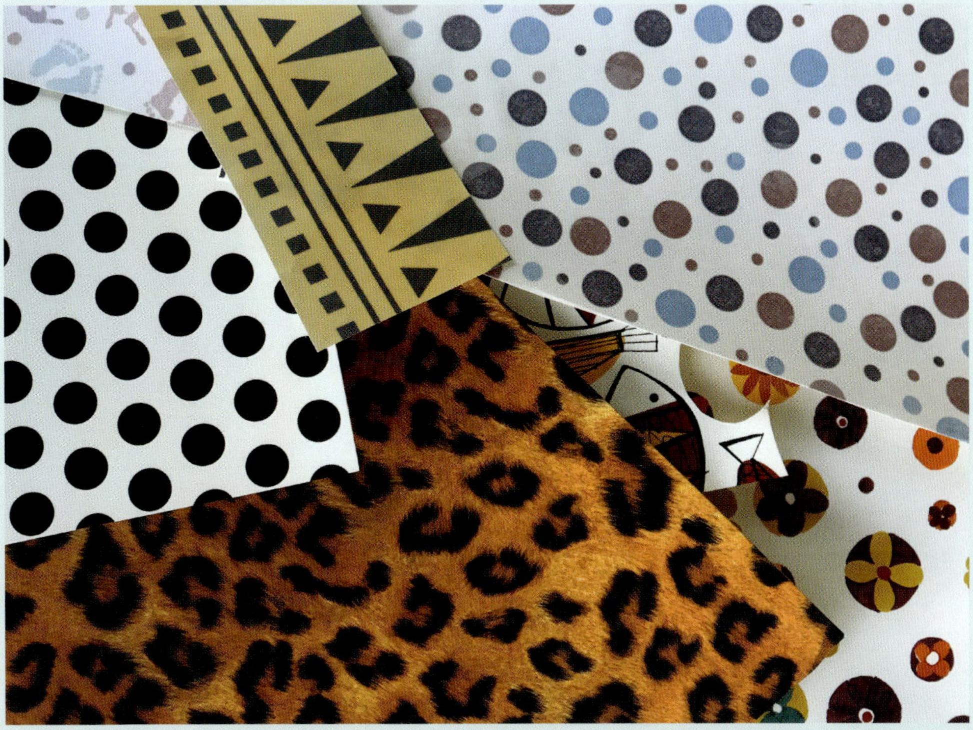

Glazes can be made from scratch, in much the same way as mixing a cake recipe. Raw materials are weighed out in specific quantities. A glaze formula has three principal parts:

- **Silica:** The main glass former, naturally occurring in flint and quartz. Silica has a very high melting point of 1700°C (3092°F).
- **Flux:** This is required to lower the melting point to a more achievable temperature.
- **Alumina:** The third part of a glaze, alumina, comes from clay-based materials, which bring stability to the glaze and aid adhesion to the pot.

Glaze is applied to a bisque surface by either dipping, pouring or submerging in a bucket of liquid glaze material. Large pieces can be glazed using a gravity-feed spray gun and compressor. Avoid painting glaze with a brush (unless it is a specifically a brush-on glaze) as this can lead to patchy results. Other points of consideration are the firing temperature of the recipe, the clay body (see Firing, p.46) and the purpose of the object – is it functional, sculptural, decorative? All these factors will impact on the suitability of the glaze you use. If you prefer not to make your own glazes, you can buy ready-made formulas and brush-ons from a fantastic selection stocked by a pottery supplier.

Enamels, lustres and transfers

Post-glaze, you may wish to enrich your surfaces further with one of these low-temperature techniques. Enamels (china paints) are a type of fritted glass that is ideal for painting fine decoration and illustrations. If you are after a more opulent effect, lustres offer bright golds, silvers or iridescent mother-of-pearl finishes. Transfers can be used to create playful patterns and imagery on your glazed surfaces.

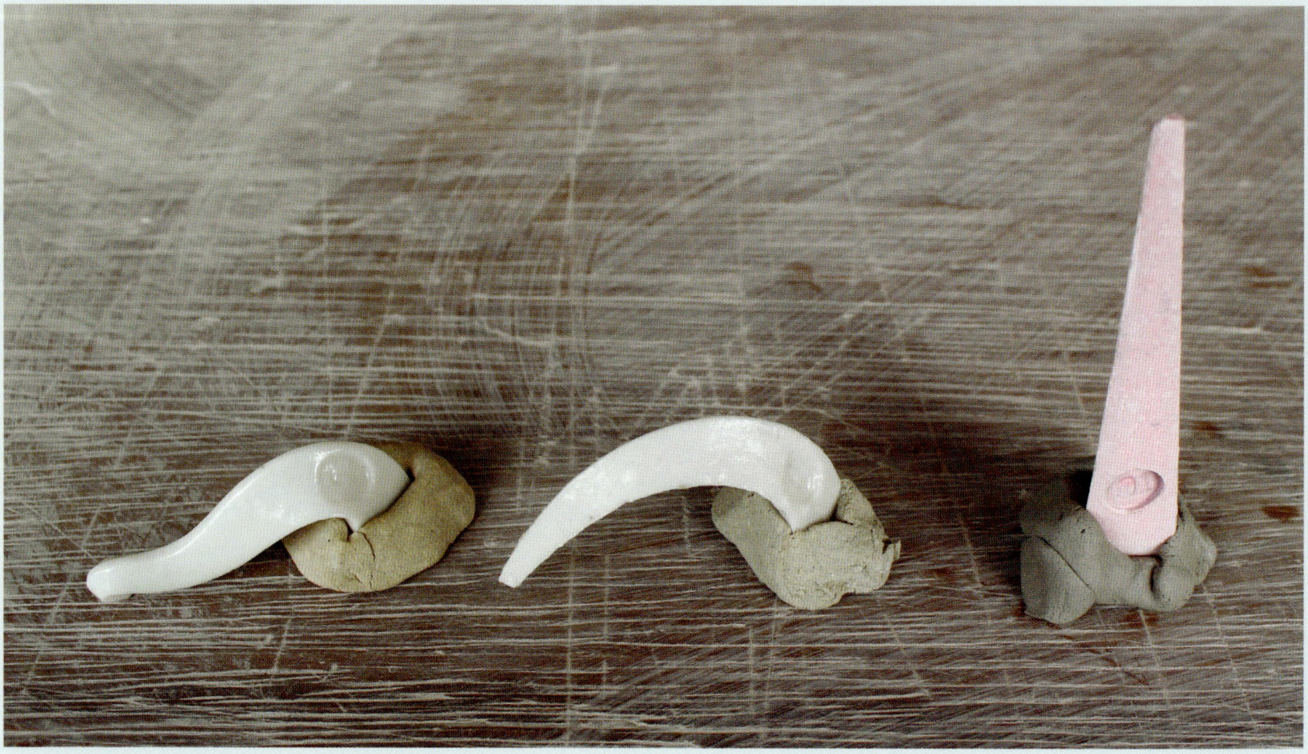

Firing

Clay is not ceramic until it has surpassed a temperature of 573°C (1063°F). This is when clay goes through a transformation called the quartz inversion. The chemical bonds between the clay structure become fixed and the process is now irreversible. Firing is a critical part of the ceramic process and can have a dramatic impact on the outcome of your work. The aim of a successful firing is to get to the point where both clay and glaze have reached maturity. A typical firing can take around twelve hours to complete, plus cooling. You should not open a glaze firing above 80°C (176°F) or you could risk cracking your work.

Bisque (or biscuit): Firing temperature 970–1180°C (1778–2156°F)

Clay can be fired from raw straight up to its final temperature. However, the bisque stage offers a point in between where the ceramic can be handled but remains porous enough to accept glaze. The temperature of the bisque is important for the next step.

Earthenware: Firing temperature 1040–1180°C (1940–2150°F)

Some clays (for example, red earthenware) have a low melting point and cannot be fired to a high temperature. Earthenware provides a point where colours remain bright and there is less strain on the work. The downside is that earthenware clay bodies are porous and can chip easily. Earthenware requires a high bisque firing (1120–1180°C/(2048–2156°F) followed by low-temperature glaze firing.

Stoneware: Firing temperature 1200–1300°C (2192–2372°F)

Stoneware is a much higher temperature firing, which can put a lot of strain and stress on a piece of work; however, the pay-off is a strong and hardy material. The clay body is now vitrified and no longer porous. Colours are generally more muted than earthenware. Bisque is low-temperature firing (1000°C/1832°F) followed by high-temperature glaze firing.

Oxidized/Reduction

The kiln environment within the chamber can greatly affect the outcome of your work. Electric kilns use radiant heat and oxygen is present throughout the firing. Kilns that use a combustible fuel source are heated by a flame that consumes the oxygen in the kiln to increase the temperature. As the oxygen is removed, this creates a reduction atmosphere. The flame draws oxygen from wherever it can, including from oxides in the glaze. Copper oxide in an oxidized atmosphere is green, whereas in reduction it transforms to a beautiful blood-red.

(Left) Pyrometric cones
Pyrometric cones placed in the kiln chamber act as a firing record and can be a useful way to track the heat work that occurred during the firing. Right: the cone is prepared for the firing with a wad of clay. Centre: the perfect arch indicates the required temperature has been reached. Left: the temperature has surpassed.

(Right) Raku firing
Raku is a rapid-firing technique. Here, the kiln was opened when the temperature reached 1000°C (1832°F). The ceramic items inside glow an intense bright orange colour. They are carefully extracted from the chamber with tongs.

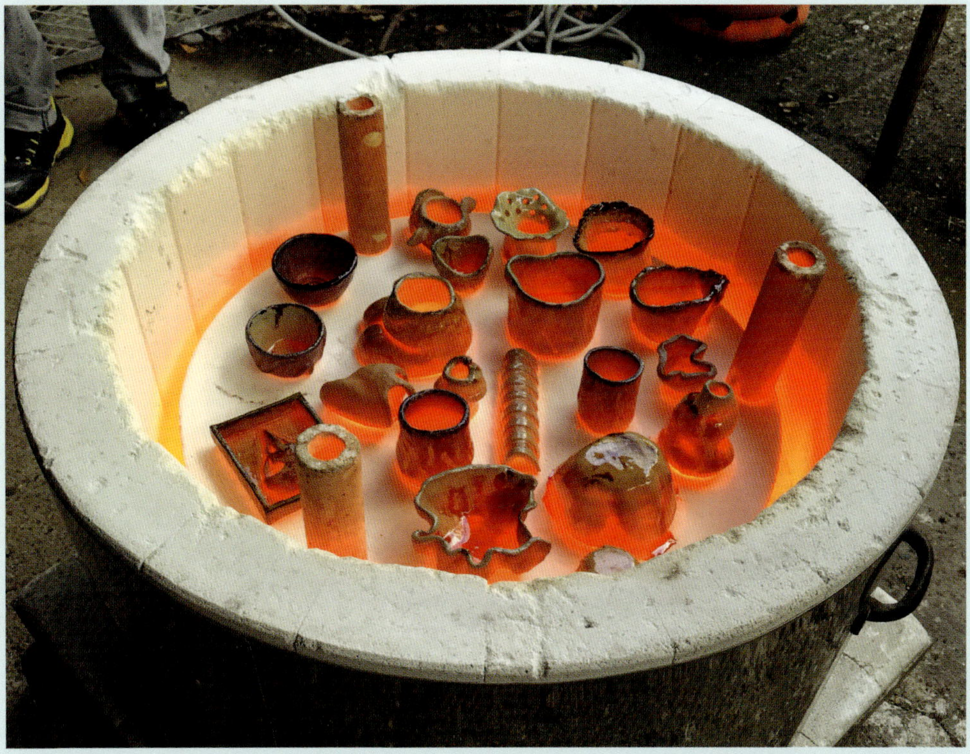

Soaking

Once the kiln has reached its top temperature, it is held at this point for a duration of time in order to even out inconsistency of temperature between the bottom and top of the kiln chamber. Soaking can help bring your glazes to a point of maturity and intensify the results.

Low firing techniques: pit, smoke and raku firing

These types of firing derive from ancient techniques and can be rudimentary ways to fire your pots. Pit and smoke firing just require a shallow chamber dug into the ground. Pots are buried in sawdust, ignited and left to smoke. This can create wonderful smoky effects. Raku stems from the traditional Japanese tea ceremony. The basis of the technique involves rapidly firing pots to around 1000°C (1832°F), after which they are taken from the kiln red-hot and placed in a bed of sawdust and left to reduce. Raku produces a beautiful crackle effect and iridescent colours.

Health and safety

Good health and safety practice within ceramics cannot be emphasized enough. Clay and ceramic materials contain silica which is incredibly harmful to your health and can lead to a serious lung condition called silicosis, so dust management is vital.

- Benches, tools and surfaces should be cleaned regularly with a sponge and bucket of water. Vacuum and mop floors at the end of the day. Do not dry sweep.
- Wash cloth aprons and overalls – consider wearing plastic/ wipe-clean fabrics that do not hold dust.
- Where contact with dry material is unavoidable, always wear a suitable dust mask with filters. It should fit flush against the skin.
- Do not eat, drink or smoke in the studio.
- Be kind to your back and avoid heavy lifting and awkward movements. Manoeuvring shelves in and out of the kiln and lifting moulds full of slip can all risk jarring your back. Bend your knees when lifting heavy items and keep the item close to your body.
- Beware hot exterior parts of kilns and wear gloves if you are removing hot kiln shelves. Make sure there are no combustible materials left in the kiln room and ensure good ventilation.
- Tie loose hair back and remove jewelry around machinery.
- Wear gloves when mixing glazes, especially if you are using toxic materials or have any open cuts/wounds.
- Ceramic materials that derive from lead and in combination with metallic oxides such as copper, have the potential to leach from glazes when in contact with acidic foodstuffs such as tea or lemon juice. It is a legal requirement in many countries to have your ware laboratory-tested for lead release.

Vesse

Objects defined as vessels are rooted in past associations with utilitarian wares used for storage, cooking and serving of food. This link can be explored in artworks, to signify the containment of meaningful thought and ideas. The vessel form shares much in common with expressions of the human body. Its various proportions are referred to as the foot, belly, shoulders, and neck. Starting with these principles in mind, you could exaggerate proportions of your vessel like the wide flared vase by Lucie Rie (p.54), or bellied shape of Gabriele Koch's smoke-fired pot (p.64). This may continue with explorations of volume, space, and containment like the sculptural pots of Toshiko Takaezu (p.56) or Hans Coper (p.58).

The vessel can be explored as an art form, for example abstracting it as seen in the works of Elizabeth Fritsch (p.60) and Alison Britton (p.72), to deconstruct and re-establish the notion of conventional form. Like Peter Voulkos (p.68), you may pursue a more physical approach to your making, in such a way that the form evolves organically as a result of spontaneous and intuitive intent. This approach could equally be very controlled and minimal like the sleek intersecting vessels by Ruth Duckworth (p.66).

The process of slip-casting appealed to the artists Monika Patuszyńska (p.76) and Matt Davis (p.78) for their vessel forms, and like them you could experiment with your moulding processes to create unique distortions. Groupings and composition could be another area to explore, learning from artists like Gwyn Hanssen Pigott (p.70), who displays vessels together in thoughtful arrangements.

William Staite Murray

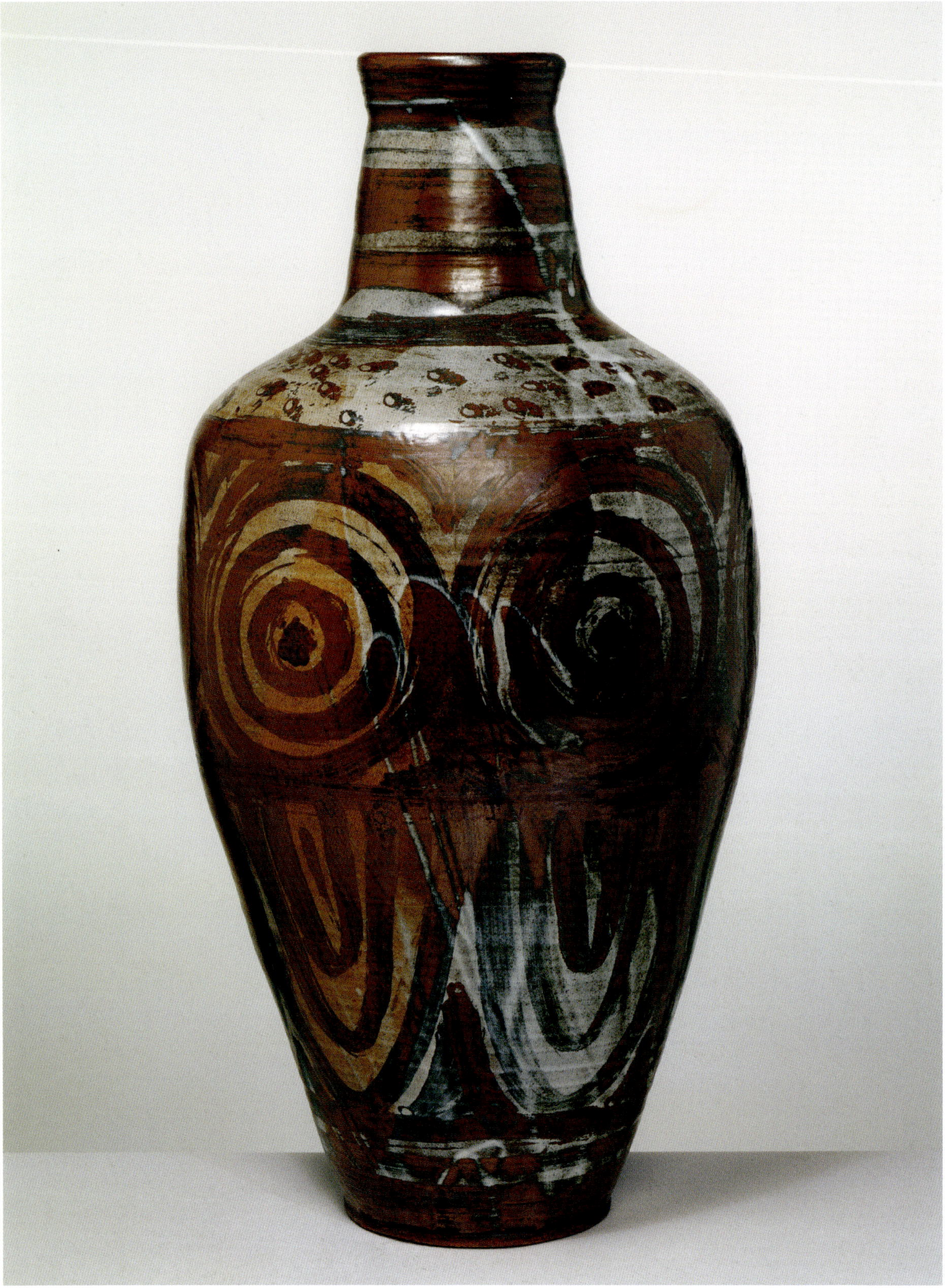

Wheel of Life *c.* 1939

Stoneware with painted decoration
63 × 30 cm (24¾ × 11¾ in.)

Like his contemporary Bernard Leach, William Staite Murray was influenced by the refinement of Chinese ceramics from the Song Dynasty (AD 960–1279). However, unlike Leach, whose ambition was to mass-produce handmade pottery, Staite Murray's works were objects of art and on a level equal to painting and sculpture. Staite Murray's close association with the abstract art movement led him to develop sophisticated gestural brush work and painterly surfaces. He was less interested in functional elements, such as handles and spouts, and his catalogue of works is predominantly made up of vase, bottle or bowl forms. In the early 1920s, Staite Murray met the Japanese potter – and Bernard Leach's friend – Shōji Hamada, who inspired him to experiment with the Chinese glaze colours that formed the foundation of his earthy palette, including glossy *tenmoku* blacks and metallic *shino* reds.

Tall in stature and elegantly thrown, this vase has a figurative quality suggested by the high shoulders and elongated neck of the vessel. Staite Murray created a lively surface by first covering the vase in a light grey glaze and then overpainting bold, abstract decoration with rich red-brown glaze. Large swirling circles are interrupted by energetic 'U'-shaped brushstrokes that generously undulate and curve around the lower part of the form. Dabs and dots of glaze speckle the neck, hemmed by thick banding lines. Scratchy marks made by individual strands of the brush are visible through the thickness of the glaze and the layering of decoration provides visual depth and an overall feeling of movement.

William Staite Murray (British, 1881–1962) studied painting in France before taking pottery evening classes at Camberwell School of Art and Crafts in London between 1909 and 1912. While at Camberwell he explored earthenware forms with painted decoration. In 1919, Staite Murray established his first studio in Rotherhithe, south-east London, and associated with avant-garde painters involved with the Vorticist movement. In 1925, he was appointed Head of Ceramics at the Royal College of Art, London. At the outbreak of World War II in 1939, Staite Murray and his wife became stranded when visiting relatives in Rhodesia (now Zimbabwe) and settled in the country, but he never made pottery again.

See also

Pippin Drysdale (p.122)
Bernard Leach (p.136)
Shōji Hamada (p.140)

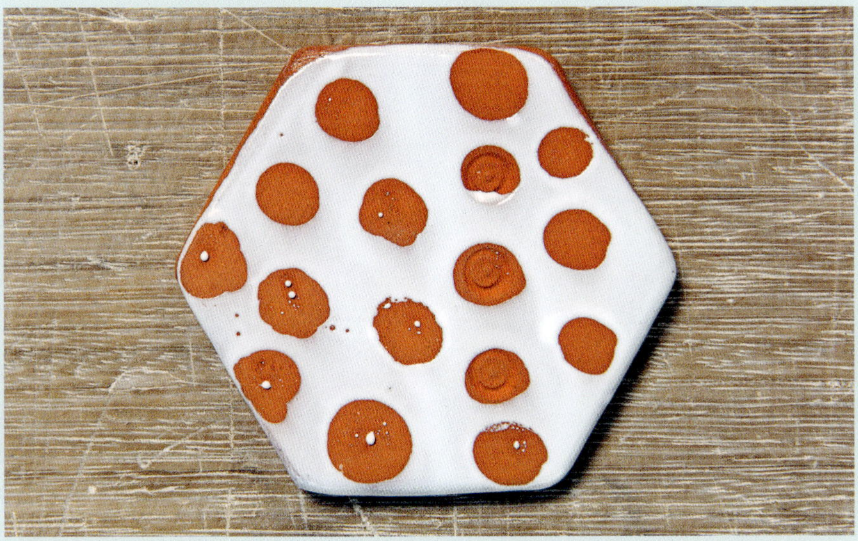

Surface

To create expressive, painterly surfaces it is wise to have some idea of your intended decoration – but try not to overthink what you are doing. Experiment with chunky brushes loaded with thick glaze or slip, and apply them liberally to your work at varying lengths of stroke and speed to create energy and movement. After firing your work, observe how the layers melt and react with one another. For example, resist (wax or latex) will burn away during firing and expose the layer beneath, producing an interesting contrast within the surface. Experiment and allow yourself to play – but keep a record of your methods so that you can repeat your results.

Lucie Rie

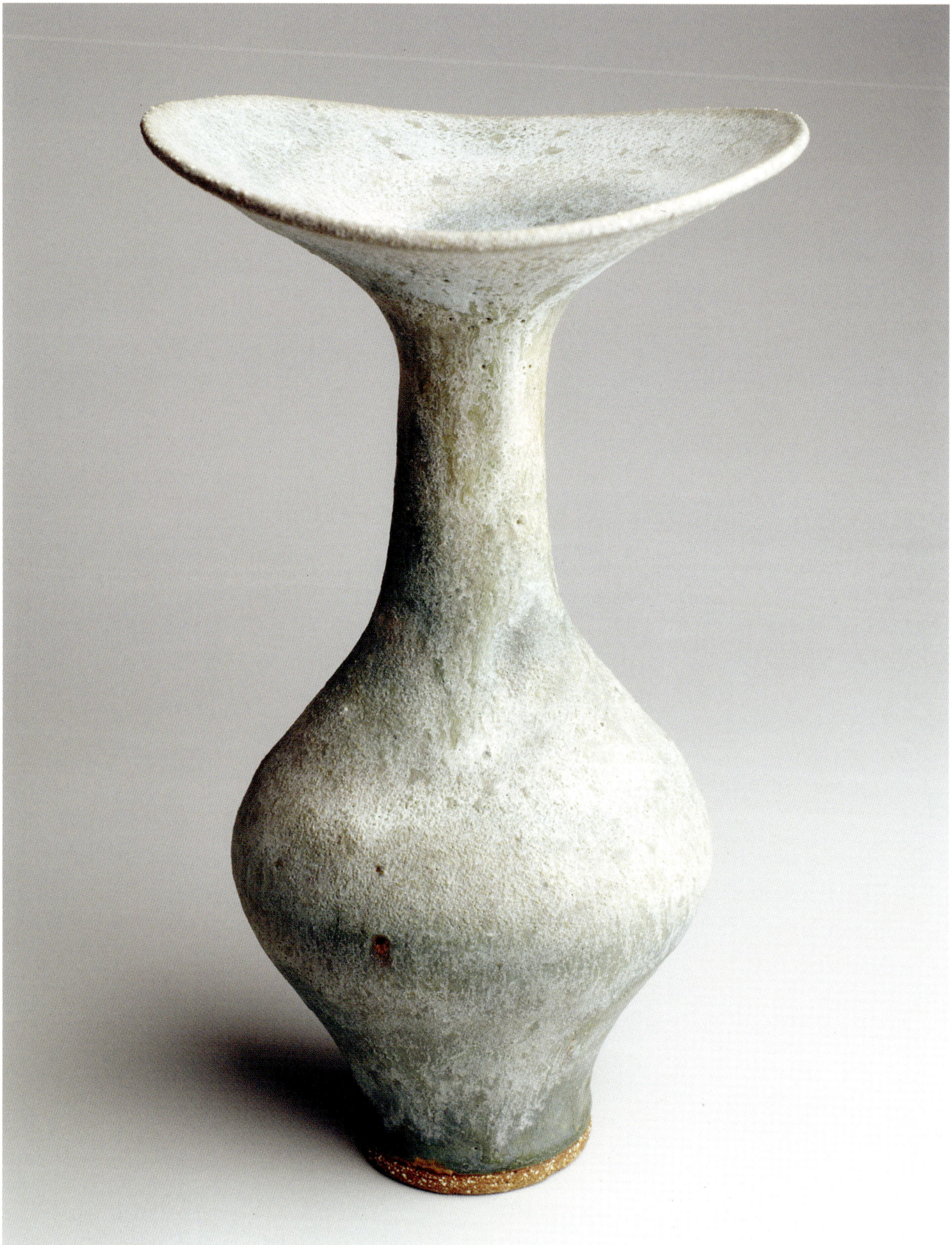

Vase *c.* 1970
Stoneware
Height: 27.5 cm ($10\frac{7}{8}$ in.)

Influenced by the Bauhaus movement and modernist designers such as Josef Hoffmann (1870–1956), Lucie Rie followed the principles of minimal form and surface, a stark contrast to the East Asian-inspired work of her contemporaries, including Bernard Leach and Michael Cardew (1901–83). Rie was known for her direct and unfussy manner, saying, 'I like to make pots – but I do not like to talk about them.' She used a kick wheel to throw her pieces and enjoyed simply exploring the qualities of the clay. Quiet but self-assured, this tall fluted vase has a confidence that reflects Rie's character and modernist ideals. The bulbous base of the vase is visually balanced by the elongated neck, which flows and expands into a rhythmic, flared rim.

Rie's ability to create a sense of tension and control within a form is further enhanced by her use of a textured grey/white glaze. An early adopter of the electric kiln, Rie preferred the aesthetics of oxidized stoneware firings and pioneered the technique, much to her advantage; subsequently others have found it very difficult to replicate her glazes. Archives of her glaze journals indicate a number of experimental approaches, such as adding metal oxides, including copper, manganese and cobalt, to the clay body prior to throwing. Rie once-fired her pots, and therefore she glazed them when they were raw, often applying different glazes on top of each other, and occasionally between layers of slip and glaze. Here, it is likely she followed these principles, which has caused the glazes to bleed through the layers, leaving inky, blue-green traces blotting the surface and softening the overall form.

Lucie Rie (Austrian, 1902–95) was born in Vienna and studied pottery at the Kunstgewerbeschule. She enjoyed considerable success before having to flee Austria due to Nazi German rule. She relocated to Britain in 1938. Rie established her studio in central London and during the post-war years produced buttons and jewelry for Bimimi Designs. She then progressed to making functional wares. Rie gained substantial glaze knowledge and the colours she used ranged from chalky whites to vivid citric yellows, electric blues and sugary pinks. In 1946, Hans Coper – a German refugee without any previous ceramic experience – joined Rie as her studio assistant, which led to an enduring friendship. The pair encouraged one another to develop their own individual styles. Rie was appointed Dame Commander of the Order of the British Empire (DBE) in 1991.

See also
Hans Coper (p.58)
Bernard Leach (p.136)
Stuart Carey (p.150)

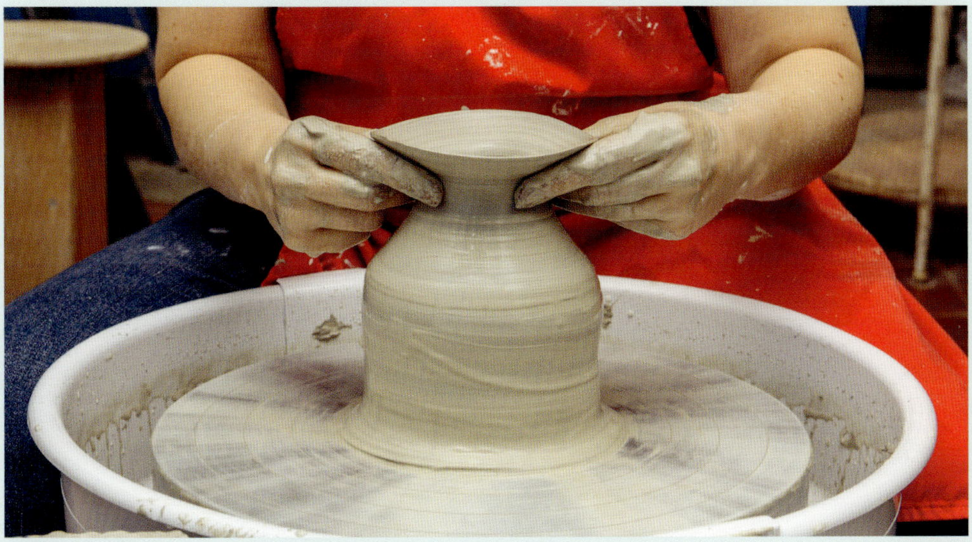

Technical
For this piece, Rie used the pottery wheel to throw a cylinder shape, which she then swelled to create the belly area of the vase. She then collared the top of the form and brought the clay in towards a narrow opening. At that point she was able to skilfully draw the neck of the vase up into a long, exaggerated shape. To complete the vase, Rie flared the rim very widely, almost to the point of collapse. Play with the rims of your thrown bottle forms and see how wide you can flare them out.

Toshiko Takaezu

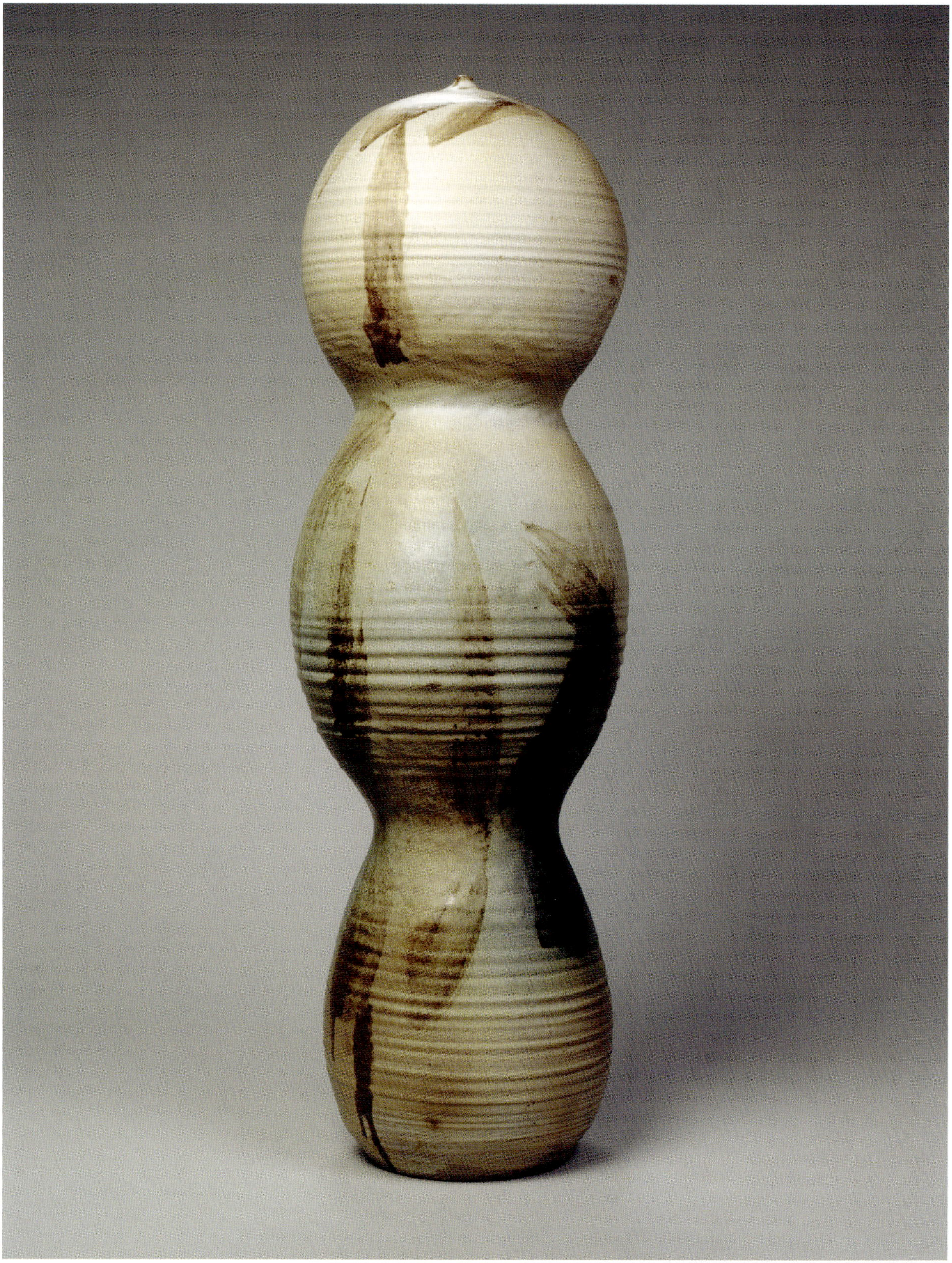

White Tamarind *c.* 1970
Stoneware
Height: 89 cm (35 in.)

The rise of the abstract expressionism movement around the mid-20th century was a strong influence for Toshiko Takaezu. Taking inspiration from nature and Hawaiian landscape, Takaezu blended a style of free, abstracted shapes with gestural brushwork and liberally applied glazes. This piece represents Takaezu's interest in organic forms, particularly fruit and vegetables. The vessel is tall and has been assembled from three separate rounded, thrown vessels. The top section is enclosed and finished with a narrow point which Takaezu called 'a nipple'. The throwing lines are still visible, capturing the moment in time when the clay was drawn and pulled to create the walls of the pot as the wheel rotated. Irregular distribution of concentric circles from the process brings movement and energy to the piece, making it appear less static.

There was integrity in Takaezu's making process. In line with the ideals of abstract expressionism, she worked intuitively and without hesitation. Bold brush marks sweep upwards and fade away. She wood-fired this piece to achieve the browns, greys and delicate blues using metal oxides, such as iron oxide.

Takaezu liked the idea of the containment inside the vessel, the air and the voluminous cavern being an important representation of the human body and soul within. As a playful gesture, Takaezu often placed a small bead of clay – wrapped in paper – inside her pots during construction, which after being fired, made a rattling noise when shaken. She also wrote hidden messages and poems on the inside of her vessels before they were sealed – a secret only revealed if the pot is broken.

Toshiko Takaezu (American, 1922–2011) was born in Hawaii to Japanese immigrant parents. She initially trained at the University of Hawaii and then at the Cranbrook Academy of Art in Michigan, studying ceramics under the tutelage of esteemed Finnish potter Maija Grotell (1899–1973). In 1956 she spent eight months in Japan, living in a Zen Buddhist monastery. She studied the traditional tea ceremony and visited several leading Japanese potters, including Shōji Hamada and Kaneshige Toyo (1896–1967). This led her work to become more sculptural. At the heart of her influences was a love for nature and the interconnection of life and art. Takaezu taught for many years at the Cleveland Institute of Art and Cranbrook, but retired in 1992 to focus on her own work.

See also
Peter Voulkos (p.68)
Shōji Hamada (p.140)
Ron Nagle (p.208)

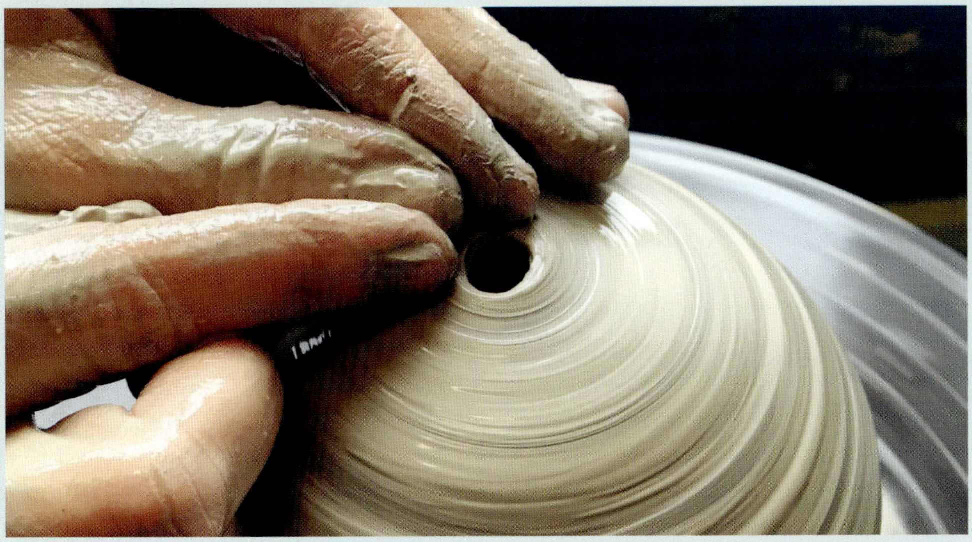

Process
Takaezu was renowned for producing enclosed forms. Enclosed forms can be coiled or wheel thrown. The process is very similar to making a bottle form, but requires tighter collaring in of the neck, bringing it closer and closer until the centre area seals over. A small hole (using a pottery needle tool will suffice) must be made in the base or another discreet area to allow air to escape and prevent the piece from exploding during firing.

Hans Coper

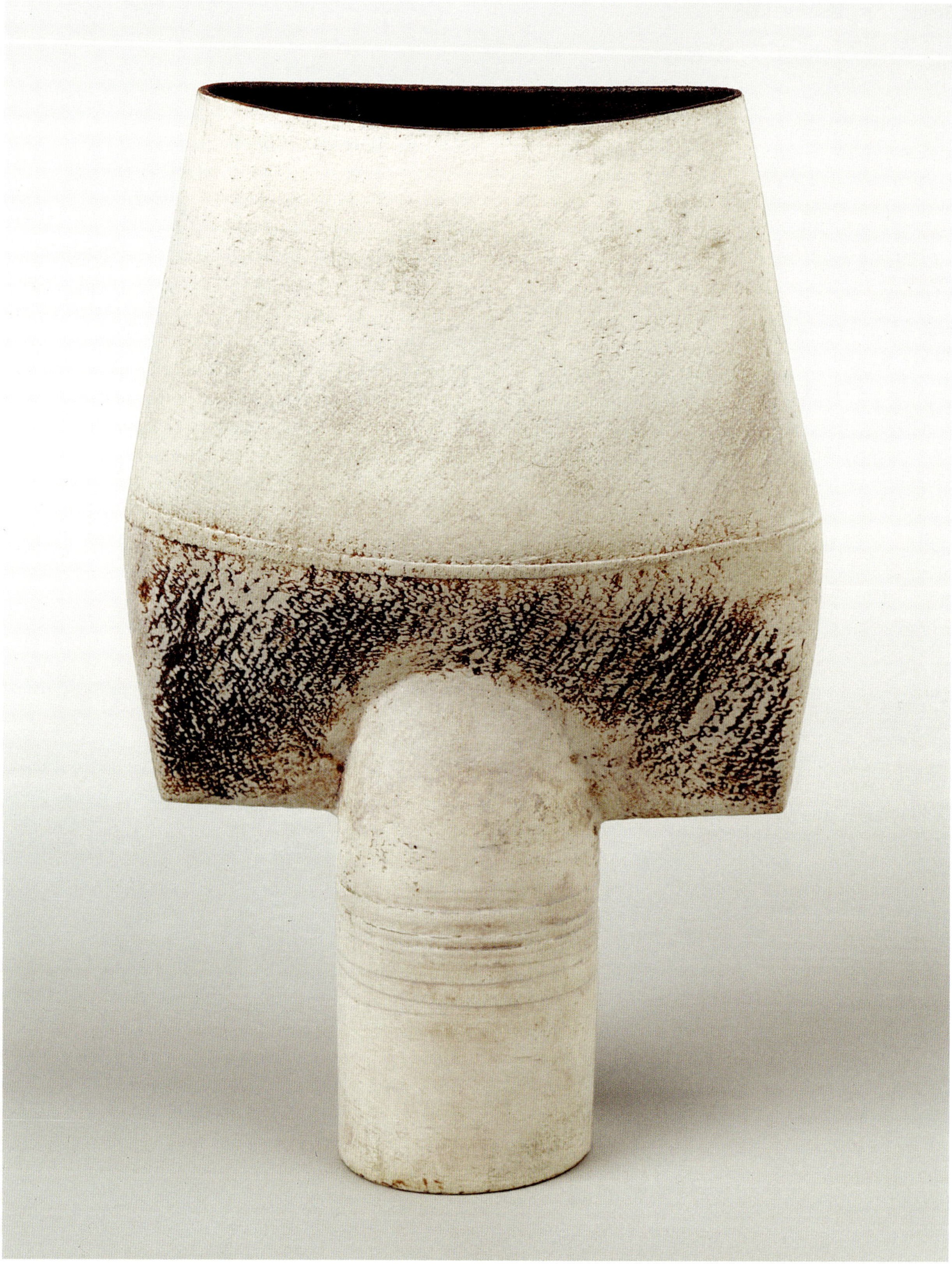

Spade Form *c.* 1971
Stoneware
Height: 25.5 cm (10 in.)

Hans Coper had a background in engineering and an interest in Egyptian and Cycladic pottery; his combined influences earned him much admiration. Minimal and crisp, the stoneware forms produced by Coper centre around a small range of shapes, which he referred to as 'Bud', 'Arrow', 'Flower', 'Egg' and 'Spade'. Coper made his work by throwing discs, cylinders and bellowed vases on the pottery wheel, which he then precisely cut apart and reassembled. His methods involved joining two separate pieces rim to rim or altering one shape by merging it with another. This example of a 'Spade' vessel is pocket-like in form, with a flattened edge along the base. A cylinder intersects the centre and holds the piece upright with poise and balance.

Coper was less interested in glaze than his studio counterpart Lucie Rie, instead preferring a more muted surface finish, working in matt whites, buff, earthy browns and black. For this piece, Coper created a strong visual contrast by abrading the surface of the lower third of the container with a scouring pad or serrated kidney tool. He then further enhanced the rough texture by painting it with black slip and rubbing metal oxides (his preference being manganese dioxide) into the crevices and grooves. For the darker areas he may have used resist techniques or wiped the area with a sponge to keep it clean from glaze and allow the exposed slip or oxide to a form a metallic sheen during firing. The interior of the vessel is heavily painted with the same black-brown slip, which unites the form and completes the overall composition.

Hans Coper (British-German, 1920–81) arrived in the UK in 1939 as a Jewish refugee from Nazi Germany, but he was considered an 'enemy alien' and was posted in Canada for military service during World War II. On his return to the UK, Coper found work in the London studio of Lucie Rie. Despite having no previous experience with ceramics, Coper assisted Rie with the production of her functional wares and button-making business, establishing a firm and lasting friendship in the process. As Coper's skills advanced, he soon developed his own very distinctive sculptural style that became quite different to Rie's finely thrown works. Historically significant to the progression of post-war studio ceramics, today pieces by Hans Coper (and Rie) are highly sought after and fetch record-breaking prices for studio pottery at auction.

See also
Lucie Rie (p.54)
Ruth Duckworth (p.66)
Pablo Picasso (p.172)

Surface
To achieve the subtle colours of this vessel, Coper once-fired his work to stoneware temperatures (1260–1280°C/2300–2336°F) using an electric kiln. Coper experimented with oxides both beneath and on top of the matt white glaze, the change of application resulting in a very different aesthetic. When oxide is beneath a glaze it softly bleeds through the glaze and will produce a colour depending on the type of oxide used. For example, in an oxidized firing, copper oxide will produce tonal greens and greys and manganese dioxide can range from dark charcoal browns to shades of plum. When oxide is applied on top of a glaze it generally melts into the glaze but any thick areas will transform into a metallic surface. Another technique Coper used to add texture was to lightly scratch the surface of the clay using wire wool or an abrasive pad as illustrated here (see right).

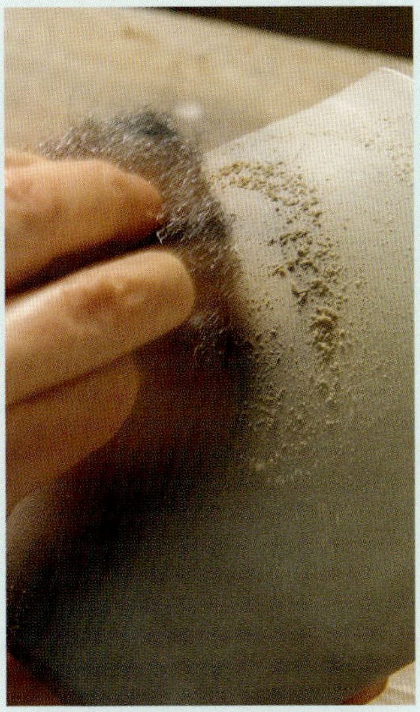

Process
Coper used the pottery wheel as a tool to create the components he needed to construct his forms. Experiment with this technique to create larger and more complex forms in your own work. Plates can be paired together to produce a wide disc shape, cylinders can be stacked to increase height and vase shapes altered by slicing the sides and pinching them together again. Intersect forms by cutting away areas of, for example, a cylinder and joining it to the main body area.

Elizabeth Fritsch

Quantum Pocket II 1992
Stoneware, coloured slips
Height: 32 cm (12⅝ in.)

At first glance, this vessel by Elizabeth Fritsch appears to be three-dimensional and to offer containment; however, it is a visual trick and the piece is actually flat, or as Fritsch calls it, 'two-and-a-half-dimensional'. At just a few inches thick, the ellipse of the rim and the undulating geometric decoration convinces us that the vessel is round. The interplay between pattern and form distorts our perception of what is true, and the result is both clever and unsettling.

In contrast to the spontaneous, abstract expressionist ceramics produced by other artists of the same period, this piece by Fritsch is more controlled and mathematical in its precision. Hand-built using coils of clay, the vessel is slightly curved on the front and the back is flattened like an envelope. Fritsch then carefully and meticulously scraped and refined the surface before decorating it with coloured slips. To create the optical effect, she aligned consistent blocks of muted reds, greens and blues together, and set the pattern against a dark background to make it appear as if it is floating. On closer inspection, some of the facets are textured and accentuated by tonal gradation to enhance the three-dimensional effect further. Like notes on a musical score, the complex cubic design is rhythmical and follows the profile of the vessel, becoming narrower and diminishing as it reaches the rim. The suggested interior space is golden in colour and beams like a beacon, which draws your eye up and around the piece.

Elizabeth Fritsch (British, born 1940) initially studied classical harp and piano at the Royal Academy of Music in London from 1958 to 1964. In 1968, she was accepted to study ceramics at the Royal College of Art and her tutors included Hans Coper and Eduardo Paolozzi (1924–2005). After graduating in 1971, Fritsch lived in Denmark and worked at the Bing and Grøndahl factory in Copenhagen. In the 1970s there was a shift away from traditional approaches to working with clay that brought exciting developments in the field. The distinctive works made by Fritsch were at the forefront of this new direction. In 1995, Fritsch was made a Commander of the British Empire (CBE) and a Senior Fellow at the Royal College of Art. She is regarded as one of Britain's leading ceramic artists and her works are held in many important collections worldwide.

See also

Hans Coper (p.58)
Alison Britton (p.72)
Halima Cassell (p.236)

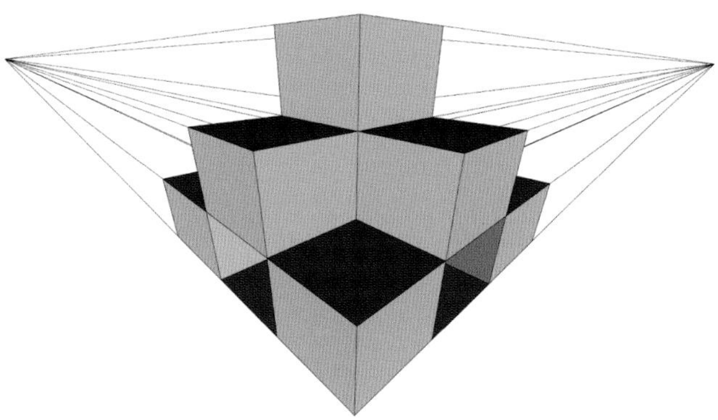

Composition
Part of Fritsch's success here is with the consistency and execution of the block design, particularly her play with scale and curves to give the illusion the piece is round. When designing an optical illusion, like the crisp geometric patterns used by Fritsch, it can be challenging to obtain the right level of realism needed to fool the eye. Therefore, it is important to understand perspective and learn the techniques and skills that will enable you to give your work a sense of depth and distance. Depending on the complexity of your design, one method is to draw a series of lines and measurements taken from vanishing points, and build your design within this framework, as illustrated here. Consider if you intend to have a repeat pattern or prefer a one-off statement design. You may find it helpful to sketch by hand or draw using computer software before you start decorating your piece.

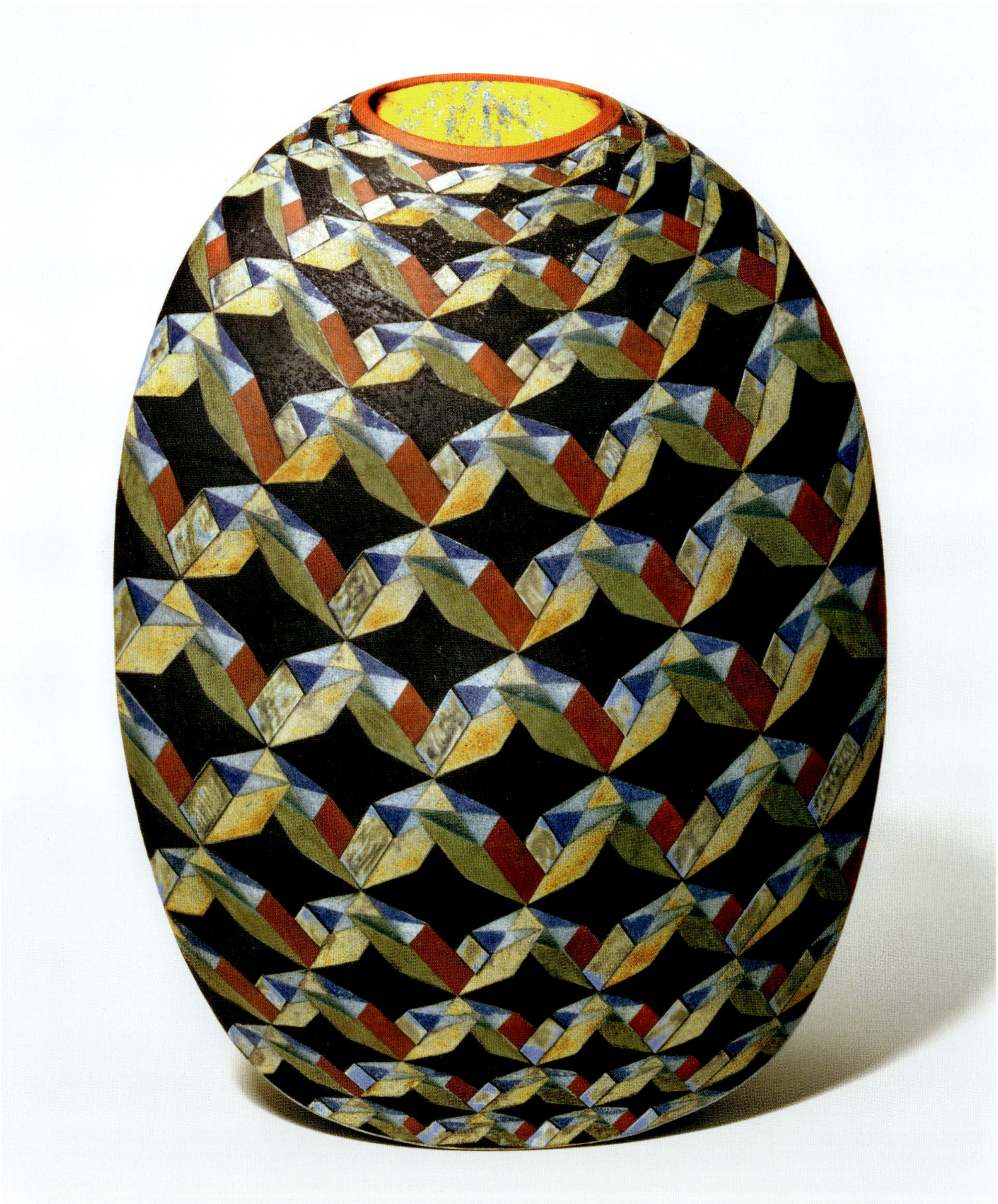

Magdalene Odundo

Vase 1995
Coiled, burnished and reduced red clay
42.5 × 33 × 31.75 cm (16¾ × 13 × 12½ in.)

Beautifully crafted and elegantly poised, the work of Magdalene Odundo is the result of an eclectic blend of influences, ranging from her Kenyan/African heritage to dance, spirituality and modern culture. The human figure and expressions of the female form are important aspects of her practice – specifically, the way the body can move and contort, and the versatility it shares with clay as a material. In this example, sumptuous curves resemble the rounded belly of a pregnant woman, bellying out and then in towards a tightly nipped waistline. An exaggerated, funnelled neck protrudes at an angle, like a wide-open mouth – offering a glimpse of the interior space and prompting us to contemplate ourselves as vessels, able to carry and contain ideas and aspirations of our own.

Decoration is minimal to allow the strength of the form to resonate. A series of small raised peaks pinched from the surface refer to Odundo's childhood in Nairobi, when she remembers looking at and touching the tribal scarification patterns that adorned her mother's body. As an adult reflecting on this experience, she is intrigued by cultural identity and perceptions of beauty.

Steeped in the traditions of African rural pottery making, Odundo coil-builds her forms using red earthenware clay. Each piece goes through a meticulous process of finishing, which involves repeated burnishing and smoothing to achieve the highly polished surface. She then low-fires her work in a reduction atmosphere, which transforms the rich orange-red colour of the clay to gunmetal black.

Magdalene Odundo (British-Kenyan, born 1950) was born in Nairobi, Kenya. She studied commercial graphic arts before moving to Britain in 1971 to do a foundation course at Cambridge College of Art. She developed an interest in ceramics and pursued an undergraduate degree at West Surrey College of Art and Design in 1976. This was followed by a master's degree in ceramics at the Royal College of Art, London (1979–82). Odundo travelled extensively, including to China, Mexico, Uganda and Nigeria. From these diverse cultural experiences, Odundo developed the sensual hand-built forms for which she is most renowned. In 2020, she was made Dame Commander of the Order of the British Empire (DBE) for services to the arts.

See also

Gabriele Koch (p.64)
Maria Martinez (p.138)
Viola Frey (p.174)

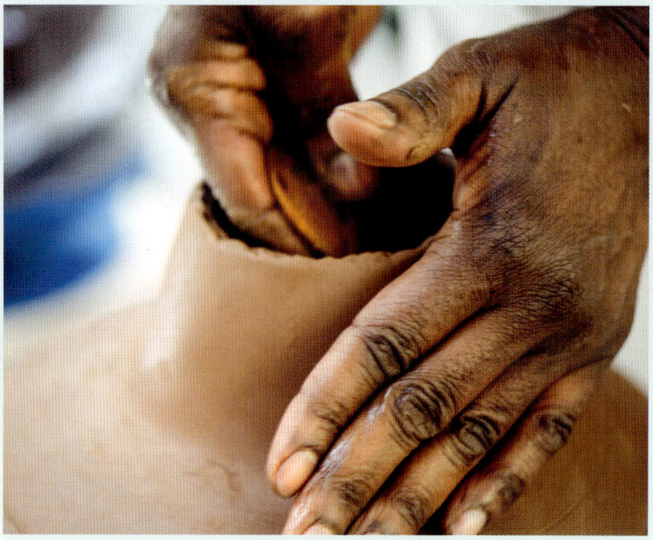

Process

Odundo constructs her voluptuous forms by first gouging out the centre of a lump of clay and then raising the main walls of the vessel to a obtain a certain height. More coils of clay are added and Odundo shapes and refines the internal profile to achieve the bellied chamber. At this point, she skilfully narrows the waist of the vessel and the elongated neck is formed and altered. Timing is critical when making a coil pot and it is very important to be aware of the stage the clay is at. Too soft and the pot will sag under its own weight; too dry and the pot will be susceptible to cracking. Cross-hatching and scoring the clay, and applying slip between the coils as you build, helps adhesion and reduce the risk of technical issues. In general, the most successful coil pots are the ones that retain a sense of freshness and have a lightness to the form. Be mindful of the opening/rim: it is the exit point for the eye and should work in balance to the rest of the profile.

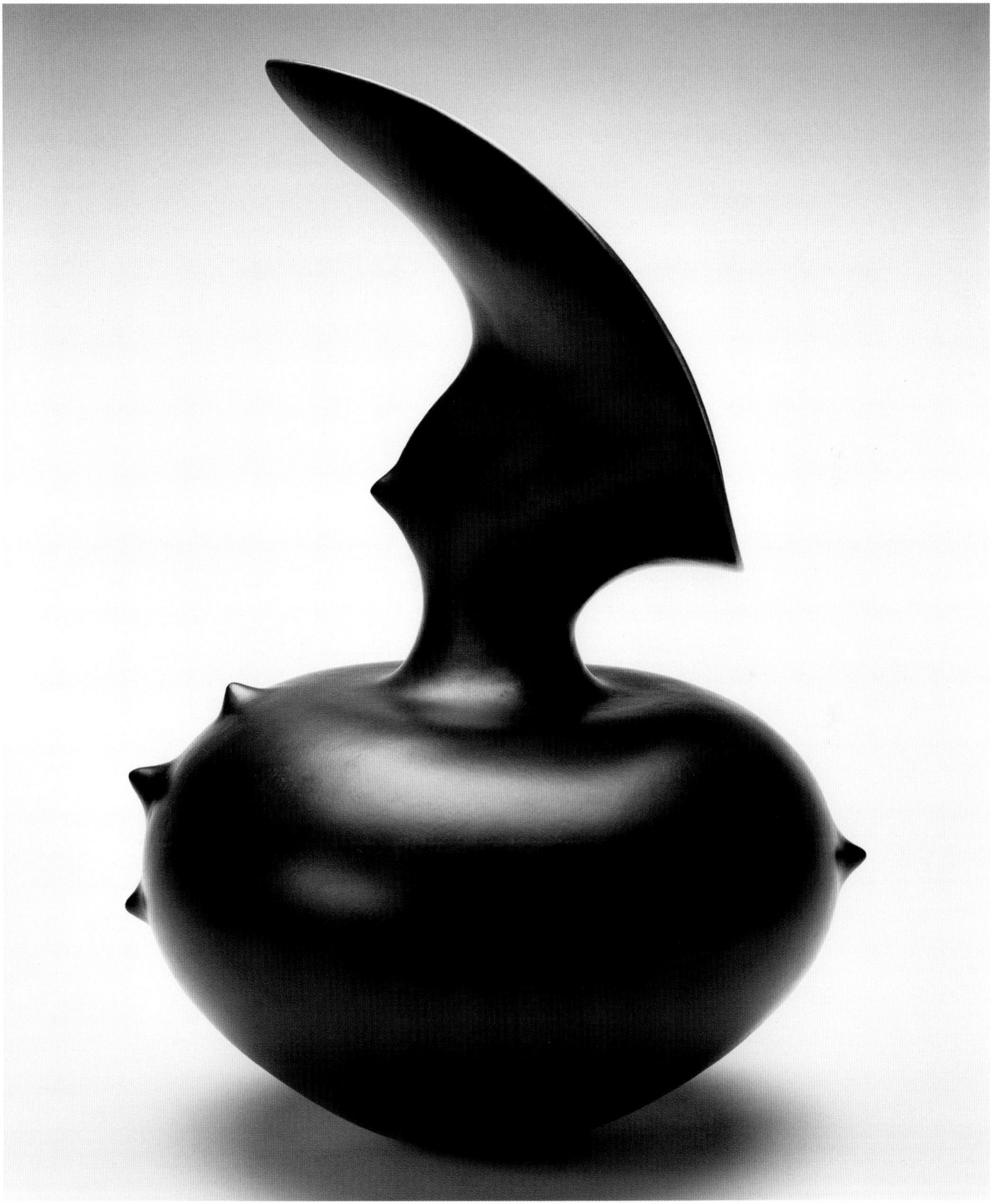

Gabriele Koch

Pot 1996
Burnished, smoke-fired earthenware
Height: 34.3 cm (13½ in.); Diameter: 43 cm (16⅞ in.)

When Gabriele Koch arrived in the UK in the 1970s, she was absorbed by the flourishing ceramics scene and felt empowered to turn her ambition to work with clay into a reality. During this period, the influence of Bernard Leach was far reaching and although Koch shared his values of simplicity, restraint and beauty within a pot, she leaned more towards the modernist, urban style of Lucie Rie and Hans Coper. As Koch says when she describes her creative journey, 'There was perhaps a meeting of the ancient and the modern, the rural and the urban that led me to the making of simple forms, trying to integrate balance and tension, stillness and movement, expansion and the containment of volume, precision and spontaneity.'

This large, voluminous pot, built from wide strips of T-material clay, exemplifies Koch's ability to respond sensitively to material and process. She developed a coil-building technique that enabled her to shape and manipulate the clay into sensual organic forms. The pot stands on a narrow base and flows freely into a vast bellowed chamber. Defined by the line of the shoulder, the form undulates towards the centre, concluding with a refined wide-mouth rim. Delicate textural marks, created by burnishing, swirl and dance around the piece.

Reflecting on the open desert landscapes and earthy tones of black and red ochres that she had seen on her travels abroad led Koch to explore the connection between form and surface. With hints of Africa and ancient cultures, Koch utilized traditional smoke-firing techniques to produce her distinctive dappled patterns of rich browns and salmon pinks, highlighting the subtle ridges and rhythm of the burnished marks.

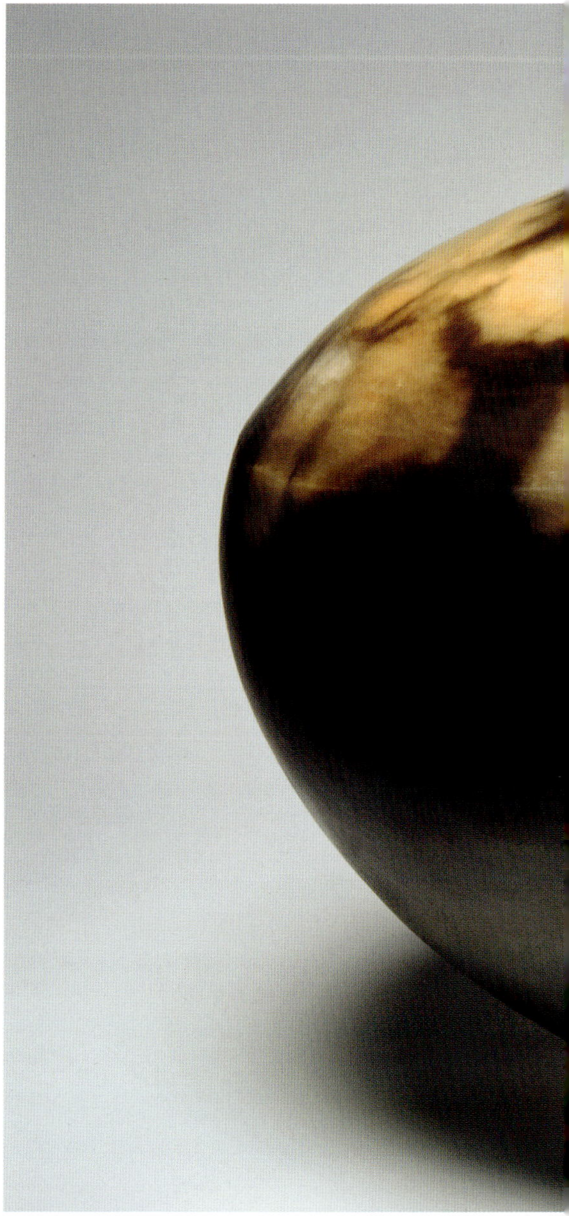

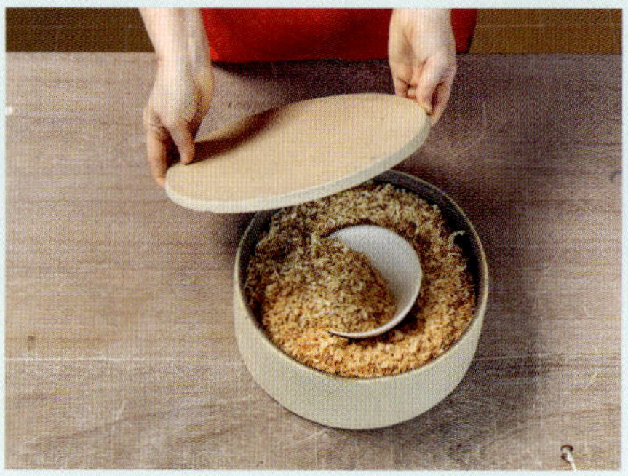

Process
Koch sawdust fires her work outside in a large oil drum; however, a saggar box made from coarse clay can be used to smoke small pieces in an electric or gas-fired kiln. Place the piece inside the saggar and cover with sawdust. Seal the lid with a coil of clay and fire to a temperature of 700–1000°C (1292–1832°F). Good ventilation within the kiln room is essential.

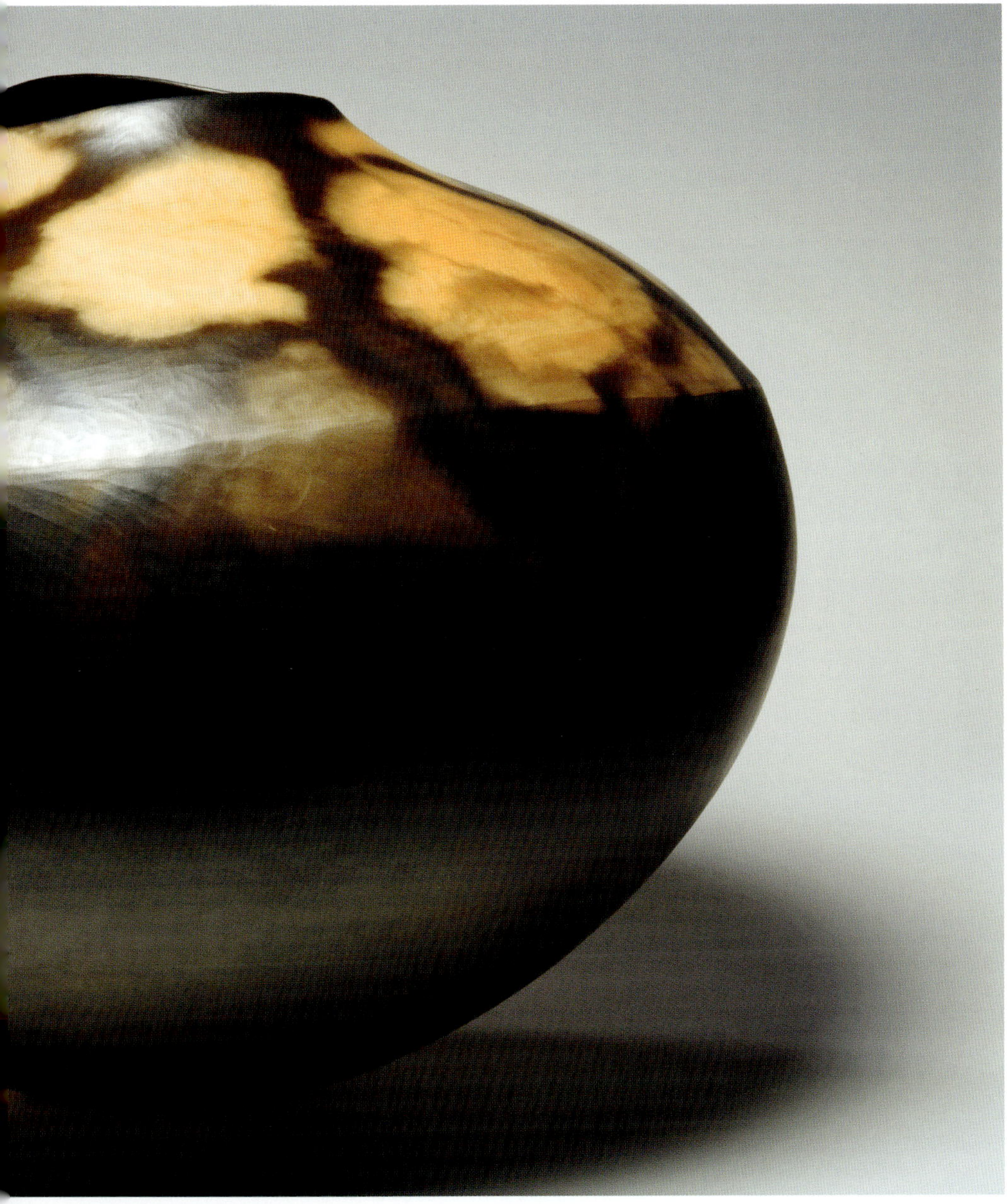

Gabriele Koch (German, born 1948) is an internationally acclaimed ceramicist. Born in Lörrach, southern Germany, Koch studied English, history and political science at university but a study trip to Zaragoza in Spain, where she discovered the beauty of unglazed pottery and surfaces enlivened by fire marks, kindled a desire to work with clay. She moved to the UK in 1974 to teach languages in London and went on to study ceramics at the Camden Institute (1974–77), followed by a degree at Goldsmith's College, London (1979–81). During the 1980s Koch developed her distinctive hand-built smoked vessels, which became synonymous with the period and led her to the forefront of the discipline. In recent years, her work has become more graphic, progressing from low-fired earthenware to high-fired black stoneware with integrated porcelain detailing, but it remains deeply rooted in her understanding of form and surface. Examples of Gabriele Koch's iconic work are held in many prestigious collections worldwide.

See also

Lucie Rie (p.54)
Hans Coper (p.58)
Magdalene Odundo (p.62)

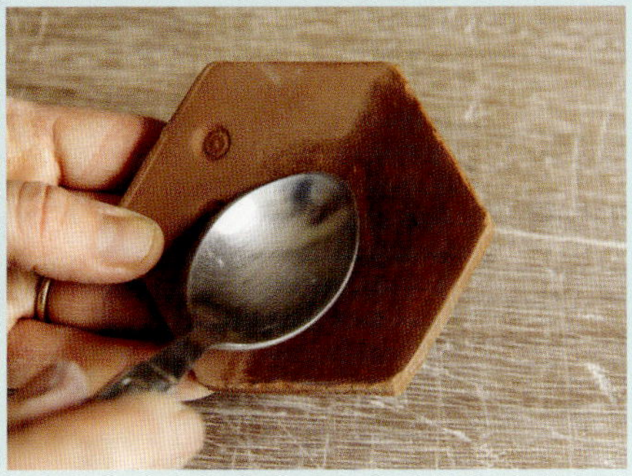

Technical

Koch used a surface technique called burnishing to give her vessels their signature polished finish. The technique involves rotating a pebble or the back of a spoon in a circular motion over leather-hard clay; this compresses the platelets in the structure, producing a delicate waxy sheen. In conjunction with the burnishing, Koch applies slips to produce subtle colours that are further enhanced by the smoke firing. Another technique you can try is to wrap copper wire or string dipped in oxide mix to specific areas, which will resist the smoke and leave behind interesting patterns and colours. When your piece is finished, enrich the smoke pattern by applying a few coats of furniture wax and buffing with a soft cloth.

Ruth Duckworth

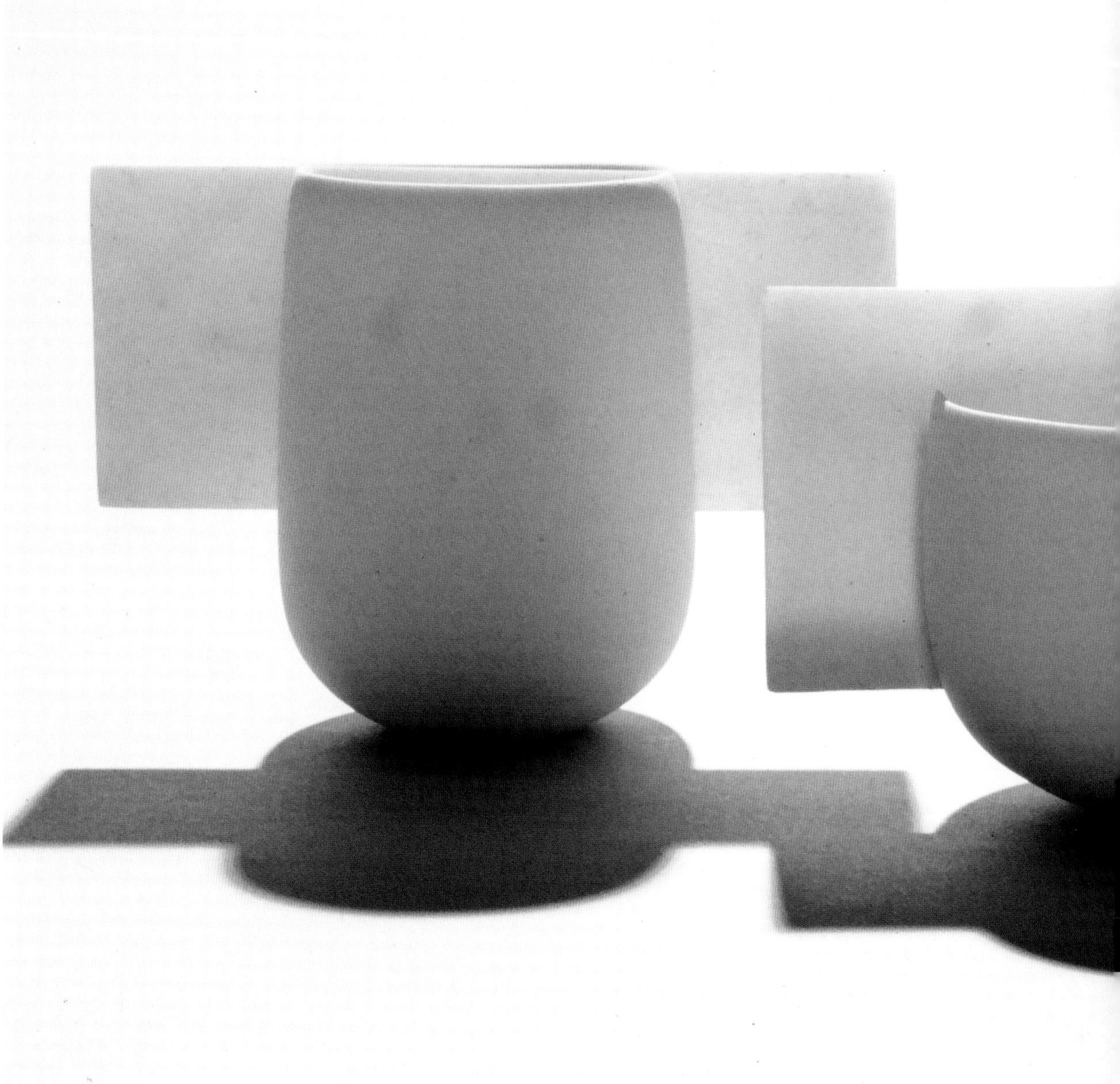

See also

William Staite Murray(p.52), **Lucie Rie** (p.54), **Hans Coper** (p.58)

Ruth Duckworth (German-American, 1919–2009) was born in Hamburg, Germany. She left Germany in 1936 as a Jewish refugee and settled in Britain. Duckworth attended the Liverpool College of Art and studied drawing and painting until 1940. She earned a living by carving gravestones and touring with a puppet theatre company. Her first major commission was to carve, in low-relief, the fourteen Stations of the Cross at St Joseph's Church in New Malden, Surrey. Duckworth moved to London in the late 1940s and, with an interest in ceramics, she enrolled first at Hammersmith School of Art in 1955 for one year, and then in 1956, at the Central School of Art, where she stayed for two years. She also taught there from 1959 to 1964. In 1964, Duckworth was offered a teaching position in the United States at the University of Chicago. Upon retiring in 1977, she established her studio and remained in the country for the rest of her life. Her work is held in many public collections worldwide, including the Art Institute of Chicago, the Los Angeles Country Museum and the Victoria and Albert Museum, London.

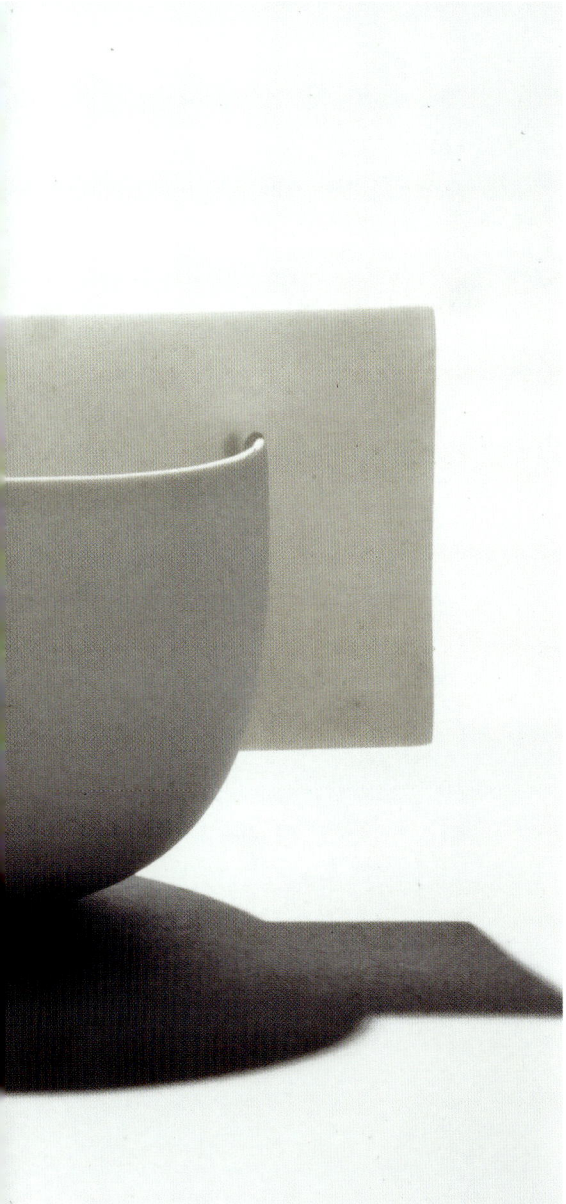

Untitled 1997
Porcelain, two elements
Left: 17.8 × 12.7 × 8.9 cm (7 × 5 × 3½ in.)
Right: 10.2 × 17.2 × 10.2 cm (4 × 6¾ × 4 in.)

The breadth of modernist sculptor Ruth Duckworth's work ranges from large-scale installations and figurative sculptures to abstract wall murals and refined vessel-based forms. Inquisitive and curious about materials, Duckworth explored a variety of media, including stone, bronze, stoneware and porcelain. During her years in Britain, she formed a lifelong friendship with fellow immigrants and potters Lucie Rie and Hans Coper and was influenced by the minimalist aesthetic of sculptors Henry Moore (1898–1986) and Isamu Noguchi (1904–88). Nature was another source of great inspiration to Duckworth and she enjoyed spending time in her garden observing seed pods spiralling down from trees in the breeze and appreciating the organic shapes and forms of flora. Her approach to making was very playful and experimental, with Duckworth commenting, 'The process is intuitive, not intellectual. You have to learn to be spontaneous and trust yourself.'

Intimate in scale and sensitively executed, these exquisite vessel forms by Ruth Duckworth exemplify her ability to exploit the translucent, delicate qualities of porcelain. Paired with minimal form, the resulting composition is balanced and beautifully proportioned. Inspired by ancient Bronze Age tools and Cycladic pottery, Duckworth called this series 'cup and blade'. A paper-thin sheet of luminous porcelain intersects the curved form across the diameter and expands on either side, strengthening the relationship between the two opposing elements. The contrast between the softness of the vessel's curve and the straightness of the blade edge extends the play with the light and throws delicate shadows. Absent of glaze, the vessels have a smooth, bone-like surface, which gently rebounds subtle tones and transitions of light.

Composition
The strength of Ruth Duckworth's abstract sculpture is the clarity of form based on her modernist ideals. When working in this way, pare your forms back to the most essential, cleanest shapes. Allow yourself to play with various combinations, stacking and joining component parts and observing the interplay between light and shadow.

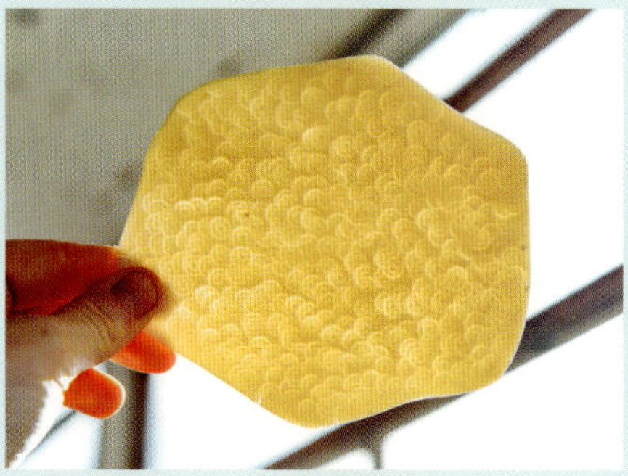

Material
As illustrated by Duckworth's sculptural vessels, you can exploit the translucent nature of porcelain to accentuate the outlines and profile of your forms. For best results, the porcelain should be only a few millimetres thick and ideally high-fired to a temperature of 1280°C (2336°F). Experiment with stamping textures or scoring lines into the surface to create a strong contrast when flooded with light.

Peter Voulkos

The Eagle Has Landed 1999
Wood-fired stoneware
87.6 × 58.4 × 58.4 cm (34½ × 23 × 23 in.)

Experimental and progressive, Peter Voulkos is considered one of America's greatest artist/sculptors who worked with clay. This large sculptural work by Voulkos is free of ceramic conventions and embodies his unrestricted and powerful approach to working with clay. The form is confrontational in stature, and stomps and asserts its place as an assemblage of chunky thrown fragments punctured by rugged lumps of torn clay. Sections are stitched and remodelled like patchwork, unafraid to hide the scars of the process. A bottle-like neck is squashed and smeared onto the top of the form. Perhaps its purpose is to return a sense of order and offer containment? However, a crudely cut hole near the base contradicts this notion and renders its function ambiguous. Freshly worked, this piece juts and slumps under its own weight, yet maintains its stance.

Random flashes of ochre yellows and muddy browns swirl and orbit the form. Voulkos achieved this effect by wood firing his pieces using a traditional Japanese *anagama* kiln. The unpredictable nature of the firing technique adds to the overall spontaneity of the piece. Voulkos's strength was his ability to improvise and be decisive – there is no sign of hesitation in the construction of this piece, or any sense it has been laboured over. He was known to work intuitively, in line with his abstract expressionist ideals, saying, 'The quicker I work, the better ... if I start thinking and planning, I start contriving and designing. I work mostly by gut feeling.' Voulkos's energetic and radical approach to clay redefined a generation and led him to the forefront of the discipline.

Peter Voulkos (American, 1924–2002) studied painting and printmaking at Montana State College in 1951, followed by an MFA in ceramics in Oakland. He established a studio at the Archie Bray Foundation for Ceramic Arts in Helena, Montana and made functional pottery to support his painting. In 1953 – while teaching a summer course at Black Mountain College in North Carolina – Voulkos was introduced to avant-garde artists Josef Albers (1888–1976), Robert Rauschenberg (1925–2008) and John Cage (1912–92). In New York he met abstract expressionists Willem de Kooning (1904–97) and Franz Kline (1910–62) – who significantly influenced the direction of his work. Voulkos was a revolutionary figure in the rise of the California Clay Movement. His phenomenal influence and contribution broke down divisions between fine art and craft, liberating the medium into unprecedented territory.

See also
Paul Soldner (p.206)
Ken Price (p.210)
Sterling Ruby (p.218)

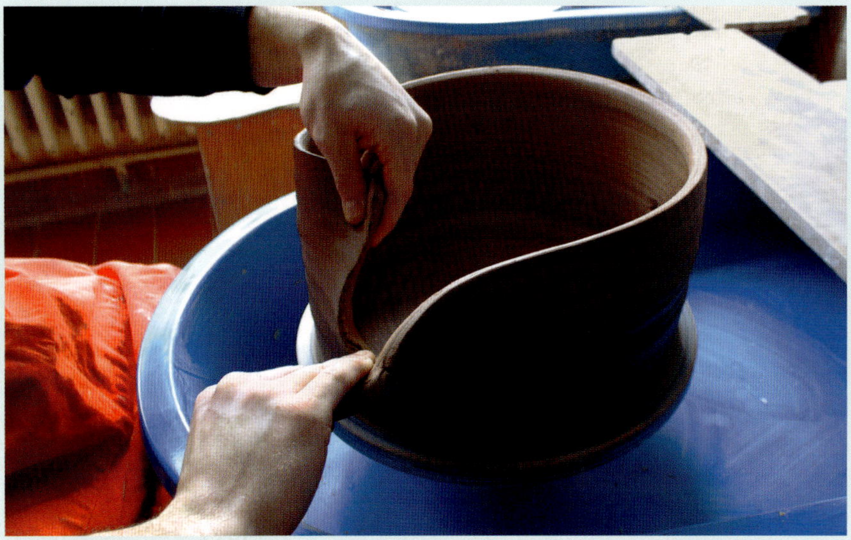

Composition
Voulkos typically worked on a very large scale, using a variety of methods to construct the works, including slab-built and thrown sections, which he freely combined and assembled. He provoked disorder and expression in his forms by slashing, piercing and splitting the clay, allowing areas to collapse and distort in the process. To work in this ethos, allow yourself to work gesturally and with spontaneous intent. Experiment with ripping sizable chunks of clay, stacking and manipulating component parts. Follow your instincts and try not to overthink your actions – the most exciting results can happen when you are totally immersed in what you are doing.

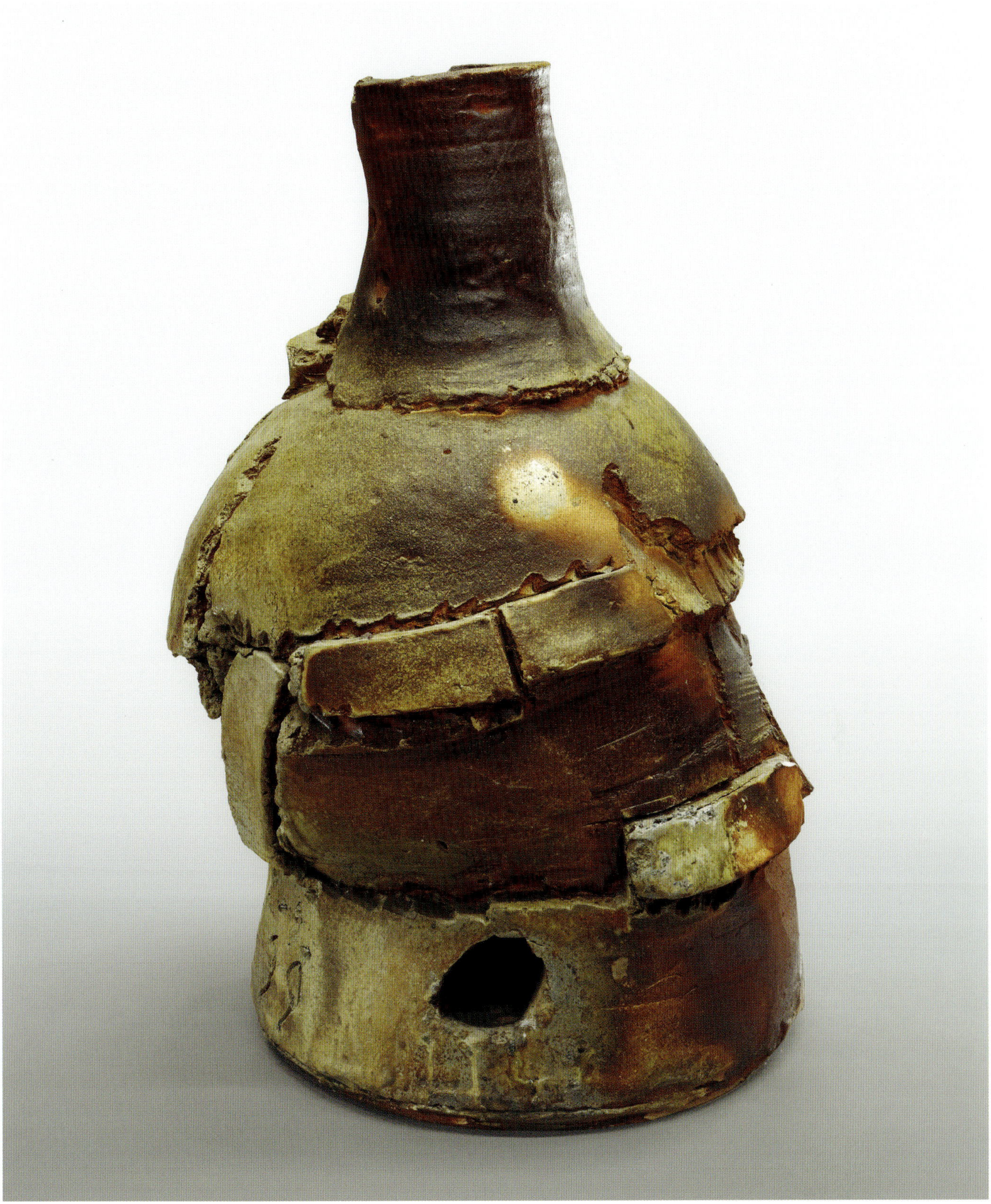

Gwyn Hanssen Pigott

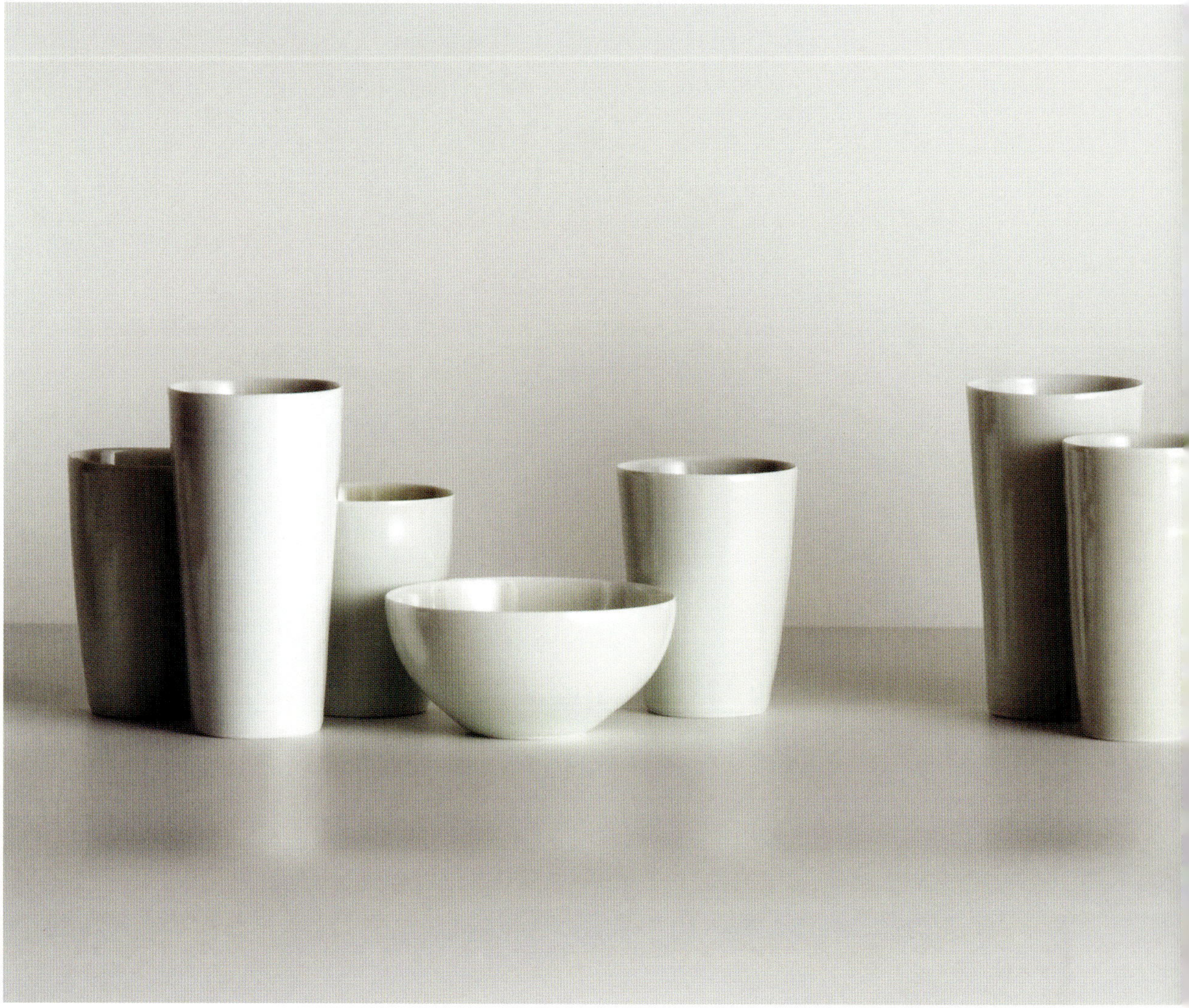

Kinder Trail 2010
Porcelain
128 × 16 × 18 cm (50⅜ × 6¼ × 7⅛ in.)

Like many potters of the Leach era, Gwyn Hanssen Pigott subscribed to the philosophy of fusing Eastern and Western traditions and admired Chinese Song Dynasty pottery (960–1279), which was renowned for its rich colours and minimal decoration. During her years in Britain Hanssen Pigott met modernist potter Lucie Rie, who became an important mentor and inspired her to create works that were fresher, poised and contemporary. As her interest in European ceramics broadened, Hanssen Pigott developed an admiration for Italian painter and printmaker Giorgio Morandi (1890–1964), whose subtle works depicted staged still-life assemblages of everyday objects, including cups, bottles and bowls. She studied Morandi's restrained approach to colour, his ability to retain the realness of what he was describing and enjoyed how he used space and intervals to strengthen the relationship of the group.

Serene and intimate, this installation comprises ten beakers and four bowls, all carefully curated in precise clusters across a linear stretch. The title alludes to the migration of child refugees, each group a family in transit, their vulnerability exposed. Thrown on the pottery wheel using porcelain, the quality of making is exceptional and deeply rooted in Hanssen Pigott's understanding of the functional form. The tranquil and meditative qualities of her work are enhanced further with the application of a delicate blue-grey celadon glaze. Fired in a wood-fuelled kiln, the process of transformation and unpredictability of the firing reveals sensitive and subtle variations and has much in common with the nuances of the human character.

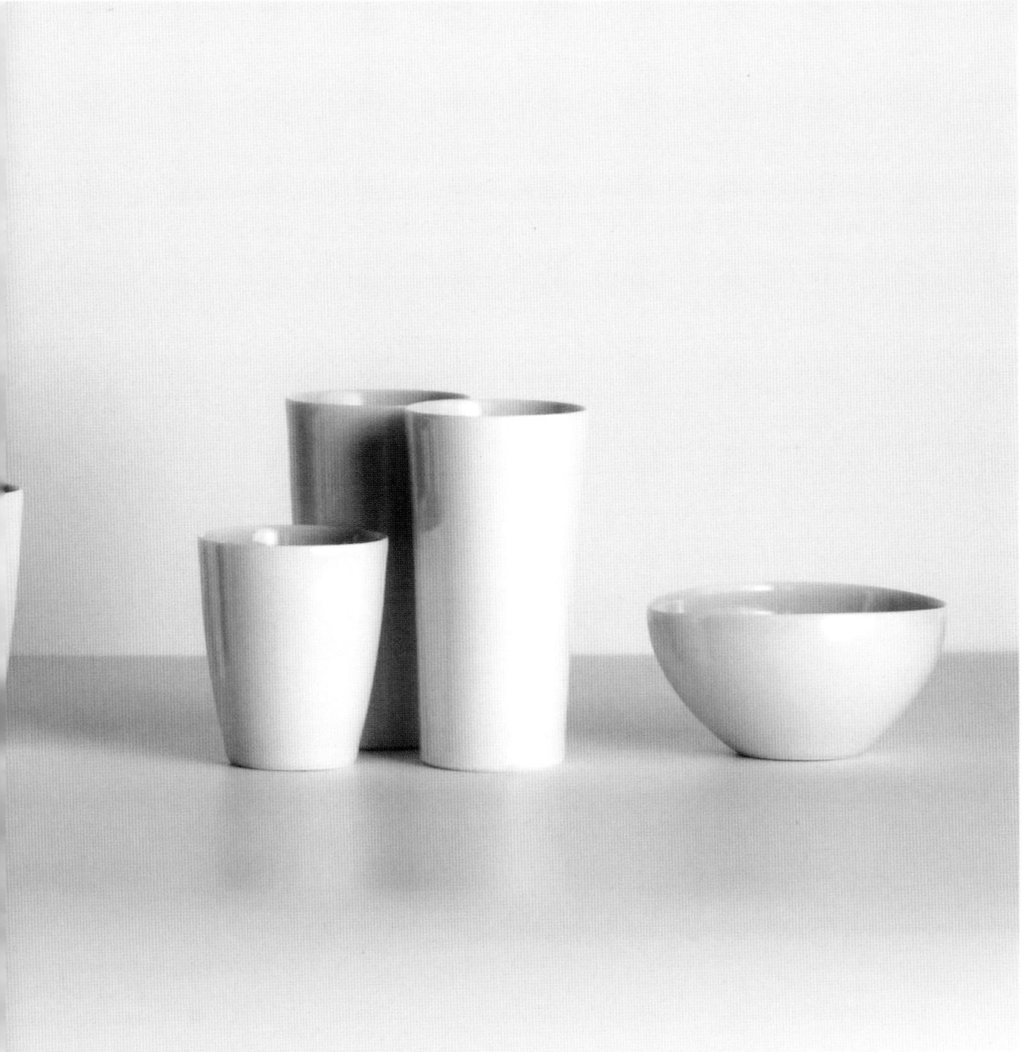

Gwyn Hanssen Pigott (Australian, 1935–2013) was born in Ballarat, Victoria, and studied Fine Arts at Melbourne University. After reading *The Potter's Book* by Bernard Leach (see p.134) she became fascinated by pottery, and in 1955 embarked on a three-year apprenticeship with eminent Australian potter Ivan McMeekin (1919–93). Hanssen Pigott immersed herself in her training, learning how to dig and process clay, throw pots on the wheel and wood-fire her work. In 1958 she travelled to Britain to work with distinguished names including Ray Finch (1914–2012), Michael Cardew (1901–83) and Bernard Leach himself. Hanssen Pigott based her first studio in London and then moved to France for a number of years before returning home to Australia in 1973. It was in Australia that she produced her most famous works, quiet still-life groupings of beautiful translucent porcelains. In 2002 she was awarded the Medal of the Order of Australia for service to the arts.

See also

Pippin Drysdale (p.122)

Kirsten Coelho (p.160)

Edmund de Waal (p.250)

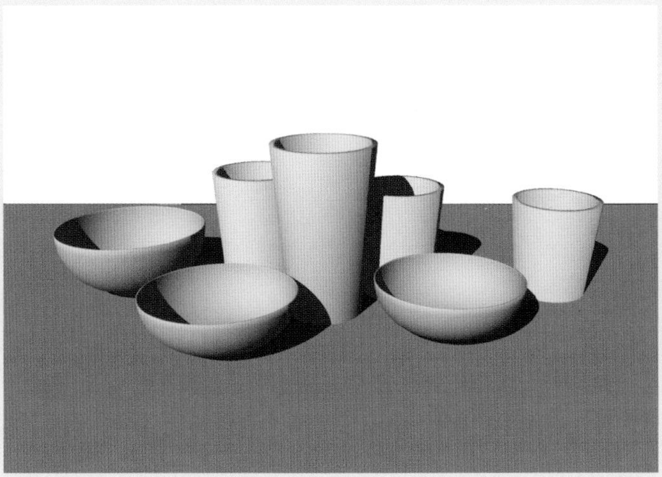

Composition

Hanssen Pigott arranged her groupings with carefully planned spaces in between, like natural pauses to heighten the contextual message of her work and allow the viewer to absorb the breadth of the installation. When composing an installation, aim to create a skyline of varying heights and work towards a pyramid formation, with the tallest item around the centre point. Arrange your works in groups of odd numbers and follow a zig-zag line, bringing lower pieces to the front and placing taller pieces at the back. Subtle differences in height and width, colour and tone, will create visual interest. Play around with combinations of arrangements and groupings, observe the installation from different viewpoints and make small adjustments until a resolution is established.

Alison Britton

Watershed 2012
Red earthenware, slab built, with poured slips and glazes
44 × 43 × 28 cm (17⅜ × 16⅞ × 11 in.)

Alison Britton is one of the defining makers of her generation. Throughout her career, Britton has continually explored the notion of 'containment' through the language of ceramic vessels. Her distinctive hand-built pots are investigations of familiar everyday objects such as jugs, bowls or dishes, but their unwieldly size and unusual handles and spouts defy functional purpose. Influences including ceramic history, ornamentation and sculptural form are integral to Britton's work and she treats the surface of her pots as a canvas to adorn with abstract painterly marks and rich decoration. The artist says, 'my main preoccupation is making the form I've arrived at also work as a painting'. The ambiguity displayed in Britton's work prompts us to question our assumptions about art and craft, by 'bridging sculpture with the domestic'.

Watershed is from a series of works that examine the themes of flow and liquidity; the title refers to the containment and movement of water. The slab-built form is asymmetrical and angular in composition and consists of two chambers – much like a trough or syphon trap. A narrow pipe extends beyond the outer wall and reveals a playful dynamic between the inner and outer spaces. The artist has placed emphasis on 'fluidity' and this is reflected in the improvized drips and pours of creamy white slip and inky glaze that spill down the facets of the piece. Britton's interest in the use of red clay followed a residency at the Shigaraki Ceramic Cultural Park in Japan in 2010. The pairing of the red clay with the loose surface decoration echoes the traditions of Devonshire slipware.

Alison Britton (British, born 1948) studied at Leeds College of Art, London's Central School of Art and Design, and the Royal College of Art (RCA). In the 1970s, she was part of the radical group whose work laid the foundations for the 'New Ceramics' movement. She makes large slab-built earthenware pots with brightly coloured glazes. Her work references domestic ware such as jugs and vases, but her gestural style and use of expressive surfaces challenges conventional assumptions about functional objects. Britton has taught at the RCA since 1984 and was awarded an OBE (Order of the British Empire) for services to art in 1990. With a career spanning four decades, she significantly challenged the course of craft practice during the late 20th century.

See also

Elizabeth Fritsch (p.60)
Simon Carrol (p.98)
Janice Tchalenko (p.110)

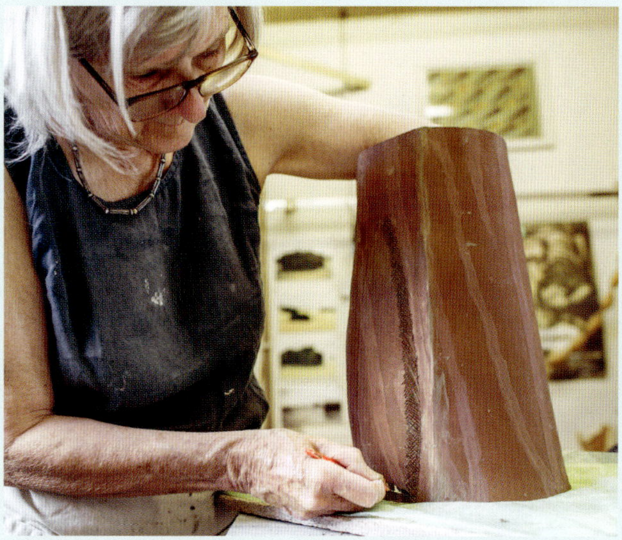

Process
Britton constructs her pots using slab-building and coiling techniques. The slabs are rolled by hand, using wooden guides to roll against to ensure an even thickness. When the slabs are leather-hard, they are manipulated and eased into position. Britton works intuitively – the slabs are often prepared first with layers of gestural slip decoration and hand-drawn surface textures, which are added to as the piece progresses. For *Watershed* Britton used a jug to freely pour slip and glaze over the red clay background. This required great intuition and confidence in the application to maintain the freshness and spontaneity of the result – a second attempt is not an option. The rich, earthy colour of red clay, as illustrated here, offers warmth and character to a piece. It is typically fired at low earthenware temperatures: 1080°C (1976°F). But if you take it to a slightly higher temperature of around 1180–1200°C (2156–2192°F), the clay colour will intensify and the surface will gain a delicate sheen.

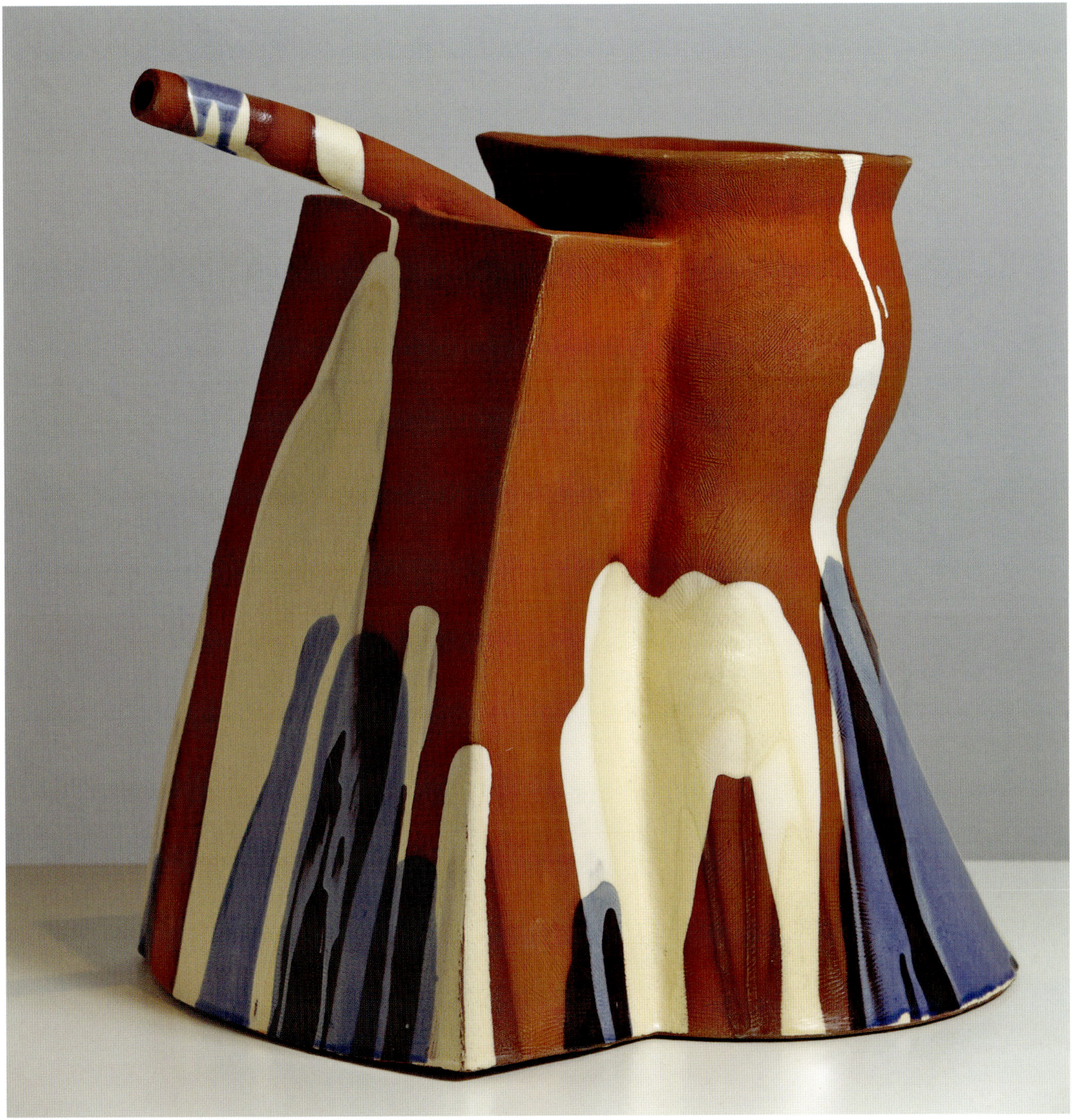

Elisabeth Kley

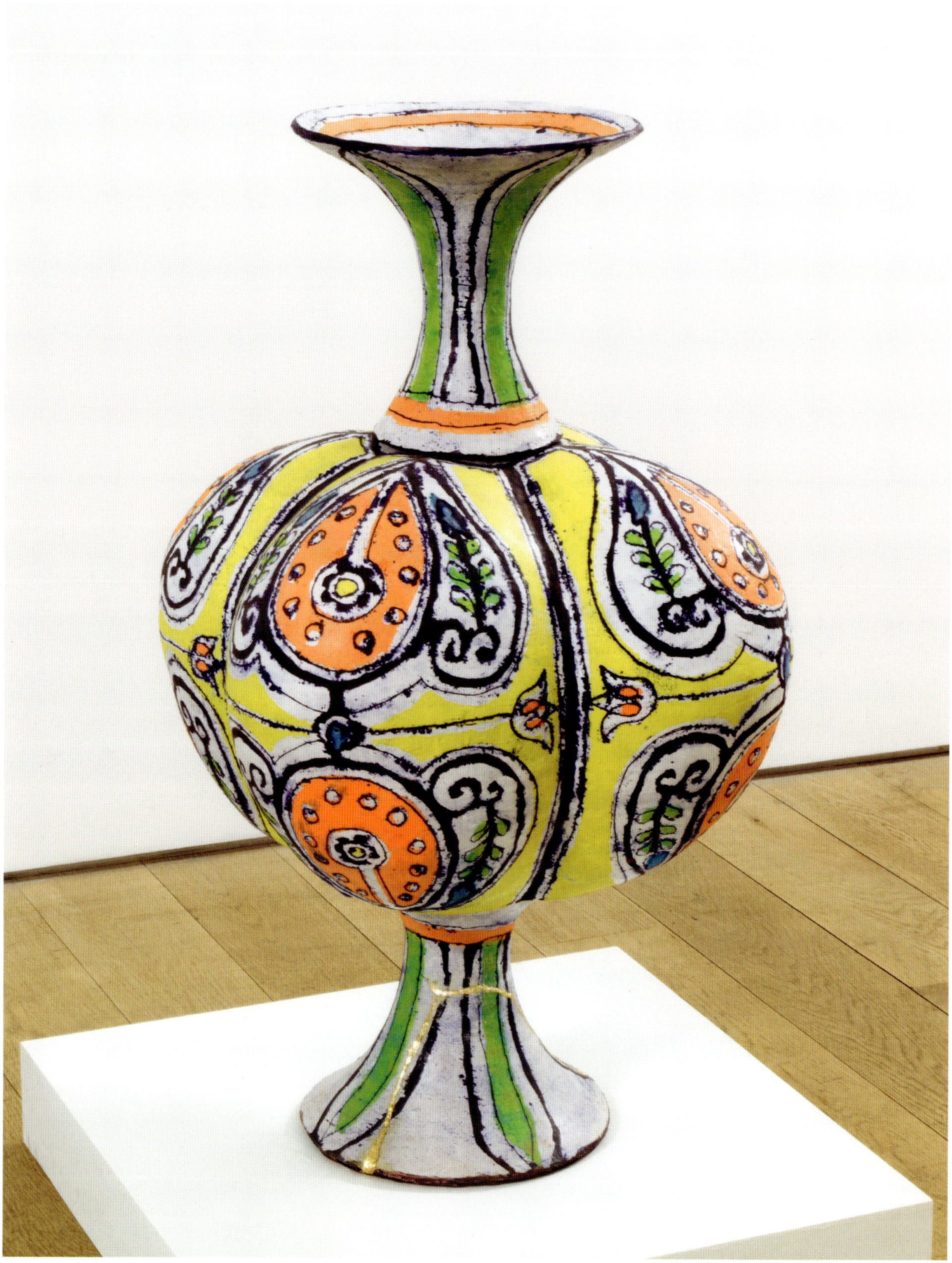

Large Yellow and Red Three-part Bottle 2012
Earthenware, glazed
Height: 90 cm (35½ in.)

Vividly bright and exuberant, the lively decorated work of Elisabeth Kley is a celebration of joyful colour and pattern. Kley draws her inspiration from many sources, from the ornamental designs of ancient Islamic and Asian art right through to studies of the flamboyant costume and make-up of drag performers. Drawing and painting is another important aspect of Kley's work and feeds directly into the surface designs for her ceramic pieces. Her bold style is typically floral and calligraphic in application and has a symmetrical element within the pattern that shares similarities with textiles.

This beguiling vessel by Kley was coil built in three parts: a pair of fluted sections top and bottom and a wide, bulbous middle area. Its undulating ridges and contours resemble a prize gourd or pumpkin. The whole form is quite loose in construction and retains an organic quality. Kley has created a pleasing sense of balance and proportion by cleverly mirroring the decoration from the centre line of the vessel. She applied colourful underglazes, wax resist and sgraffito techniques over a white glazed background and deliberately left areas of white exposed to heighten the impact of the yellow and orange block colours. The whole decoration has been overpainted with varying thicknesses of cobalt oxide lines, which pull the composition together. On the fluted neck and base areas, Kley has painted long leaf-shaped strips of luminous green. This visual trick elongates the vessel and allows for the middle area to carry the weight of the decoration.

Elisabeth Kley (American, born 1956) studied etching at Hunter College and painting at SUNY Empire State College, New York; however, she later focused her practice on drawing and ceramics. She works mostly in clay, creating densely ornamented decorative objects such as bird cages, bottles, fountains, peacocks and urns. Kley covers her vessels with hand-printed underglazes that she scrapes away to reveal patterns and provocative narratives. Her work references a wide range of cultural influences, from Japanese textiles and drawings by Aubrey Beardsley (1872–98) to Egyptian hieroglyphs and antique French tapestries. Her pieces often have elaborate shapes that evoke both ancient and modern structural forms.

See also
Pablo Picasso (p.172)
Viola Frey (p.174)
Ramesh Mario Nithiyendran (p.190)

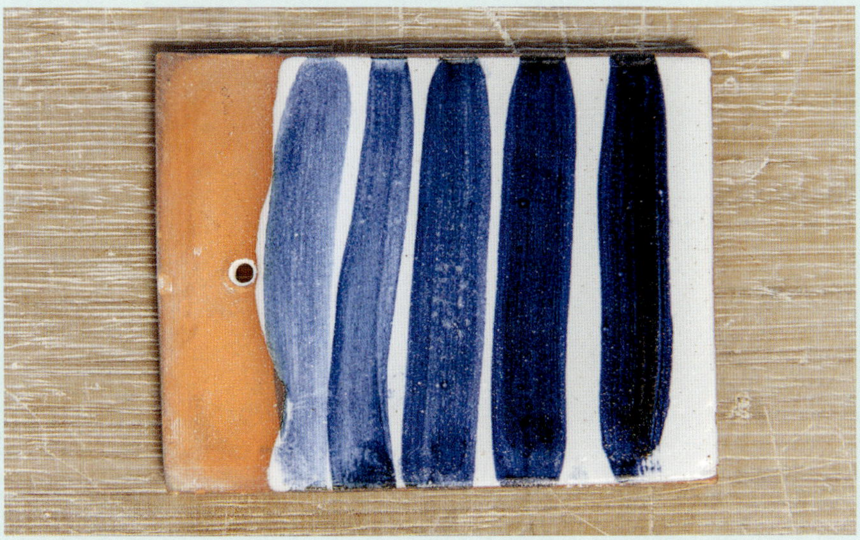

Technical
Painting an outline using an oxide brings a dense tone of colour to decoration without the harshness of pure black. It can also create an inkiness and smudgy line, as seen in Kley's work. To emulate these graphical qualities, follow a technique called majolica painting. Cover your piece with a white tin glaze and apply underglaze colours or oxide mix directly on top, then fire to earthenware temperatures (1080–1120°C/1976–2048°F). The tin oxide in the glaze aids the melting of the colour decoration, creating a smooth, bright surface. As you can see from this tile example (painted with cobalt oxide), the more water you add to the stain or oxide, the lighter the tone will be.

Monika Patuszyńska

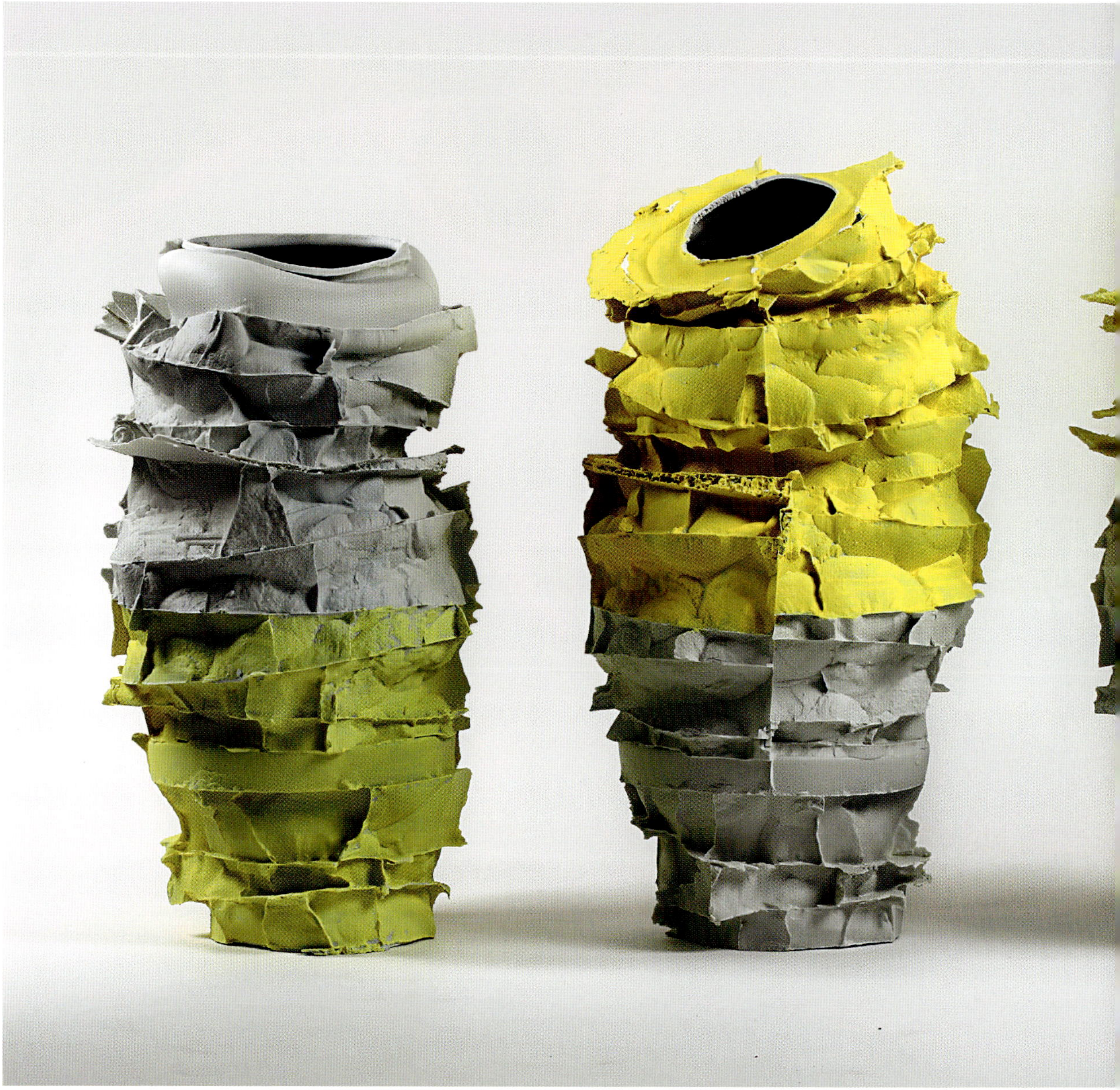

See also

Piet Stockmans (p.144), **Torbjørn Kvasbø** (p.258)

Monika Patuszyńska (Polish, born 1973) is known for her inventive and contemporary slip-cast forms made using porcelain. She was born in Warsaw, Poland, where she now lives and works (based in Milanówek). Patuszyńska received her master's in ceramic design from the Wroclaw Academy of Fine Arts, Poland, in 1999. She has been a member of the International Academy of Ceramics since 2009 and has won numerous awards and distinctions at international ceramic competitions, including the Taiwan Province of China Ceramics Biennale in 2008 and the Master Prize, European Prize for Applied Arts, Mons, Belgium, in 2015. Patuszyńska was the Artistic Director at the Institute of Design, Kielce, Poland, from 2014 to 2016. She has been a lecturer at the School of Form, Poznań, Poland, since 2014.

Surface

Patuszyńska creates a colour contrast by decorating the vessels with a yellow engobe. This helps preserve the moulded texture on the surface and enables her to decide where and how much colour it needs. You could also try to paint or trail coloured casting slip in the mould prior to taking a cast. The slipped marks will transfer from the plaster mould onto the clay surface and give a printed effect.

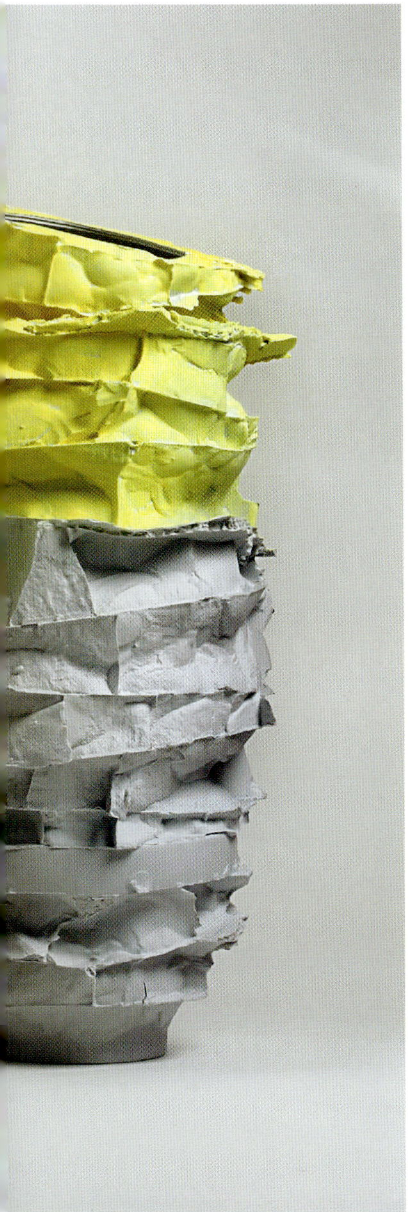

From the series TransForms Plus (Bernese stories) 2015–16
Porcelain, high-fired, unglazed
Height: 70–75 cm (27½–29½ in.)

Unconventional and highly experimental in approach, the irregular slip-cast, porcelain forms of Monika Patuszyńska challenge plaster moulding techniques that have been used for centuries with an innovative rethink. As illustrated with these three angular vessel forms from her *TransForms Plus* series, Patuszyńska has created a playful inside-out structure by exploiting the moulding process itself.

Typically, a standard plaster mould is made by first casting from a model, resulting in a drop-out or multipart mould, which is then used to take a slip cast. Through much experimentation and 'playing with the nature of mistakes', Patuszyńska developed an inventive new technique based on these principles. This process involves her sawing, smashing and breaking up found or redundant plaster moulds and reassembling the broken pieces into a non-defined form or structure. Patuszyńska then pours casting slip into the void inside, sometimes adding more pieces from other moulds and manipulating the cast itself. Patuszyńska comments, 'The process of breaking up and reassembling the broken pieces allows me to define the object again, depriving it of its earlier designed character and giving it a new, different meaning.'

Here, the fluffy, powdery quality of the broken plaster shards of the mould have been delicately transferred onto the clay cast. Patuszyńska creates dynamic surfaces by exploiting the joins and spaces between her plaster assemblages, which allow the slip to seep through, defining the 'negative space' of the vessel. When the pieces are fired the porcelain distorts and crumples under its own weight, resulting in a series of uniquely scrunched and contorted forms that are a testament to materiality and process.

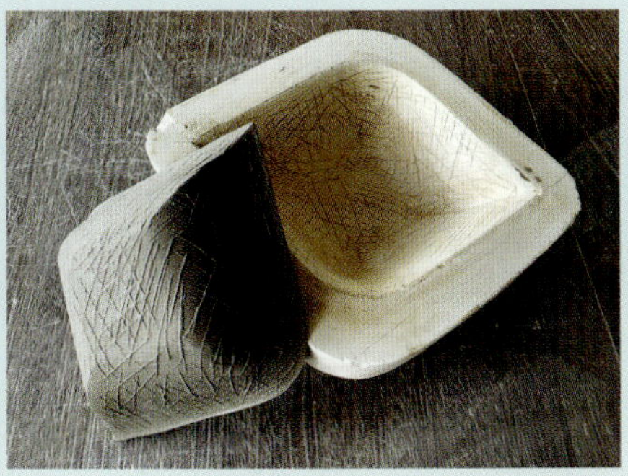

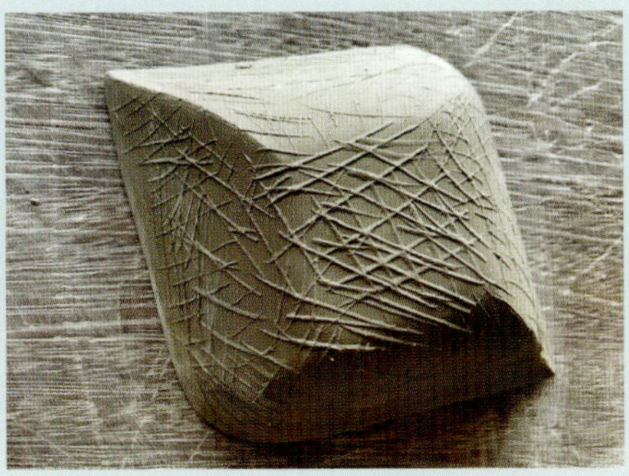

Process
Plaster is traditionally used for ceramic moulds due to its absorbent properties, which draw the water from the casting slip, leaving behind a thin wall of clay. Alter a mould by scratching and carving in to the plaster wall to create a relief texture on your casts. You could also emphasize the seam lines of the cast by creating a mismatched alignment in the mould, which will cause the slip to seep through.

Matt Davis

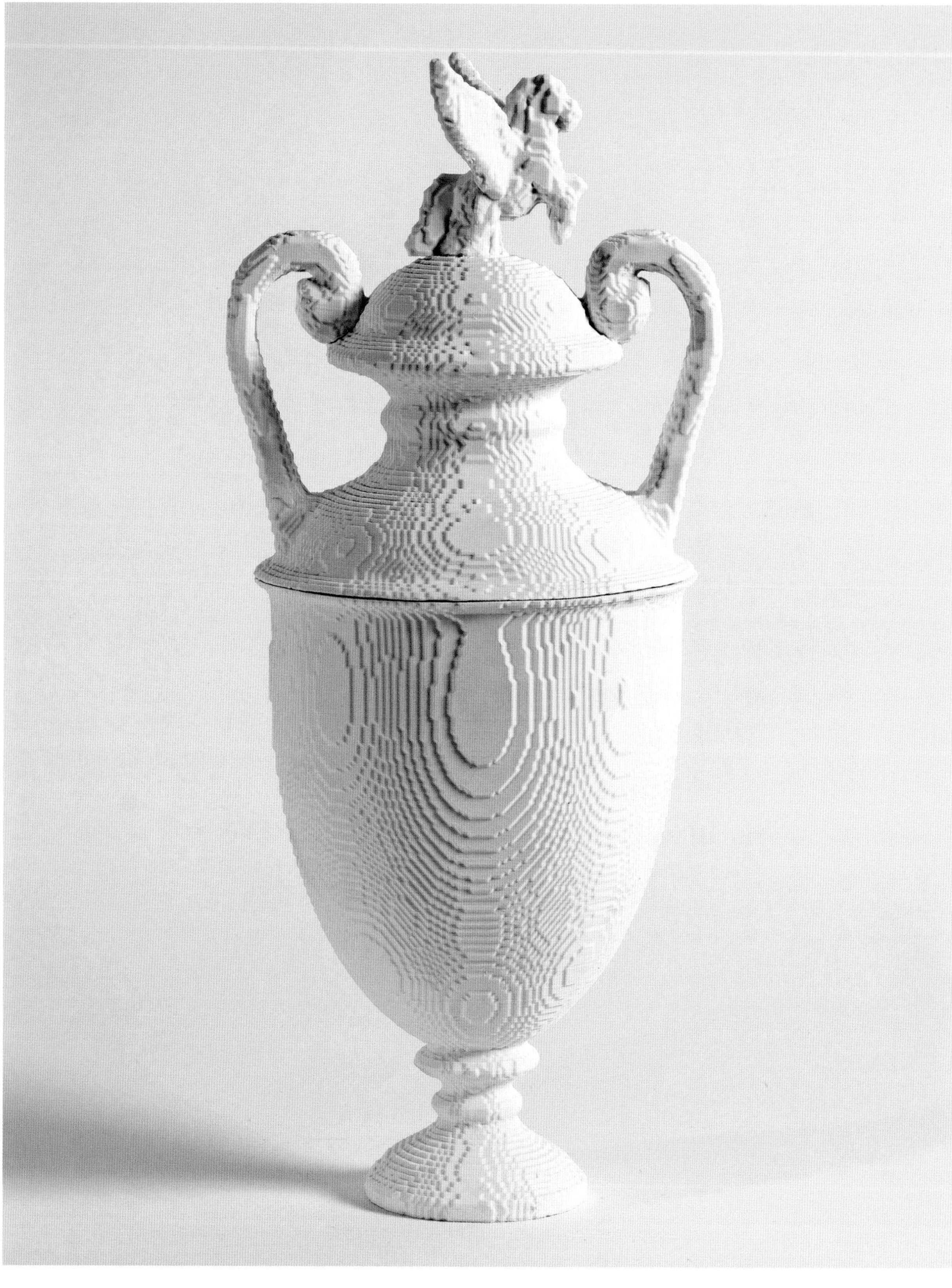

Wedesus Urn 2017
Bone china, slip cast
38 × 17 cm (15 × 6¾ in.)

Drawing inspiration from historical British and East Asian vessels, Matt Davis distils his interpretation of the archetypal vessel into digitally processed forms. Davis combines computer-modelled design with handmade craft, as he says, 'to challenge our preconceptions on the relationship between technology and traditional craft'. This example, entitled *Wedesus Urn*, is a reference to the iconic shape of a Wedgwood urn (the title itself is a wordplay of Wedgwood and Pegasus). Davis has distorted and blurred the outline of the urn: tactile ridges and lines trail across the vessel like a digital fingerprint, bringing the virtual visualization into solid form.

Davis uses CAD (computer-aided design) software to model his pieces and prepare the files for 3D printing. Interestingly, in much the same way as an artist sculpts and manipulates a physical form, Davis experiments with the process in the virtual plane. This interaction led to the development of the pixellated, blocky surface of the urn, which emphasizes its digital credentials. Higher resolutions generate a finer surface, but ultimately it is Davis who decides how the final vessel will appear, commenting, 'When working on the computer I produce multiple versions of each form, often to the point of total degradation in the surface, then make an aesthetic judgement on the final texture. During this stage of the process I need to take into consideration how it will eventually be moulded.' Davis slip casts his vessels in small batch series, using bone china and black stained porcelain.

Matt Davis (British, born 1977) came from a background in graphic design when he returned to study a master's degree in 3D design and craft at the University of Brighton, graduating in 2016 with a distinction. It was at Brighton that he discovered a passion for ceramics and began to explore ideas of digital/physical hyperrealistic objects. Davis is now based in Birmingham. His work has won numerous awards for innovation and is in the permanent collection at the Potteries Museum and Art Gallery, Stoke-on-Trent. The digitally created ceramics made by Davis represent a new generation of makers and artists who embrace new technologies to push the boundaries of contemporary practice.

See also
Ruth Duckworth (p.66)
Bouke de Vries (p.260)
Paolo Polloniato (p.262)

Material

The *Wedesus Urn* is made from bone china, which is a slip-casting clay body. As a material it offers beautiful translucent qualities and can be very finely cast. Bone china is notoriously tricky to work with and items made from it need a careful drying and firing schedule to prevent warping and distortion of the form. This piece by Davis is unglazed and fired to a stoneware temperature of 1220°C (2228°F) with a ninety-minute soak time.

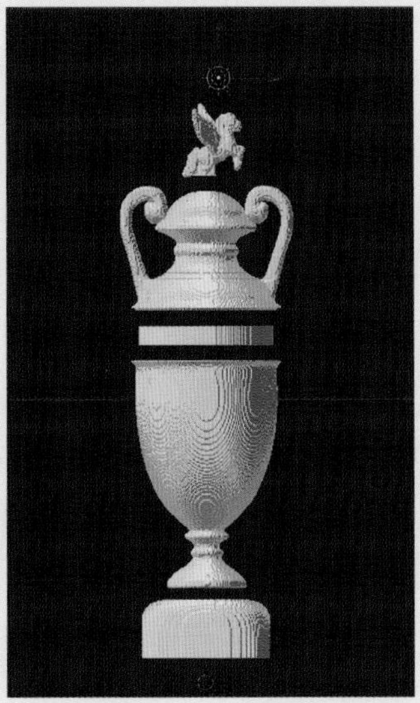

Process

Rapid prototyping and 3D printing has become widely accessible in recent years, and is an indispensable tool for artists and makers creating objects that would otherwise be very time consuming or difficult to achieve. The process frees the artist from limitations and allows more room for play and experimentation. Once the digital drawing has become a 3D printed object, it can then be used as a model and a mould taken from it. This digital drawing of the *Wedesus Urn* (see left) was made prior to it being 3D printed. As Davis's work has evolved, the prototypes have been split into parts to accommodate more complex designs. The biodegradable plastic prints require a surface clean-up and go through a construction process in preparation for manually moulding in plaster. When making designs to be moulded, consider the most efficient shapes to avoid overly-complex multi-part moulds and technical issues such as undercuts or areas where the cast could get stuck.

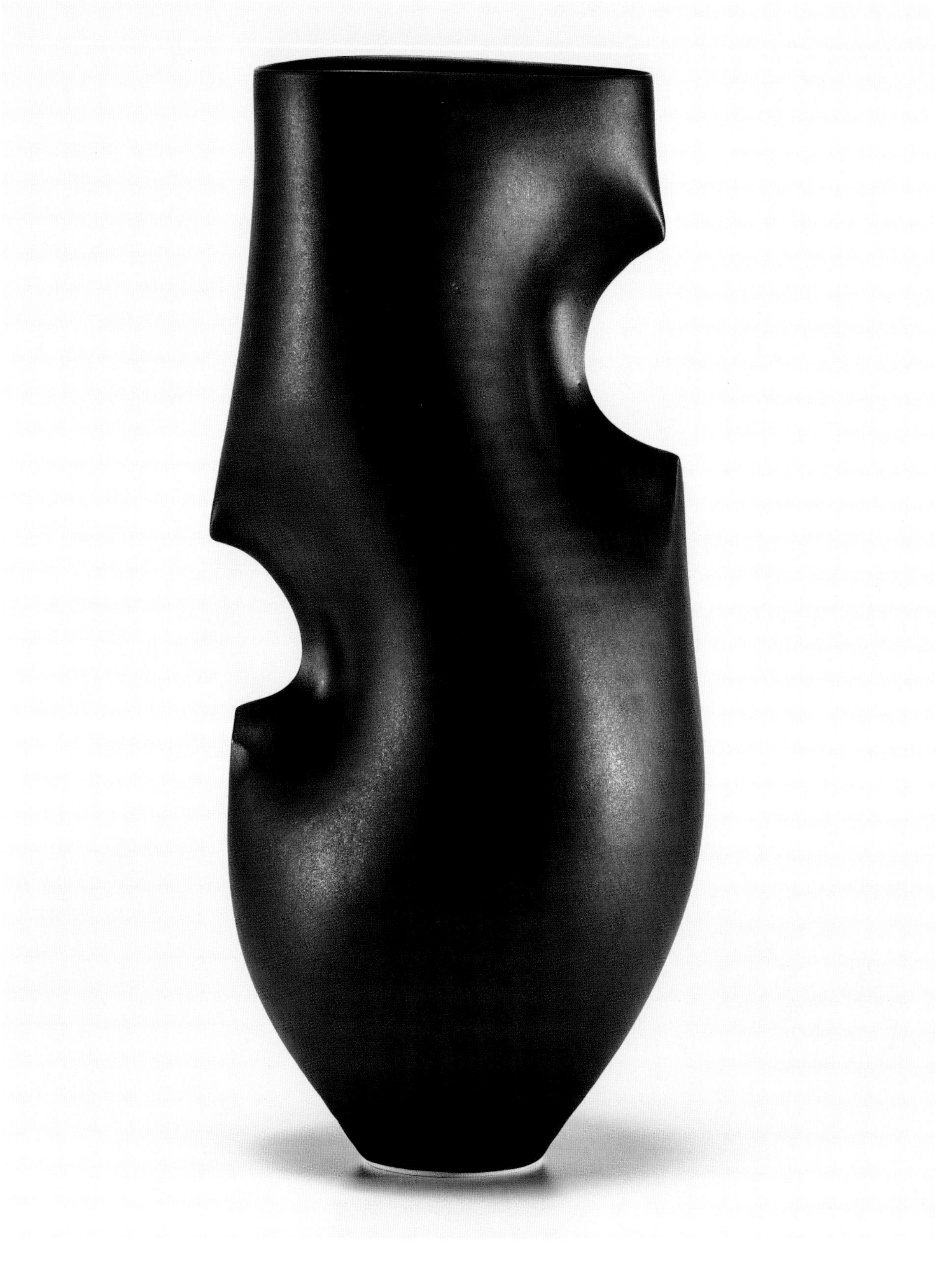

Hipped Vessel 2019
Thrown, cut and reassembled porcelain
Height: 33 cm (13 in.)

With their undulating curves and crisp, cut lines, the sensual forms made by Sara Flynn are the epitome of sophistication. Process is crucial and underpins her creative thinking, coupled with a constant exploration of form, volume and silhouette. Another important part of Flynn's approach and development involves 'play' – experimenting and taking risks in order to establish new ground. She says of this process, 'I try things out, which often initially don't work. This uninhibited part of my making-cycle involves risk-taking, failure and critical understanding. It is fundamental to my way of understanding and resolving ideas'. To create her works, Flynn throws each piece in porcelain using the pottery wheel. In this example, the resultant shape was distorted by the artist pushing the clay out from the inside, using the profile of her hand to define the contours that delicately ripple across the surface. A pair of sweeping cut lines – like huge bites – clamp the sides of the vessel, contorting and twisting the shape in the process. The resulting piece is meticulously finished, yet retains a freshness and conviction of form.

Flynn does not limit her choice of glaze options and chooses whether to fire her work in a reduction and oxidized environment depending on the overall colour she feels best suits the form. Here, the use of metallic black glaze allows for gentle refractions of light, accentuating the contours. Flynn describes the balance of achieving the right mix of form and surface as absolutely crucial to the success of the piece. She researches extensively to find the best glaze for the form and vice versa.

Sara Flynn (Irish, born 1971) began her career making small-scale functional pots before concentrating solely on producing one-off vessels that are purely sculptural in their intent. Born in Cork, Ireland, Flynn trained in ceramic design at Crawford College of Art & Design, where she experimented with porcelain, which she continues to use exclusively. She established her first studio in Kinsale in 2000, and then moved to Leap, West Cork, in 2006. She now lives and works in Belfast, Northern Ireland. In 2017, she was shortlisted for the inaugural edition of the Loewe Foundation Craft Prize and her work is held in many major collections, including The Gardiner Museum, Toronto, and The Art Institute of Chicago.

See also
Toshiko Takaezu (p.56)
Sun Kim (p.154)
Anne Marie Laureys (p.232)

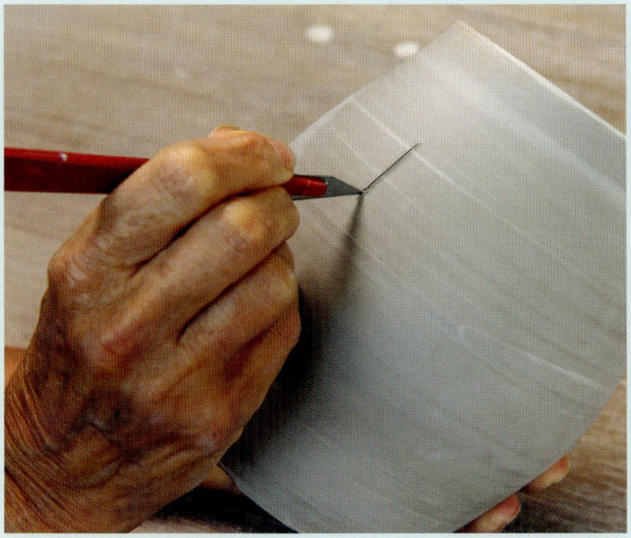

Composition
When planning a new form, Flynn will first loosely sketch out her ideas – but she does not let this dictate the design of the overall piece. She works intuitively and responds to the challenges of the material as the form develops. Flynn uses cutting and pinching techniques to adapt and alter her forms. This is a really simple and effective way to change the profile of a piece, but the skill lies in being decisive in order to retain the freshness of the cut and avoid fussy joins. Use a pottery knife or scalpel to slice sections of your work, and experiment with the stages of clay from very soft to leather-hard. Observe how the clay responds to being pulled back together and the impact on the overall form. A sharp scalpel will give you a crisp cut in the clay (see left). You could exploit these qualities further by pairing your forms with a suitable glaze that will draw out the textures and subtleties of the surface.

Decor

ative

The term 'decorative' is used quite loosely in this chapter. The intention is not to tie the featured artworks to 'ornamentation' but instead explore the links between form and surface, and the many ways decoration or applied surfaces can be used creatively as a means of artistic expression.

The fluid properties of slip can provide an opportunity to treat your raw clay surface as a canvas, perhaps to convey a narrative like the characterful charger plate by Thomas Toft (p.88), or more freely, like the robust works of Simon Carroll (p.98). Clay and glazes are brilliant for mimicking realistic, natural qualities such as the watery colours of Bernard Palissy's dioramic plates, teeming with life (p. 86), or the leafy troll persona, created by Malene Hartmann Rasmussen (p.106). You can be very experimental and uninhibited with your surfaces, by incorporating mixtures of combustible or non-organic materials into your clay body to impact your form. Adopting an inquisitive approach can directly influence your glazing and surface application methods too, like Bente Skjøttgaard (p.108) and Brian Rochefort's (p.128) heavily saturated, oozing forms.

Feature glazes could offer you an interesting dynamic to your surface, from the metallic, lustrous glaze of Hideaki Miyamura (p.104), to Kate Malone's crystalline glazes that complement her geological shapes (p.116). Matt surfaces can enhance a form, such as the curvy, thrown assemblages of Wouter Dam (p.114) or interplay of crisp pattern and sharp lines of Bodil Manz's work (p.96). Like Grayson Perry (p.94), you could exploit the familiarity of archetypal ceramic form to convey unsettling themes through rich decoration.

Bernard Palissy

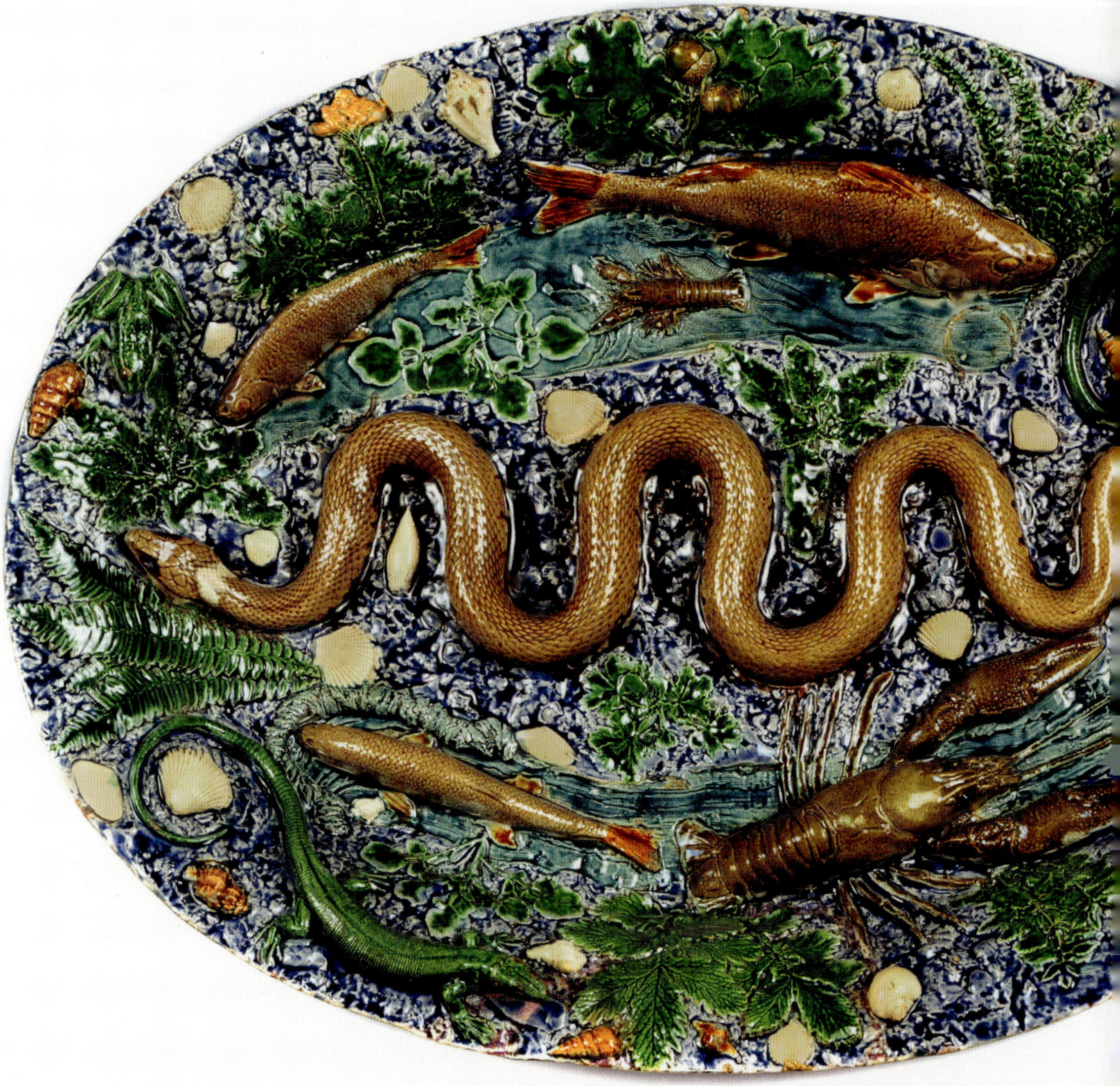

See also

Malene Hartmann Rasmussen (p.106), **Bertozzi & Casoni** (p.228)

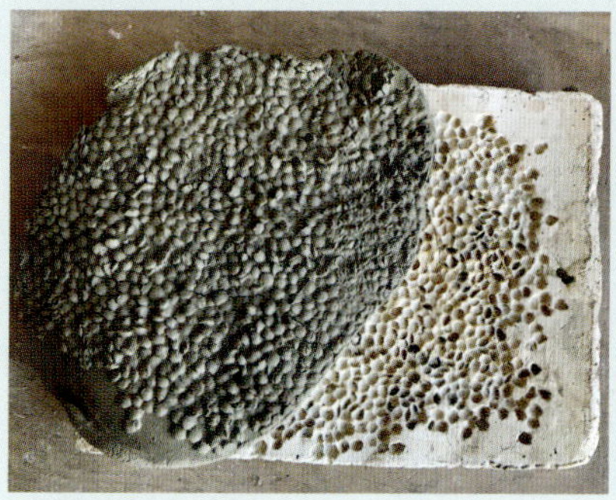

Bernard Palissy (French, 1510–90) was a Renaissance artist with interests spanning science, natural history, palaeontology and stained glass. Palissy is most famous for producing large dioramas on plates and sculptural vessels that depict pond scenes teeming with life and curiosity. During his career, he earned a notable reputation and was extremely popular among royalty and distinguished members of society. In 1545 he was commissioned by the Queen Mother of France, Catherine de Medici, to create a large-scale grotto in the grounds of the Tuileries Palace in Paris. Although this project was never completed, Palissy enjoyed huge success during his lifetime but his luck ran out in 1588 when he was imprisoned for his Calvinist beliefs. He died of mistreatment at the Bastille in 1590.

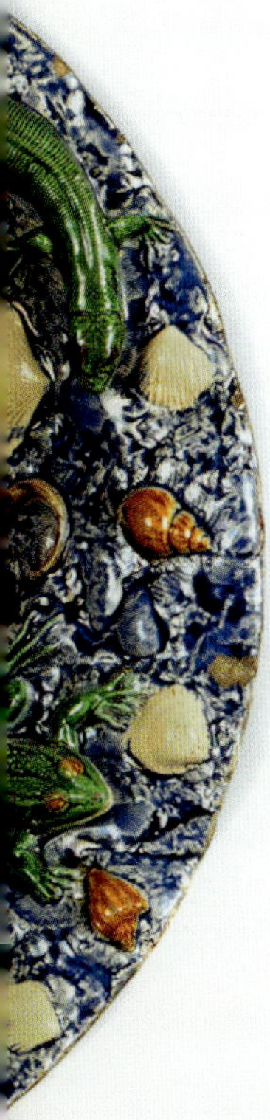

Rusticware Platter 1575–99
Lead-glazed earthenware
Length: *c.* 50 cm (19¾ in.); Width: *c.* 40 cm (15¾ in.)

This oval platter is a typical example of Palissy's imaginative scenes, often referred to as *pièce rustique* (rusticware). A grass snake undulates in the centre of the platter, a trickling stream bubbles and twists, fish darting along it and a snipping crustacean emerging from its banks. Lizards, shells, fern leaves, acorns and pebbles adorn the rim. A frog perches on the edge of the platter, his hind legs tucked in, poised to leap. Palissy's great skill was his ability to convey movement and imply that the creatures in his scenes could come to life and scuttle away. Following his work with stained glass, Palissy set out to mimic the brilliant shine and gloss of enamels and sought to translate these qualities into ceramic earthenware glazes. Through much experimentation, he emulated watery realism by painting his ceramics with rich cobalt blues, purples, green and honey lead glazes to complete the scene.

The subjects in Renaissance art often centred around religion, and symbolism was used to convey coded messages to the viewer about anything from fertility and wealth to immortality. Rabbits represented lust, goldfinches embodied the soul and snakes were considered evil, due to connotations with the manipulative serpent in the garden of Eden. It is unclear whether Palissy sought to embed a deeper level of symbolism into his dioramas, although he was particularly intrigued by frogs. To him they represented the generation of new life. What is also curious is the relationship between the specimens he chose for the display. An undulating snake in a pond with a crayfish seems at odds with how the animals would inhabit the wild. It seems likely that the scenes he created were imaginative representations of his interest in the natural world and his creative intention was purely decorative.

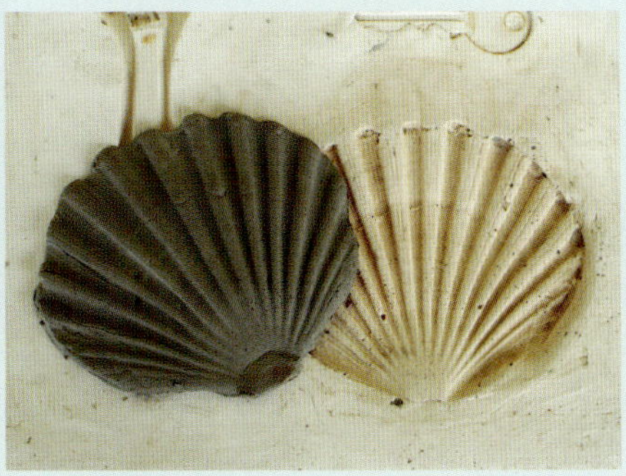

Technical

Palissy experimented with press-moulding techniques after he was inspired by bronze casting processes. Like Palissy, you can take simple plaster moulds of natural artefacts such as shells (left). A textured plaster panel (far left) can be made by embedding small stones or even lentils onto a clay sheet with raised sides. To capture the imprint, press wads of clay into the mould and compact down with your thumb or a wooden tool. Scrape away any excess clay, so that the surface is flush with the mould. Allow the clay to firm a little before carefully removing it from the mould and arranging the cast on a prepared form. Secure the piece in position by cross-hatching the points of contact and applying slip. Use a wooden tool to seal the cast to the surface of the form, followed by a light tidy-up with a damp sponge.

Thomas Toft

Charger *c.* 1680
Earthenware, slipware
Height: 8.9 cm (3½ in.); Diameter: 50.2 cm (19¾ in.)

Freely illustrated and playful, this large charger bears the royal coat of arms supported by a lion and a unicorn. Within the heraldic imagery there are other more subtle symbols: behind the lion's shoulder, a rose represents England and a Scottish thistle climbs and twists around the unicorn. An oak tree occupies the centre of the dish. Peeping out from within the tree is a portrait of King Charles II (1630–85), identifiable from the initials C. R. – for Charles Rex – inscribed between the arms of the rearing animals. This illustration is a reference to a popular true story that the young future king climbed into an oak tree in Boscobel Wood in Shropshire, UK, to escape the Roundheads following his defeat at the battle of Worcester in 1651. As he was hiding, one of the soldiers passed directly beneath the tree without noticing him.

To create this piece, Toft press-moulded a large dish shape using a coarse, iron-rich red clay, dug from the local area. He then applied a layer of white slip to prepare a 'canvas' on which he slip-trailed his motifs. The simple, earthy colour palette was produced mainly using variants of iron oxide; in the 17th century, ceramic pigments would have been very limited compared to the range available to a modern potter. The dark outline of the illustration, infilled with a lighter orange slip, is enriched further with intricate white dots. Around the outer edge of the dish is a broad trellis pattern, the opposing directions of lines trailed in a different tone to create the illusion of depth. To complete the charger, Toft glazed the front of the dish with a honey-coloured lead glaze to enhance the detail and enrich the slip colours.

Thomas Toft (British, active 1660–80) created work that has become some of the most recognizable in ceramic history due to his ambitious use of slip and lively motifs. Toft's subject matter ranged from royalty and cavaliers to mythology and mermaids. Thought to be of Scandinavian descent, Toft was based in Burslem, a district of Stoke-on-Trent. Little is known about his life other than that he had a number of relatives who all produced pottery in the same slipware tradition. The pieces by Toft and his family are easily identifiable because their signature is proudly emblazoned on the rim and incorporated into the overall design. There are very few pieces of his work in existence – approximately thirty to forty. It's possible they survived because they were made as display pieces to showcase his skill and promote his other utilitarian wares.

See also
Simon Carroll (p.98)
Bernard Leach (p.136)
Shōji Hamada (p.140)

Technical
Thomas Toft was the master of the slip-trailing technique, a method that involves piping slip into decorative lines and marks (see right and far right). In the 17th century, Toft's tool would have been made from a cup-like container pierced with a reed or quill to allow the slip to flow freely. Modern slip trailers are usually made from rubber and are bulb shaped, with interchangeable pen nibs that the user can change to draw lines ranging from very fine to thick.

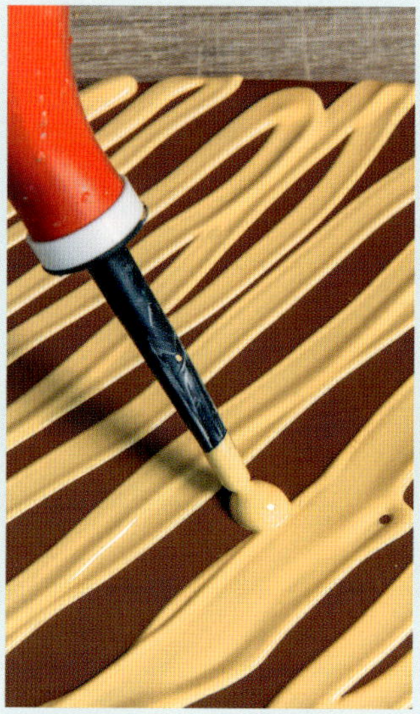

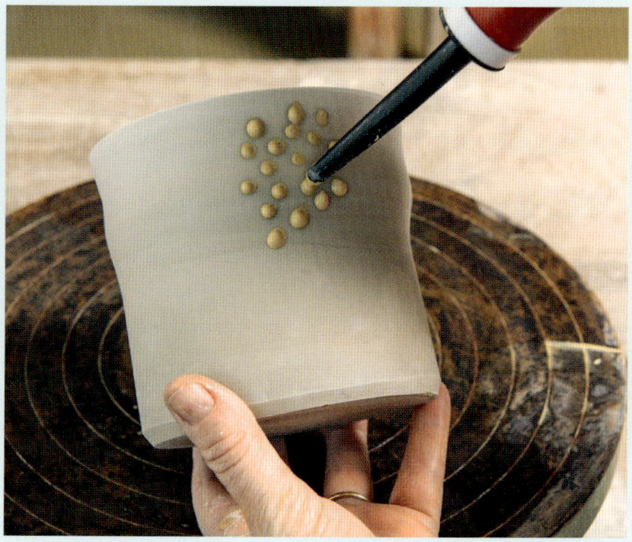

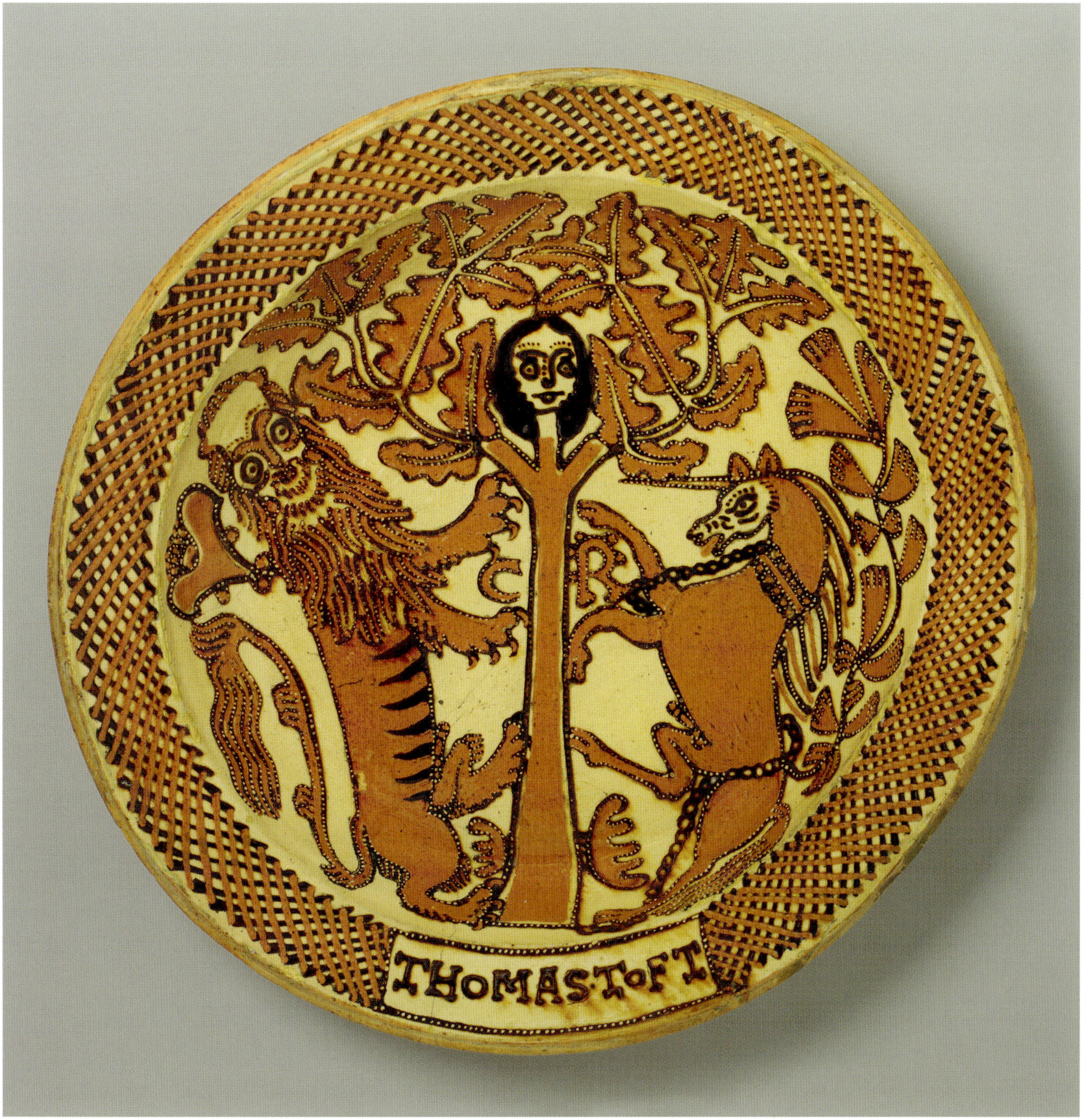
C R
THOMAS·TOFT

George Ohr

Vase 1910
Earthenware
11.1 × 14.6 × 14.6 cm (4⅜ × 5¾ × 5¾ in.)

By the end of the 19th century, art nouveau was an influential art movement sweeping across Europe and the USA. It was around the height of this period, from 1895 to 1910, that George Ohr was at his most prolific, and the elements that define art nouveau – such as flowing lines based on natural forms and ornamental style – are clearly evident in his experimental pottery forms.

Ohr sourced his materials locally, digging iron-rich clay from the Tchoutacabouffa River and transporting it by canal to his workshop in Biloxi, Mississippi. He was an exceptional thrower and had the skill to throw paper-thin walls, which he crumpled and distorted beyond recognition. This example of a vase by Ohr demonstrates his playful approach to form and surface. Here, he has swelled out sections of the vessel to create an organic, flower-like shape; the softness of the clay can still be seen in the free-flowing pleating of the rim. Ohr juxtaposed the rich glossy interior with an austere metallic earthenware glaze on the external surface. He continuously experimented and explored new glazes that were completely unique to him. His techniques ranged from sponging and dabbing oxides to spattering effects and textured, blistered glazes that evoked repulsion.

Ohr's wacky and maverick approach to using clay was quite the contrast to the traditional utilitarian wares made by potters of the same era. He never made two pots alike and found it incredibly difficult to part with his work. On the rare occasion that he sold a pot, he would often chase the new owner down the street and ask for it back! When the collection of Ohrs' pottery came to market in 1972, it was viewed with fresh enthusiasm and appreciation for his talent. Ohr is regarded as a contributing influence to the rise of the American expressionist studio potters and sculptors, including Peter Voulkos. Famously, his work was collected by iconic artists of the day, including Andy Warhol (1928–87) and Roy Lichtenstein (1923–97).

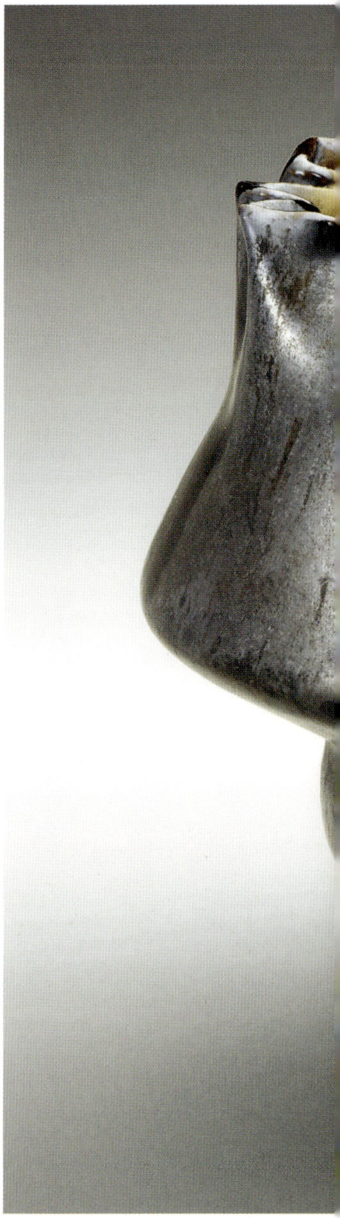

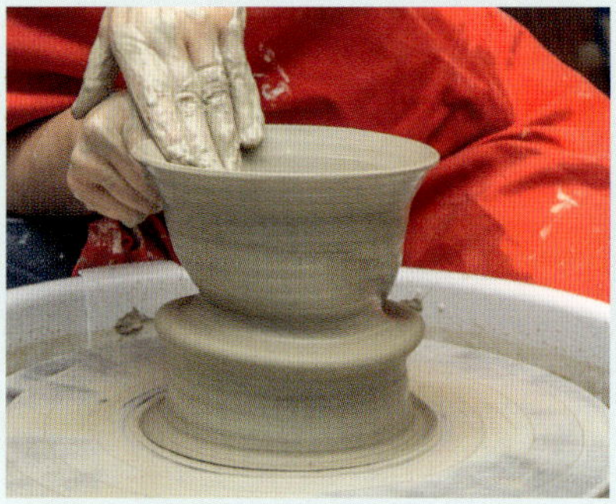

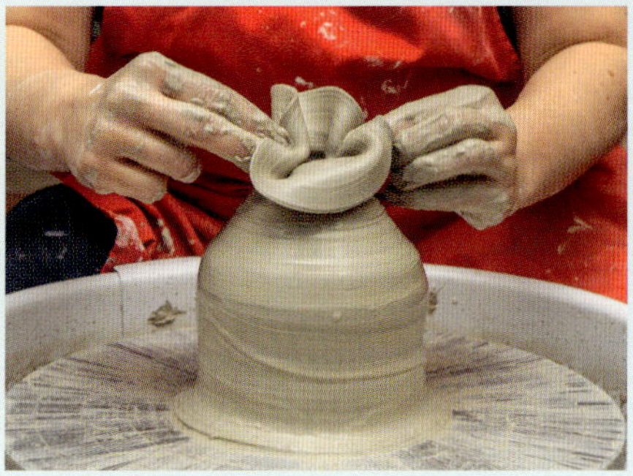

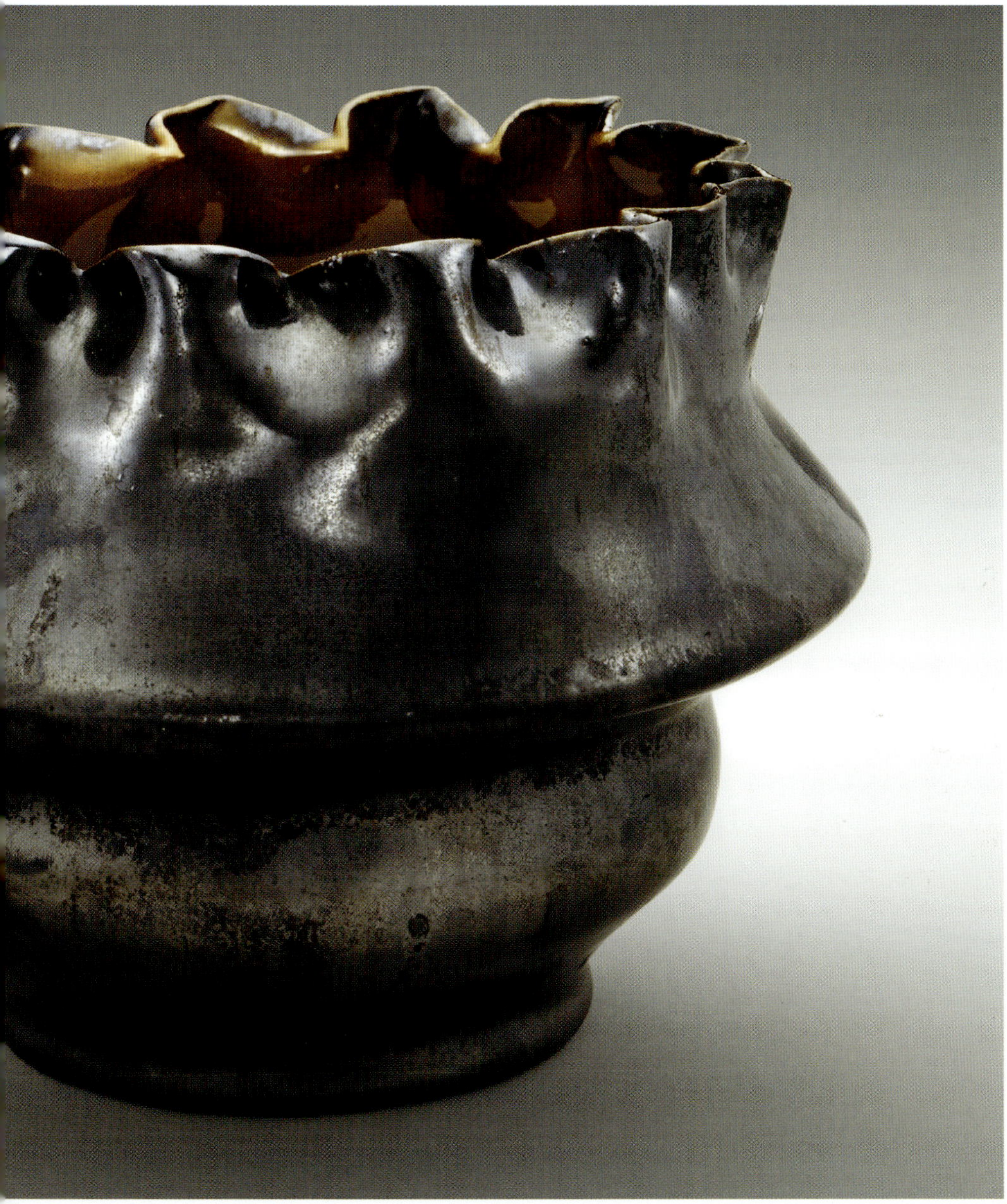

George Ohr (American, 1857–1918) had a wildly coiffed hairstyle and a distinguished eighteen-inch moustache – his eccentric appearance and behaviour earned him the title of the 'Mad Potter of Biloxi'. He was the son of German immigrants who arrived in New Orleans *c.* 1850. He first followed his father's trade as a blacksmith, but at the age of twenty-two he trained as a potter with Joseph F. Meyer (1848–1931). Ohr proclaimed himself 'The Greatest Art Potter in the World'; however, his audience were less appreciative of his works and Ohr was largely misunderstood during his lifetime. After his death at the age of sixty, his studio was converted into a motor garage and fuel station by his sons. His collection of more than 7,000 pots was put into storage and that is where they remained for more than fifty years. It was not until a chance discovery by an antiques dealer that Ohr's originality and brilliance was at last truly recognized. In 2010, The Ohr-O'Keefe museum was built in Biloxi to showcase Ohr's extraordinary works and preserve his legacy.

See also

Peter Voulkos (p.68)
Takeshi Yasuda (p.158)
Anne Marie Laureys (p.232)

Process

To emulate the buckled, contorted forms of George Ohr, try experimenting with throwing very fine forms and allowing your fingers to snag the internal wall to force a twist in the vessel (see far left). Compress a cylinder from the rim and observe how the clay walls crumple under the weight (see left). A smooth plastic clay will behave differently to a grogged clay and this variation could be explored further to best suit your intended work. Ohr was very experimental with his glazes and strived to create unique results. He often flicked oxides and glazes over the top of a base colour. A toothbrush is an excellent tool for recreating this effect (see right). You could also use a natural sponge dipped in oxide to produce softer textured effects.

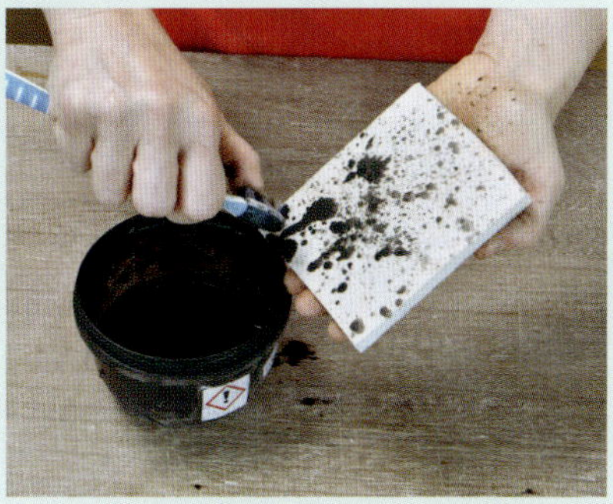

Jun Kaneko

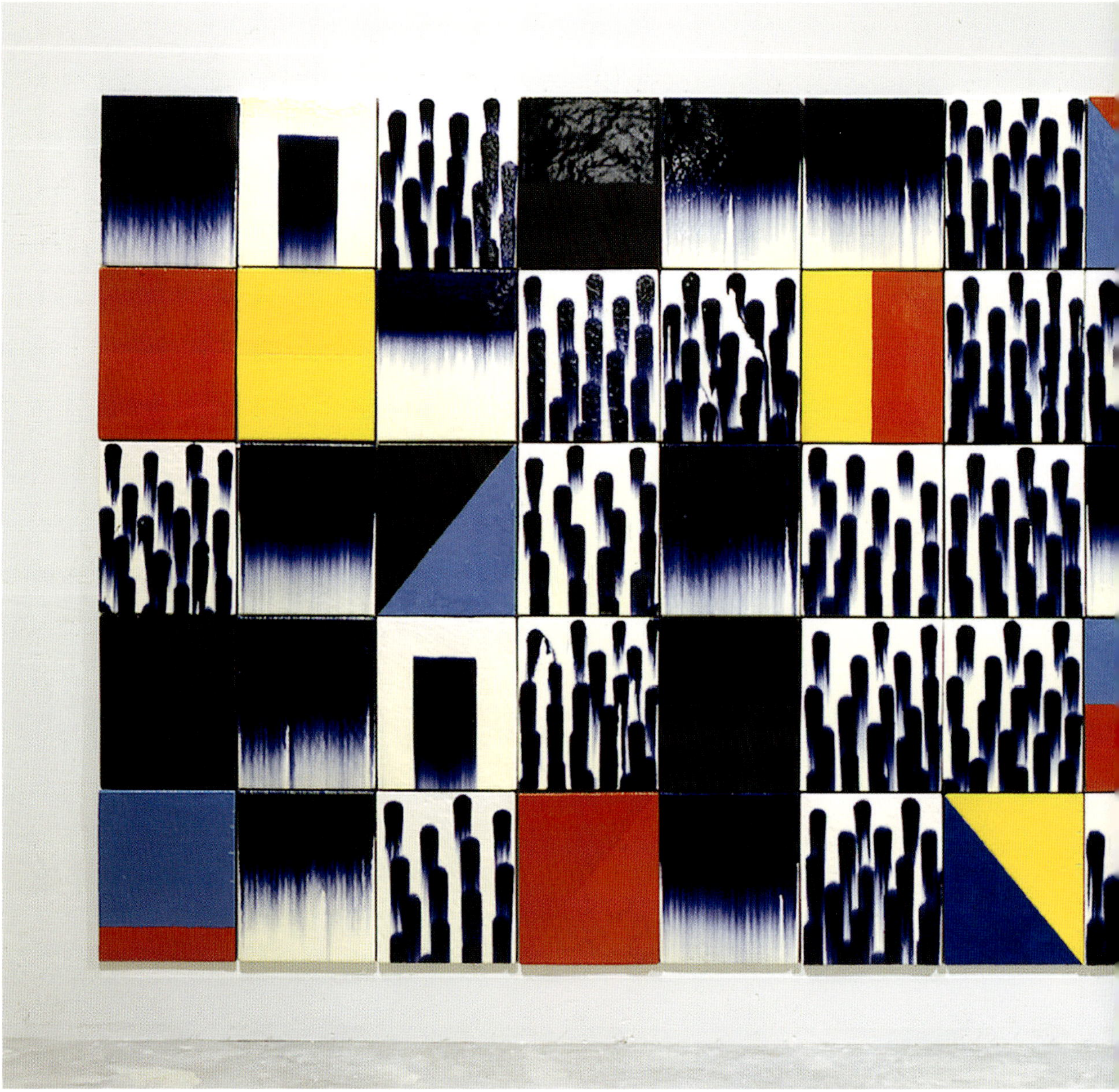

See also

Elisabeth Kley (p.74), **Janice Tchalenko** (p.110)

Jun Kaneko (Japanese, born 1942) was born in Nagoya, Japan, where he studied painting until he moved to the United States in 1963 to continue his studies at the Chouinard Institute of Art in Los Angeles. There, he was drawn to sculptural ceramics. He studied under Jerry Rothman (1933–2014), Paul Soldner (see p.206) and Peter Voulkos (see p.68), who formed the California school of ceramic arts that combined Western materials and technology with Japanese techniques and aesthetics. Kaneko is known for his experimentation with raku firing and his large, hand-built and glazed sculptures covered in abstract imagery.

Technical

When making tiles from slabs take care with the drying and firing to prevent them from warping or becoming uneven. Make sure you have thoroughly wedged, kneaded or pug milled your clay first, and when the tiles are drying in their raw state avoid draughts, which will cause the edges to curl up. Firing should be steady but you can stack tiles on top of one another in batches of six to eight.

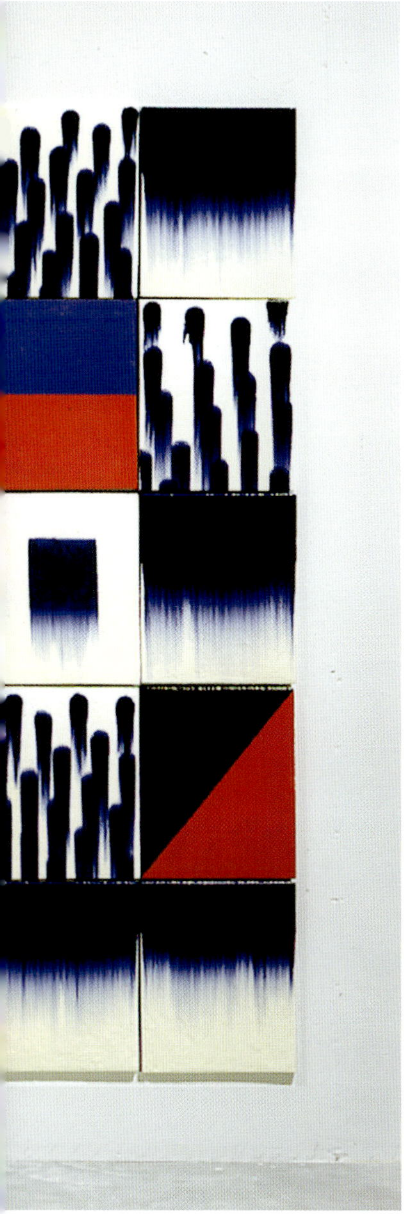

Untitled, EKWC Wall 1996
Hand-built and glazed ceramics
233.7 × 368.3 × 2 cm (92 × 145 × ¾ in.)

Jun Kaneko is world renowned for his monolithic, hand-built Dango sculptures and colourful, abstract works in many other mediums. He has successfully designed for three opera productions and created formidable works for public art commissions. With a career spanning more than fifty years, Kaneko initially trained as a painter and he uses the ceramic surface as a canvas for his timeless designs. Kaneko comments, 'I find it difficult to leave the surface of my sculpture as it is. I almost always have a need to paint on it.... When I can hear what a form has to say, I start seeing marks and colours on the surface.'

This lively tile wall composition was made from hand formed and glazed ceramic slabs, during his second residency experimenting with low fire ceramics and glazes at the European Ceramics Work Centre (EKWC) in the Netherlands. Kaneko's interpretation is free in application and he mixes up the impact of the bold colours with painterly polka dots and bleeds of cobalt oxide. Another interesting aspect of this piece is how Kaneko has played with subtle shifts in the light refracting from the glazed surface of some of the tiles by juxtaposing a matt glaze with a shiny version of the same colour. Using a masking technique, Kaneko has differentiated between the horizontal, vertical and diagonal plane arrangements as well as the proportions of colour within the tile, bringing a graphic element to this dynamic surface. Kaneko's repeats of colour mixed with abstract decoration unite this wall panel into one sophisticated resolution. In the book on this body of work he remarks, 'To me, a pattern or a color repeated, makes some kind of visual order [and] the spaces between the marks contribute a great deal to the tonality of the finished work.'

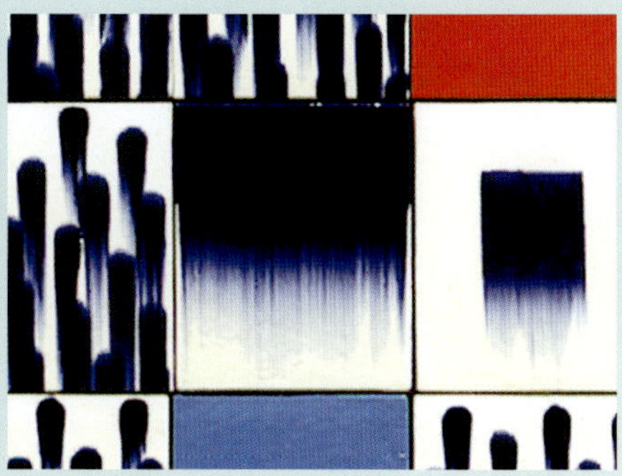

Surface

Kaneko explores the flowing quality of cobalt oxide to create organic, expressive results in his surfaces. If you have made tiles and like this effect, you could fire them upright in a support to allow gravity to force the oxide to cascade as it melts. Another way is to dip your brush in a washy mix of oxide and, as you drag the brush across the unfired glaze background, lift your hand away and ease the pressure to allow the brush to just lightly stroke the surface. Play with the variety of marks that can be made using a brush, from small dabs to big gestural strokes. Try overlapping variable strengths of oxide wash to give depth to your composition. You could also layer matt and glossy glazes over sections of your decoration and cause the oxide to react differently.

Grayson Perry

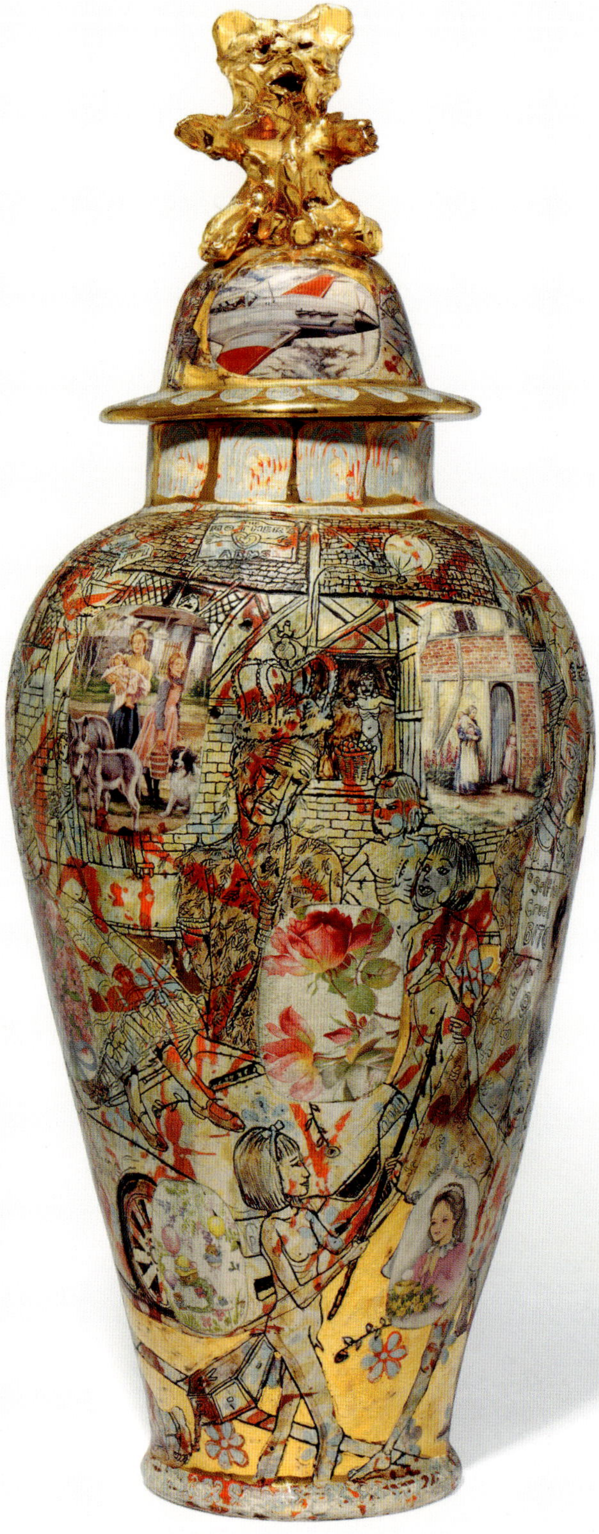

Triumph of Innocence 2000
Earthenware
70 × 23 × 23 cm (27½ × 9 × 9 in.)

Grayson Perry's pots are classical in form and richly decorated. Reminiscent of ancient Greek pottery and folk art, they feel familiar and invite closer inspection. However, the subjects that adorn these vessels are seemingly at odds with their classical appearance. Perry's work tackles uncomfortable themes and draws on diverse influences, from popular culture to highly charged social and political topics – always using humour and satirical commentary to soften the controversial and provocative subject matter. His work is heavily autobiographical, with frequent depictions of his transvestite alter ego, Claire, and childhood teddy Alan Measles. Perry plays upon this divergence between the object and its message to engage the viewer.

This lidded urn portrays images of prepubescent children marching with their captured adult prisoners on their way to execute them. In pursuit is teddy Alan Measles driving a car with Perry's female self, Claire, sprawled on the bonnet. The scene parodies the historic Dutch Renaissance painting *The Procession to Calvary* (1564) by Pieter Bruegel the Elder (*c.* 1525/30–69), whom Perry cites as an influence. Beneath the dense visuals of flower motifs, cutesy children and animals lies a heartfelt expression of Perry's difficult childhood and the coping mechanisms he used to seek mindful refuge. The saturated clash of colours and exuberant use of gold are characteristic of Perry's style. Through the approachable medium of clay, Perry amplifies the interplay between beauty and obscenity, stating, 'no matter how brash a statement I make, on a pot it will always have [a] certain humility'.

Grayson Perry (British, born 1960) studied fine art at Portsmouth College of Art and Design. He came to prominence in the 1990s for his ceramic pots, which adopted a classical form but depicted narratives of contemporary themes. Frequently, Perry's work takes the form of social commentary on issues ranging from child abuse to environmental disaster – all tackled with his signature irony and wit. His oeuvre covers themes of identity, gender, sexuality, art history, politics and class. Perry's work has been recognized with numerous awards, including the prestigious Turner Prize in 2003. He was awarded a CBE in 2013.

See also
Robert Dawson (p.100)
Ramesh Mario Nithiyendran (p.190)
Vicky Lindo (p.240)

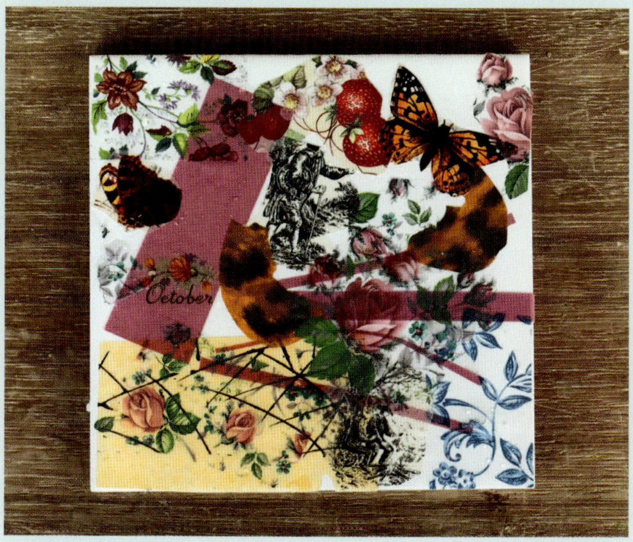

Process
Grayson Perry's subversive pots are made using the traditional method of coiling. The irregularity of the technique gives the pots an authentic, handmade feel that accentuates Perry's crafted aesthetic. His complex surfaces are accomplished using many techniques. Starting at the raw stage, Perry applies relief moulds, slip decoration, inlay and sgraffito to define the initial content. After the piece is bisque fired, it is glazed with a glossy, clear earthenware glaze to bring out the depth of colour. The rich surface decoration is achieved by dense layering of photographic transfers and metal lustres, which are fired at a lower temperature of around 820°C (1508°F). As this tile demonstrates, you can build up a lively collage with ready-made ceramic decals of, for example, chintzy flowers, fruits and butterflies. The overlaps and clash of patterns can produce a striking visual effect.

Bodil Manz

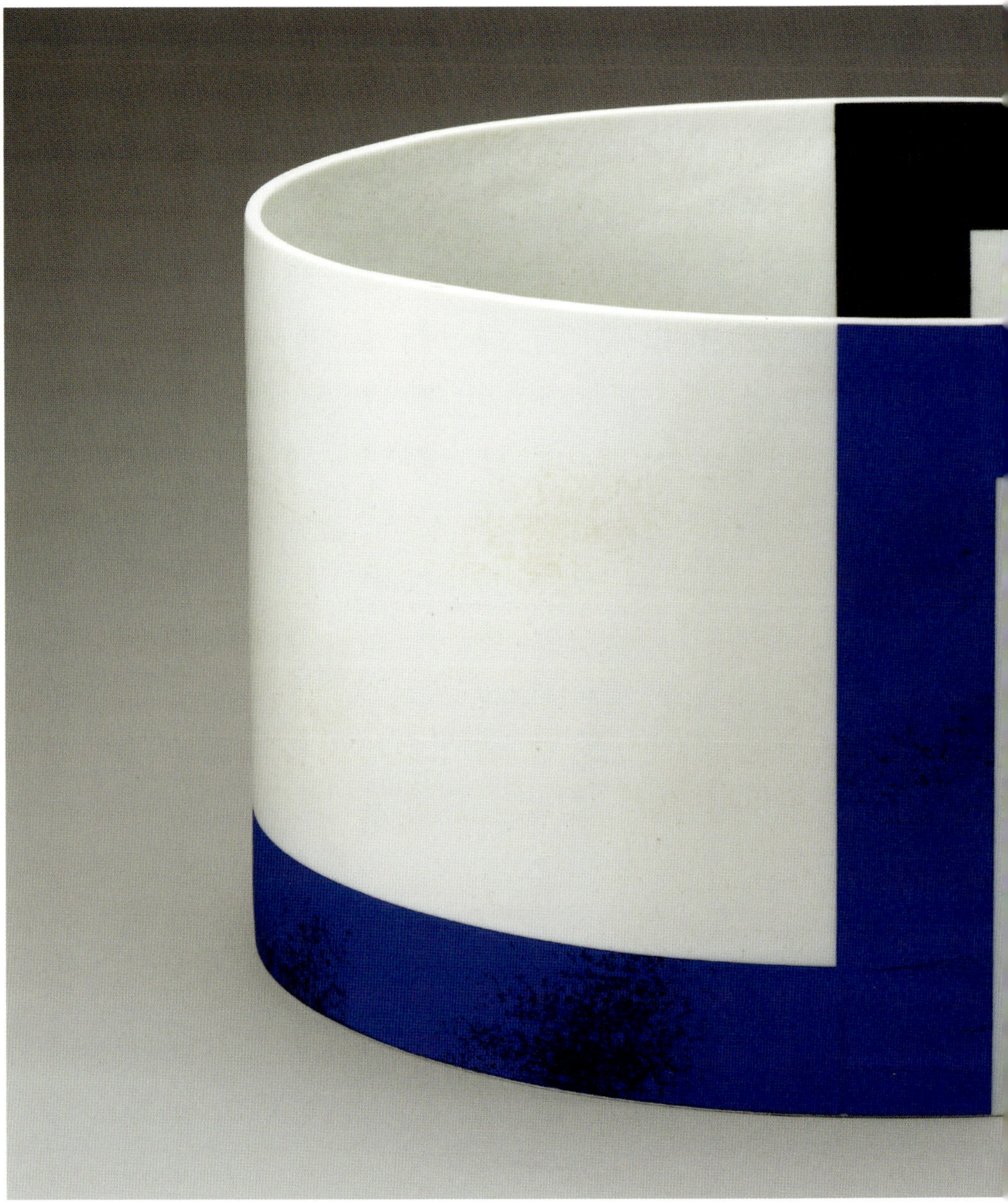

Bodil Manz (Danish, born 1943) studied ceramics at Copenhagen School of Arts and Crafts; the Escuelo de Diseño y Artesanias in Mexico; and then at the University of Berkeley, California. Manz set up a workshop in Horve, Denmark, with her husband Richard (1933–99) in 1967. Initially, she created traditional servingware, but from the 1990s onwards she began experimenting with ways to produce ultra-thin, translucent eggshell porcelain to create cylindrical forms. Her signature vessels have bold, colourful geometric designs on the exterior and interior that evoke De Stijl, Cubism and Russian supremacism. In 2006 she was awarded the Grand Prize at the 4th World Ceramic Biennale, Korea.

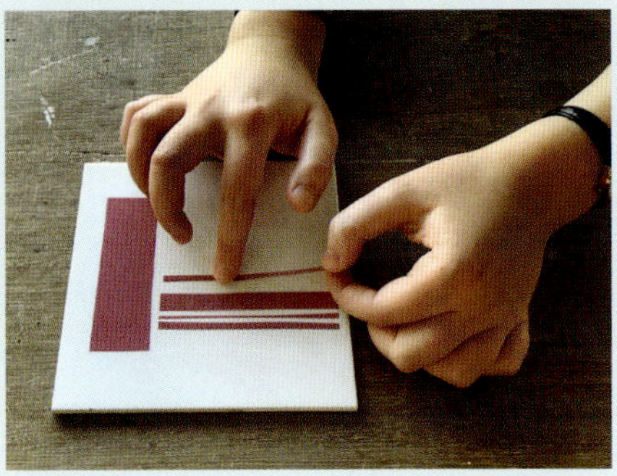

Technical

Manz initially plans her compositions on paper to ensure a successful design. She then cuts out strips of coloured ceramic transfer paper, which she applies to the unglazed piece. The artist uses the high temperature of the firing to allow the transfer to melt into the ceramic surface. Transfers can be made via screen printing or you can have them digitally printed. You could experiment with a collage effect or try your hand at more structured designs like Manz. Typically, transfers are fired to a temperature of 820°C (1508°F), but you could apply them to a glazed surface and high-fire to stoneware temperature, which will cause them to fade and bleed into the glaze.

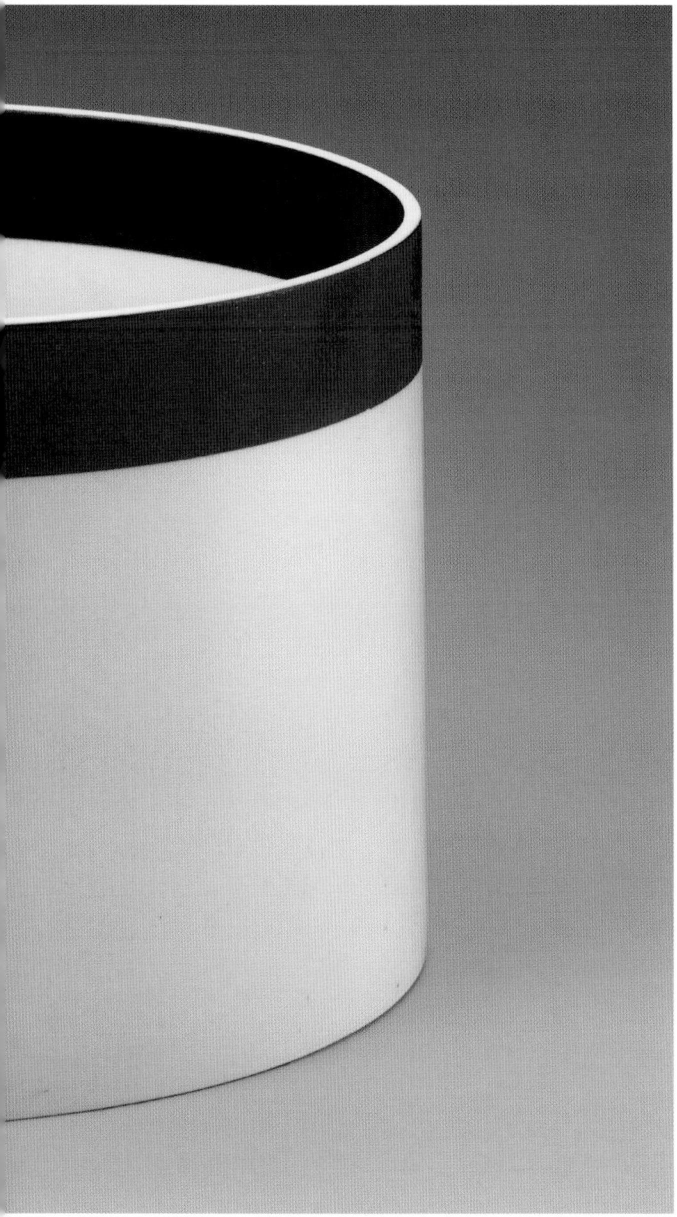

Vessel 2001
Porcelain
22.2 × 37.1 × 25.7 cm (8¾ × 14⅗ × 10 in.)

Danish ceramicist Bodil Manz is world-renowned for her ultra-thin, translucent porcelain cylinders. Inspired by modernist architecture and painters such as Piet Mondrian (1872–1944) and Kazimir Malevich (1879–1935), Manz has developed a unique style, in which she constructs abstract linear compositions from strips of black and the primary colours. This aesthetic, combined with a high level of refinement, results in pieces that exhibit a wonderful interplay between the interior and exterior decoration as light floods through the walls of the vessel.

This flawless cylinder by Manz exemplifies her ability to command the form with a striking geometric design. It is very simple but incredibly effective. In this piece, a blue line follows the base before turning ninety degrees vertically and then turning back on itself. This is echoed by a black line that follows an identical path on the interior. The strength of line and the remarkable quality is impeccable, forcing an optical illusion and an interesting play on light and shadow.

The piece was finely slip cast from a mould and a thick linear motif was applied as a transfer to the unglazed bisque surface. This is an unusual method because transfers are typically applied to a glazed surface to ensure a good melt. Manz, however, has pioneered a technique in which she exploits the semi-glazing properties of porcelain to enable the transfers to adhere to the surface by melting the glaze into the clay body itself. Manz high-fires her work to a temperature of 1300°C (2372°F) and it can take several firings to achieve the desired effect.

See also
Robert Dawson (p.100)
Piet Stockmans (p.144)
Ruth Duckworth (p.66)

Simon Carroll

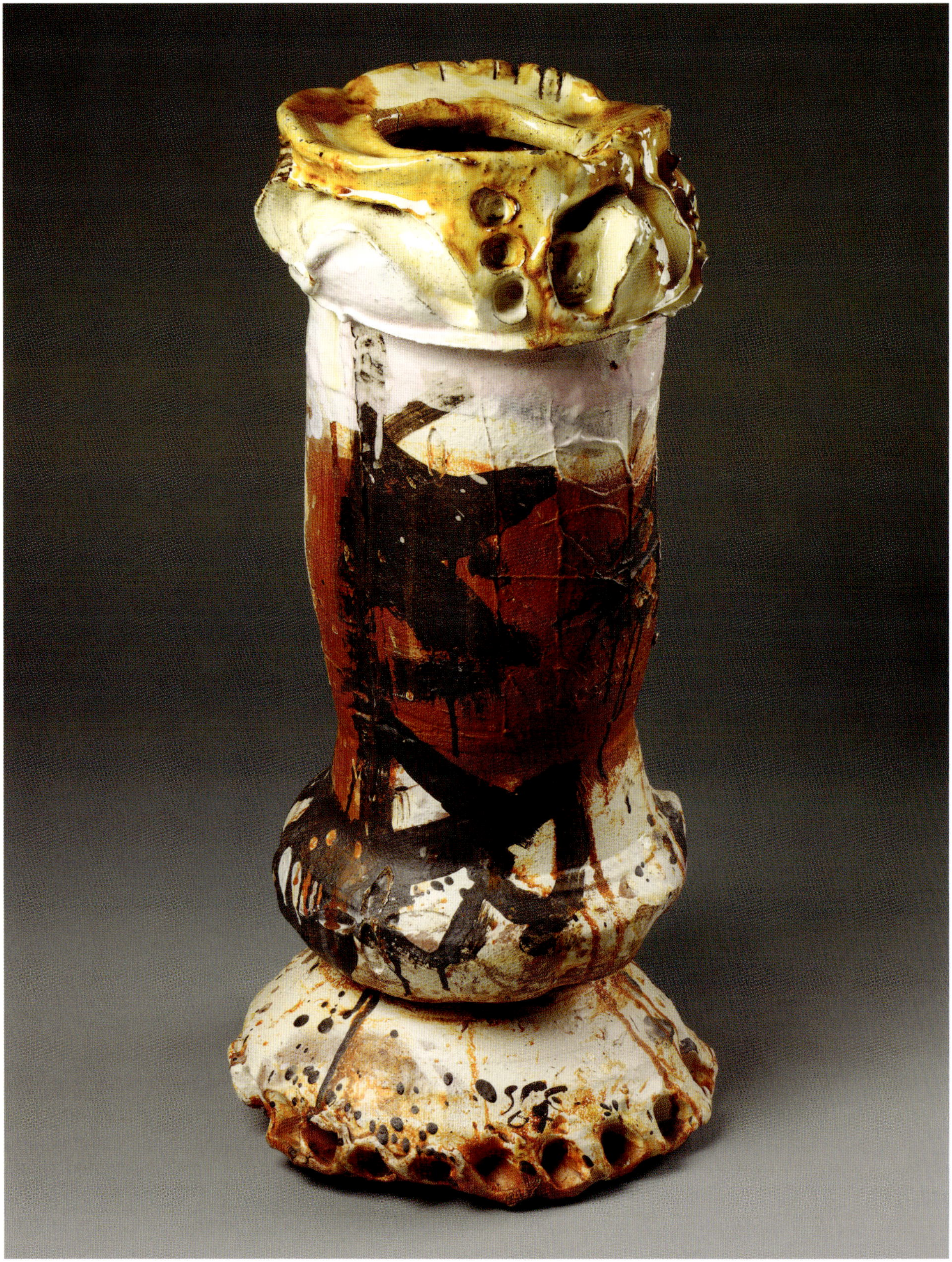

Tall Thrown Pot 2004
Thrown and press moulded with slip decoration and honey glaze
63.5 × 30.5 cm (25 × 12 in.)

Drawing upon the influence of traditional slipwares of the 17th and 18th centuries, this tall thrown vessel breaks all established conventions and encompasses Carroll's uniquely exuberant style. Rugged and robust, the chunky form asserts a powerful presence. The piece encapsulates the moment in time in which it was created, displaying spontaneity of mark marking, freedom of process and unrestricted playfulness with texture and decoration. What it is, exactly, is rather ambiguous. It feels familiar, like a jug or a vase, but defines itself as neither; instead the intended purpose resides in its sculptural elements. It is a celebration of materiality.

Carroll was very experimental with his working methods. One of his techniques involved encasing a thrown vessel in a mould lined with scratched marks and drawings. The mould was clipped onto the pottery wheel and Carroll continued throwing the vessel to force it to take the new profile and transfer the embossed imprint in the mould onto the clay surface. This piece likely started as a series of thrown components, which he freely assembled and joined. Expressive drips and splashes of creamy slip drench the form with colour and energy; bold brush marks painted on with oxide zigzag and pivot across the vertical surface. Carroll liberally applied a golden honey lead glaze around the rim, intensifying the yellow colour of the slip. The resulting build-up of layers is intensely rich and dynamic. Carroll's pounded thumb marks can be seen at pulsed intervals, defining the making process and retaining the softness of the clay in a state of permanence.

Simon Carroll (British, 1964–2009) grew up in Hereford and trained in ceramics at the University of the West of England, Bristol, under the tutelage of Walter Keeler and Mo Jupp. In the early 1990s, Carroll assisted in the art department at the Royal National College for the Blind in Hereford and was inspired by the intuitive methods the students used to create their works, which heightened his own awareness of touch and haptic sense. Carroll was particularly interested in historical collections of 17th- and 18th-century slipware produced in Staffordshire and enjoyed the playfulness of the decoration. Carroll was an artist of many great talents, ranging from painting and print to giant beach drawings. In 2004, he was awarded the prestigious Arts Foundation Prize. Carroll died prematurely at the age of forty-five.

See also
Alison Britton (p.72)
Walter Keeler (p.142)
Mo Jupp (p.178)

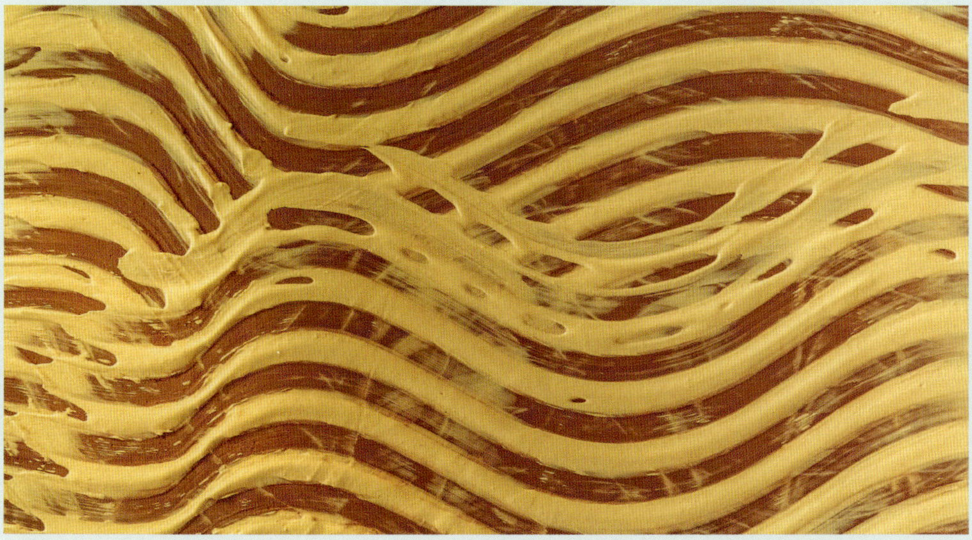

Surface
Carroll freely trailed, poured and splashed slips onto his ceramic vessels. Try combing your fingers through slip at variable speeds. Allow drips and pours to spill over edges and run down the sides of your piece for a lively effect. Textured plaster panels are an excellent way to bring surface interest and embossed detail to clay. You can also experiment with textured wallpapers, which can be wrapped around a vessel to transfer the imprint.

Robert Dawson

Spin 2010
Print on bone china
Each plate: Diameter: 27 cm (10⅝ in.)

Willow pattern, with its familiar blue-and-white chinoiserie design, was developed and manufactured in Stoke-on-Trent, UK, in the early 19th century. Representing a traditional Chinese tale, the iconic scene tells a story of forbidden love, forced separation and reprisals, with the protagonists forever immortalized as a pair of flying doves. Referring to his practice as 'aesthetic sabotage', Robert Dawson takes the willow pattern and playfully manipulates the imagery to subvert and skew our interpretation.

Spin, a collection of six plates bearing the willow pattern, is a brilliant example of Dawson's interplay with image and form. Here, he has achieved a dramatic feeling of intense speed and motion, all contained within a stationary dinner plate. The series starts with a plate that seems to be rotating gently. The pace progresses, with each plate appearing to spin faster and faster until the final plate is just a blur – inducing a dizzying effect. The spinning motion captured by Dawson represents processes integral to the production of ceramics, from throwing on the pottery wheel to jigger and jollying methods associated with industrial manufacture of plates and functional wares. Dawson creates his works by using computer software to manipulate the images. His method requires precision and accuracy to achieve the desired effect. The completed image is made into a digitally printed transfer, which is applied to a manufactured dinner plate and fired to a temperature of around 800°C (1472°F). The result is an abstracted image that remains accessible.

Robert Dawson (British-American, born 1953) was born in New York and grew up in Geneva, Switzerland. Now based in London, Dawson studied painting and ceramics at Camberwell College of Art from 1990 to 1993 and then completed a master's degree at the Royal College of Art between 1997 and 1999. Dawson's practice centres around visual illusions such as trompe l'oeil and plays on perspective. Through digital processing techniques, he distorts and skews imagery to prompt intrigue and interaction with the viewer. Dawson has designed and produced a number of large-scale public art installations on architectural facades. Another facet of Dawson's practice involves successful collaborations with industry, including Ceramica Bardelli in Milan, Italy, and Josiah Wedgwood & Sons in Stoke-on-Trent, UK.

See also
Matt Davis (p.78)
Bodil Manz (p.96)
Clare Twomey (p.246)

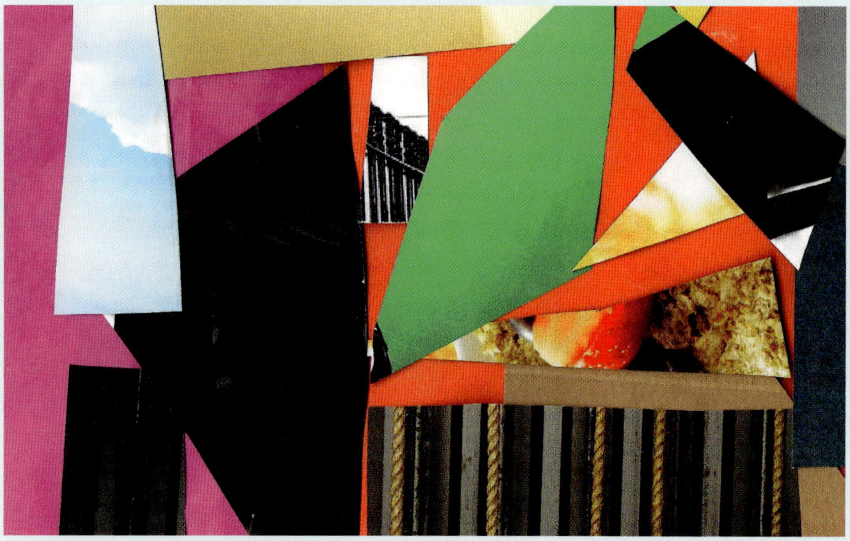

Technical
Computer software programs such as Adobe Photoshop offer a number of tools that can be used creatively to alter and distort images. Alternatively, you could create a collage from magazine cuttings, photographs or drawings, which you then scan into a computer as illustrated here. Once you are satisfied with your design, it can be made into a digital ceramic transfer by sending the file to a specialist company who will prepare the transfers for you. To apply a transfer, cut it out from the sheet, soak it in a little water and slide it away from the backing paper and onto your piece. For best results, apply to a glazed surface and fire to a suggested temperature of 820°C (1508°F).

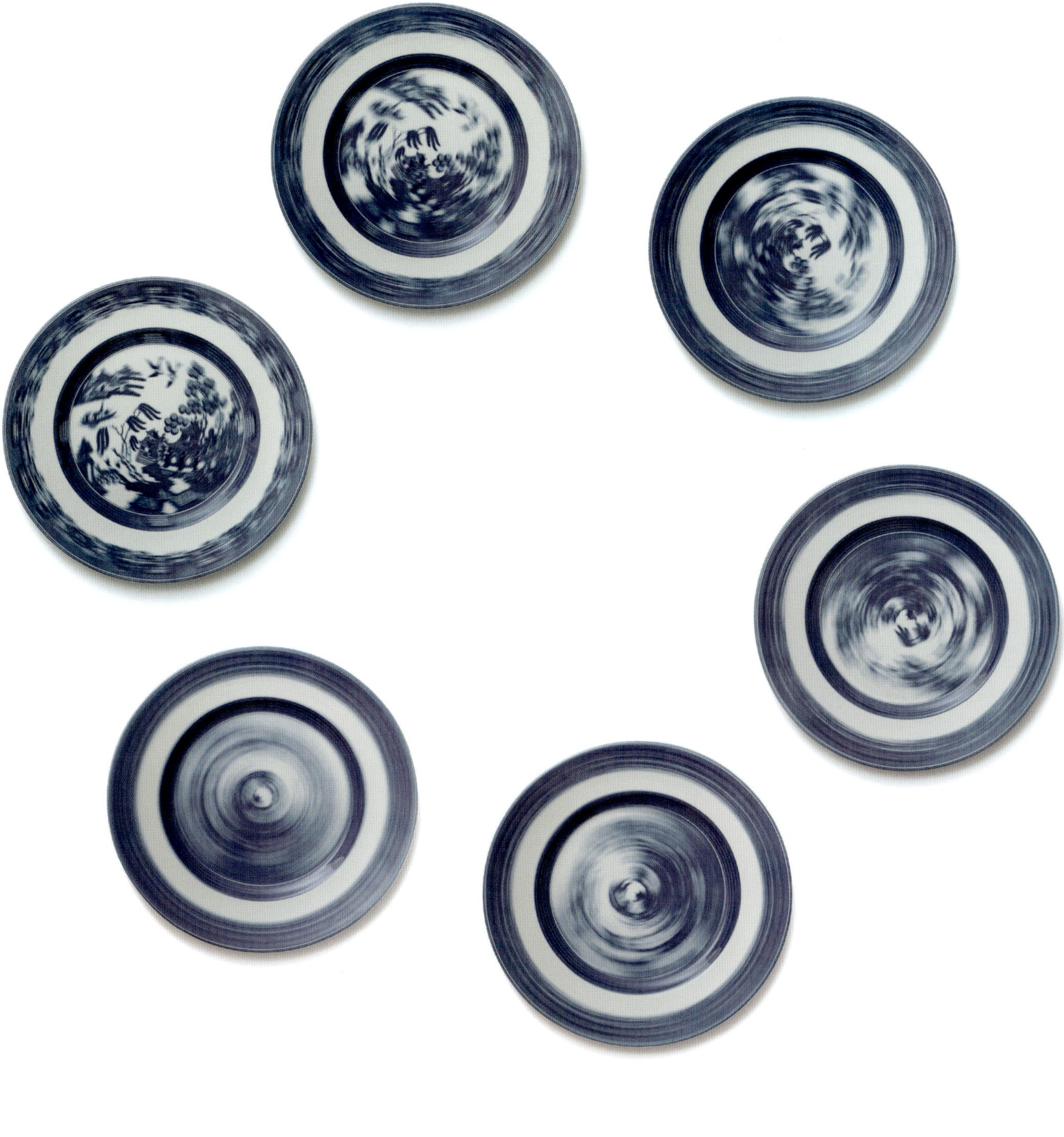

Aneta Regel

Open Metamorphosis 2 2012
Stoneware, slips, incorporated mixed materials, rock
Approx. 33 × 25 × 22 cm (13 × 9⅞ × 8⅝ in.)

This wonderfully vivid sculpture sparks with energy and life. It's a visual feast of sumptuous surfaces and textures, where rich, craggy and dry surfaces are juxtaposed with elements of bright, oozy glaze. The piece has a powerful sense of momentum – like an animal concealed in ceramic form – appearing to twist and contort with every stride. Regel's work carries anthropomorphic references and autobiographical narratives. She says: 'I create objects that exist neither in the natural or in the manufactured world but which, once brought into being, can reflect and transmit information and feelings about nature and my own existence'.

Regel takes inspiration from cracked, sun-baked riverbeds, weathered glaciers and volcanic stones. Her methods are highly experimental and material led: she sources rocks such as granite, basalt and feldspar from her travels, smashing them up into sizeable chunks and fragments, which she then kneads and incorporates into the clay body. Regel works intuitively, using the hand-building techniques of coiling and pinching to construct and define the structure. During the extensive making process she does not dictate the overall form, but instead allows the piece to emerge and flourish until she feels 'it works'. This can involve multiple firings at high and low temperatures; each time she adds more components and overloads the surface with thick pastes of dry, colourful slips and raw glazes. Areas where stone material has been combined with clay break out and push through, resulting in complex, tactile and visually dynamic surfaces.

Aneta Regel (Polish, born 1976) has a passion for materials that stems from her childhood experiences growing up in rural Poland, where she was surrounded by wild landscapes and beautiful natural environments. Regel initially studied sculpture at the Fine Art Academy, Gdansk, before moving to the UK in 2000 to pursue a ceramics degree at the University of Westminster. This was closely followed by a master's degree in ceramics and glass at the Royal College of Art, London, graduating in 2006. Regel's studio is based in Stoke Newington, north London. She exhibits her sculptures throughout Europe and internationally and has been shortlisted in many high-profile competitions, including the Loewe Craft Prize (2018) and the World Ceramics Biennale in Korea (2019).

See also
Takuro Kuwata (p.124)
Ken Price (p.210)
Rafa Pérez (p.214)

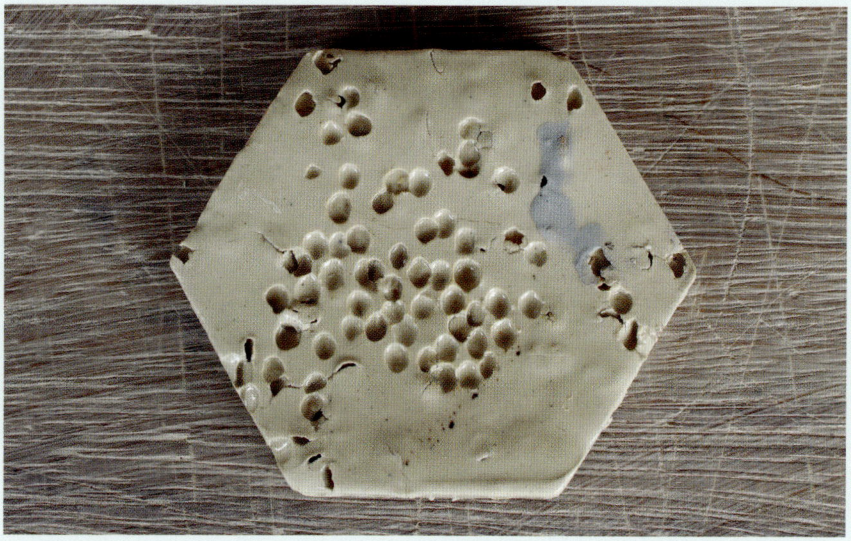

Material

Regel throws the rule book out of the window and employs a refreshing approach to working with clay. She simply enjoys materiality and allows material 'to do what it wants to do'. With this in mind, challenge yourself to think differently about your own methods. You could try adding combustible food stuffs to your clay, such as lentils, rice and pasta. When burnt away during the firing, the residual imprint will bring visual interest and texture to your work. Experiment with metal wire and filings, imbed glass and found items. Dab colourful and bright glazes, matt or shiny, to highlight particular areas or to encourage a potential interaction with the surface.

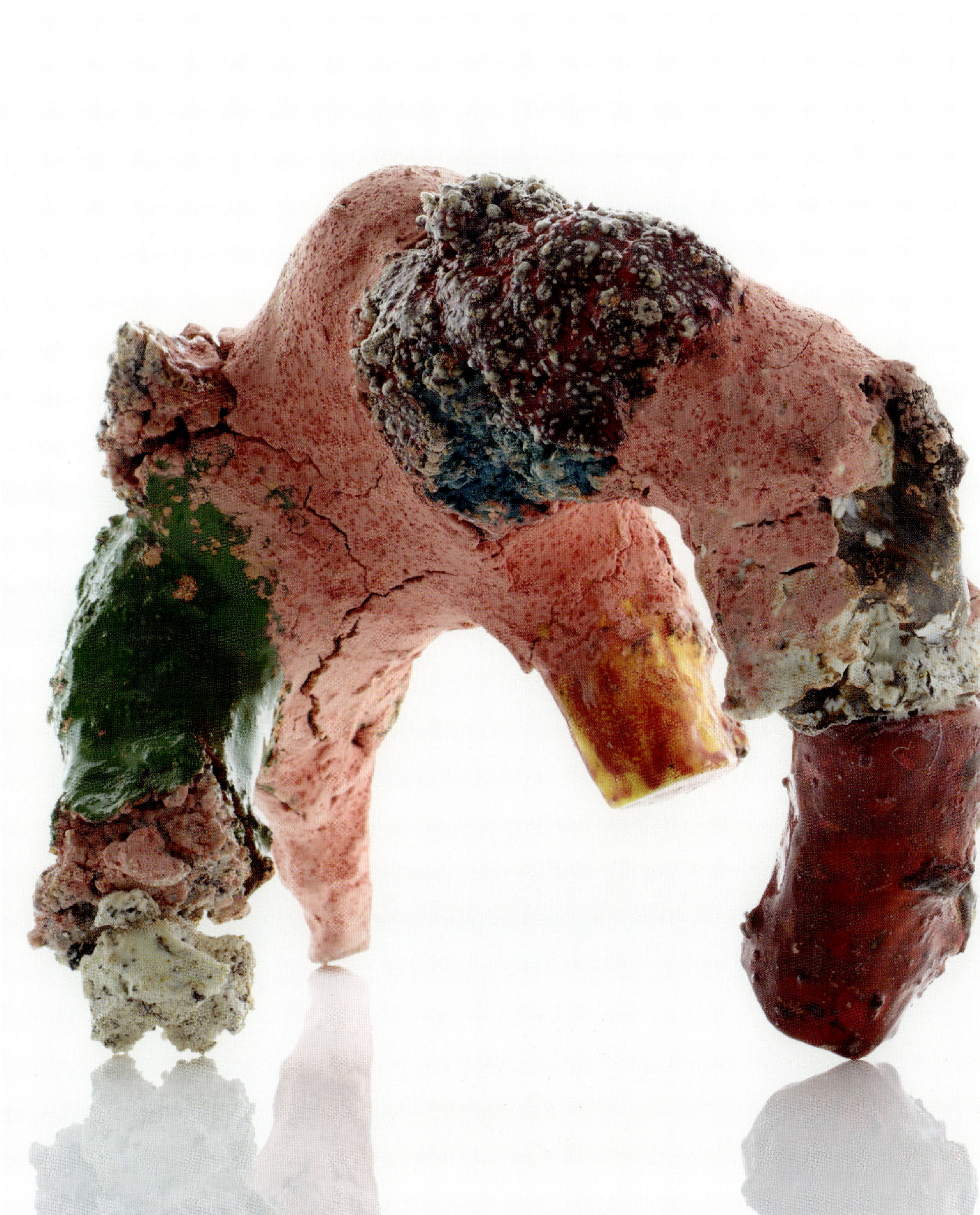

Hideaki Miyamura

See also
Thomas Bohle (p.112)
Kate Malone (p.116)
Nick Weddell (p.120)

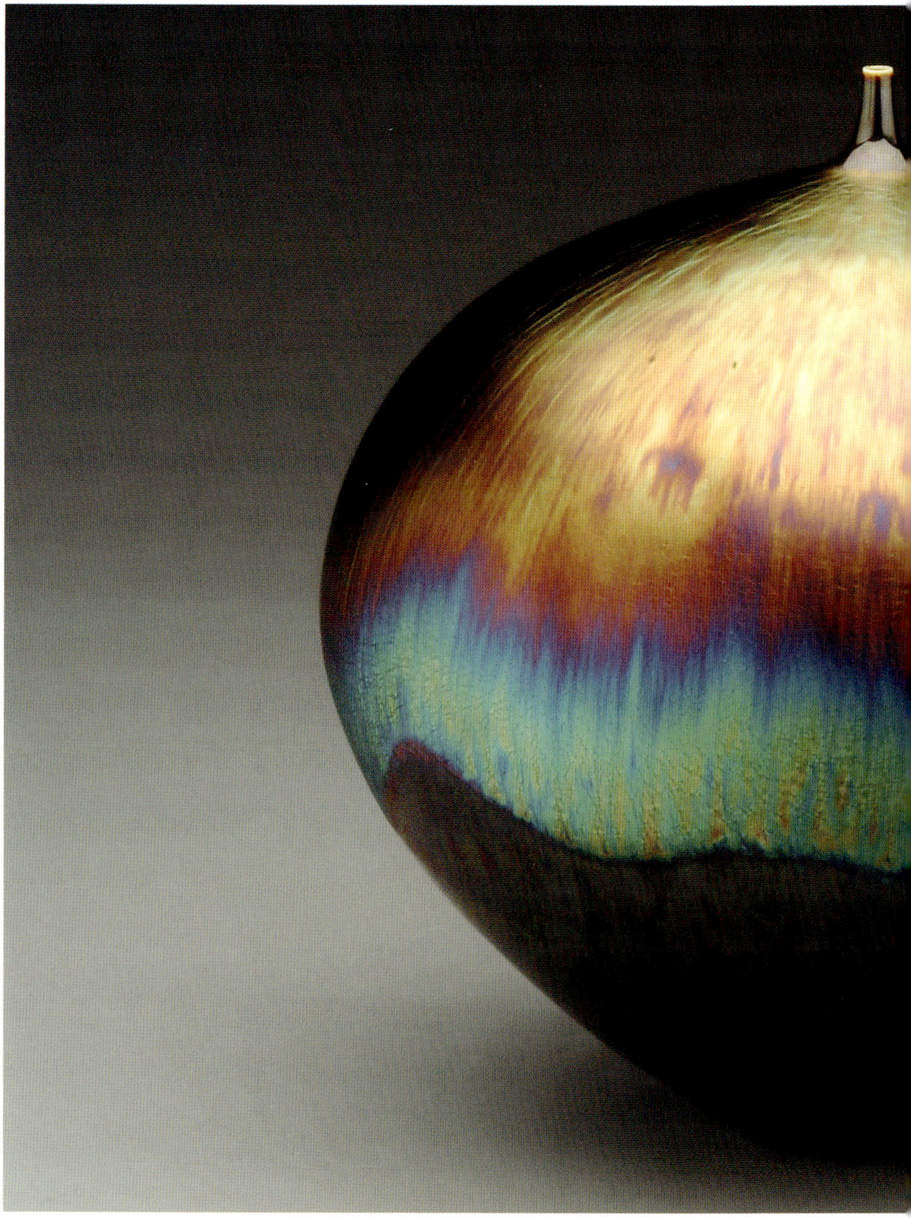

Hideaki Miyamura (Japanese-American, born 1955) was born in Nigata province, Japan and travelled to the United States in 1979 to study art history at Western Michigan University. With ambitions to be a potter from a young age, Miyamura returned to Japan in 1987 and began a five-year apprenticeship with master potter Shurei Miura (born 1942) in Yamanash. Miura is renowned for his rich tenmoku glazes and exquisite pottery forms. The apprenticeship with Miura instilled an industrious work ethic in Miyamura and he refined his skills by throwing thousands upon thousands of identical shapes and spent endless hours glaze testing. After completing his apprenticeship, Miyamura emigrated to the United States in 1997. His current studio is based in New Hampshire. Examples of his beautiful, luminous pottery are held in many public collections, including the Asian Art Museum of San Francisco and the Victoria and Albert Museum in London.

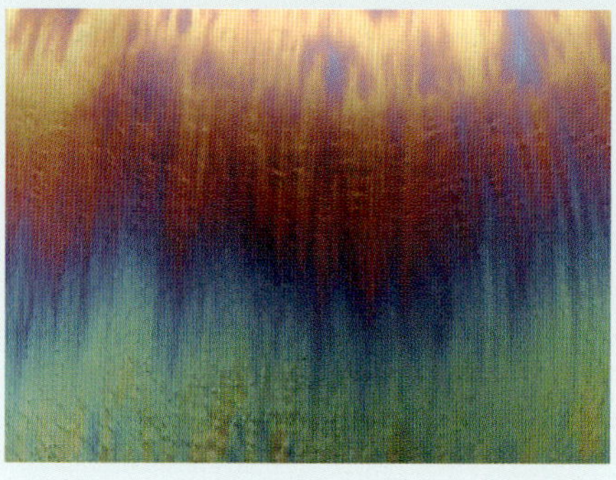

Technical

Adding rutile and/or titanium dioxide in amounts of 6–8% to a suitable stoneware base recipe can produce iridescence in a glaze. See Chun recipe in glaze section (p.275). You could also achieve a similar effect with a low-fired 'titanium' lustre applied over the top of a neutral-coloured glaze background. This particular lustre will give a rainbow/spectrum sheen to your work.

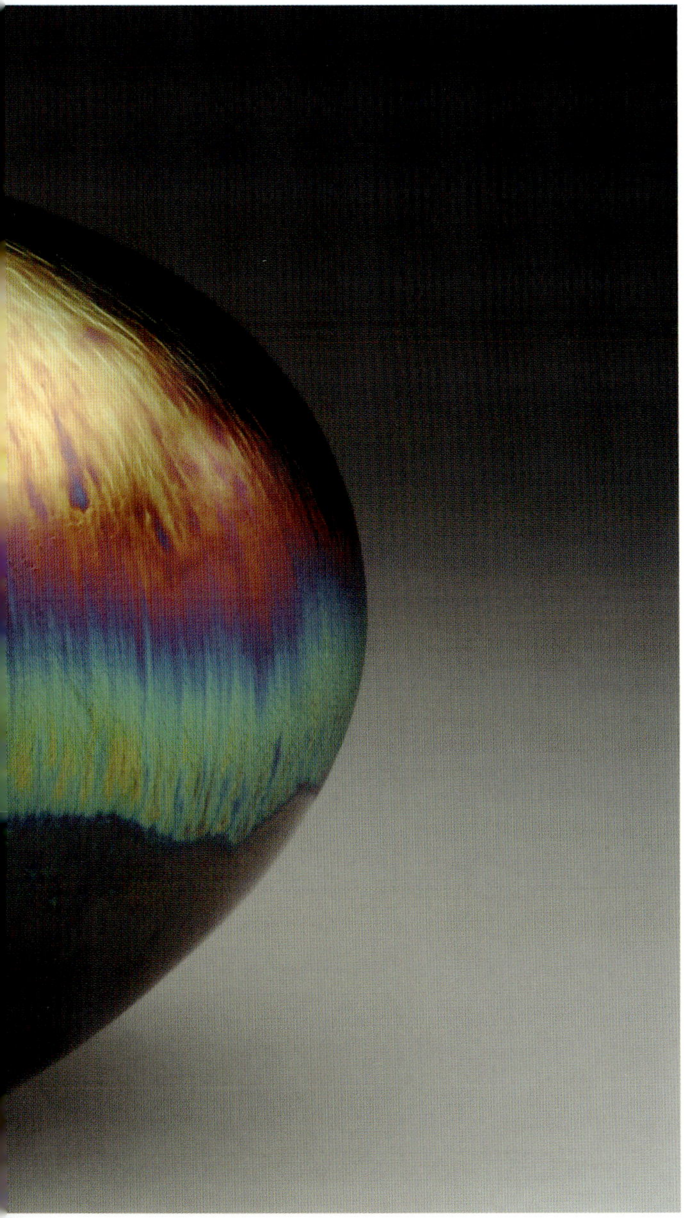

Vase *c.* 2015
Porcelain with gold and blue hare's fur glaze
27.9 × 25.4 cm (11 × 10 in.)

The pristine, lustrous ceramics created by Hideaki Miyamura are a testimony to his drive and determination to develop glazes of sublime quality. His passion for glaze originates from a research project he conducted into 12th-century Chinese Song Dynasty pottery – specifically, pieces glazed with rare 'yohen' tenmoku, which is characterized by an iridescent glaze on a rich black background. To replicate the glaze required many years of refinement and perseverance.

Miyamura takes inspiration for his shapes from Venetian glass vases, the work of Italian master Lino Tagliapietra (born 1934) is a particularly strong influence. His aim is to emulate the fluid, ethereal nature of molten glass in his forms and surfaces. Miyamura begins by sketching the profile and proportions of a shape, which then leads him to decide on an appropriate glaze to suit the form. Using porcelain, he throws his pieces on a pottery wheel and fires them in a reduction kiln to a very high temperature of 1300°C (2372°F). His years of training and experience have given him the critical judgement skills to gauge when the glaze has reached full maturity and achieved the desired qualities.

For this vase piece, Miyamura paired the dainty teardrop vessel shape with a beautiful cascading glaze, which he refers to as 'hare's fur'. A vibrant array of iridescent hues, resembling the psychedelic spectrum of a kaleidoscope, gush and stream down from the fine neck of the vase to the waist, culminating in an intense, feathery turquoise blue. Streaks of brilliant gold shimmer and radiate within the glaze, bringing delicacy and softness to the overall surface.

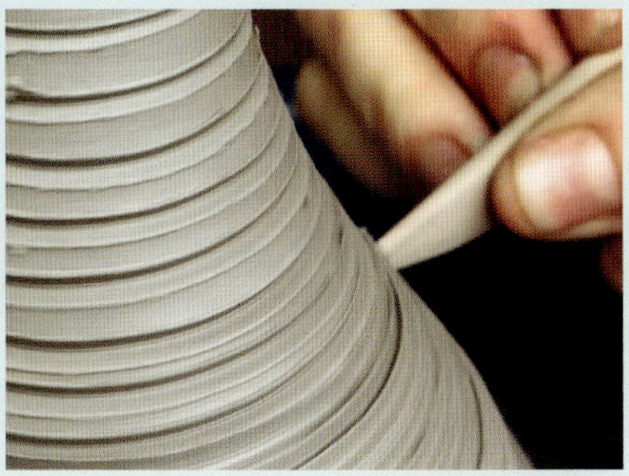

Surface

Miyamura meticulously plans his forms to accommodate the glaze. He adds texture to the surfaces of some of his sleek vessels to force the glaze to pool and become translucent as it breaks and cascades over edges. When making your own forms, consider how the glaze will interact with the surface or shape of the form itself. Experiment with wide, flared rims, roundness, flatness, ribbing and protrusions to provide a 'stage' for the glaze to run into the creases and crevices and enhance the texture and surface quality. You will need to experiment with the kiln firing itself and how this impacts the glaze surface, especially 'soaking' the top temperature (holding the temperature for a specific amount of time) to allow the glazes to fully mature and intensify.

Malene Hartmann Rasmussen

Troll #7 2017
Ceramic, earthenware
51 × 42 × 11 cm (20 × 16½ × 4⅓ in.)

The intricate, surreal sculptures of Malene Hartmann Rasmussen initially appear sweet and toy-like, but on closer inspection they reveal a darker narrative. A recurring subject in Hartmann Rasmussen's work is the forest as a setting for ancient cults, pagan rituals and folklore in European literature. This has led her to conjure fantastical imaginings of the forest and the mythological creatures that lurk within. As she explains, '[the forest] … simultaneously embraces the sinister darkness in which the savage and beastly thrive [… and] the supernatural, romantic, and nostalgic world of the fairy-tale'. She also cites the naturalistic works of 16th-century potter Bernard Palissy as a significant influence and elements of his imagined depictions resonate strongly with her work.

This enchanting piece is from a series of work entitled *Troldeskoven* (*In the Troll Wood*). Here, the artist reflects on her childhood memories of growing up in rural Denmark, where she retreated to the forest to immerse herself in daydreams and escapism. The notion of the troll is represented here in the shape of a mask and Hartmann Rasmussen says such things 'echo ancient rituals, where the mask was a powerful object for connecting with the spiritual world'.

What is extraordinary about the piece is the playfulness of the leafy composition and the array of sumptuous colours. The organic textures and lush glaze invite the viewer to examine the bright flora, foraged berries and spiralled shells that make up the facial features of the mysterious character. Another curiosity is the dainty butterfly, resting on the mouth of the creature. Symbolic of the embodied soul, it is this boundary between the 'living and non-living, animal and human, plant and creature, fact and fiction' that makes this piece so compelling.

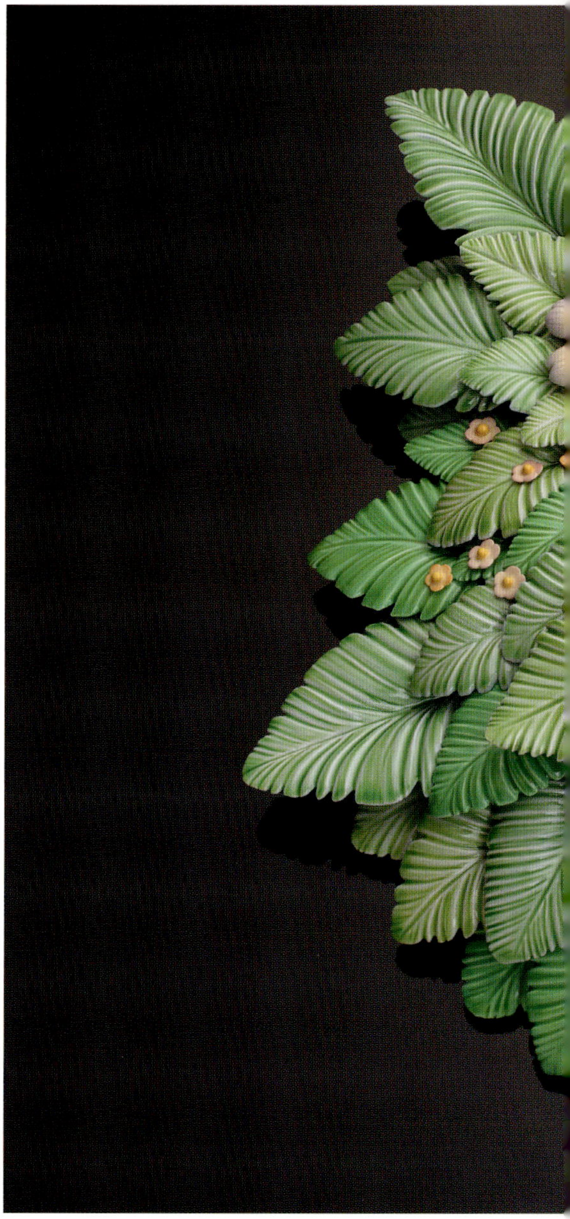

Technical
The artist created this work by hand-modelling hundreds of component parts rather than using a press mould. The individual parts are fired separately, then glazed and assembled on a base of clay – much like a flower arrangement. This is a technique that the artist developed herself and it enables her to assemble complex and fragile works that would otherwise be very difficult to make.

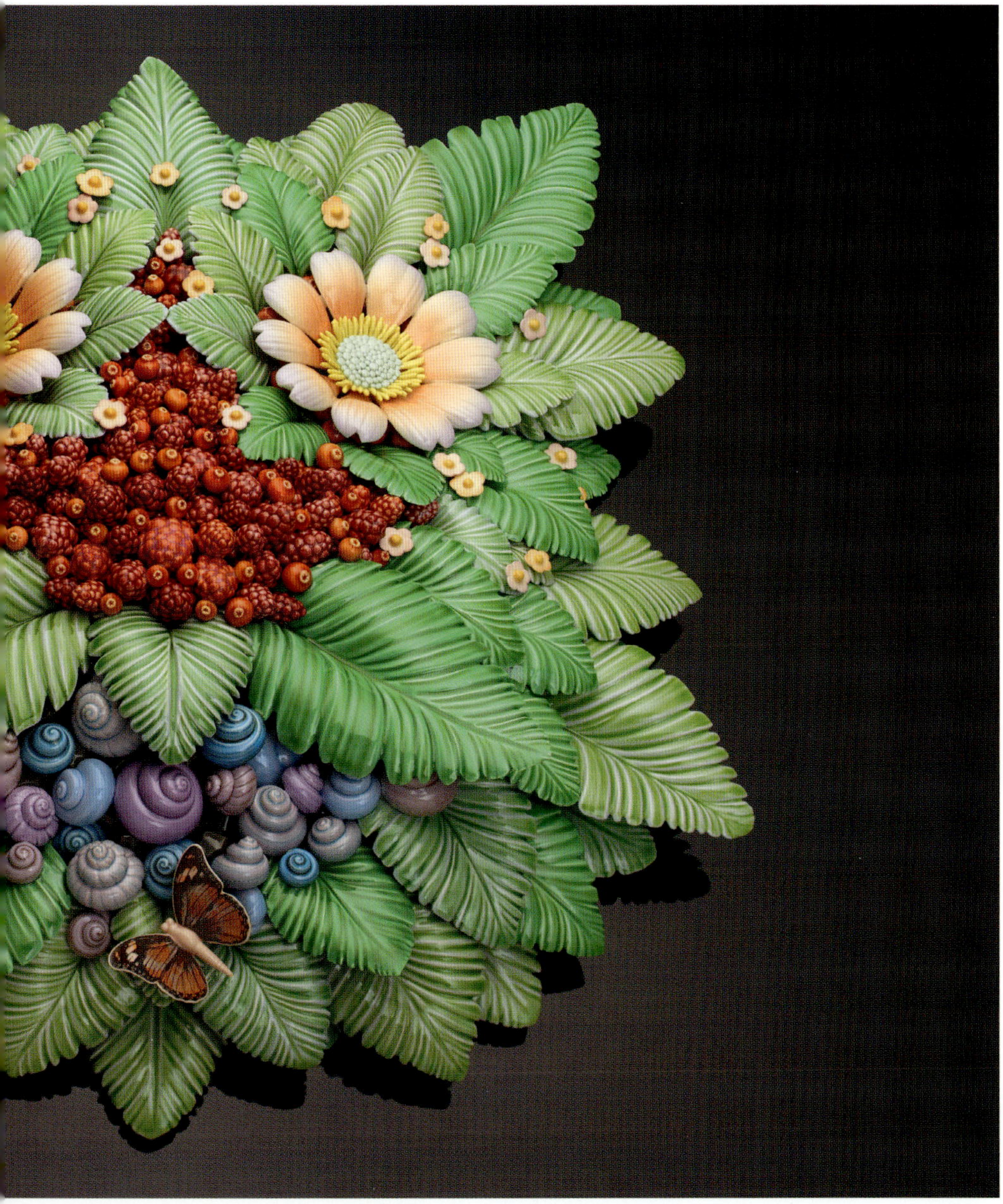

Malene Hartmann Rasmussen (Danish, born 1973) initially worked as a cinema projectionist, but after joining a pottery evening class her focus turned to ceramics. She then studied at the Royal Danish Academy of Fine Art, Bornholm, and at London's Royal College of Art. She now lives and works in London. Hartmann Rasmussen experiments with traditional craft skills to create mixed-media sculptures inspired by folktales and mythology connected to everyday life in pagan Scandinavia. Her complex still-life scenes initially appear playful but, on closer inspection, feature absurdist dark narratives.

See also

Bernard Palissy (p.86)
Kim Simonsson (p.192)
Carolein Smit (p.198)

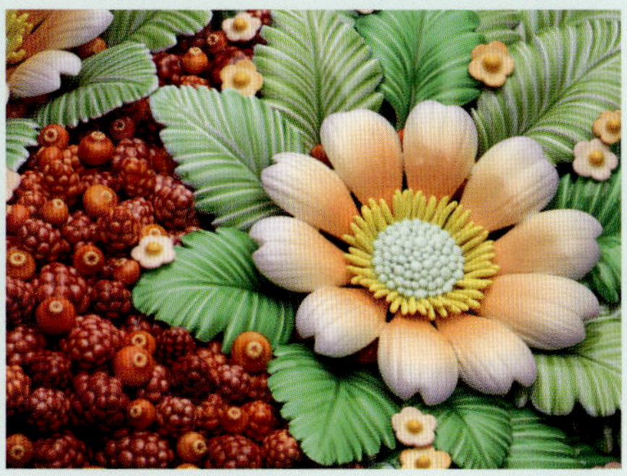

Surface

The jewelled colours and surfaces of this piece were achieved with low-fire glazes developed by Hartmann Rasmussen. The artist has created a stylistic, graphical aesthetic by carving bold lines into her modelled components that exploit the glossy traits of the glaze. Note the incredible attention to detail, such as the flower 'eyes' where Hartmann Rasmussen has added touches of soft purple to the tips of the pink petals, and the vibrant mix of red and orange berries, which appear tantalizingly real. The rich assortment of textures and colours are carefully curated, with contrasts of tones rather than lots of different, opposing glazes. This gives the work a strong identity and visual impact whether viewed close up or from afar.

Bente Skjøttgaard

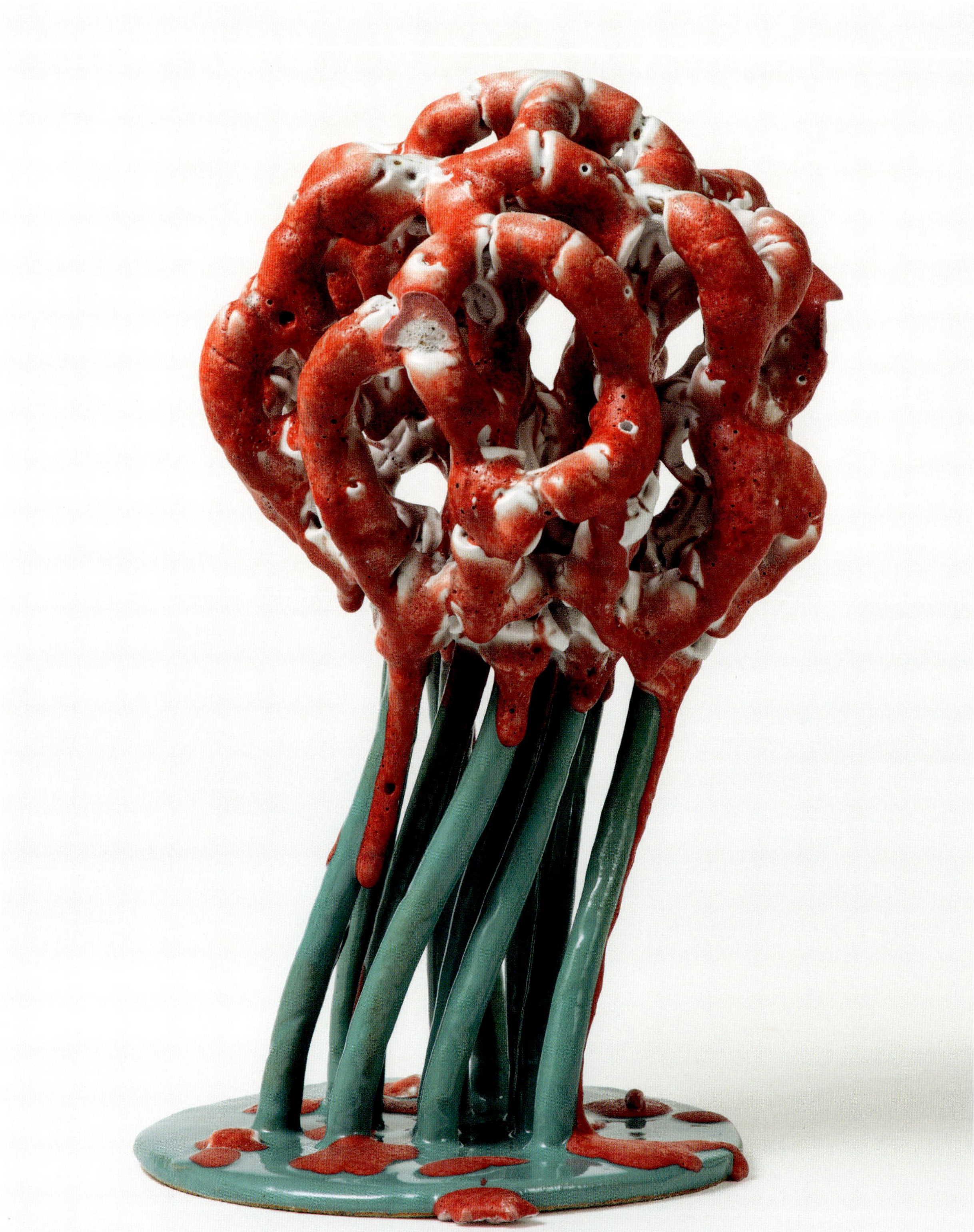

Cloud #1796 2017
Stoneware and glaze
47 × 27 cm (18½ × 10⅗ in.)

Pushing material and form to the extremes, Bente Skjøttgaard sets out to mimic the voluminous, ethereal nature of cloud formations through her densely textured surfaces and looped structures. Skjøttgaard seeks to convey the natural thermal rising of clouds in the heavy and hard medium of clay. As she explains, 'Clay is initially soft, then hardens during the firing, while a cloud remains unattainable, vaporous and constantly in motion, retaining the ability to transform into something else. This "non-static-ness" makes clouds interesting to explore sculpturally and to relate to as volume, material, motion and colour.' Within her imaginative compositions Skjøttgaard plays on the ambiguity of familiar shapes and outlines that we perceive when observing clouds.

Skjøttgaard typically builds her tall forms into a 'lollipop' structure, starting with a series of clay uprights attached to a supporting base. She then proceeds to shape rings of clay that she links together with adjoining coils, repeating the process until the frothy mass is complete. For this piece, Skjøttgaard experimented with milky, viscous glazes to express the ambient colours of the sky. The heavy richness of the surface was achieved by dipping and pouring opposing glazes over the top of existing layers, and refiring each time. Skjøttgaard also exploits the transformative impact the high firing temperatures have on the final outcome – gentle shifts and movements in the form are reminiscent of the transience of clouds in the sky. Skjøttgaard's aim is to obtain a feeling of weightlessness, defying the physicality of clay yet at the same time retaining highly ceramic qualities.

Bente Skjøttgaard (Danish, born 1961) studied at the Design School Kolding in Demark and then the Bezalel Academy of Arts and Design in Jerusalem. She worked in the product development department at Danish porcelain manufacturer Bing & Grøndahl from 1986 to 1990 and had her debut solo show at the Royal Copenhagen gallery in 1990. Her work is characterized by an experimental approach to glazing and form. In 2001, she created a series of pots named *Glazed Pieces*, which are suited to carrying several layers of glaze. Two years later she followed it up with *Ramifications*, a series of abstract constructions consisting of multiple joined curves.

See also
Morten Løbner Espersen (p.126)
Gitte Jungersen (p.222)
Matt Wedel (p.226)

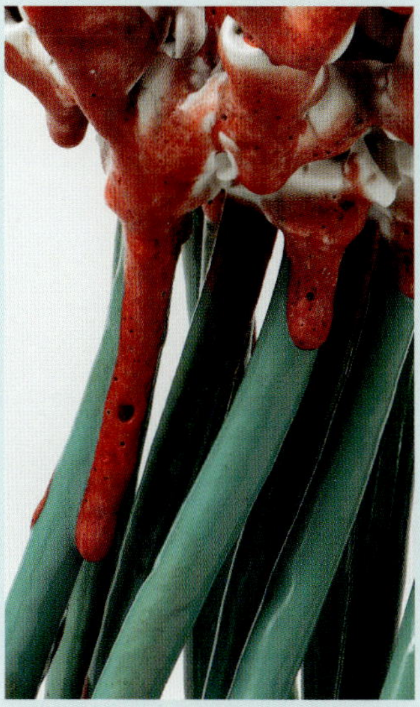

Surface
Skjøttgaard has an inquisitive approach and enjoys engaging in expressive experiments that test the boundaries of materiality and form. Here, she has saturated the cloud form with multiple layers of thick glaze, which ooze and dribble, creating tension and drama within the structure. Like Skjøttgaard, be curious about the possibilities of glaze. Perhaps you could accommodate points in the structure to force the glaze to behave in a specific way.

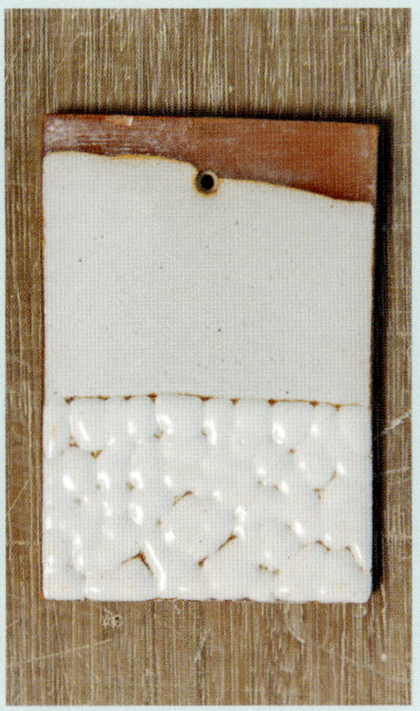

Technical
Thickness of glaze has a massive impact on the final outcome. As illustrated here, the top section of the tile shows normal application but when applied thickly the glaze has repelled the clay body and formed tight globules across the surface. This is a technical fault referred to as 'crawling', but you can exploit this tactile quality for visual effect. For example, you could pair a crawled glaze surface with a coloured clay body, creating a dynamic contrast.

Janice Tchalenko

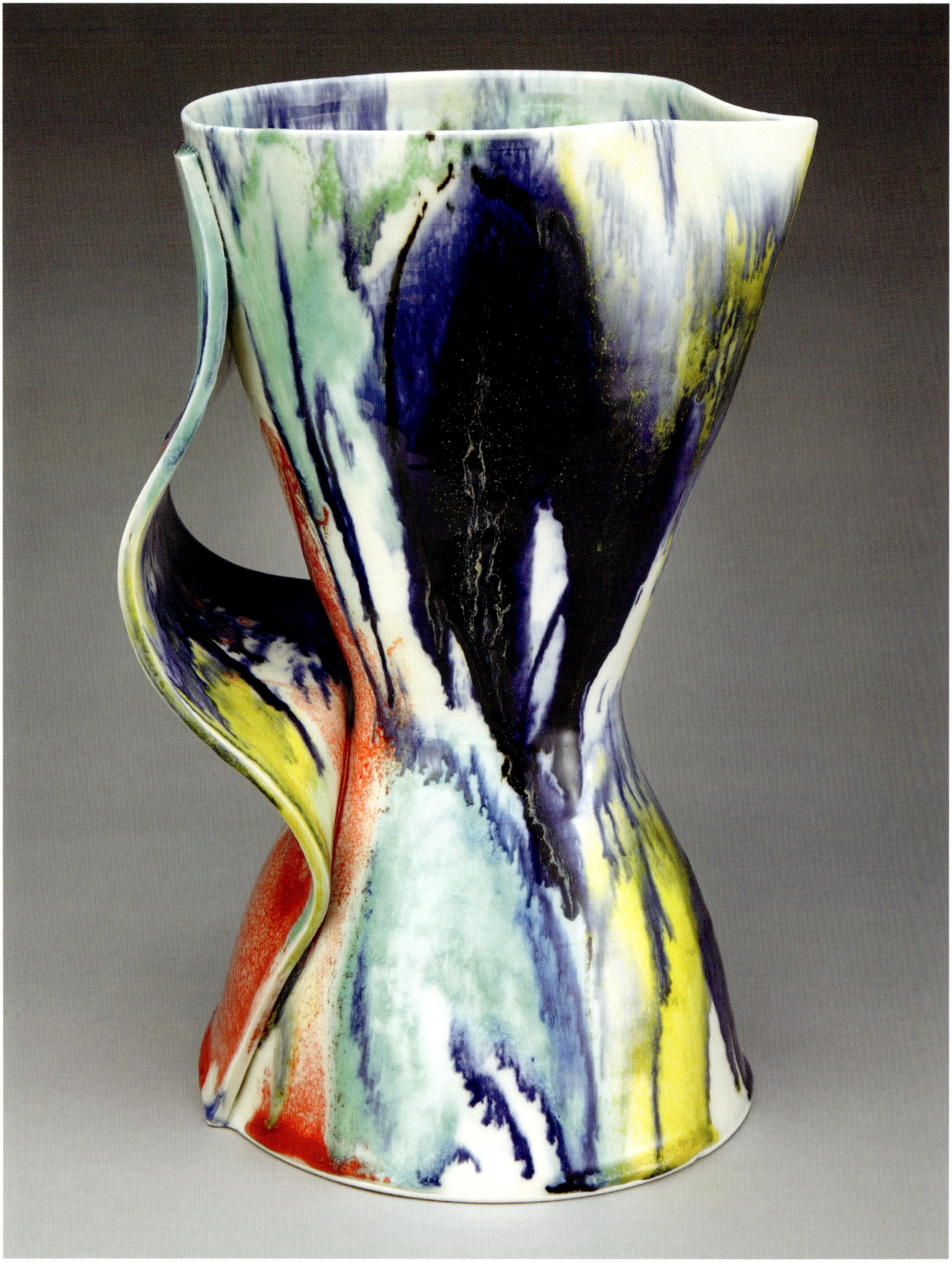

Jug 2017
Porcelain, thrown, oxidized glazes
39 × 25 cm (15⅜ × 9⅞ in.)

Janice Tchalenko travelled extensively and visited Morocco, Russia and the Middle East. Her travel experiences introduced new possibilities for colourful decorative surfaces to her work. She combined these influences with an appreciation for the graphical scribbles and free brush marks of abstract contemporary painters Cy Twombly (1928–2011), Roger Hilton (1911–75) and Jackson Pollock (1912–56). Tchalenko sought methods to translate the work's graffiti-like qualities into her own painterly compositions. With a flair for glazes, she experimented with high-fired reduction recipes and produced colours of great depth and richness – a stark contrast to the more conventional, earthy tenmokus and ash glazes being used by other studio potters of the same period.

This example of a large jug by Janice Tchalenko was made during the later years of her life, after she had moved from the studio in her home of forty years in Dulwich, London, to a new studio in Forest Hill in 2014. The move meant she no longer had access to a gas reduction kiln, so she had to overhaul her glazes and relearn all she knew to adjust to oxidized firings in an electric kiln. Undeterred, she applied her inventive and free approach to glaze technology and created a new range of dynamic glazes in the same exuberant manner as before. When using porcelain, the material intensifies the richness of the glaze, allowing the punchy combination of turquoise, blues, yellows and reds in this jug to resonate. Tchalenko fired her work to 1260°C (2300°F), soaking the top temperature in the kiln for fifteen minutes to force the glazes to cascade and merge harmoniously into one confident composition.

Janice Tchalenko (British, 1942–2018) initially worked as a civil servant at the British Foreign Office before training as a studio potter at Harrow College of Art in the late 1960s. She became a proficient thrower – going on to teach the skill at Harrow – and for the next ten years she produced fashionable, muted tableware in the Leach tradition. A Crafts Council bursary in 1980 enabled Tchalenko to experiment with bold decoration and vivid colours, unleashing a fresh, exciting new direction that revolutionized the studio pottery movement. From 1984 to 2010 she was chief designer for Dartington Pottery. Tchalenko was elected as a fellow of the Royal College of Art in London and taught there from 1981 to 1996. Examples of her studio work and industrial ranges are held in many prestigious public collections, both nationally and internationally.

See also

Jun Kaneko (p.92)
Stuart Carey (p.150)
Betty Woodman (p.252)

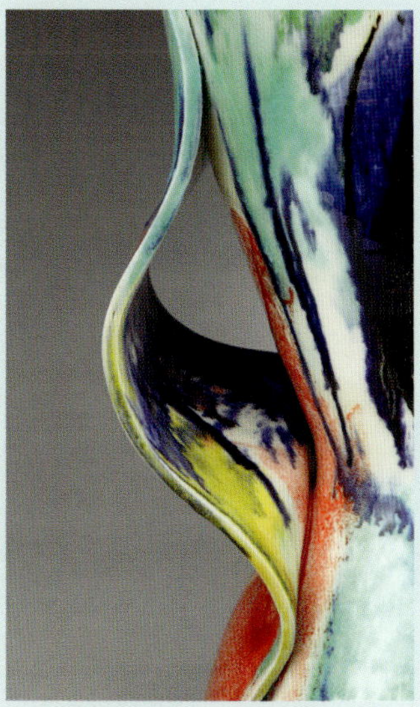

Composition
To achieve the hourglass shape of this jug, Tchalenko made two separate bowls and then turned one upside down and joined it to the other to obtain the height. The shape and size of a handle is another important element in regards to the overall success of the piece. Here, Tchalenko has complimented the free-flowing decoration with a wide strap handle that is in perfect proportion to the body of the jug and flicks through the air like a gymnast's ribbon.

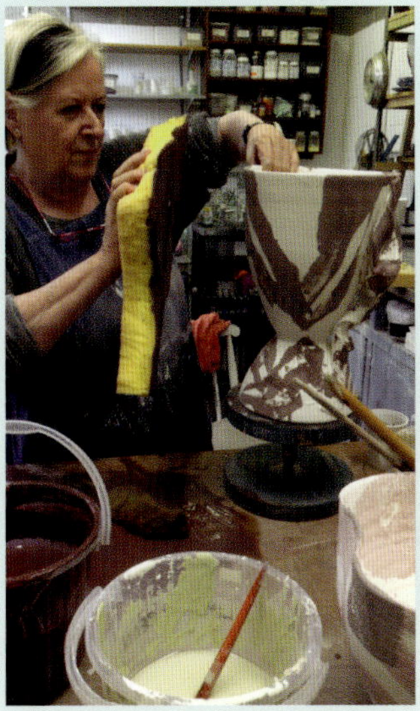

Surface
Tchalenko decorated her pieces with semi-abstract patterns resembling flowers, leaves and organic shapes. For this piece she cut a leaf-shaped stencil out of a large chunk of foam, which she then dipped in glaze and stamped onto the surface of the piece. She continued to overlap layers of contrasting glazes to create visual depth. She then highlighted the outline of the leaf shapes with oxide and more dabs of glaze. The resulting surface is lively and expressive.

Thomas Bohle

Mushroom Form 2018
Exterior ox blood red, interior black glaze
Height: 18 cm (7 in.); Diameter: 22 cm (8⅗ in.)

Precisely thrown and skilfully made, the double-walled vessels of Thomas Bohle express an ongoing dialogue between interior, exterior and hidden surfaces. Bohle's sophisticated work draws inspiration from ancient artisanal pots and forms in nature. Architecture, sculpture and music are also contributing factors and resonate strongly within his work. Bohle is motivated by the interplay between form and surface, which leads him to continuously explore new shapes and colours.

Mushroom Form illustrates Bohle's extraordinary ability to hold all elements of a piece in perfect balance: the form, the glaze and the engineering required to make the piece are all vital to its success. A sense of lightness was achieved through the process of throwing a double-walled vessel, where an interior and exterior wall are formed and joined to create one form. The technique allows Bohle to create wide, complex shapes that defy apparent limitations.

Bohle has a passion for East Asian glazes and his vibrant colour palette centres around traditional tenmoku, celadon and ash glazes. Here, Bohle has paired his crisp form with an intense red oxblood (*sang de boeuf*) glaze on the exterior and a black glaze on the interior – which he fired in a gas reduction kiln at 1280–1300°C (2336–2372°F). During the firing the exterior glaze became incredibly fluid and forced a cascade of beautiful red and white colouration. As a result, pools of glassy drips congregate around the bottom rim, bringing extra tension and movement to the overall form.

Thomas Bohle (Austrian, born 1958) studied to be a nurse before undertaking a pottery apprenticeship. He then worked in various studios until he opened his own in 1991. He came to international attention for his double-walled vessels. He then went on a study trip to Japan accompanied by German ceramicist Uwe Löllmann (born 1955) and held successful shows in Tokyo and Shanghai. His work is inspired by ancient forms and glazes and aims to show the connection between traditional and contemporary ceramic art. He has won several awards, including the Bavarian State Prize in 2006 and the Vorarlberg State Prize in 2014.

See also
Hideaki Miyamura (p.104)
Theodor Bogler (p.134)
Walter Keeler (p.142)

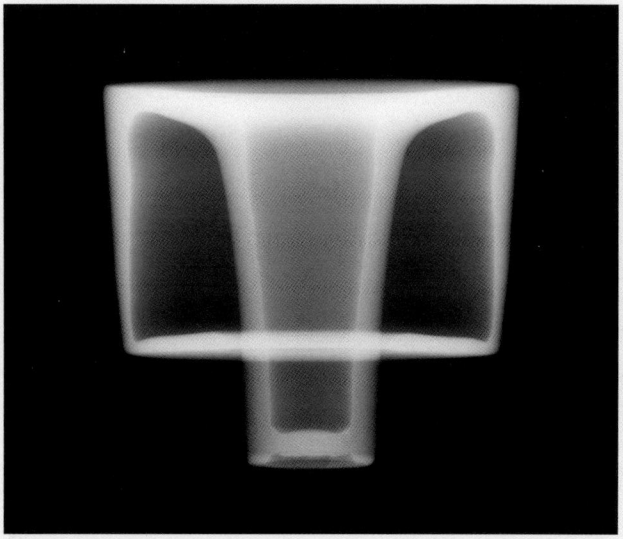

Technical
As this fascinating X-ray image of the piece reveals, Bohle's double-walled vessels are technically very challenging to make. Thrown from a single piece of clay, Bohle initially makes the form upside down and has to strongly rely on the power of his imagination and intuition to achieve the desired shape. Bohle also has to consider the drying phase and firing process to accommodate the inner and outer walls drying at different rates. The benefit of this technique is to give the illusion of width and chunkiness to a form. At a basic level, you could try making a simple doughnut shape from a thrown ring of clay before progressing to more challenging forms. The principle is to divide the clay wall into two sections, proceeding to pull the inner and outer walls until they meet. The join is compressed with a rubber kidney, and the profile shaped and refined at the trimming stage.

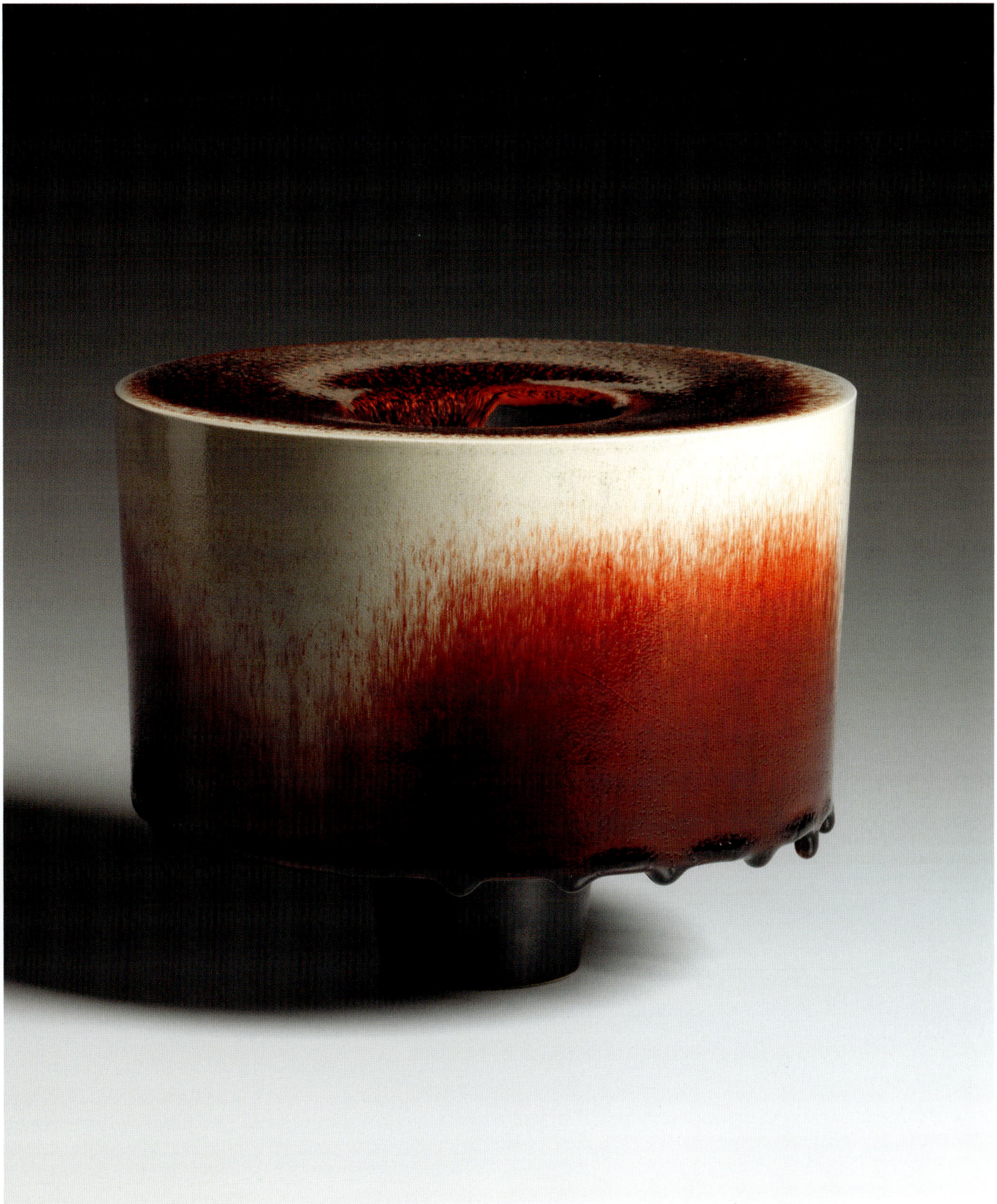

Wouter Dam

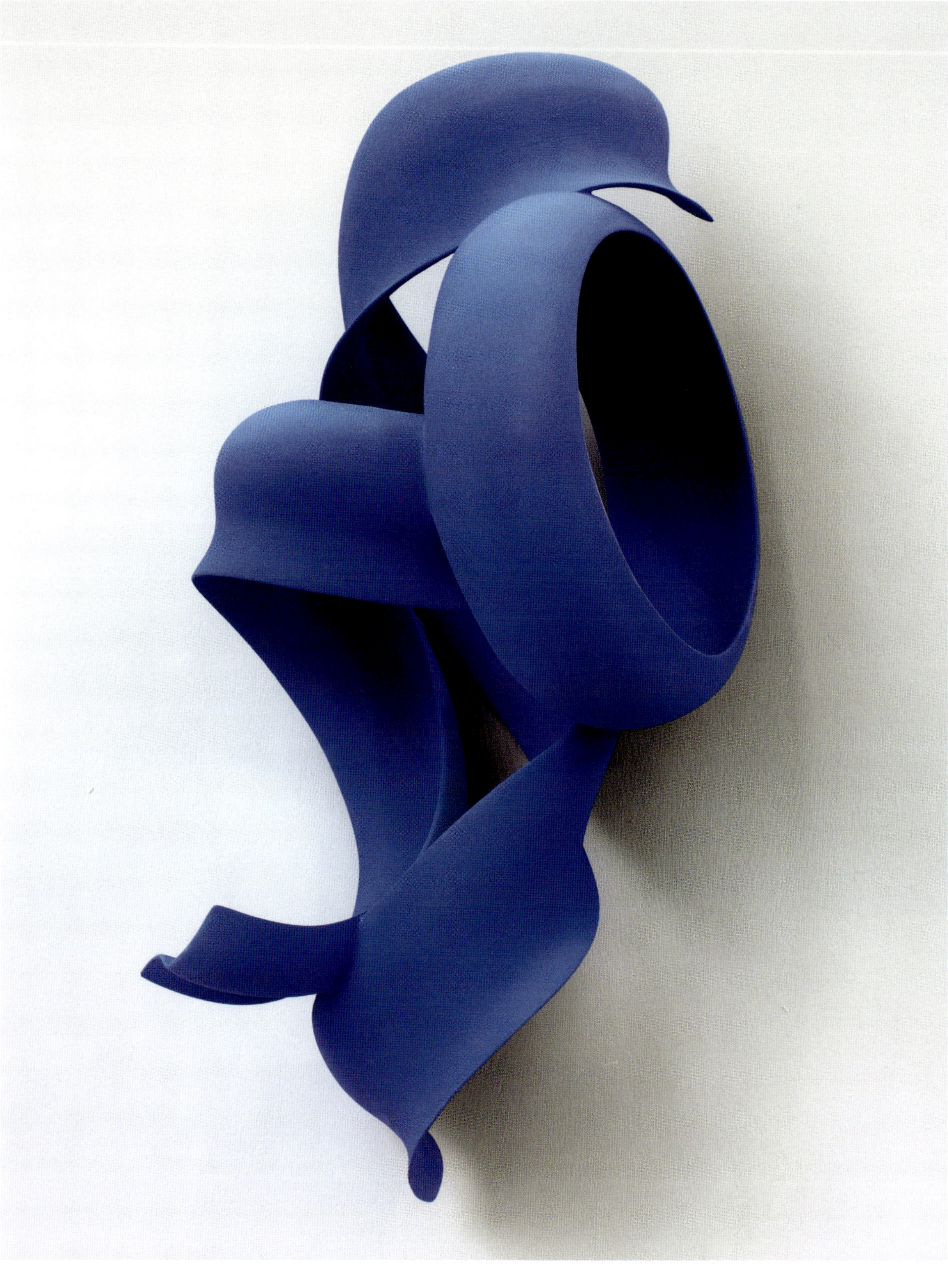

Blue Wall Sculpture 2018
Westerwald stoneware clay
52 × 22 × 33 cm (20½ × 8⅝ × 13 in.)

With elegant twists and descending curves, the sculptural assemblages made by Wouter Dam allude to forms of the body, landscape and water. His intriguing compositions share a connection with classical and modern sculpture, with Dam taking inspiration from the intricate, baroque wood carvings of Grinling Gibbons (1648–1721) and the purity of form achieved by modernist sculptor Barbara Hepworth (1903–75).

This flowing sculptural piece by Dam has no obvious beginning or end. Gentle undulations and sweeping contours lead the viewer to discover new angles around, over and through the complex piece. Intimate in scale, the domestic size of the piece intensifies the energy contained within the directional pull of the curves, bringing movement to this static form.

Dam's approach to making this free-flowing piece began at the pottery wheel, where he made a series of cylindrical component parts. After waiting for the clay to firm to leather-hard stage, Dam proceeded to cut and unravel the cylinders into long strips. He then skilfully built the structure with precise positioning and regard for composition, retaining a delicate balance of concave and convex shapes. The process of making the thrown vessels can still be felt within the structure and Dam plays on the familiarity and unfamiliarity of the abstracted form. To complete the piece, Dam sprayed it with an engobe, coloured with a blue commercial stain, to achieve the silky matt finish. The calming quality of the colour, paired with its smooth texture, accentuate the delicate subtleties of light and shadow projected by the form.

Wouter Dam (Dutch, born 1957) trained in ceramics at the Gerrit Rietveld Academy in Amsterdam, graduating in 1980. Dam is renowned for his curved, undulating sculptures that are firmly rooted in ceramic traditions. He says of his work, 'Every object I create is slightly different, each one a step in a long line of development, a subtle variation on the same theme. My search is for a very personal kind of perfection, I look for a certain tension in the work, beautiful and fascinating in equal measure.' Wouter Dam exhibits extensively throughout Europe and internationally. Examples of his work are held in numerous collections, including in Amsterdam, Paris, London and Detroit.

See also
William Staite Murray (p.52)
Janice Tchalenko (p.110)
Matt Wedel (p.226)

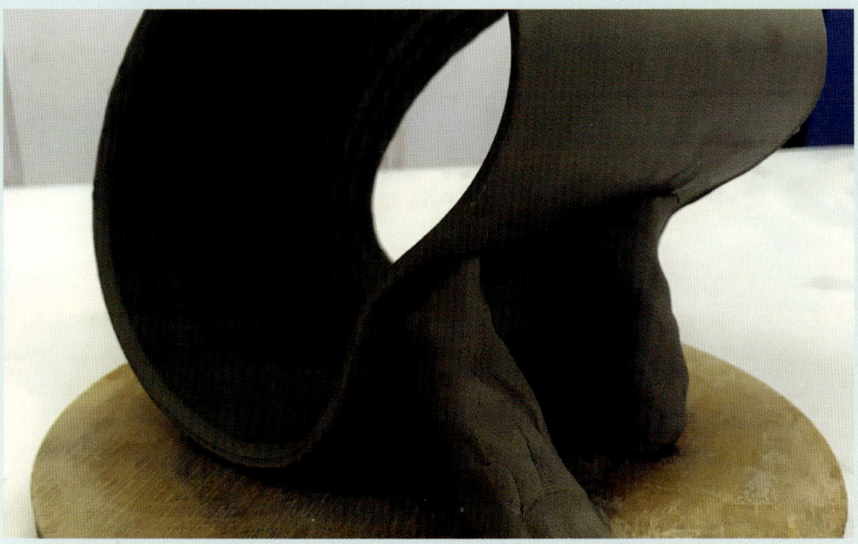

Technical
As Dam's work demonstrates, the pottery wheel can be used to make forms beyond functional purpose. Constructed from a series of wheel-thrown cylinders, Dam cuts and reassembles sections to build his ribbon-like structures. To preserve the freshness of the curve, Dam builds a supporting frame in leather-hard clay, which he places underneath and around the shape to prevent it from sagging and distorting during firing. When building a delicate structure, prop the form up with supports made from the same clay and leave them in position during the drying and firing stages to help maintain the shape.

Kate Malone

A Pair of Striped Magma Vases 2018

Crystalline-glazed stoneware

Height: 36 cm (14⅛ in.), Diameter: 26 cm (10¼ in.)

Throughout her thirty-year career, the natural world has been a continuous source of inspiration for Kate Malone. She creates exuberant, richly decorated forms that 'brim with a sense of growth and abundance and aim to communicate the "life force" to the viewer'. Her work is frequently inspired by fruit and vegetables, including pineapples, gourds, pumpkins and many more. More recently, her attention has turned to the Earth's crust and the molten, fiery magma beneath. This interest led Malone to explore crystal formations in both her shape structures and lustrous glazes.

To create these works, Malone hand built an archetypal vase shape using the coiling technique. She then encrusted the exterior with a scattered composition of modelled geometric blocks, faceted shapes and spheres. The light positioning of the components prompts imaginings that the form is magnetic and the crystal structures are drawn to it by an invisible force.

Malone says that she relies on her intuition and subconscious rather than a prescriptive approach when making her forms, and this organic progression of development and individuality resonates strongly within her practice. Another important aspect of the work is Malone's sophisticated approach to glazing – she has a style that is unique to her and stems from years of dedicated glaze research and rigorous testing. Here, Malone has successfully paired the constructed vessels with cascades of shimmering and dazzling crystalline glazes. Within the iridescent glaze colours small growths of splintered crystal strands are clearly visible and spread across the surface, bringing a sense of tremendous energy and liveliness.

Kate Malone (British, born 1959) studied at Bristol Polytechnic and London's Royal College of Art. Her work focuses on themes in nature: in the 1980s she examined the sea, in the 1990s the land and in the 21st century under the Earth's crust. Her pots draw on organic shapes found in nature, such as gourds, pineapples and pumpkins. She is known for her pioneering research into glazing techniques. This has resulted in her signature vibrant, crystalline glazes, as well as collaborations with architects and designers to create large-scale, sculptural works for public-art projects. In 2019 she was made a Member of the British Empire (MBE) for services to ceramic art.

See also

Hideaki Miyamura (p.104)

Janice Tchalenko (p.110)

Brian Rochefort (p.128)

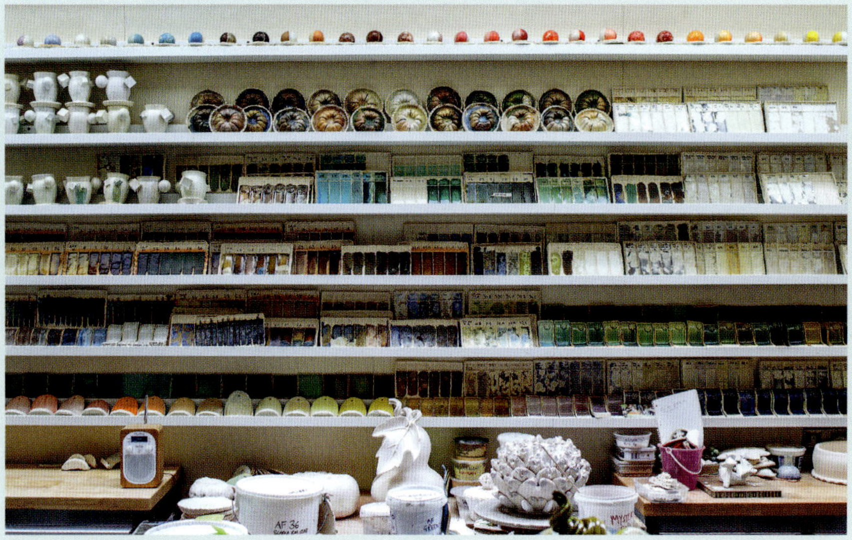

Technical

Kate Malone uses crystalline glazes for their 'unique, uncontrollable beauty'. In general, this type of glaze is fired to stoneware temperatures of between 1280 and 1300°C (2336 and 2372°F). It requires a precise firing schedule of cooling and holding the temperature at specific points in order to establish successful crystal growth. Sizes of crystals can typically range from a few millimetres to 4 or 5 centimetres (⅛–2 in.) wide, depending on the recipe you use. This type of decorative glaze can be very runny and fluid, so you need to allow for this by making a sacrificial tray or placing your work on stilts to avoid unwanted drips or sticking to the kiln shelf.

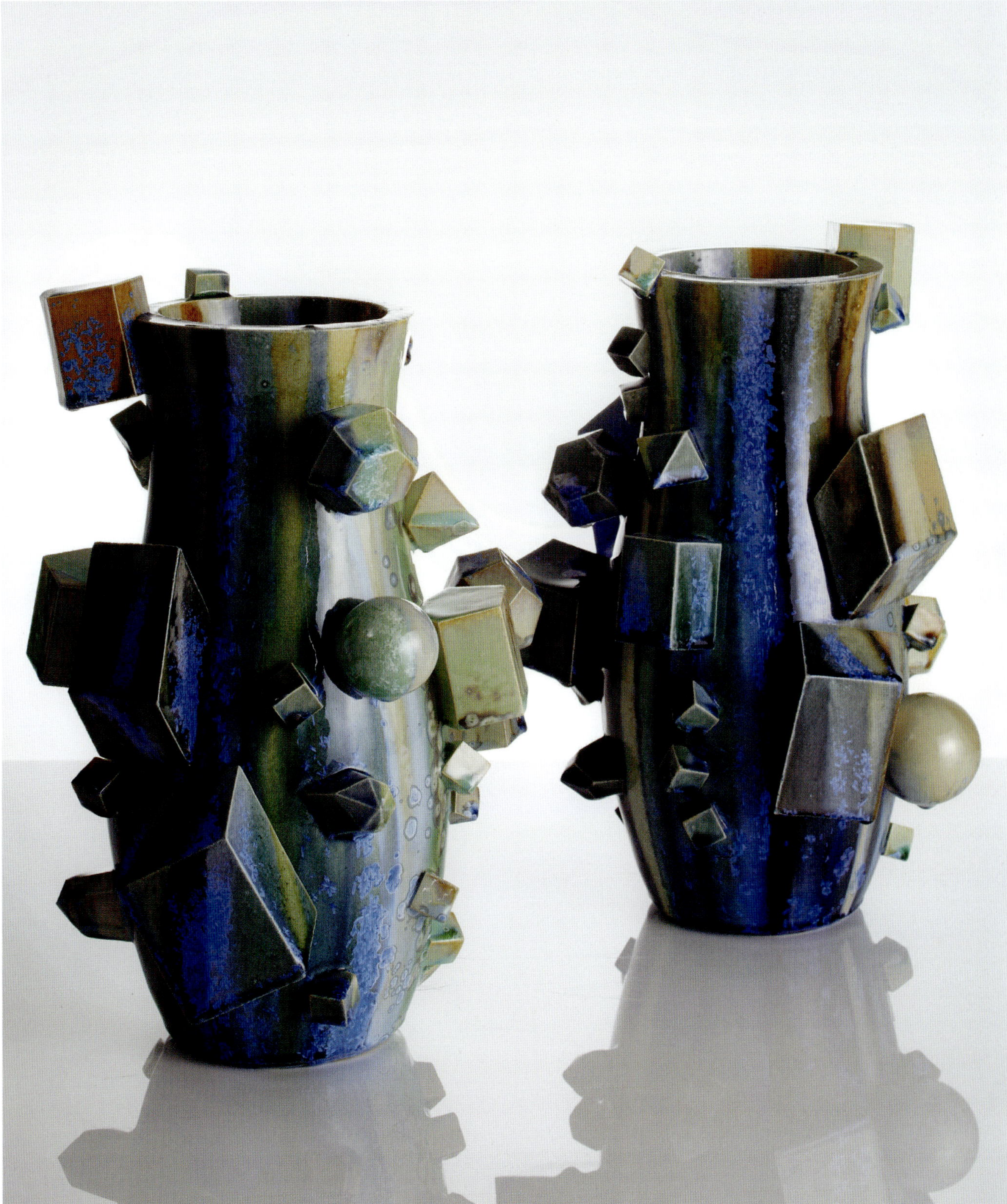

Judy McKenzie

Nerikomi Plaque 2018
Porcelain, ceramic stains and oxides, silver
Diameter: 27 cm (10 3⁄5 in.)

This exuberant, decorative plaque by Judy McKenzie follows the principles of traditional Japanese agateware, referred to as *nerikomi* (or *neriage*). The artist brings the technique into contemporary application by using the process freely to emulate the formation of natural rock. The overlaps of contrasting colours and bold linear compositions induce a dynamic effect.

To construct this piece, first McKenzie coloured porcelain clay with amounts of body stains to achieve gradations of pinks, orange, greens, blues and greys. She proceeded to stack, fold and press thin slabs of different colour combinations into lengths that were then sliced to reveal unique pattern structures. The pieces were then artfully arranged and rolled flat to create one sheet. McKenzie has brought depth to this piece by varying the widths and shapes of the patterned material, set against block areas of cool green and grey colours. This successfully draws the eye into the composition, bringing movement and energy. The piece was fired to 1000°C (1832°F), polished with grades of diamond pads (a fine sanding tool) and fired without glaze to 1200°C (2192°F) to enhance the colours.

McKenzie embraces the imperfections that can occur during the construction and firing of her works. Here, she has implemented *kintsugi* – the Japanese art of repair, whereby faults and cracks are accentuated by an infilled line of resin and precious metal dust. For this piece, McKenzie used solid silver to enhance the flaws that occurred.

Judy McKenzie (British, born 1955) made the audacious decision at the age of sixty to change direction from a successful career as a designer in the design and printing industry, to study a BA (hons) degree in Three-dimensional Craft and Design at Havering College, London (2012–15). This was followed by a master's degree at the Royal College of Art (2016–18). During her studies, she became very inspired by a technique making ribbons of multi-coloured clay. This prompted further investigation into the Japanese processes of *nerikomi* and *kintsugi*, using online video sharing sites and reading books on the subject. Now an emerging artist, McKenzie is already making a substantial impact with her vibrant ceramic creations by winning international awards and gaining the attention of galleries and press.

See also
Kate Malone (p.116)
Michelle Erickson (p.212)
Honor Freeman (p.268)

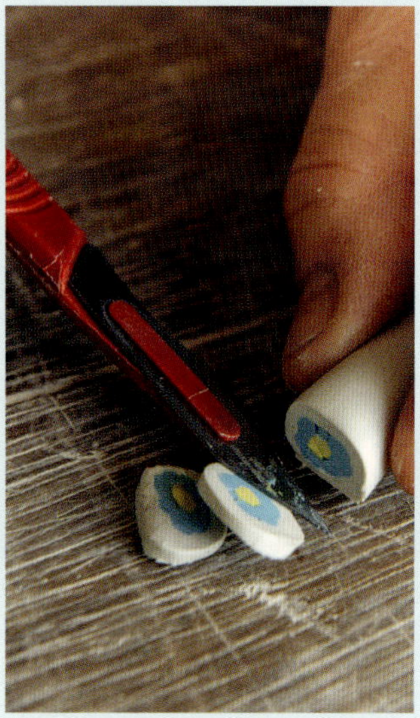

Process
Nerikomi is a time-consuming technique that involves rolling fine layers of coloured clays and then cutting and reassembling them in formation to create beautiful ornate patterns. With an infinite number of possible outcomes, the technique is incredibly addictive. For best results, use two or more coloured clay bodies. To make an attractive pattern such as the design seen here, roll one long thin coil of yellow clay and eight blue coils (or a colour of your choice). Arrange the blue coils around the yellow coil and lightly roll to compress together. Prepare a thin sheet of white clay, wet lightly and encase the coil in the sheet, then roll again to seal. Allow to firm slightly before cutting thinly with a sharp knife, as illustrated here. Lay the sliced pieces side by side, cover with fabric and use a rolling pin to integrate everything into one patterned sheet. You can then use this sheet for press moulding and hand-building your forms.

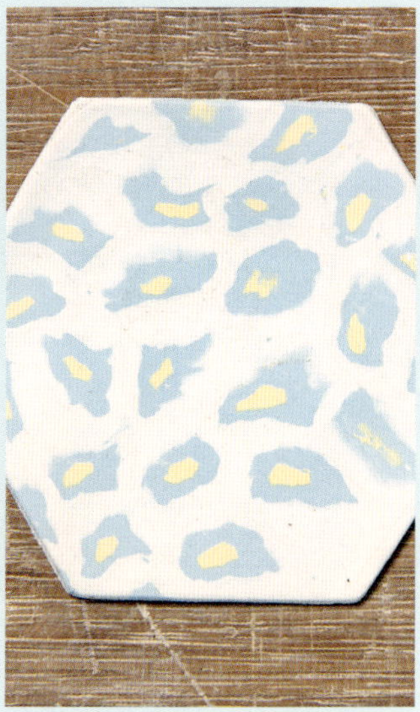

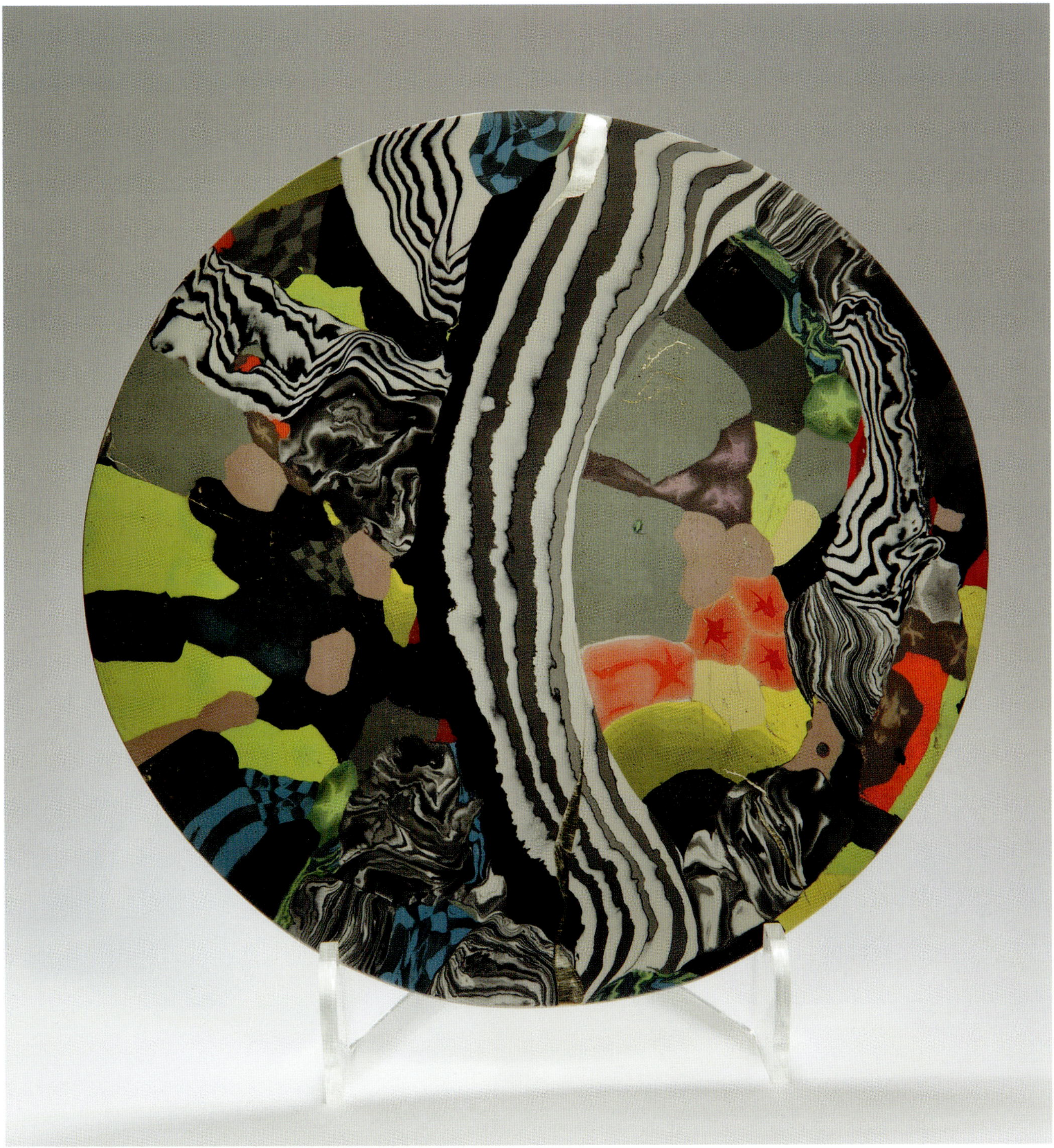

Nick Weddell

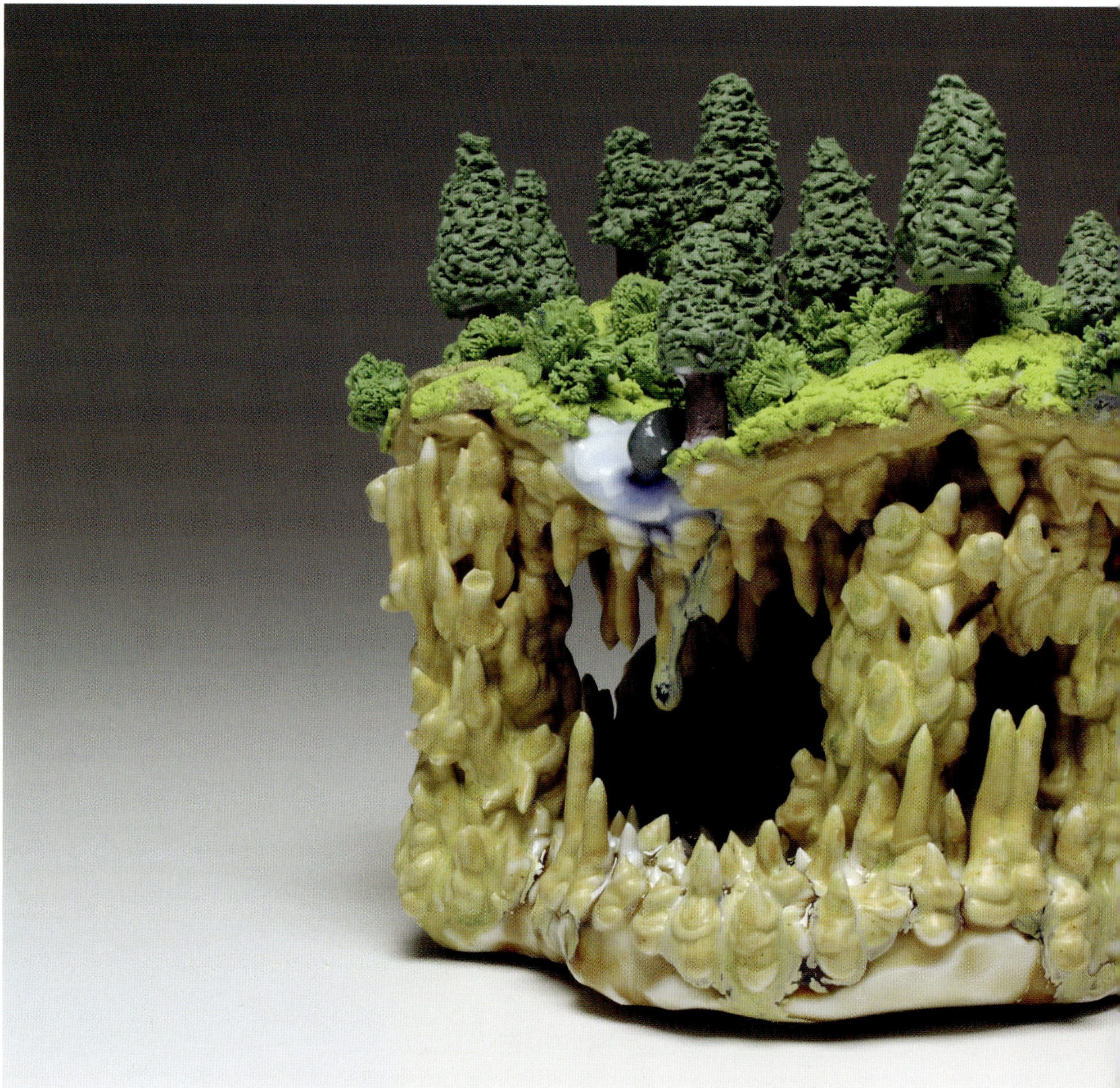

See also

Bernard Palissy (p.86), **Barnaby Barford** (p.266)

Nick Weddell (American, born 1994) studied ceramics at Texas State University, going on to gain a master's degree from the New York State College of Ceramics at Alfred University. He experiments with glaze and surface to challenge what is possible with ceramic material. The result is pots in bright, sometimes acid, colours with highly tactile surfaces. His vessels draw on natural forms, such as coral and tropical fish, yet appear to be whimsical creations that would not be out of place in a cartoon. He continues to push boundaries by producing metamorphosed versions of everyday objects, ranging from cups and armchairs to chaise longues and bathtubs.

Surface
Weddell used an array of matt and semi-matt glazes to convey the naturalistic qualities of the forest, capturing the freshness of the stream that runs through the piece by using an icy blue glaze with glossy properties. In your own work, exploit the surface texture of a glaze to draw your viewers' eyes to specific areas of your piece and emphasize the contrast in tone.

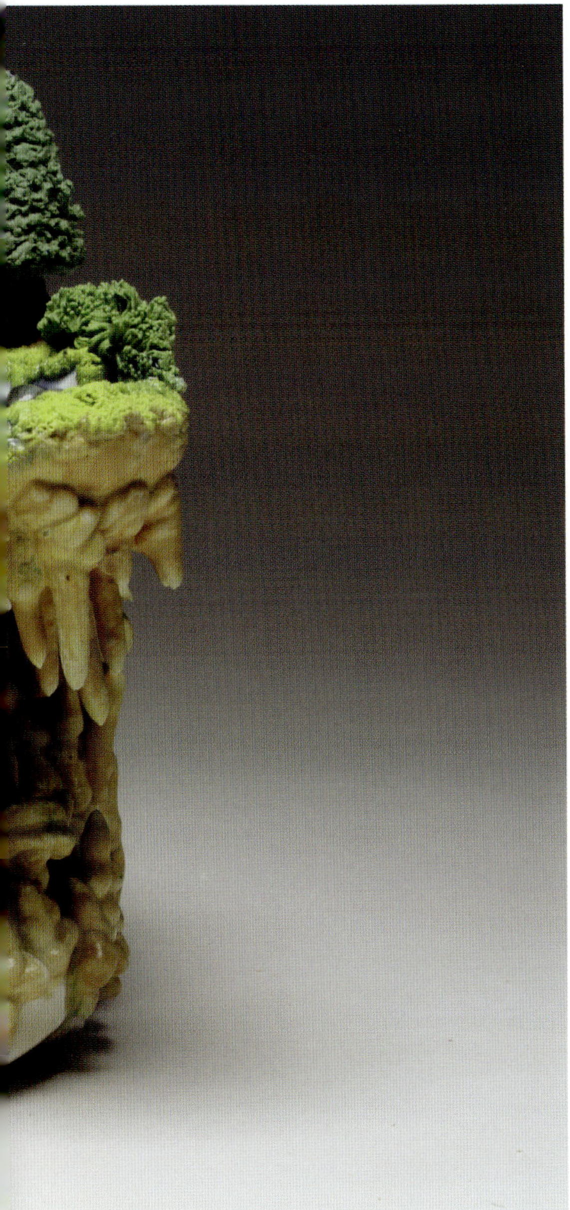

Minor Meteor 2018
Clay and glaze
16.5 × 17.8 × 17.8 cm (6½ × 7 × 7 in.)

This subterranean world depicted by Nick Weddell has a curious explorative element, which encourages the viewer to delve into the cavernous retreat. A profusion of stalactites and stalagmites plays with our perception of scale, making us feel like giants in a world of small domain. With its toy/model-like qualities, the piece is a dioramic portrayal of a forest glade and flowing stream, brimming with nature and wilderness. Capturing a perfect moment in time, the idyllic scene prompts the viewer to consider the world that lies beneath their feet and the potential for new discovery.

What is intriguing about *Minor Meteor* is that it evokes the senses beyond its pleasing visual aesthetic, tricking you into believing that you can actually smell the fresh pine resin of the trees and hear the light bubbling and trickling of the stream. The feeling of inner calm and serenity in the above-ground landscape is starkly contrasted with the hidden depths of the cave beneath, which has a rather unsettling and mysterious ambience. Weddell says it's his intention to create something to 'metamorphose into experiences of wonder and strange joy'.

Another aspect to this piece is the attention paid to the surface decoration. Weddell's background is firmly rooted in natural sciences and this has resulted in an interest in glaze alchemy. He experiments endlessly with what is possible and he thinks of glaze as a form rather than just a surface.

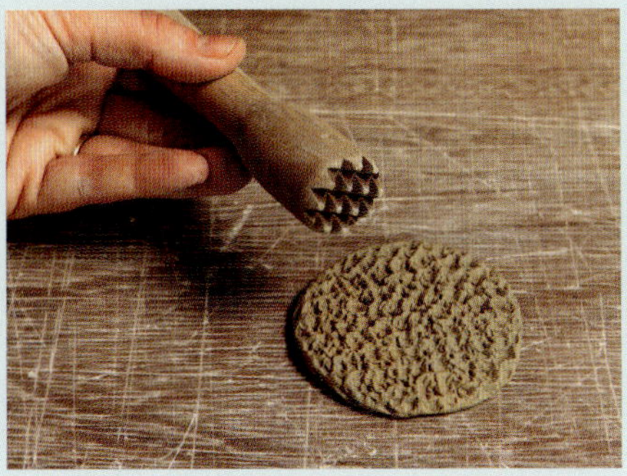

Technical

A carved wooden tool such as this one is great for stamping texture onto your clay surfaces. Weddell has used a similar technique to define the leaves and foliage within his composition. You can be very resourceful with how you create texture on clay, using, for example, a meat tenderizer for chunky, pitted surfaces, a fork for scratchy rough marks, an old hacksaw blade for fine lines and light abrasion or an assortment of textured wallpaper samples to roll clay onto for embossed decorative pattern. Pebbles, shells and other organic materials are all excellent for transferring rich textures into your clay creations. Consider using a fluid glaze or barium-type recipe, which will enhance the texture by pooling or highlighting raised detail rather than cover it up.

Pippin Drysdale

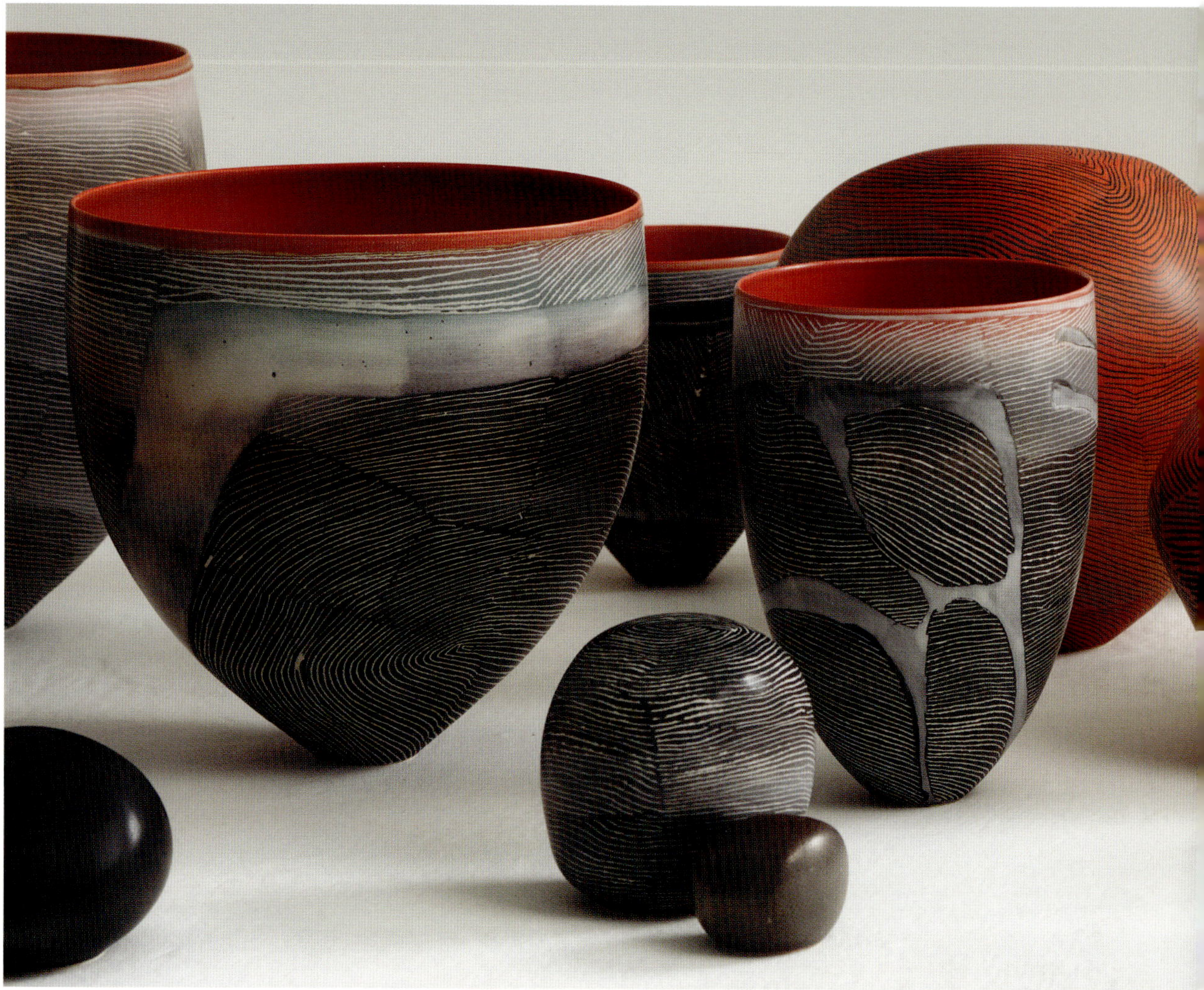

Splendour at Black Rock, East Kimberley (detail) 2019
Porcelain
Dimensions variable

Pippin Drysdale draws inspiration for her vibrant and evocative colour palette from the vast expanse of the Australian landscape. Her sensitive installations of beautiful vessels and tactile, enclosed forms take the viewer on a journey through wind-swept deserts and arid lands. Mapped within her vivid forms are intricate lines and pathways, resembling the patchwork integration of landscape when viewed from an aerial position.

The collection shown here is part of a much bigger installation of more than thirty pieces (Drysdale's largest to date), entitled *Splendour at Black Rock, East Kimberley*. Drysdale made the installation for the show *An Idea Needing to be Made* and it was exhibited at the Heidi Museum of Modern Art in Melbourne in 2019. Drysdale encapsulates the richness and ambience of the Kimberley Desert through her use of colour, employing sandy yellows and seductive tones of red and black.

What is striking about this installation is its expanse and scale. Beginning from the left, the colour palette changes dramatically, like a dawn sunrise, gently transitioning from deep hues of red and burnt orange to subtle pink-greys and delicate whites. Drysdale brings greater variety to the installation with boulder-like forms. These enclosed forms forge a direct link to the geological landscape that inspired the work. The variety in shape and colour breaks up the openness of the vessels, encouraging the eye to wander and absorb the breadth of the installation and reconnect with the landscape.

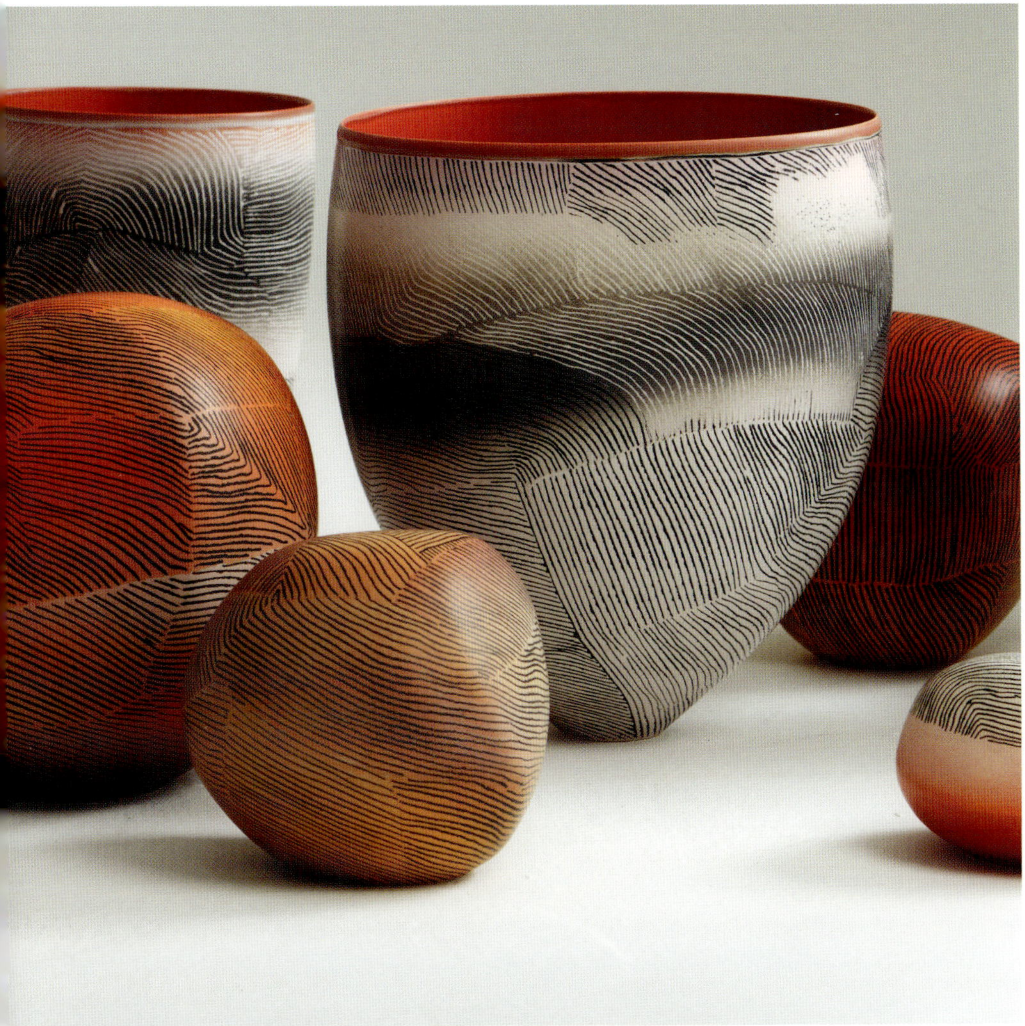

Pippin Drysdale (Australian, born 1943) is one of Australia's leading ceramic artists, with a career spanning more than forty years. Drysdale is based in Fremantle, Western Australia, and works in collaboration with a team. Her elegant forms are made by master potter, Warrick Palmateer, and Drysdale decorates them in her distinctive style. She began her training in 1982 at Western Australia School of Art and Design, studying a diploma in advanced ceramics. This was followed by a bachelor's degree at Curtin University of Technology in 1985. Drysdale has travelled and taught extensively all over the world, including in Canada, Italy and Siberia. Examples of her work are held in numerous collections nationally and internationally. In 2007 she was awarded a Master of Australian Craft and in 2015 the Western Australian Government bestowed on her the prestigious State Living Treasure Award.

See also

Toshiko Takaezu (p.56)
Gwyn Hanssen Pigott (p.70)
Sara Flynn (p.80)

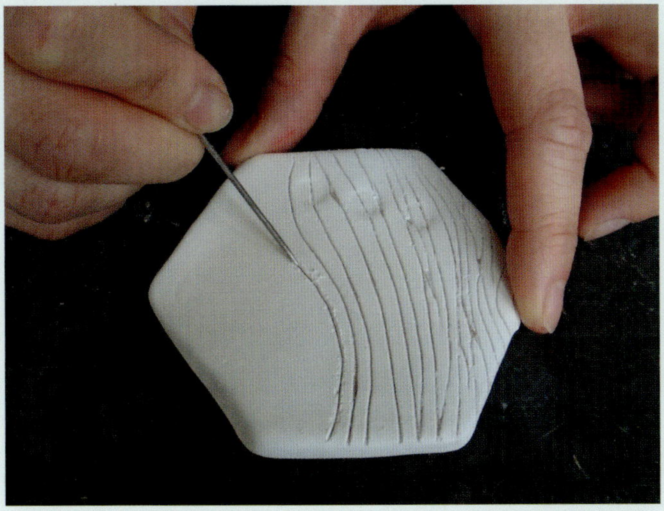

Surface
Drysdale inscribes fine contoured lines using masking and resist techniques. Experiment with painting wax resist or a coating of shellac over the top of a glaze and, with a scalpel or sharp tool, drawing a design through the layers. Spray or paint a coat of a different coloured glaze to cover the lines and fire to your desired temperature. The aim is to create a contrast between the line and background colour.

Composition
Drysdale carefully planned this composition so that the flow of intense crimson red takes the viewer's gaze on a journey around the undulating contours and spaces of the installation. Think how you can build in repeats of colour into your pieces: perhaps you could apply a hint of colour in the rim of one vessel and the foot of another, or apply flicks of the same colour within the surface decoration itself.

Takuro Kuwata

Tea Bowl 2019
Porcelain, glaze, pigment, platinum, steel
35 × 35 × 39 cm (13¾ × 13¾ × 15⅜ in.)

Takuro Kuwata has gained an international reputation for his radical, experimental techniques. He challenges the conventions of historic Japanese craft traditions with his innovative practice, although, as Kuwata says, 'I'm not trying to break the rules. I just want to apply a contemporary sensibility to pottery. I believe I can create something truly new, work that reflects our time.'

This globular tea bowl by Kuwata is grounded in the tradition of *kairagi* – a type of shino ware, originating from the Momoyama period (1574–1615) in Japanese history. This is a method of intentional glaze shrinkage, which is characterized by a thick glaze that crawls and repels, exposing the clay body beneath it. Kuwata has playfully exaggerated this glaze effect by overloading and saturating his form with handfuls of feldspar glaze, which he applied to the pot. Also visible are a number of partially buried steel pins, their purpose being to attach the glaze material to the surface. The glaze technique is pushed so far that during firing the material peels and falls away from the pot in great globs, clinging on by mere strands in some areas. Post firing, Kuwata applied a brilliant platinum lustre coating to the fragmented glaze, resulting in a vessel that appears as if molten metal is squeezing out from within. Underneath the melted chunks, the ceramic form is quite loose in its construction and we can see the marks of Kuwata's fingers where he smudged and smeared the profile. This deliberate roughness is contrasted with the vibrant blue colour of the pot, which brings freshness and vitality to the work.

Takuro Kuwata (Japanese, born 1981) studied ceramics at the Kyoto Saga University of Arts and Tajimi City Pottery Design and Technical Center. Kuwata is best known for his reinterpretations of the traditional Japanese tea bowl. He has broken with the conventional aesthetic of *wabi-sabi* to create highly colourful ceramics with fractured forms and peeling glazes. In 2015, he received a grant from the Arts Council Tokyo, which led to him creating an object for the *Heaven* indoor stone garden, created by artist Isamu Noguchi (1904–88) for the Sogetsu headquarters in Tokyo. In 2018, he won a special mention as a finalist for the LOEWE Craft Prize.

See also
Bente Skjøttgaard (p.108)
Morten Løbner Espersen (p.126)
Brian Rochefort (p.128)

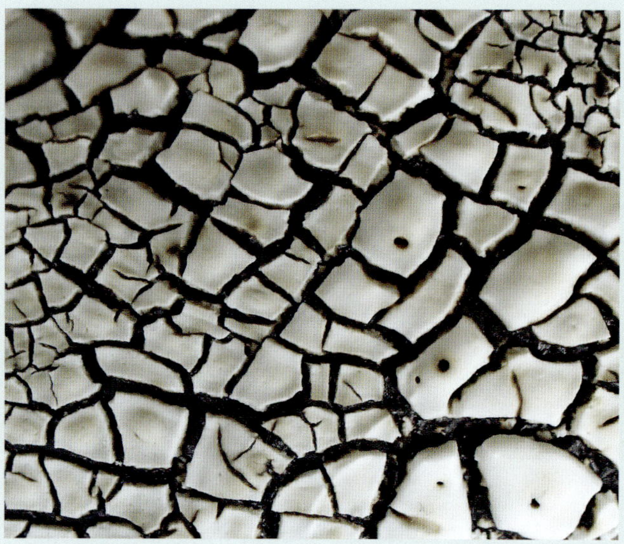

Process
Kuwata sensitively reflects on ancient Japanese traditions/philosophies and combines this with a contemporary aesthetic. Alongside *kairagi*, Kuwata also practices *wabi-sabi* – the acceptance of transience and imperfection. Glaze flaws, warped rims and uneven surfaces are all part of the pot's unique beauty to be celebrated. You can bring this approach into your own work by creating unconventional forms and surfaces that become defined through specific processes.

On the sample shown here, a heavy crackle surface was created by painting very thick, dry matt slip/glaze (see p.276) over a black clay stoneware body. It was fired to 1280°C (2336°F), and during the firing the glaze fragmented and split apart, causing an effect not dissimilar to a dried-out river bed. The stark contrast between the white glaze and black background is particularly dramatic and highly tactile.

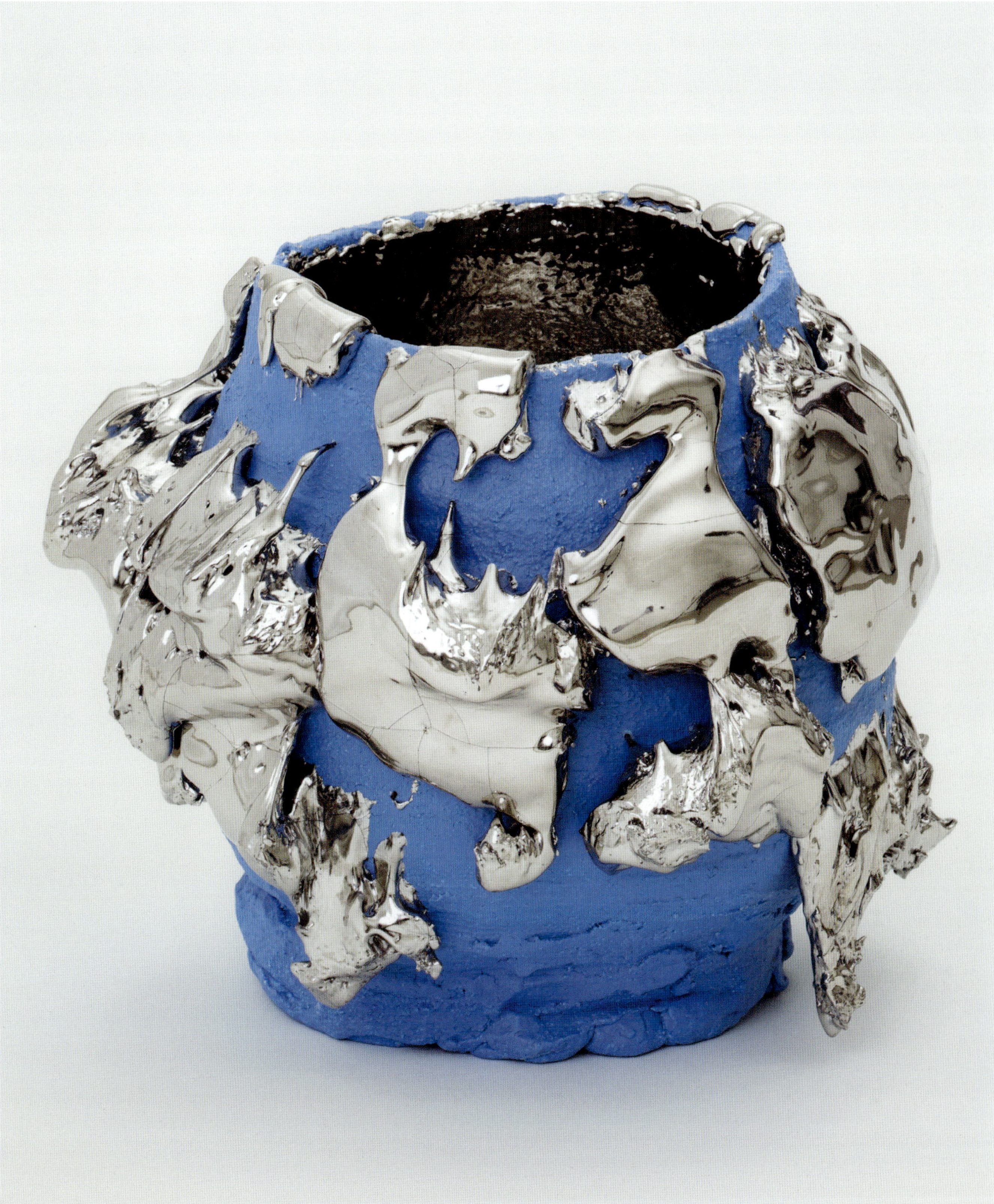

Morten Løbner Espersen

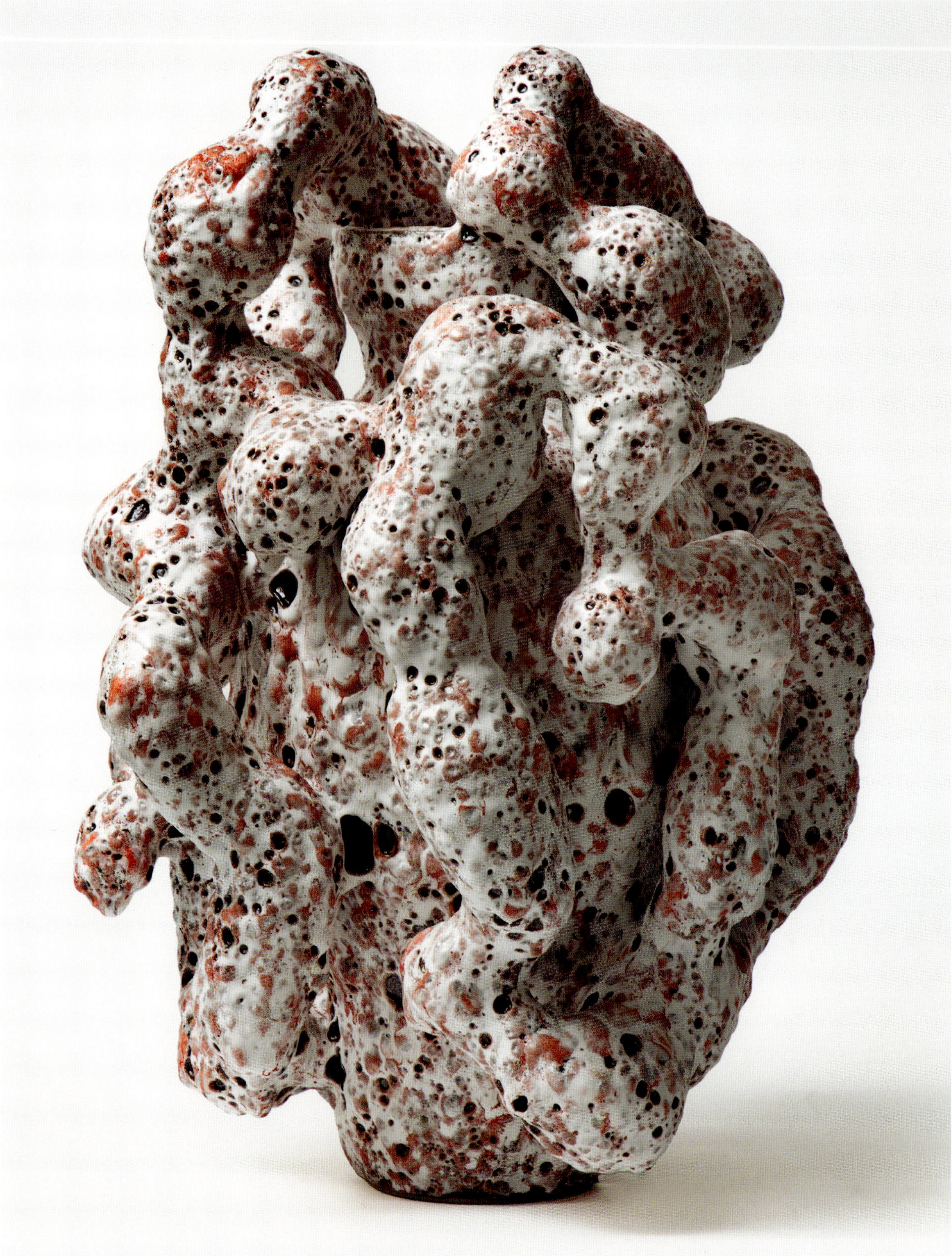

Horror Vacui #2160 2019
Stoneware and glazes
62 × 50 cm (24⅜ × 19¾ in.)

Horror Vacui – 'fear of empty spaces' – is a term used to describe filling the entire surface of an artwork with intricate detail and decoration. Morten Løbner Espersen takes this idea and ramps it up another notch with his series of works that explore the relationship between complex, vivid glazes and archetypal form. Reflecting on the history of ceramics, Espersen comments, 'My vases are classical forms entwined in an anarchic form: a three-dimensional ornament that is liberated from the vessel and camouflages the vase whilst amplifying and paying homage to it.'

On the piece shown here, bubbling and frothy appendages writhe and twist on a vase profile that's hidden within. Resembling a mass of spilled intestines and oozing flesh, the surface initially evokes revulsion – but after further observation, the true beauty and astonishing depth of the glaze becomes apparent. The fine balance between control and unruliness achieved by Espersen is held in a perfect state of equilibrium, resulting in a piece that is wildly expressive and compelling.

Taking inspiration from the refined colour palette of East Asian glazes, Espersen applies layer upon layer of opposing glazes. He fires the work multiple times – up to seven in some instances – with Espersen saying, 'My goal is to create rich, complex surfaces ... I never have a precise image of the final glaze in mind, but every time I empty the kiln I hope to be surprised and see something I've never seen before.' Espersen's skilful and curious approach exemplifies the endless possibilities of glaze and interface with form.

Morten Løbner Espersen
(Danish, born 1965) lives and works in Copenhagen. He has been practising for more than twenty years and is renowned for his experimental, highly saturated glazed vessels. Espersen specialized in craft at the Royal Danish Academy of Fine Arts, School of Design in Copenhagen from 1987 to 1992, followed by intensive training in ceramics at Duperré School of Applied Arts in Paris from 1989 to 1990. Espersen is drawn to the malleable, unpredictable nature of clay, commenting, 'Clay is my material of choice, because it contains so many possibilities: a plastic, amorphous material of incomparable formability that can be fired into imperishable, precise forms.' Espersen's work is exhibited throughout Europe and internationally and his works are included in collections in London, New York and Rotterdam.

See also
Bente Skjøttgaard (p.108)
Gitte Jungersen (p.222)
Matt Wedel (p.226)

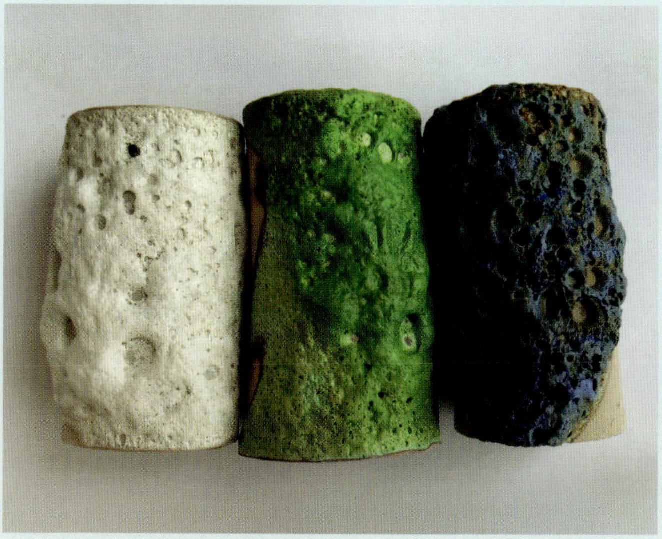

Surface
To achieve foamy, effervescent glazes such as this, use a crater glaze recipe (see p.275) with the active ingredient silicon carbide. This material volatizes during the firing (best results high temperature) and produces deep moon-like craters and pits in the glaze. Add oxides or stains to colour the glaze; when it is fired, you can further enhance the bubbly texture by sanding the surface lightly with sandpaper.

Process
When experimenting with glazed surfaces, allow yourself to take risks and be inquisitive about what exciting results could emerge from the kiln. You can fire a piece multiple times, building up layers of shiny, dry, textured glazes between each firing until the ultimate outcome has been reached. To apply new glaze on top of a fired glazed surface, mix it with a little wallpaper paste or PVA glue to aid adhesion. This will burn away in the firing, leaving the glaze behind.

Brian Rochefort

Paint Can 2019
Ceramic, glaze
11 × 11 × 11 cm (4⅓ × 4⅓ × 4⅓ in.)

Brian Rochefort creates heavily decorated, experimental sculptures that explore the realms of glaze and surface. Overflowing with thick, oozing glazes and textured, crackling effects, this piece from the *Paint Can* series projects energy and visual delight. Spills of luscious, gloopy material flow and pour from the rims and sides of the vessel. Beneath the dense overlay of heavy globular decoration, a chequered gingham pattern forms the background on which everything else is built. In contrast to the fluid areas, thick sugary pink and yellow dollops cling on to the rim and intensify the tactility and richness of the surface. The piece gives the illusion that it is in constant flux and movement, yet it remains preserved in a fixed state.

Rochefort draws his inspiration from his adventures travelling to remote places, including the Sierra Negra Crater in the Galapagos Islands and the cloud forests of the Bolivian Amazon. He channels his experiences and emotions into his artwork by 'amplifying colours and textures to the point where they became totally alien'. To create this piece, Rochefort formed the main cylindrical shape on the pottery wheel. He then used the form as a three-dimensional canvas. He achieved the molten glazed surface by carefully applying layer upon layer of glaze and firing the piece between each stage. The process can take several firings to create the perfect composition. It is this inquisitive approach and rigorous investigation that has led Rochefort to establish a playful blend of innovative material exploration and abstracted surface.

Brian Rochefort (American, born 1985) studied at the Rhode Island School of Design and then participated in the Lillian Fellowship Residency at the Archie Bray Foundation for the Ceramic Arts in Montana. He is known for his experimental approach to glazes, which he uses to create playful pieces covered in colourful abstract patterns. He has travelled extensively to remote locations in South and Central America and East Africa, and become inspired by natural phenomena, such as volcanoes, cloud forests and barrier reefs. Since 2016 he has been building a series of ceramic vessels called *Craters*, which are reminiscent of geological formations found in Belize, Tanzania, Nicaragua and the Galapagos Islands.

See also
Aneta Regel (p.102)
Bente Skjøttgaard (p.108)
Takuro Kuwata (p.124)

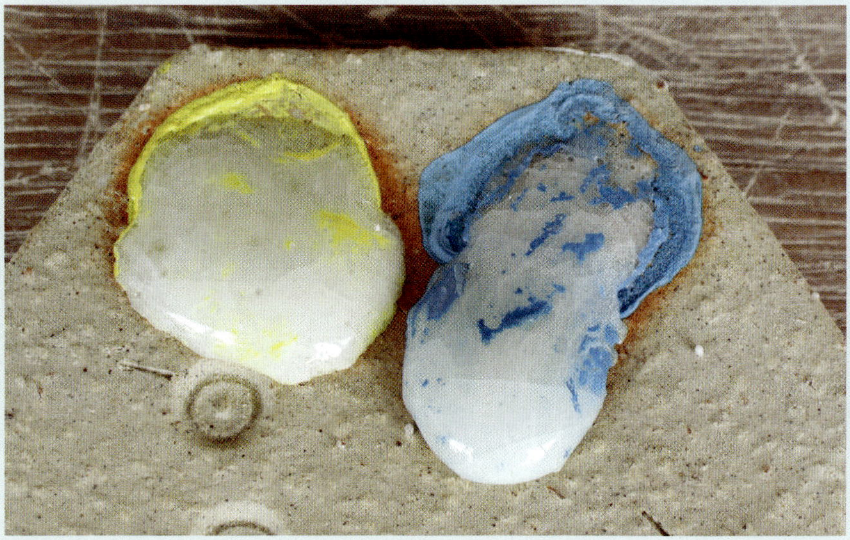

Surface
Rochefort experiments with combinations of ceramic materials to achieve his vibrant, fluid surfaces. Even though there are a lot of different elements at play in this piece, the artist has limited the colour palette to pink, yellow, black and blue. If you are interested in this type of effect, you could experiment with feldspar materials (see p.276). Feldspars are the flux element in a glaze recipe and, by themselves, they create thick gloopy liquids when fired to stoneware temperatures of between 1220 and 1300°C (2228 and 2372°F). Oxide and stain washes can be brushed over the top to encourage a crackled colouration on the glaze surface.

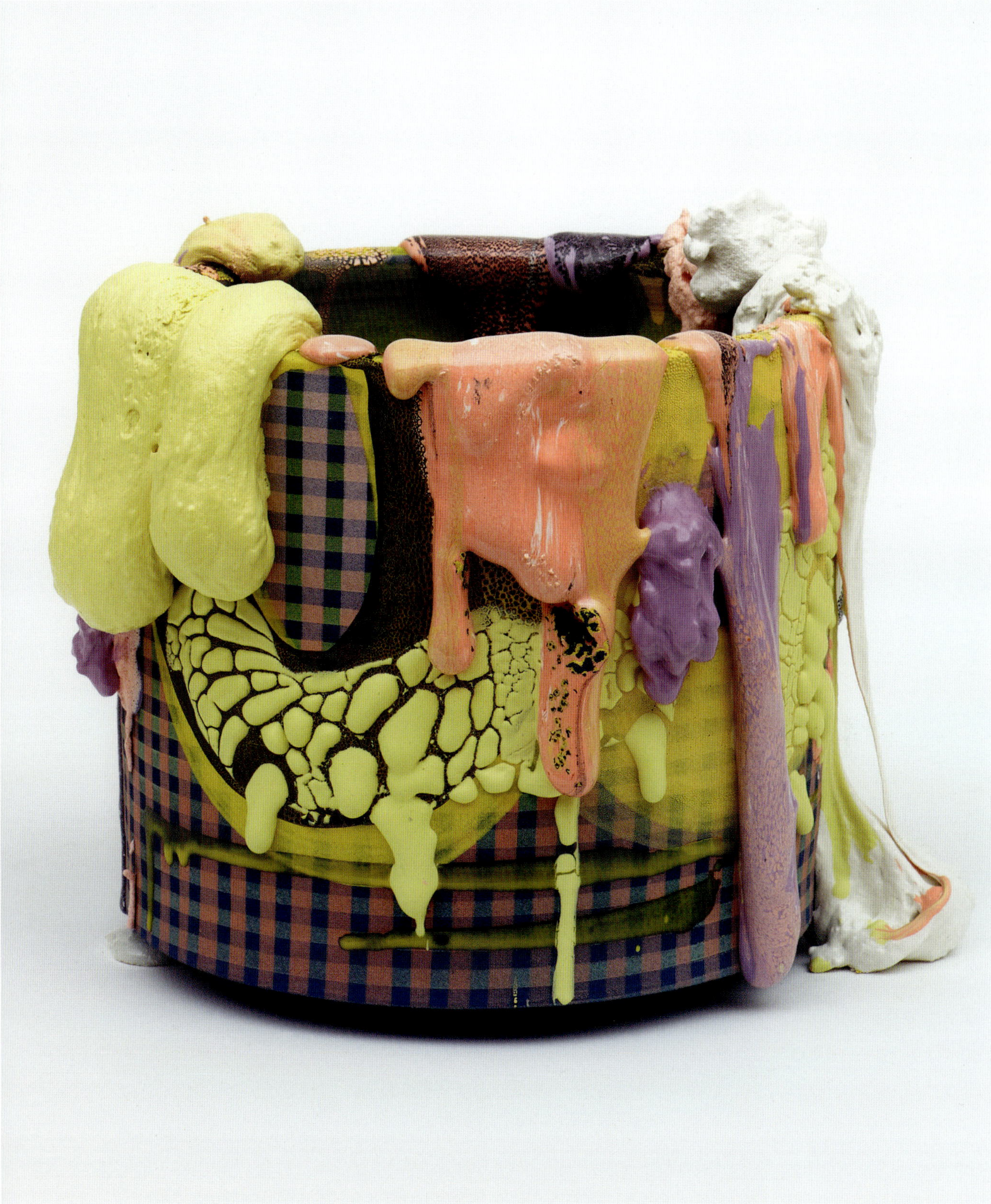

Funct

ion

One of the great joys associated with ceramics is that it can be used, and making functional pieces can be a way to explore and encourage human interaction. Certainly, drinking a cup of tea from a handmade mug is one of life's simple pleasures that uplifts the everyday experience. When creating functional wares, you should first consider the type of clay body you plan to use and the method of construction.

Thrown tableware such as the work of Anne Mette Hjortshøj (p.146) or Stuart Carey (p.150) invites use by offering wonderful tactile forms that are generous in scale and connect the user with the maker. With function comes the association of rituals and ceremony, a theme explored by Kiho Kang's pinched tea-tools sets (p.148) – which may prompt you to think about multi-use sets, whereby the function is ambiguous and left open for interpretation by the user. Like Bernard Leach (p.136) and Shōji Hamada (p.140), your design principles might align closer with the Anglo/east Asian aesthetic dictating that hand-crafted pots should be both beautiful and useable.

By contrast, the notion of what we define as functional is challenged by Ikuko Iwamoto's spiky table sculptures (p. 152) that appear to repulse and welcome at the same time. Function can extend beyond use and into decorative application, exemplified by Sun Kim (p.154), whose crisp geometric vessels function as stand-alone artworks yet can enhance a display of flowers. By creating beautifully designed pieces to enrich our daily experiences, functional ceramics can be as meaningful and engaging as other artforms.

Theodor Bogler

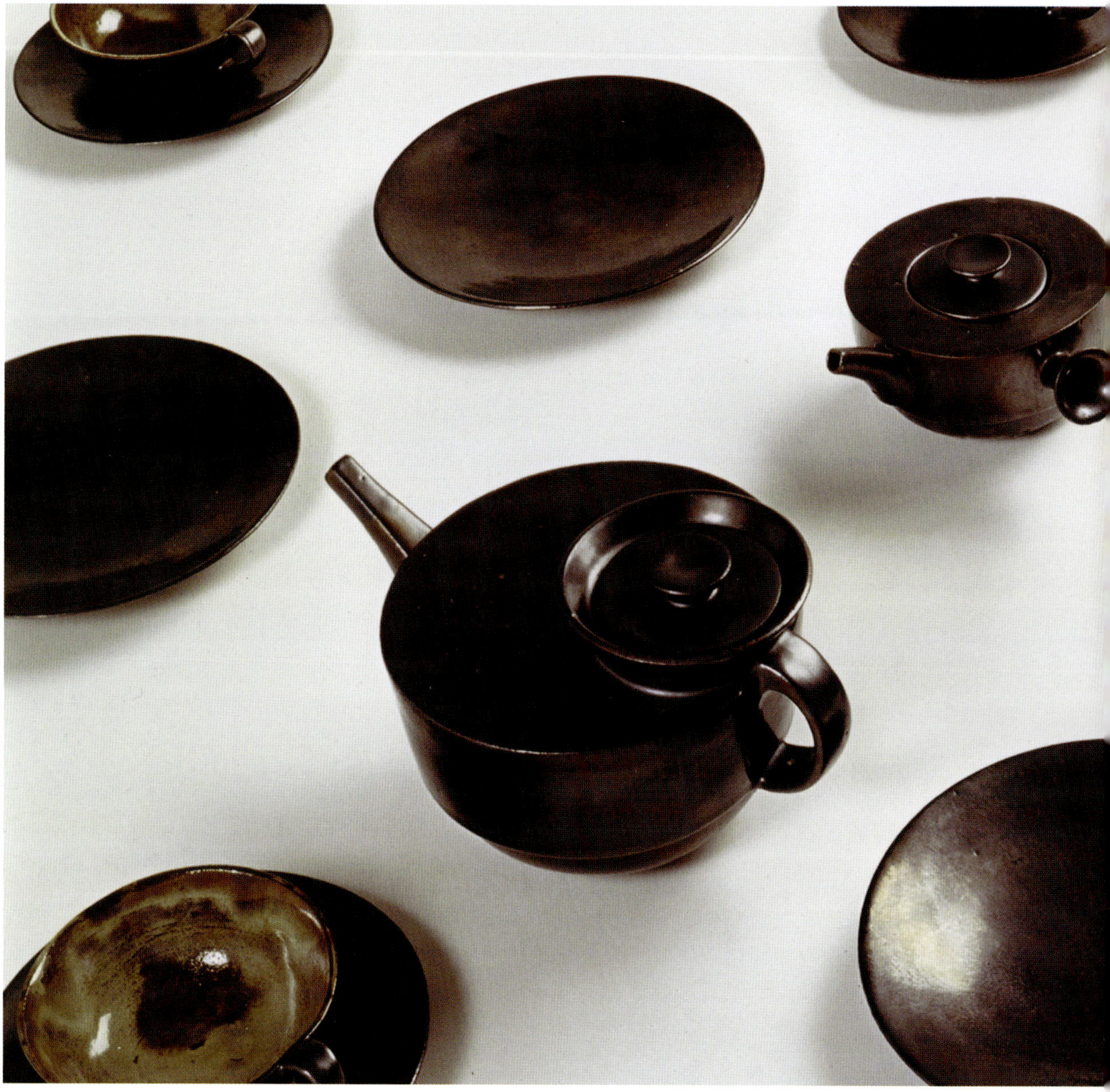

See also

Jill Shaddock (p.156), **Adam Frew** (p.164), **Clare Twomey** (p.246)

Theodor Bogler (German, 1897–1968) attended the ceramics workshop of the Weimar Bauhaus in Dornburg, Germany, from 1920 to 1924, completing an apprenticeship under the direction of sculptor Gerhard Marcks (1889–1981) and Crafts Master Max Krehan (1875–1925). In 1923, Bogler became the business manager of the ceramics workshop but left the Bauhaus in 1924. From 1925 he led the Velten model and casting workshop at the Velten-Vordamm factory, north of Berlin. Bogler had a prominent career ahead of him, but his ambition came to a sudden halt in 1925 when his wife committed suicide. In 1927, Bogler converted to Catholicism and became a Benedictine monk. After World War II he continued to make ceramics for the Karlsruhe Majolika-Manufaktur and Höhr-Grenzhausen factories.

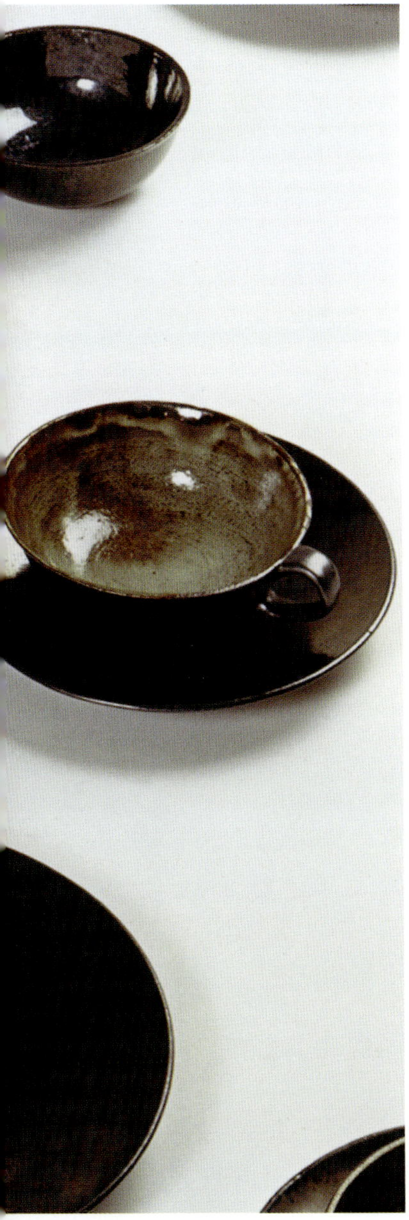

Tea Set (consisting of 'combination' teapot, a small teapot, a sugar bowl, six cups and saucers, and six plates) 1923
Slip cast, earthenware with black metallic glaze
Teapot height: 10.5 cm (4⅛ in.)

The Bauhaus was a German art school founded by the architect Walter Gropius (1883–1969) in 1919, existing until 1933. One of the main principles of the Bauhaus philosophy was to unite the arts: fine art, craft, design and architecture. Gropius stated, 'there is no essential difference between the artist and the craftsman', going on to explain, 'Our guiding principle was that design is neither an intellectual nor a material affair, but simply an integral part of the stuff of life, necessary for everyone in a civilized society.' The emphasis of the Bauhaus ideology was placed on 'form follows function' and 'fit for purpose'. The resulting designs and products were efficient and stripped of any ornamentation or fussiness, allowing the purity of the form to resonate.

The aim of the pottery workshop at Dornburg during the Gropius years was to be an income-generating entity for the Bauhaus, with ambitions to produce ceramics on an industrial scale. The machinery in the workshop was updated from pottery wheels in favour of new slip-casting methods to produce prototypes for industry. Theodor Bogler worked alongside his brother-in-law, Otto Lindig (1895–1966), an influential Bauhaus designer himself.

Bogler's bold ceramic wares represent the radical 1920s Bauhaus style: solid forms, emphasis on functionality, and clean aesthetic designed for modern living. The unique aspect of this design was a modular system of individual component parts comprising the main body, lid, funnel trim, spout and handle, which allowed for a greater variety of combinations within assembly to create different products. For example, the mould for the teapot body was also used to make a lidded bowl. In practice, the design was too complicated and expensive for mass production, but Bogler's principle of modular components is widely regarded as ambitious and highly innovative.

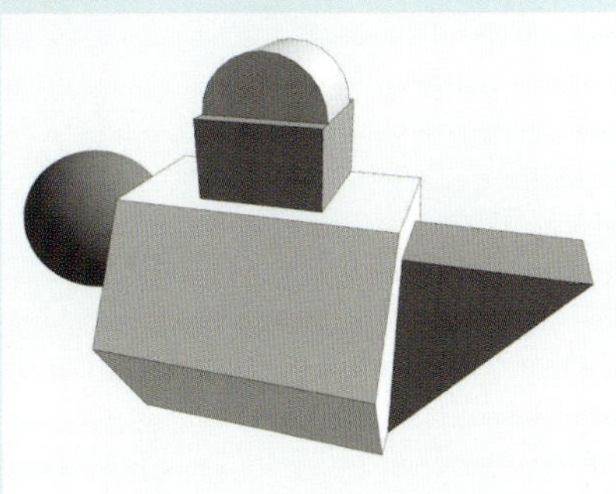

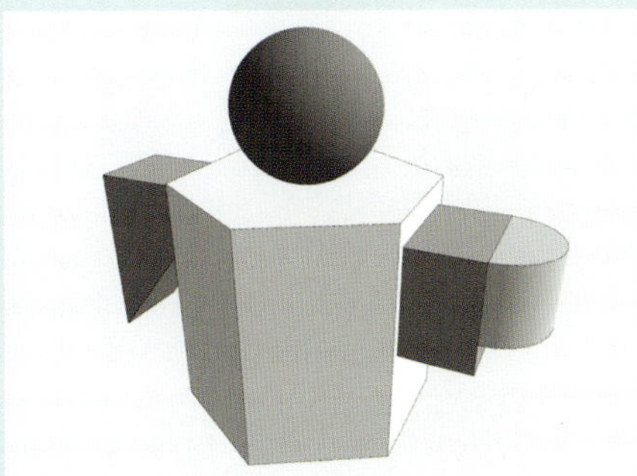

Composition
The Bauhaus was one of the most influential art and design schools in history. To follow the ideology of the Bauhaus, start by paring your forms back to key essential principles: simple form, minimal or no decoration, emphasis on functionality. You could set yourself a limit of five component parts and experiment with the various combinations that can be produced from one set.

Bernard Leach

Vase *c.* 1931
Stoneware
Height: 26.3 cm (10⅜ in.); Depth: 21 cm (8¼ in.)

Modern studio ceramics would not be where it is today without the significant contribution of Bernard Leach. Through his traditionalist philosophy and teachings, Leach pioneered the concept of the artist-potter. The ideology and ethos of Bernard Leach aligned with the core principles of the designer William Morris (1834–96) and the Arts and Crafts movement. Heavily influenced by Japanese, Chinese and Korean pottery forms, Leach fused a cultural blend of restrained East Asian aesthetic with the liveliness of English slipware. He used the pottery wheel to throw simple, individual forms in stoneware or porcelain and occasionally produced large decorated earthenware dishes in homage to the playful style of Thomas Toft.

Bulbous in shape and neatly proportioned, this thrown bottle by Bernard Leach combines his interest for East Asian illustrative qualities with modest form. Using a buff stoneware clay body, sourced from the local area, Leach applied grey-blue slip over a layer of white slip. He then used sgraffito to incise a stylized carp motif in the central panel of the piece. Around the rim and base, bold brush marks flick and dash, framed by neat banding lines. To finish, the piece was covered in a clear glaze to enhance the slip colours and an area of clay body near the base was left exposed to display a rich toasted clay colour. The piece was high fired to a temperature of around 1280°C (2336°F) in a reduction environment, most likely using the three-chambered Japanese climbing kiln built on site at the Leach Pottery – the first of its kind to be used in the West.

Bernard Leach (British, 1887–1979) was born in Hong Kong (China) and raised in Japan. He was sent to school in England at the age of ten to be prepared for a career in banking. However, by age sixteen he was disillusioned with this and decided to pursue his passion for drawing by enrolling at the Slade School of Art in London, and later, the London School of Art. Leach returned to Japan in 1909 with the intention of teaching etching, but after encountering a traditional Japanese raku tea ceremony, he was so enthralled by the process that he decided to become a potter. In 1920, Leach left Japan to establish a pottery in St Ives, Cornwall, with help from his friend the Japanese potter Shōji Hamada. The venture achieved mixed financial success; however, in 1940, Leach earned high acclaim for his publication, *A Potter's Book*, which is still regarded as the go-to manual for the studio potter.

See also
Thomas Toft (p.88)
Shōji Hamada (p.140)
Doug Fitch (p.162)

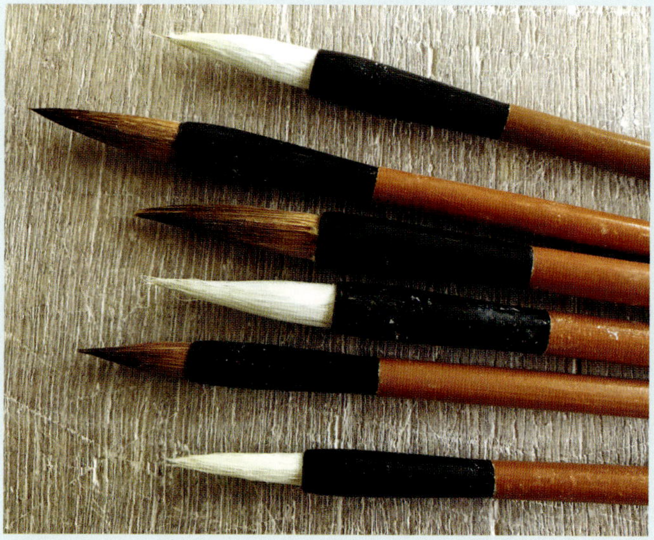

Surface
The typical Leach glaze colour palette was earthy in tone and ranged from speckled whites and *temmoku* browns to subtle green ash glazes. Leach developed 'Standard Ware' – forms intended for everyday life – as well as handcrafted one-off signature pieces: large dishes, tall jars and bottle forms that he decorated freely with illustrations of subjects such as fish, birds and plants using oxides and slips. Leach used soft Chinese calligraphy brushes to apply decoration and painterly marks to his pottery forms. Try dipping calligraphy brushes into a watery oxide mix and allow the pigment to flow across the clay surface in a painterly and expressive manner. You can recreate a similar grey-blue colour to this Leach vase by mixing a combination of one-third cobalt oxide with wo-thirds manganese dioxide. Dilute with water to achieve your desired strength of tone.

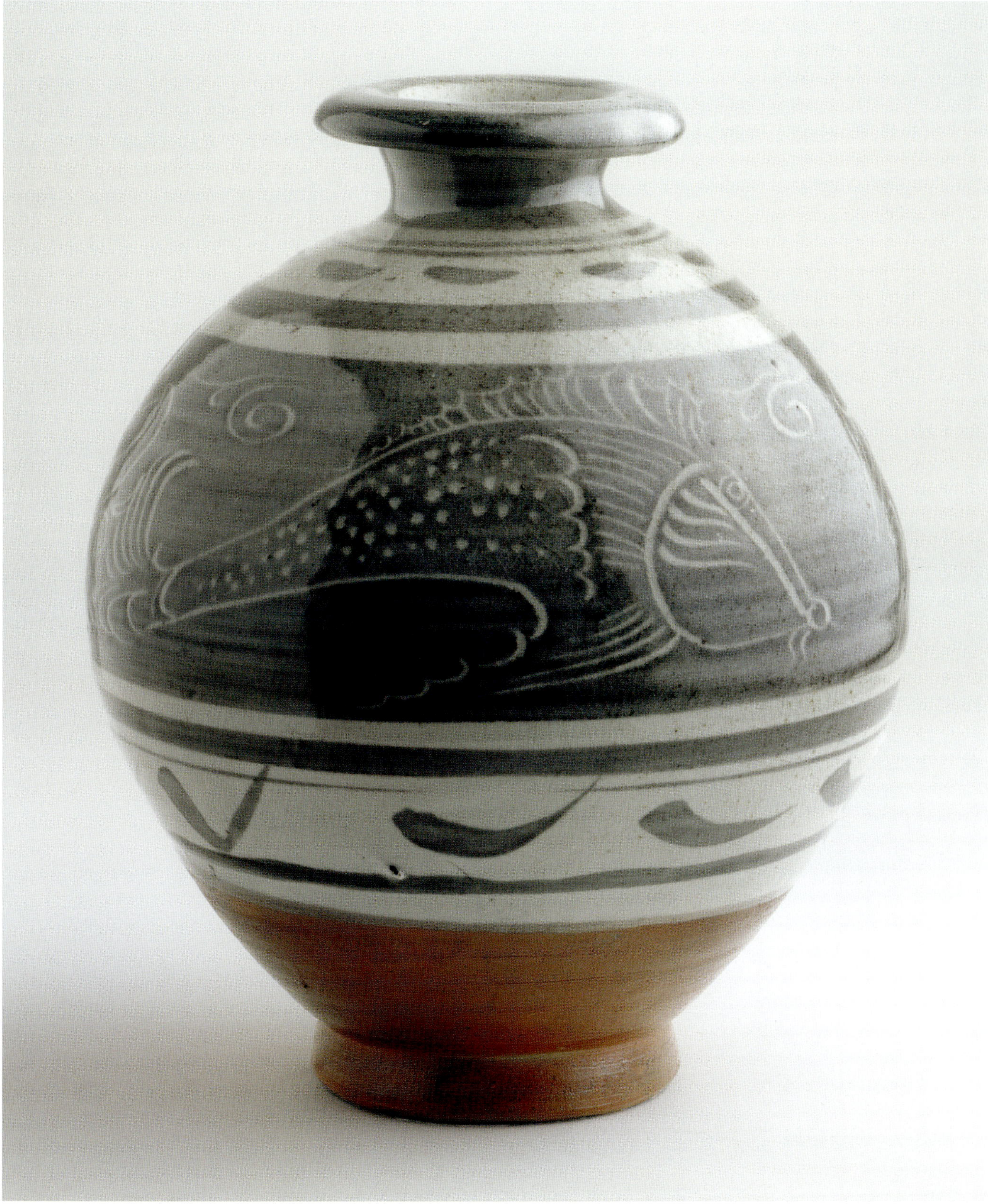

Maria Martinez

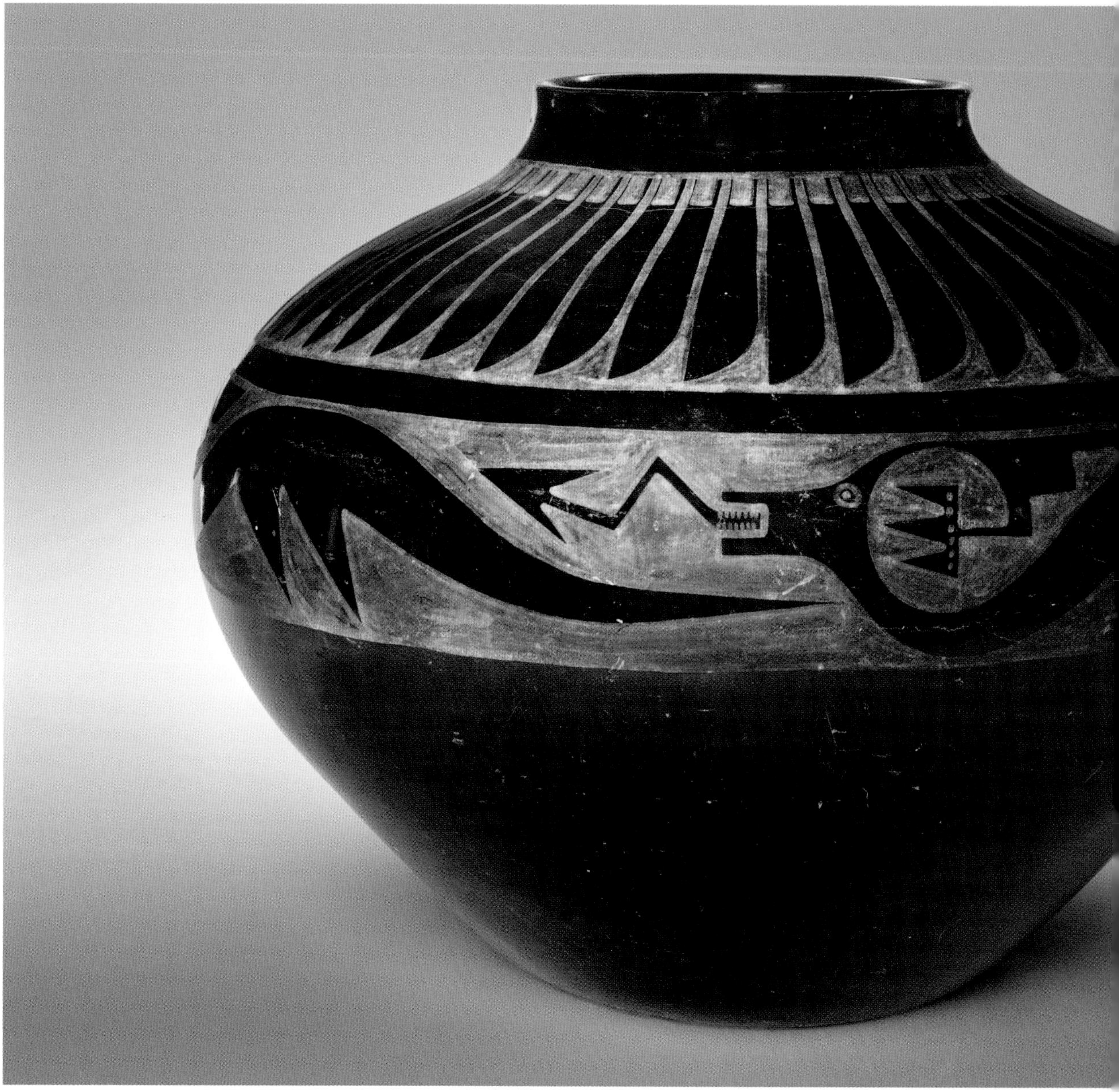

See also

Magdalene Odundo (p.62), **Gabriele Koch** (p.64)

Maria Martinez (American, 1887–1980) is considered one of the most influential Native Americans of the 20th century. Based in the San Ildefonso Pueblo, New Mexico, she learnt her craft from a young age by observing her aunt and grandmother making traditional pottery shapes. In 1908, archaeologist Dr Edgar Lee Hewett was excavating the local area and discovered black shards of pottery dating from the 12th to the 17th centuries. He advertised for local potters to recreate the pottery from the found shards and Martinez responded. After a long period of trial and error, she perfected the technique that created the distinctive blackened surface and began producing the wares commercially to sell to non-native audiences in retail outlets based in National Parks.

Jar *c.* 1956
Earthenware slip, black-on-black finish
15.24 × 17.78 cm (6 × 7 in.)

Pueblo pottery making was a communal affair and Maria Martinez collaborated with her family members. Her husband Julian was a skilled decorator and painted the graphic motifs that adorned her vessels. After his death in 1943, she continued to produce blackware with her sons Popovi Da and Adam and her daughter-in-law, Santana. This jar piece is a later example and demonstrates Martinez's command and skill with the process. The clay started as a rich red colour and Martinez formed the pot by hand, using traditional pinching and coiling techniques. Once she obtained the basic shape, Martinez used a rib carved from a dried gourd to scrape and refine the pot. When dry, she applied an iron-rich slip and burnished the pot by rotating a stone in a circular motion against the clay, creating a highly polished surface. .

The black, mirrored decoration has much in common with the bold, geometric designs of the art deco movement popular around the time Martinez was producing her works. Martinez did not decorate the pieces herself, leaving the task to her sons. Decoration ranged from bird feathers to rain clouds and rivers. On this example, the motif element illustrates the Avanyu, a horned serpent with an arrow – a Tewa deity known as a guardian of water and rain. It was painted in slip on top of the burnished surface using an extremely fine brush made from a yucca leaf. The slip resists the smoke during the firing and gives the pot its unique matt black design against a shiny black background.

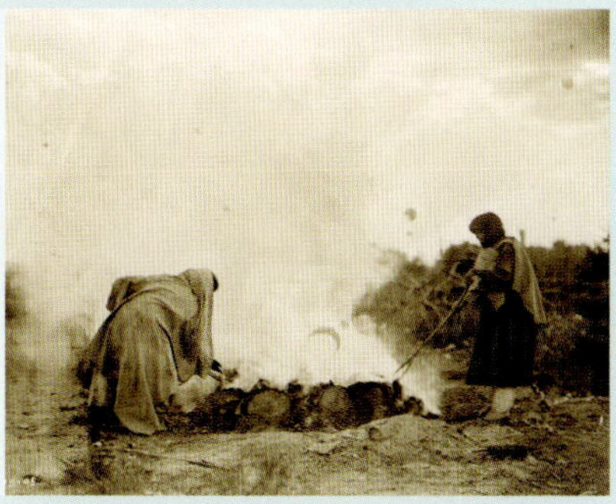

Process

Martinez did not have access to a kiln and she fired her pieces using the traditional method in a pit dug in the ground. The preparation and firing of the wares involved a very long process and many days' labour. Wood and organic material were placed in the base of the pit and the pots nestled within. More organic material was placed on top and the fire was lit. When the fire was established, Martinez covered the wares in dry cow manure to smoother the flames, trapping the smoke and creating a reducing effect (removal of oxygen). The pit fire achieved temperatures of around 600–800°C (1112–1472°F); once the cycle was complete, it was left to burn out and the pit opened a few days later.

Shōji Hamada

Plate Decorated with Geometric Patterns *c.* 1958
Stoneware, iron rust glaze, trailed decoration, reduction
Diameter: 27.2 cm (10¾ in.)

During the three years Hamada spent with Bernard Leach at the Leach pottery in St Ives, he closely studied early English slipware and medieval pottery in the British Museum. Like Leach, Hamada's ideas aligned with the Arts and Crafts movement. The movement centred around simple, functional design without excessive decoration and was a reaction against mass-industrialization. Building on these principles, Hamada took the theory back to Japan and became one of the key figures to establish the *Mingei* movement. *Mingei* translates as 'folk art', otherwise known as 'the people's crafts'. The character traits of the movement are defined by simple, practical objects with restrained decoration for everyday use.

Hamada was a potter of immense skill and precision. He made his works sitting crossed legged at a wooden pottery wheel embedded into the floor of his studio, which he propelled using the momentum generated by the shunt of a stick. This striking plate by Hamada reflects his modern outlook on traditions of the past. The clarity of shape demonstrates a competency and ease for its creation. It is glazed very simply, with just two colours – an iron rust background and freely trailed white decoration applied on top. The depth and tone achieved within the surface is intensively rich and dynamic, particularly in areas where the rust-black glaze breaks over thin edges and burns into the expressive marks, creating a three-dimensional shadow effect. In line with the philosophy of *Mingei*, Hamada did not sign his creations, believing the pots were signatures in themselves.

Shōji Hamada (Japanese, 1894–1978) was born in Misonokuchi, Kanagawa prefecture, Japan, and trained in chemistry and geology at Tokyo Technical College (now Tokyo Institute of Technology). After graduating in 1916, he worked at the Ceramic Testing Institute in Kyoto and in 1919 he was introduced to Bernard Leach. The meeting ignited a lifelong friendship, and in 1920 Hamada accompanied Leach back to the UK with the agenda being to establish the Leach Pottery in St Ives, Cornwall. He returned to Japan in 1924 and set up a studio in Mashiko. Hamada and philosopher-critic Soetsu Yanagi (1889–1961) became the founding members of the Japanese folk craft movement *Mingei*. Hamada was designated a National Living Treasure in 1955 and awarded the Order of Culture in 1968.

See also
William Staite Murray (p.52)
Bernard Leach (p.136)
Kirsten Coehlo (p.160)

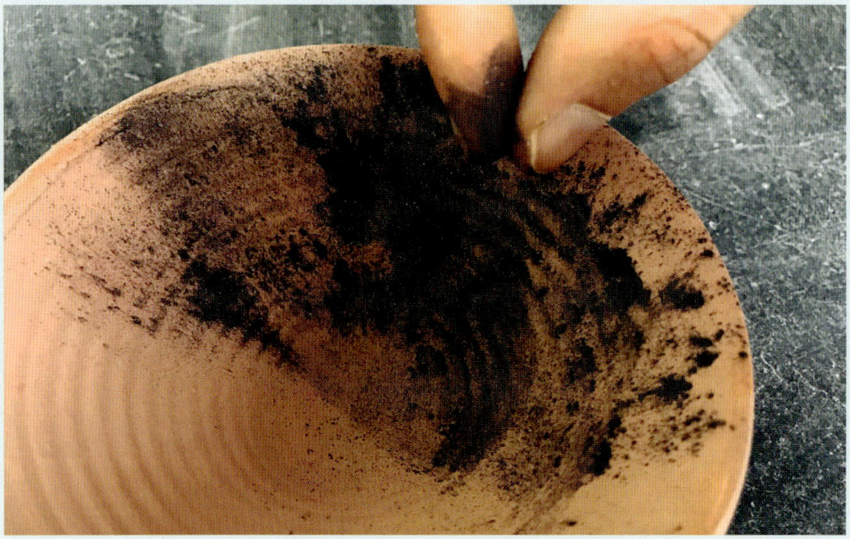

Surface
To make his signature black-red *tenmuko*, Hamada used iron rust from a local blacksmith. Nuka, a creamy white glaze was made of rice husk and the subtle, greeny-grey tones of Hamada's ash glaze came from a variety of wood, straw and reed ash. You can make a very simple glaze just from ash because it is naturally high in silica, which is the key 'glass' component in a glaze. Try sourcing your own organic materials and experiment by adding the ash to your glazes to create different variants. You could also try sprinkling iron dust or spangles on top of the glaze before firing to produce cascading effects in the surface.

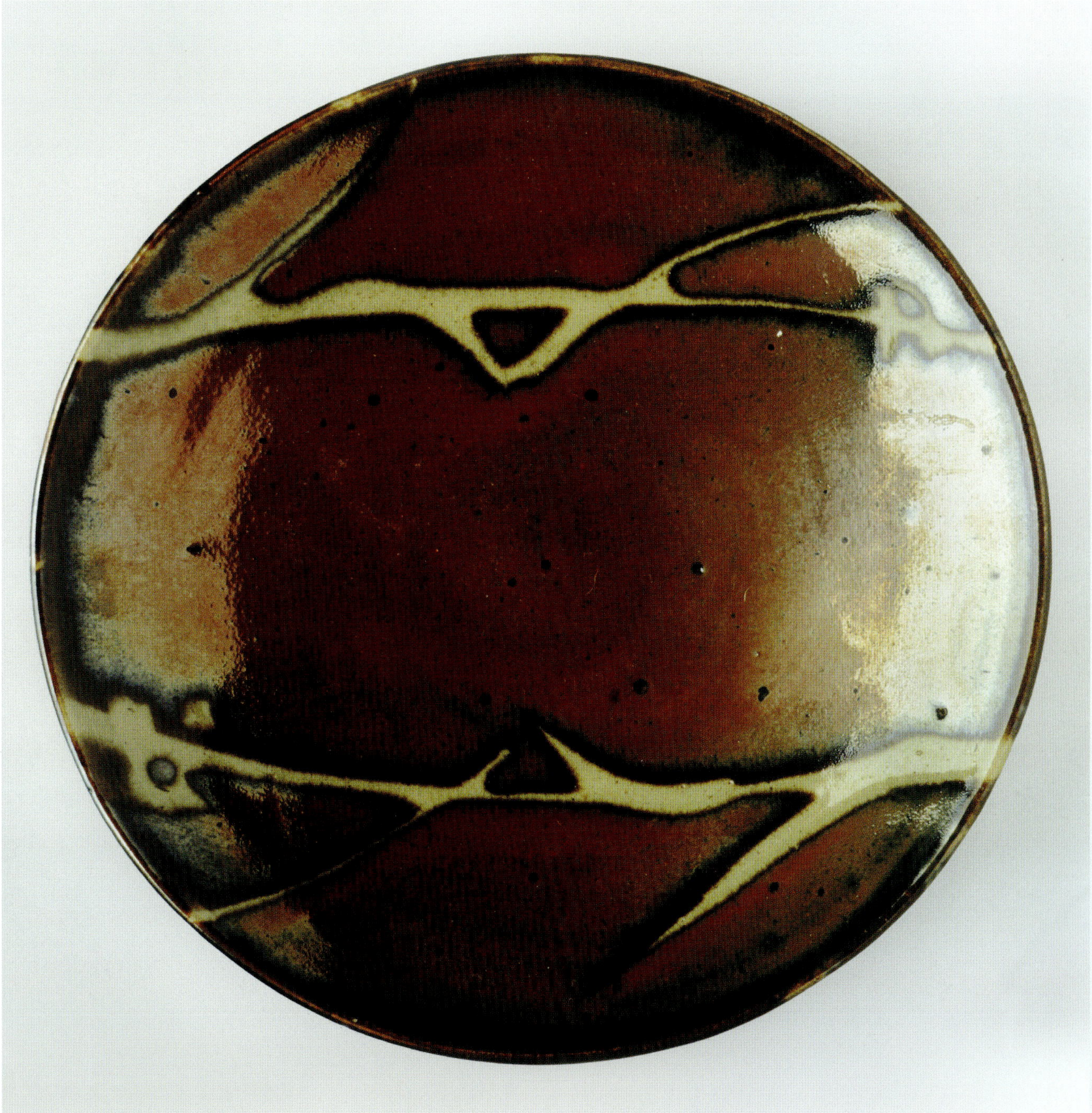

Walter Keeler

Five Branch Dish 2007
Blue and green Whieldon-glaze earthenware
Height: 29 cm (11⅜ in.); Diameter: 45 cm (17¾ in.)

Function and the pottery tradition is at the heart of Walter Keeler's practice. His inventive and characterful pots combine sculptural design with functional purpose. Keeler's interest in clay began from a young age when he enjoyed 'mudlarking' along the river Thames in London, searching for fragments of ancient pottery.

This link with the past is strongly reflected in Keeler's forms, which take inspiration from Greek pottery, Roman glass, 18th-century Staffordshire wares and tin oil cans. A skilled thrower, Keeler's handling of the clay is crisp and precise; what truly brings Keeler's pieces to life, however, is the addition of extruded, lathed and hand-built components, which, along with the thrown sections, he assembles into one accomplished resolution.

Five Branch Dish demonstrates Keeler's lively engineered approach, which imbues his work with charm and intrigue. Here, a series of truncated branch appendages twist and protrude from the rim of a doughnut-shaped bowl. With reference to 18th-century crabstock pottery – a type of functional ware that resembled gnarled twigs and branches – Keeler has reimagined the design into a stylized, honed aesthetic. To complete the piece, it was glazed in a vibrant Whieldon lead glaze, which is characterized by intense colour and a mottled tortoiseshell pattern. Keeler has used the glossy richness of an emerald green (copper) glaze on the outside with a warm honey (iron) glaze on the base and on the tips of the branches. The resulting composition reflects processes of the past but with a modern interpretation.

Walter Keeler (British, born 1942) is a studio potter and was professor of ceramics at the University of the West of England from 1994 to 2002. Keeler attended Harrow School of Art in London from 1958 to 1963 and was trained there by Michael Casson (1925–2003). Keeler set up his first pottery at Bledlow Bridge, Buckinghamshire, in 1965; eleven years later he moved his studio to Penallt in Monmouthshire, Wales. He makes salt-glaze pottery influenced by early industrial pottery, such as Staffordshire creamware, and is known for innovative sculptural works that reinterpret domesticware and draw on the history of ceramic processes. His pots are thrown on the wheel and then hand-altered. He is the president of the South Wales Potters and in 2007 was named Welsh Artist of the Year.

See also
Thomas Bohle (p.112)
Catrin Howell (p.184)
Sterling Ruby (p.218)

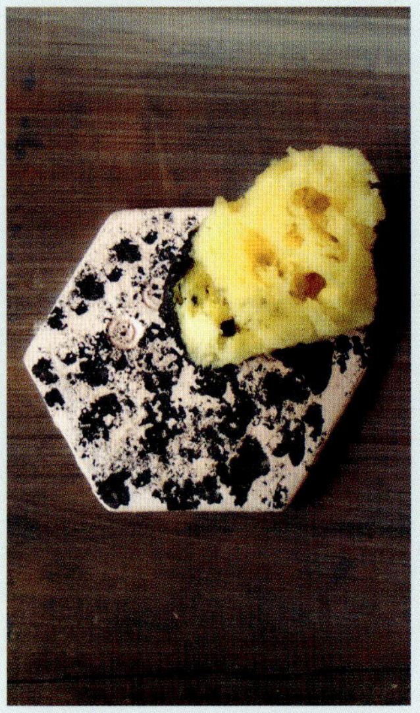

Surface
Keeler has two prominent strands to his glaze aesthetic: high-temperature salt glaze and low-temperature earthenware/creamware. In *Five Branch Dish*, he has paired the form with a traditional earthenware Whieldon glaze. To recreate this tortoiseshell effect, you could use a natural sponge to dapple black stain or oxide (try manganese dioxide or iron) mixed with a little water to your piece prior to applying a glaze on top.

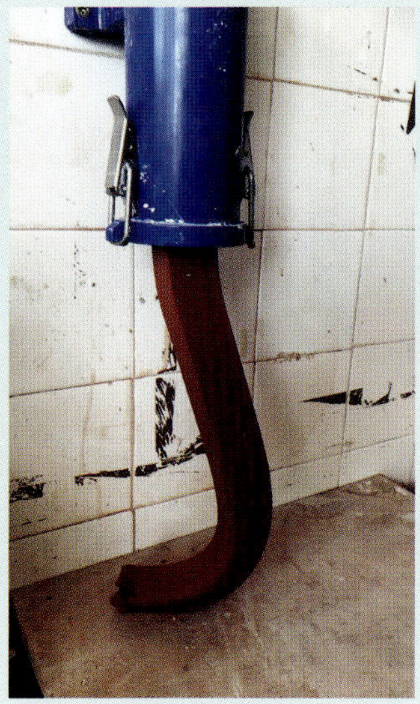

Process
The extrusion process involves compressing clay through a die, the shape of which will determine the outcome. Extrusion can be very useful for creating component parts for your work – for example, handles, trim details and surface embellishments. Extruded tubes can also be made into containers and you can also extrude coils to speed up hand building. Extrusion can achieve a crispness and consistency that would be difficult to achieve another way.

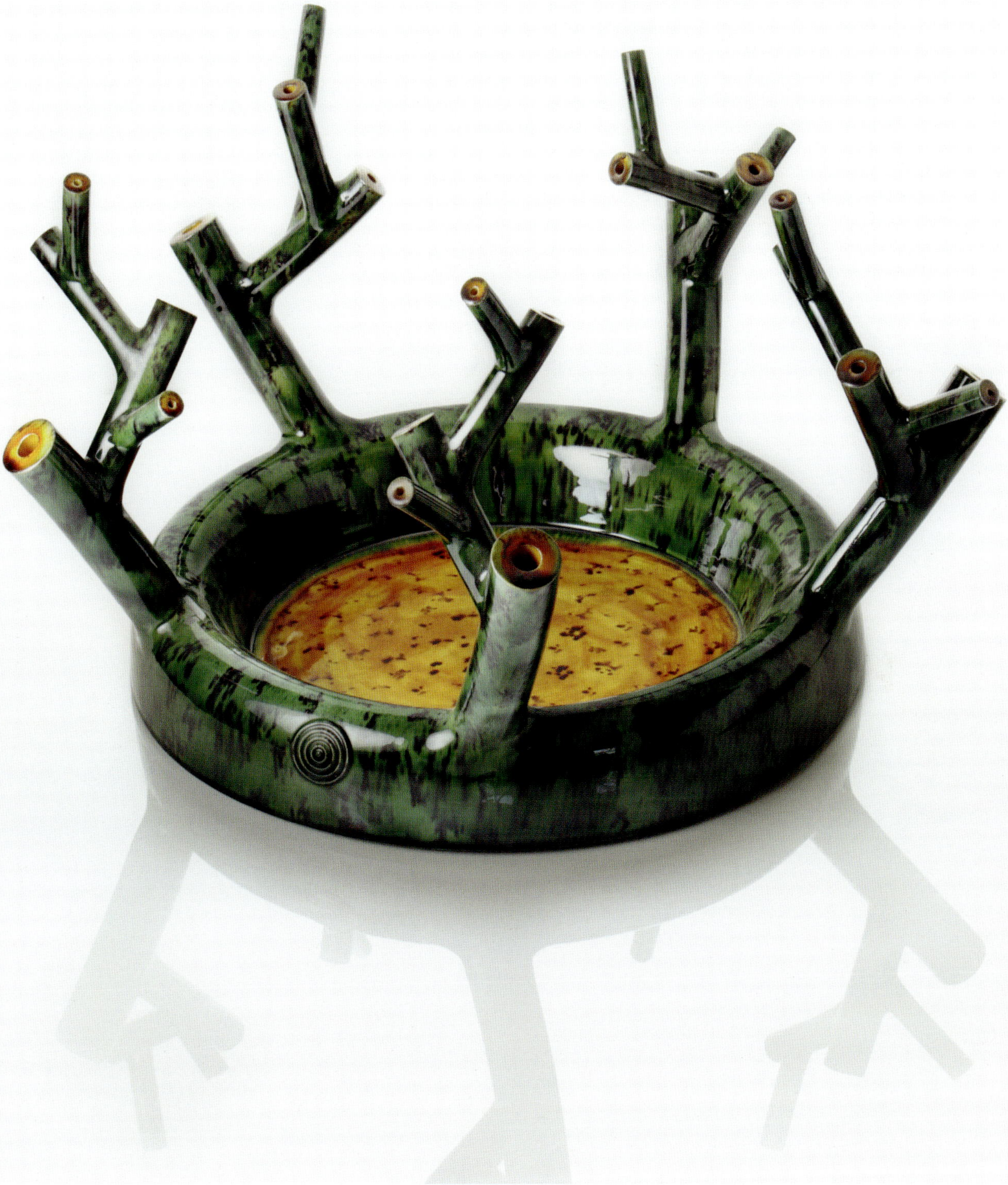

Piet Stockmans

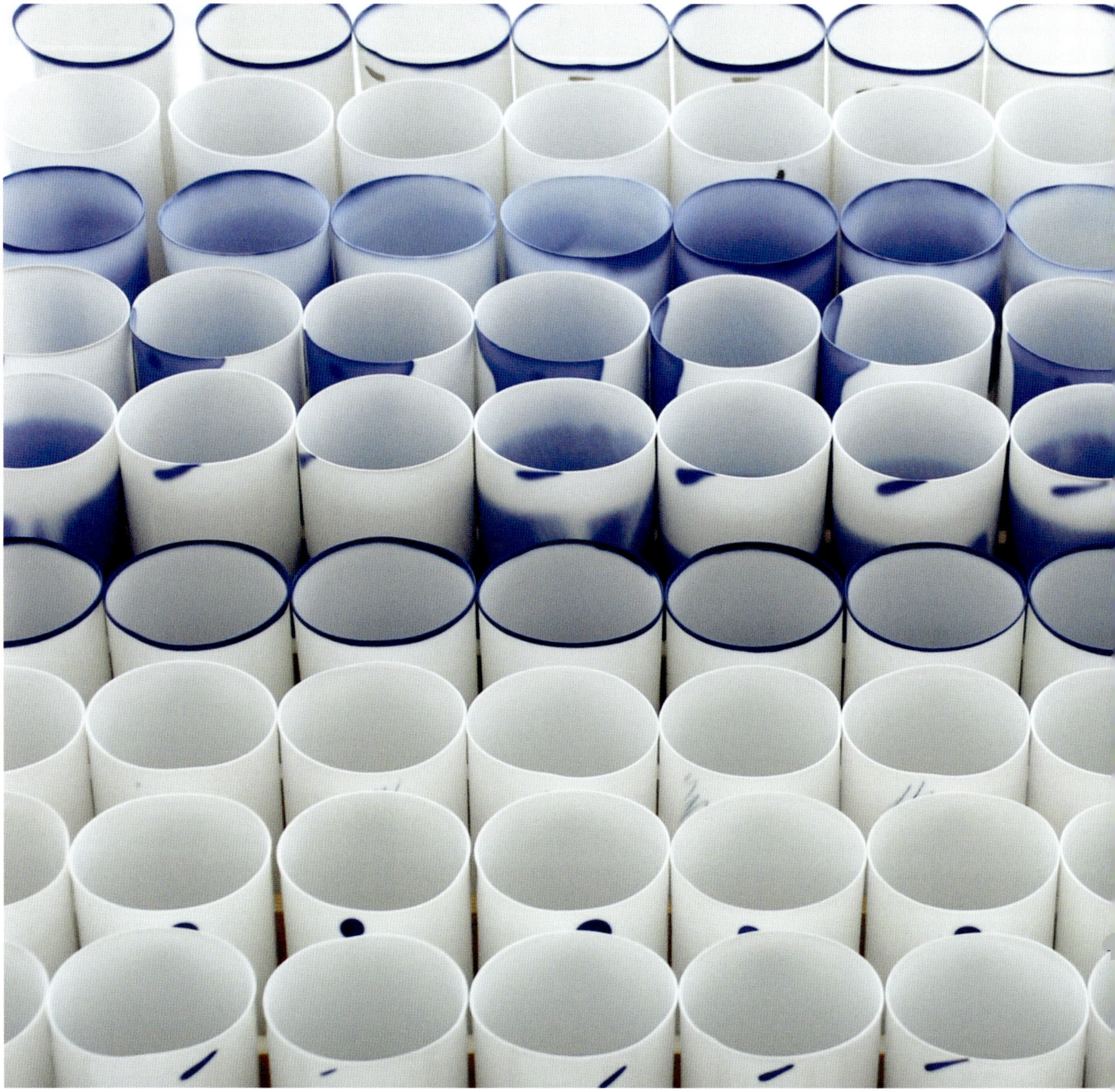

See also

Theodor Bogler (p.134), **Torbjørn Kvasbø** (p.258)

Piet Stockmans (Belgian, born 1940) studied sculpture and ceramics at the Higher Institute of Architecture and Applied Arts in Hasselt, Belgium, and the Technical School for Porcelain in Selb, Germany. He was an industrial designer at the Royal Mosa B.V. porcelain factory in Maastricht, the Netherlands, for twenty-six years. While there, he designed more than 150 different pieces of china, including, in 1969, the *Sonja*, a thin, stackable coffee cup of which more than 40 million were sold. He also taught at the Luka School of Arts in Genk, Belgium, and at the Design Academy Eindhoven, in the Netherlands. In 1987 he established Studio Pieter Stockmans, which specializes in hard porcelain.

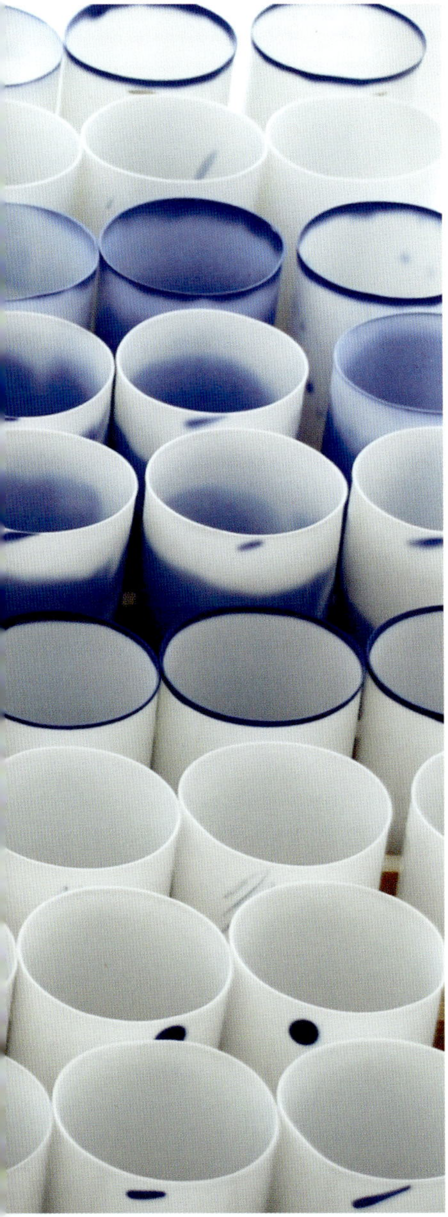

Dishes and Cups 2007
Porcelain
100 beakers – dimensions variable

When we think of the slip-casting process in terms of industrial manufacture, it conjures up visions of a conveyor belt system where identical objects – all consistent in size and shape – are churned out, devoid of any sense of individuality. However, Piet Stockmans firmly quashes that notion and his sophisticated collections of crisp, translucent porcelains are full of expression and unique character.

Stockmans has worked with porcelain exclusively throughout his long career and is renowned for his signature blue-and-white colour combination (to the point where the colour is named after him – Stockman's Blue). Here, row upon row of slip-cast porcelain beakers follow standard principles of form and proportion – yet, what sets these beakers apart from one another is the touch of numerous hands throughout the making process. This human contact brings a greater sense of individuality to each piece. During manufacture, the forms were lightly distorted when removed wet from the plaster moulds. Random dabs and flecks of cloudy blue stain on the sides and rims of the pots distinguish them from one another, along with blended tones of blue and white. As a collection, they sit comfortably and playfully together.

The beakers are unglazed and fired to the incredibly high temperature of 1400°C (2552°F). This renders the pots completely vitrified, producing a self-glazed quality that is very practical for day-to-day use. Striking in their simplicity and clarity, the resulting objects lie somewhere between the realm of art practice and industrial design.

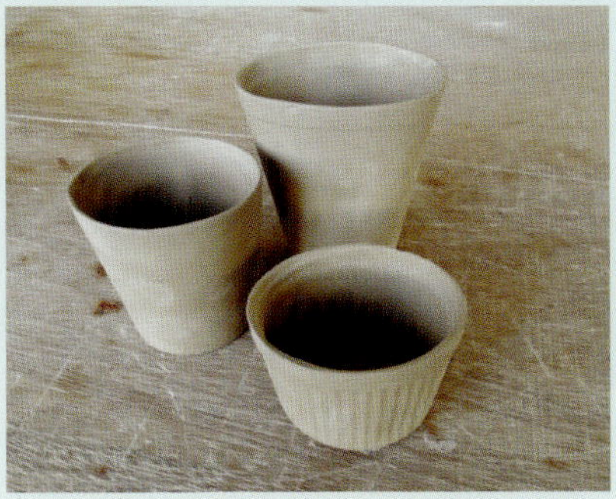

Process

When making a batch of identical pieces – slip-cast, thrown or hand-built – consider the subtle differences you could put into each one to bring greater variety and intrigue to the collection. At the raw stage you could experiment with lightly squeezing the form, leaving finger indentations or distorting the overall shape. You could colour your clay body and marbleize the slip. This is a simple but effective technique and involves adding a small quantity of coloured slip to white or contrasting colour casting slip. Avoid the temptation to mix at this stage. Instead, the slip colours will marbleize and swirl together when poured from the jug into the mould. To complete the pieces, apply dabs of slip or glaze with a brush or sponge to liven up the surface and inject some personality into the work.

Anne Mette Hjortshøj

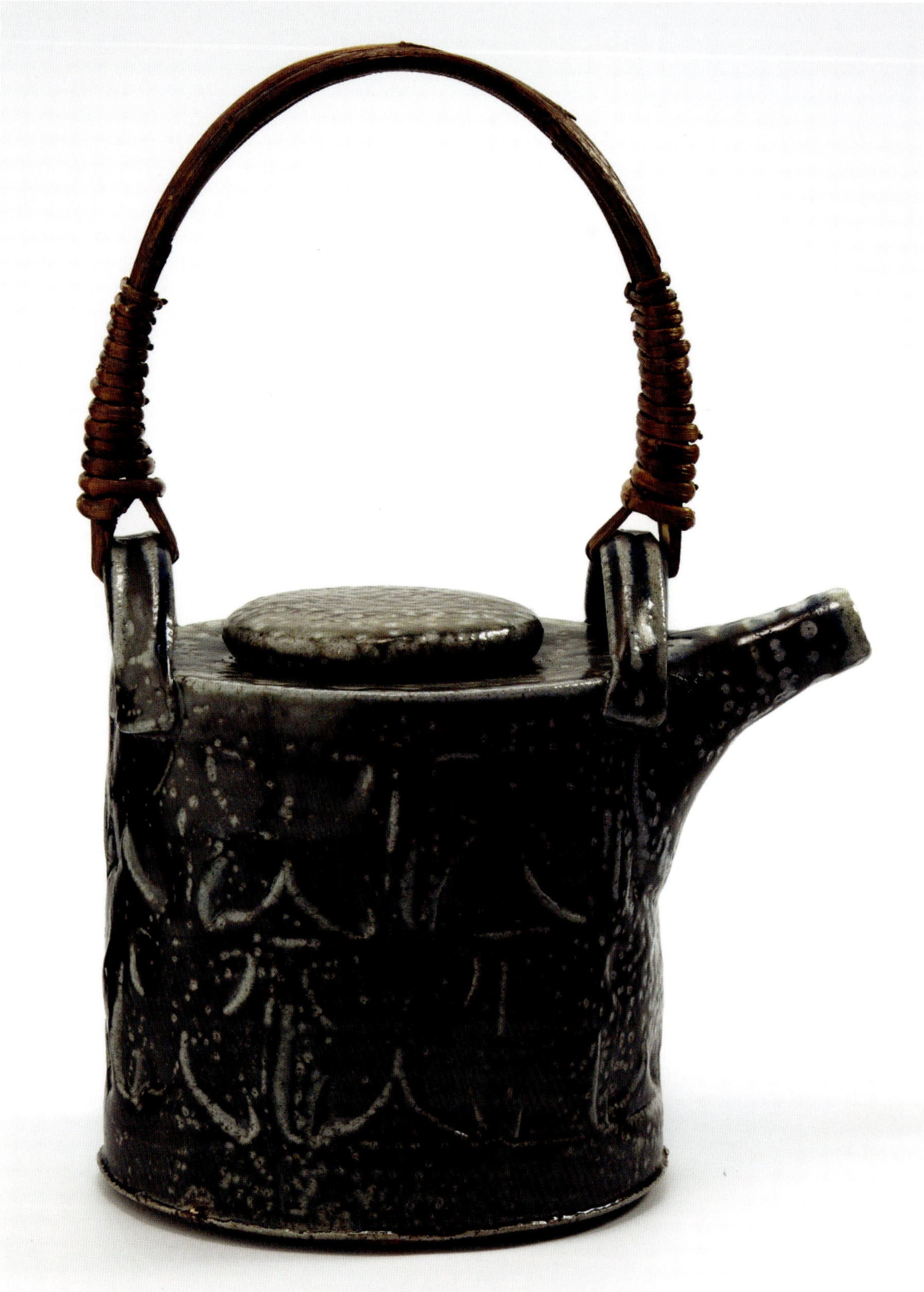

Teapot 2015

Thrown and altered stoneware, salt-glazed, willow handle
Height including handle: 25 cm (9⅘ in.); Width: 16 cm (6⅓ in.)

Anne Mette Hjortshøj's pots are solid, hardy, modest pots, imbued with the artist's sheer passion for clay. Hjortshøj draws her influences from her wild, natural surroundings on the island of Bornholm. Her daily routines involve collecting clay from the local beaches to make into slips and glazes to decorate her wares.

This charming, salt-glazed teapot by Hjortshøj was thrown on the pottery wheel in parts. First, she made a cylinder, which she cut and lightly shaped into an oval. This was attached to thrown disks of clay to make the top and base of the teapot. The lid was made by cutting it away from the top section as the piece rotated on the wheel. Hjortshøj then shaped the lid by hand and a rim was thrown on to it. She added little straps of clay to act as a location point in preparation to attach a hand-made willow handle (made by local basket maker, Pia Rasmussen). The sides of the vessel were stamped and a spout added.

The lively, pitted glaze finish was created by Hjortshøj's two-chamber *noborigama* wood-fired kiln. The whole exhausting process takes more than twenty-four to thirty hours to fire and reaches temperatures exceeding 1300°C (2372°F). At top temperature, Hjortshøj introduced parcels of salt to the second chamber of the kiln – approximately 4 kilos (almost 9 pounds) over the course of three hours to achieve the desired amount of salting. Hjortshøj explains why she finds the process so appealing: 'The fundamental magic occurs at the moment when wood, fire, salt and ashes combine with the clay to change the shaped surface. The image of perfection disappears – the piece obtains its identity.'

Anne Mette Hjortshøj (Danish, born 1973) lives and works on the small Danish island of Bornholm, situated in the Baltic Sea. She studied ceramics at the Royal Danish Academy, Bornholm, from 1997 to 2000. In 1998, during her second year, she came to the UK to begin an apprenticeship with master potter Phil Rogers (born 1951) who was based in rural Wales. She stayed for eighteen months and travelled to the USA, Korea and Australia to exhibit her works. The apprenticeship with Rogers had a profound effect on her practice and shaped her approach to making and firing her pots. Hjortshøj continues to exhibit her work throughout Europe and internationally. Her beautiful wood-fired pots have garnered high acclaim and even resulted in a royal visit to her farmhouse studio by Margrethe II, Queen of Denmark.

See also
Martin Brothers (p.170)
Paul Soldner (p.206)
Michelle Erickson (p.212)

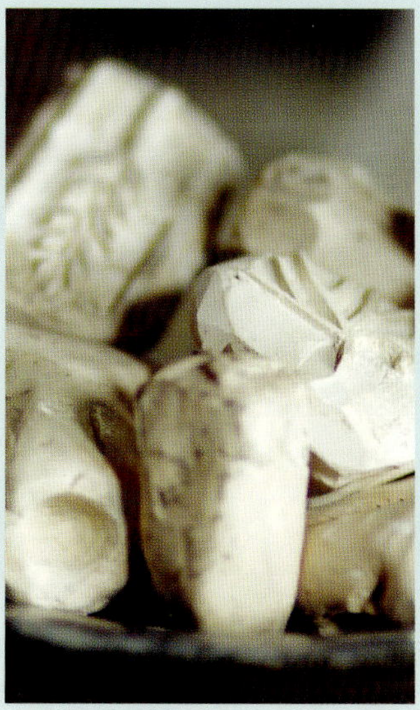

Surface
Hjortshøj stamped the surface of this teapot with a distinctive square petal pattern that she carved herself. The salt glaze has emphasized the outlines and textures of the pattern and the repeat around the body of the teapot is particularly effective. You can create your own stamps by carving into a block of plaster or leather-hard clay – the clay will require bisque firing. Fine metal tools, such as dental tools, are very good for carving intricate detail.

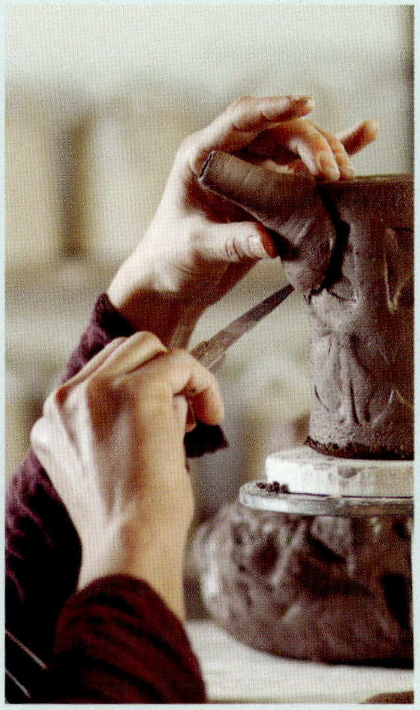

Technical
Teapots are highly engineered and can really test a potter's skill. There are lots of different elements to consider: the shape of the lid; the position of the spout; the type of handle; how it pours; and overall weight. One of the most critical considerations is the position of the spout. As illustrated here, the tip of the spout should be located above the teapot body, otherwise the user will not be able to fill the pot to the top and liquid will spill out from the spout.

Kiho Kang

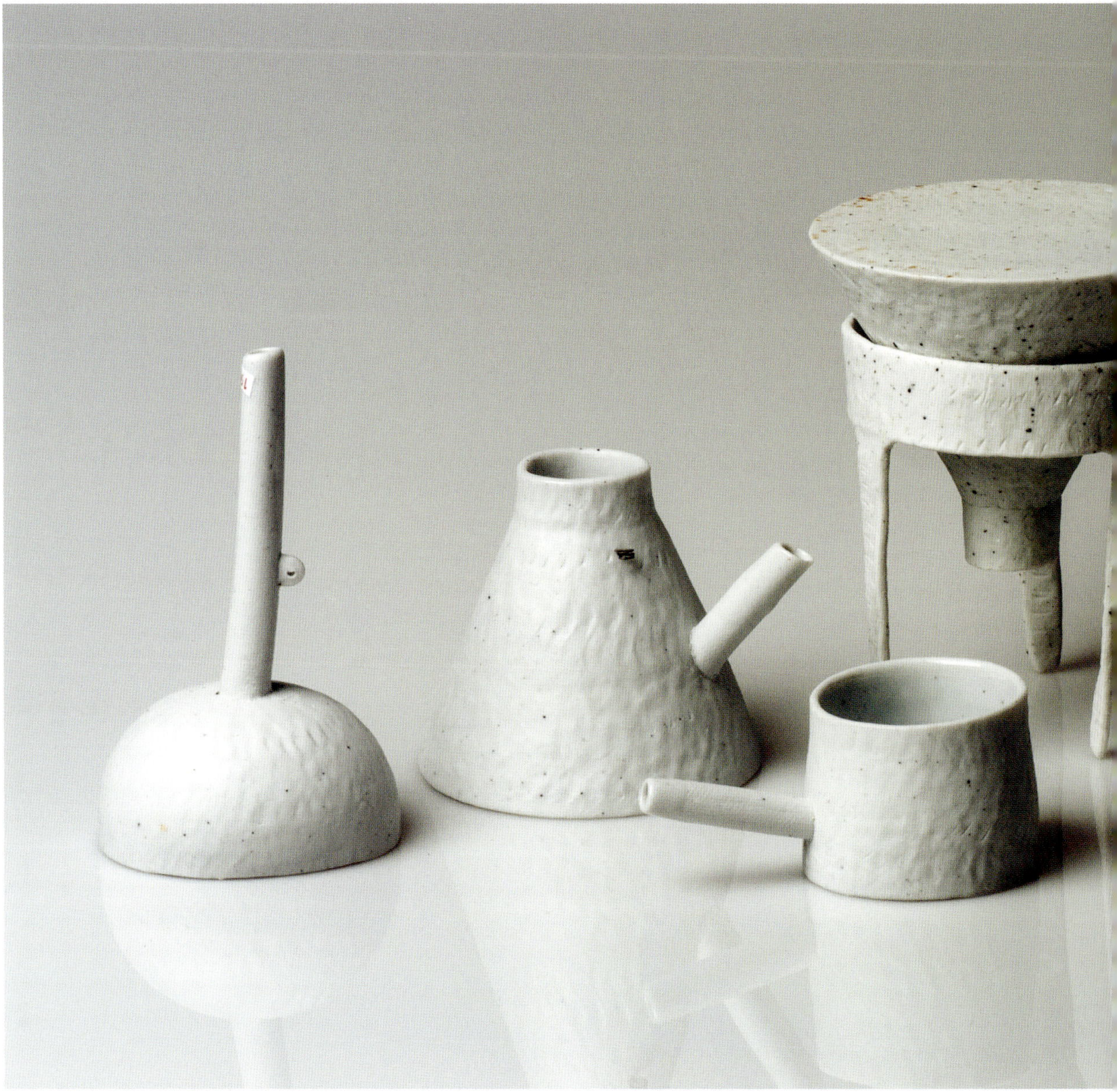

See also

Aneta Regel (p.102), **Kim Simonsson** (p.192)

Kiho Kang (Korean, born 1980) is a Munich-based ceramicist who was born in Jin-Hae, South Korea. From 1999 to 2006, Kang studied a bachelor's degree in ceramic art at Kookmin University in Seoul, followed by a master's degree in 2009 from the same institution. In 2014, Kang undertook a further master's in artistic ceramic and glass at Koblenz University of Applied Sciences in Germany. Kang has won numerous accolades, including the World Ceramic Exposition Foundation Award (2008) and the Award of the Justus Brinckmann Gesellschaft (2013). Kang has earnt a reputation for making exquisite hand-built, functional forms that celebrate and enhance the day-to-day dining experience. He exhibits his collections throughout Europe and internationally.

Process

Kang combines coil-building techniques with pinching, allowing a fine, even wall thickness. Use your fingertips and thumb to apply steady pressure from inside and outside the clay wall. The aim is to manipulate the clay in an upwards direction while obtaining a sense of pace. Try varying the pressure you apply to create a range of effects, from refined marks through to more gestural marks.

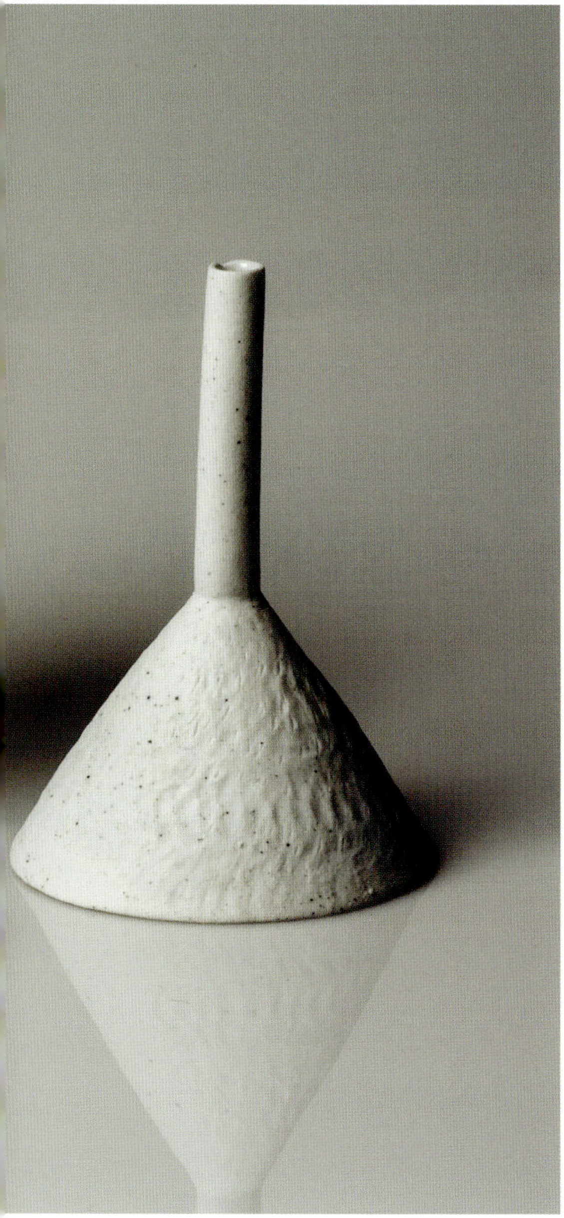

Tea Tools 2016
Porcelain, coil built
Dimensions variable

The rhythmic, tactile surfaces of Kiho Kang's beautiful tableware and functional ceramics evoke a feeling of stillness and inner calm – as Kang says, 'the beauty of slowness; the beauty of imperfection; the beauty of naturalness. These are my guidelines and working philosophy to this day. I am not a robot or machine that makes ceramics cut and dry. I make ceramics with my hands. They are beautiful and have humanity.'

Inspired by memories, architecture and the user experience, this collection by Kang, entitled *Tea Tools*, comprises a series of ambiguous functional forms that playfully encourage interaction. Tall funnels, spouted vessels and obscure apparatus lead the user to create and invent their own ritual and drinking ceremony. Coil building his pieces from porcelain, Kang has developed a method where he captures a lightness of touch through gently pinching the clay as he constructs the piece. He begins by softly pounding a flat, even base, which he cuts into a perfect circle. Next, Kang rolls neat coil lengths and gradually builds up the height of the walls. He uses his fingertips and a wooden modelling tool to smooth and blend each coil, producing the distinctive dappled surface.

Loosely based on geometric shapes, the clean, essential forms are neatly paired with the purity of the porcelain. Kang has removed any unnecessary ornament, his intention being to allow the simplicity of the construction process to resonate. He completes his work by glazing the interior of the vessel for functional purpose, leaving the outside unglazed. He then fires his ceramics in a reduction kiln to 1280°C (2336°F), which gives his work its signature pale grey-blue colour.

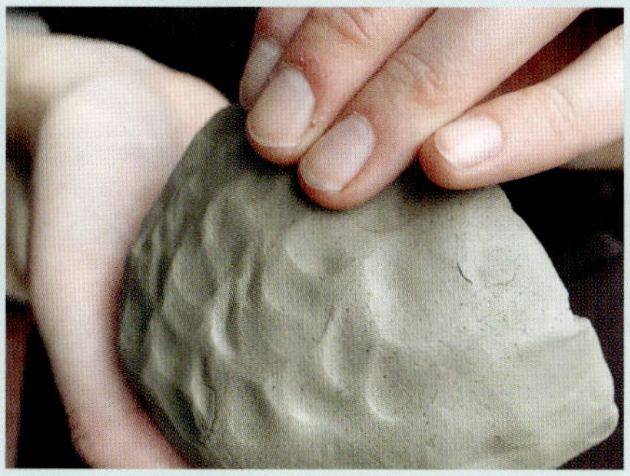

Material
On closer inspection, note how the clay body of this piece is speckled. This gives a subtle character to the surface and was achieved by adding iron-rich grit to the clay body prior to construction. You can experiment with mixing percentages of fine coloured grog or molochite sand into your clay body. The granular quality of the sand is particularly effective when used in combination with porcelain or coloured clay bodies.

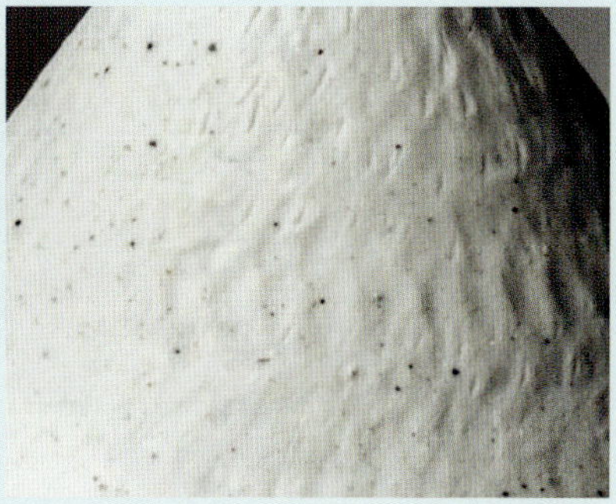

Stuart Carey

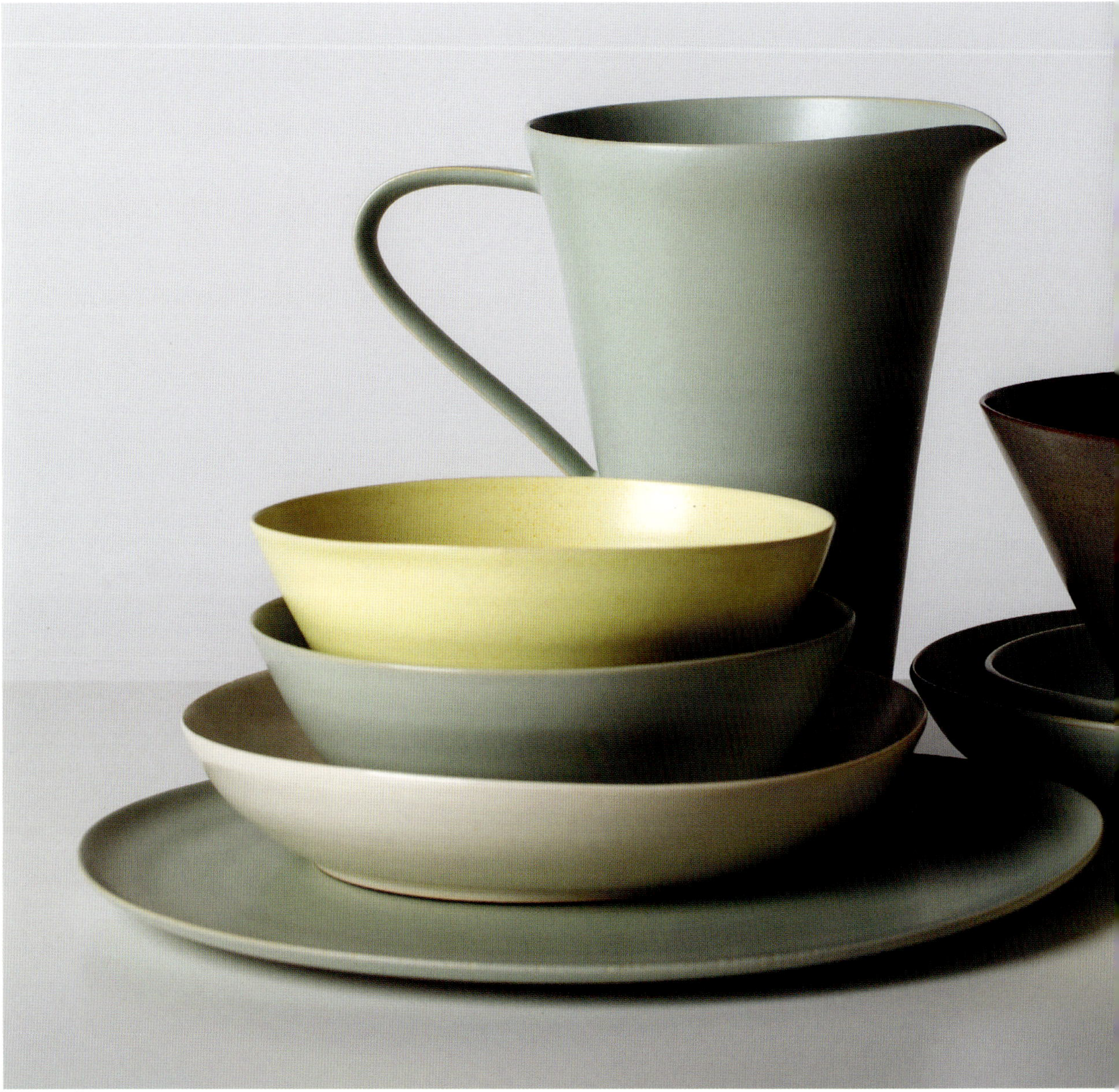

See also

Gwyn Hanssen Pigott (p.70), **Janice Tchalenko** (p.110)

Stuart Carey (British, born 1987) was born in Newcastle-upon-Tyne and studied ceramics at Glasgow School of Art, after which he completed a master's degree at the Royal College of Art, London. During his MA studies, he developed his finely honed collection of tableware, which he officially launched in 2011 and which now has an international following. In 2015, Carey was awarded the Homes and Gardens designer award for Use of Materials and the ELLE Decoration British Design Award for Best Craft Maker. Carey regularly writes for trade publications and has a strong stance on the redevelopment of the crafts, which informs his writing and teaching practice. Carey is the co-founder of the Kiln Rooms in Peckham, London – an open-access ceramics studio and education space designed to make ceramics available for everyone.

Process

The design and shape of a handle can be critical to the success of a piece. Here are some typical examples (Left to right): rolled coil - suits hand-formed shapes; slab – for chunky strap handles; pulled handles - from a lump of clay, rounded or U-shape, typically used for thrown work; extruded – you can make your own engineered shapes. You can also press mould a handle of your own design.

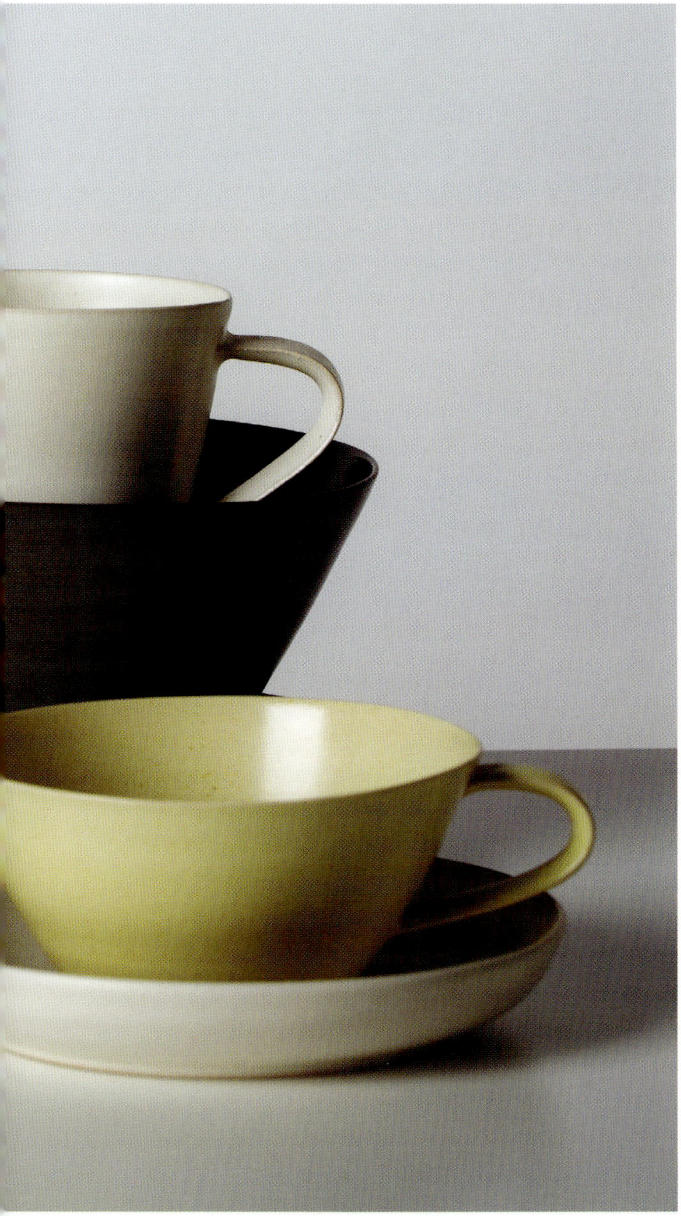

Tableware 2018
White stoneware
Dimensions variable

Stuart Carey creates beautiful collections of hand-thrown tableware that enhance and uplift day-to-day life. Made from semi-porcelain stoneware, the timeless range is driven by feel and tactility, enticing the user to interact and take pleasure from using the items. Carey is influenced by the tranquil vessel installations of Gwyn Hanssen Pigott (1935–2013), and shares her ideals of clarity of form and command of the functional vessel. He combines this with an interest in the classical shapes of the historical Korean pottery in the British Museum collections.

The utilitarian items made by Carey range from conical jugs, flared cups and plates to serving bowls of various sizes. When making a batch, he applies a set of principles to follow: a certain weight of clay, a common aesthetic and a consistency of scale. Carey lifts each piece from the wheel while wet to bring individual movement and distinctions between forms, but retains a feeling of continuity within the collection. He considers all aspects of form and function to suit modern life. Rims and openings are generous in proportion and exaggerated, looped handles fit comfortably in the hand. The hardy properties of stoneware make it an excellent material for absorbing the knocks and heavy demands of daily use.

Carey's choice of glaze palette includes delicate, muted shades of cool blues, warm creams, lemon yellows and beiges. He achieves a smooth coverage of glaze by spraying (with a paint gun and compressor) or dipping his wares in a bucket. The matt and gloss glazes work harmoniously together, not overpowering one another or the food that is being presented.

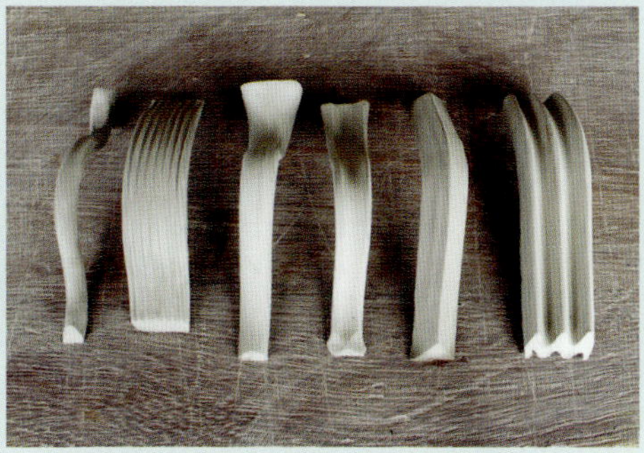

Technical

The strength of Stuart Carey's tableware lies in its simplicity and uncomplicated design. There are many aspects to consider when making functional vessels:

- Size of the vessel – will it hold a suitable portion/volume?
- Shape – can your pieces stack or be stored easily?
- Durability – will your pieces withstand day-to-day use? Think about washing up or placing in the dishwasher – rims are particularly vulnerable.
- The placement of the handle in relation to height of the vessel – does it feel comfortable to hold?
- Sturdiness – the piece should not be too narrow in the base or top heavy, otherwise it could tip over.
- Does it complement the food being presented without being overbearing?

Ikuko Iwamoto

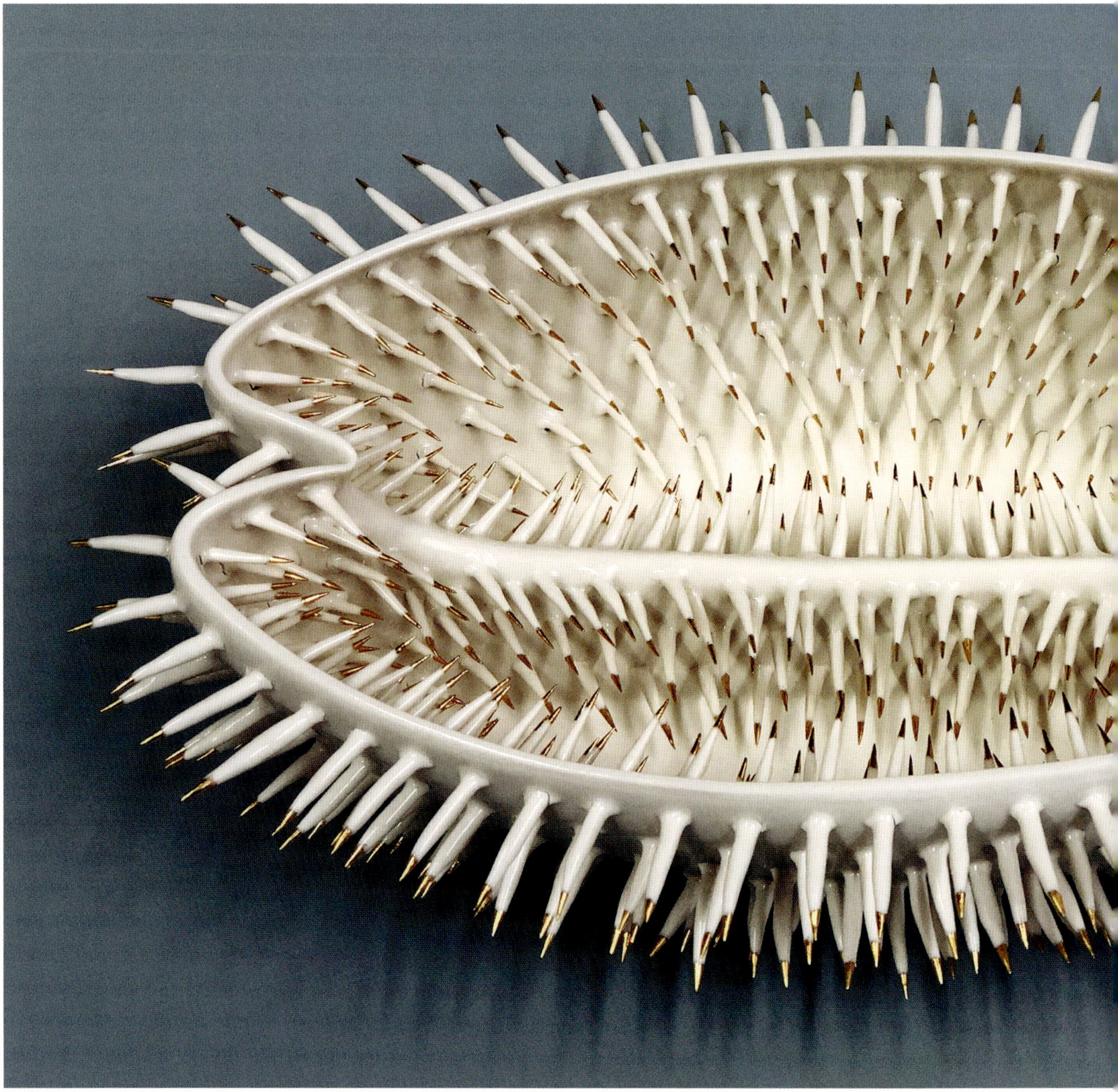

See also

Shary Boyle (p.194), **Hitomi Hosono** (p.238)

Ikuko Iwamoto (Japanese, born 1971) began working with clay in 1990 at Tezukayama College in Nara, Japan. She moved to the UK in 2001 to study ceramics at Camberwell College of Arts, London, followed by a master's degree at the Royal College of Art. Her studio is based in Stoke Newington, north London, where she makes curious, functional wares, sculptures and wall art. Iwamoto says of her work: 'I make exquisite cups and other objects for a bizarre tea ceremony. They suggest the everyday, the ordinary, but are in fact extraordinary. They are the vehicle to make visible an invisible, microscopic world. A world of intricacy and detail, of mathematical pattern and organic chaos, of beauty and repulsion.' Examples of Iwamoto's work are held in the UK in London, Rochdale and Manchester.

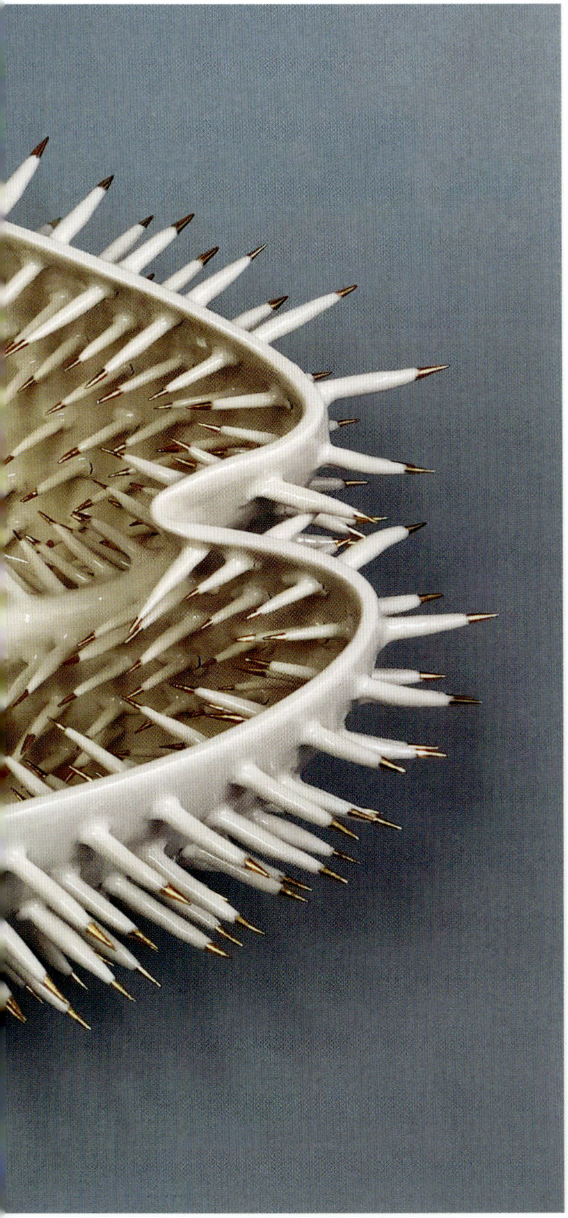

'Spiky Twins' Tabletop Sculpture 2018
Porcelain, slip cast, gold lustre
8.5 × 32 × 22 cm ($3\frac{3}{8} \times 12\frac{5}{8} \times 8\frac{5}{8}$ in.)

With jaws open wide like a Venus fly trap waiting to snare an unsuspecting meal, this spiky porcelain tabletop sculpture by Ikuko Iwamoto is rather curious, if not unsettling. Iwamoto plays with our perception of function and the tension between usability and fragility. The seedpod-shaped bowl appears welcoming and invites use, but at the same time, hundreds of gold-tipped spikes scream danger. Our immediate response is repulsion, but also intrigue about the texture and sensation of the spikes becomes too tempting to resist and the user is encouraged to interact with the piece.

Inspired by nature, cells and organic forms, Iwamoto's pieces resemble living, breathing creatures. Her interest in tactile surfaces stems from a research project undertaken during her master's studies where she designed tableware for visually impaired users. She was intrigued by the use of contrasting textures and how this can improve the functionality of a vessel and enhance the overall sensory experience.

Iwamoto uses slip-casting techniques to produce her organic forms. She first sculpts a blank model (without spikes) from a plaster block and then takes a mould from which she can generate multiple casts. Once the clay cast has been removed from the mould and firmed, Iwamoto drills dozens of tiny holes all over the surface. She prepares double-ended spikes of porcelain and painstakingly threads each one through the holes and secures them with slip. The process requires incredible patience and control, and can take her many hours from start to finish.

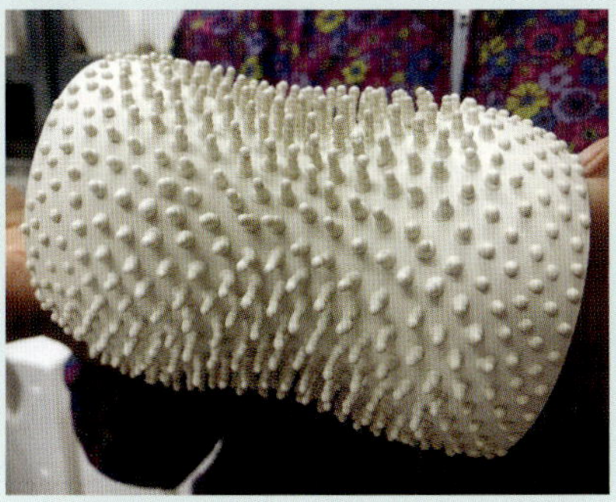

Process

Slip casting is a brilliant technique for producing a batch of the same form all identical to the next. Iwamoto combines slip casting with hand-building skills to bring greater individuality and interest to each of her pieces. When working in this way, start by designing a generic 'blank' shape, which you can embellish with added components, such as a sprigg or dabs of slip. You can also use a sharp tool to carve or pierce the surface to allow light to pass through it. Another aspect is to consider the tactile experience the piece can offer the user. For instance, a raised, dotted texture could provide a grip area on a beaker instead of a conventional handle. To finish the piece, Iwamoto applied gold lustre to the tips of the spikes to suggest the form is 'poisonous'.

Sun Kim

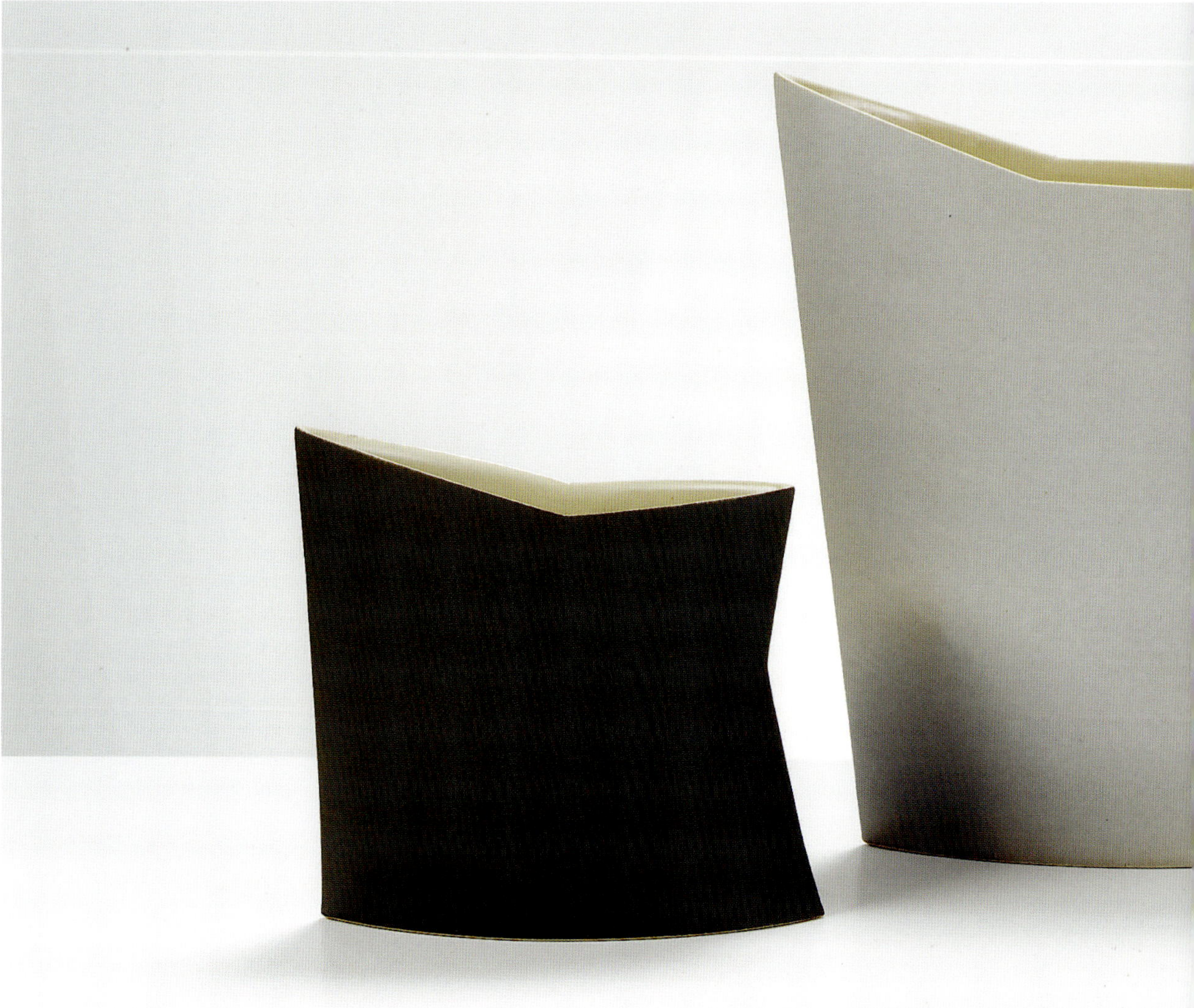

Geometric Vessels 2018
Stoneware
Overall: 28.5×50×15 (11⅕×19⅝×6 in.)

Sun Kim produces sophisticated and elegant functional wares that explore traditional and contemporary aesthetics. She takes inspiration from her surroundings: objects and their historical context, architecture, texture, colour, design and nature. They all continually feed her visual language and open up new paths of investigation into form, shape and volume. As Kim says, 'Making is not only a personal journey, but also my interest in generating interaction and a narrative within the environment'.

With their sharp outlines and satisfyingly crisp shapes, this collection of angular vases by Kim emphasizes volume, tension and expansion within a form. Resembling sheets of precisely folded paper, there is a feeling of lightness and airiness in the construction of each piece. The vases are made from stoneware clay and thrown very finely on the pottery wheel. Kim then uses a variety of hand-building techniques to alter the form. She begins by cutting a series of seam lines into the clay walls, which she proceeds to manipulate, stretch and assemble – retaining a sense of immediacy and confidence throughout the process. On closer inspection, the fine concentric lines created by throwing are just visible on the surface, running at a diagonal axis. This allows the viewer to begin to understand the process of construction the form has gone through to get to its final shape.

To finish her pieces, Kim has paired the sweeping angles of the rims and tailored edges with a delicate colour palette of pale, stony greys and greens. The soft, muted tones of the matt glaze gently rebound light and shadow, accentuating the creases and lines present in the forms.

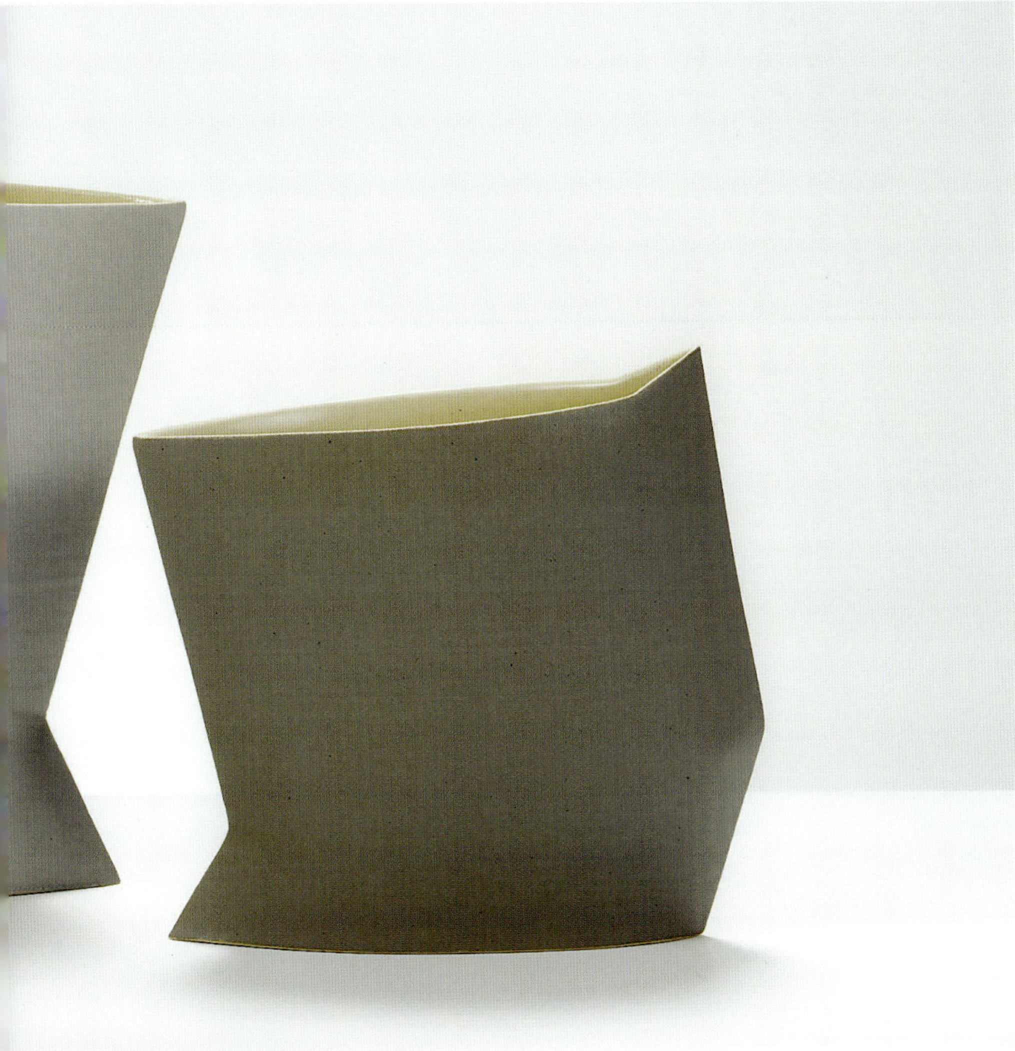

Sun Kim (Korean, born 1977) was born in Saudi Arabia and grew up in Sao Paulo, Brazil. She studied for a degree in fine arts in Sao Paulo, and then in 2003 moved to New York to continue her studies in ceramics at Alfred University. After graduating, Kim arrived in the UK in 2004 to begin a studio assistantship with Edmund de Waal. She subsequently settled in the UK and in 2007 she established her own studio in south London, where she is currently based. Kim exhibits widely throughout the UK and internationally. Exhibitions include Cheongju International Crafts Biennale in Korea, European Ceramic Context in Denmark and The Clay Art Centre in the USA. Examples of her work are in the permanent collections of the Museum of Northern Ireland and Mashiko Museum of Ceramic Art, Japan.

See also

Sara Flynn (p.80)
Ron Nagle (p.208)
Edmund de Waal (p.250)

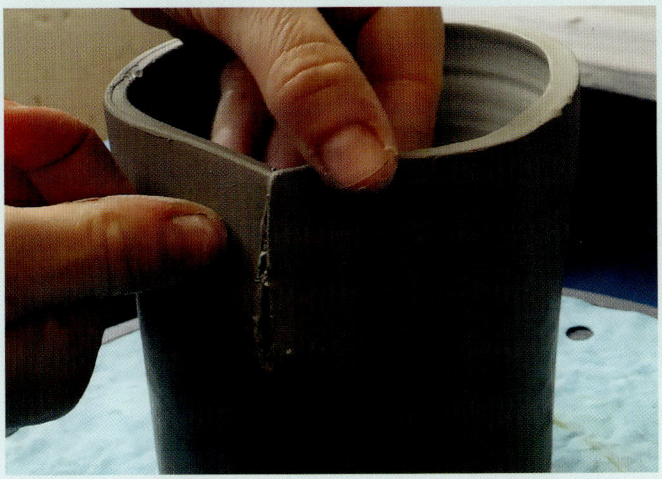

Process

Kim enjoys problem solving through the process of making. She uses cutting and assembling techniques to create her delicate and precise forms. Working intuitively, she slices, folds, joins and alters the shapes – each piece is different from the next. Consider how you might take a simple form – for example, a flared cylinder – and how you could alter it by slicing it into sections and attaching new parts. Perhaps you could squash the form into a pocket shape, turn it upside down and attach a new base to make a rocking form. Or you could experiment with the leather-hard stage and score a number of lines into the interior wall to push out the clay and give the appearance of crumpled paper. Aim to capture the feeling of volume and containment in your forms by swelling out the clay wall into a rounded shape prior to cutting and altering.

Jill Shaddock

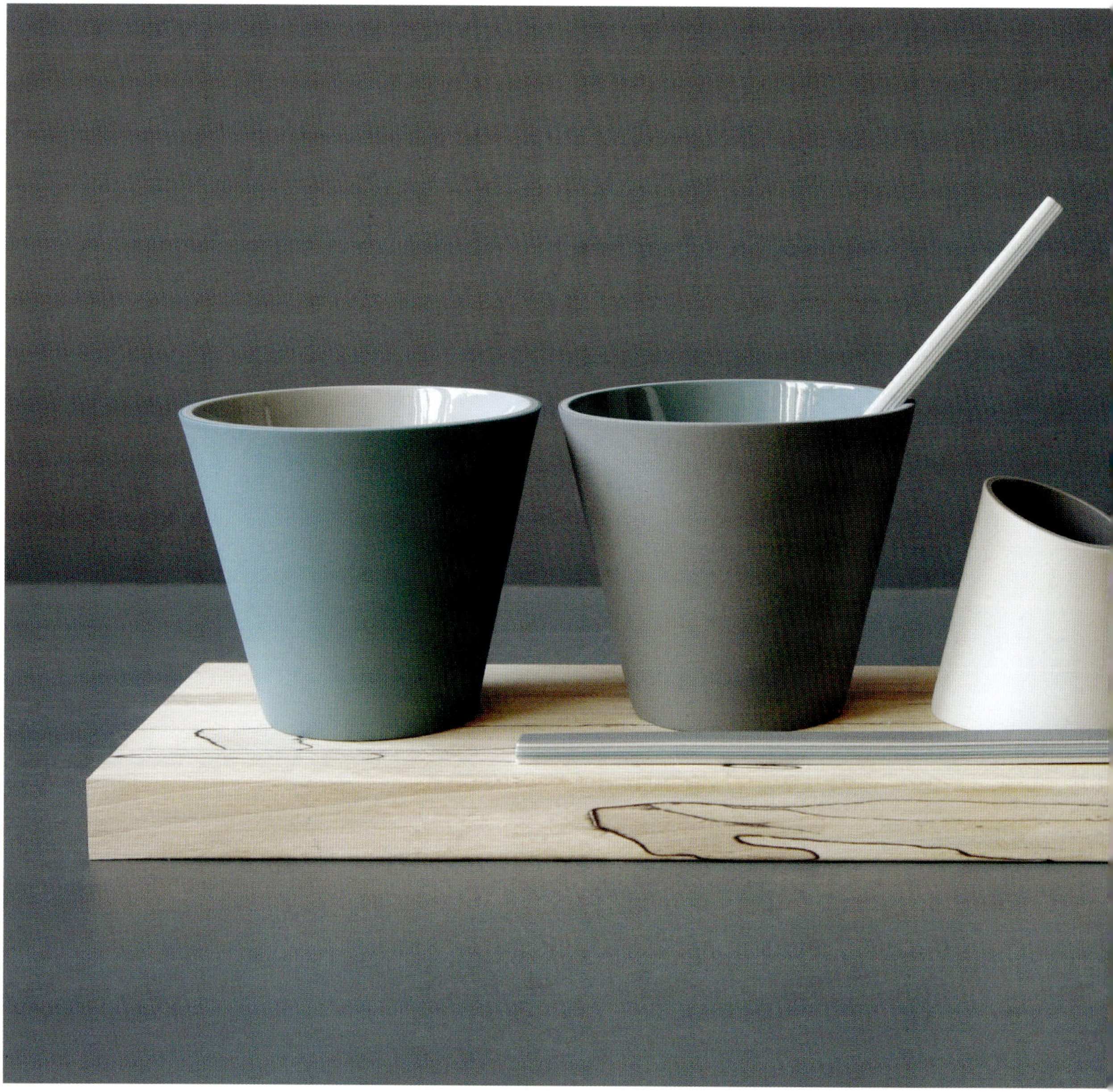

See also

Kiho Kang (p.148), **Kirsten Coelho** (p.160)

Jill Shaddock (British, born 1989) is a multi-awardwinning ceramicist who produces stylish tableware collections designed for contemporary living. She specialized in ceramics when studying her undergraduate degree in 3D design at Manchester School of Art, UK (2008–11). She works from her studio in West Yorkshire, where she creates her ceramics for exhibitions, galleries and collectors.

In 2012 she participated in Project Network, a residency at Guldagegaard, Denmark, and in 2013 she was a recipient of the Crafts Council Hothouse scheme. Shaddock is a professional member of both the Craft Potters Association and Contemporary Applied Arts, London. The Victoria and Albert Museum, London, acquired an example of her coffee set for their permanent collection in 2018.

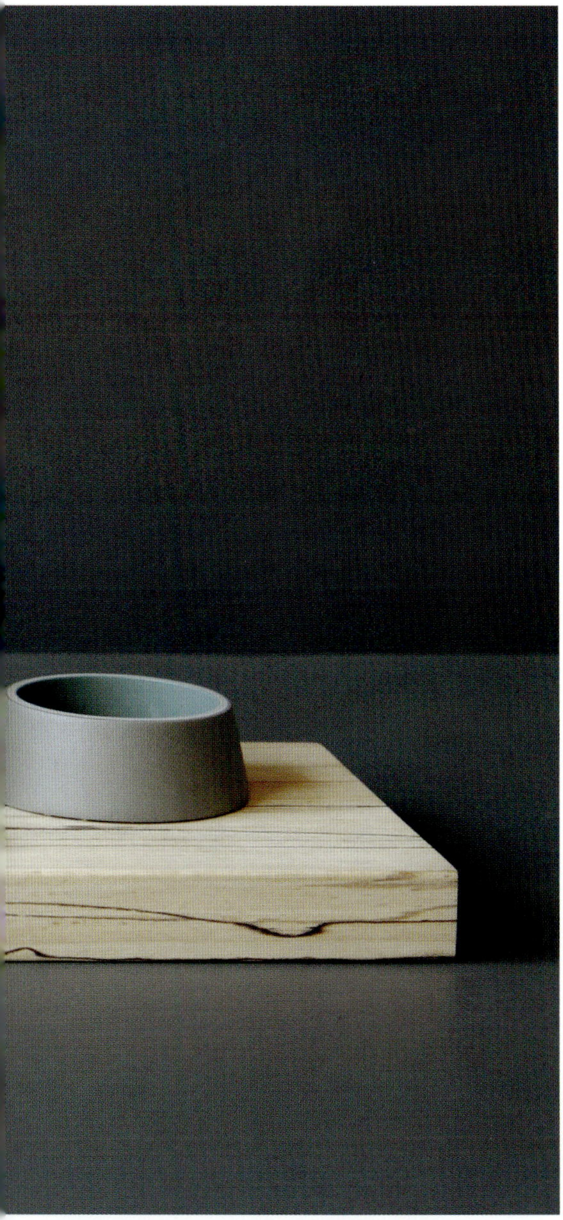

Coffee Set 2018

Parian porcelain with body stains, slipcast in layers
Dimensions variable

Without handles or any unnecessary details to disrupt the clean lines of her considered forms, the minimal and precise tableware sets by Jill Shaddock strip function back to its purest sense. This coffee set for two presents pairs of beakers and stirrers plus a sugar pot and a milk pourer – all neatly aligned on a plinth of spalted beech wood. Designed with modern living in mind, Shaddock's work blurs the boundaries between the functional and the purely decorative, allowing the user to choose whether to interact with the pieces by using them or simply to display the set for aesthetic enjoyment.

A cool, refined palette of teal, grey and matt blues, inspired by photographs taken during Shaddock's travels abroad, sit comfortably together. Shaddock enjoys the scientific experimentation and methodology of working with colour and it is a key starting point when developing her works. For this set, Shaddock has created a visual dialogue between the individual components by echoing exterior colours in the interior colour of a neighbouring piece, resulting in a family of related objects.

Shaddock uses slip-casting methods to produce her tableware and is fascinated by the idea of elevating and enhancing a process typically associated with mass production. The striking linear strata effect visible on the rims of the beakers and the side profiles of the stirrers is produced by a skillful process of multilayered slip casting. This complex lamination technique involves pouring coloured slip into a mould using precise casting times, allowing each layer to firm before pouring the next. The combination of minimal aesthetic, honed form and refined colour palette is highly tactile and engaging.

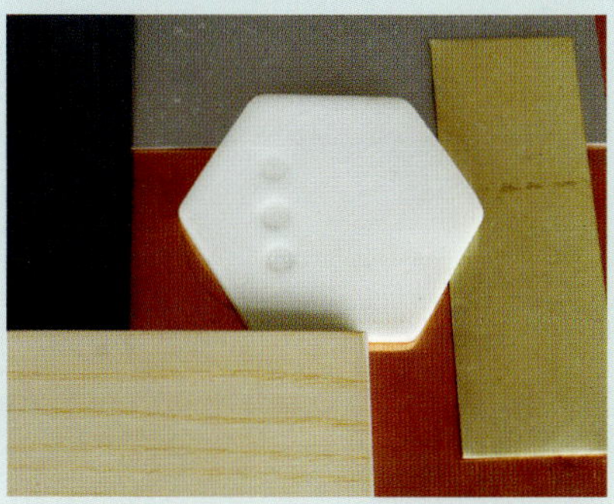

Material

This coffee set by Jill Shaddock successfully demonstrates how a contrasting material such as wood can complement ceramic forms. Here, she exploits the spalting in the wood – black streaks caused by fungus – to echo the strata effect in the rims of her pieces. Consider how you might incorporate other materials into your work. For example, the harsh, inflexible properties of metal could be juxtaposed with softly thrown vessels. Tableware does not have to follow the conventional norms to function effectively. The 'spout' element of the jug made by Jill Shaddock is simply a sloping rim and pours perfectly. There are no handles, either, but the wide rims of her beakers allow for the shape to fit comfortably in the hand.

Takeshi Yasuda

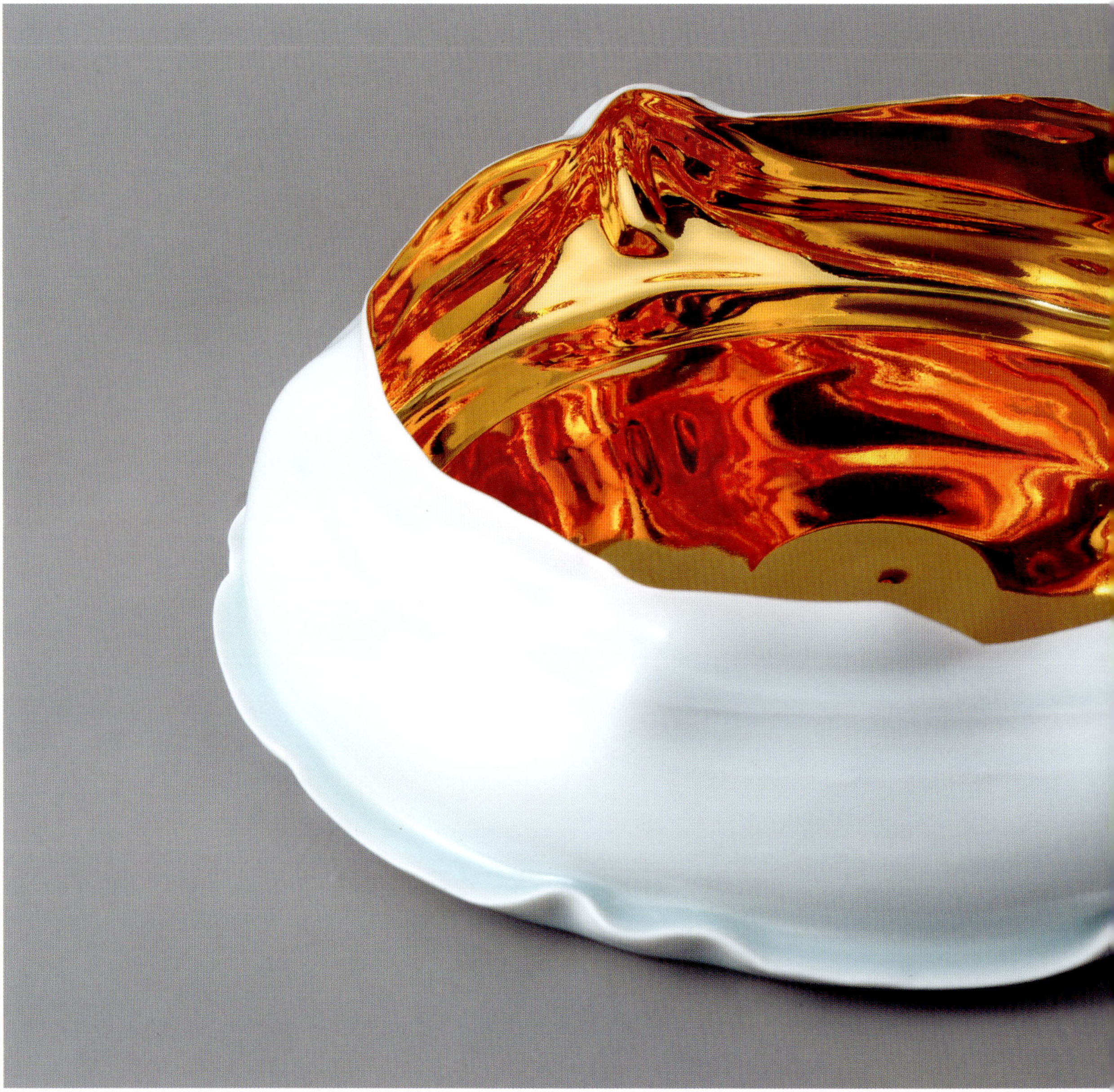

See also

Paul Soldner (p.206), **Anne Marie Laureys** (p.232)

Takeshi Yasuda (Japanese, born 1943) trained at the Daisei-Gama Pottery in Mashiko, Tochigi Prefecture, and set up a studio there. In 1973, Yasuda moved to the UK, where he taught in art schools and universities. He makes wheel-thrown pots for domestic ware. His early work was in stoneware clay glazed with a white slip then, in the late 1990s, he developed his creamware and started to use celadon glazes. In 2010, he became director of the Pottery Workshop in Jingdezhen, Jiangxi Province, China, where he began to use moulds. A year later, he co-founded the Red House Studio in Jingdezhen.

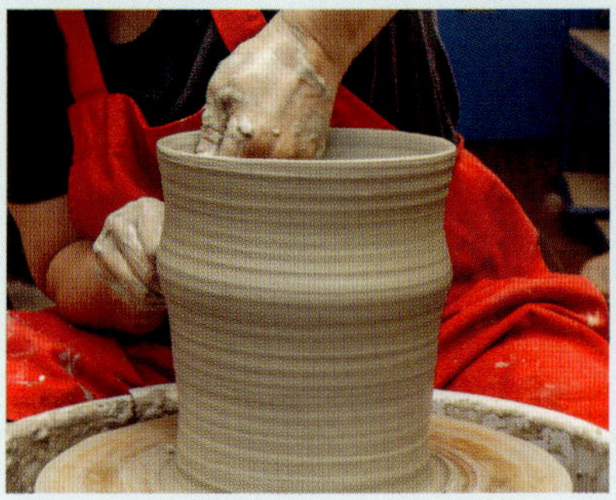

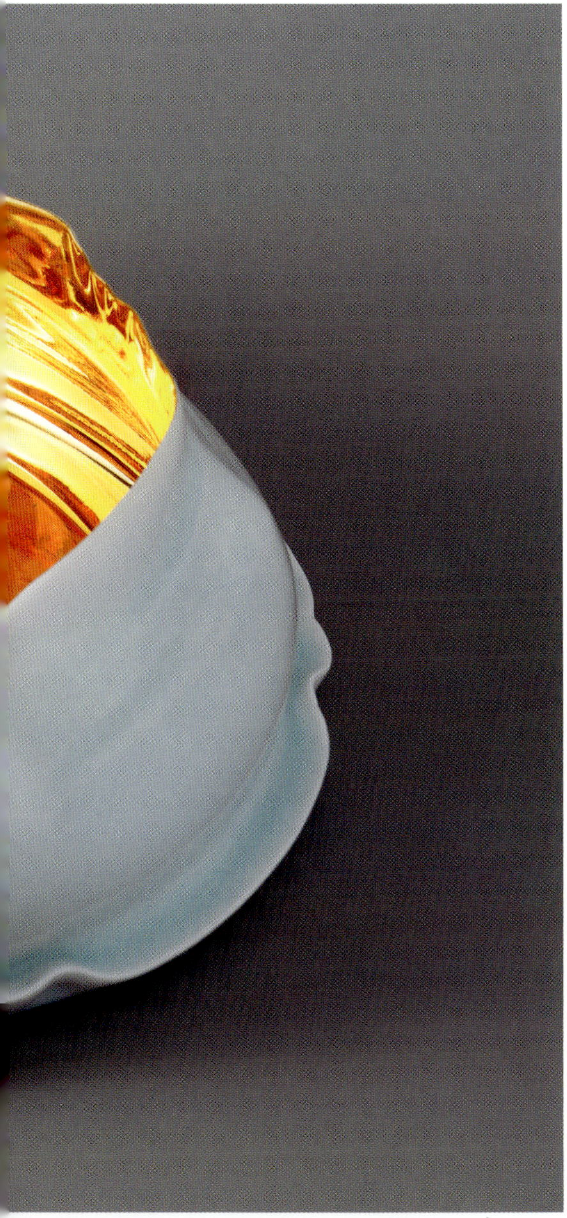

Qingbai Gold Bowl 2018
Hand-thrown porcelain clay, qingbai glaze and hand-painted colloidal gold
38 × 38 × 10 cm (15 × 15 × 4 in.)

'Clay is such a magical material – you are playing with mud', says Japanese-born potter Takeshi Yasuda. With an international career of more than fifty years, his endless enthusiasm and passion for clay is truly evident. Through his magnificent works, Yasuda explores the unlimited potential of ceramic processes and their relationship with form. Function is an important aspect of his practice, his philosophy being to create special, celebratory objects that become deeply integrated into the rituals of daily life. As Yasuda explains, 'I like people to discover using my pots, the user makes the function.'

Yasuda predominantly throws his studio works and in recent years has developed a range of dynamic celadon-glazed porcelains (coinciding with his move to Jingdezhen, China). This luscious piece exemplifies Yasuda's loose and expressive approach to clay. Softly thrown and retaining a feeling of casual ease, the sensuous handling of the clay flits between tension and control, with its free-flowing lines showing the interruptions of Yasuda's finger marks.

At play is Yasuda's spontaneous decision making and inquisitive approach. For this piece, he experimented with turning the work upside down, attached to a wooden bat. He then proceeded to swing the work with such great force that it caused the clay to shift and tear away. He continued to work the piece by lightly stretching and manipulating the clay walls to cause further distortions. Yasuda paired this fluid form with a pale blue Qingbai celadon glaze – a glaze closely associated with the ancient Chinese Song dynasty (960–1279). Yasuda has complemented the delicacy of the celadon glaze with a striking gold lustre interior, which gives the piece a sense of opulence and occasion.

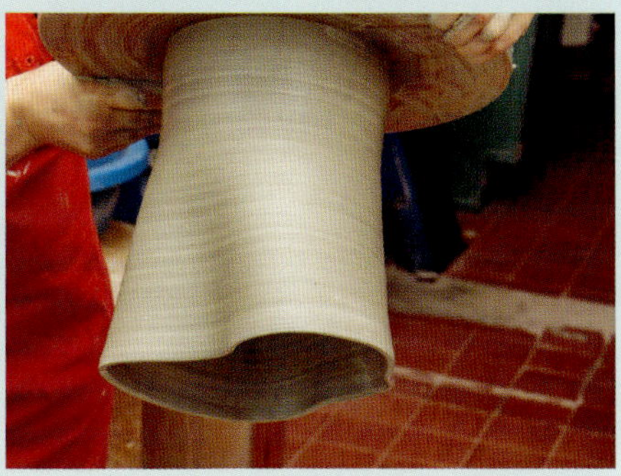

Process
Wooden bats attached to the wheel head are useful for moving your work without disrupting the form; however, you could use them to deliberately affect your form. First, throw your piece and remove the bat from the wheel. Don't wire the base off just yet. Turn the bat upside down and give it a shake. This will cause the clay to stretch and ripple. To retain the shape, leave it upside down in a supporting frame and either dry with a heat gun or gas torch or allow it to firm to leather-hard before turning over and wiring off. If your piece is shallow, you can turn the piece back the right way while it is still fresh and continue to manipulate the clay walls. Spin the pottery wheel very fast and the centrifugal force will impact the form by flaring it outwards, resulting in further distortions.

Kirsten Coelho

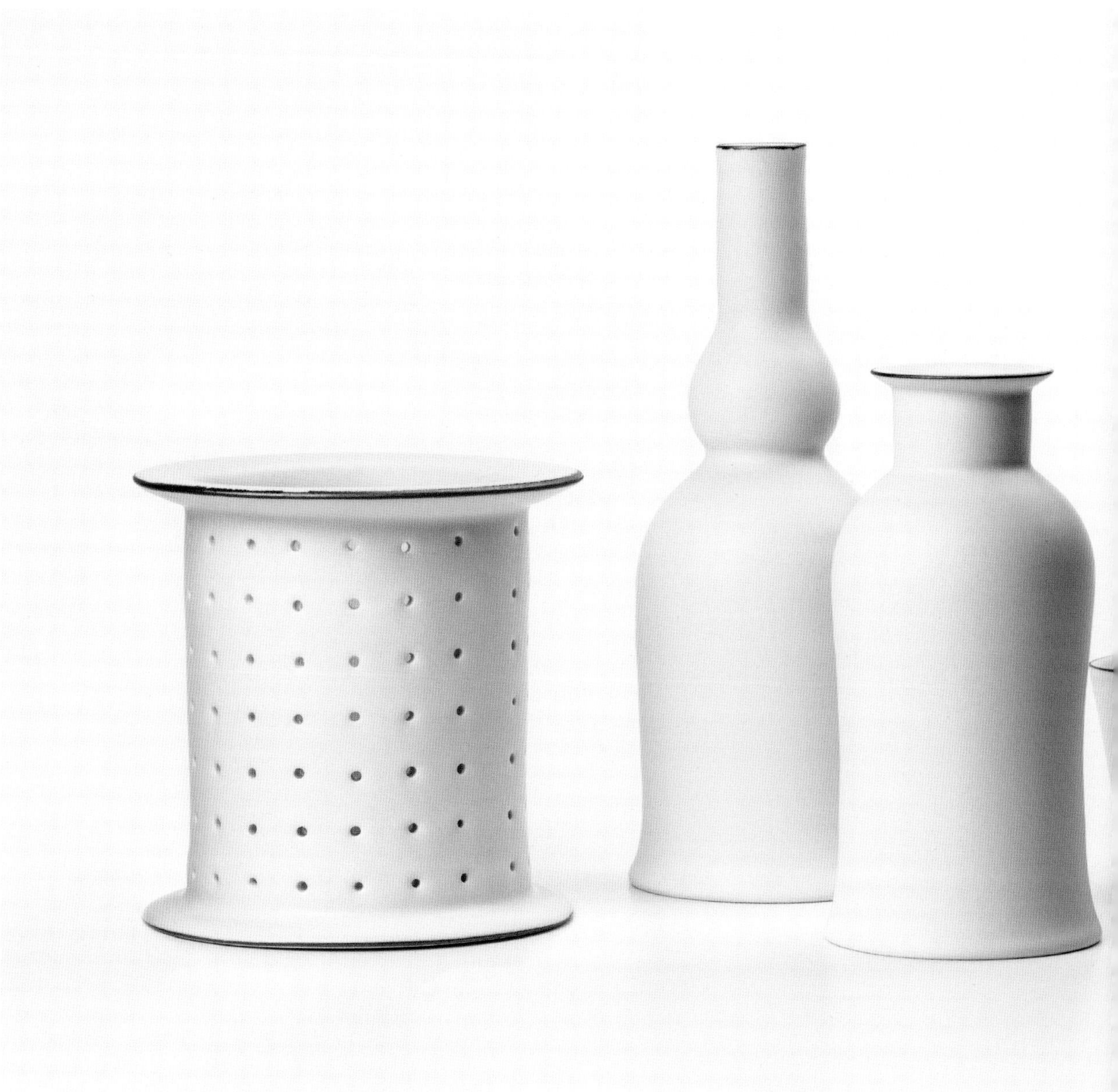

See also

Gwyn Hanssen Pigott (p.70), **Adam Frew** (p.164)

Kirsten Coelho (Danish, born 1966) was born in Denmark and now lives and works in Adelaide, Australia. From 1984 to 1988, she studied an undergraduate degree in design at the South Australian School of Art, Adelaide. In the early 1990s Coelho moved to London and worked in a ceramic studio, making and selling her wares. She returned to Adelaide in 1998 and studied for a master's degree in visual arts at the South Australian School of Art from 2000 to 2004. Coelho has achieved high acclaim for her beautiful, tranquil ceramics and her work is represented in numerous institutional collections. She has been the recipient of the Sidney Myer Ceramic Award in 2012 and the City of Hobart Art Prize in 2015.

Composition

Within the display, Coelho has considered the relationship between the height and proportions of each component: the dark iron-oxide line painted around the rims leads the eye across the forms and in between the carefully planned spaces. These subtle details bring continuity to the collection and allow the forms to stand out when placed in neutral-coloured spaces.

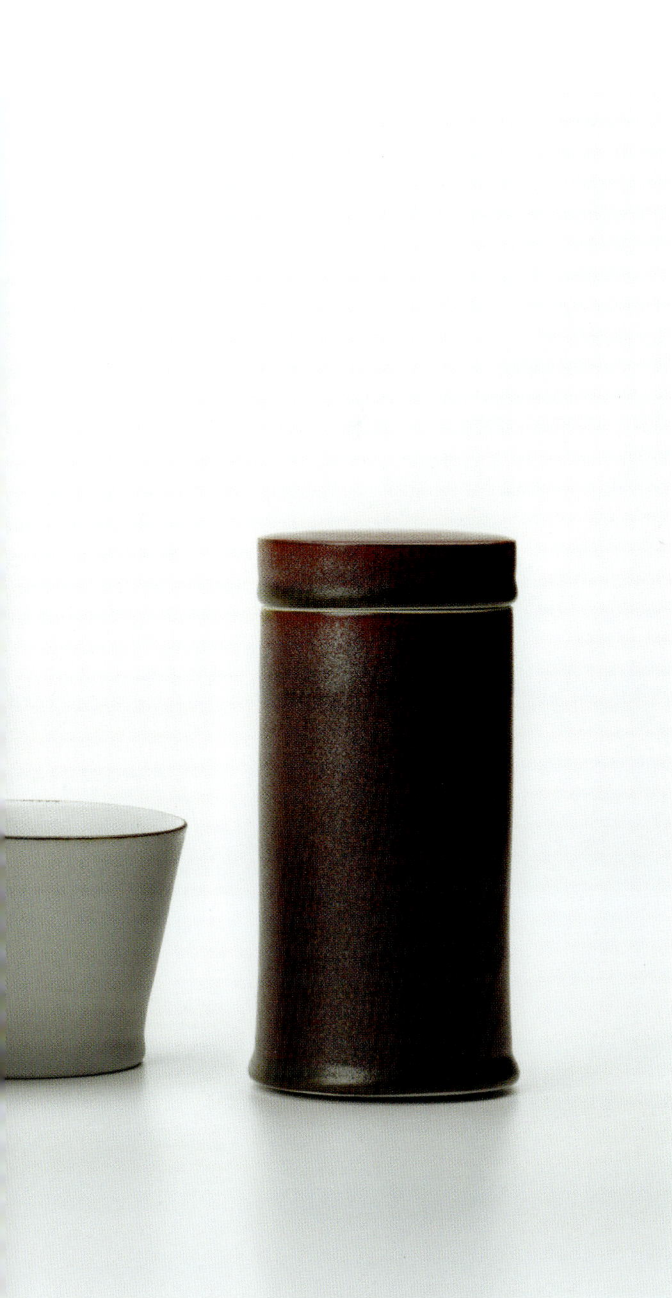

Deliberation 2019
Porcelain, matt white glaze, iron oxide, saturated iron glaze
25 × 60 × 25 cm (9⅞ × 23⅝ × 9⅞ in.)

Grounded in the migrant experience of colonial Australia during the 19th and early 20th centuries, the immaculate, serene forms of Kirsten Coehlo evoke memories of the rituals and routines of daily life. Coehlo is influenced by the chipped and worn surfaces of domestic enamelware, referencing familiar utilitarian objects such as jugs, flasks, beakers and bowls. Made in porcelain and thrown on the pottery wheel, touches of rusty iron oxide outline the rims and blemish the perfect white forms. Coehlo's intention is to echo the weathering of iron and decay within the urban landscape. These subtle abstractions create a juxtaposition between the precious and the commonplace.

This collection of curated forms by Coehlo, entitled *Deliberation*, connects to her ongoing investigation of migration, exile and social history. She imagines what sort of objects are taken on a journey, what compels the choice and how the context of that object can be transformed when placed in a new cultural setting. Her work aims to explore and reinterpret the cultural history imbued in these utilitarian wares in ceramic form.

Having thrown her forms in porcelain on the pottery wheel and high fired them in a reduction environment, Coelho accentuates their silhouettes with a beautiful soft, matt glaze. She adds further visual interest by displaying her pieces alongside a variety of related functional objects, each one with its own intricate details, from the pierced holes in the colander to the undulating profile of the bottle neck. A fine iron-oxide line bleeds from the rims and the rust colour is reflected in the intense, flecked red glaze of the lidded jar, which neatly punctuates the whole composition.

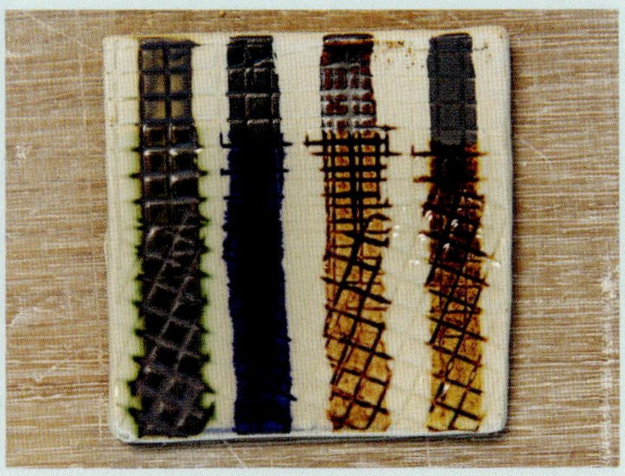

Surface
Coelho exploits the rich, metallic colour of iron oxide to mimic the rusty tones of urban decay. In terms of decoration, metal oxides are incredibly versatile when used in conjunction with a glaze or simply applied to an unglazed surface. As this tile illustrates, without a glaze, oxides have a dense graphite quality, but when covered with a glaze, the true colour is revealed. You can exploit the diverse tonal qualities of an oxide to enhance texture, particularly when recreating organic or natural surfaces.

Left to right: Copper oxide, cobalt oxide, manganese dioxide, iron oxide. Three-quarters covered with a shiny stoneware transparent glaze.

Doug Fitch

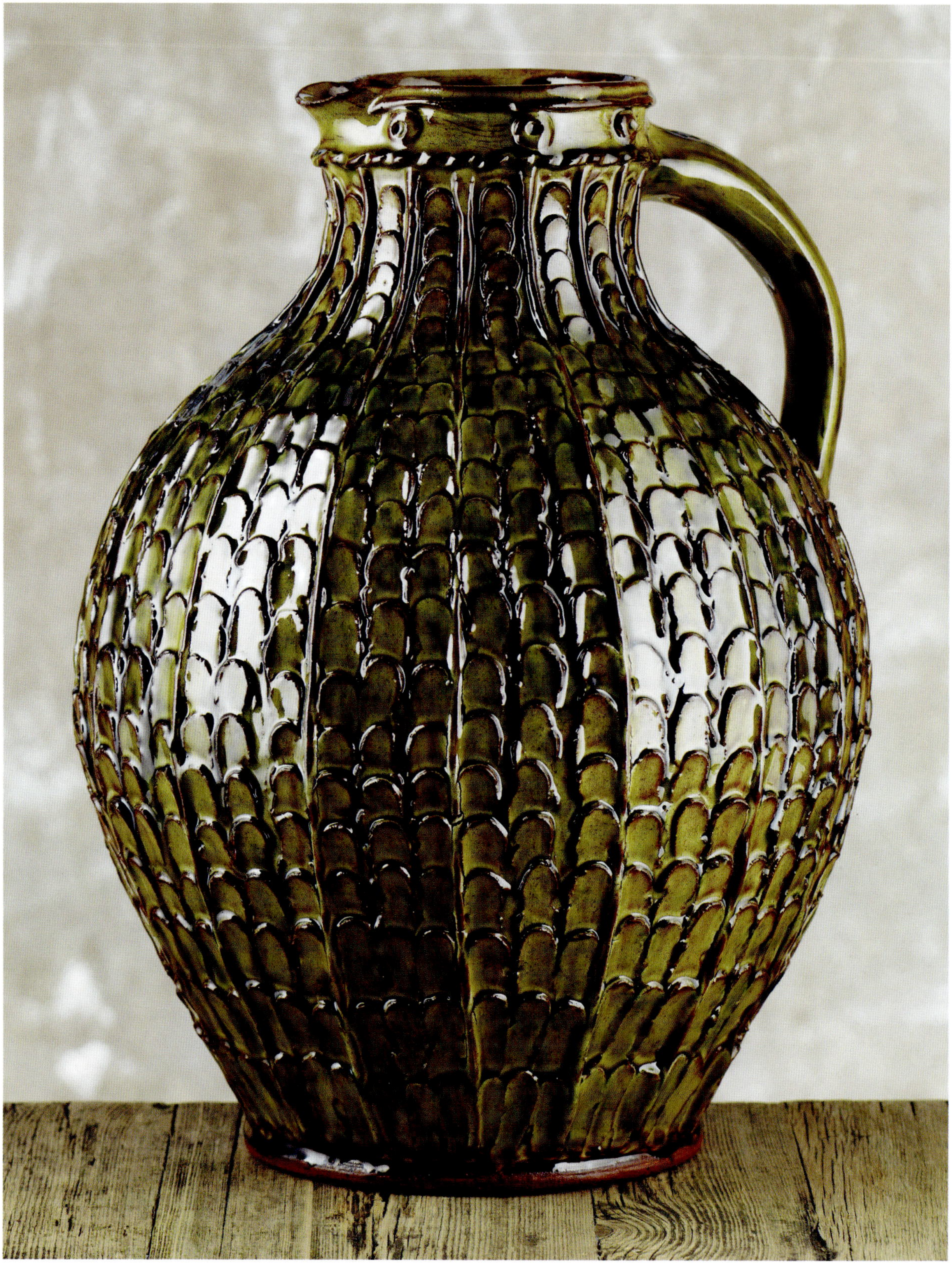

Large Green Pellet Jug 2019
Red earthenware, slip, wood fired
Height: 33 cm (13 in.)

Drawing on centuries-old traditions of Staffordshire slipware techniques, Doug Fitch creates modern interpretations of heritage pottery forms that are richly decorated and inviting to use. His rustic, functional wares range from large pitchers and lidded storage jars to bowls and teapots. Fitch uses a blend of red earthenware clay mixed with brick clay to give it a gritty texture and 'tooth'. He predominantly throws his work, but uses press moulds to make dishes and platter forms. Inspired by the earthy colours of his local landscape, Fitch's pots are simply decorated using slip trailing, sgraffito and appliqué techniques. A depth of colour and warmth is brought to the decoration by glazing the slip-covered surface with an oily green or honey-coloured glaze and low-firing in a wood-fuelled kiln to a temperature of around 1100°C (2012°F), oxidized.

This striking example of a pellet jug by Doug Fitch is intensely rich and tactile. Fitch has applied vertical seams of clay to the surface and infilled them with a rhythmic pattern of smeared 'pellets', which change in scale as they progress down the belly of the pot. The strap handle was pulled directly from a lump of clay attached to the side of the vessel and echoes pottery techniques of the past. As this piece clearly demonstrates, what distinguishes Fitch's work from that of others is his ability to inject genuine charm and character into every piece. The sincerity and sense of personality held within his pottery forms establish a deep connection between the maker and user.

Doug Fitch (British, born 1964) trained in ceramics at the Derbyshire College of Higher Education. Starting in 1986, he worked at a flowerpot factory where he gained experience in production throwing, jollying and press moulding. In 1988 he left to establish a company in Liverpool making slip-cast lighting products. From 1990 to 1992 he worked as a ceramics and sculpture technician at the University of Plymouth. In 1990 he joined the kiln-firing team for a number of Devon-based potters, comprising Svend Bayer (born 1946), Clive Bowen (born 1943) and Nic Collins (born 1958). In 2003, Fitch established Hollyford Pottery in Devon, specializing in wood-fired slipware. He and his wife Hannah McAndrew work together in their isolated studio in Scotland, specializing in slipware.

See also
Thomas Toft (p.88)
Bernard Leach (p.136)
Anne Mette Hjortshøj (p.146)

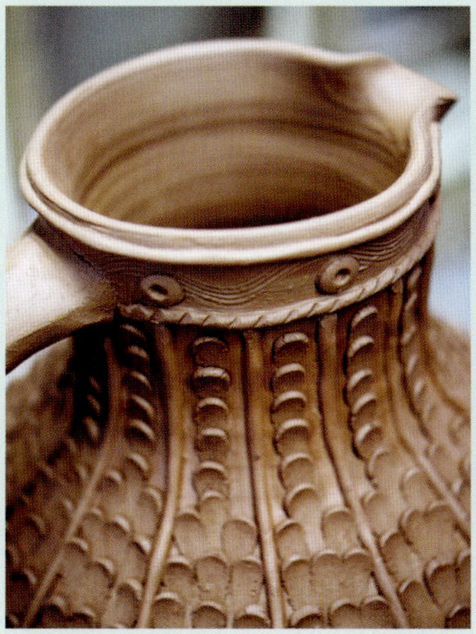

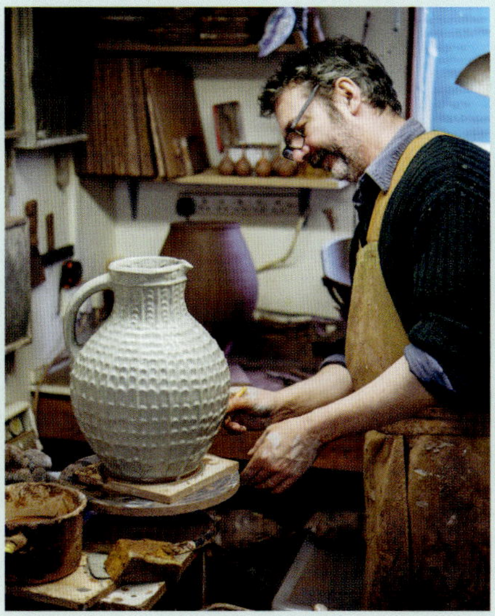

Surface
Alongside slip decorating his work, Doug Fitch also constructs a relief pattern on the clay surface by using an appliqué technique. As illustrated here, Fitch applies individual pellets of clay and smudges them into a scaly texture with his fingertips. You can bring liveliness and tactility to your own work by rolling or extruding thin strips of clay and arranging them in a pattern on the surface of your work. You could use small sprigs or stamps to break up the design. Consider the overall symmetry and repetition of the decoration; the strength of this type of decoration lies in its simplicity and conviction of line.

Adam Frew

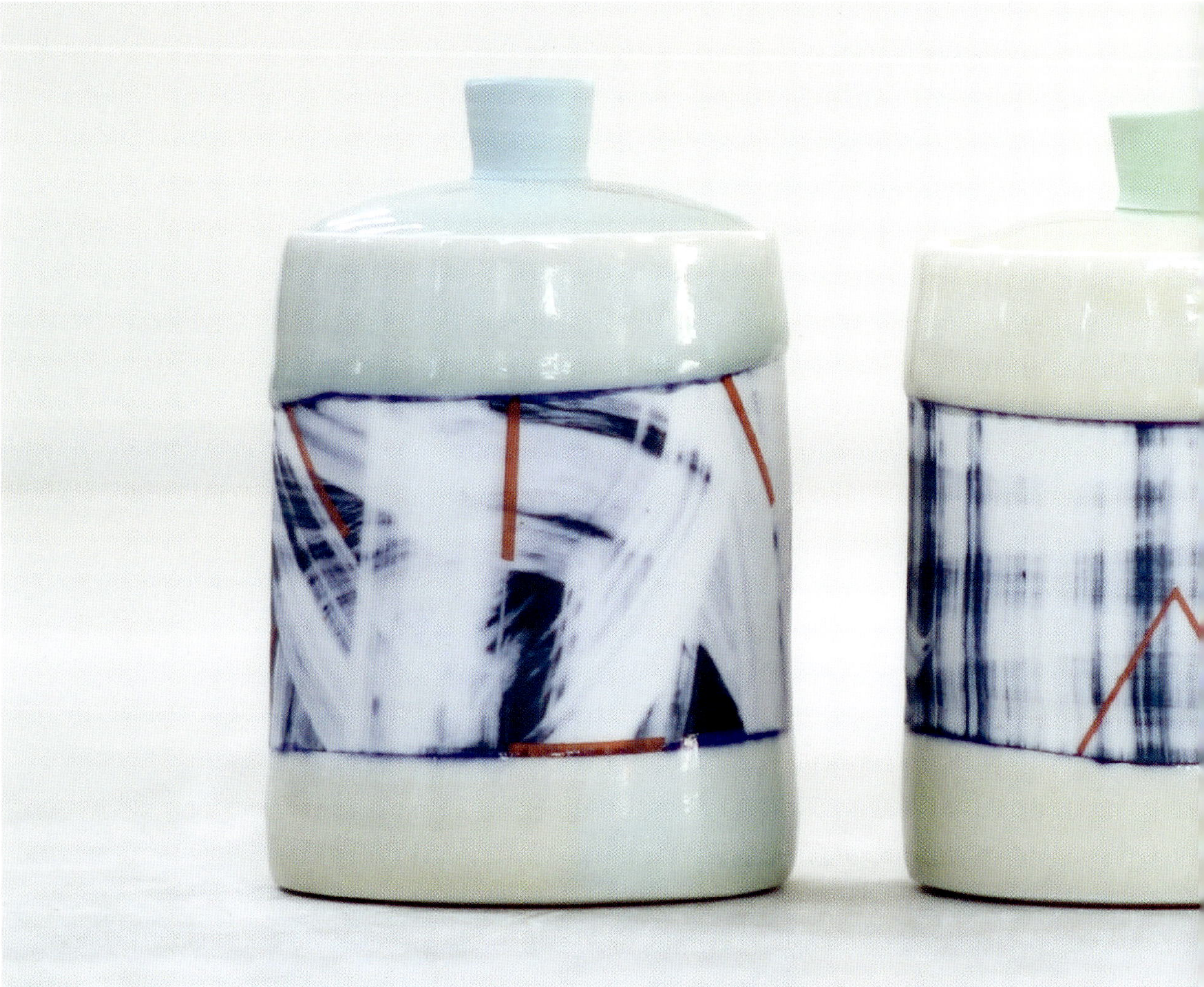

Lidded Jars 2019
Porcelain with reduction
Height: 13 cm (5 in.)

Adam Frew uses the pottery wheel to throw forms that echo the traditions of East Asian pottery. His aim is to capture the exuberance of the act of throwing in his work and retain the energy and spontaneity of the process. There is a continuous dialogue from one piece to the next and Frew ensures individuality by constantly experimenting with his methods and forms. These three lidded jars demonstrate Frew's ability to create a canvas for rich abstract painting on a functional form, elevating the status of the vessel beyond its practical purpose.

Frew conveys the evocative colours of the wild Northern Irish coastline with rich panels of painterly decoration on his wares. With an interest in drawing, he enjoys the interplay between form and surface. Mark making is gestural and intuitive: strong contrasts between scratched lines, crayon scribbles, expressive brush work and sponged sections are contained by the delicate pale hues of celadon glaze. Flecks of orange retain some sense of order amongst the chaos of the decoration and reconnect with the precise proportions of the overall form. Frew uses masking techniques to create his richly decorated surfaces. He tapes sections and freely applies coloured slips using brushes, sponges or any method he feels appropriate for that moment. Frew continues to push the surface by wiping areas back, re-masking and overlapping with even more decoration, resulting in dynamic and energetic qualities.

All his work is made from porcelain – the whiteness of the material provides the perfect canvas to paint against. To complete his works, Frew fires them in a gas- or wood-fired kiln in a reducing atmosphere.

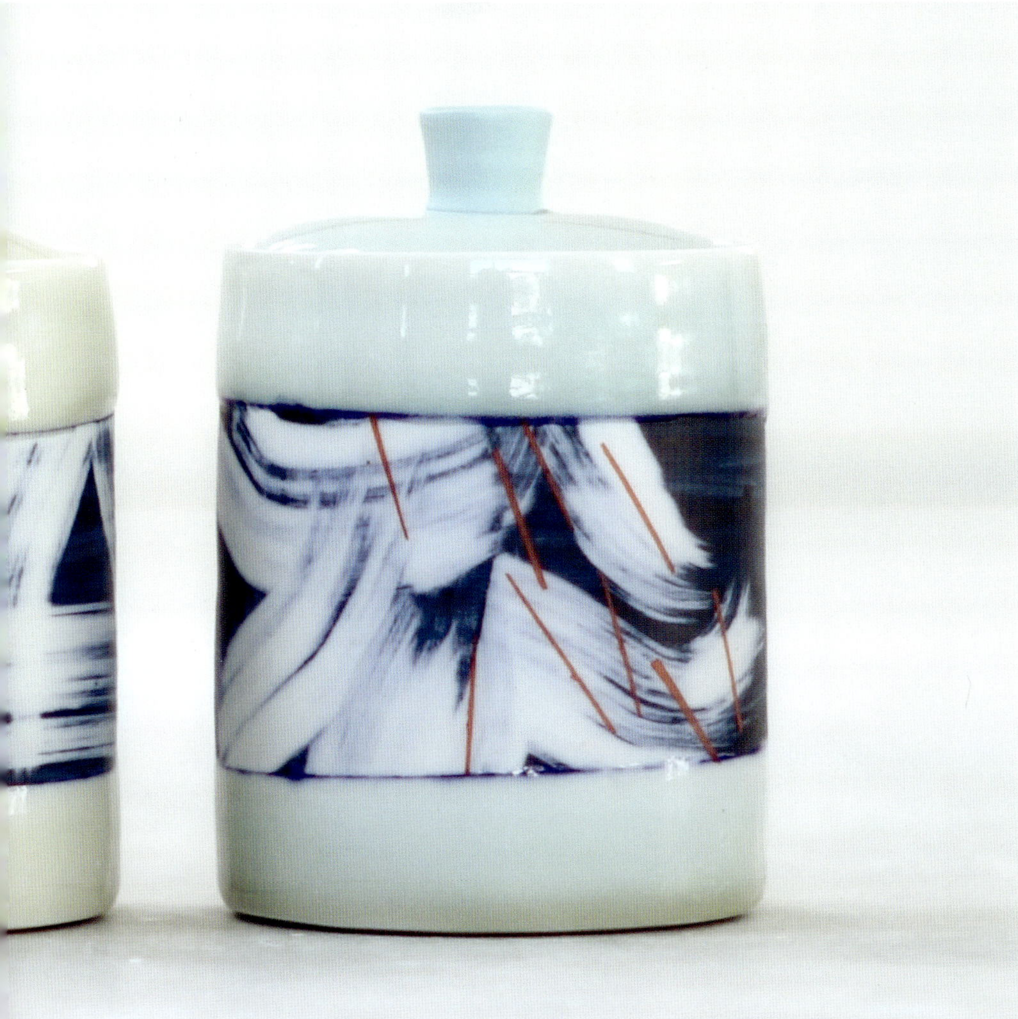

Adam Frew (Northern Irish, born 1981) is based in county Londonderry, Northern Ireland, and produces his collection of decorative porcelains for shops, galleries and collectors worldwide. He works closely with chefs and restaurants and creates bespoke ceramic items ranging from plates to sinks. Frew trained at Belfast Art College and furthered his skills at the historic Winchcombe Pottery in Oxfordshire, followed by work experience with Judy Makela in Finland. After graduating in 2004, Frew undertook a two-year apprenticeship with renowned potter Lisa Hammond at her pottery in Greenwich, London. In 2006, he returned to Northern Ireland and was resident potter at Flowerfield Arts Centre for twelve years. Frew now works from a purpose-built studio within the grounds of his home. Examples of his work are held in several major collections, including the Mungyeong Ceramic Museum in Korea, the University of Ulster and the Arts Council of Northern Ireland.

See also

Toshiko Takaezu (p.56)

Bodil Manz (p.96)

Kirsten Coelho (p.160)

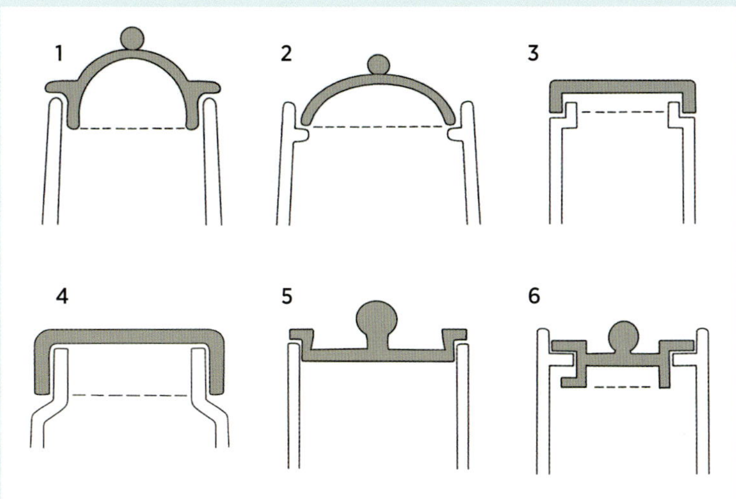

Technical

There are several different lid designs you can make for your thrown forms. It is important to ensure a good fit and that the design works together as a whole.

1. Dome-shaped lid with flange that sits on the rim of the pot. The lid has a gallery to fit the pot internally to prevent it from slipping.
2. Curved inset shape, sits on an internal gallery.
3. Shallow lid, sits on an external gallery to look flush with the main container wall.
4. Overhang cup lids are easy to make and suit pots with a narrow neck and no gallery.
5. Inset lid with turned knob, raised flange to sit on rim.
6. Internal inset lid and gallery, with lock piece to prevent the lid from falling out – for example, when pouring a teapot.

Figur

From the representation of the embodied soul, to communicating fertility, status and power; the figure – be it human, animal, hybrid or mythical – has been a constant source of inspiration throughout history and continues to inform the work of artists today. There are a number of different aspects to this genre that you could incorporate into your own work, many of which centre around anthropology or the exploration of the human condition – and what it means to be human. Starting with yourself can be an intriguing subject of investigation.

Autobiographical themes are prevalent in the work of Robert Arneson (p.176) and Tip Toland (p.188) who draw on their life experiences to inform their work. Expression of character resonates strongly throughout all the featured works in this chapter – particularly the application of material to convey emotions such as humour and profound human spirit, to the sculpting and moulding of clay to mimic life-like qualities of skin and limbs, as seen in the work of the Martin Brothers (p.170) and Daphne Corregan (p.180).

Another area of investigation that may interest you is the topic of social and gender issues, explored by Viola Frey (p.174) and Shary Boyle (p.194). Artists Catrin Howell (p.184) and Claire Curneen (p.196) play out a narrative from ancient Welsh manuscripts, creating hybrid forms which convey a powerful message of resilience and positivity. The body can act as a metaphor for containment, a vessel as such – which connects back to the notion of the archetypal ceramic form. Figurative artworks challenge the way we perceive the figure and the form it entails, questioning our interpretation and understanding of the world around us.

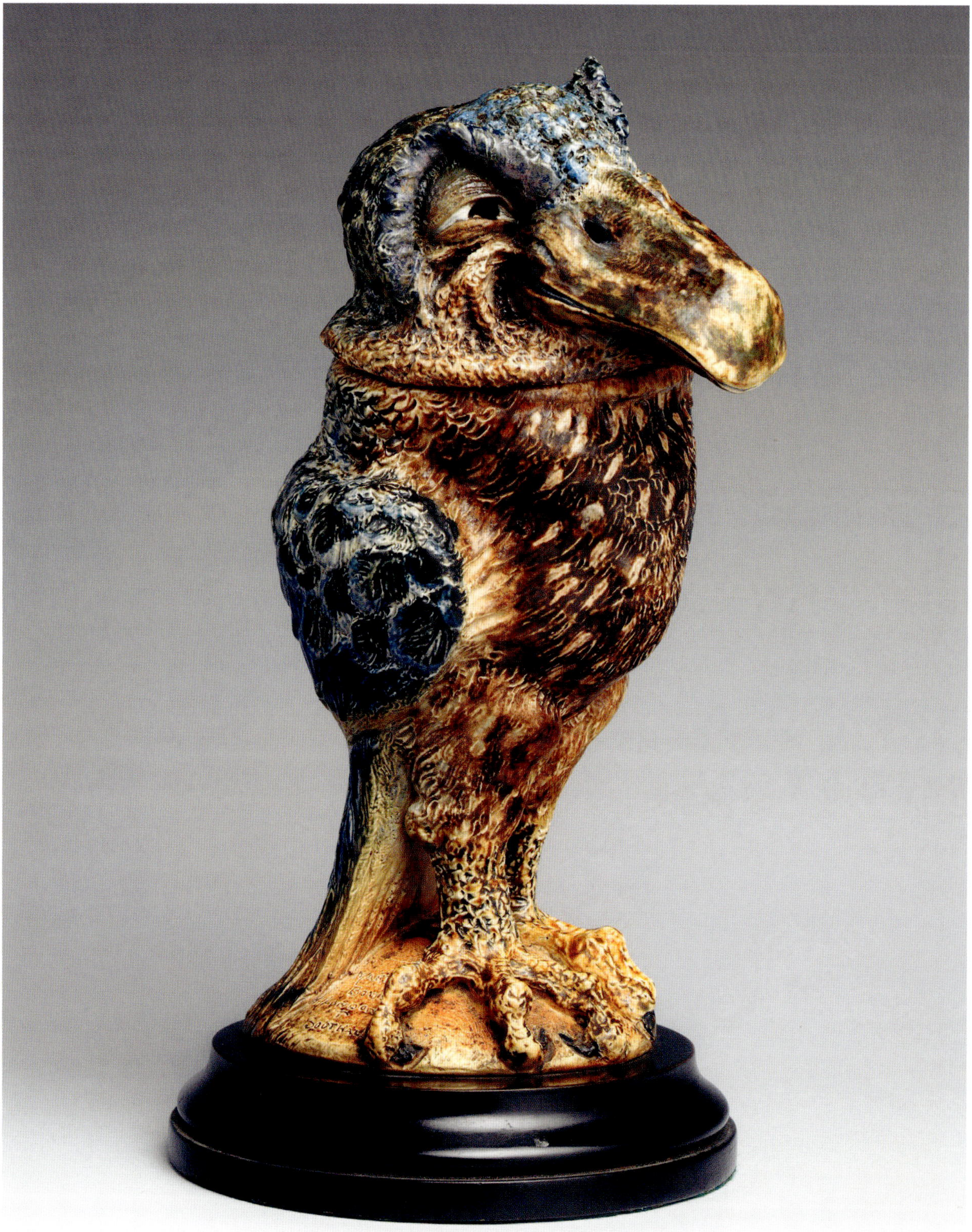

Wally Bird Jar 1888

Martinware

31 × 16.4 × 16.4 cm (12¼ × 6½ × 6½ in)

Inspired by an eclectic mix of the naturalistic works of 16th-century artist Bernard Palissy and medieval gothic revival, this Wally Bird jar is a typical example of the whimsical and imaginative work created by the Martin Brothers. The idea for the Wally Bird was conceived by Wallace Martin who had previous experience carving stone gargoyles for iconic London landmarks, including the Houses of Parliament in Westminster. This skill enabled Wallace to understand the subtleties of expression and character, which he was able to translate into clay with convincing realism. The bird itself was a purely fantastical creature, a representation of the Martin Brothers' eccentric ingenuity. Each piece was hand modelled and sculpted individually rather than batch produced from a mould, as this allowed for greater variety and experimentation between the works.

Perched on a round wooden plinth with steep, arching eyebrows and a wry glare, this Wally Bird has a knowing expression. The slightly upturned grinning beak and the tilt of the head imply a mischievous character. Delicate, flecked marks on the bird's crest and tucked wings create softness against the pitted skin texture of the gnarly feet and talons. From a functional point of view the head of the bird can be lifted away from the body, which serves as a container. It is thought the jars were intended for storing tobacco, but they are not airtight, so it's more likely that they were used for ornamental purposes.

The Martin Brothers' (British) pottery was founded in Fulham, London, in 1873 by Robert Wallace Martin (1843–1923) and his three siblings: Charles (1846–1910), Walter (1857–1912) and Edwin (1860–1915). Each brother had a particular role within the business. Working together as a team, they created experimental collections of pottery ranging from decorative bowls and vases inspired by Japanese art to eccentric 'Wally Bird' jars. The pottery relocated to Southall, Middlesex, in 1879 and continued production until 1923 when Robert, the last brother remaining, died. The Martin Brothers' work is considered important because it signifies a shift from industry manufactured ceramics of the Victorian period to the beginnings of the art-pottery studio movement.

See also

Bernard Palissy (p.86)
Walter Keeler (p.142)
Carolein Smit (p.198)

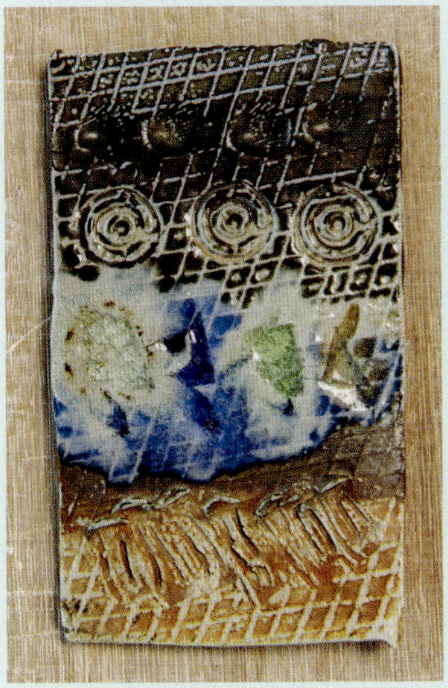

Surface

The Martin Brothers made stoneware pottery and used a firing technique called salt firing to glaze their work. This type of firing meant that the pots did not have to be glazed prior to firing – all that was required was a painting of slip and dabs of oxides. During a typical salt firing, parcels of salt are put into the kiln at the highest temperature (around 1280–1300°C/2336–2372°F) in a reduction atmosphere. The salt parcels instantly vapourize and cause the sodium to react with the silica in the clay body and slips to create a distinctive orange-peel glazed surface. Here is a salt-glaze sample tile with distinctive orange-peel texturing. Note how the lines and details have been highlighted by the salt effect. The glossy blue areas in the middle of the tile are from shards of glass that were embedded in the clay prior to firing.

Subject Matter

The Martin Brothers were masters of conveying character through the medium of clay. To help understand the complexities of human expression, hold a small mirror (or take some selfies) and play around with grimacing and contorting your face. Observe the slight changes between movements and how this reads as an emotion. Sketch or take a photo of the expressions that interest you and explore translating these qualities into clay.

Pablo Picasso

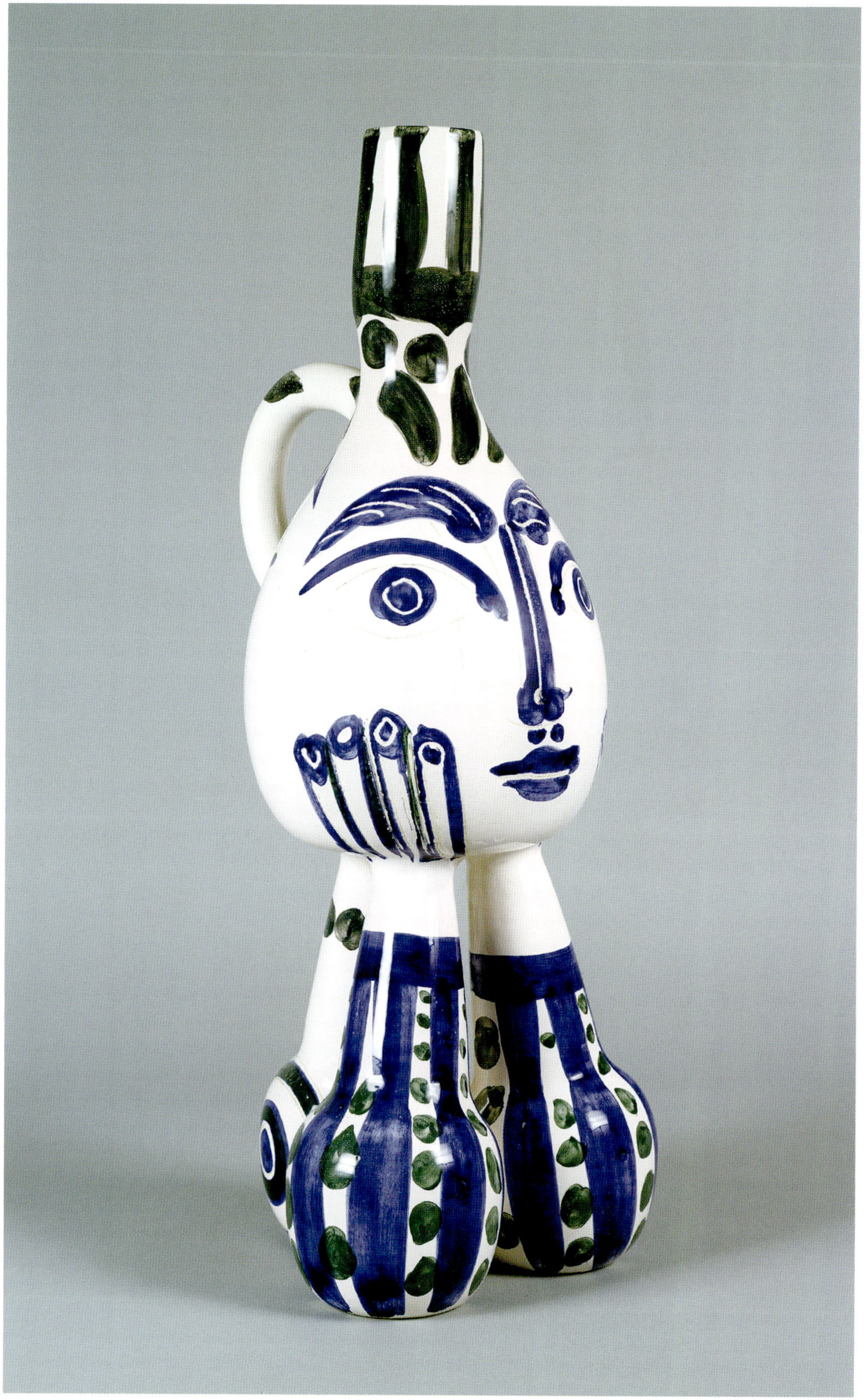

Pitcher Depicting Two Faces 1951
Ceramic
Height: 77 cm (30 ⅓ in.)

Lively and expressive, this abstracted figurative piece demonstrates Pablo Picasso's exceptional ability to represent the broad range of human emotions, with just a few strokes of a brush. With origins in cubism and surrealism – just some of the influential artistic movements instigated by Picasso – the face motif is stripped to its most essential features. Picasso has assembled the piece in such a way that the three bulbous vase forms at the base have become an essential part of the decoration, whereby they depict the character's clothing and make it look as if the hands are bearing the weight of the head in a contemplative stance. Freely decorated with oxides in Picasso's signature playful style, the pared selection of colours – whites, blues and greens – is very bold and engaging.

Picasso worked in collaboration with the potters at the Madoura workshop who made the pieces to his specification, often supplying them as separate shapes and vessels to allow him to experiment with the assembly and construction of the final piece. Picasso played with the likeness of pottery shapes to the human figure – for example, the belly, shoulders and neck of a vase – and painted his characters in response to how he positioned these components in the overall piece. Picasso did not have much previous experience of working with clay and learned a lot through trial and error. His experimental and dynamic approach was very different to the traditional Leach style of the same era and inspired a new generation of potters who were seeking an alternative aesthetic.

Pablo Picasso (Spanish, 1881–1973) is widely regarded as one of the greatest artists of the 20th century. In the later years of his life – and already phenomenally successful – he turned his attention to clay after a visit to Vallauris (France) in 1946. The small coastal town was known for its pottery production and Picasso established a friendship with Suzanne Ramié (1905–74) and Georges Ramié (1901–76) who owned the Atelier Madoura. The couple allowed Picasso to work alongside them in the studio and introduced him to Jules Agard (1905–86), a local potter who made the vessels that Picasso decorated using slips and oxides. Picasso was a prolific worker and produced more than 3,500 pieces ranging from plates and bowls to jugs and pitchers. His intention was to create functional wares that were more accessible and affordable to everyday people.

See also
Peter Voulkos (p.68)
Viola Frey (p.174)
Robert Arneson (p.176)

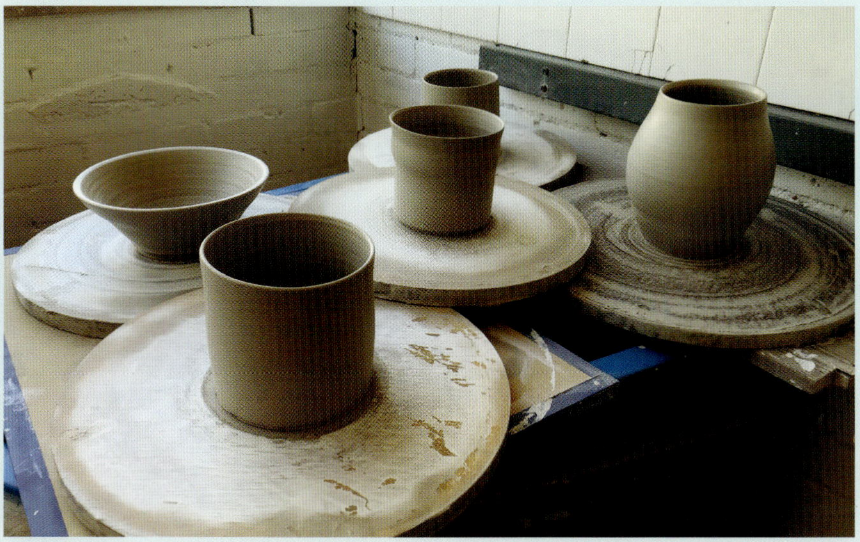

Technical
Picasso constructed his works from a series of thrown shapes. This assembly technique is a useful way to construct larger forms, and it can lead to greater freedom with the outcome. Throw or hand build a number of component pieces, such as bowls, cylinders and bellied vessels. One of the most important considerations is to make sure the pieces will align when fitted together. Therefore use callipers or a ruler to measure the rims and openings to ensure a good fit. Play with turning them upside down, stacking one on top of the other or cutting and re-attaching to form new shapes.

Viola Frey

See also
Mo Jupp (p.178)
Tip Toland (p.188)
Betty Woodman (p.252)

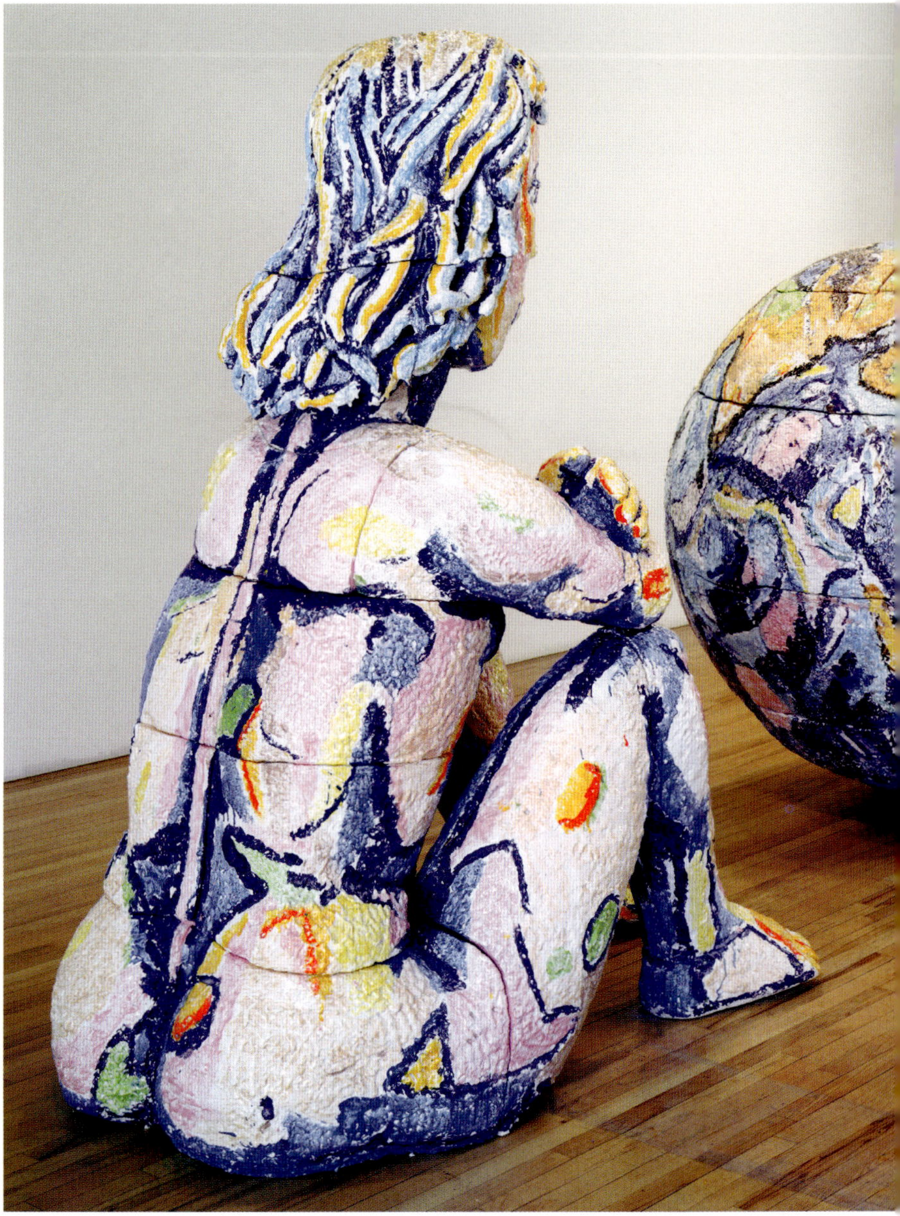

Viola Frey (American, 1933–2004) studied painting and ceramics at California College of Arts and Crafts. She then went on to do a master's degree at Tulane University in New Orleans, studying under painter Mark Rothko (1903–70) and ceramicist Katherine Choy (1929–58); however, she moved to New York before graduating. In New York, Frey worked with Choy at the Clay Art Center, where artists were in the vanguard of using clay as a fine-art medium. Frey then returned to California where she became known for her brightly coloured, monumental ceramic sculptures and figurines that explored issues of art history, cultural iconography and gender.

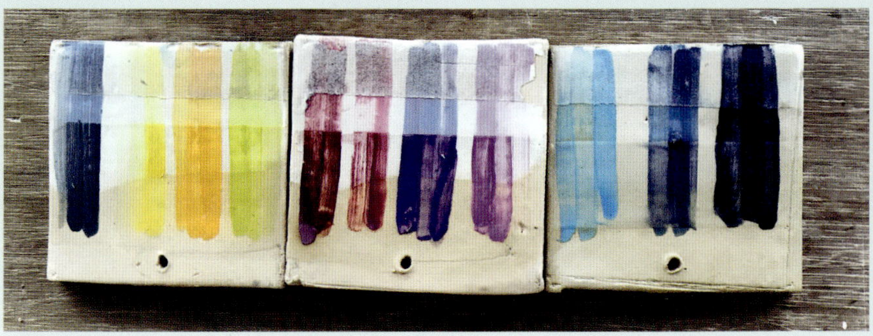

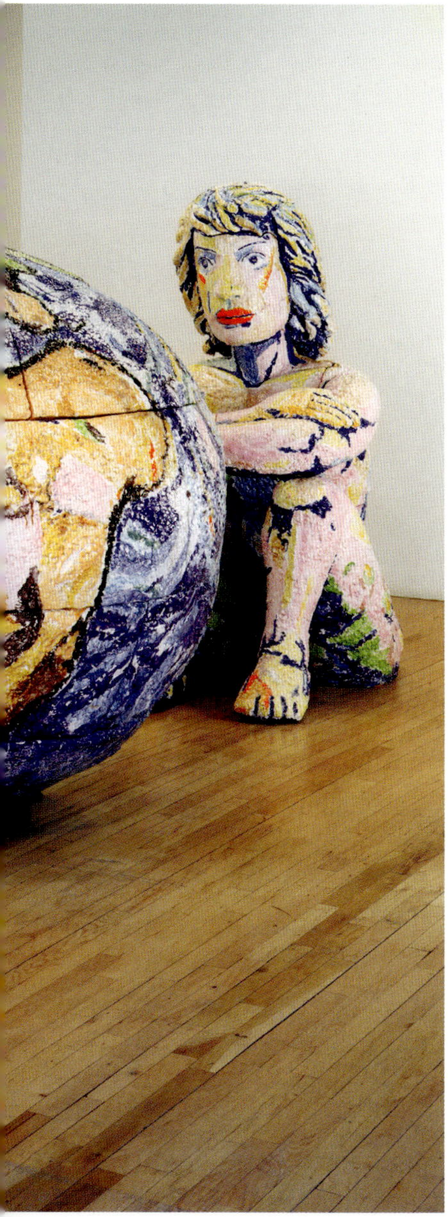

Two Women and a Globe 1990–91
Glazed ceramic
212 × 604.5 × 172.7 cm (83½ × 238 × 68 in.)

American artist and sculptor Viola Frey worked across painting, drawing and sculpture. In the 1960s and 1970s, her colourful, larger-than-life ceramic sculptures were instrumental in bridging the divide between craft and fine art. Frey, initially influenced by the abstract expressionism of the 1950s, became closely aligned with pop art in the 1960s, and later, Funk art – a cohesive movement that was emerging from the San Francisco Bay Area of California at the time. A key aspect of Frey's work was her exploration of the figure, through which she reflected on themes including cultural iconography, power and gender dynamics.

Frey was an avid collector of bricolage and she was fascinated by ceramic figurines. She sought to recreate these objects in her sculpture and paintings. Frey explains their appeal in relation to her work: 'Figurines function in order to make acceptable those things that our culture finds unacceptable. They might deal with old age, with menace, or with women. My work is figurative, but it's as far towards the abstract transformation as it is possible to go and still retain the integrity of the image or the information.'

The notion of the figurine is apparent in *Two Women and a Globe*. Straight away we are confronted by its monumental, supersize scale – a key feature in many of Frey's works. This dominating sculpture portrays two women reflecting on their place in the world. Frey, an ardent feminist, believed that 'in contemporary society the female nude symbolized power and control'. True to the Funk style 'outsider art' aesthetic, Frey decorated the piece in vivid, brazen colours and bold, painterly lines. The abstract use of colour communicates the human spirit and represents the strong, independent women that Frey admired.

Surface
Frey achieved her bold, colourful aesthetic by using low-fired, on-glaze decoration techniques. The piece was first coated in a white glaze (likely a tin glaze) and coloured pigments were applied directly on top, as if painting on a canvas. Frey's aesthetic centred around blues, pinks and yellows. She emphasized painted lines with a strong tone aligned next to a lighter tone – for example, dark cobalt blue, against powder blue. The tiles shown here emulate Frey's bright colour palate and demonstrate how commercial stains behave when applied at variable strengths. The top half of each tile has been coated with a transparent glaze and the bottom half with a white glaze. The middle section is left unglazed. In combination with a specific glaze, the colours can intensify or become pastel.

Technical
Frey's large-scale works are made up of sections that fit together. Her process was to first construct the sculpture as a whole, then, once it had dried to the greenware stage, it was cut up into blocks using an electric saw. This allowed Frey to fit the components into the kiln for firing without compromising on the final size. When the piece was displayed, it was reassembled like a jigsaw puzzle.

Robert Arneson

Golden Triangle/Us Guys 1991
Earthenware
50.8 × 53.3 × 12.7 cm (20 × 21 × 5 in.)

With origins in Dada and surrealism, Funk art was a progression from the loose spontaneity and macho gestures of abstract expression towards a more radical attitude, often with sensational and outrageous intent. Funk can perhaps be best described as a way of thinking rather than a defined aesthetic, typified by an eclectic approach ranging from crudely made sculptures that play on humour and shameless vulgarity right through to works that explore the illusional aspects of trompe l'oeil and hyperrealism.

Robert Arneson was an artist at the forefront of the Funk movement and his early works of the 1960s explored provocative themes that acted as a commentary on the social and political events of the time. Later in his career, around the 1970s, Arneson's work became more autobiographical and focused on self-portraiture, which playfully mocked the role of the artist in the world.

This large wall piece was made a year before Arneson's death. Diagnosed with terminal cancer, Arneson portrays sentiments of melancholy and reflections about his own mortality. The piece is quite simple in construction (the loose way Arneson has sculpted the hair and beard is true to the Funk aesthetic), and there is a naivety to the making that is fully intentional. Arneson has used the three points of the glazed triangle to focus the viewer's attention on the centre of the piece and question why two of the self-portraits tenderly kiss and embrace one another while the third looks on. Arguably, it could have been Arneson's intention to display a united symbol of self-reliance, defiant in the face of death, and perhaps, with a subtle tongue-in-cheek dig at his ego.

Robert Arneson (American, 1930–92) is considered the pioneer of the Funk art movement that came to prominence in the Bay Area of San Francisco between the early 1960s and late 1970s. Born in Benicia, Arneson studied at the College of Marin in Kentfield, California, from 1949 to 1951. This was followed by a bachelor's degree from the California College of Arts and Crafts in Oakland and by a master's degree in fine art from Mills College, Oakland. As an ex-student of Peter Voulkos, Arneson's early works were influenced by abstract expressionism; however, by the beginning of the 1960s, Arneson had abandoned the 'abstract' element and moved towards a more figurative, personal narrative within his work. In 1991, Arneson was awarded the American Academy and Institute of Arts and Letters award for Fine Art, and in 1992 a fellowship from the American Craft Council.

See also
Viola Frey (p.174)
Sergei Isupov (p.186)
Bertozzi & Casoni (p.228)

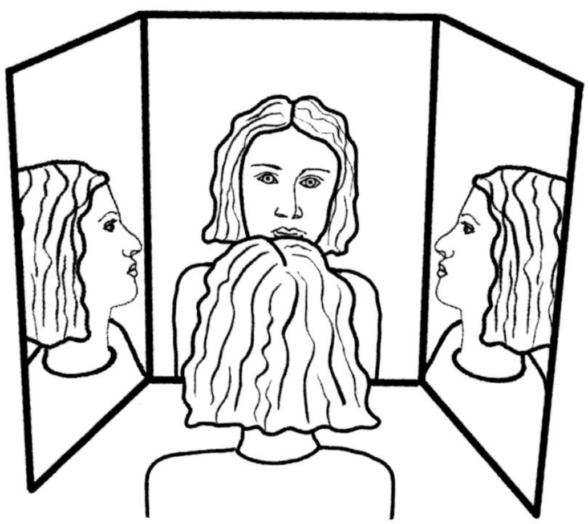

Subject Matter
When sculpting a self-portrait, a hinged mirror or three mirrors placed in a U-shape formation will help you to gauge facial proportions in three dimensions. You could also take lots of pictures of your face at different angles – for example, straight on, looking up, looking down and side profile. The more familiar you are with the intricacies of your head and face, the easier it will be to interpret them in clay.

Material
One of the defining traits that separated Funk from abstract expressionism was the choice of materials. Rough and rustic stoneware was the preferred clay of the likes of Peter Voulkos; however, Funk artists, including Arneson, moved on to smooth, white earthenware, which was more in line with Funk 'hobbyist' values. Arneson fired his pieces at a low temperature in a gas kiln to produce the toasted colour.

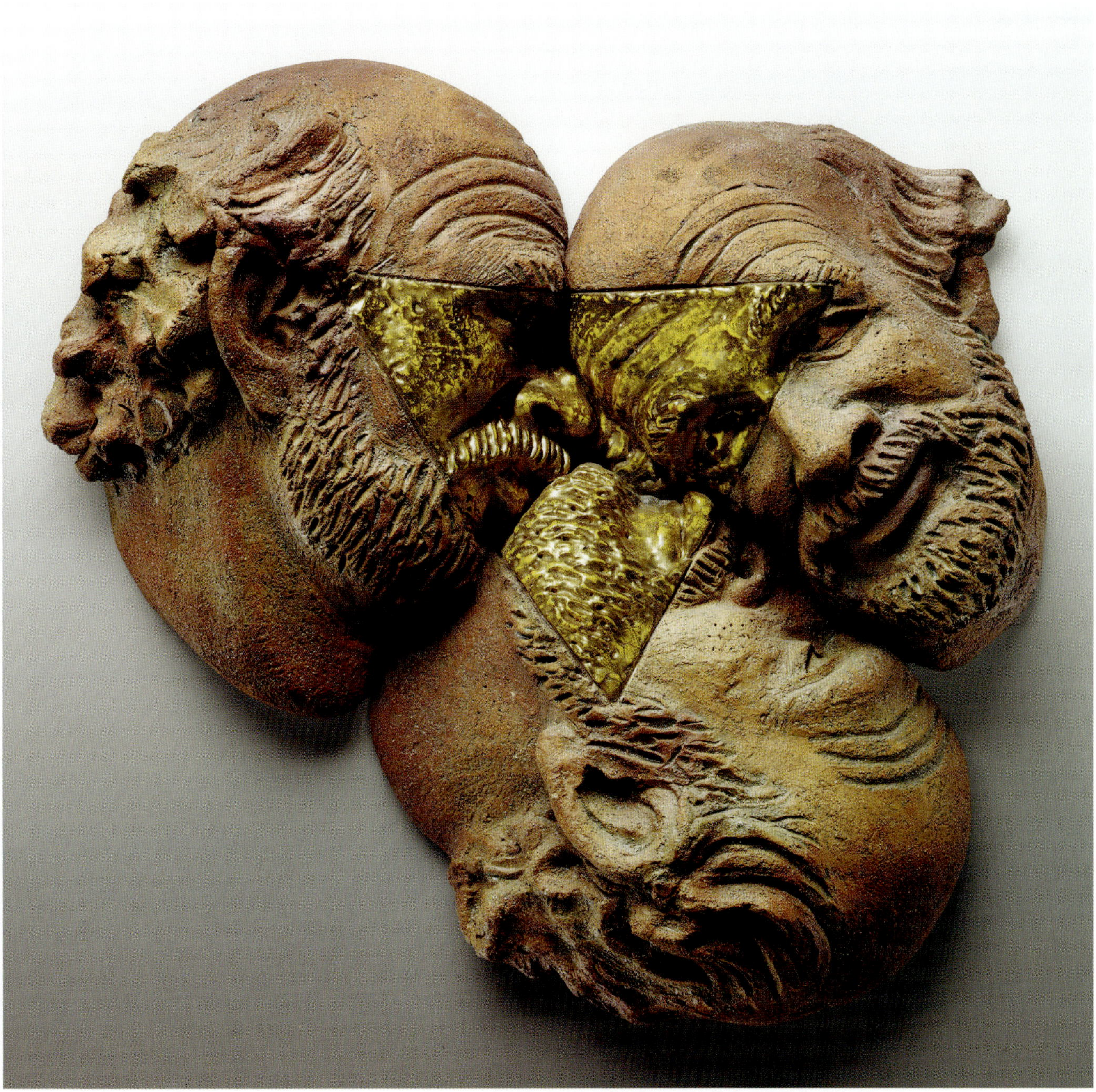

Mo Jupp

Figure 2012
Terracotta: unglazed, waxed
Height: approx. 15 cm (6 in.)

This relaxed, semi-kneeling female figure sensitively captures the gentle silhouette and feminine curves of the nude form. A long, thin torso with humble peaks for breasts is poised upright, with a slight twist held in the hips. The visual weight of the figure's posture can be felt by the casual recline of the legs, not only from an aesthetic point of view but also practically: the retracted left leg and right knee anchor the piece to the base.

Jupp took much of his inspiration for his female figures not directly from life drawing but rather from photographs or magazine clippings that interested him. He was fascinated by posture and he observed women going about their day-to-day business and questioned how he could interpret the ordinariness of their stance and position in clay. Jupp never included the head, because he was not interested in who the person was or their specific character. His primary focus was always the body, the shape and the feeling of movement and expression of the female form.

One of Jupp's direct influences were the tall and spindly figures made by renowned artist and sculptor Alberto Giacometti (1901–66). Jupp's sculptures share traits with Giacometti's work, such as the elongated limbs and exaggerated torso. Built from a series of thin sheets and tubes of pressed and rolled clay, there is an element of tailoring and patchwork to the construction of this piece. During assembly, Jupp used a sharp knife to score a line down the torso and across the legs, emphasizing the curvature of the body. With such a genuine affection for the female form, Jupp's enchantment and admiration are evident.

Mo Jupp (British, 1938–2018) trained in ceramics at Camberwell College of Art, London, where he was taught by prestigious names including Hans Coper and Lucie Rie. This was followed by a master's degree at the Royal College of Art, graduating in 1967. Jupp's early works from the 1970s centred around the theme of helmets; however, from 1978 onwards, he concentrated almost entirely on the female form. A respected educator throughout his career, Jupp maintained long-running teaching posts at Harrow (Westminster, London), Bristol Polytechnic and Bath Academy of Art. Major exhibitions include the Primavera Gallery, London and Cambridge; Arts Council Shows in Japan and the USA; a solo show at the ICA Gallery London; and a solo show at Oxford Ceramics Gallery.

See also
Lucie Rie (p.54)
Hans Coper (p.58)
Lawson Oyekan (p.224)

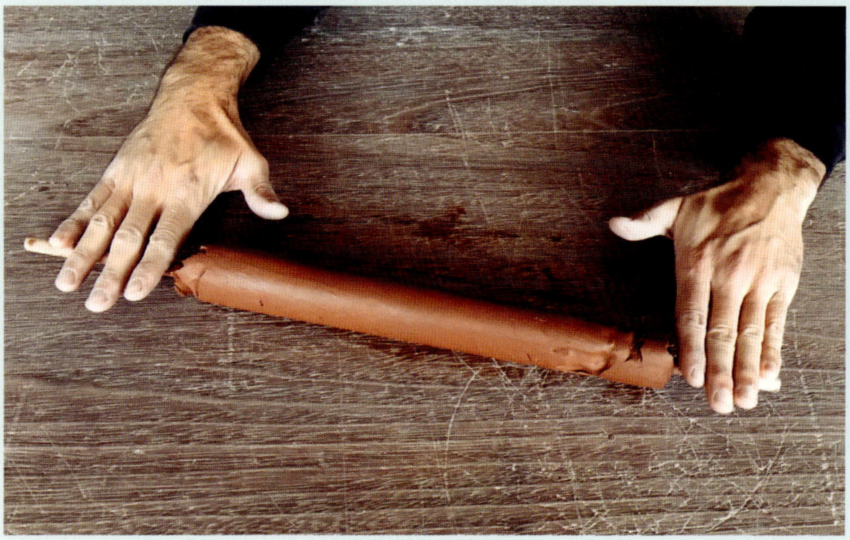

Process
Jupp made this female figure by squeezing terracotta clay around the length of a wooden dowel. He then proceeded to roll the clay on the dowel to create a hollow, irregular tube. After removing the clay tube, Jupp crushed it into a flattened cylinder shape. He repeated the process to make a number of 'body parts', which he used to construct and assemble the overall form. Consider how you could work in component sections: these could be thrown, pinched or rolled – the key is understanding your subject and focusing on the essential elements that describe the overall form.

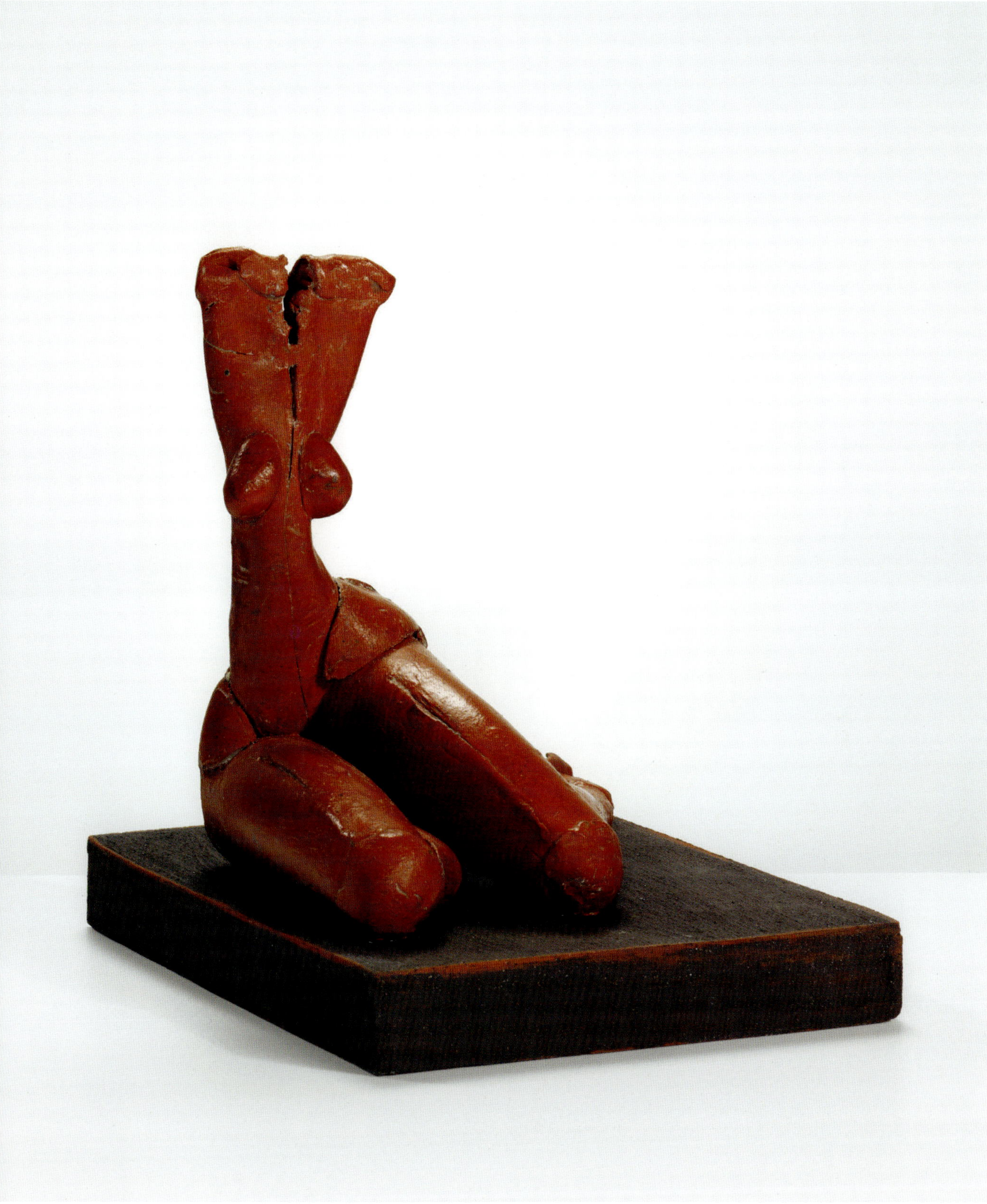

Daphne Corregan

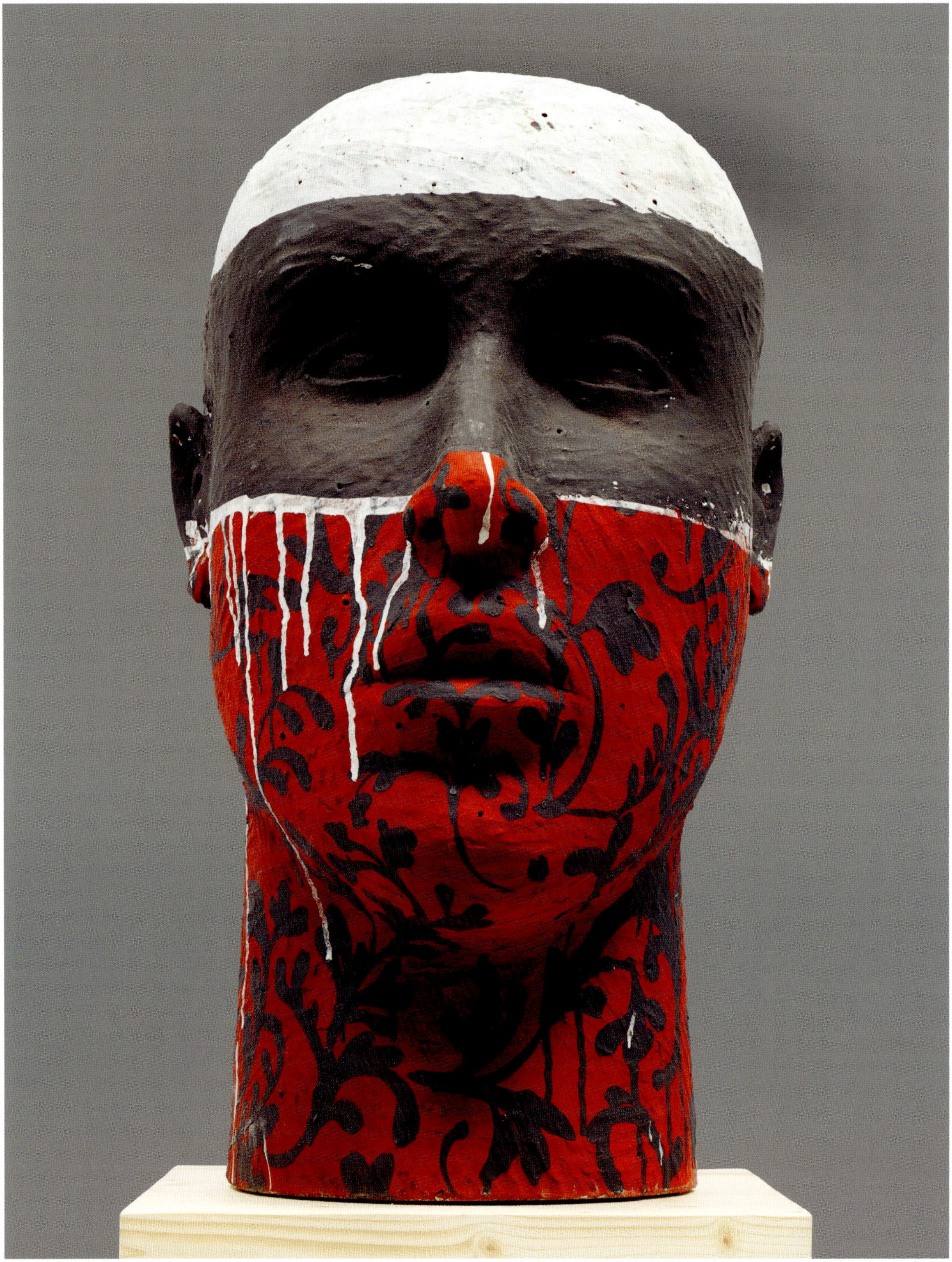

Masked Head 2014
Ceramic with wooden base
Head height: 57 × 45 × 194 cm (22⅘ × 17¾ × 76⅓ in.)

The body – whether presented as a whole or in its parts – has been a great source of inspiration in Daphne Corregan's work, reflecting the defiant, resilient power of the human spirit. Through her travels to parts of the world including North Africa, West Africa, China and Egypt, Corregan observed and learned about traditional craft techniques, taking inspiration from the vibrant textiles and adornment worn by tribes and indigenous people.

This piece amalgamates all these diverse references into one sculptural resolution. The piece itself is large in stature, but its weight is borne on a precariously constructed wooden base – a subtle reference to the weight and fragility of the conscious mind and human psyche. The head is displayed at a height designed to match the viewer's eye level. Its confrontational gaze is paired with little facial expression; however, it still allows the viewer to sense the scope of emotions and the resigned attitude of the character within.

Working on a large scale, Corregan hand modelled the head from coils of stoneware clay. She smoothed and defined the facial features with the pressure of her fingertips, leaving subtle traces of movement within the surface. Drawing inspiration from intricate body painting seen in Africa, Corregan freely decorated the head with earthy coloured slips and engobes, allowing drips and splashes to disrupt the composition. The lower half of the head is decorated with an intricate floral pattern, which echoes the baroque floral motifs of historical European textiles and links Corregan's own cultural identity to this androgynous form.

Daphne Corregan (French-American, born 1954) was born in Pittsburgh in the USA but relocated to the South of France in 1970. With a passion for ceramics from a young age, Corregan studied art and design, ceramics and sculpture, first at the École des Beaux Arts in Toulon in 1972, followed by a year at Marseille and finally three years at the École des Beaux Arts in Aix-en-Provence. In 1977, Corregan joined the ceramics studio of Jean Biagini and was introduced to the raku technique and smoke firing methods, which she continues to use in her work. Corregan has been teaching at the Art School of Monaco since 1989 and is a member of the International Academy of Ceramics.

See also
Maria Martinez (p.138)
Kiho Kang (p.148)
Tip Toland (p.188)

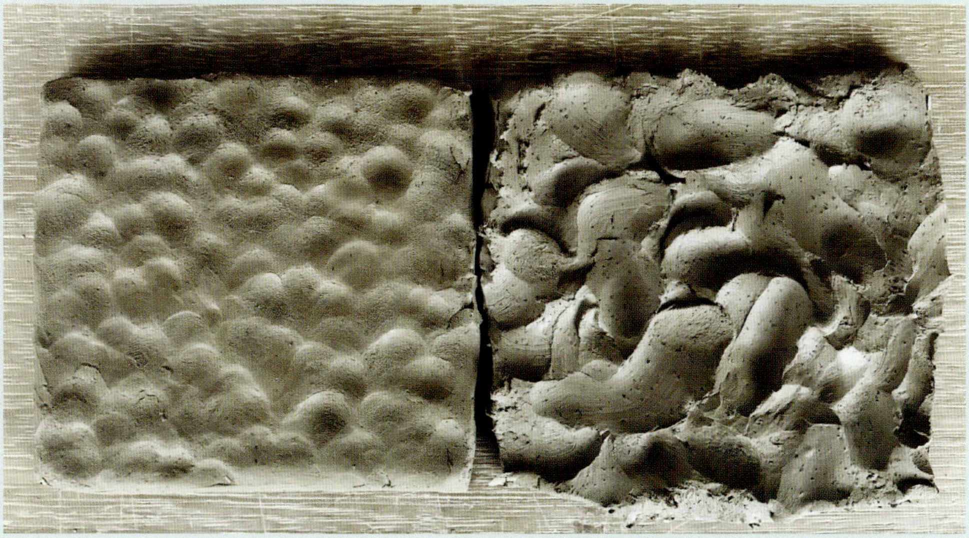

Process
Corregan enjoys using the malleable properties of clay to convey sensitive and emotive qualities. When modelling facial features, you can exaggerate certain expressions by texturizing and sculpting the clay with your fingertips or with a suitable tool. Large, energetic marks can express a wide range of emotions from anger or fury to laughter and enjoyment. Delicate, tightly modelled marks can convey vulnerability or sensitivity.

Rita Gudiño

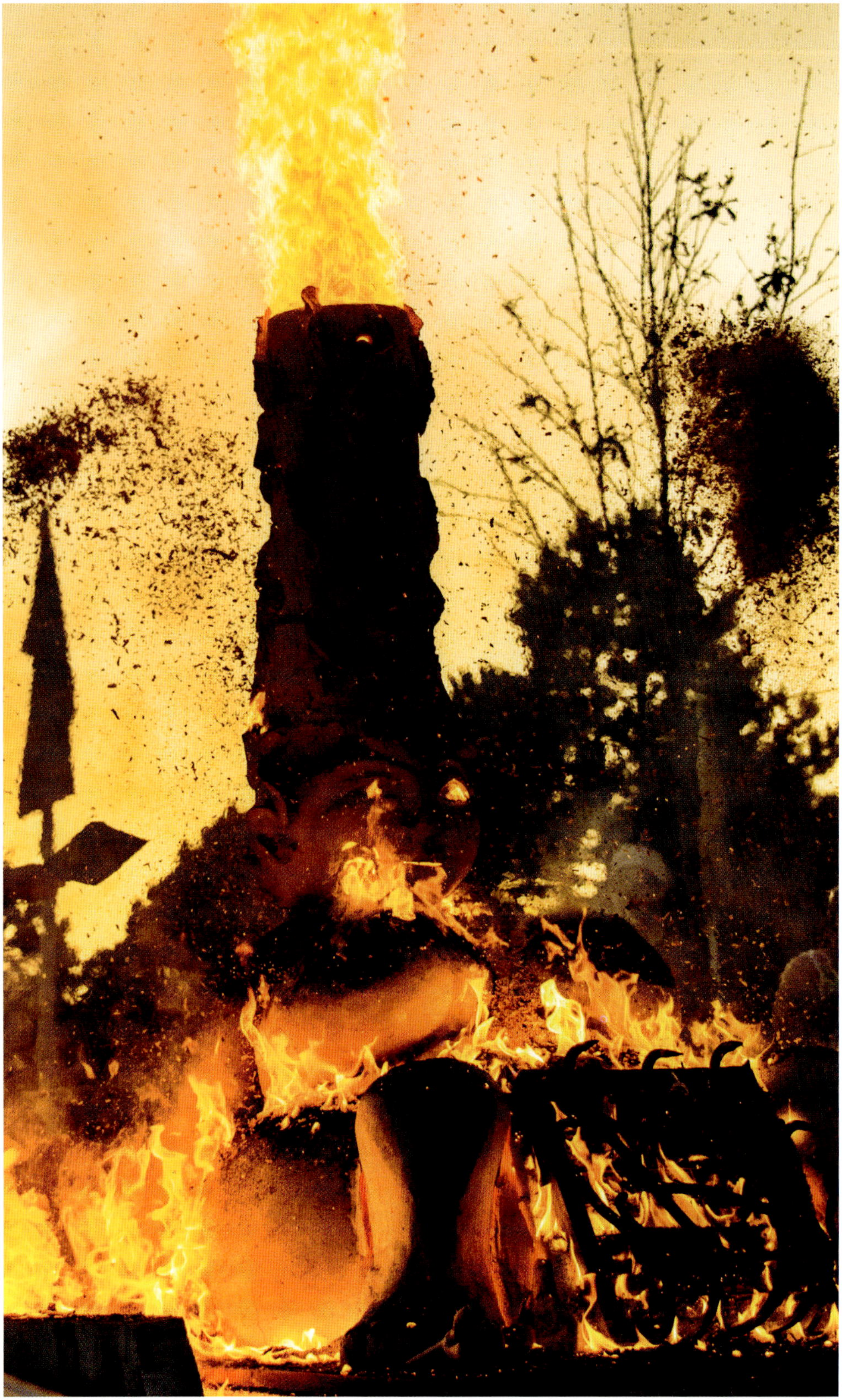

LUAL Kiln Art 2015
Clay, mixed media
Dimensions variable

Rita Gudiño created the *LUAL* kiln as a metaphor for childbirth and new life. *LUAL* – which translates as 'birth' – is a performative piece that centres around the ceremonial aspect of building and firing a raku-type kiln in the shape of a birthing goddess. The kiln is opened and 'gives birth' to clay babies, which Gudiño calls *Sibol*. Gudiño's objective is to turn the firing process itself into an art form and represent 'the woman's role in bringing forth life, which is nothing short of being a miracle, offering life to yield life'.

This version of the *LUAL* kiln was built for the International Ceramics Festival in Aberystwyth (Wales, UK) in 2015. Using more than a tonne of strong stoneware clay, a team of people helped Gudiño to build the kiln on site and together they made *Sibol* babies to place inside the 'womb' kiln chamber. On the night of the performance, the *LUAL* kiln was encased by a 'kumot', a large metal frame structure lined with a ceramic blanket, which acted as a secondary kiln. Once the firing began, ceremonial rituals were carried out, involving feasting, music, chanting prayers and presenting offerings to the kiln goddess. The thrilling spectacle came when the 'kumot' doors were opened, revealing the fiery, blazing kiln inside. Paper packets in the shape of flowers, filled with oxides and salt, were thrown as gifts to *LUAL*, as well as handfuls of sawdust. After removing the kumot completely, *LUAL* was opened and the *Sibol* babies were 'birthed' (extracted using tongs). They were then sprayed with water and placed in a bed of sawdust, following the raku method. The whole firing process took twelve to fourteen hours to complete.

Rita Gudiño (Filippino, born 1969) studied Industrial Design at the University of the Philippines College of Fine Arts while also working as a designer for a ceramic manufacturing and exporting company. She then joined the faculty of the university in 1993. In 1999 she learned how to throw on a potter's wheel and a year later she participated in the International Ceramic Arts Workshop in Tokoname, Japan. She is known for *LUAL*, a sculptural raku kiln that she built and fired in situ in a performance in 2012. The kiln takes the shape of a birthing woman, who 'gives birth' to the clay figures fired within it. Gudiño rebuilt and fired *LUAL* at the International Ceramics Festival in Wales in 2015.

See also
Paul Soldner (p.206)
Maria Martinez (p.138)
Jessica Stoller (p.248)

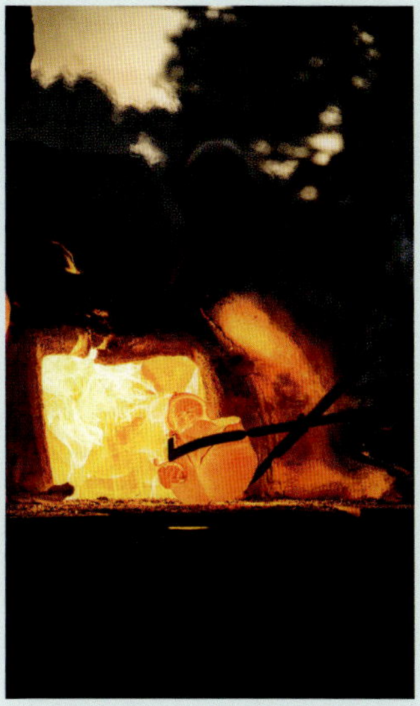

Subject Matter
Gudiño's research stemmed from an interest in the representation of maternal gods in other cultures, including Tlazolteotl in Aztec mythology and Minaden in Philippine mythology. This led her to connect her own experiences of childbirth with that of the kiln firing itself. Much like the stages of labour, the whole performative experience of *LUAL* shares emotions ranging from anticipation and apprehension to transformation and deliverance.

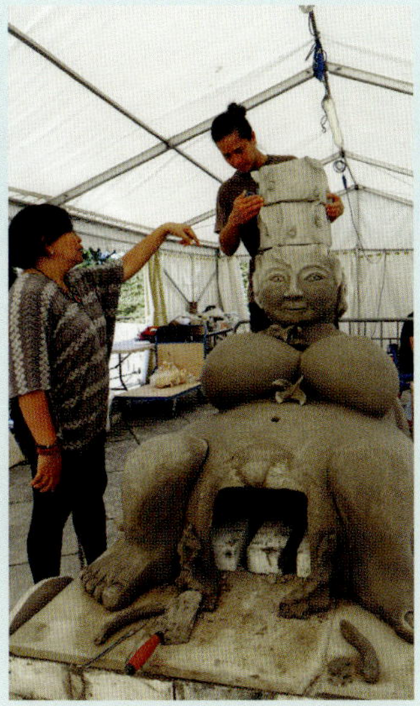

Technical
The design for this piece was meticulously planned, using computer software to calculate the best fuel efficiency and airflow throughout the kiln. Gudiño followed a template and built the kiln on site. She had to accommodate firing chambers and fuel boxes in order for the kiln to fire effectively. If kiln building is an area you are interested in, the most basic of kilns can be made from a metal dustbin or even an old supermarket trolley lined with ceramic fibre.

Catrin Howell

Dryslwyn 2016
Red and black terracotta clay
30 × 28 × 8 cm (11⅘ × 11 × 3 in.)

Animal mythology and the interpretation of ancient symbolism are constant themes in Catrin Howell's beautifully modelled work. As she explains, 'I am fascinated by animals and the way they are used to convey narratives. From the roles they play in mythology, as iconic symbols, and their ability to trigger memories and emotion. I am drawn to myth because it allows the impossible to happen; challenging perceptions by playing with assumptions of the real and the supposed.' A strong influence on Howell's practice is the *Mabinogion*, a collection of eleven prose stories based on medieval Welsh manuscripts. Howell is interested in the portrayal of animals as the hero and recurring themes such as metamorphosis and transformation. This source of inspiration led her to create shape-shifting creatures in hybrid forms, questioning our understanding of what is true and what is not.

Dryslwyn (Welsh for 'thicket') appeals to the imagination. Hidden within the dense scrub, a beast – part hare, part hound – lies poised and alert. There is a desperate feeling of suspense and tension, as if a dramatic scene of survival is just about to unfold. Howell has cleverly engineered this lingering sense of danger and anticipation with an array of subtle visual clues, including the pricked position of the beast's ears and the slight tilt of the head peering through the entangled branches. The spiky thicket conceals the creature, making it inaccessible and offering a place of safe retreat. Another striking feature of this piece is the emptiness of the creature's eye socket. The dark void bears an eerie presence, yet the creature remains characterful and highly expressive.

Catrin Howell (British, born 1969) was brought up on a farm in Ceredigion, Wales. She studied ceramics at the Royal College of Art in London and the University of Wolverhampton. Howell draws inspiration from Welsh folktales and myths, exploring ideas around metamorphosis and transformation. Animals feature prominently in her work. She employs a hand-building technique to make figures of beasts akin to hounds, deer and hares that are hybrids of the real and the fantastical. She has won various prizes, including a Fletcher Challenge Merit Award (New Zealand, 1994) and the gold medal for Craft and Design at the National Eisteddfod of Wales in 1999.

See also
The Martin Brothers (p.170)
Mo Jupp (p.178)
Claire Curneen (p.196)

Material
As illustrated so effectively in *Dryslwyn*, Howell has used a very simple combination of two contrasting earthenware clay bodies to represent the opposing elements of the composition (figure and thicket). The rawness of the unglazed surface relates to the naturalistic wildness of the creature itself and the habitat in which it resides. Howell made the creature by carefully pinching out clay into a thin, hollow form. Drops of glaze fuse the animal and branches together.

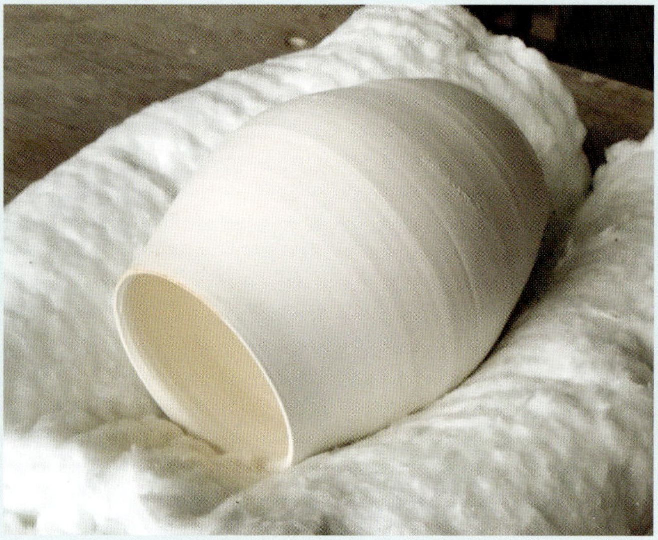

Process
Howell built this piece from component parts. The branches were made individually and assembled around the creature. When constructing a fragile work, consider building your piece around a supporting armature. It may help to lay the piece on a large sponge block, packed out with crumpled balls of newspaper. Another tip is to build directly on a kiln shelf and/or ceramic fibre blanket to enable you to transfer the piece to the kiln without disturbing the form.

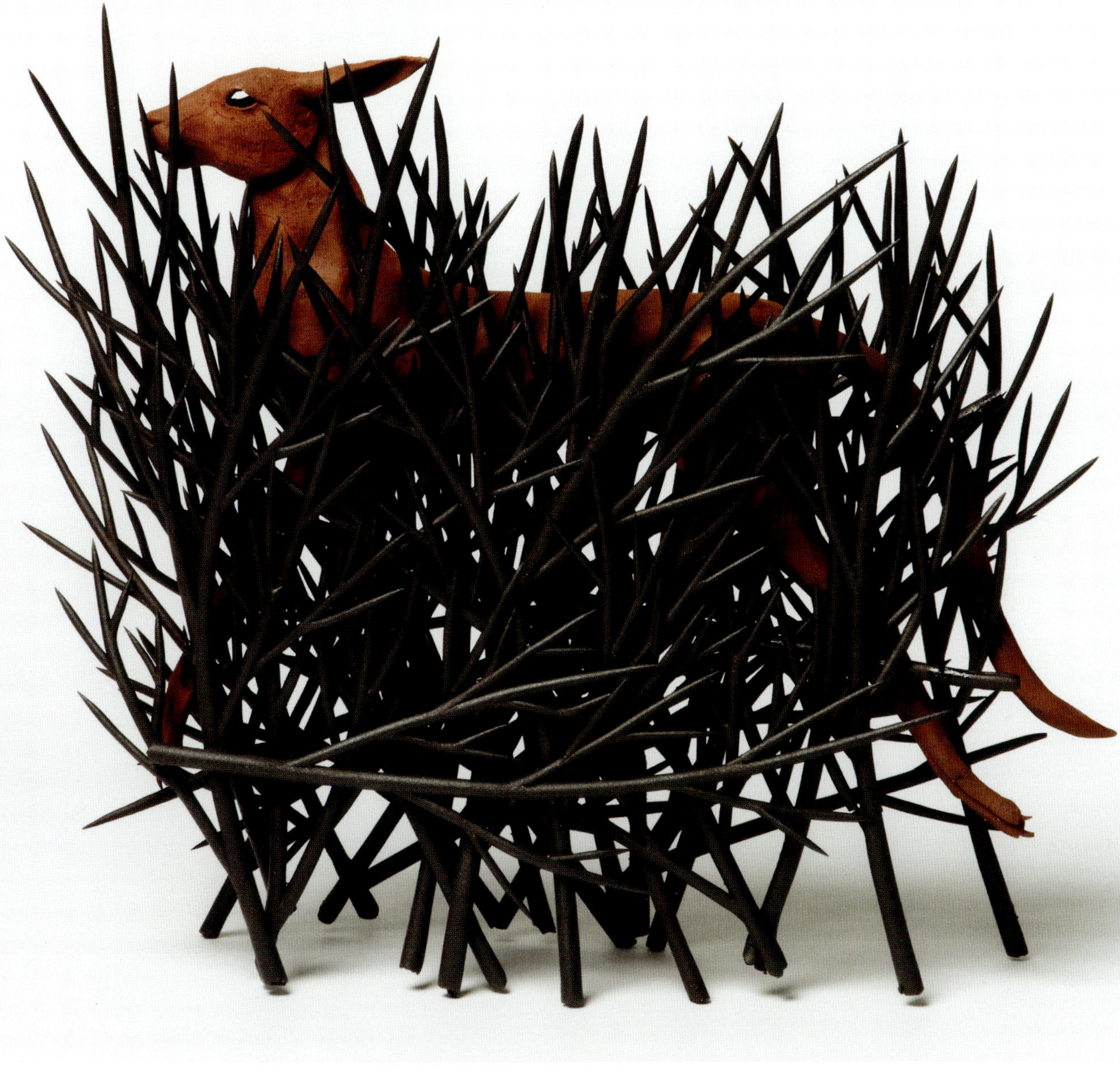

Sergei Isupov

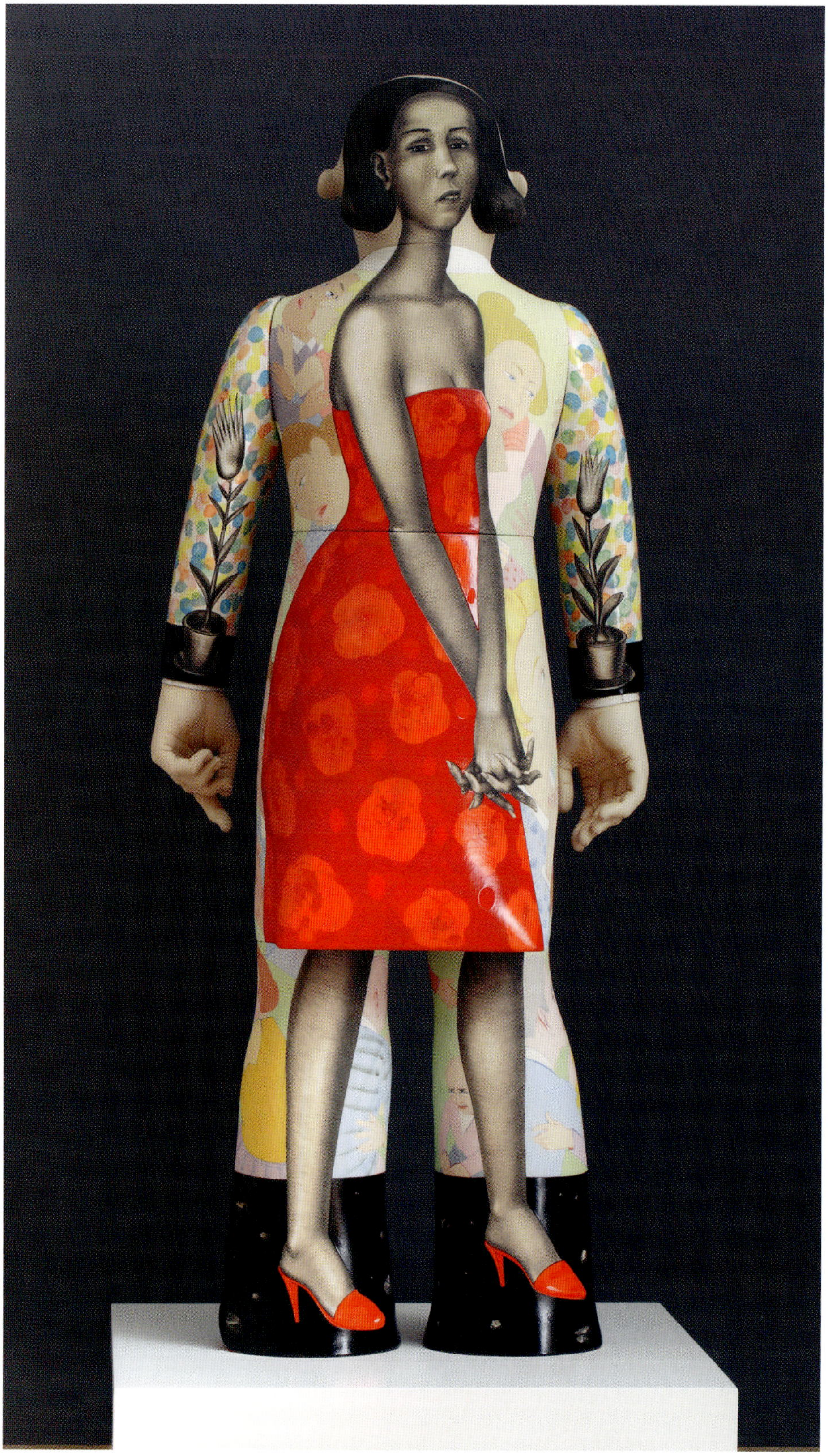

Risen 2016
Stoneware, slip, glaze
243.8 × 101.6 × 50.8 cm (96 × 40 × 20 in.)

Towering at a colossal 2.4 metres (8 feet) tall, *Risen* by Sergei Isupov is an impressive figurative sculpture in the form of a standing male. Within his silhouette there is a painting of a young woman wearing a red strapless dress. Her body language appears anxious – her arms are crossed and her fingers are fidgety. Her gaze seems absent, as if she is troubled by her thoughts. Behind her are a number of smaller illustrations that depict a narrative of romance, betrayal and emotional exchanges between the couple.

The viewer is encouraged to walk around the sculpture, and on the other side the story deepens. A man in just his underwear is pleading, with his hands clasped, looking up to the main character (standing male). Could this be a sordid affair or bitter love triangle between the characters? Isupov leaves this question open for the viewer's own interpretation, explaining his motivations: 'My work portrays characters placed in situations that are drawn from my imagination but based on my life experiences. My artworks capture a composite of fleeting moments, hand gestures, eye movements that follow and reveal the sentiments expressed.'

Isupov's work is often compared to the dreamy worlds of surrealist artists Salvador Dalí (1904–89) and René Magritte (1898–1967). This can certainly be felt in the way Isupov has achieved a graphical, stylized quality in his paintings, and in the interplay between the two-dimensional content and three-dimensional form. The scene-within-a-scene concept brings great depth to the work, allowing Isupov's investigation of the human condition to be told through rich and complex surfaces.

Sergei Isupov (Russian, born 1963) comes from an artistic family and was trained from an early age as a painter. His father Vladimir and brother Ilya are painters; his mother Nelli is a sculptor working in ceramics. Sergei studied art and ceramics at the Ukrainian State Art School in Kiev and the Art Institute of Tallinn, Estonia. He emigrated to the United States in 1994. He works in porcelain using traditional hand-building and sculpting techniques that combine surface and form with narrative painting. He is known for his figurative pieces, such as the *Androgyny Heads* (2008) series. He continues to create painted heads that draw upon religious iconography and indigenous art traditions with surreal, and sometimes disquieting, results.

See also
Pablo Picasso (p.172)
Viola Frey (p.174)
Shary Boyle (p.194)

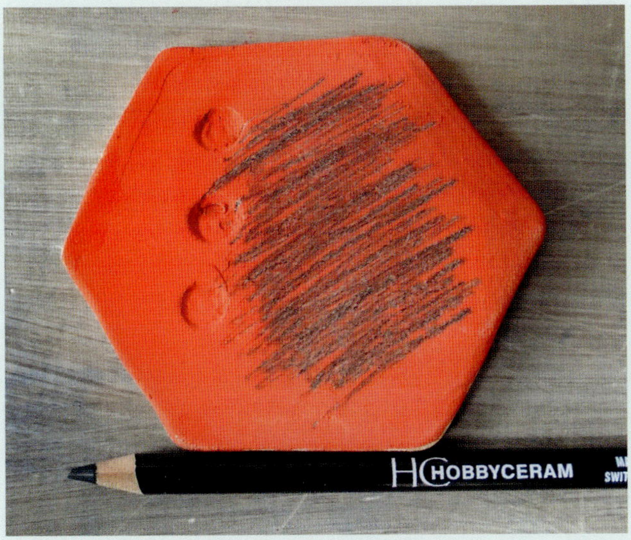

Surface
Isupov accentuates light and shadow through his use of sketchy graphite lines. This contrasts boldly with the bright colours, giving the illusion that the figures are three-dimensional. To achieve illustrative qualities in your own work, underglaze pencils and crayons are brilliant for drawing outlines and shading. They can be purchased (or made, see p.176) in a range of colours but, unlike conventional colouring pencils, they do not burn away when fired and can even be used in conjunction with glaze.

Technical
Isupov hand built the figure from stoneware clay in several interlocking sections. This enabled him to achieve the huge size of the figure without compromising due to the restraints of the kiln. When displaying work on this scale it's wise to have an internal frame made from a strong material, such as steel, that your components can slot over and be secured to, including a fixed base, hidden from view. Use this as a way to counterlever or support complex works.

Tip Toland

Beauty Parlour 2017
Stoneware clay, paint, chalk pastel, synthetic hair
Length: 91 cm (36 in.)

The uncanny and incredibly lifelike figures of Tip Toland explore themes concerned with the essence of humanity, the vulnerabilities and the fragilities of the human condition. Her subjects are typically either very young or very old, which means, as Toland says, 'they both can portray innocence as well as extreme complexity'. With an autobiographical narrative (and likeness), this piece portrays a tender moment when the artist's young goddaughter played hairdressers using Toland as the model. The expression held within the face is resigned, eyes closed, with a slight upturn at the corners of the mouth suggesting that the character is enjoying the interaction. Decorated with an array of cutesy clips and intricate plaits and ponytails, the sculpture conveys undertones of sentiment and humour, prompting the viewer to reflect on their own cherished experiences and memories.

To create her convincing figures, Toland first starts drawing from a life model or herself. Using a stoneware clay, she constructs the head or figure around an armature made from plumbing pipe. She uses this to take all her measurements off and help gauge proportions accurately as she builds. Toland brings character to the figure by carefully defining the bone structure, wrinkles, teeth and facial features. Once the piece is complete, she cuts it into segments, hollows it out and removes the armature before firing. Toland mimics the subtle sheen of skin and flesh by using an encaustic technique involving hot wax and pigment. This is further enhanced with flecks of paint and chalk to heighten the realistic nature of her subject.

Tip Toland (American, born 1950) is a ceramic artist and sculptor based in Seattle, USA. Toland studied ceramics at the University of Colorado, Boulder, receiving her bachelor's degree in 1975. This was followed by a master's degree from Montana State University in Bozeman in 1981. As her career progressed and she became more interested in the figure, Toland attended sculpting classes based on classical observational training at the Gage Academy in Seattle. She has received many prestigious accolades, including an Artist Trust GAP grant and the Virginia A. Groot Foundation Grant. Toland splits her time between her studio and teaching workshops across the United States and internationally.

See also

Robert Arneson (p.176)
Marilyn Levine (p.204)
Bertozzi & Casoni (p.228)

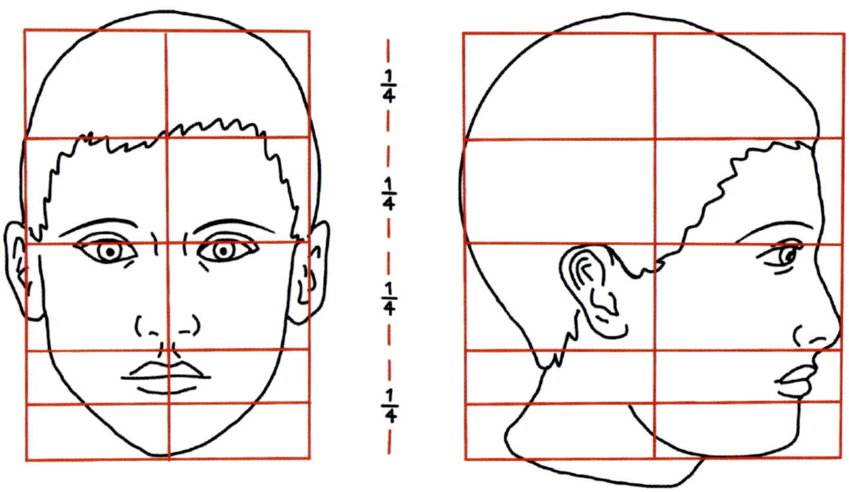

Technical
When sculpting a head, follow these basic principles. Take the length and width measurements of your subject's head and divide it into quarters. Divide the bottom quarter into two parts again to obtain the proportion of the lips in relation to the chin. Following the grid system, align the tops of the ears with the eyelids and the tip of the nose with the bottom of the ears. The forehead and eyebrows should reside in the top two quarters of the grid.

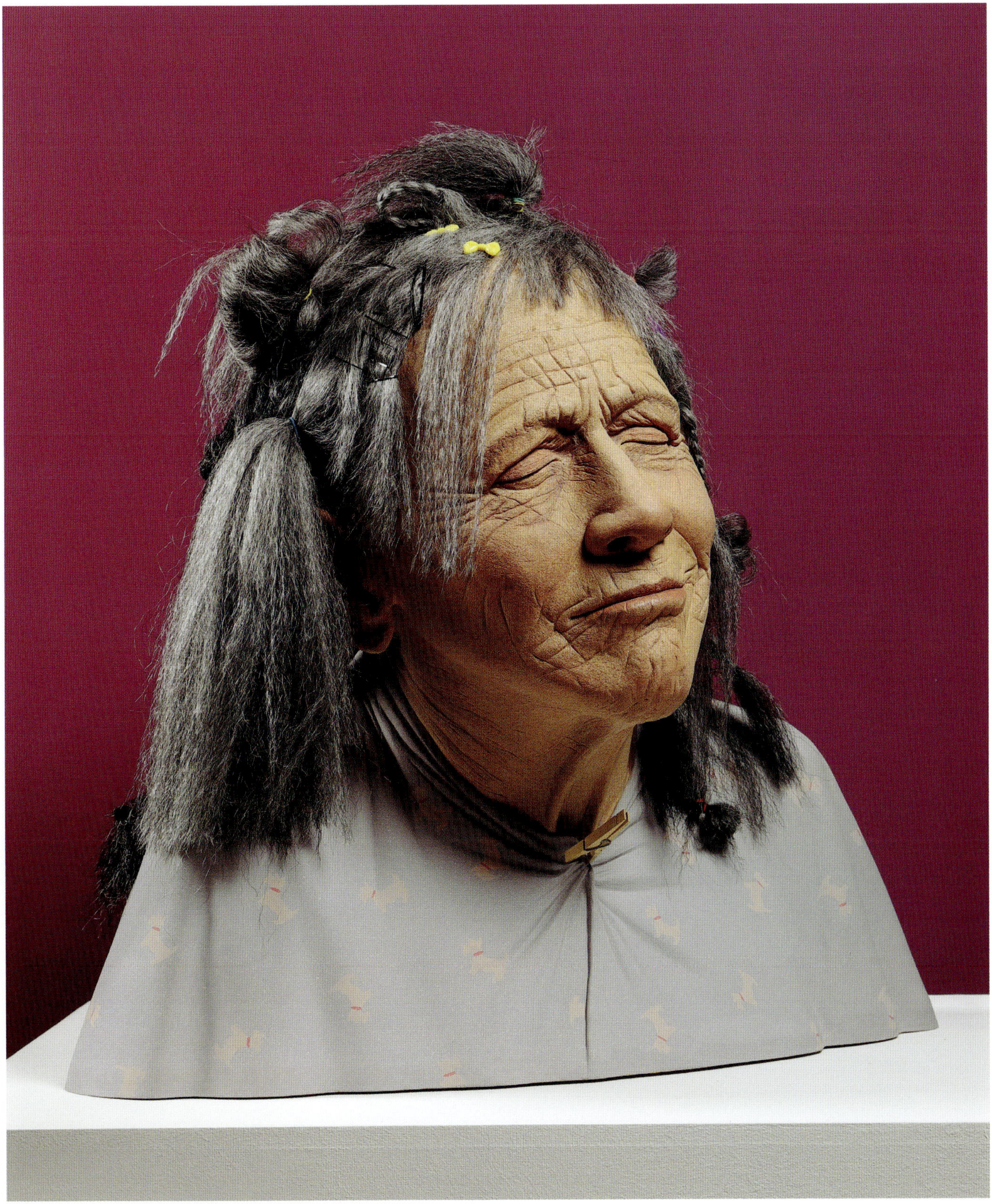

Ramesh Mario Nithiyendran

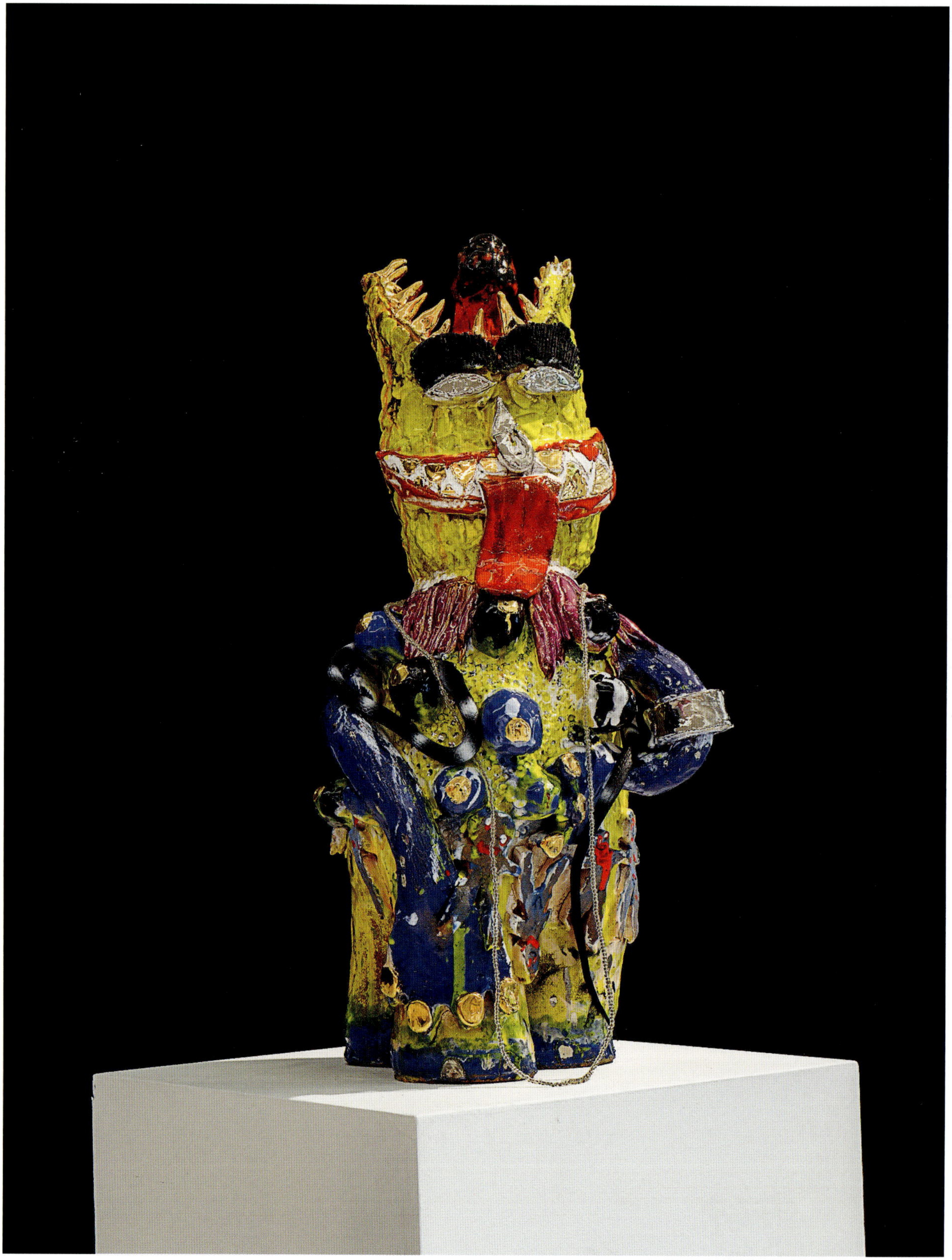

Snake Charmer 2018
Earthenware, glaze, lustre and rubber snake
75 × 37 × 32 cm (29½ × 14½ × 12⅗ in.)

Ramesh Mario Nithiyendran creates garish, rough-edged 'new-age idols', which explore the politics of sex, the monument, gender identity and religious iconography. Self-portraiture and self-representation are recurrent themes in his work. A staunch atheist, Nithiyendran draws upon his Hindu and Christian heritage as a reference, but not necessarily from the perspective of his own cultural identity as is so often assumed. Rather, a subject he researches is the cultural connotations of colour.

This vibrant, flamboyant figure, from the *R@MESH Volume II* series, beams with a toothy grin and cheeky demeanour. In this piece, the artist explores gender, popular culture, exoticism and outsider aesthetics. A set of jaws on the figure's head are held wide open and a phallus emerges from within. The figure's tongue sticks out quite indignantly, as if to say 'so what?' With this piece, Nithiyendran engages with the realms of gender fluidity and the non-binary aspect of his figures.

Nithiyendran formally trained as a painter and is a self-taught ceramicist – he considers himself as an artist who uses clay. He hand built this piece using coiling and slabbing techniques and freely decorated the surface with bold and varied glaze colours. The figure's nails, teeth and clothing have been further embellished with gold lustre, which brings a feeling of exuberance and opulence to the piece. The use of such lurid colour acts as a self-parody, but Nithiyendran also plays along with the idea of the artist as a brand in modern culture.

Ramesh Mario Nithiyendran (Australian, born 1988) was born in Colombo, Sri Lanka, and a year later his family moved to Australia. Nithiyendran studied at the College of Fine Arts, University of New South Wales. In 2015 he won the premier national award for ceramicists, the Sidney Myer Fund Australian Ceramic Art Award. He creates figurative sculptures that experiment with form and scale and explore themes of sexual politics, the monument, gender and religion. When he exhibited his mixed-media installation of five large-scale sculptures, *Mud Men*, at the National Gallery of Australia in Canberra in 2016, he became the youngest artist ever to hold a solo show at the gallery.

See also
Elisabeth Kley (p.74)
Brian Rochefort (p.128)
Pablo Picasso (p.172)

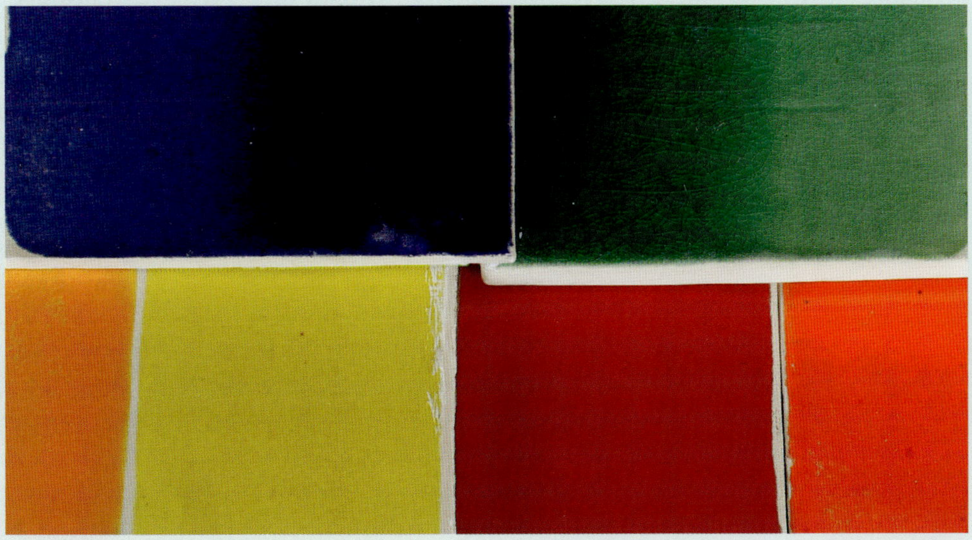

Material
The surface of this piece is a riot of clashing hues and brash tones. The result is so over the top and flamboyant – but its garishness works visually. Experiment with mixing bright glaze stains in qualities of 8-10% into a transparent base glaze (earthenware will provide the best results). In your decoration, you could combine vivid pink with citric orange or try overlapping a bright green against an electric blue colour for startling effect.

Kim Simonsson

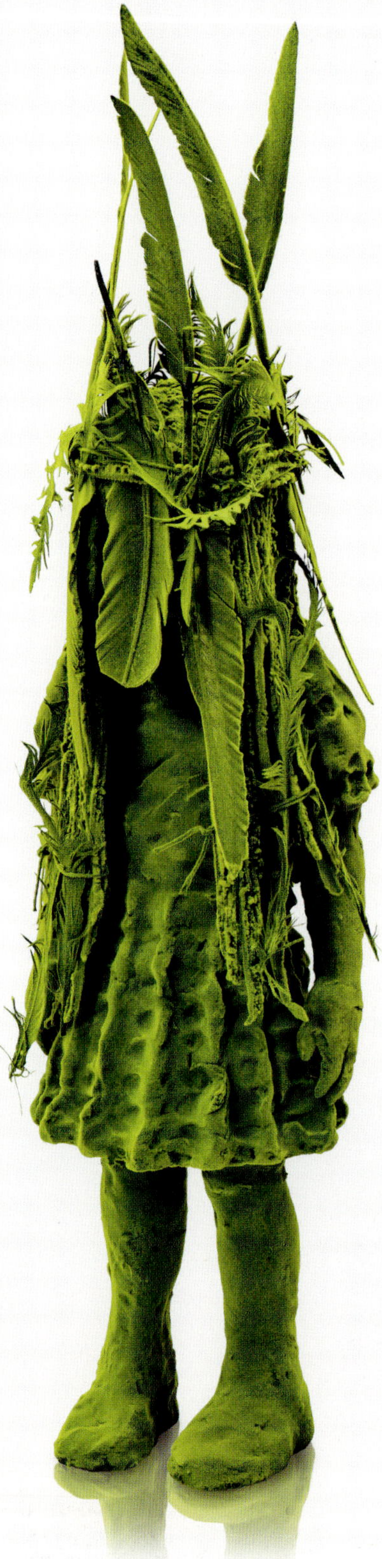

Moss Girl with Feathers 2018

Ceramics, feathers, rope, nylon fibre
115 × 45 × 45 cm (45¼ × 17¾ × 17¾ in.)

Kim Simonsson imagines a post-apocalyptic world, one hundred years in the future, where only young, prepubescent children have survived. They are self-reliant and have had to quickly adapt to this strange and unforgiving domain. Simonsson refers to these camouflaged characters as *Moss People*, explaining, 'The moss-green figures blend perfectly into their natural surroundings, just as a soft carpet of moss covers the ground, rocks and tree trunks and acts as a sort of protection. In the Moss People world, lost and disconnected children, evoking different characters, gather in a Shaman Party, choose leaders and end up creating false idols.' Simonsson draws inspiration from an eclectic range of sources: from Nordic fairy tales and folklore to *Mad Max Beyond Thunderdome*, the 1985 dystopian action film. What unites all these themes is an interest in fantastical, subversive narratives that comment on societal collapse and the disruption of normality.

Lifelike in stature, *Moss Girl with Feathers* stands quietly, her arms and hands held loosely as if she is trying to blend into her surroundings to avoid being noticed. Her face is obscured by her long, dishevelled hair and feathered headdress – adding an element of intrigue to her persona. The dainty little dress she wears evokes sweetness and innocence, but this is starkly contrasted by her feathered headpiece, which implies she is part of a tribe. Although the character appears mysterious, she is not evil – but rather, a solitary type who has to protect and assert her place in this unruly, adult-less world.

Kim Simonsson (Finnish, born 1974) studied at the University of Art and Design in Helsinki. In 2004 he was the recipient of the Tampere Art Museum's Young Artist of the Year prize and was invited to work as guest artist for the Arabia Art Department Society – a society of Finnish ceramic artists. Simonsson's output is influenced by traditional Nordic storytelling, including the fairy tales of Danish writer Hans Christian Andersen (1805–75) and the paintings of Norwegian artist Edvard Munch (1863–1944). His ceramic sculptures are usually sleek and smooth, but he is also known for his series of life-size figures, *Moss People* (2015), which he created using a technique that combines stoneware, paint and green nylon fibre, giving the figures a mossy surface.

See also
Malene Hartmann Rasmussen (p.106)
Kiho Kang (p.148)
Daphne Corregan (p.180)

Surface
Kim Simonsson achieved convincing mossy colour and texture on his sculptures by experimenting with a process called 'flocking'. He coated the entire piece with a black paint, and then proceeded to overspray it with electrically charged neon-yellow nylon fibres. Flocking is a process that you can do yourself with the right equipment and safety gear; an easier option is to source a specialized company who will do this for you.

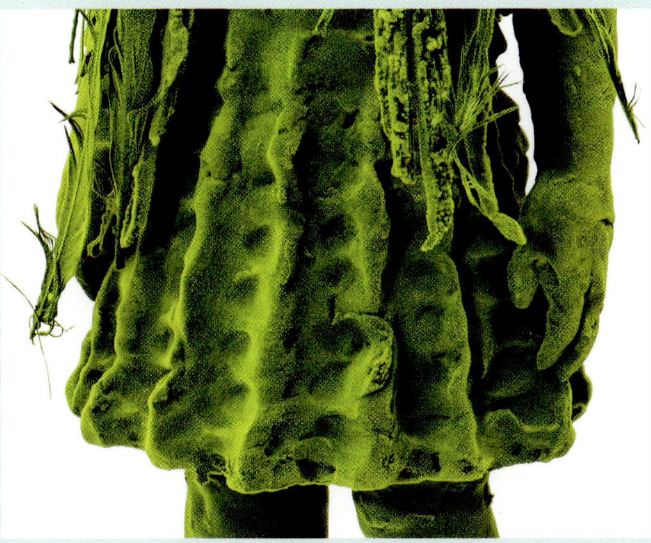

Technical
Simonsson deliberately left the surface quite textured and expressive. Pummel marks from his hands and fingers can be seen on the clay surface, which adds to the roughness of the character's composition. The sculpture was fired to 1200°C (2192°F), painted and then flocked with nylon fibre. The velvet quality of the flock accentuates the loose texture of the figure by projecting dramatic shadows and highlights over its contours.

Shary Boyle

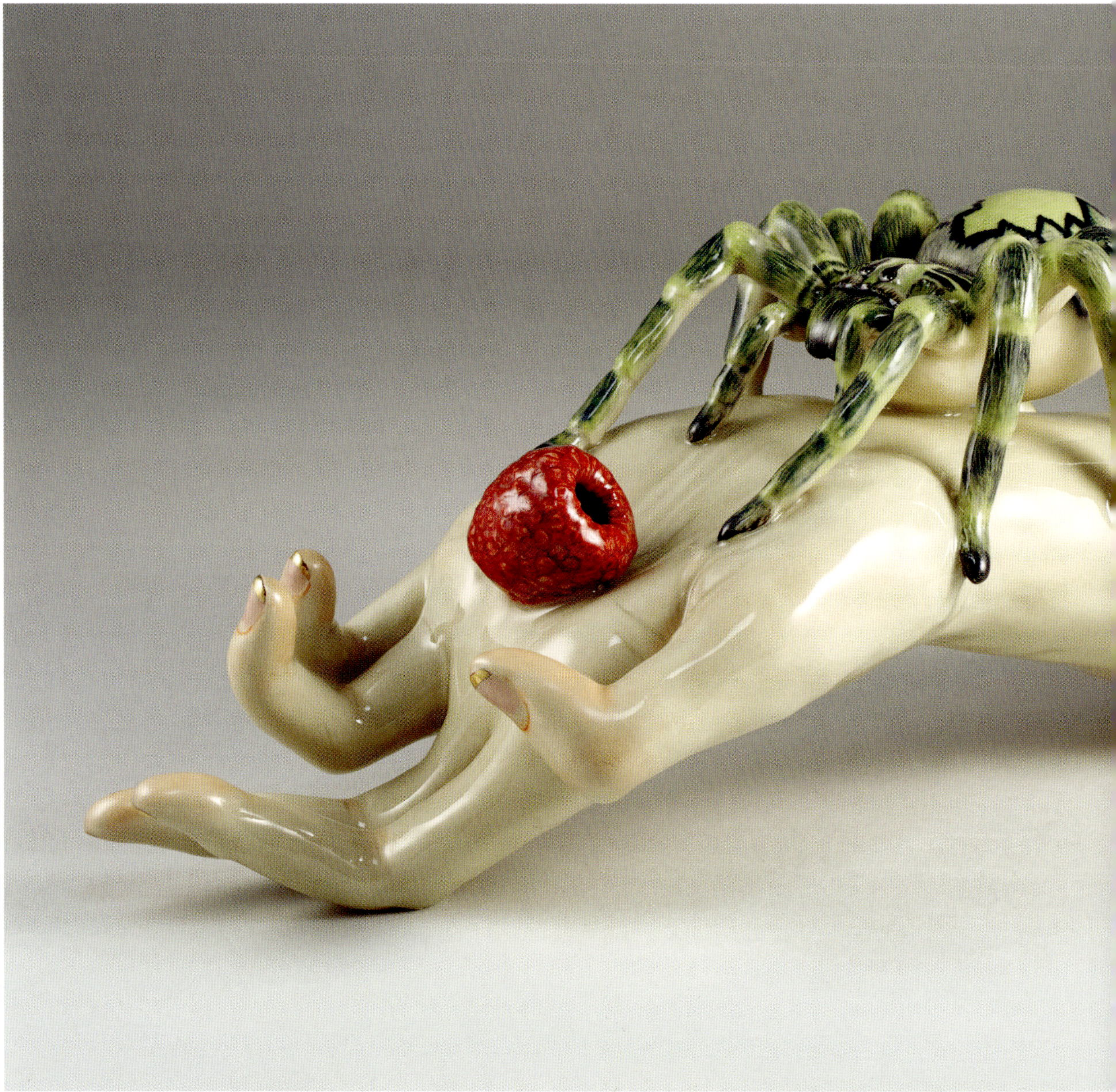

See also

Claire Curneen (p.196), **Jessica Stoller** (p.248)

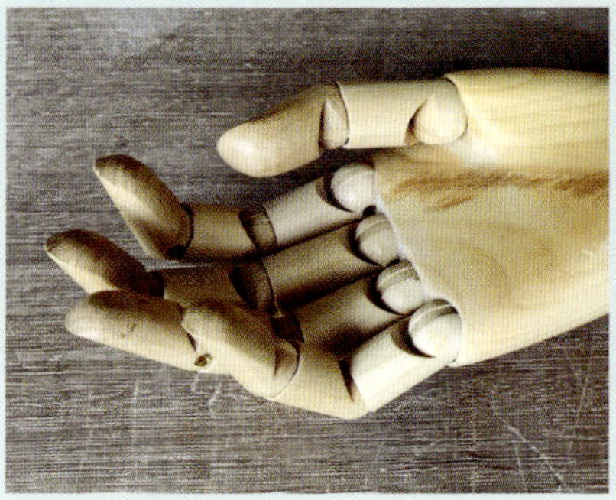

Shary Boyle (Canadian, born 1972) graduated from Ontario College of Art. She is a visual artist who works across various media, including sculpture, painting, performance and drawing. Boyle is best known for her porcelain figurines that explore themes of gender and sexuality. She came to prominence with her series *Lace Figures* in 2006, for which she used commercial moulds and traditional porcelain lace techniques to examine the historical relationship between decoration and women. She has garnered numerous plaudits, including the Gershon Iskowitz Prize in 2009 and the Hnatyshyn Foundation Award in 2010. She represented Canada with her project *Music for Silence* at the 55th Venice Biennale in 2013.

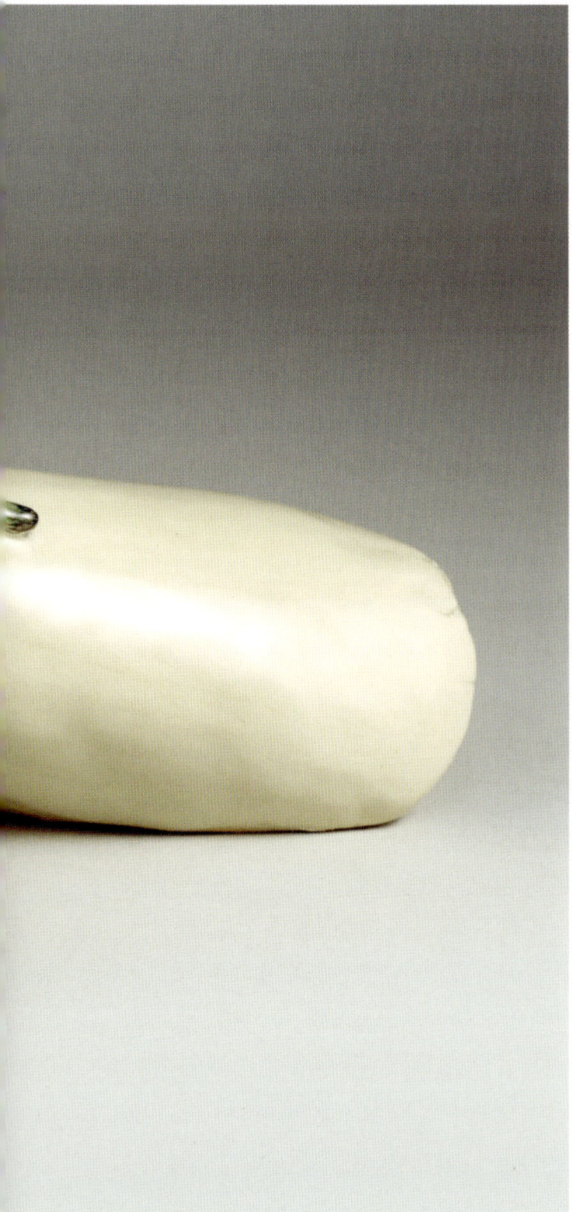

Raspberry 2019
Porcelain, china paint, gold lustre
50 × 20 × 20 cm (19⅗ × 7⅘ × 7⅘ in.)

Contemporary visual artist Shary Boyle works across a broad range of media. Focusing on the human figure, Boyle is drawn to the fragility of ceramics to convey confrontational and revealing themes that explore gender, identity and social history narratives. Boyle makes all her pieces by hand, the process being an integral part of her practice.

Boyle's interest in the fantastical and surreal is reflected in this transgressive piece, entitled *Raspberry*. A giant tarantula creeps towards a succulent raspberry that waits in the palm of an open hand. Boyle has embedded allusions to religious iconography in the piece, which are revealed as we study it in more depth. The position and style of the sculpted hand were inspired by the ecstatic hand gestures of medieval Christian 'stigmata' paintings. These commonly depict a saint with palms upturned or held out in front to show bodily wounds in locations corresponding to the crucifixion of Christ. This notion is further supported by the position of the raspberry within the palm and its intense blood-red colour.

Ultimately, the tension within this artwork lies between the tarantula – a creature closely associated with our darkest fears and phobias, but so often misunderstood – and the raspberry, a symbol of healthy desire and pleasure. The work evokes an array of complex emotions, from sexual desire, fear and repulsion to repression. The tarantula represents these dark desires we might hold or try to contain, but the lure of the delicious fruit is too hard to resist as we surrender to its sweet offering.

Technical

Sculpting a hand or digits can be a very challenging task to complete using clay. Fingers can easily appear limp and lack any sense of convincing movement. Here, Boyle has skilfully modelled the fingers of her piece to appear elongated and slim. The result is very stylized and reduces the need to be exacting in anatomical terms. When sculpting a hand, it can be useful to refer to an artist's model or sketches from life to help you gauge proportions and positions. Begin by modelling the basic shape in soft clay – but don't worry about being too accurate at this stage, as you can refine the profile when leather-hard using wooden modelling tools to add texture and detail. Support fingers with wads of tissue beneath and between each one to retain their fragile shape and prevent cracking.

Surface

Boyle uses china painting techniques to decorate her works. She completed this piece using the traditional method of crushing pigments into clove oil and lavender oils to act as a medium to bind the colour. China paints (enamels) can give strong vibrancy to a piece at low firing temperatures of 600–850°C (1112–1562°F). Boyle also added touches of gold lustre to the tip of each fingernail.

Claire Curneen

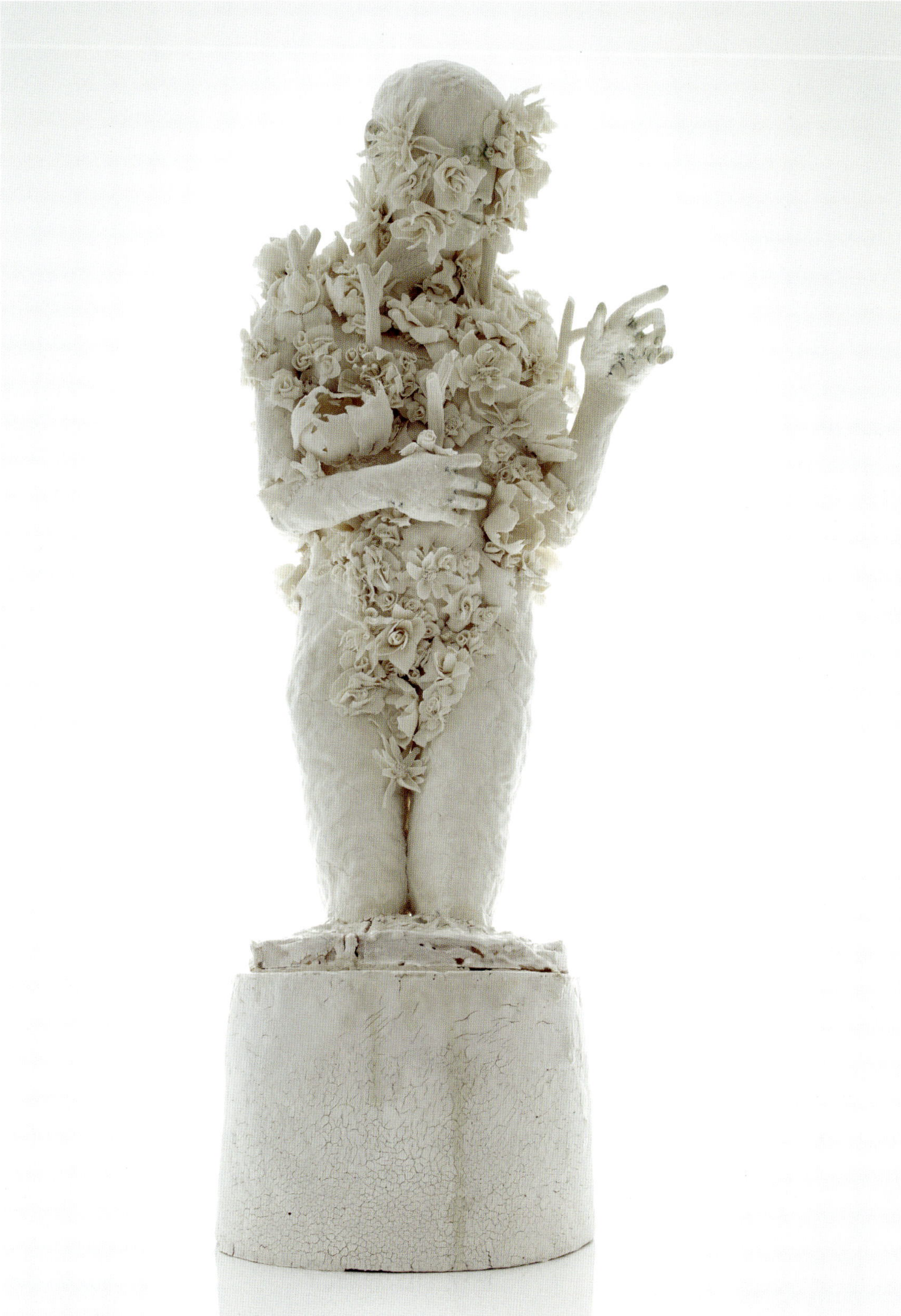

Still Life 2019
Porcelain, glaze, oxide
98 × 40 × 30 cm (38½ × 15¾ × 11⅘ in.)

The figurative sculptures of Claire Curneen make manifest enigmatic, serene and poignant reflections on humanity. Through her ethereal depictions, Curneen explores profound themes, including loss, suffering and rebirth. As the artist explains, 'My work with the figure is grounded in the exploration of the human condition, focusing on aspects of the religious and the ceremonial. With semi-autobiographical references, the figure serves as a vessel for the physical and spiritual being.'

An important aspect of Curneen's approach is her sensitive use of porcelain. She exploits its precious, translucent virtues to express the nuances and complexities of the human disposition. This piece makes a subtle reference to the Welsh *Mabinogion* legend of *Blodeuwedd*, the 'woman made of flowers'. Curneen explores the notion of the flower as an emblem full of pathos and loss – a signifier of life and death.

The position and stance of the figure encapsulates a divine presence. An abundance of flora and foliage creep and engulf the resigned figure as she accepts her inevitable transformation. From within her torso branches sprout and emerge, suggesting the potential for regeneration or something new to happen. This influence originates from Curneen's interest in the Greek mythical tale of the naiad Daphne, who is turned into a laurel tree as she flees the god Apollo. Through this piece, Curneen has conveyed a feeling of transcendence. The figure appears mournful and elegiac; the overarching message is one of positivity and hope.

Claire Curneen (Irish, born 1968) studied at Crawford College of Art and Design in Cork, Ulster University in Belfast and the University of Wales Institute in Cardiff. From 1999 to 2000 Curneen undertook a residency at the Crawford Arts Centre at the University of Saint Andrews in Scotland. The human figure is central to her work and at Saint Andrews she focused on Catholic depictions of martyrdom and the saints. Her highly stylized ceramic figures often draw on Christian iconography and imagery from the early Italian Renaissance. She uses floral patterns and gold lustre – found on mass-produced crockery – to reference the everyday.

See also
Mo Jupp (p.178)
Kim Simonsson (p.192)
Shary Boyle (p.194)

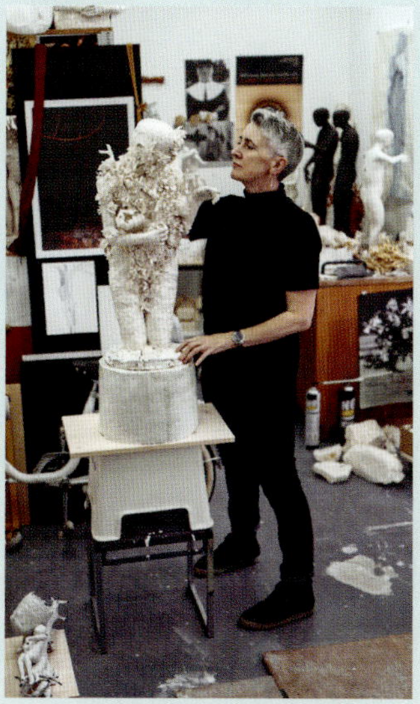

Process
Curneen constructed the figure from thin pads of porcelain, which she made by smearing and pressing the clay between her hands and fingers. She built the form freely and the joins and overlaps of the making process are deliberately left visible, mimicking skin-like qualities and enhancing the apparent fragility of the figure's character. The paper-thin flowers that adorn the figure were individually modelled and applied to the surface in the green state.

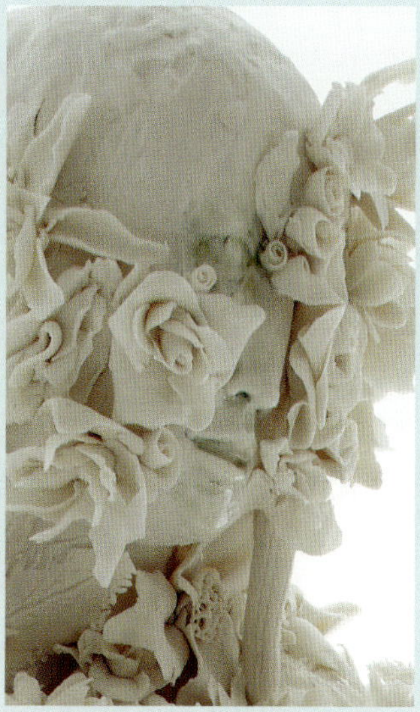

Surface
Curneen has enhanced the hands and facial features by applying a light touch of black stain mixed with red iron oxide. This was followed by applying a transparent stoneware glaze on top. This process has created an inky, tonal effect that reinforces the figure's haunting presence. Light dabs and rubs of oxide mixture can bring greater depth to your work without running the risk of overpowering the details with a heavy glaze colour.

Carolein Smit

Bello Tattoo Hond 2019
Earthenware with coloured glazes and lustre
70 × 32 × 63 cm (27½ × 12⅗ × 24⅘ in.)

Curiosity cabinets, scientific collections and museum displays of religious devotional items are all sources of inspiration for Dutch artist Carolein Smit, whose figurative works push the boundaries between what we view as adorable and sweet and the grotesque and uncomfortable. With its high level of refinement and endearing expression, this exuberant piece is reminiscent of a precious Meissen porcelain figurine. Smit wants you 'to love her sculptures', but says, 'At the same time I don't want to make this loving too easy. It's painful, fragile, unfulfilled, and sometimes dangerous.'

The rearing stance of *Bello* signifies power, but there is also an overarching feeling of melancholy implied by the animal's resigned and mournful gaze. The richly embellished fur and gilded collar seem to embody baroque opulence. On closer inspection we see that the skin and fur of the creature is actually made from hundreds of intricately moulded ornaments and trinkets (sourced by Smit from flea markets). From roaring lions and a heart motif to imprints of ornate brooches and flowers, the effect is captivating.

Smit draws upon biblical and mythological tales that caution against greed, vanity, power and impotence in her work. Here, amongst all the heavy decoration, on the hind leg of the creature, is a moulding of a skull. This is reminiscent of the 16th- and 17th-century *vanitas* tradition, which sought to symbolically represent the ideas of life and death and the passage of time through the imagery of skulls and decaying food. The richly detailed surfaces of the piece prompt us to contemplate our superficial material obsessions and the impermanence of our existence.

Carolein Smit (Dutch, born 1960) studied graphics and lithography at the Academy of Art and Design St Joost in Breda, the Netherlands. She worked as an illustrator for thirteen years before completing a residency at the European Ceramic Work Centre in Den Bosch in 1995; while there she became interested in working in clay. Smit is now based in Belgium and her highly detailed sculptural ceramics are inspired by fairy tales, myths and religious iconography. She is known for works that depict animals such as sheep, hares and dogs, often with symbolic significance referencing *memento mori* and *vanitas* paintings of the Dutch Golden Age.

See also
Claire Curneen (p.196)
Bertozzi & Casoni (p.228)
Barnaby Barford (p.266)

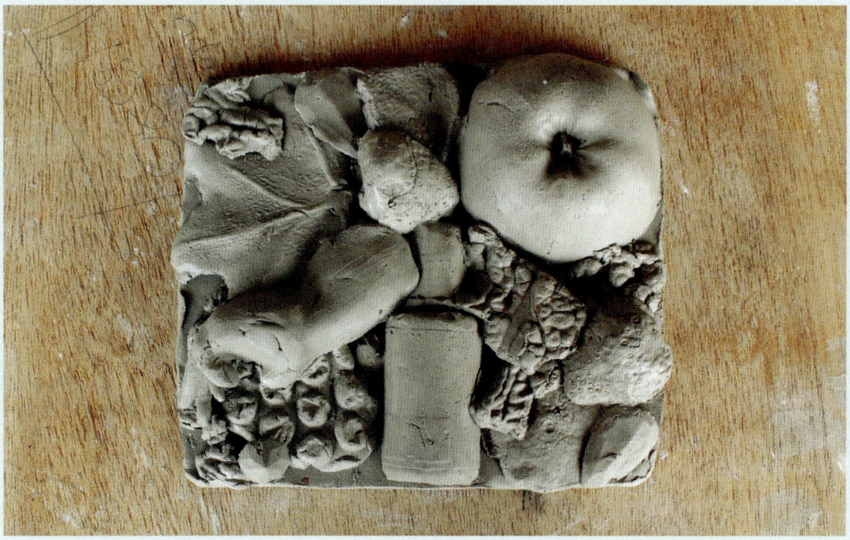

Technical
Smit constructed this piece using a fine-grogged white clay body. The added grit in the clay body provides strength, which allows Smit to build complex hollow structures. She then moulded and hand sculpted detailed embellishments to replicate skin and hair. These elements are all made separately, applied with slip and fused together by the glaze. The collage effect of intricate mouldings and sprigs layered on the body of the creature is very engaging. On this sample tile, simple moulds of found items such as fruits and leaves were made, and the clay casts were assembled freely as a lively composition.

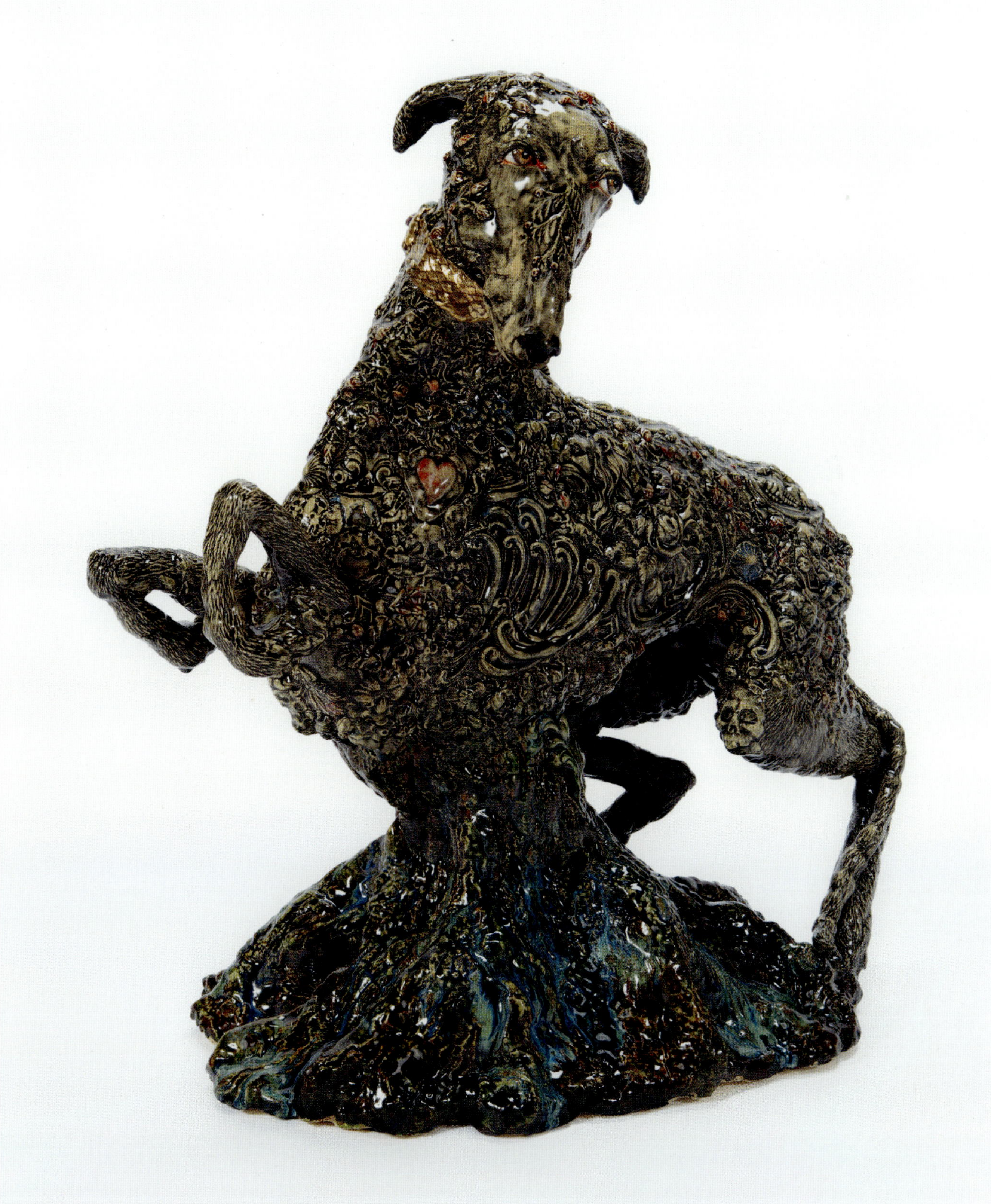

Conc

eptual

At the heart of all great artwork is an idea – a unique concept which drives the artist to explore and delve into new territories. 'Conceptual' doesn't necessarily mean you need to have a clever or 'out-there' idea. In fact, it can simply relate to the creative process – whereby personality and research interests are represented through the material, leading to a strong identity. The focus of this chapter centres around works that are predominantly one-off, either existing individually or as part of a series/line of enquiry.

This can be addressed in a number of ways, from a sculptural aspect as seen in the biomorphic forms of Ken Price (p.210) and the expressive works of Sterling Ruby (p.218), through to realistic, satirical works that skew our perception of reality, or comment on society in some way, such as

Richard Slee's carrot umbrella (p.216) or Bertozzi & Casoni's still-life portrayal of a consumed feast (p.228). You could explore scale, either incredibly large and dominating like Matt Wedel's entangled forms (p.226), or more intimately, such as the exquisite cup series by Ron Nagle (p.208). You may feel encouraged to take a material-led approach to your work, whereby you allow the material to respond and react to processes that are instigated by you, but the end result is completely left to chance – represented in the expanded works of Rafa Pérez (p.214) and Jongjin Park (p.234). Achieving movement and expression through the clay like Anne Marie Laurey's sensual forms (p.232) could be another source of investigation, or you could convey a personal narrative through the surface of the piece, as demonstrated by Vicky Lindo (p.240).

Marilyn Levine

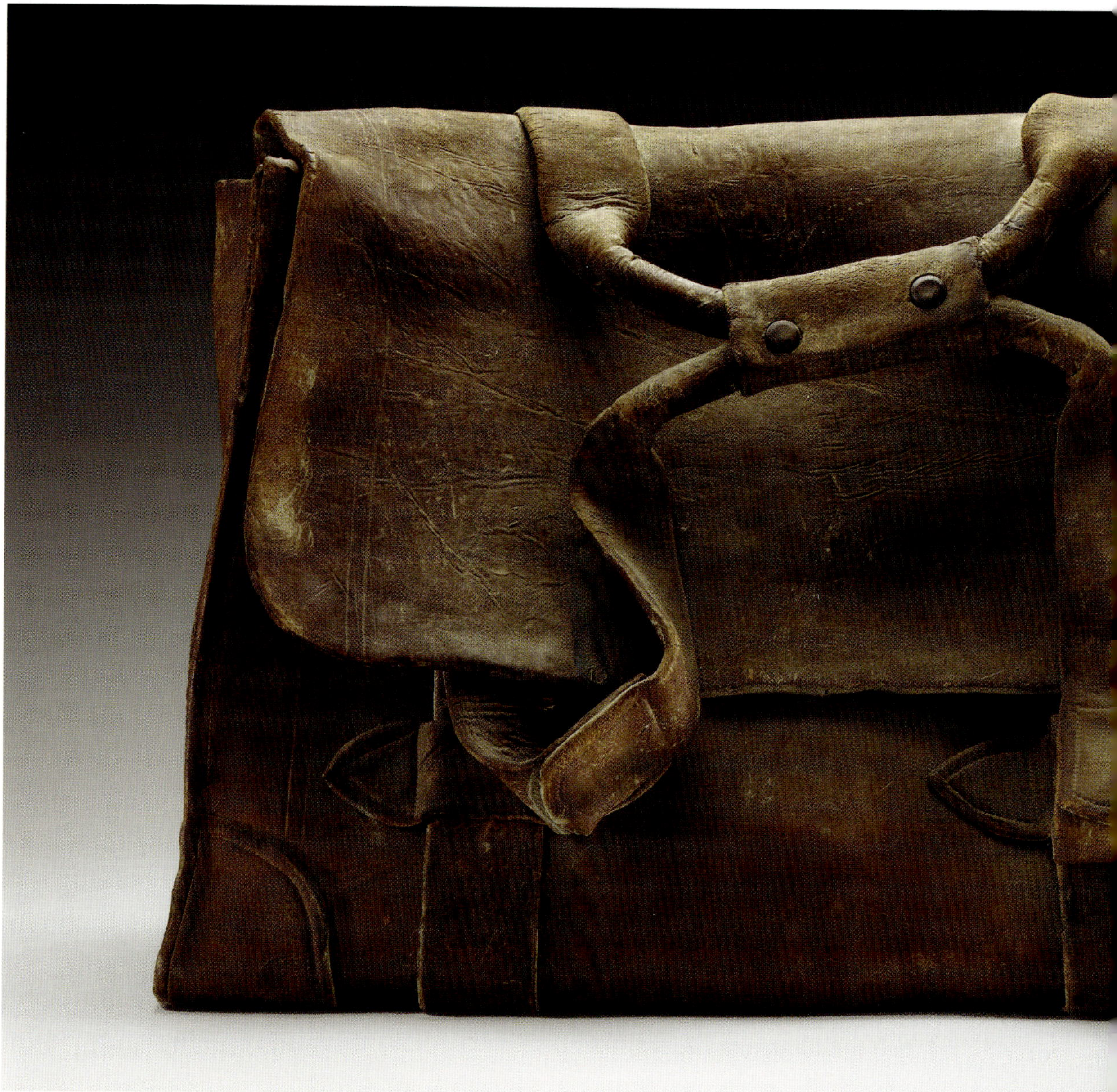

See also

Peter Voulkos (p.68), **Robert Arneson** (p.176), **Ron Nagle** (p.208)

Marilyn Levine (Canadian, 1935–2005) trained as a chemist and spent a number of years surveying geological rocks. Unable to find new work, Levine pursued her passion for the arts and enrolled at the University of Saskatchewan extension programme. There she learnt how to pot and, in 1968, received a travel grant to visit the University of California, Berkeley, where she was impressed by the work of Peter Voulkos, Robert Arneson and Ron Nagle. This prompted her to relocate to California in 1969 and study for a master's degree in ceramics at Berkeley. During the late 1960s and early 1970s Levine was introduced to the vibrant California Funk art scene, an emerging creative movement that was a reaction against the non-objectivity of abstract expressionism, creating works that were more figurative or 'real'.

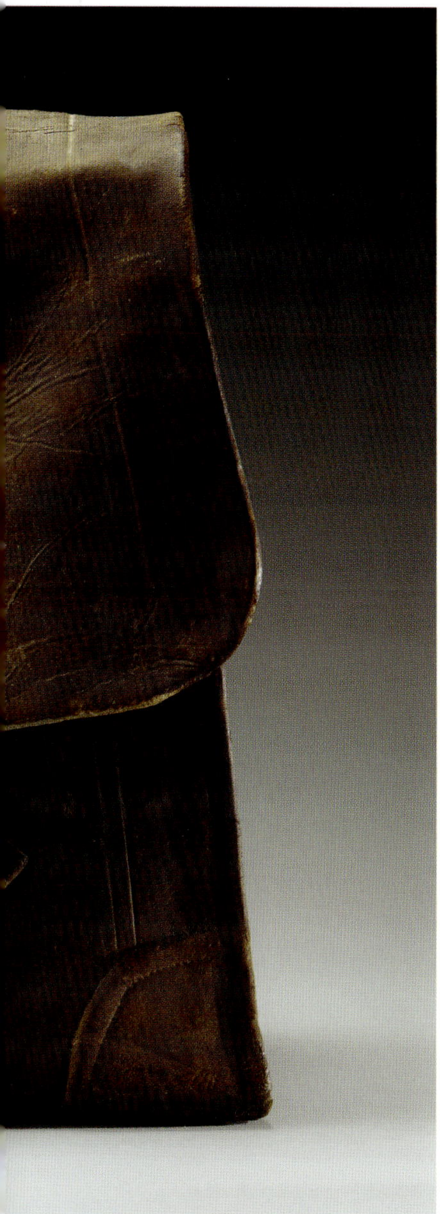

Flea Market Bag 1971
Stoneware and string
32.4 × 43.8 × 22.9 cm (12¾ × 17¼ × 9 in.)

The super-realistic works by Marilyn Levine convincingly imitate scuffed and worn leather bags, belts, boots and even jackets hanging loosely on hooks. The resemblance is truly uncanny and it is hard to believe the items are actually made from clay. This piece, *Flea Market Bag,* presents the illusion of a well-used bag, bearing the signs of the wear and tear of daily life. The sturdy handle slumps over the front of the bag, and has a sense of weight that implies it has just been placed down. There is a feeling of melancholy about this piece: creases, abrasions and the overall shabbiness of the leather record the transitions of time and communicate themes of human absence and loss.

Levine made her work by hand from slabs of stoneware clay. She exploited the versatile properties of clay by developing a process where she added finely cut nylon fibre to the clay to strengthen it; when the nylon burnt away during the firing, the resulting texture mimicked the wrinkly qualities of leather. Inside the bag form, she constructed a supporting structure of clay coils to brace the shape and prevent cracking. Details such as buckles and rivets were mostly made by Levine intricately carving them by hand, but occasionally she used a press mould if she required a specific component. The convincing leather colour was achieved by rubbing commercial stains and glazes onto the surface and firing to stoneware temperature. The pieces could take her many months to complete and involved incredible patience and a scrupulous eye for detail.

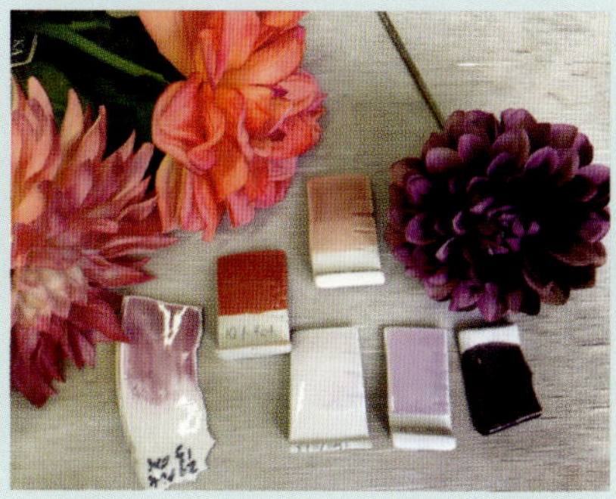

Subject Matter

To achieve the convincing realism of *Flea Market Bag*, Marilyn Levine carefully observed folds and creases of leather and understood how to depict the visual weight of the material in clay. When creating works that mimic real objects, accuracy and authenticity are key. Consider the scale and proportion of the object you are copying; analyse the feel, touch, weight and density and think about the colour of the item and how best to approach the glazing and surface finish. For example, plastic can be imitated by using a matt earthenware glaze; metallic surfaces, such as aluminium foil, can be replicated with platinum lustre; and stoneware glazes brushed with oxides are very good for mimicking organic items, such as fruit.

Paul Soldner

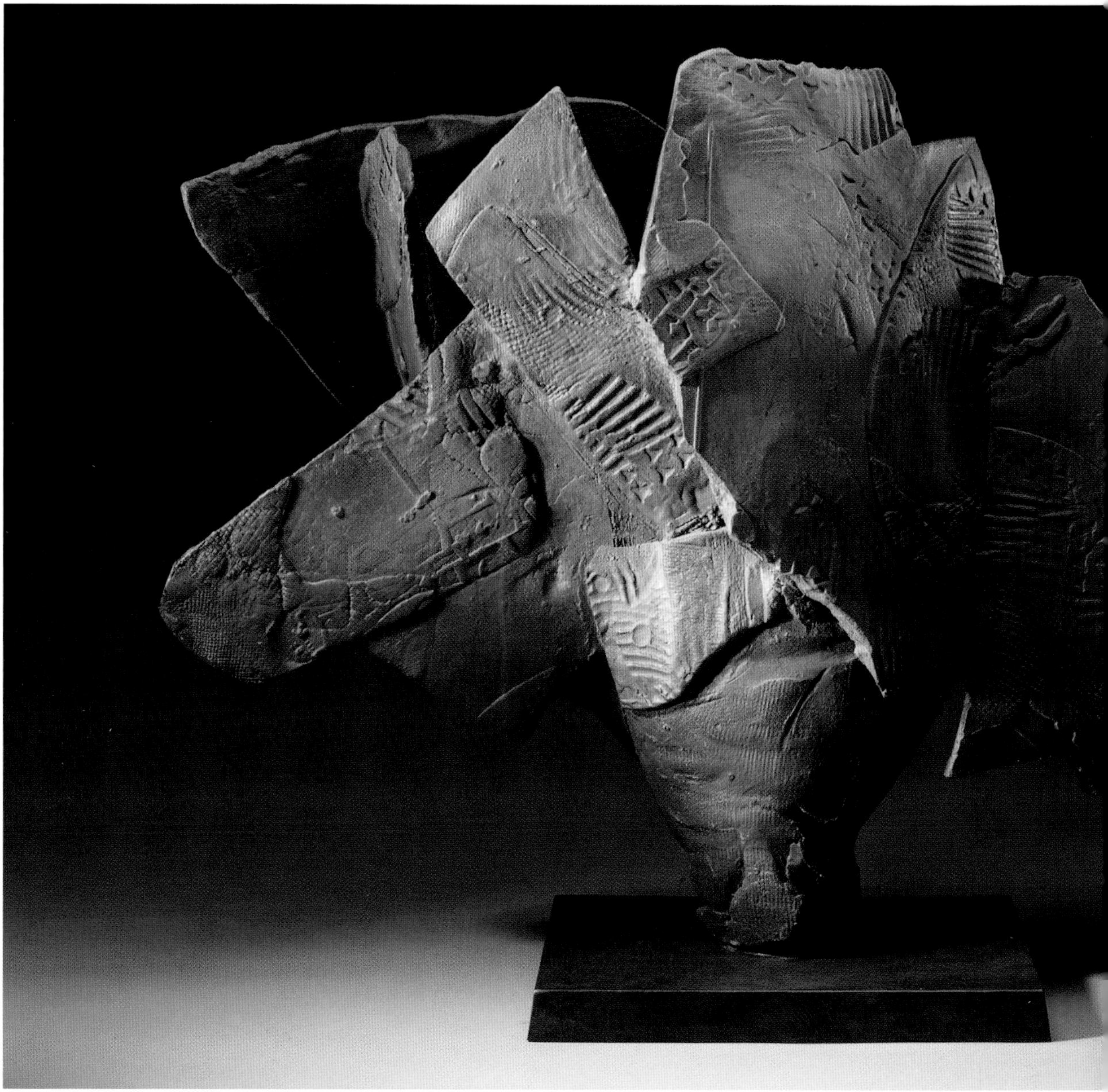

See also

Peter Voulkos (p.68), **Bernard Leach** (p.136), **Michelle Erickson** (p.212)

Paul Soldner (American, 1921–2011) initially served as a medic in the American army corps; however, after World War II, he decided he wanted to pursue his interest in art and sculpture and, in 1954, he enrolled at the Los Angeles County Art Institute (now Otis Art College of Art and Design) at which Peter Voulkos (1924–2002) had established a new ceramics programme. It was here that Soldner was influenced by abstract expressionism and explored clay as an expressive, gestural medium. Voulkos's dynamic and unrestrained approach to the material encouraged Soldner to follow his instincts and take risks with his work, leading him to develop experimental firing techniques. This earned Soldner a reputation as the 'father of American raku' for his innovative and ambitious use of the traditional Japanese low-firing technique and for inventing a new low-fire salt fuming method.

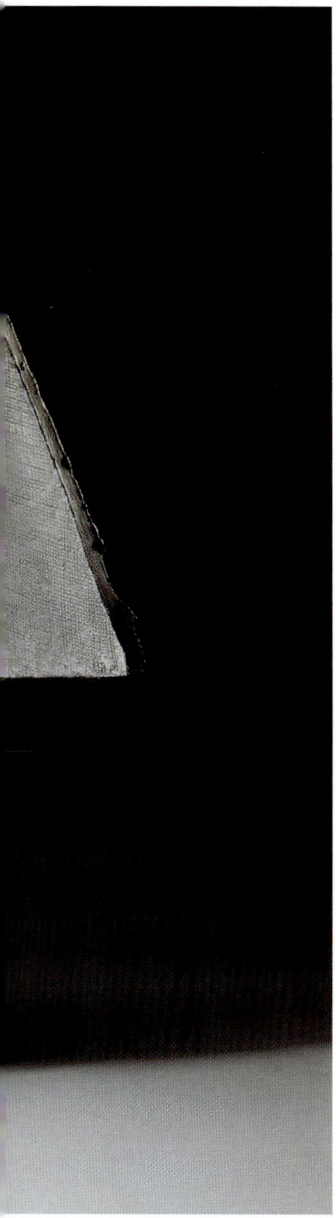

Pedestal Piece (87-6) 1987
Wheel-thrown and altered raku clay, copper slip, unglazed, low-temperature salt vapour fired
73 × 96.5 × 31.8 cm (28¾ × 38 × 12½ in.)

Monumental in scale and precariously balanced, this pedestal piece conveys a raw, powerful energy and conviction of process. Slabs of torn, rugged clay overlap and surround a thrown base that has been squashed and manipulated to further disrupt the vessel form. Stamped within the clay are the imprints of found materials and the tread of a running shoe, suggesting an immediate physical connection where Soldner has pounded and worked the clay during the construction. Soldner relied on his intuition to dictate the composition of the piece, commenting, 'I like to discover what is happening with the clay, I'm more comfortable not knowing what to expect than with knowing.'

During the early 1960s, Soldner was inspired to use raku after reading *The Potter's Book* by Bernard Leach. In traditional Japanese raku, the piece is fired to around 1000°C (1832°F) and left in the open to cool after being removed from the red-hot kiln. The unpredictability of the technique and bright metallic colours appealed to Soldner. Employing his maverick approach to experimentation, Soldner introduced a post-reduction method that involved submerging the piece in leaves or combustible material in a closed container, producing a heavy reduction atmosphere and thick smoke. This results in a distinctive blackened surface with flashes of metallic sheen from applied copper slip.

For this pedestal piece, created in the 1980s, Soldner developed a new low-fired salt fuming technique based on his experiences using raku. His radical new technique involved introducing salt into the firing, placing it directly onto the flame of the burners rather than in the kiln chamber, which volatized and contributed a delicate, pitted quality to the clay surface. After surviving this brutal process, the piece retains the spontaneity and energy of its creation.

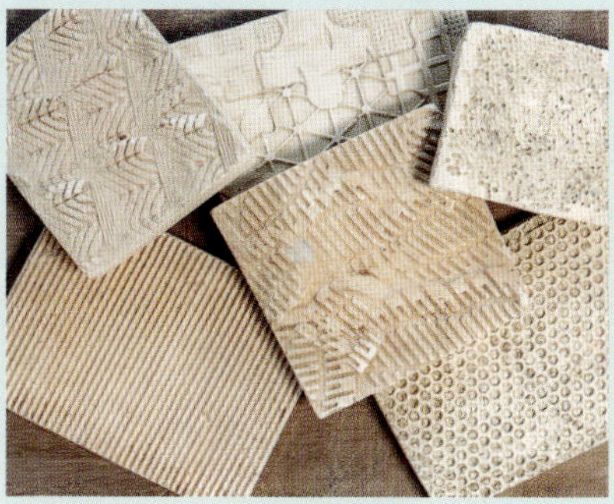

Process

Soldner had a very physical and expressive approach to making his work. He explored the potential of spontaneous actions, such as throwing a large vessel and then immediately slamming it into the floor to disrupt the form. To work like Soldner, you could experiment with tearing and folding slabs of clay and stamping and pressing found textures, such as textured plaster panels or wallpaper samples, into the surface. You could prepare sheets of clay that you take out into the environment and press against brickwork, tree bark or concrete paving to capture the print. Observe how the clay responds to your actions, and consider the transition point when the clay no longer retains its freshness and slips into looking overworked and laboured.

Ron Nagle

Cardworthy 2001
Earthenware
14.9 × 15.6 × 10.2 cm (5⅘ × 6⅕ × 4 in.)

The vibrant ceramic sculptures of Ron Nagle are intimately scaled and typically explore the vessel format – specifically the cup form. *Cardworthy* is a super-slick, ultra-styled assemblage of slip-cast and embellished surfaces. The shape is partially enclosed, with just a small vented opening at the top. An ear-shaped 'handle' is melded to the side of the piece as if it has pushed itself out from within the form. With his pieces abstracted beyond any recognizable shape, Nagle's primary concern is 'silhouette rather than volume'; he aims to have a graphical two-dimensional quality to the work just as much as a three-dimensional aspect. This graphical element stems from his interest in drawing and painting, underpinned by influences including still-life painter Giorgio Morandi (1890–1964), artist Philip Guston (1913–80) and American cartoonist George Herriman (1880–1944).

Nagle, a former apprentice of Peter Voulkos, was very much inspired by the abstract expressionist movement of the mid-20th century; however, his work does not share the usual gestural, macho traits that commonly defined this movement. Instead, his practice fits more comfortably with the biomorphic work of sculptor Ken Price, whom Nagle cites as a significant influence. Like Price, Nagle exhibits a commanding use of colour and this is demonstrated in *Cardworthy*, where a vivid purple is set against an airbrushed halo of yellow around the piece's central panel. The flawless finish of the piece is inspired by Nagle's enthusiasm for highly lacquered and polished paint jobs on American hot-rod cars.

Ron Nagle (American, born 1939) is a sculptor, musician and songwriter. His mother introduced him to ceramics when he was young. Initially he studied English at San Francisco State College, but then switched to studying fine art, graduating with a focus on ceramics. He is known for making small objects, mostly out of clay, and employing a range of techniques, including slip casting, airbrushing and hand moulding. He taught ceramics for almost fifty years at the University of California, Berkeley, San Francisco Art Institute and Mills College, Oakland. He has garnered numerous awards, including the Guggenheim Fellowship Award in 2012, and thirty of his pieces were included in the 55th Venice Biennale in 2013.

See also

Toshiko Takaezu (p.56)

Alison Britton (p.72)

Ken Price (p.210)

Composition

The strength of Nagle's precise works is their small scale, which provides a more intimate experience when viewing them. Small pieces can be incredibly engaging, absorbing the viewer's interest and offering up surprises – they demand close-up examination. You may find small scale your only option if you are restricted by kiln size, but with precision and care, you can produce works of exceptional quality that demand close-up examination.

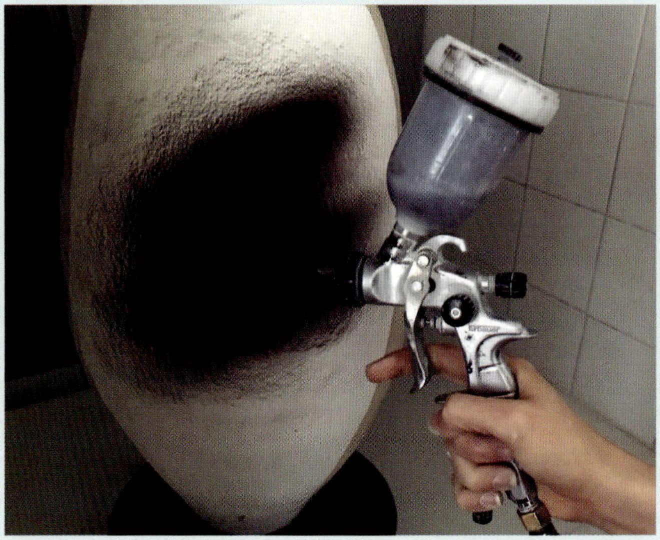

Surface

Airbrushing can give you a gradient finish and stylized aesthetic. To get started, you could source a small handheld kit – the type used for graphic design – or a spray gun and compressor for more substantial jobs. Fill the gun with underglaze pigment or oxide mixed with water and diluted to the desired strength. Experiment with masking areas off with tape or latex to produce a halo outline, as seen in Nagle's work.

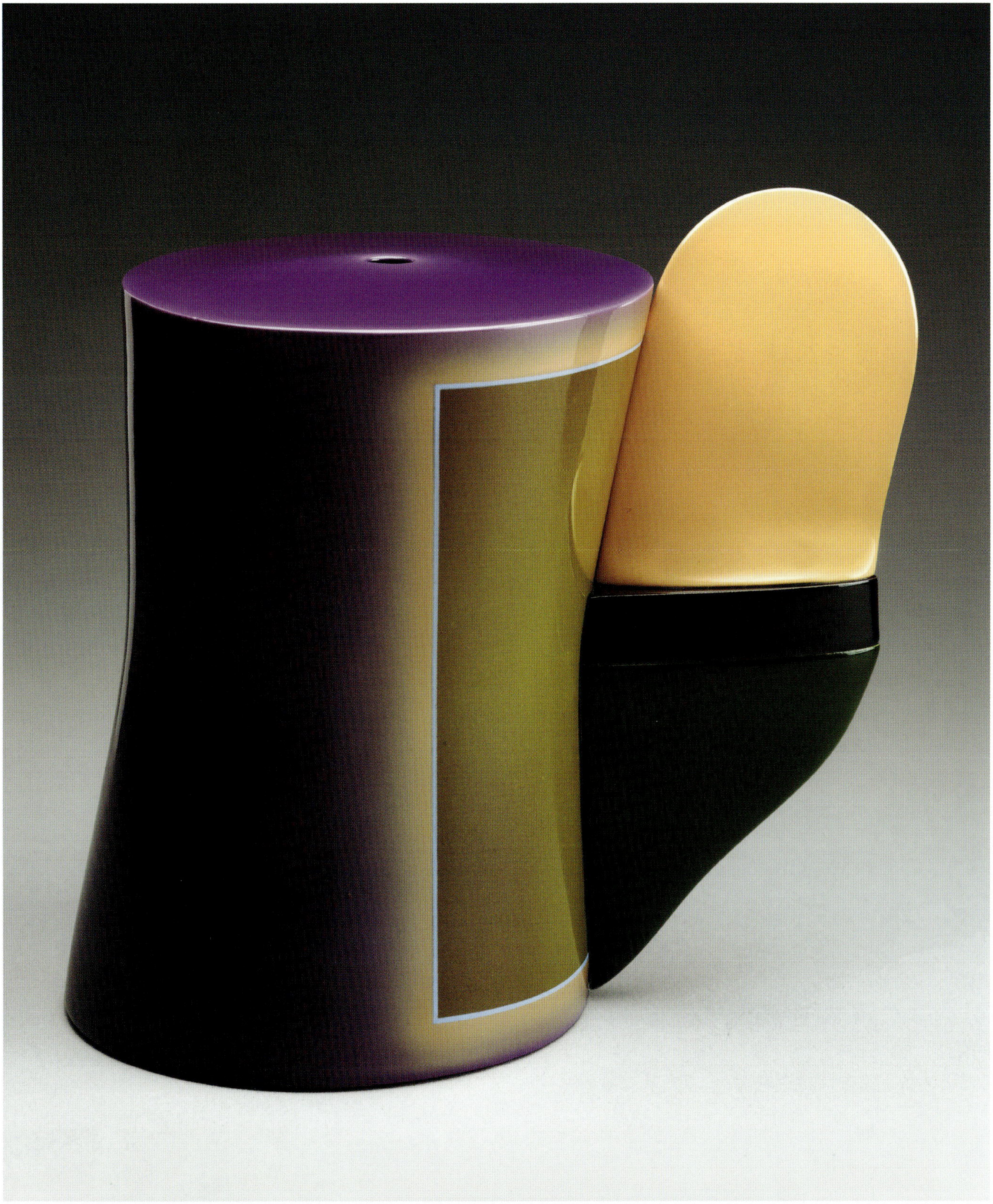

Ken Price

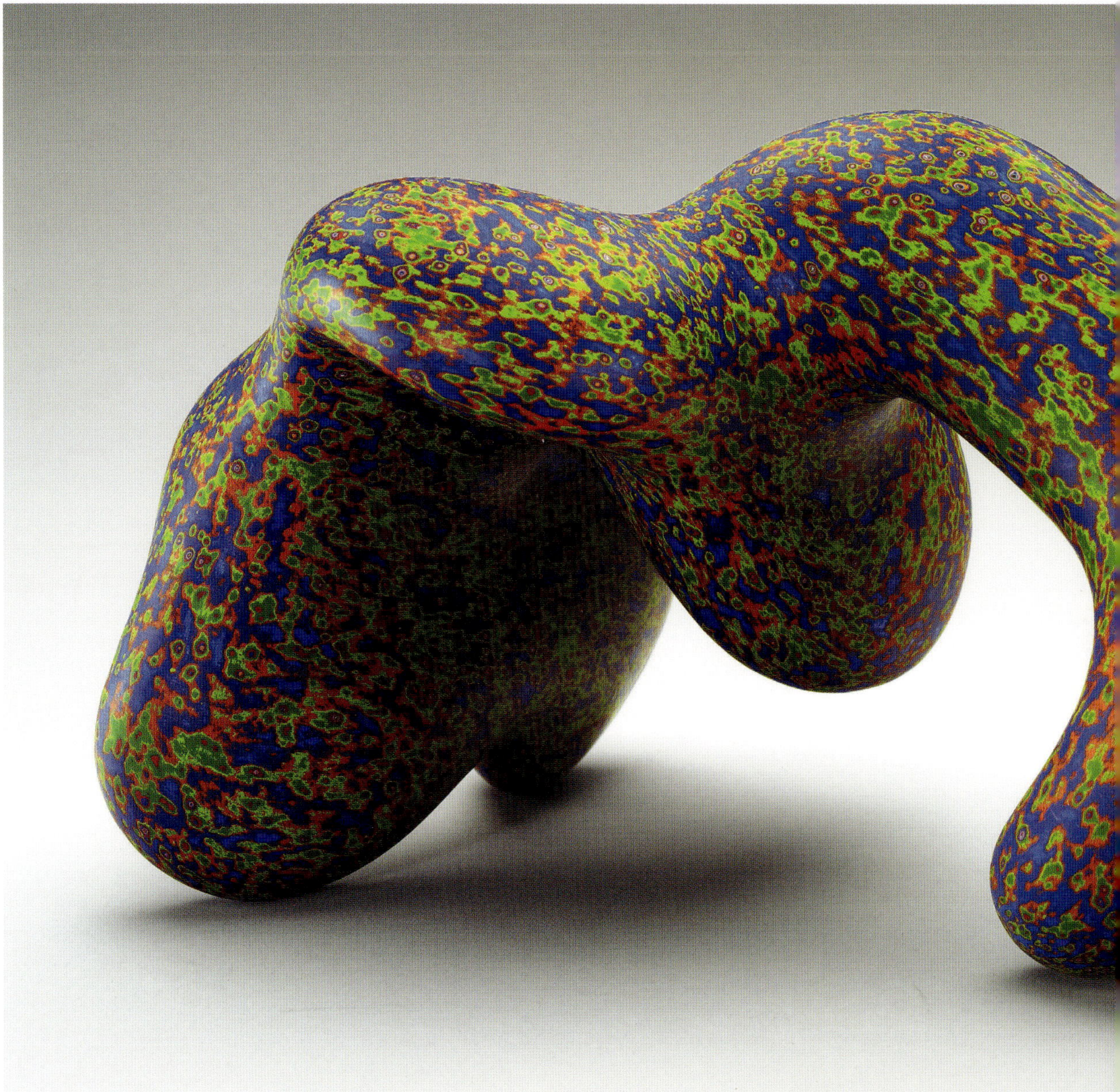

See also

Peter Voulkos (p.68), **Aneta Regel** (p.102)

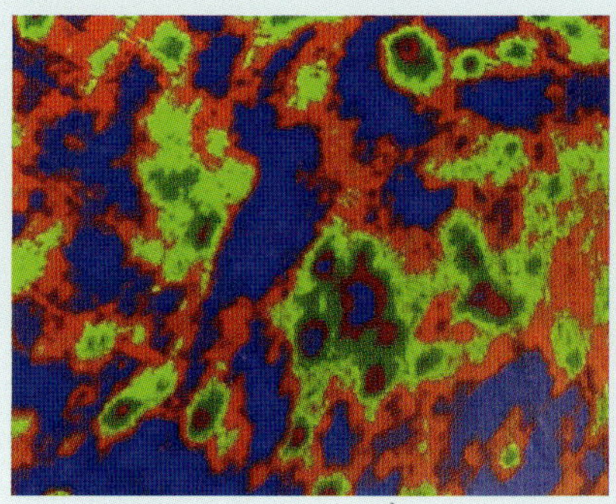

Ken Price (American, 1935–2012) studied at the Chouinard Art Institute and Otis Art Institute in Los Angeles and New York State College of Ceramics at Alfred University. At Otis he studied under Peter Voulkos and was inspired by Mexican folk pottery. He is best known for his abstract, small-scale sculptures and cups constructed from fired clay. He did not usually glaze his pieces but painted them with multiple layers of bright acrylic paint, which he then sanded down to reveal the colours beneath. The process results in playful ceramic forms with glossy surfaces of variegated colour.

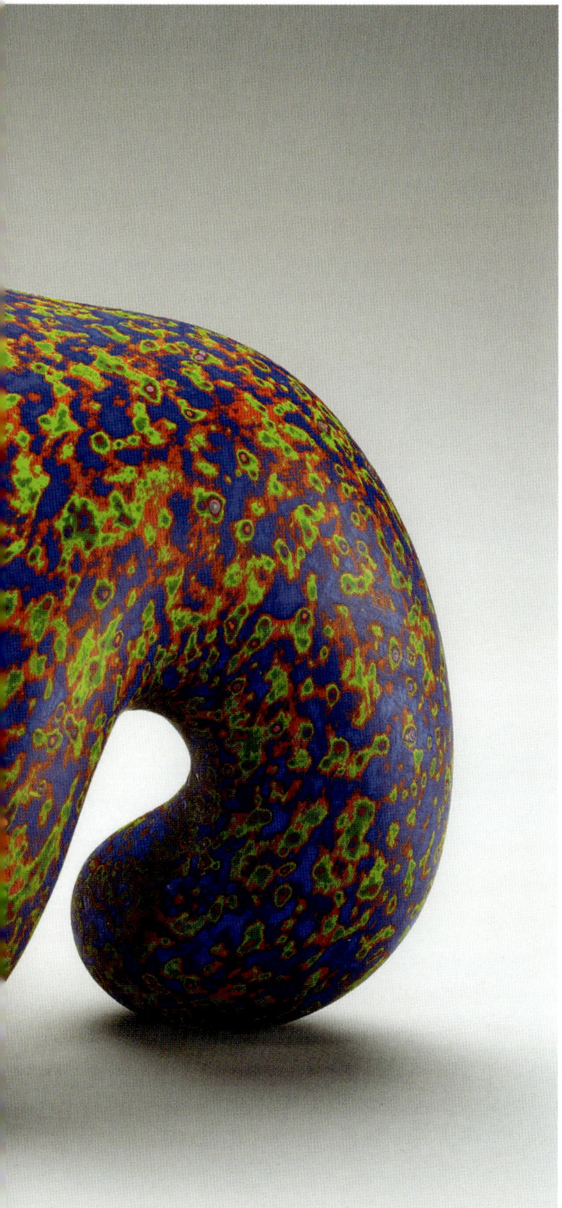

Morpho 2001
Acrylic on fired ceramic
15.2 × 30.5 × 18.4 cm (6 × 12 × 7¼ in.)

American artist and sculptor Ken Price emerged from the vibrant West Coast ceramics scene in the 1960s. This was a time of immense energy and experimentation, which saw attitudes shift from viewing clay as a craft material towards bringing it into the realm of fine art. Price's revolutionary works explored eclectic themes, ranging from the vivid colours and shapes of Mexican folk pottery to geology, eroticism and even his love of surfing. His use of bright, psychedelic colours was unique to him and he freely experimented with unconventional methods and did not limit himself. Price felt his work was 'strictly for pleasure' and he rarely discussed the conceptual meaning behind it.

This biomorphic, globular form embodies an organic fluidity that breathes life and movement. Like a liquid in flux, the evolving shape is strange and compelling. As with the majority of Price's works, he hand built this piece on an intimate, human scale. This allowed him to sensitively manipulate and sculpt the form; however, it still retains a commanding presence to rival that of a large-scale sculpture.

Up until the 1980s Price finished his works with glaze, but he began to find it too restrictive and sought a different aesthetic. As an experienced painter, he developed an innovative technique whereby he applied multiple, thin layers of acrylic paint and/or lacquer to the fired ceramic. Over the course of many hours, he proceeded to wet-sand back through the layers to reveal a complex, animated surface. As so colourfully illustrated by *Morpho*, the resulting mottled finish is gloriously resplendent and extremely accomplished.

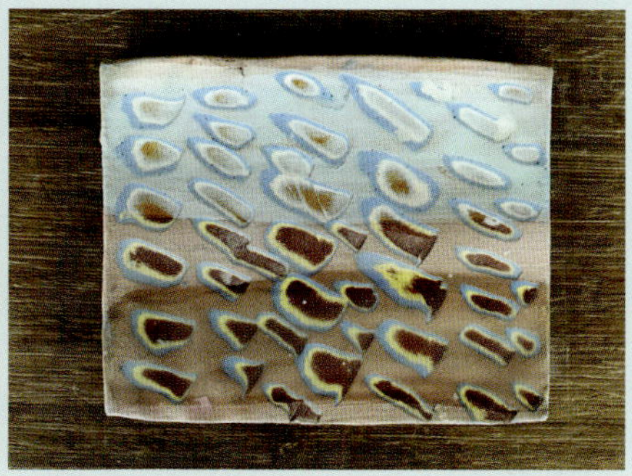

Surface
You can emulate the blotchy, speckled qualities of Price's surfaces in a number of ways. This tile example demonstrates a technique using decorative slips. Layers of alternative coloured slips were applied to a leather-hard surface using a large hake brush. Each layer was left to dry to a matt sheen before the next coat was applied. A metal kidney was used to scrape back through the layers to create a strata effect where the outline has multiple colours. Another technique to try involves painting layers of matt glaze or engobe slips onto a bisque surface. Once the piece is fired, use a sandblaster or a wet-stone grinder to polish away areas and expose the layers of colours. Like Price, you can even use car paint and/or lacquer as a decorative surface to experiment with, instead of glaze.

Michelle Erickson

Koi Junk Teapot 2009
Porcelain, coloured earthenware agate, indigenous clays
31.75 × 28 cm (12½ × 11 in.)

Ancient shipwrecks and archaeological salvage are sources of inspiration for Michelle Erickson's *Koi Junk Teapot*. Here, Erickson has created an imagined discovery excavated from a sunken Chinese junk sailing boat.

Encrusted with marine detritus, shells and sealife, the jumbled mass of pottery forms reflects the appearance of actual shipwreck finds that have become fused by mud and barnacles after spending many years on the seabed. Inspired by the naturalistic works of 16th-century potter Bernard Palissy, Erickson took casts from real-life subjects and added dabs of ceramic material to imitate silt and ocean sediment. The composition consists of a precarious stack of porcelain beakers and dishes that replicate early Chinese wares – Erickson hand-decorated each one with traditional motifs of koi fish and Chinese text.

The focal point of the sculpture is the pecten shell-shaped teapot, recreated by Erickson in the style of 18th-century Staffordshire agateware. The technique of creating multicoloured layers of clay within a pattern formation originated in 8th-century China and was adopted by British ceramic manufacturers. In this piece, Erickson has combined references to the past with contemporary practice. Her impressive range of skills as a maker enable her to create works that rival authentic artefacts. On the back of the piece Erickson has added a digital decal that says 'made in China'. This catapults the piece straight back into the 21st century and serves as a comment on modern consumerism and the globalized economy.

Michelle Erickson (British, born 1960) studied at the College of William and Mary in Williamsburg, Virginia, USA. After graduating, she worked for a year as a potter in the Busch Gardens theme park in Williamsburg. She also ran the ceramics studio at the Jamestown Settlement in Williamsburg, where she started to recreate pottery from the collections of early colonial excavations at the site. In 2012, she was artist in residence at London's Victoria and Albert Museum, where she was able to continue her investigation of lost techniques. She is known for using 17th- and 18th-century ceramics techniques to create narratives about historical and contemporary political, social and environmental issues.

See also

Bernard Palissy (p.86)
Malene Hartmann Rasmussen (p.106)
Judy McKenzie (p.118)

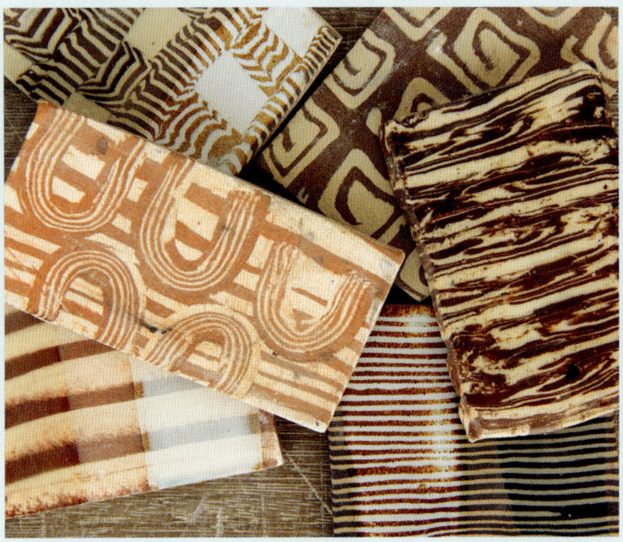

Process

Erickson refers to her practice as 'experimental archaeology'. She is an exceptional maker, able to investigate and rediscover lost ceramic techniques. The surface pattern of the teapot in this sculpture was made using a traditional method called agateware. The technique is similar to Japanese *neriage* or *nerikomi* and involves using two or three different-coloured clay bodies. This can be as simple as red and white earthenware or you can make your own coloured clay. As these tile samples illustrate, you can produce marbled effects, stripes and stylized patterns. Start by layering multiple sheets of thin coloured clay and compressing it with a rolling pin to make one sheet. Experiment with cutting the agate into small squares, then line them up in opposing directions and re-roll. This will create a zigzag effect similar to the pattern in Erickson's teapot. Red and white agate can turn black and white when fired to a temperature of 1200°C (2192°F).

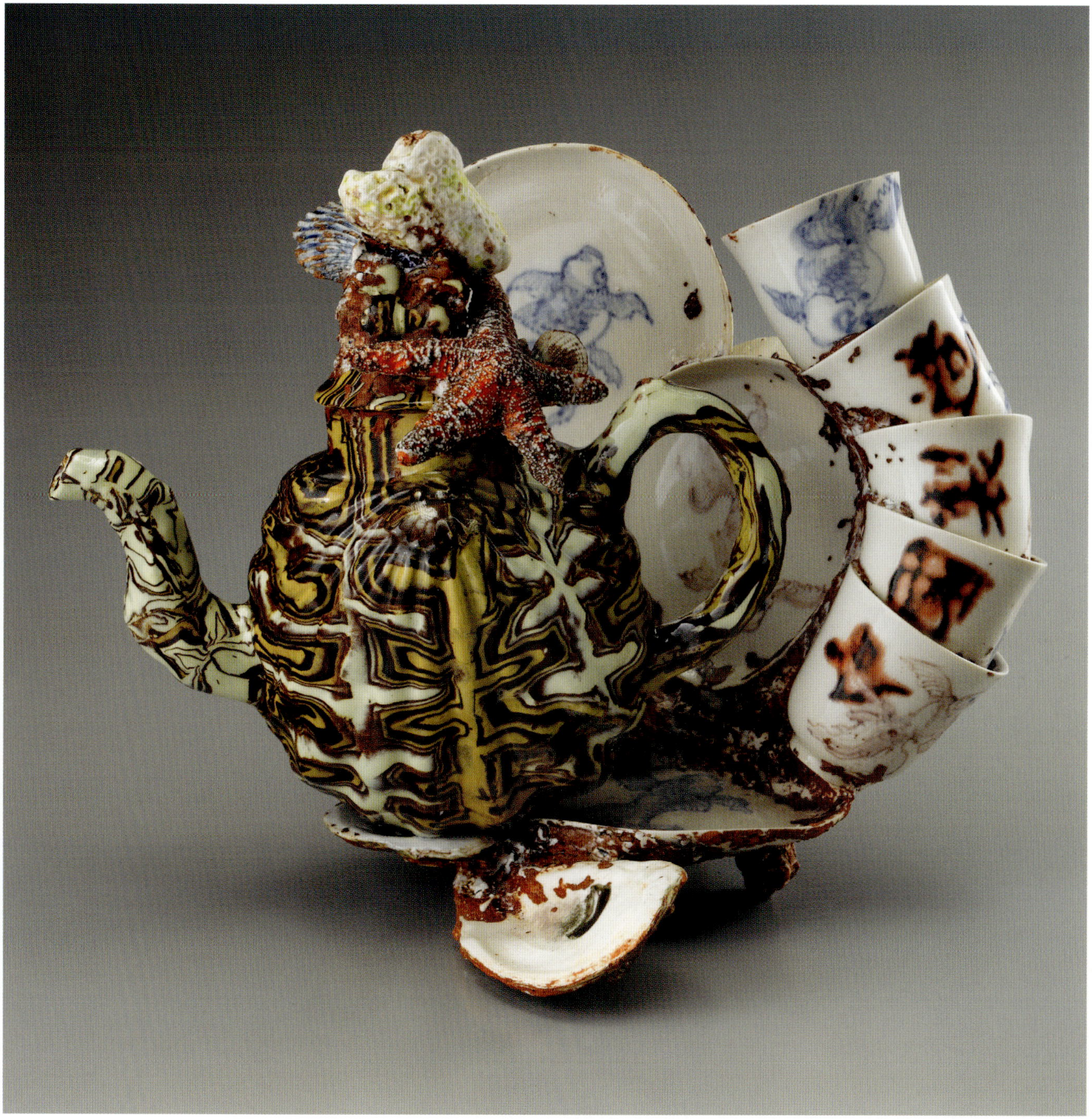

Rafa Pérez

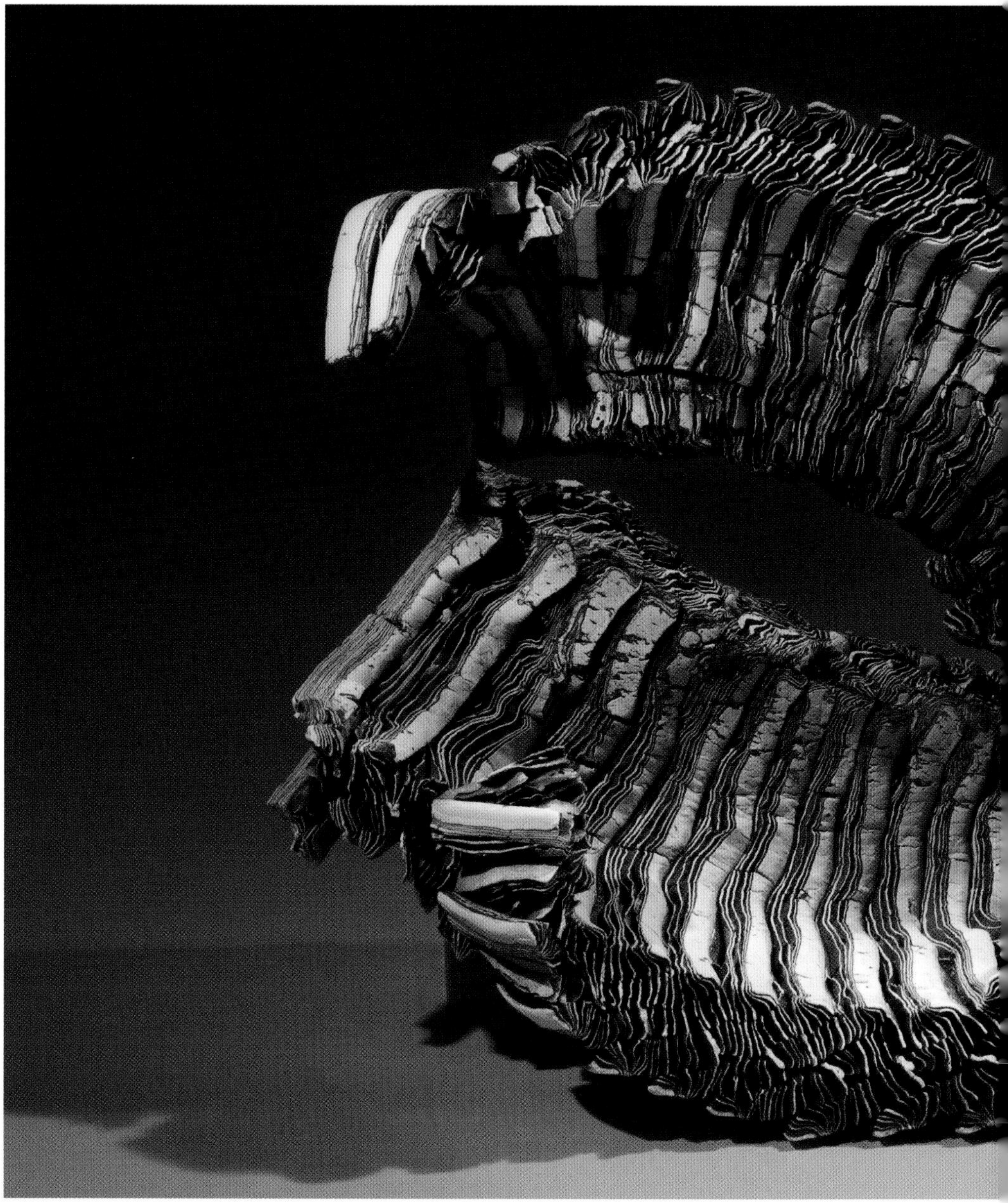

Rafa Pérez (Spanish, born 1957) studied at the Escuela Massana in Barcelona. He has garnered numerous national and international awards for his abstract geometric works that experiment with texture and surface. He fires white porcelain and black earthenware clay together at a high temperature to exploit the fact that the materials respond differently to the kiln and expand at different rates. The earthenware erupts to create what he calls a 'volcanic landscape', while his glazes crack, split and peel away to reveal the material through a crust. In 2007, he was elected a member of the International Academy of Ceramics.

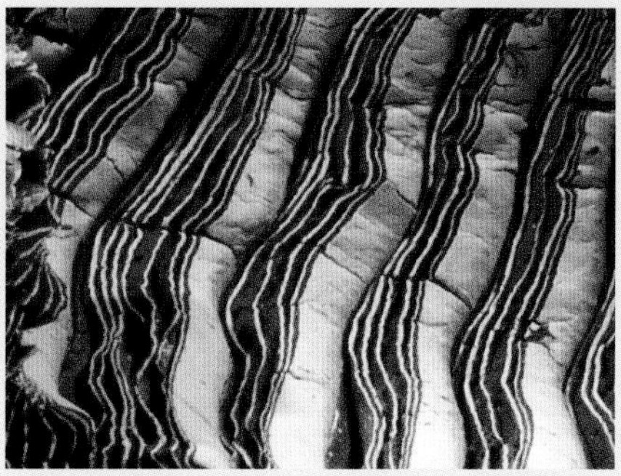

Technical

Pérez carefully orchestrated the outcome of firing this piece by carrying out many tests prior to making the work. He adds organic material to the black clay, which causes it to grow and expand during firing. Another advanced decision Pérez makes is where he cuts and slices the form to force it to unfold in a certain position. This piece was fired once to 1200°C (2192°F) in a gas kiln. Pérez carefully watched and checked on the piece in the kiln. For some of his works, Pérez lightly sandblasts the piece after firing to distress the surface further and reveal more unique qualities. A similar technique to explore is to apply shellac (lacquer) or wax resist to your piece and wipe the clay surface multiple times with a damp sponge. The areas without resist will wear down and give the illusion that your piece has eroded away.

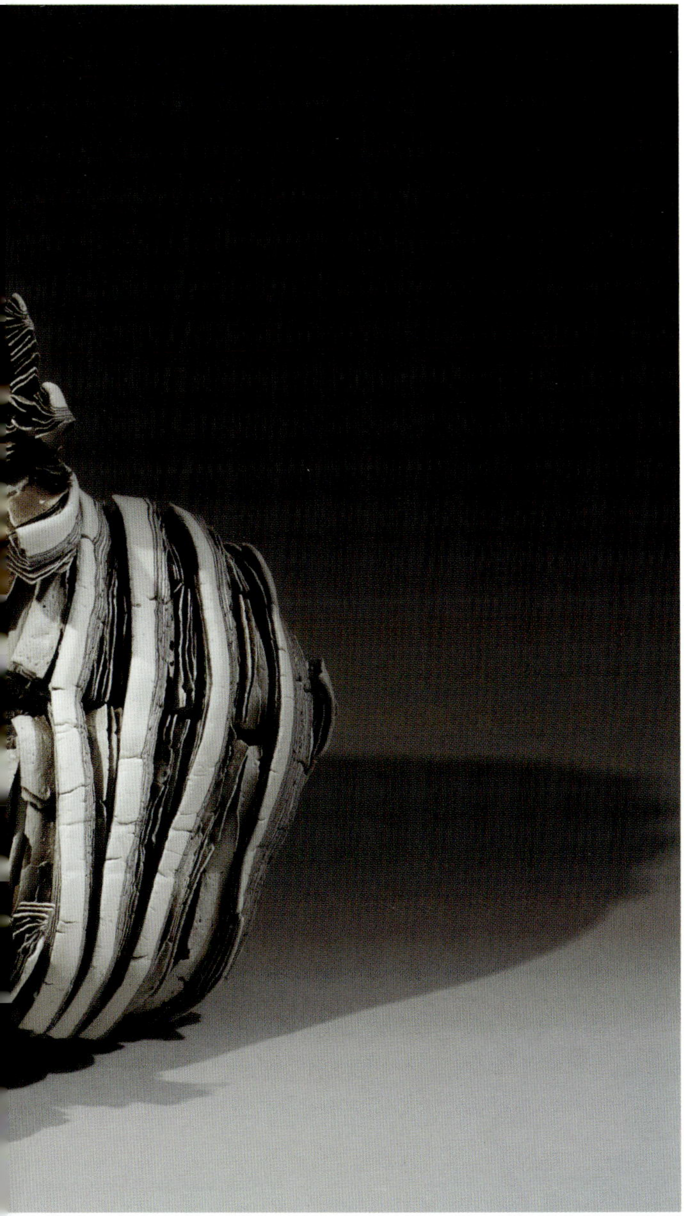

Untitled 2010
Porcelain and black earthenware combination, unglazed
40 × 20 × 50 cm (15¾ × 7⅞ × 19⅝ in.)

Rafa Pérez is excited by the element of surprise and unpredictability he is faced with each time he opens his kiln. He can never be quite sure how his ceramic creations will react to the heat they are subjected to during the firing. This thrill-seeking attitude is the driving force behind his experimental practice and has earnt him a maverick reputation. For this large, expansive piece, Pérez experimented from the very beginning of the process, starting with the materials. He rolled and layered alternating slabs of porcelain and black earthenware clay together to form one stripy block. He then proceeded to slice the block into long, thick strips and reassemble them into a cylindrical structure.

Pérez exploits the opposing properties of the two clay bodies, understanding that they will respond very differently to the firing temperature. The black clay expands and erupts away from the more stable porcelain clay, creating thin, papery sheets and ruffles. Although there is a strong element of uncontrolled interaction within Pérez's work, he states, 'What emerges from the fire is not mere chance or just a happy accident. That is because it is directed by me. I impose my will on the materials to the extent that I create the cuts and layers that interact within the kiln.' When creating this piece, before firing, Pérez slashed the side of the cylinder form with a knife and this caused it to split open during firing, resulting in a shape that looks like a splayed ribcage from an animal carcass.

See also
Pippin Drysdale (p.122)
Paul Soldner (p.206)
Jongjin Park (p.234)

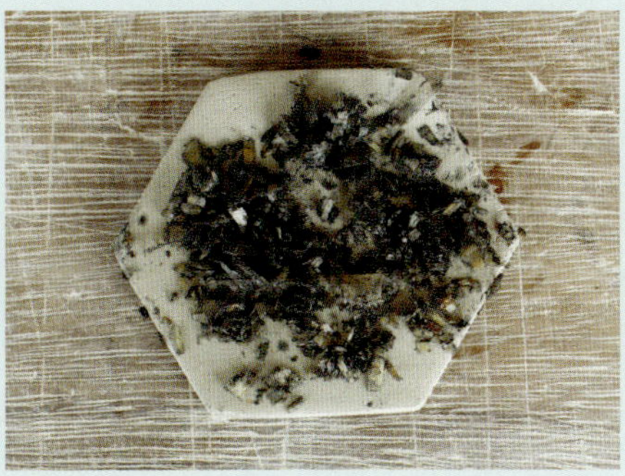

Material
You can create your own material experiments by thoroughly mixing organic substances, such as paper pulp, fabric fibre or sawdust, into the clay body. These will burn away during the firing, causing your piece to radically change beyond your control. For this sample tile, fine sawdust was pre-soaked in a copper oxide and water mix and then pressed into the clay.

Richard Slee

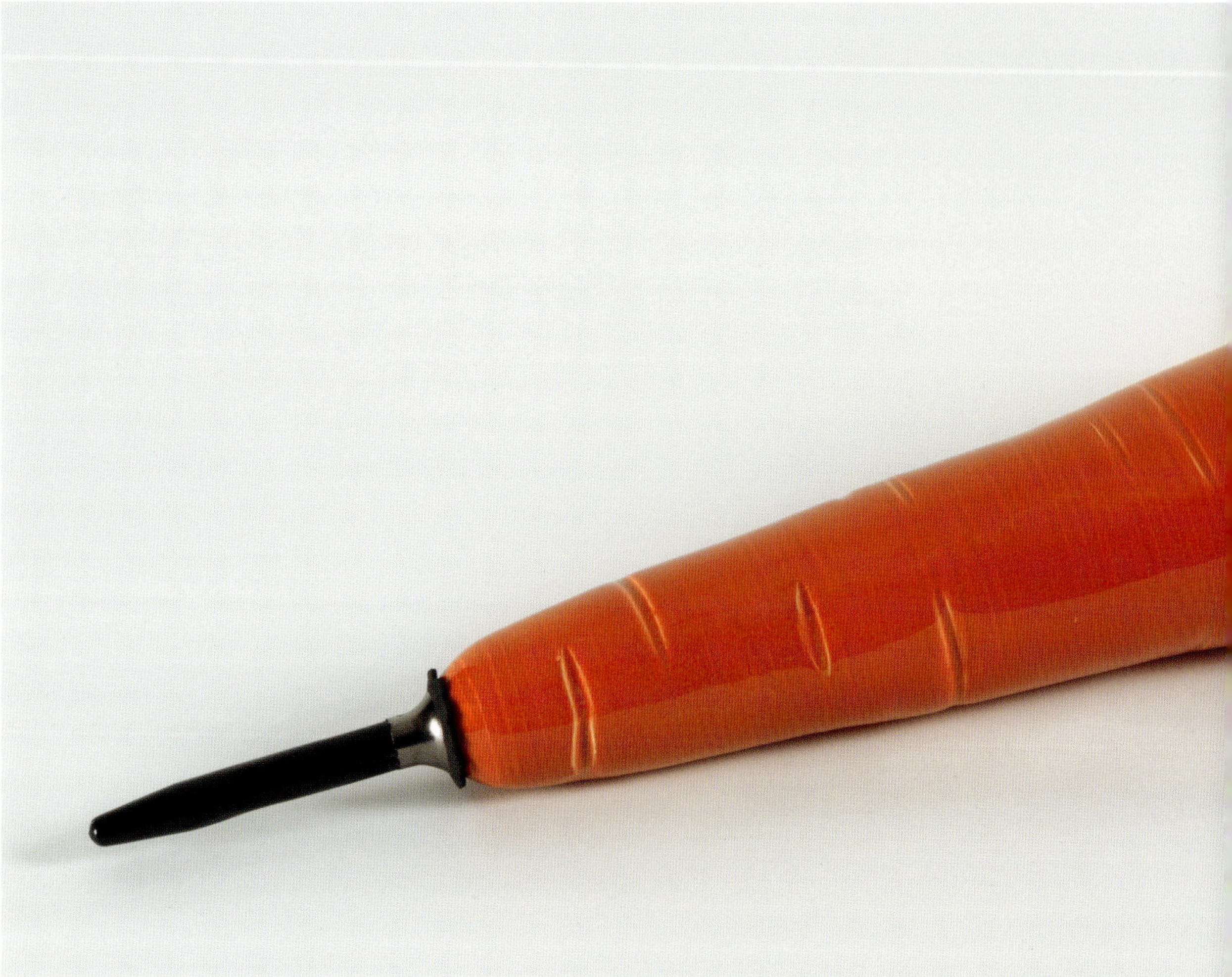

Carrot 2012
Glazed ceramic with umbrella parts
10 × 66 × 15 cm (4 × 26 × 5⅞ in.)

Richard Slee is widely considered to be one of the most influential ceramic artists working in Britain today. His imaginative sculptures blend dry wit and irony with exceptional technical accomplishment. Slee's practice reflects the domestic and familiar by playfully investigating subversive themes that transcend ornamentation and utilitarian traditions. By specializing in ceramics, Slee's practice has, in his words, 'evolved from studio pottery to a contemporary craft debate with reference to the current positioning of material specializations in visual creativity'. In his recent works, such as this wry piece entitled *Carrot*, Slee combines ceramic and non-ceramic materials which, as he says, 'question past loyalties towards a single material'.

The origins of Richard Slee's recent works lie in his fascination with commonplace and everyday objects, such as radios, brooms, spades, saws and hammers. With its cartoonish appearance and bright aesthetic, *Carrot* – in the guise of an umbrella – alludes to a capability to protect from the rain, but in application would be absolutely useless. This irony-tinged dysfunction renders the piece somewhere between the uncanny and the absurd.

Another playful aspect left open for the viewer's interpretation is Slee's seemingly innocent hint to male anatomy. The comic silliness of the carrot pokes fun at itself and the sexual connotations we might assign to it. Attached to the ceramic carrot is a plastic umbrella handle and tip. Slee deliberately avoids using secondhand and junk ready-mades in his assemblages, saying, 'I use new and shiny components, the manufactured things that carry no romanticism. It's also a commentary on modern consumerism'. With values shared with post-modernism and pop art, Slee's modern take on ceramic art remains distinctively his.

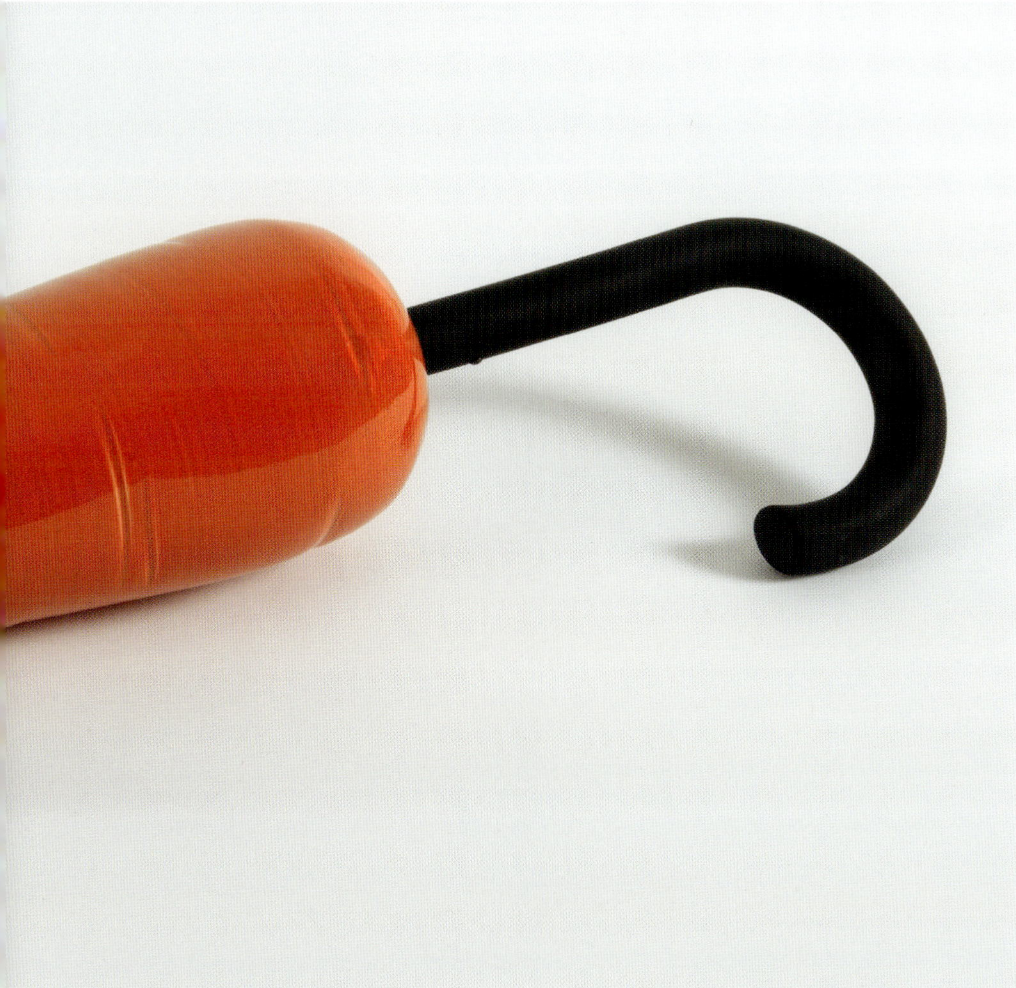

Richard Slee (British, born 1946) studied at Carlisle College of Art and Design and then at London's Central School of Art and Design and the Royal College of Art. He is known for his brightly coloured, glazed earthenware pieces inspired by photographs, souvenirs, pop art and cartoons as well as for witty and subversive works like his 1991 *Toby Jug* series – outsize ceramics that relate to the domestic realm. His dexterity with clay and glazing skill have led to him being nicknamed the 'Grand Wizard of Studio Ceramics'. He became professor of ceramics at Camberwell College of Arts, London, in 1992 and won the Jerwood Prize for Ceramics in 2002.

See also

Kate Malone (p.116)
Ramesh Mario Nithiyendran (p.190)
Marilyn Levine (p.204)

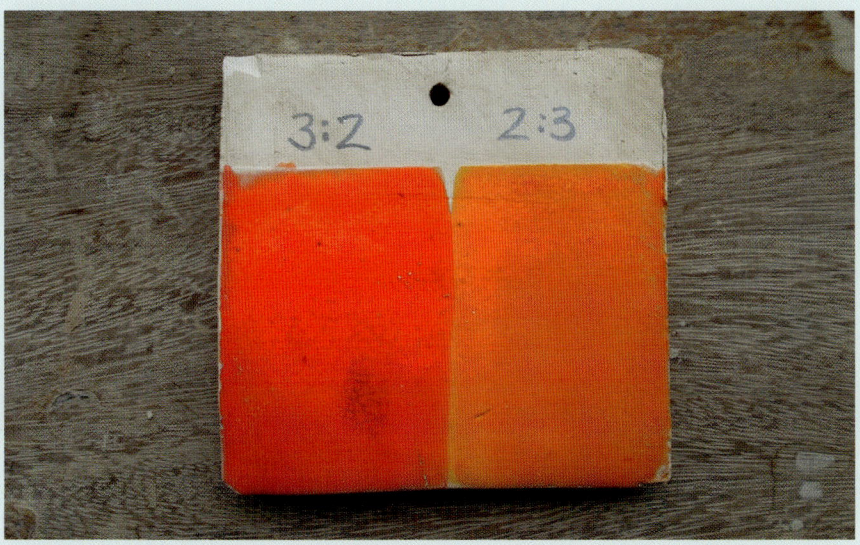

Technical

Slee's refined ceramic works are ultra-crisp and appealing in their style and high degree of precision. He commonly hand builds and press moulds his forms to such effect that it is often difficult to distinguish between the specific processes he used. Here, it is likely Slee hand built the carrot as a hollow form, giving the piece a greater sense of individuality and connection with the organic nature of the subject. The artist has incised the surface with light cuts and deeper lines suggestive of carrot skin. Paired with a vivid orange earthenware glaze such as the colours shown here (made with 10% stain), the completed piece has a stylized, 'pop' aesthetic.

Sterling Ruby

Basin Theology/THE PIPE 2013
Ceramic
101 × 110.5 × 111.8 cm (39¾ × 43½ × 44 in.)

Thick, chunky and rudimentary – the archaeologic-like ceramic sculptures by Sterling Ruby engage a highly physical and expressive approach to the material. Commanding in scale, this extravagant piece from the *Basin Theology* series resembles a rather obscure and curious excavation site. A long, extruded pipe section extends beyond the height of the vessel like a chimney or car exhaust of some sort, suggesting the vestiges of an industrial or urban history. Within the pit of the basin, broken fragments and detritus from years of past failures are fused and embedded into the form. Resembling a waste heap of shrapnel and smashed shards, the piece presents a cleansing ritual of past attempts regenerated into something new. As Ruby comments, 'I like the opportunity for chance, the reclamation and recycling through materials. It becomes an autobiographical excavation, my own archaeology'.

With firm origins in the gestural qualities of abstract expressionism, Ruby was fundamentally influenced by the freeform ceramic sculptures of Peter Voulkos. He also cites the Italian artist Lucio Fontana's (1899–1968) craggy ceramic crucifix series as a significant influence. For Ruby, 'clay has always been about malleability as opposed to vulnerability'. He is drawn to clay as a responsive material. To create this tactile form he rolled, pummelled and squeezed great lumps of clay between his hands. Working intuitively, he loosely shaped a high-sided 'ashtray' (as Ruby calls it), and from there pulled and tore at the sides to expose the central area. Glazed in a shock of red, the rich intensity of the basin is a record of Ruby's visceral explorations.

Sterling Ruby (American, born 1972) works in an extensive range of media, including ceramics, painting, drawing, collage, sculpture, video and textiles. Ruby graduated from the Pennsylvania College of Art and Design, Lancaster, in 1996. He received a bachelor's degree in fine art from the School of the Art Institute of Chicago in 2002. This was followed, in 2005, by a master's degree from the ArtCenter College of Design in Pasadena, California. Based in Los Angeles, Ruby's practice draws upon themes of marginalized societies, urban culture and autobiography. In all his work there is implied violence and a sense of destruction. Ruby has designed interiors for the fashion brand Calvin Klein, and in 2019 he launched his own label of unisex clothing and accessories under the guise of S. R. STUDIO. LA. CA.

See also

Peter Voulkos (p.68)
Simon Carroll (p.98)
Linda Sormin (p.264)

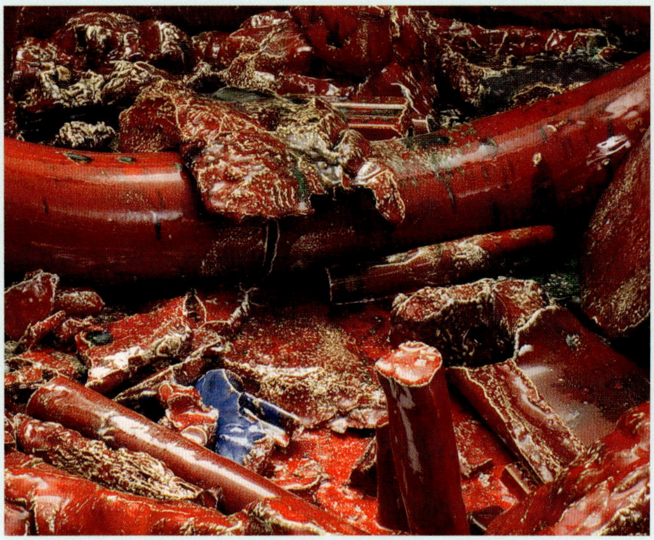

Process

Here, frenzied and expressive marks made by Ruby's fingertips manipulating and sculpting the clay convey an acknowledgment of established craft traditions. Ruby has made a visual link between the exterior wall and the interior by piercing small pipe sections through deep holes in the lower side of the piece to draw the viewer's eye. He has contrasted the red expanse of glaze by including a very small blue fragment – which immediately draws our eye into the centre.

Technical

A vast and complex piece such as this requires a slow and careful ring schedule to allow for the expansion of the clay body and glaze during the firing. A typical firing for a small object is around twenty-four hours – compared with one to two weeks for a piece of this size, which includes a steady cooling programme to avoid cracking. Ruby will often glaze-fire his pieces multiple times, occasionally adding more fragments to the pit. A piece can take him many months.

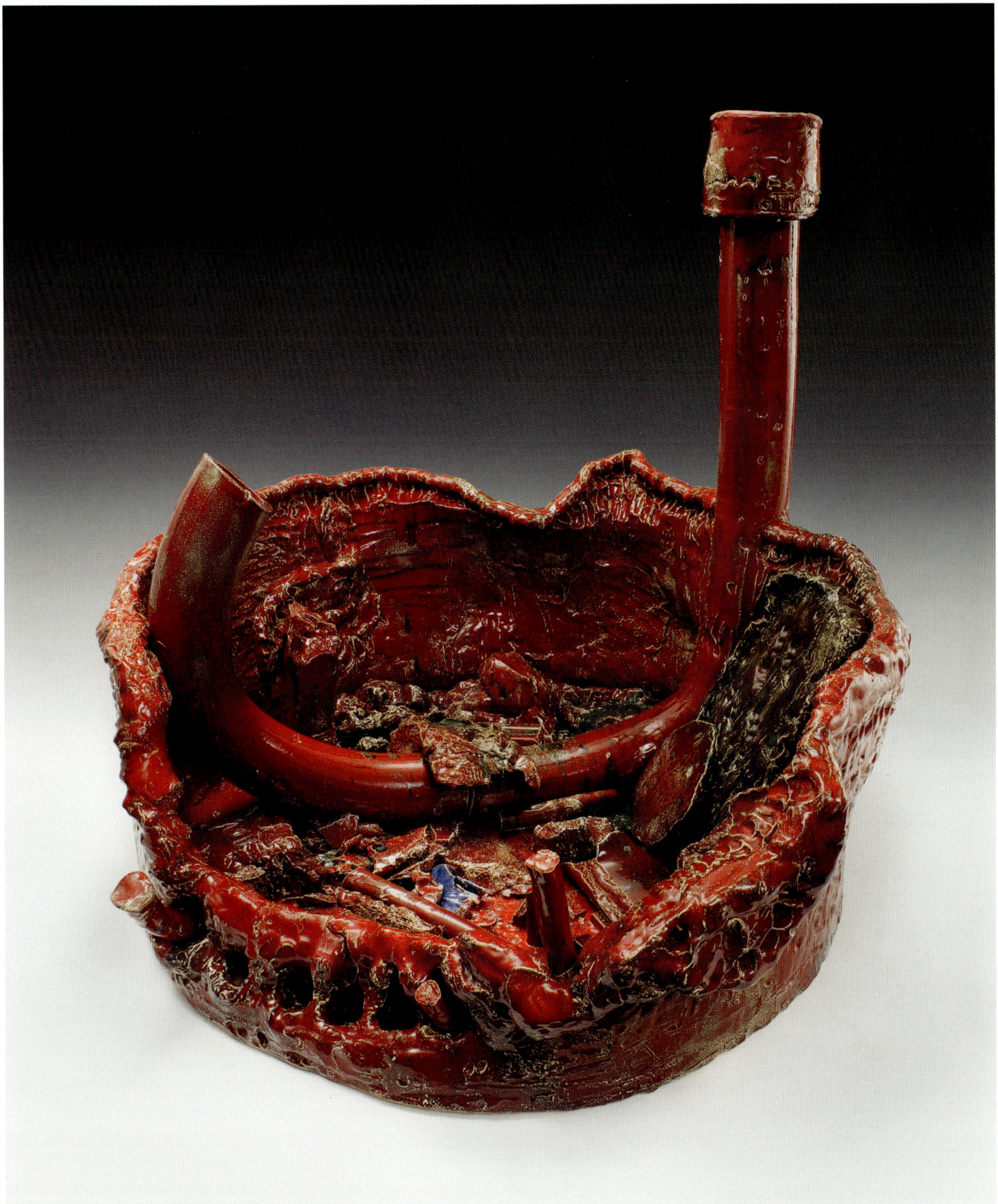

Astrid Dahl

White Matter 2014
White earthenware, unglazed
Approx. 65 x 45 x 45 cm (25 ⅗ x 17 ¾ x 17 ¾ in.)

Astrid Dahl takes inspiration for her sensuous, organic sculptures from the extraordinary photographs of 19th-century artist and botanist Karl Blossfeldt, who was famous for his magnified images of flowers, buds and seed pods. Dahl was drawn to the way he captured complex structures and the unique intricacies of his subjects. The monotone colours and simplicity of his prints would also inspire her use of white earthenware clay to construct her pieces. For Dahl, the neutral ceramic surface acts as a canvas to accentuate the projection of light and shadow against the gentle curves and soft expanses of her floral shapes.

This large, free-flowing piece, entitled *White Matter*, is reminiscent of a wild orchid or exotic plant that Dahl has enlarged and pushed almost to the point of abstraction. The frilled tendrils and paper-thin petals evoke a sense of fragile beauty and share a sensibility with the feminine *White Flower* paintings by the eminent American artist, Georgia O'Keeffe. To create this piece Dahl coil-built the initial shape, mindful of the relationship between the inner and outer profiles. The rhythmic motion of the coiling process is captured in the smooth texture of the clay, accentuating the organic quality of the form. Dahl completed the work by sanding down the clay in its green state, carefully refining the edges to sharpen its undulating contours and curls. The piece was then low fired and left unglazed, resulting in a silky, wax-like finish that allows the innate beauty of the piece to fully resonate.

Astrid Dahl (South African, born 1977) studied at the Technikon Natal in Durban, where her ceramics lecturer, Hendrik Stroebel, encouraged her to explore clay and she learned the traditional South African methods of coiling and hand working clay. After graduation she moved to Nottingham Road in South Africa's Midlands to work in a bronze casting foundry. There she met designer Neville Trickett, who introduced her to the photography of 19th-century German botanist Karl Blossfeldt (1865–1932), who magnified his subjects to thirty times their original size. Dahl began to use white clay to create sensual objects inspired by plants and flowers that have drawn comparisons to the paintings of US artist Georgia O'Keeffe (1887–1986).

See also
Annie Turner (p.230)
Phoebe Cummings (p.256)
Paolo Polloniato (p.262)

Technical
Clay forms and shapes can be refined at any stage of the making process, although the easiest stage is when clay is raw or in green state (wear a dust mask). You can use a pottery knife, metal scraper or sandpaper to rub away lumps and bumps and define the form. A further wipe-down with a damp sponge will smooth the surface and remove any minor flaws. Fold a circular sponge over your thumb, forming a neat 'v' shape, which is excellent for crisping up rims and edges.

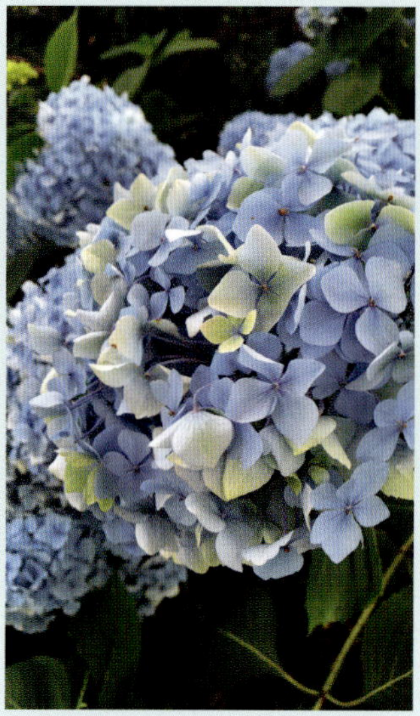

Composition
Enlarged photographic shots and close-up details can be a good place to start your creative investigations, as they allow you to study your subject from a different perspective and focus your attention on a detail you may not have noticed before. Likewise, you could draw a series of preliminary sketches from life subjects such as flowers, shells or other natural forms. Architecture can also be a fantastic source of inspiration, from modern to historical. Observe any sharp outlines, exaggerated proportions or sweeping angles of a building that catch your eye. Another technique to try is to make a simple viewfinder by cutting a rectangular hole in the middle of a sheet of paper. Hold it up in front of you to frame a specific area of interest and identify compositions that you could interpret in ceramic form. Get into the habit of taking photographs or drawing regularly to help you develop a stronger awareness of your artistic motivations.

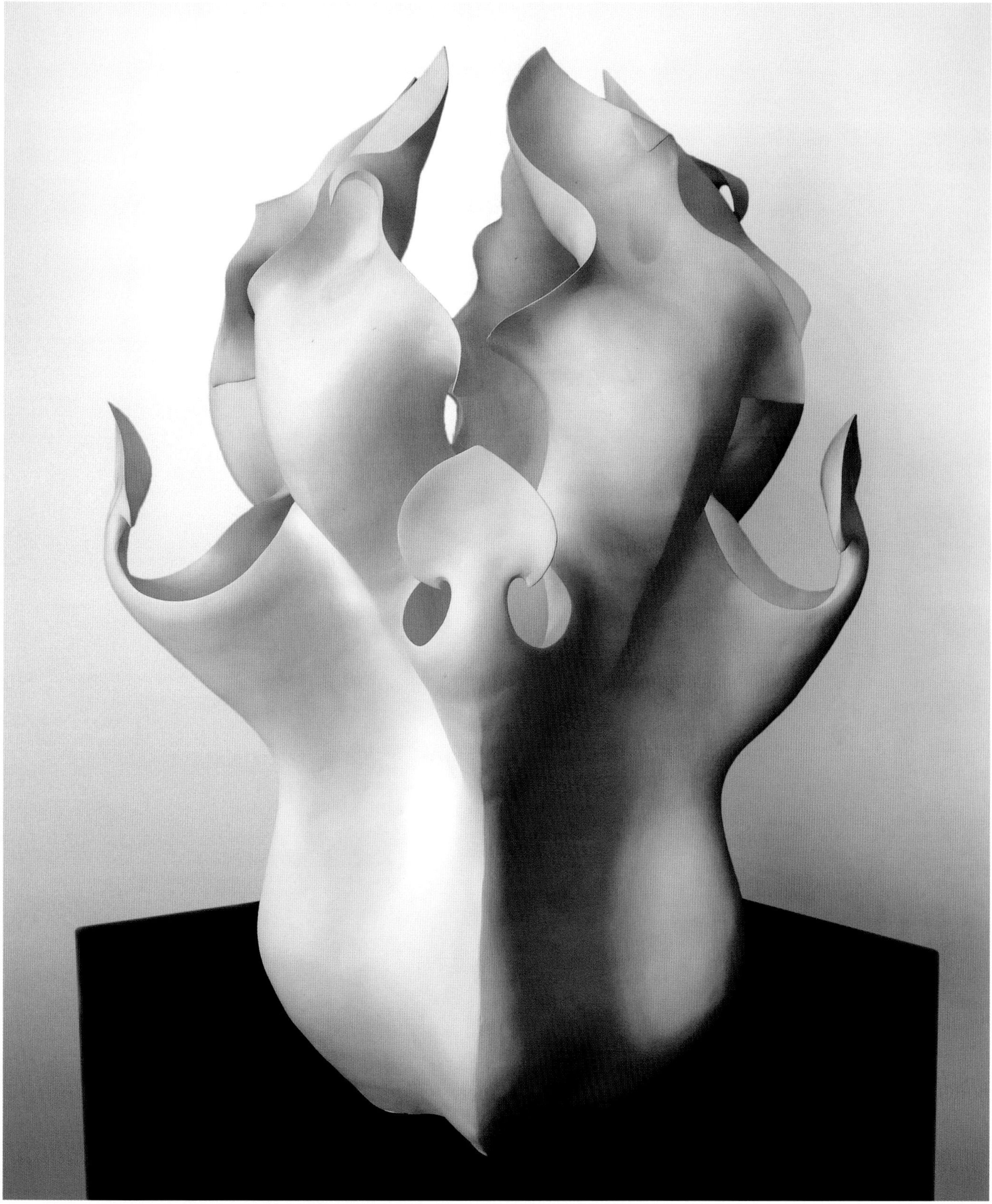

Gitte Jungersen

All is Flux #3 2015
Several glazes in layers
114 × 86 × 5 cm (44⅘ × 33⅘ × 2 in.)

All is Flux #3 by Gitte Jungersen is ceramic, but not as we conventionally think of the term – for there is no clay present here at all. In fact, this large rectangular panel is made entirely from several layers of dense glaze that have melted and solidified into one dynamic composition. Highly experimental and innovative, Jungersen 'pushes the tactile possibilities of ceramics to the limit, and investigates ceramic glaze as a phenomenon in itself'.

With its frothy, congealed mass and oily colour the piece appears otherworldly, as if it was transported here from another realm. Its physicality was defined by the immense heat and transformation produced by the kiln firing, which places the piece somewhere between unruly chaos and ultimate control. As Jungersen says, 'The works trigger a feeling of the uncontrollable and the catastrophic, despite the fact that the ceramic materiality appears as beautiful and alluring to the senses. Whether it is imminent dissolution that waits, or a new narrative about to take shape, remains open'.

Through much experimentation, Jungersen has rigorously tested the chemical properties of glaze, developing and refining specific traits that will enable the glaze to respond effectively to extreme heating and cooling. She has mastered the techniques needed to encourage desirable textures and qualities, such as bubbly and pitted surfaces that swirl and ripple like waves. The unpredictable nature of the process is a physical record of experimentation, control and chance. When all these elements are brought together, it leads to an exciting and extraordinary outcome that is incredibly beautiful and tactile.

Gitte Jungersen (Danish, born 1967) studied at The Royal Danish Academy of Fine Arts, School of Design, in Copenhagen. In 2000, Jungersen was awarded the prestigious Danish National Art Foundation's three-year working grant. She aims to push the tactile possibilities of ceramics to the limit and treats ceramic glaze as a material in itself. She creates objects that consist of several layers of glazes that have fused together when melted in the kiln. The result is pieces made entirely of glaze, with complex and ambiguous textures that spark associations with both primordial matter and man-made materials. The works appear to capture a moment in time in the lifecycle of a material.

See also
Takuro Kuwata (p.124)
Morten Løbner Espersen (p.126)
Matt Wedel (p.226)

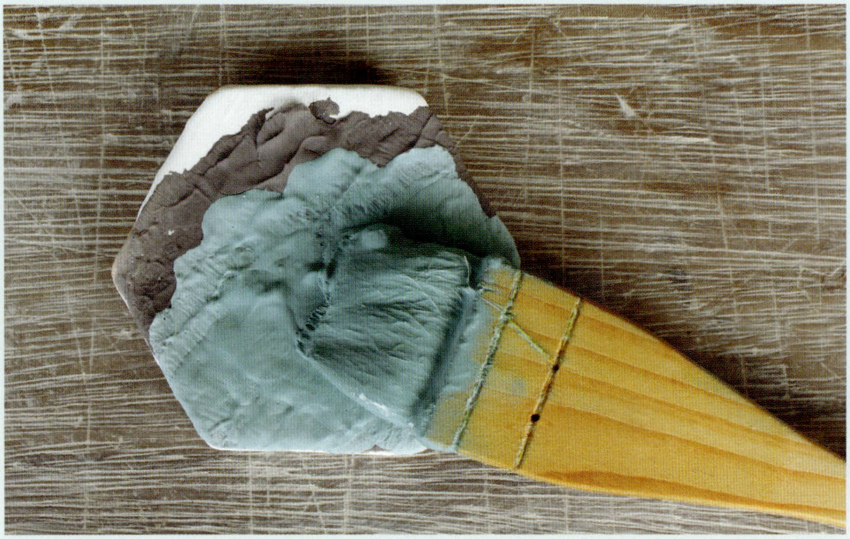

Technical
To create this piece, Jungersen poured a series of different glazes into a rectangular mould in four thick layers and kiln fired the piece at 1280°C (2336°F). During the firing the glaze melts and boils, transforming the texture and appearance of the material and softening the straight edges of the rectangle. Like cooled volcanic magma, the glaze retains its liquid appearance but as a solid form. Consider how you could be more experimental with your glazes to bring movement and tactility to your work. You could apply thick layers of different glaze types on top of each other just to see how they interact and respond together.

Lawson Oyekan

Bonnie Charlie 2015
Terracotta
Left: Height: 36 cm (14⅛ in.); Diameter: 14.5 cm (5⅝ in.).
Right: Height: 36 cm (14⅛ in.); Diameter: 13.5 cm (5⅜ in.)

Having spent several years in both the UK and Nigeria, Oyekan now resides in France. This diverse blend of cultural references can be felt in his emotive forms and they powerfully convey his life experiences and upbringing. Earlier works explored the physicality of nature and were often a response to a specific place. Constructed on a monolithic scale, their earthy, unglazed surfaces resembled huge termite mounds. Oyekan's pieces are typically adorned with piercings and frenzied crisscross lines and markings. Oyekan's intention is to 'express human endurance and deliver a message of reassurance: that human suffering can be healed'.

Bonnie Charlie – a pair of intensively dynamic terracotta forms – is an expression of Oyekan's abstract articulation of clay as a material. These pieces are intimate in scale compared to previous works and here Oyekan addresses 'the modernity of falsehoods as an evolutionary blindfold'. Oyekan handles the clay in a very direct and intuitive manner, building his forms using pads of clay that he has flattened out between his hands and assembled into a loose column shape. He then repeatedly perforates the surface of the clay, creating the squared-off holes that allow light to pass through – suggesting breath and the power of healing and regeneration. *Bonnie Charlie* is about the absence of empathy in modern culture and Oyekan's intention is to prompt contemplation about the foibles of the domineering cultures of today.

Lawson Oyekan (British-Nigerian, born 1961) was born in London but grew up in Ibadan, Nigeria. In 1983, he returned to London and studied at the Central School of Art and Design and the Royal College of Art. He won the Darwin Scholarship Award in 1989 and was the first recipient of the Grand Prix Award for the 1st World Ceramic Biennale in 2001 in Korea. He was recognized for his hand-moulded, monolithic terracotta structure *Healing Being*, from his series *Coming up for Air* (1999–2002). His work often consists of towering clay vessels with dry, unglazed surfaces, which are adorned with piercings and sometimes include text in English or his native language, Yoruba.

See also
Simon Carroll (p.98)
Halima Cassell (p.236)
Vicky Lindo (p.240)

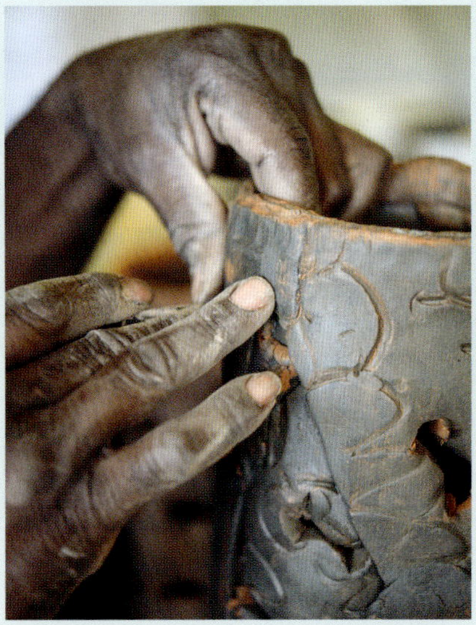

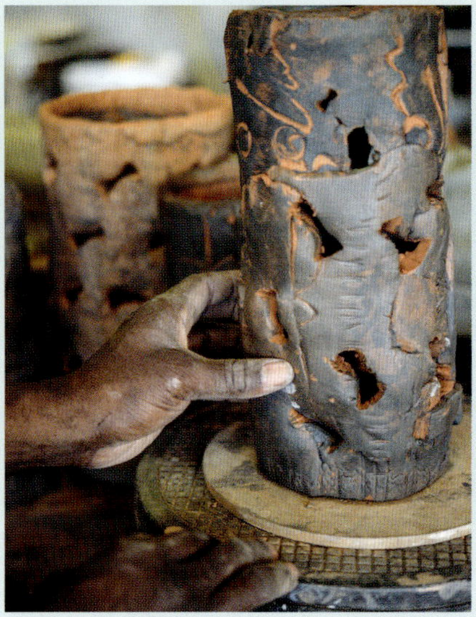

Surface
Without any glaze or surface adornment, Oyekan has allowed the rawness of the clay to speak his complex themes. The richness of the terracotta clay body complements the deliberate, scratchy knife marks and the smears made by his fingertips, which are left on the surface. Note how the marks and piercings are intentional and expressive, without dominating the overall composition. This can be a difficult balance, but the skill lies in being confident with your approach and maintaining a sense of energy and free gesture. You may find it beneficial to complete a series of preliminary charcoal or ink drawings to discover qualities to translate into your clay surface.

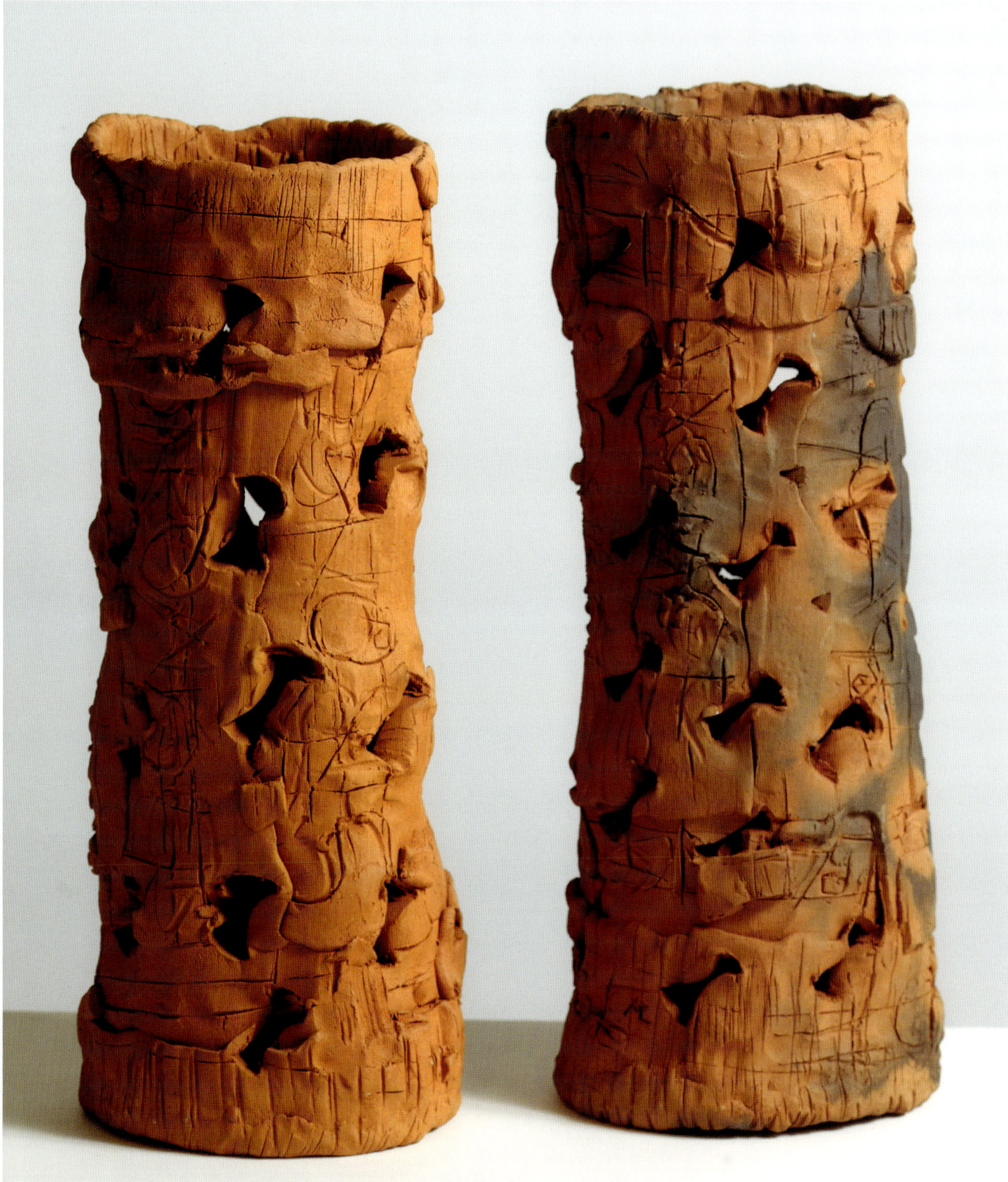

Matt Wedel

Banana Tree 2015
Ceramic
182.9 × 200.7 × 147.3 cm (72 × 79 × 58 in.)

Inspired by landscape, culture and mythology, Matt Wedel creates large-scale sculptures that explore figurative, botanical and organic themes. As he explains, 'My work is about becoming, about existing, about finding hope. I am interested in learning from my work. It is a kind of making to find understanding rather than the work as a product of understanding'.

With many of his works exceeding two metres (six feet) in height, a consistent element in Wedel's practice is his use of colossal scale. *Banana Tree* is impressive in stature and has a commanding presence, allowing the viewer to fully absorb its complex surfaces and wild composition. It is an impossible object that lies somewhere between reality and the imagined. Entangled arms and tubular structures twist and interconnect. Giant pompom flowers and branches, heavily laden with bunches of ripe fruit, overtake and pull the piece to the verge of collapse. The points of tension and suspense held within the opposing parts suggest the fragility of nature and a potential for destruction.

Wedel's approach to creating his work not only brings the physical challenges of making a piece on such a vast scale, but also relies heavily on his ability to retain a sense of delicacy and intimacy within the piece. He hand builds in a gestural manner, pinching and manipulating chunks of clay, and carries this hands-on approach into his glaze application by squirting syringes full of pastel-coloured glaze all over the entire piece. The resulting glazed surfaces are expressive and painterly and reconnect the abstracted form to its organic beginnings.

Matt Wedel (American, born 1983) grew up around ceramics because his father was a potter. He studied at the School of the Art Institute of Chicago and at California State University, Long Beach (CLUB). He travelled to Italy as part of his master's degree and became interested in the history of figurative sculpture. Wedel's oeuvre encompasses both the figurative and the abstract. He is known for his twisting, colourful porcelain sculptures that celebrate natural forms, while his small, terracotta and stoneware portraits reference classical Greek sculpture as well as the shapes of more modernist work, such as that of Italian painter and sculptor Amedeo Modigliani (1884–1920).

See also
Bente Skjøttgaard (p.108)
Ikuko Iwamoto (p.152)
Rita Gudiño (p.182)

Technical
When making pieces on a large scale, there are a number of challenges to overcome: where to store the work while it dries, the restraints of the kiln size, and the physical manoeuvrability of the work. Wedel's gigantic pieces can weigh as much as two tonnes and can take many weeks to dry before they can be fired. He has devised a method where he uses an engine hoist and forklift to manoeuvre the piece in and out of the kiln.

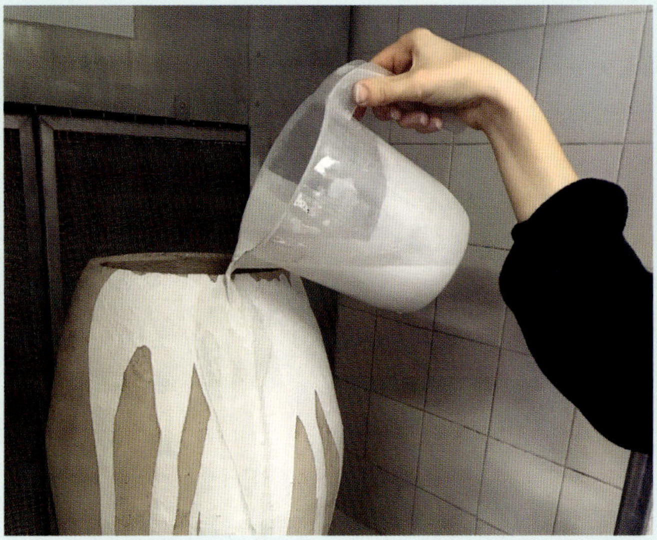

Surface
To achieve painterly surfaces like this in your work, you could use a ladle or jug to pour glaze over sections of your work (see left). Build up the layers, allowing for overlaps and allowing colours to merge. You could deliberately leave areas of clay body exposed to provide a contrast. If your piece is large, place a cement mixing tray or a small paddling pool beneath it to catch the spills and allow for more space when working.

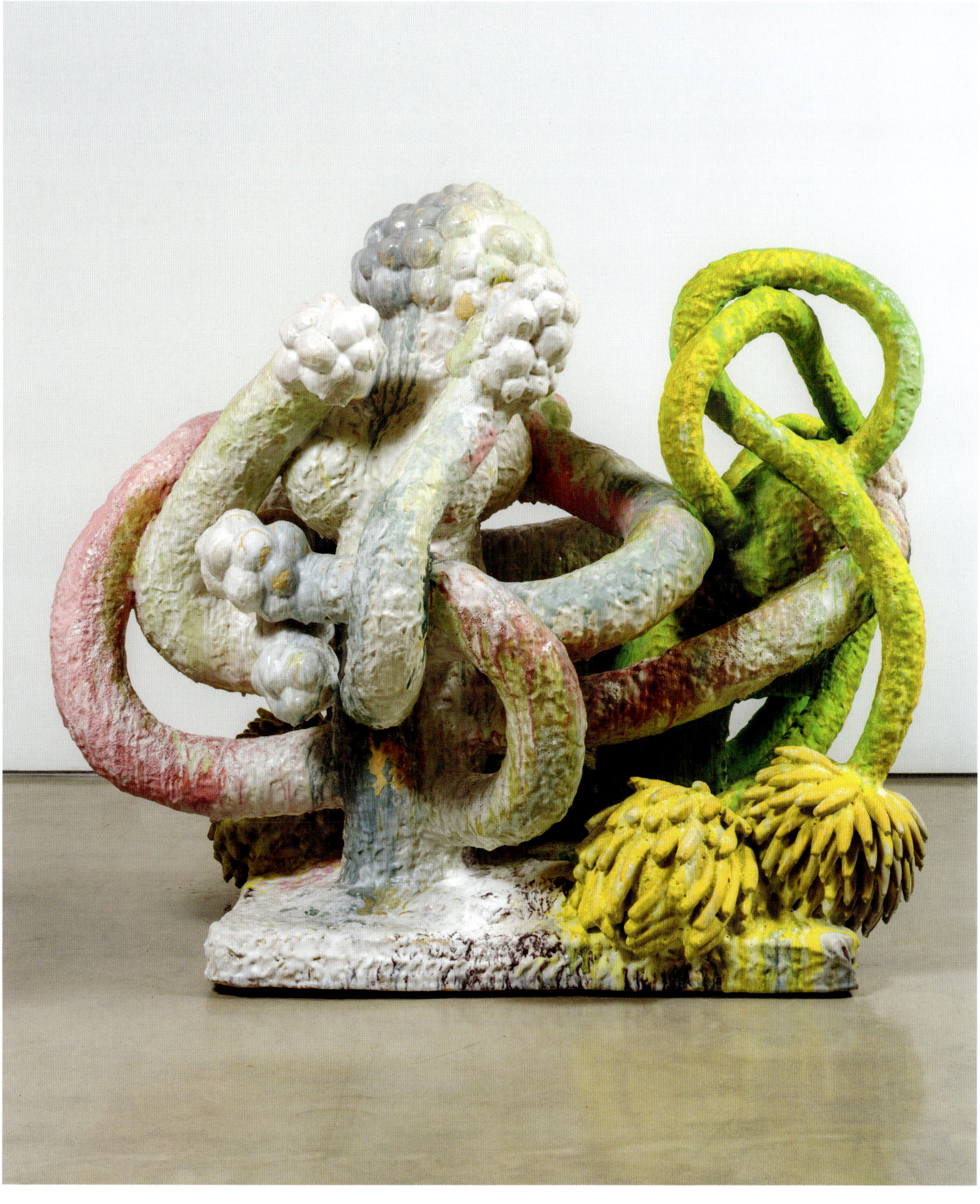

Bertozzi & Casoni

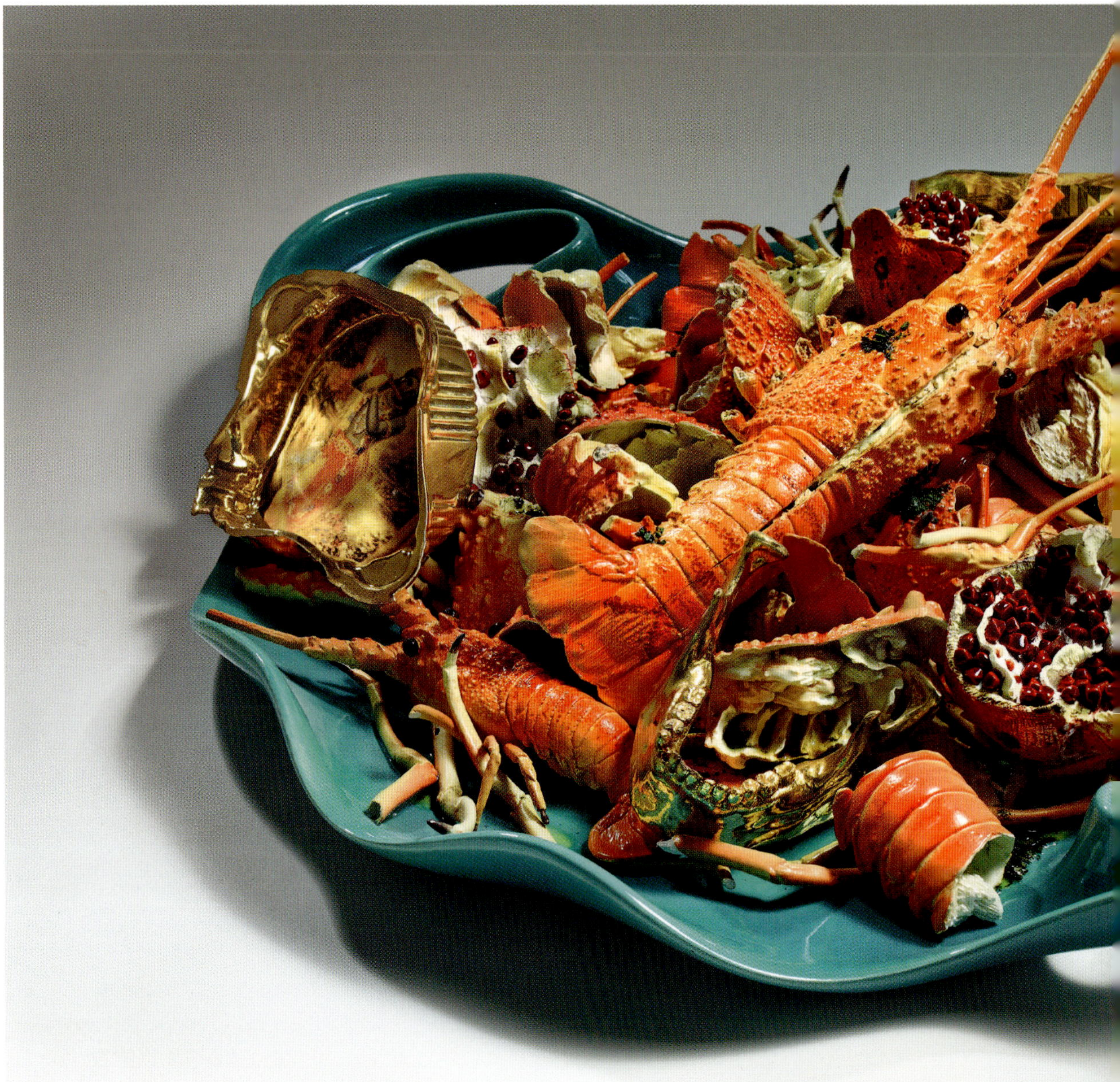

See also

Shary Boyle (p.194), **Jessica Stoller** (p.248)

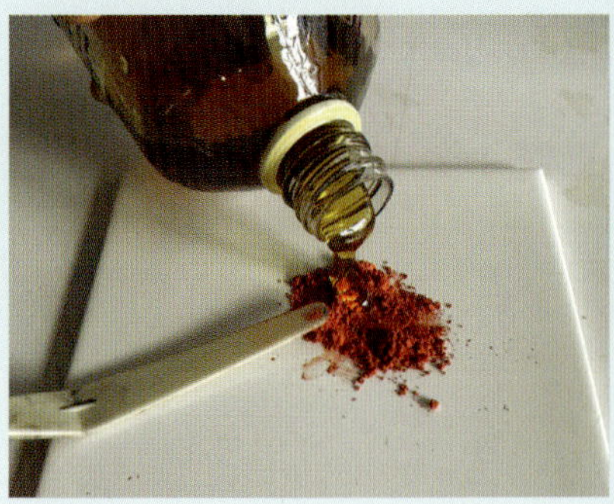

Giampaolo Bertozzi (Italian, born 1957) and **Stefano Dal Monte Casoni** (Italian, born 1961) met while they were studying at the Gaetano Ballardini Ceramic Art Institute of Faenza, Italy. They went on to study at the Academy of Fine Arts in Bologna and participated in exhibitions that focused on creating a 'New Ceramics' that bridged the gap between ceramics and painted sculpture. In 1980 they founded the Bertozzi & Casoni ceramics production company. Since then, they have created surrealist and hyperrealist sculptures that explore themes of cultural and artistic waste in contemporary society. In 2004 the artists exhibited at Tate Liverpool. Their work was also featured in the Italian Pavilion at the Venice Biennale in 2009 and 2011.

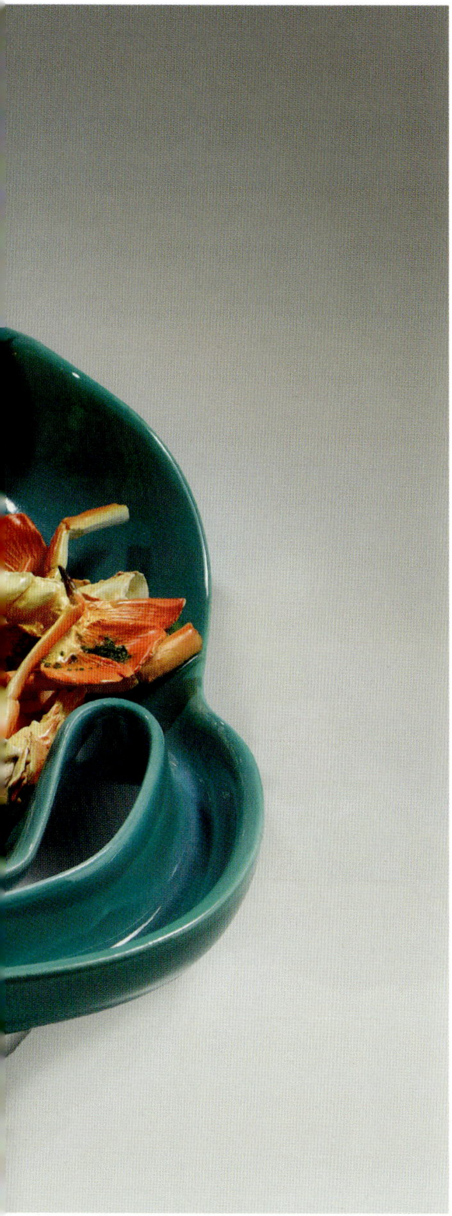

Mediterraneo 2016
Glazed ceramic
17.5 x 58 x 47 cm (6 4/5 x 22 4/5 x 18 1/2 in.)

Giampaolo Bertozzi and Stefano Dal Monte Casoni – better known as Bertozzi & Casoni – create imaginative assemblages that appear so true to life they belie their ceramic medium. The duo's masterful creations explore satirical themes that playfully subvert contemporary culture and frequently reference the *vanitas*, a 17th-century Dutch genre where symbols of death are represented in still-life painting. Their deceptive works provoke reactions from intrigue right through to repulsion and include plates of cracked egg shells with spilled and congealed yolks dripping down, tatty cardboard boxes emblazoned with the familiar 'Brillo' logo – the contents inside including crumpled money and an assortment of trash, and borderline kitsch animal sculptures that explore environmental concerns and share sentiments of melancholy.

This hyperrealistic piece appears to portray the aftermath of an exuberant feast. Mixed among the heaps of food scraps are the remnants of cans, rotting lobster carcasses and discarded pomegranate husks. Plump, ruby-coloured seeds evoke the juiciness of the fruit, eliciting a response from the viewer's sense of taste and smell as well as vision. A fragment of a human jaw bone encrusted in gold glistens and gleams from within this whimsical bricolage, serving as a *memento mori*. Bertozzi & Casoni employ a degree of symbolism in their work, their depictions of decay and impermanence a commentary on the fleeting nature of human existence.

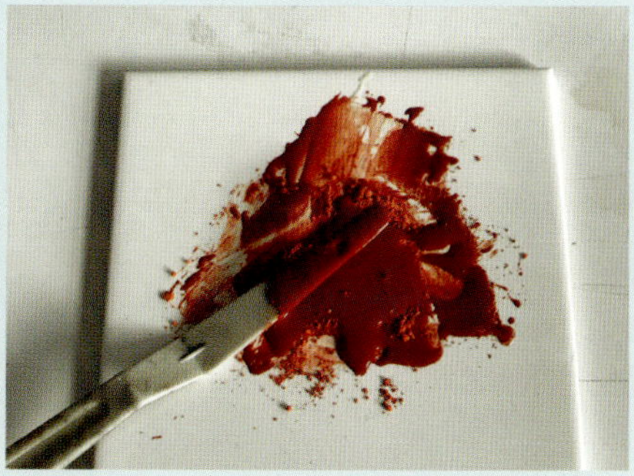

Technical

Bertozzi & Casoni construct their pieces from individual components using moulding and hand modelling techniques. You can achieve similar aesthetics in your own work by casting plaster moulds from readymade or found items – children's plastic toys in the shape of food are a good place to start. The richness of colour can be recreated by using glazes within the earthenware firing range (1080–1120°C/1976–2048°F), such as tin glazes and smooth matt pastel shades. You could also explore low-fired enamelling techniques to emphasize specific food qualities – for example, egg yolk.

Far left and left: Enamel pigments are mixed with a binder such as fat oil or milk before being applied to a glazed surface.

Annie Turner

Drift Net 2016
Red grogged clay
59 × 48 × 25 cm (23¼ × 18⅞ × 9⅞ in)

Drift Net encapsulates Annie Turner's memories of fishing with her late father, catching shellfish and scouring the muddy banks of the River Deben for fossils and remnants of the past. This is an object with a strong personal narrative, one that explores themes of recollection and the passage of time. The mesh structure of the piece shares a physical connection with the waterscape and resembles the weathered herring traps used by local fishermen that are suspended in free-flowing channels of water and subjected to the powerful currents of the river. The tonal colours are evocative of decaying jetties and corroded metal jutting out from the foreshore and are created through Turner's sensitive use of dry, rust-like surfaces created with a lithium carbonate-type glaze and a wash of yellow iron oxide. The effect is so convincingly real that is it easy to forget this piece is made from clay.

Turner made the structure by drawing a gridded template onto a sheet of canvas and then hand building fine coils of red grogged clay in a series of small vertical lines contained by horizontal supports. Through experimentation, Turner brought the form to the brink of collapse by exploiting the interaction of heat and work during the firing to pull, twist and reshape the piece. She has learned how the construction of the work can promote warping and distortion. These shifts are only revealed when the kiln door is opened, as Turner says, 'mirroring the effect of the current as it pushes and rotates nets in flow.' The piece responds uniquely to the making process, following subtle rhythms and transitions reminiscent of the natural landscape that inspired it.

Annie Turner (British, born 1958) draws her inspiration from the river Deben in Suffolk, where her family have lived and worked for generations. Growing up surrounded by transcendent landscape, she is inspired by fossils, flotsam and the detritus hauled in by the tidal pull of the water. Turner studied three-dimensional design and ceramics at Bristol Polytechnic and later, a master's degree in ceramics at the Royal College of Art, London (1980–83). Her work has been widely exhibited across the UK and globally, including at the European Triennial for Ceramics and Glass in Belgium. Turner was shortlisted for the prestigious Loewe Craft Prize in 2019.

See also
Marilyn Levine (p.204)
Lawson Oyekan (p.224)
Honor Freeman (p.268)

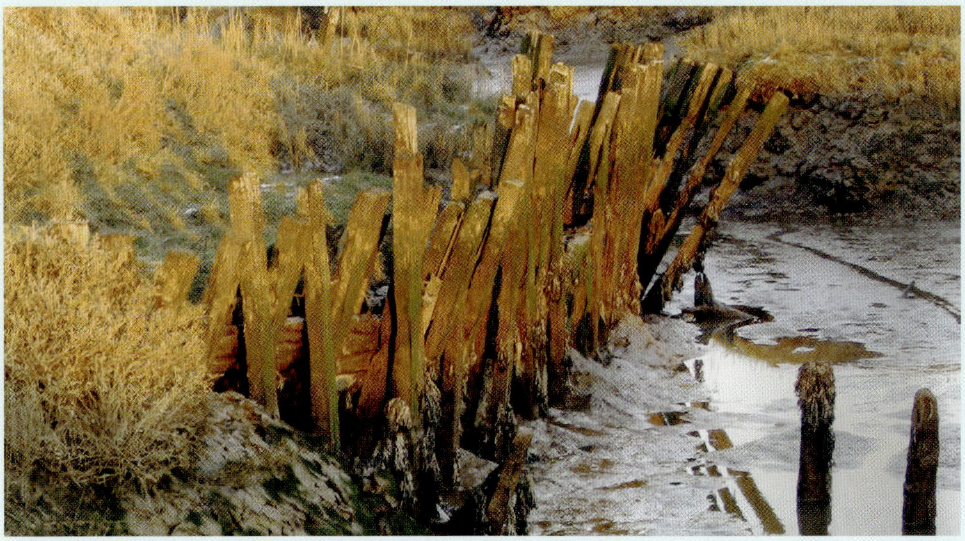

Subject Matter
Turner uses the visual language of photography to document the tones and delicate hues of the Suffolk landscape. The images she captures are as integral to the creative process as the outcome itself. Keep a photographic journal of visual subjects that interest you, from landscape to architecture. Reflect on colour combinations, interesting textures or structures that you could interpret into your own ceramic creations.

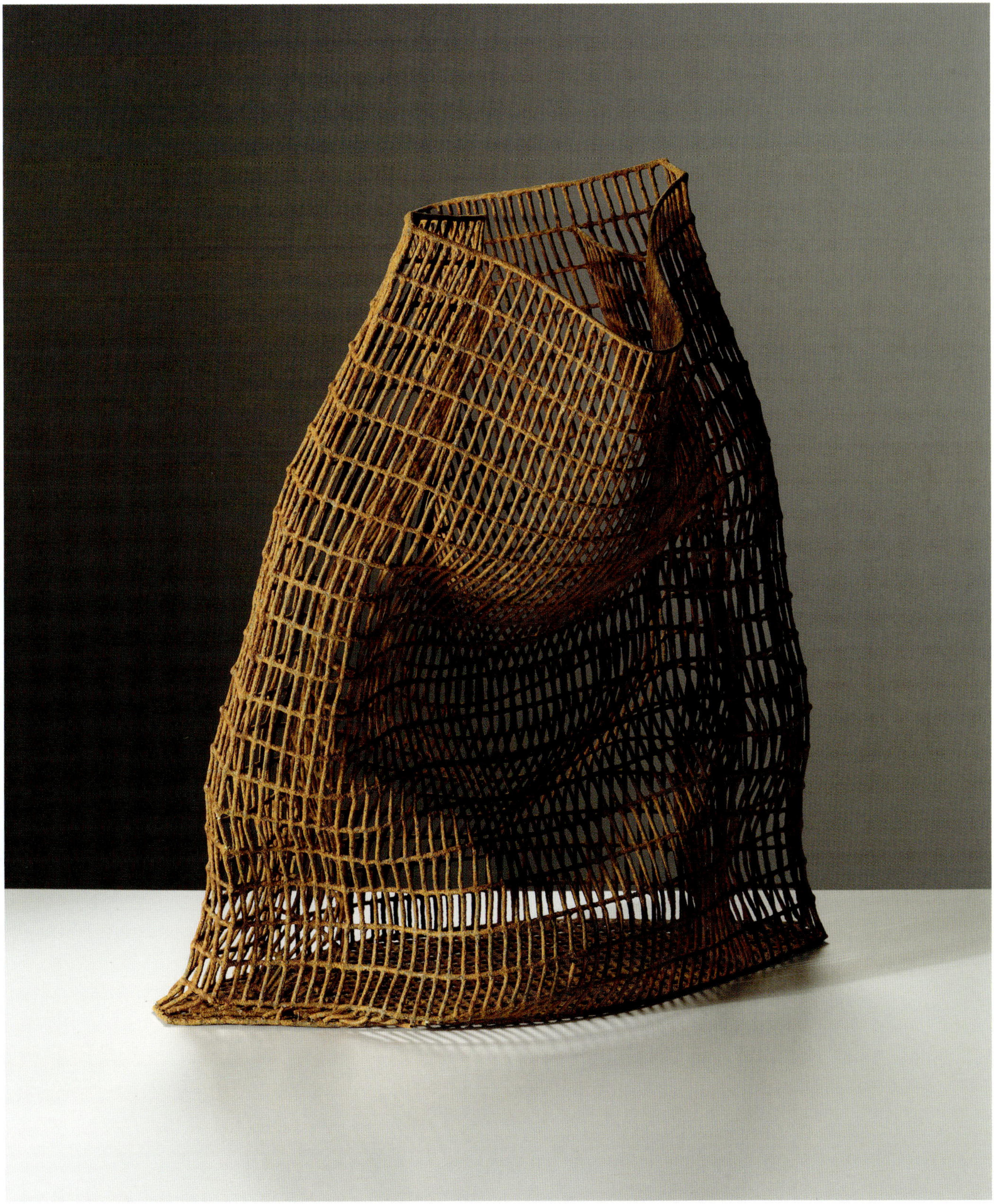

Anne Marie Laureys

Push 2018
Earthenware with coloured slip
46 × 34 × 28 cm (18 × 13⅖ × 11 in.)

Anne Marie Laureys' fluid, undulating forms convey an organic sensibility, alive with physical animation that belies their static disposition. *Push* is a writhing, fleshy mass that contorts and pulls in on itself – the boundary between the interior and exterior is seamlessly blended. With references to nature and the human form, Laureys thinks of her anthropomorphic vessels as 'metaphors for feelings', containing rich expression and spirited gesture.

Laureys aims to explore, in clay, 'the possibilities of what seems impossible', by sculpting with pots thrown on the wheel. Starting with an archetypical thrown form, Laureys then proceeds to manipulate and alter the shape by pushing, pinching and folding the clay walls to cause exaggerated distortions. As she explains, 'the plasticity of the material invites me to go beyond the thrown wall. To meet my sensual involvement with the material I test and explore its physical boundaries. After altering a series of forms, I assemble them to create an organic abstraction as an open invitation to feel the constraint tension, to discover the vivacity and the altered touch.'

Evoking the individuality of American potter George Ohr – whom the artist cites as an influence – Laureys emphasizes the directional pull of the throwing lines, transporting our gaze across the ripples and furrows of the form. To complete the piece she sprayed the surface with a light pink slip, followed by another spray of a darker shade to highlight the curves. The skin-like texture of the surface is very dry and allows light and shadow to gently rebound across the waves and folds of this sensuous composition.

Anne Marie Laureys (Belgian, born 1962) studied at the LUCA School of Arts in Ghent, Belgium. She is inspired by the work of US potter George Ohr (1857–1918) and makes energetic sculptures that play with form. She says that her ceramics are 'metaphors for "feeling"'. When she throws pots she experiments with the process using a gestural style, pulling, folding, pinching and puncturing the clay – and using the tension of the clay beneath her fingers to dictate the way the folds take shape. The result is abstract works, such as her series *Clay-e-motion* (2001–08).

See also

George Ohr (p.90)
Takeshi Yasuda (p.158)
Astrid Dahl (p.220)

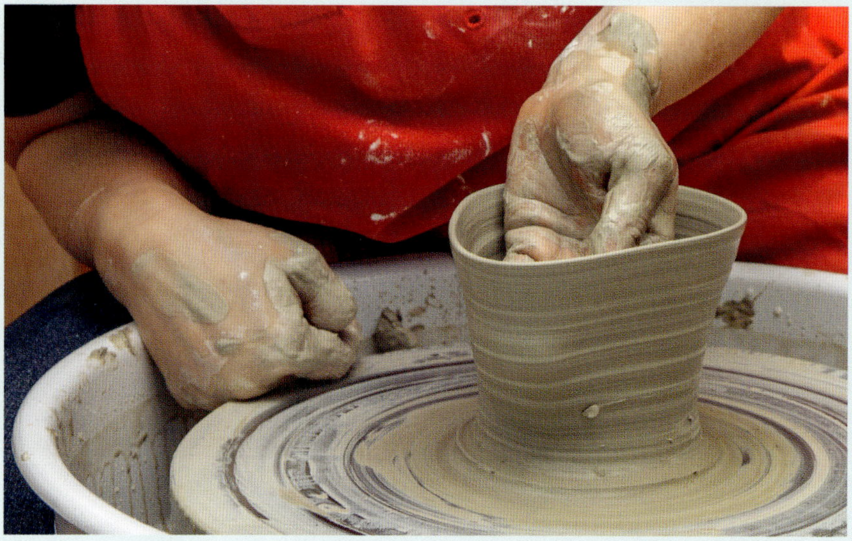

Process
Laureys composes her tactile forms by pinching, ruffling and folding the outer clay walls while they are still relatively wet and soft from the wheel. She continues to add new components and alter the form until she is satisfied with the final result. You could experiment with distorting the clay walls of your own forms. This is particularly effective on thrown work. Use your fingers to push the form out from the inside; observe how the throwing lines swell and bulge, transforming the profile of the shape. The skill lies in retaining a sense of freshness and rhythm and not overworking the piece.

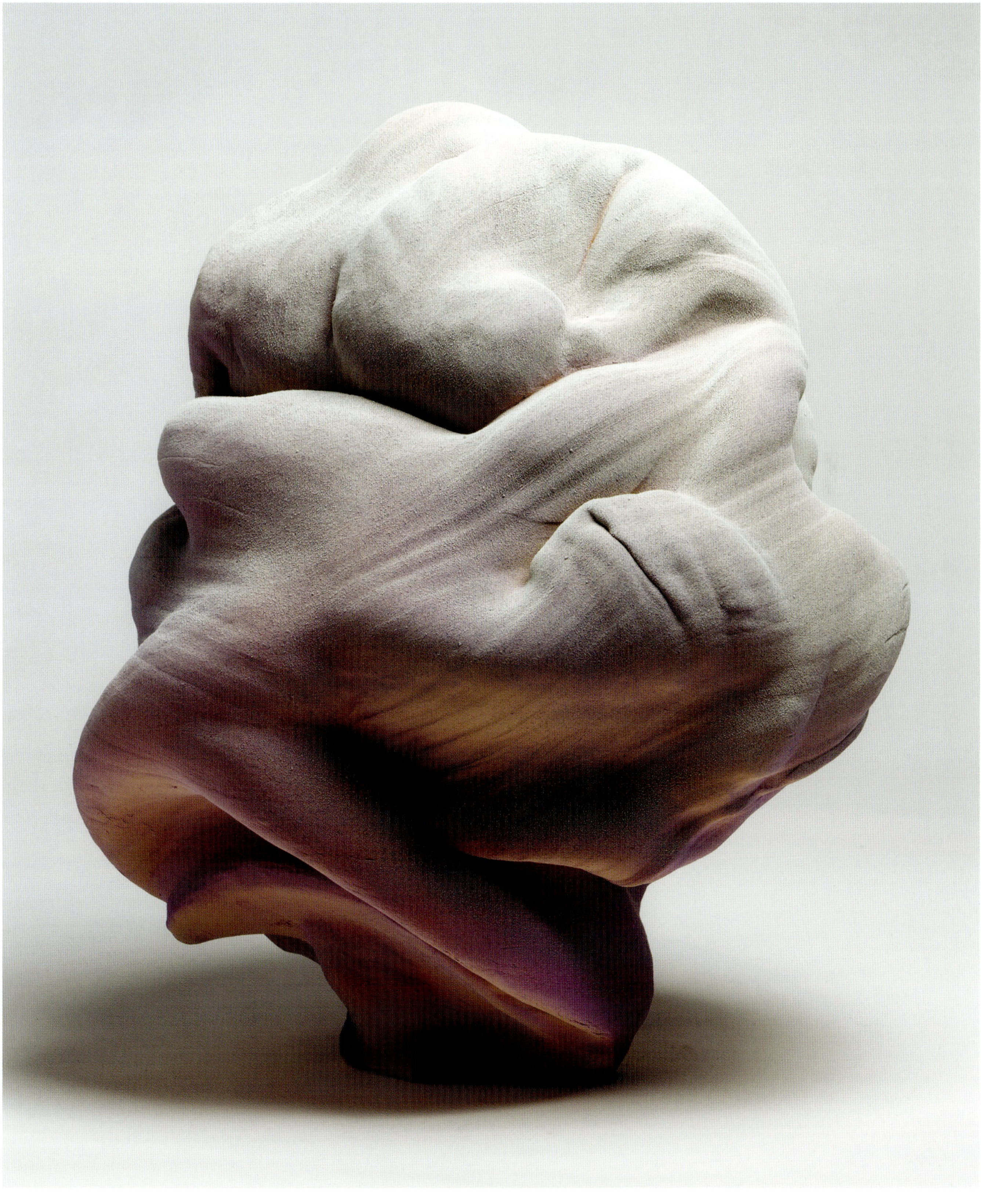

Jongjin Park

Artistic Stratum 2018
Paper, porcelain slip, stain
28 × 22 × 23 cm (11 × 8⅝ × 9 in.)

When first viewing the layered, papery constructions of Jongjin Park, it is hard to believe they are entirely ceramic. The expanded structure appears fragile and extremely delicate, but they are in fact quite the opposite and can withstand heavy-duty cutting and finishing by Park in order to achieve precise shapes. Park first developed this body of work during his studies at Cardiff University. Drawn to the materiality of clay and its ability to imitate, Park established a technique that involves painting multiple sheets of paper kitchen towel with coloured porcelain slip, which he proceeds to fold and layer into square stacks or cylindrical formations.

Resembling a pile of crisp, folded linen, this experimental piece by Park is highly tactile and visually engaging. With intricate wavy folds and multidirectional layers, the piece is buzzing with colour and texture. As Park explains, 'My work asks us to consider what is real... These effects meet with simple shapes and structures, contrasting with porcelain. I'm interested in relational art and applying it to ceramics. As ceramic artists we have the advantage of understanding our materials and processes directly and can manipulate these in interesting ways to spark a dialogue with the viewer.' A piece such as this can use as many as 1000 sheets of kitchen paper and take many days of labour to create. Park fired the piece to a temperature of 1280°C (2336°F) and the firing itself is an integral part of the finished outcome. As the paper sheets burn away, the clay slip expands and the form contorts under the strains and heat of the kiln, rendering the temporary nature of the original material into a state of permanence.

Jongjin Park (Korean, born 1982) has been studying ceramics and perfecting his art for many years. From 2000 to 2007 he pursued a bachelor's degree in ceramics from Kookmin University in Seoul, Korea, followed by a master's at the same institution. Park came to the UK in 2013 to complete a further one-year master's degree in ceramics at Cardiff Metropolitan University in Wales. He now lives and works in Guri, Seoul, and is currently working towards his Ph.D in ceramics at Kookmin University. Park's innovative material explorations have earned him significant recognition within the field. His exhibition at the 7th Cheongju International Craft Competition in Korea in 2011 was awarded the Gold Prize.

See also
Monika Patuszyńska (p.76)
Jill Shaddock (p.156)
Rafa Pérez (p.214)

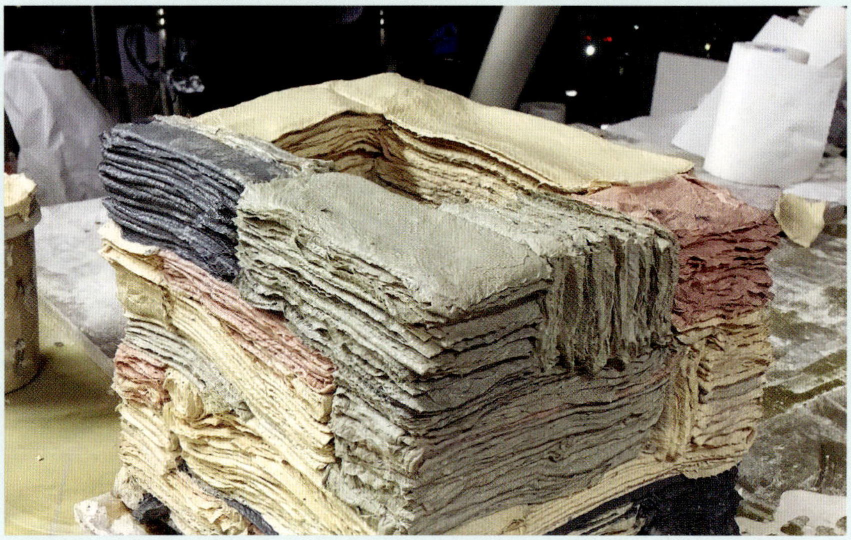

Technical
As illustrated by this piece of Park's work in its raw state, you can experiment with organic/combustible materials dipped in casting slip and play with creating patterns and textures that would otherwise be difficult to achieve. Some suggestions for things to soak in casting slip: cotton wool balls, leaves, bread (a hollowed-out loaf or slices), paper pulp or sheets of fabric (knitted panels work particularly well). The organic material will burn away during the firing, leaving a unique ceramic replica behind. Remember, good ventilation in the kiln room is essential if you use this technique.

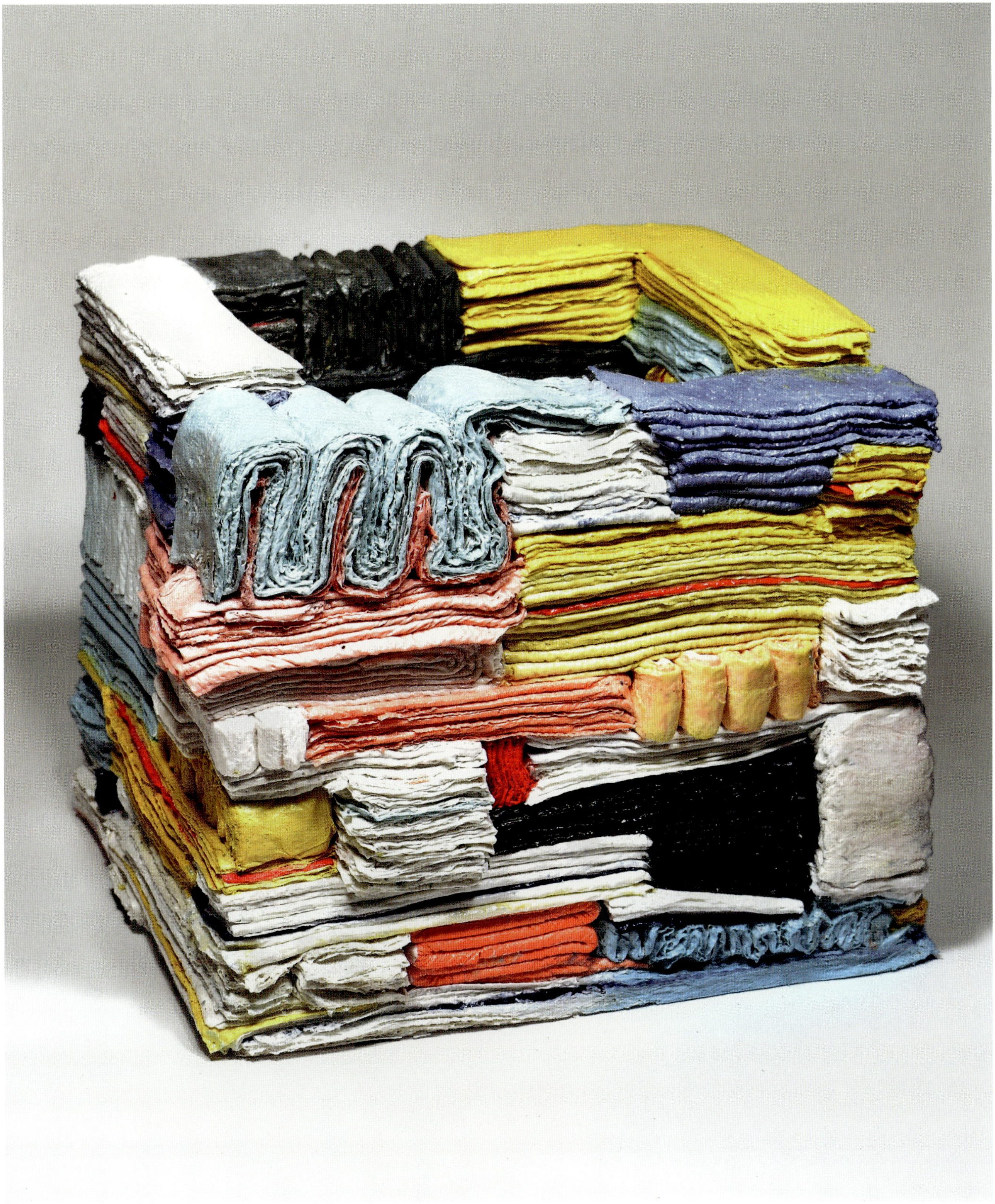

Halima Cassell

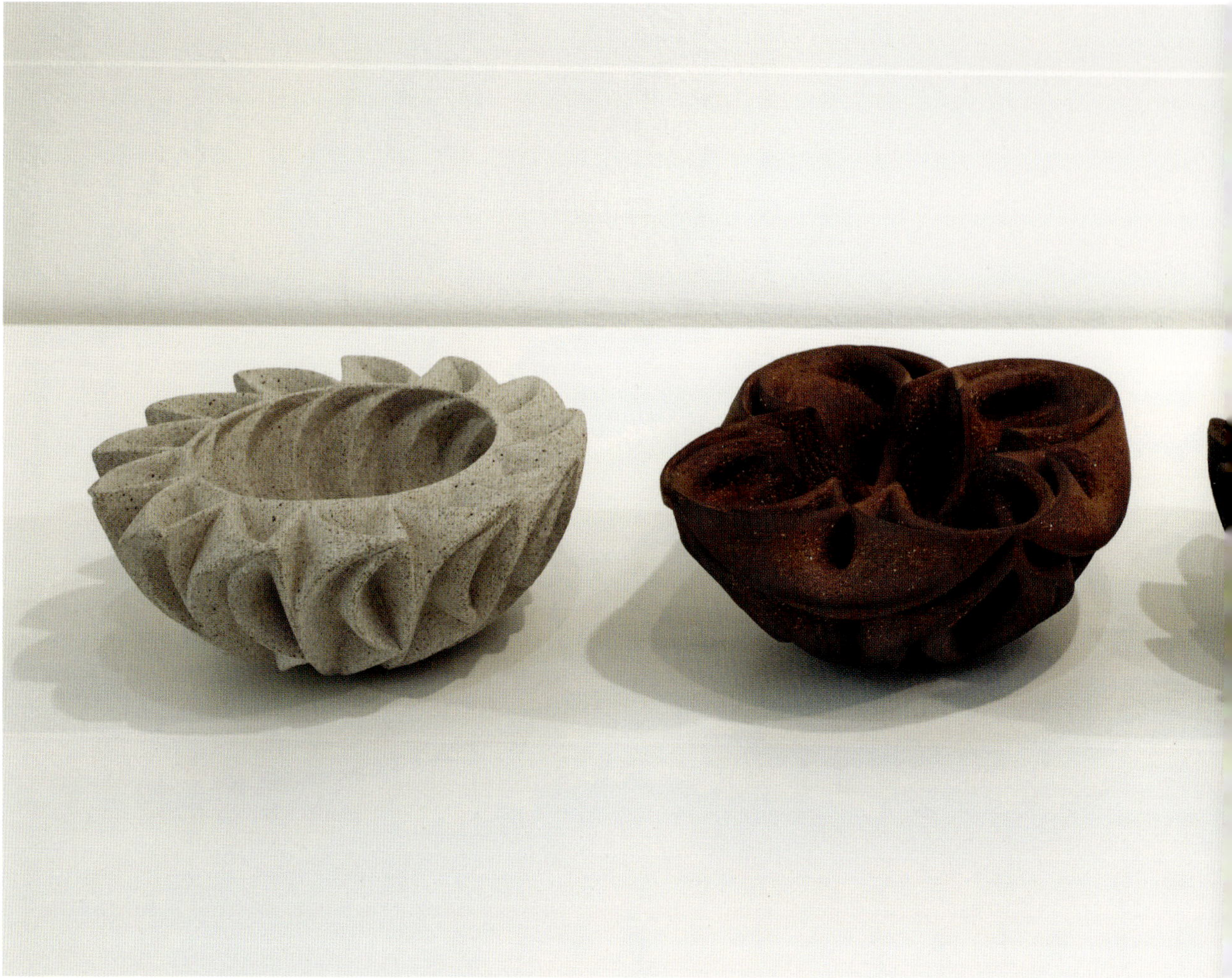

Propel, Quadri, Pulsar, Arabesque 2019
Hand carved, unglazed stoneware
Each bowl form: Height: 11.5 cm (4½ in.); Diameter: 22.8 cm (9 in.)

Artist and sculptor Halima Cassell creates beautifully carved forms inspired by Islamic architecture and the repetitive pattern motifs of North Africa. Geometry is the starting point for her designs and she plays with the illusion of movement and distortions of light. Her intricate compositions are highly engaging and invite exploration. As Cassell says, 'I create a mood and feeling of dynamic tension in my work by playfully manipulating the planes and facets of the patterns against each other. The stresses that this creates helps me to achieve the maximum impact within the overall design and also to push the boundaries of the material to its limits'.

This set of neatly incised bowl forms demonstrates Cassell's incredible skill and attention to detail. With arching curves and oscillating turns, each piece is a powerful expression of pattern and symmetry. Cassell rarely colours her work, preferring instead the rawness of the clay body itself. Here, the individual bowls are each made from a different clay body – some obtained from sites across the world. The subtle variations between coarse textures, colour and tone reflect Cassell's intention to make objects that comment on humanity: 'from clay, we come and to clay, we return'.

To make these pieces Cassell hand built and formed a very thick bowl shape to give her the suitable depth to carve into. Using precise measurements and marking grids to map out her design, she used a series of bladed tools to remove specific areas and define the unique profile. The resulting composition is held in perfect balance and symmetry – but with dramatic effect.

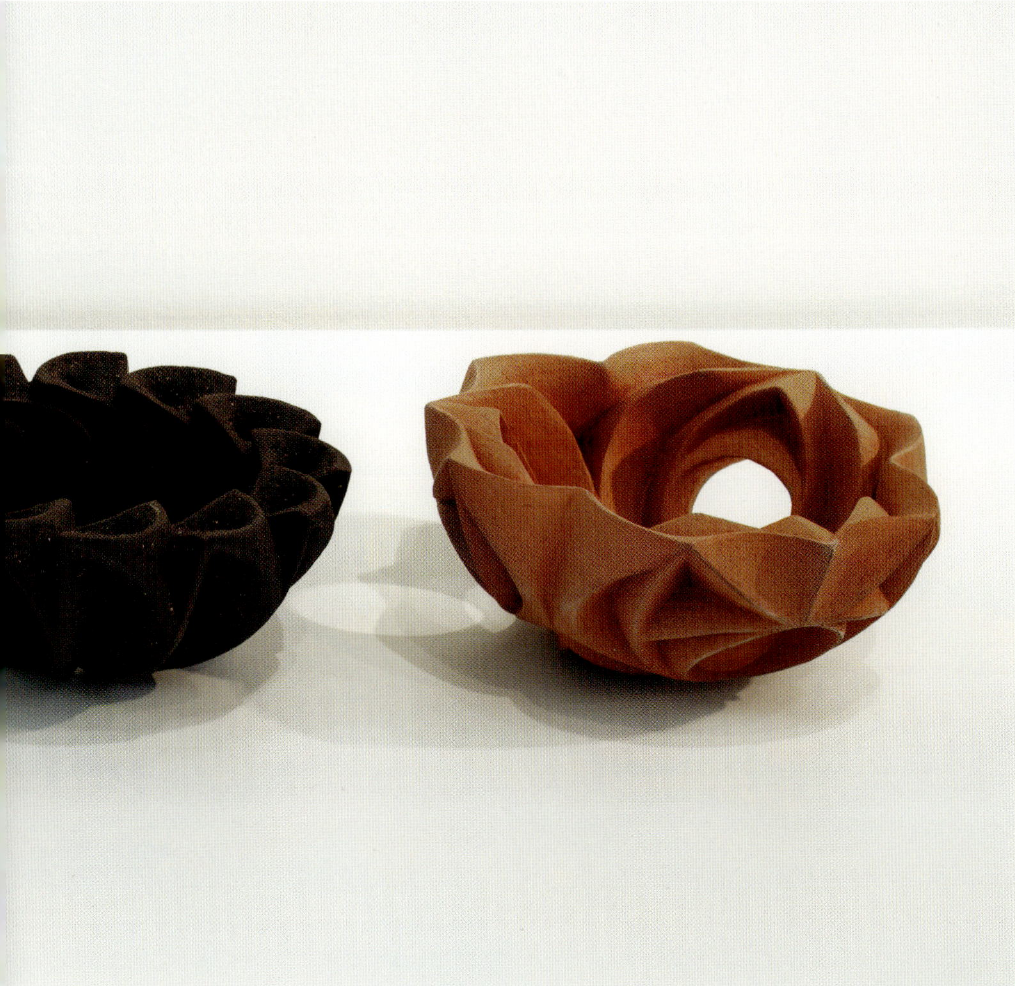

Halima Cassell (British, born 1975) was born in Pakistan and grew up in Lancashire. She studied at the University of Central Lancashire and Manchester City College. After graduating, Cassell took up a residency in a brick factory in Lancashire, where she completed a brick-carving project. Her work has a sculptural character thanks to her technique of carving directly into near-dry, heavy clay. She decorates her work with geometric patterns in high relief, inspired by the strong geometric elements and recurring patterns found in Islamic architecture and North African surface design. She has undertaken numerous public art commissions, from outdoor and indoor installations to wall friezes and smaller sculptures.

See also

Elizabeth Fritsch (p.60)
Pippin Drysdale (p.122)
Astrid Dahl (p.220)

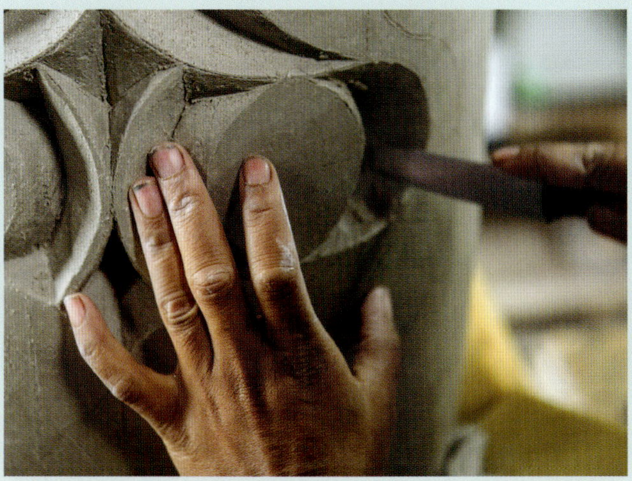

Technical

Depending on the complexities of the design and size, it can take as long as eighty to 280 hours – or more – for Halima Cassell to complete one of her pieces. Here, she has mapped the form with an outline of her pattern. Then, using a sharp knife tool, she skilfully carves areas away to reveal the beautiful profile. If you plan to use a similar method, you will get the best results if your clay walls are thick enough to accommodate the removal of clay – at least 5 cm (2 in.), depending on your design. The clay should ideally be leather-hard to very firm. Too soft and the clay will smear and smudge; too dry and your piece is at risk of cracking. Before you begin cutting, plan out your design on the clay surface with a soft pencil or needle tool. After your piece is fired, use wet-and-dry paper to sand edges and sharpen up your design.

Hitomi Hosono

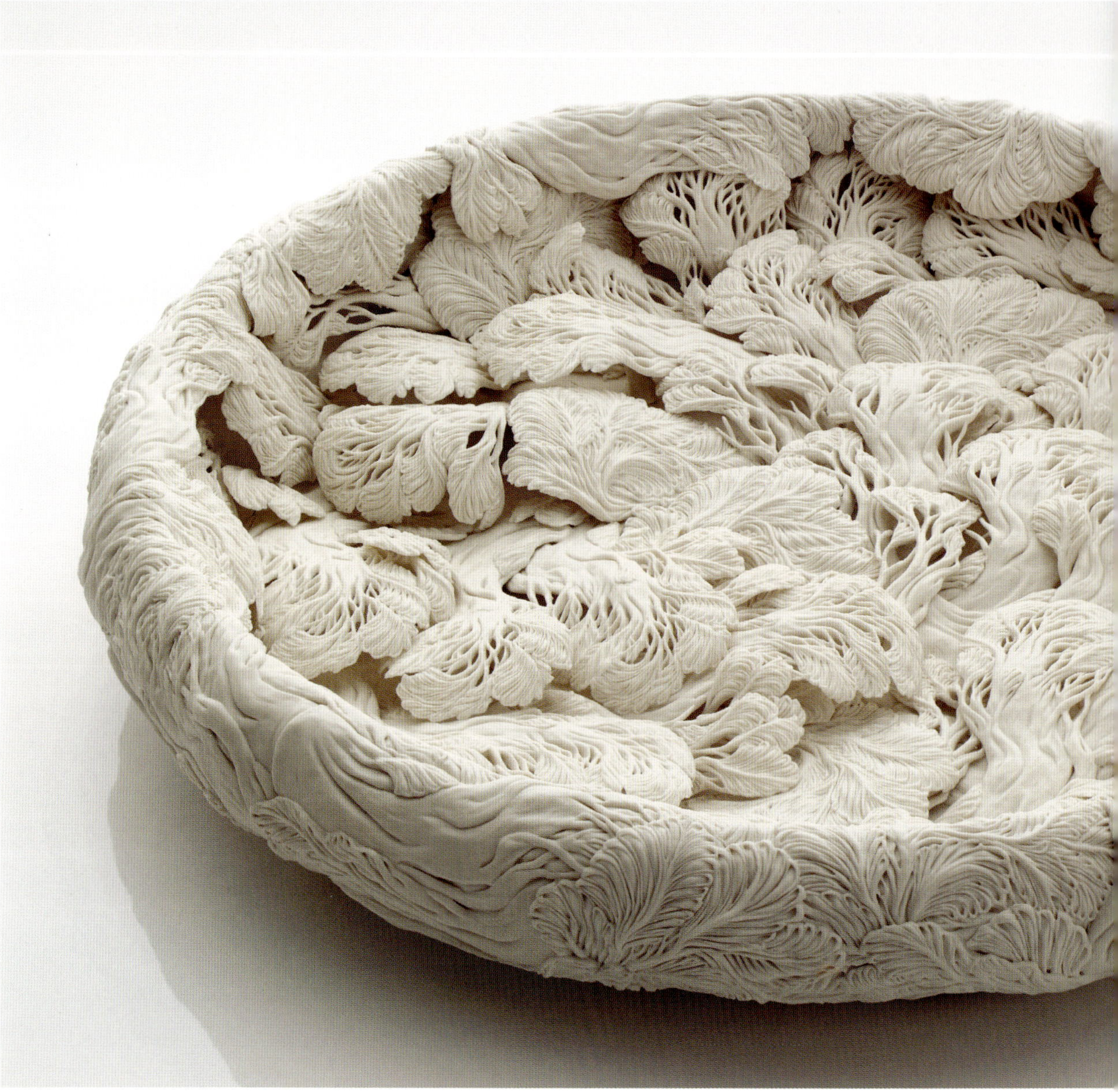

See also

Carolein Smit (p.198), **Phoebe Cummings** (p.256)

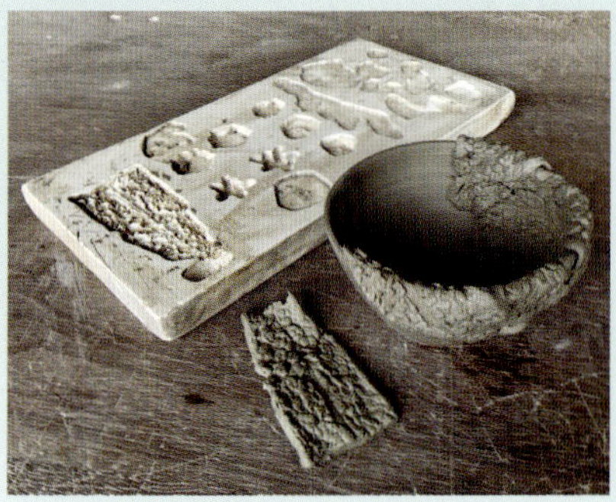

Hitomi Hosono (Japanese, born 1978) was born in Tajimi, Gifu Prefecture, which is known for its ceramics. The daughter of rice farmers and the granddaughter of a plaster and ceramics worker, Hosono grew up surrounded by tiles, pottery and nature. She studied ceramics at Kanazawa College of Art in Ishikawa Prefecture, where she became familiar with the *Kutani* style and the use of gold leaf, which she adds to the interiors of her porcelain pieces. She then studied at Danmarks Designskole in Copenhagen and London's Royal College of Art (RCA). While at the RCA she interned at the Wedgwood factory, where she gained experience of sprig moulding; she has gone on to use the jasperware technique to create bowls and vases with intricate botanical reliefs. In 2018, she became the first ever artist in residence at Wedgwood.

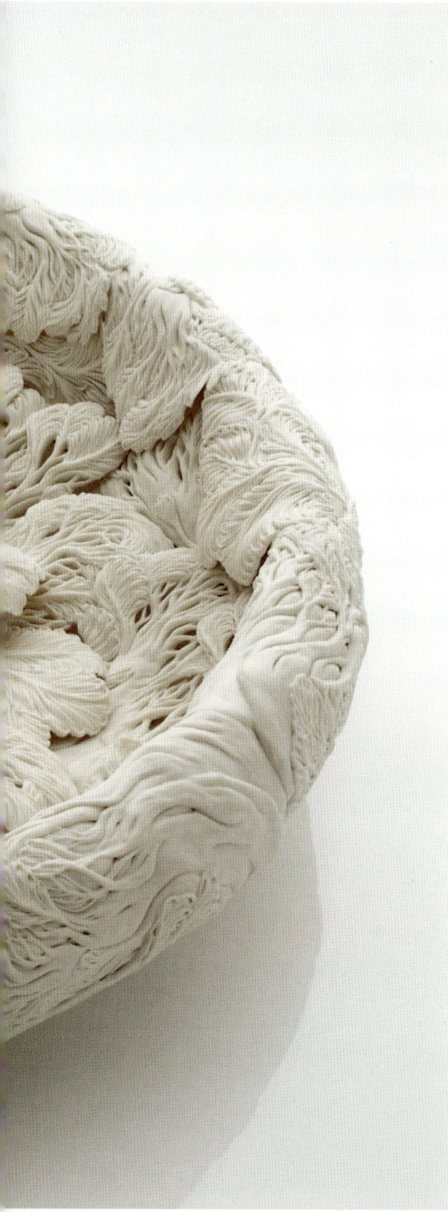

A Very Large Pine Tree Pool 2019
Moulded, carved and hand-built porcelain with an interior of dancing and pierced sprigs
Height: 7.8 cm (3 in.); Diameter: 43 cm (16⅞ in.)

Leaves, flora and the natural world are the subject of Hitomi Hosono's exquisite works. Fascinated by the intricacies of botanical forms, Hosono develops her initial ideas using a series of analytical drawings and observations, examining specific details such as the branching of veins in a leaf structure or the curves and jutting ridges that define its profile. Hosono then sensitively translates these tactile, organic qualities into porcelain. As she explains, 'It is my intention to transfer the leaf's beauty and detail into my ceramic work, using it as my own language to weave new stories for objects.'

This magnificent example is a testament to Hosono's incredible skill and patience in creating a piece of such tremendous quality and beauty. Through her innovative application of the sprigging technique, Hosono has instilled a wonderful sense of growth and movement that captures the imagination. We can almost hear the rustling noise as the ornate foliage and tendrils lift and emerge from within.

To achieve this mesmerizing effect, Hosono overlapped and layered hundreds of intricately moulded and carved leaf shapes over the profile of a shallow dish form. The density and sheer complexity of the sprigged decoration is very engaging and offers a different aspect depending on which angle you view the piece from. Hosono has pierced through some of the sprigs and manipulated spacing between the stalks and branches of the leaf shapes to allow for the interplay of light and shadow. This is enhanced further by the translucent properties of the porcelain. The purity of the material reflects the fragility of nature and captivates with its fine delicacy.

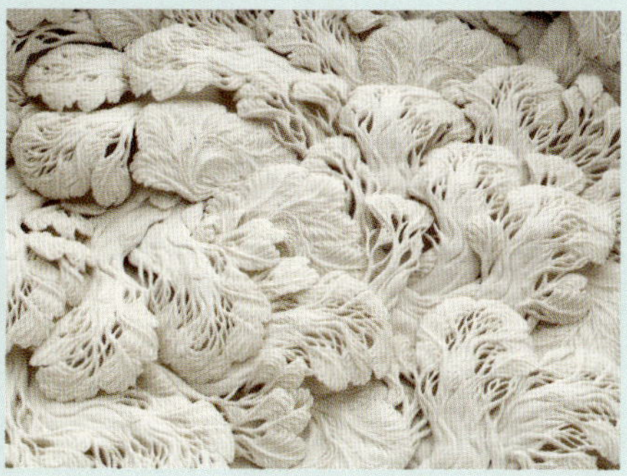

Technical
Hosono begins each piece by throwing a shape on the pottery wheel; this provides the foundation to attach the foliage to. The shallow relief (sprig) foliage was made by taking a plaster cast of a leaf shape that she had finely sculpted in clay. This method enables Hosono to press mould numerous copies of the same piece and build up the ornate layers. She adapts each moulded leaf to add individuality and mimic organic qualities. For a complex piece like this, it can take her around one month just to create the mould, followed by a number of weeks to attach the foliage. When complete – in order to reduce the risk of cracking – the piece is left for up to five months to dry before firing. The work is unglazed and high fired to stoneware temperature.

Vicky Lindo

Mother and Father (Love and Kaos) 2019
Slipcast earthenware, underglaze and glaze
Height: 34 cm (13⅓ in.)

Mother and Father (Love and Kaos) is based on Vicky Lindo's research into her British, Chinese and West African heritage and is part of a larger, poignant collection of work, entitled *Dead Dad Book*. The piece tells a touching personal story about the life of Lindo's late father, an immigrant from Jamaica who left the family home and disappeared while battling with alcoholism and trauma. After many years of no contact, Lindo discovered her father had died. He had been living alone in a wood in County Wexford, Ireland. The *Dead Dad Book* was a diary kept by Lindo's mother and sisters about the journey they took to Ireland to visit their father's grave and find out what had happened to him when he had been missing.

Mother and Father (Love and Kaos) consists of a pair of slip-cast grinning cat forms. Lindo has been making cats continuously since she was a child, and here she uses ornamentation effectively to convey significant events from the lives of her mother and father. Beautifully illustrated using the sgraffito technique, the design is built around the open-hand motif because, to Lindo, this signifies 'truth and honesty'; however, from here the pieces differ. *Mother* (left), with the heart in the centre, refers to love and the happy childhood Lindo spent with her mother and three sisters. *Father* (right) is more complex: the eye in the centre of the hand is about seeing and knowing, referring to the chaotic and solitary life he led. What is uniquely compelling about these works is how Lindo's playful, graphical style successfully communicates a deeply personal story with such sensitivity and compassion for the subject matter.

Vicky Lindo (British, born 1980) first became interested in ceramics when she was working at the Burton Art Gallery and Museum in Bideford, Devon, and saw a collection of North Devon slipware that they held. She co-founded the Pigeon Club studio in 2013 with Bill Brookes; and he casts the forms before Lindo decorates them – they both fire them. She is known for her highly decorative, narrative-driven pieces that explore themes of migration, racism and identity. In 2019 she won the top prize at the British Ceramics Biennial for her series *Dead Dad Book* – ceramics inscribed with sgraffito images and texts that explore the life of her late father, Mick, who travelled to England from Jamaica as part of the Windrush Generation.

See also

Alison Britton (p.72)
Elisabeth Kley (p.74)
Grayson Perry (p.94)

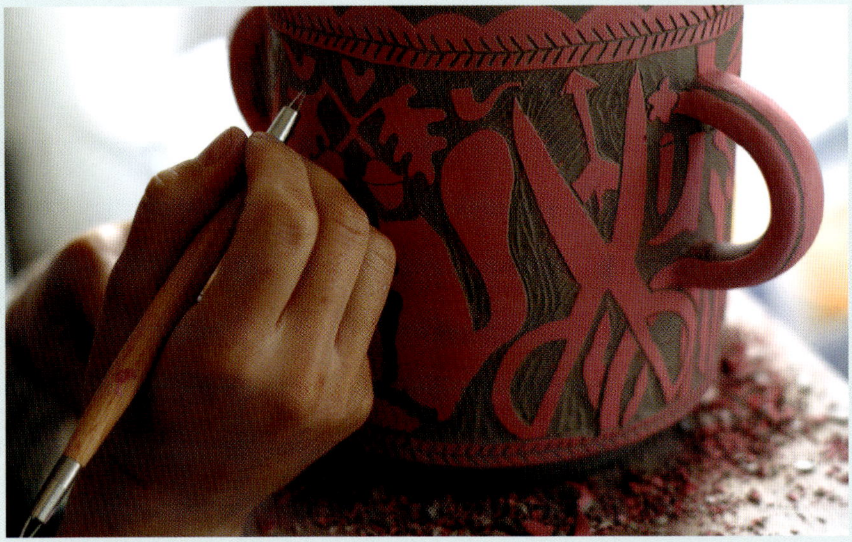

Surface
Lindo follows the traditions of North Devon pottery by decorating her distinctive work using a technique called sgraffito. This method involves coating the unfired, leather-hard clay surface with a layer of coloured slip or underglaze and using a point or hoop tool to scratch through the top layer to reveal the clay body colour beneath. This process has produced light grooves in the surface which brings added texture to the piece. Note how Lindo has only used one colour to decorate the cats. This creates a striking contrast with the white clay background, enhancing the intricacy of the pattern and the exceptional quality of line.

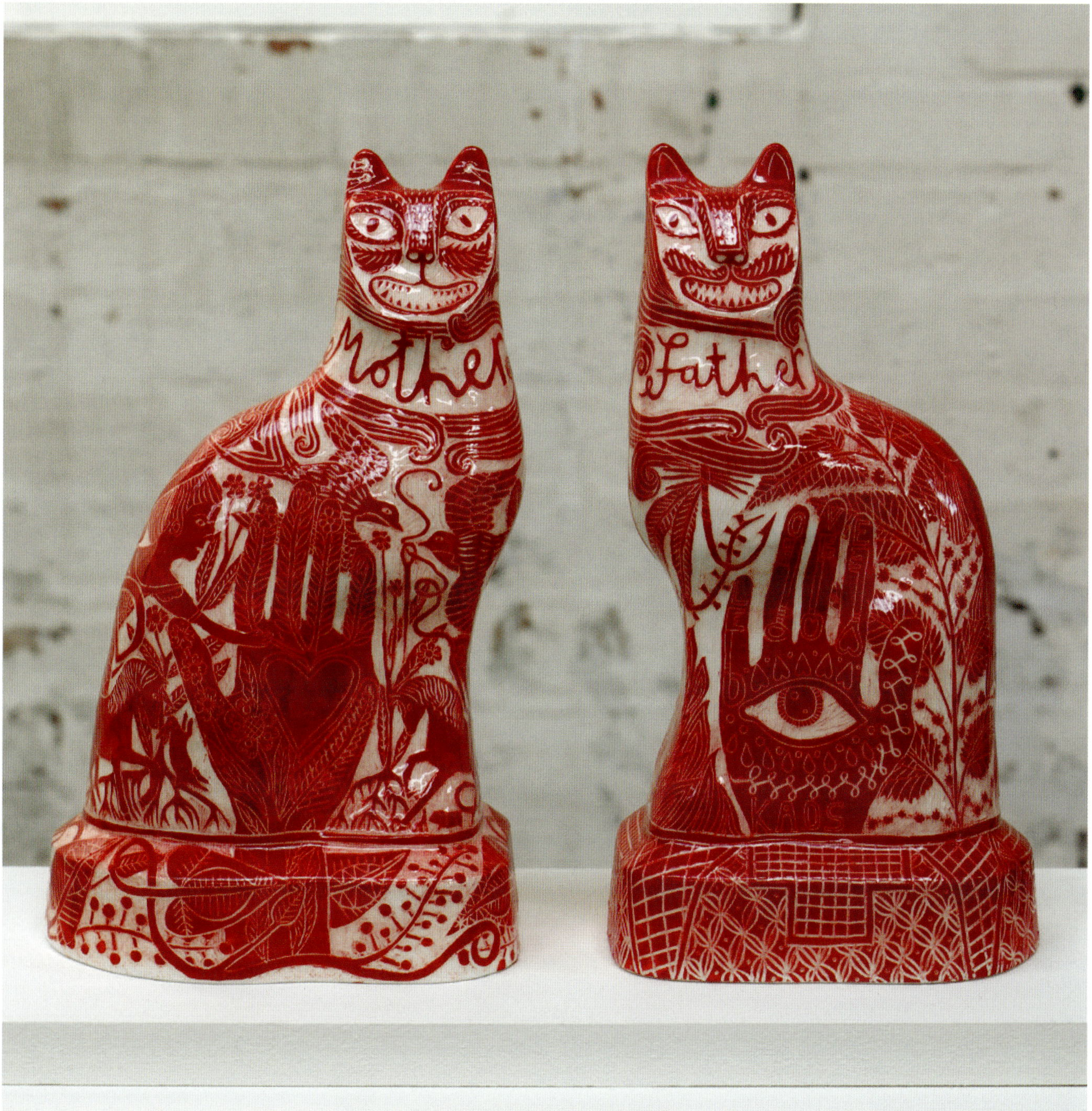
Mother
Father

Instal

lation

Installation artworks can encompass large-scale, three-dimensional mixed media assemblages, often designed for a specific place or for a temporary period of time. An installation can offer a cohesive experience, in that it might occupy an entire room or gallery space and invite the viewer to walk through or interact in some way.

If this is an area that you find appealing, you could start with a location in mind and examine your response to this environment. Edmund de Waal's featured work (p.250) echoes the transient light and changing landscape that surrounds the gallery site. You may instigate a lasting legacy into your piece, like Clare Twomey (p.246), whereby the potential for interaction extends beyond the duration of the exhibition. There could be a theatrical element to the work, evident in the work of

Betty Woodman (p.252) – combining painting with ceramics to skew our perception between two-dimensional and three-dimensional space.

Installation could embrace a performative aspect, like the unfired works of Phoebe Cummings (p.256) or Paolo Polloniato (p.262). Both these artists use unfired clay that gradually breaks down and returns to dust – representing the fragile nature of its existence. Linda Sormin (p.264) encourages the viewer to walk through the assemblage to recreate feelings of the migrant experience. Your creative message could centre around social and political themes that prompt thought and contemplation, as seen in Barnaby Barford (p.266) and Tana West's (p.270) subversive works that engage the viewer to interact and think about their moral responsibilities.

Clare Twomey

Exchange 2013
Ceramic
Dimensions variable

Exchange by Clare Twomey was a large site-specific installation commissioned by the Foundling Museum, London (UK). Established in 1739, the Foundling Hospital offered refuge for infants at risk of abandonment. Through the project Twomey explored themes concerning charity, responsibility and acts of philanthropy that are central to the Foundling's history as the UK's first children's charity and England's first public art gallery.

The installation consisted of more than 1,000 china cups and saucers spread across five trestle tables. On the base of each set Twomey inscribed individual 'good deeds' – from simple requests, such as 'make someone a cup of tea in this cup' or 'mow your neighbour's lawn' to more challenging requests like 'sign up for a 5K charity run' or even 'adopt a child'. On each day of the exhibition, ten visitors were invited to choose one cup from the hundreds on display. After reading the message, they could decide whether to accept the good deed in exchange for the cup or decline and return the cup to the table. If they chose to keep the cup, the saucer remained behind as a record of the exchange and to signify their commitment to fulfil the good deed.

This simple act of exchange instigated by Twomey is a powerful and implicit reflection of the exceptional charitable work of the hospital and the Foundling Museum today. Twomey encourages the visitors to become philanthropists themselves by acting on their good deeds. The positive impact on the wider community instils a ripple effect of enduring kindness, which is perpetuated long after the installation has finished.

Clare Twomey (British, born 1968) studied at the Edinburgh College of Art and the Royal College of Art in London. In 2011, she became a research fellow at the University of Westminster. She works with clay in large-scale installations, sculptures and site-specific works that explore themes of permanence and inheritance. She is known for her installations that incorporate transience, such as *Conscience/Consciousness* (2003), which consisted of thin ceramic tiles that covered the floor of a gallery and broke when they were walked on. She also works in collaboration for some projects, such *as Factory: the Seen the Unseen* (2017–18), for which she transformed the Tate Exchange in London into a factory making everyday objects from clay to investigate ideas about production.

See also
Piet Stockmans (p.144)
Torbjørn Kvasbø (p.258)
Barnaby Barford (p.266)

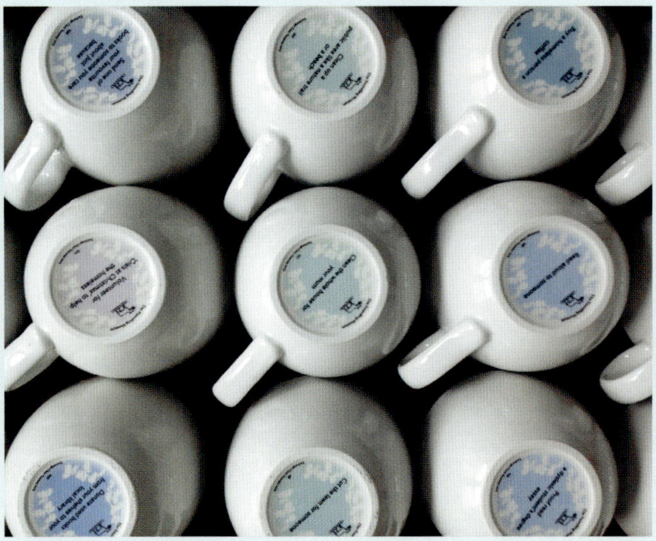

Subject Matter
Social engagement and interaction are at the heart of Twomey's practice. For *Exchange*, she collaborated with children in care, former pupils of the Foundling Hospital School, local residents, celebrities and many others to devise the more than 1,000 individual good deeds. On accepting a cup, the participant was asked to report back to the museum the outcome of their good deed via social media, written messages or photographs – creating a touching account of personal and collective narratives. As this project by Twomey demonstrates, a 'call to action' request embedded in a work can be very engaging and builds longevity into your concept, opening and expanding dialogue to digital platforms and beyond. A very simple but effective method is to instigate a written or video blog whereby you document your project and ask participants to contribute to the content.

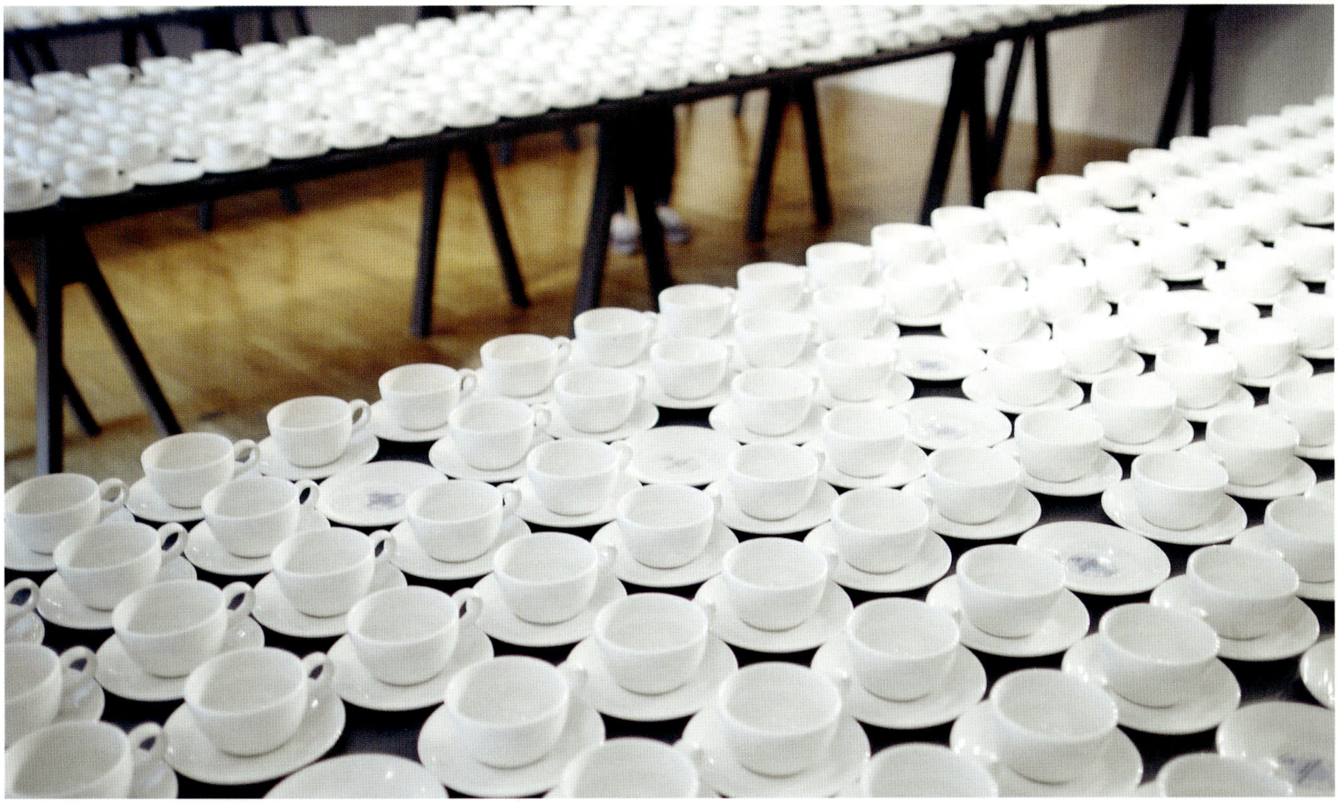

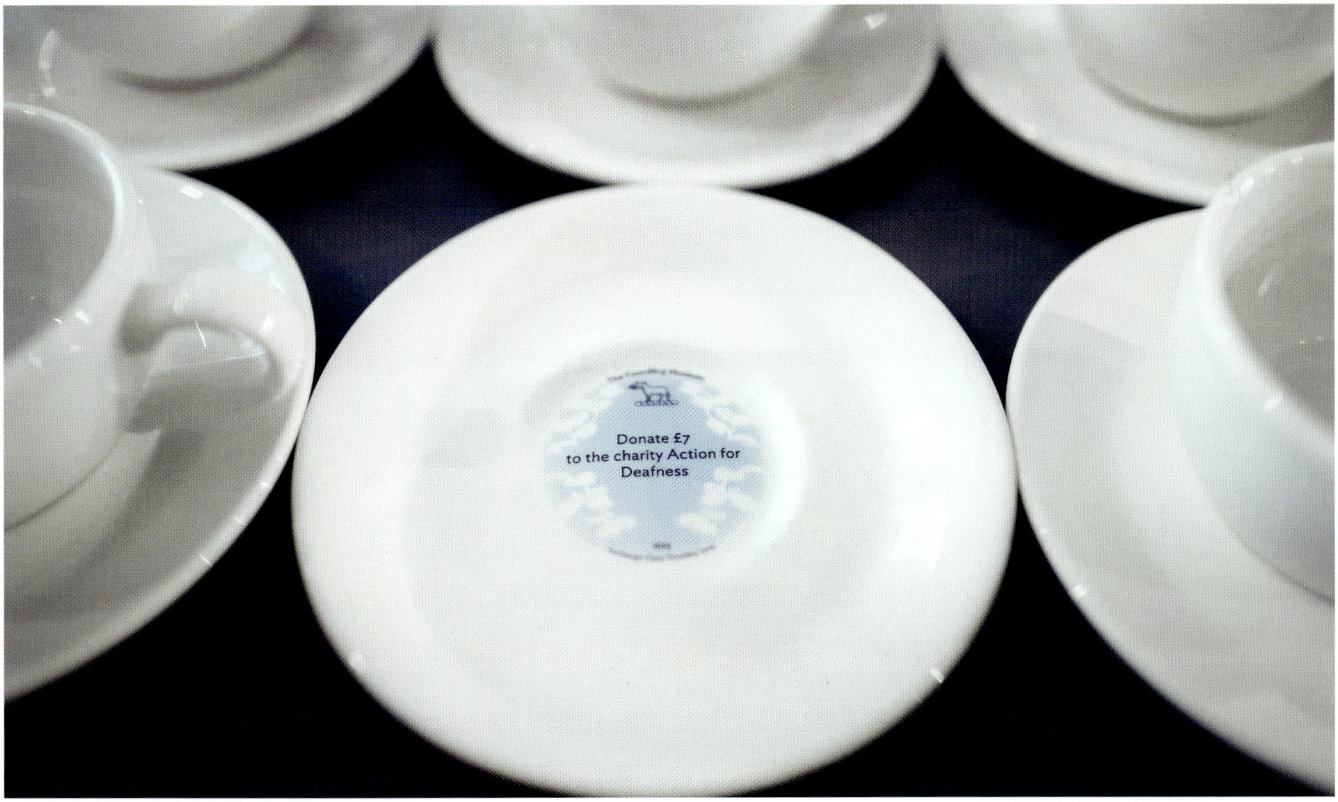
Donate £7
to the charity Action for
Deafness

Jessica Stoller

Untitled (Still Life) 2014
Ceramic, glaze
160 × 152.4 × 67.3 cm (63 x 60 x 26 ½ in.)

This debauched tableau depicts a wildly decadent feast of tantalizing cakes, ice-cream sundaes and delicious-looking sweet treats – but all is not quite what it seems. Among the drippy sauces and decorative icing sit disembodied hands, crawling ants, nipple-shaped macarons and a cake decorated with a ring of breasts.

The installation evokes the grandeur of the 18th-century French dining rituals, where porcelain eventually replaced sugar as the coveted material to depict mythological and allegorical displays. Stoller subverts this decadent tradition to something more sinister, combining varied references from *vanitas* painting to Marie Antoinette's breast cup. Elaborately constructed with naturalist detail, Stoller's ceramic objects juxtapose extremes in both content and surface, marrying a delicate balance of the corporeal and the imagined, the idealized and the grotesque.

Stoller created the components for this installation from porcelain. The artist comments that this is a significant material choice for her: 'I focus on porcelain as my primary medium, creating sculpture which mines the material's complicated past and its long-held associations with beauty, taste, and consumption. Drawing from multiple histories the work weds surrealist wit to a feminist understanding of the body as a political site. I employ notions of the "feminine," often undervalued and dismissed as lacking content; under my hand these emblems synthesize, becoming powerful tools that crack open preconceived tropes from the inside out.'

Jessica Stoller (American, born 1981) studied at the College for Creative Studies, Michigan, and Cranbrook Academy of Art, Michigan. She sculpts, drapes, carves, moulds and pipes clay to create sensuous, yet grotesque, porcelain pieces that explore notions of the symbolic, cultural and idealized female form. She works in a variety of forms, from tabletop-sized vessels, busts and figures to elaborate multi-piece tableaux that investigate porcelain's associations with desire, taste and consumption. Her works are surreal hybrids, utilizing the historic language of porcelain and the still life, while creating new and unfamiliar forms that arrest the viewer's eye with their beauty and abjection.

See also

Nick Weddell (p.120)
Viola Frey (p.174)
Bertozzi & Casoni (p.228)

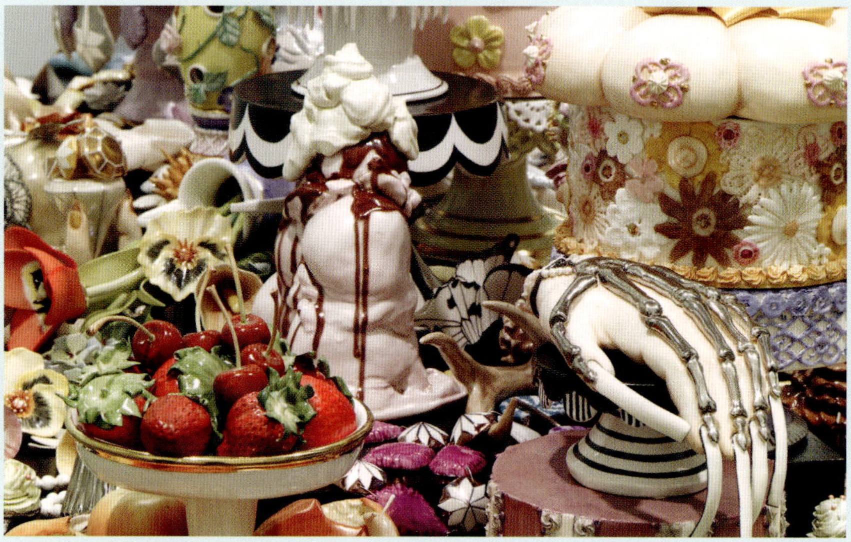

Technical
Stoller used a variety of techniques to create this highly detailed work. She hand built the ceramic forms, using coils, slabs and wheel-thrown parts. The draped fabric in the centre of the composition is actually ceramic but was achieved by dipping a sheet in slip, which subsequently burnt away in the firing, leaving a ceramic version behind. Stoller finished the confectionery elements in the same way you would a cake – by piping clay through a pastry bag. The sculptures are mostly china painted, which is an over-glaze firing process where colour is painted and fired numerous times at a low temperature to create subtly hued surfaces.

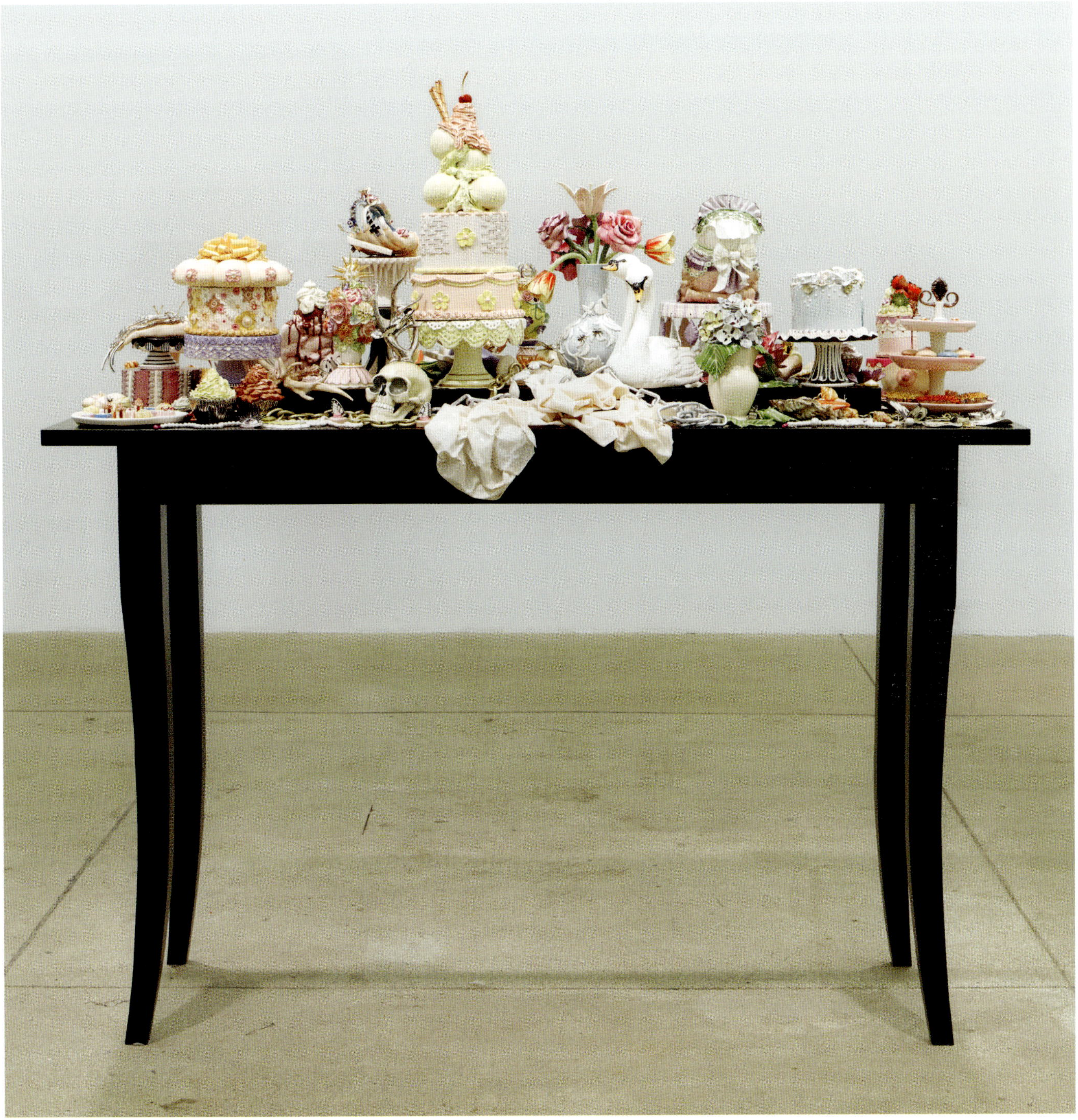

Edmund de Waal

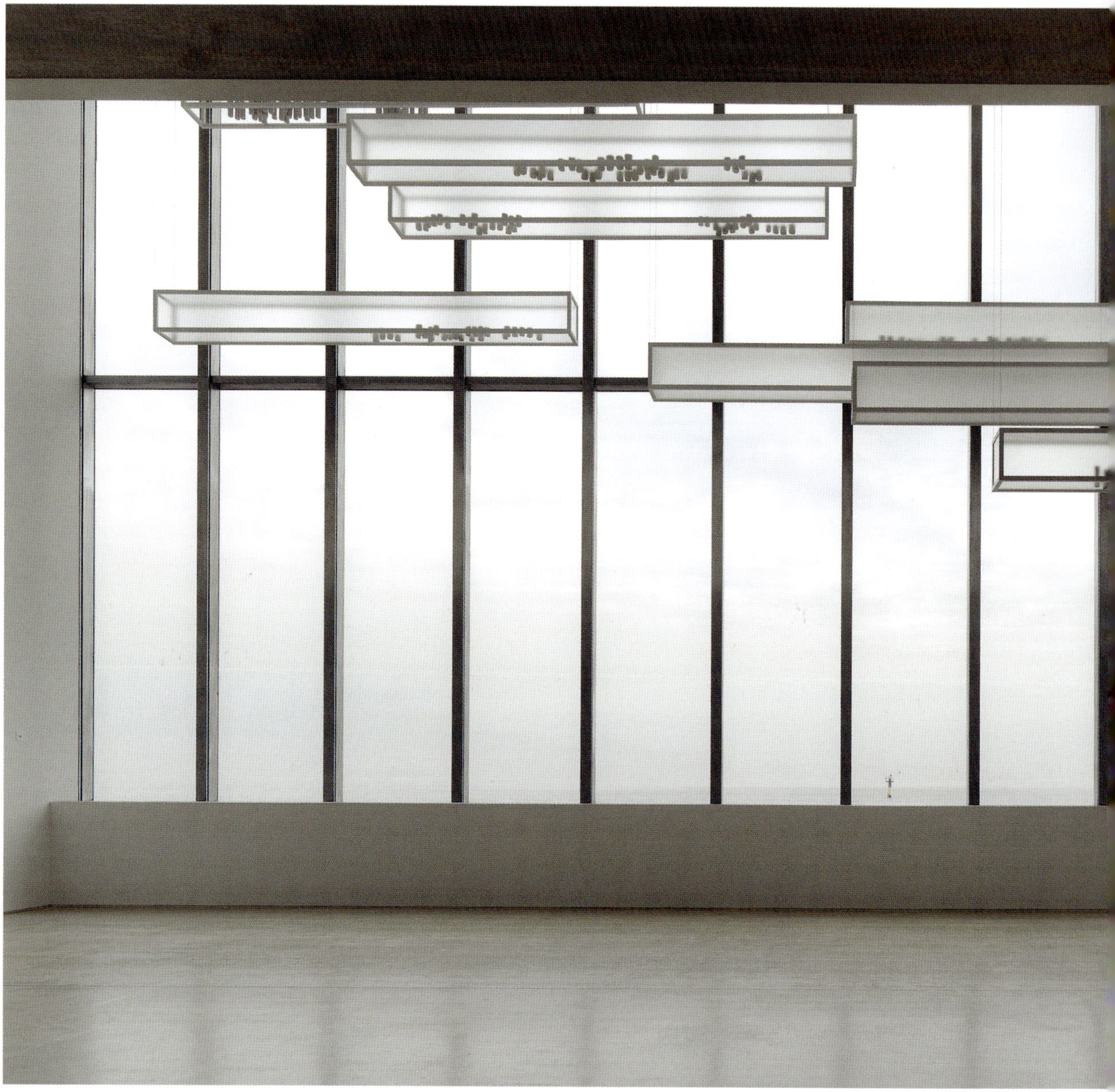

See also

Gwyn Hanssen Pigott (p.70), **Bernard Leach** (p.136)

Edmund de Waal (British, born 1964) is an internationally acclaimed artist and writer who was drawn to the expressive qualities of clay from an early age. At seventeen, he undertook a two-year apprenticeship with Geoffrey Whiting (1919–88) in the traditional Leach style and he progressed to setting up his own studio making functional domestic pottery. De Waal studied English at Cambridge University, followed by a postgraduate degree in Japanese. He spent a period of time in Japan, continuing to explore his interest in clay. In recent years, de Waal has become best known for his large-scale installations of thrown, celadon-glazed porcelains which explore themes of collecting and collections, memory and displacement. In 2011, he was awarded the Order of the British Empire (OBE) for his contribution to the arts.

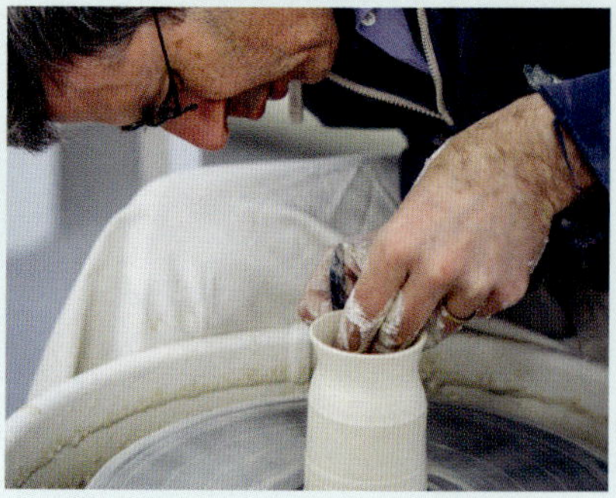

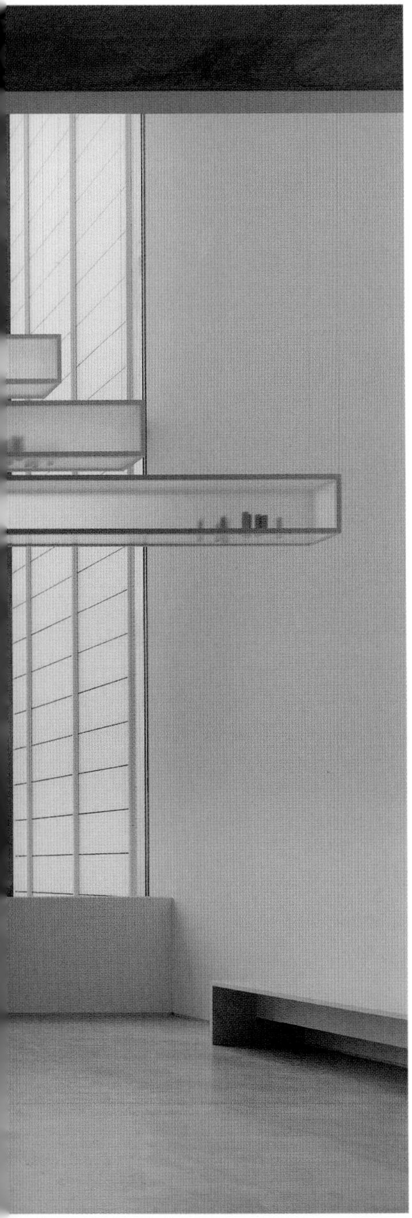

Atmosphere 2015
286 porcelain vessels in nine aluminium and plexiglass vitrines
Each: 30 × 300 × 25 cm (11¾ × 118 × 9¾ in.)
Overall dimensions variable

Suspended high in the air, nine large horizontal vitrines – filled with partially obscured arrangements of more than 200 celadon and grey porcelain pots – occupy the vast Sunley Gallery space of the Turner Contemporary in Margate, Kent (UK). The installation is a site-specific response by de Waal to the cloud formations, transitions of light and the changing landscape of the North Sea, in relation to the architecture of the gallery. The only way to view the vitrines is by looking up in the same way as we view clouds. De Waal refers to this as 'skying', an expression used by the naturalist painter John Constable (1776–1837) to describe the simple pleasure of lying down on your back and observing the sky. When this piece was displayed in 2015, mats were laid on the floor of the gallery to allow visitors to immerse themselves in their own 'skying'.

Influenced by the work of minimalist artist Donald Judd (1928–1994) and architect Ludwig Mies van der Rohe (1886–1969), these series of cloudscapes convey de Waal's restrained response to the endless movement of light and experience of weather. Positioned at alternating heights, the vitrines layer and overlap each other. Inside, carefully arranged groups of simple thrown forms are shrouded by different levels of opacity in the vitrines. One is clear, four are semi-transparent and the remaining four are opaque. The installation is named after a quote by painter J. M. W. Turner (1775–1851), who famously said, 'Atmosphere is my style.' Together, these subtle distinctions in tone and variation reflect the changing landscape and ambience created by light.

Material
Porcelain offers beautiful translucent qualities and purity of colour. De Waal throws each pot individually using a pottery wheel to create fluid and sensitive forms. Porcelain is notoriously temperamental to work with: it snags, collapses, cracks and warps, but the pay-off is a luscious clay body that is responsive and elegant. De Waal fires his pieces in either an oxidized (electric kiln) or reduction (gas kiln) environment.

Composition
De Waal explores the architectural quality of the vitrine and combines this with groupings of curated pots. The vitrines are constructed from an array of materials – from painted steel, aluminium, blackened oak and acrylic. De Waal plays with sections of frosted glass or acrylic to distort and skew our perception of the contents inside, conveying his interest in containment and distilling memory.

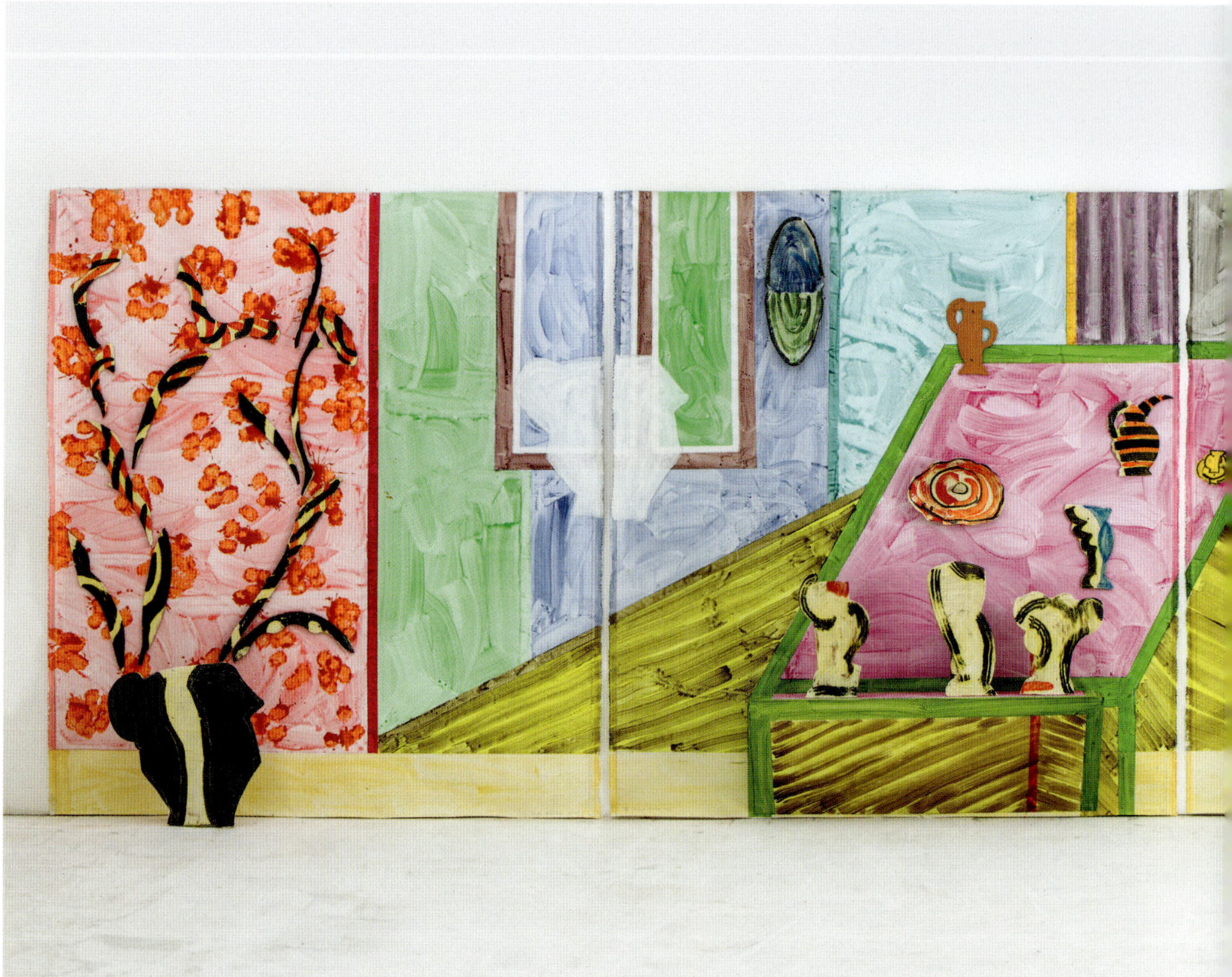

The Summer House 2015
Glazed earthenware, epoxy resin, lacquer, acrylic paint, canvas, wood
860 x 240 x 30 cm (338½ × 94½ × 12 in.)

The late American artist Betty Woodman is world renowned for her pioneering approach, which moved sculpture, painting and ceramics into unprecedented new ground. This vast installation, *The Summer House*, from her solo show, *Theatre of the Domestic* at the ICA London, consists of four joyful coloured panels that span a distance of 8.5 metres (28 feet) across the gallery wall. The painterly still-life scene alters perspective by depicting a domestic interior, with a dining table adorned with ceramic vessels that appear to jut out beyond its boundary. This interaction between a flat canvas suggesting a three-dimensional space, with physical objects that are quite two-dimensional in form is rather intriguing. Essentially, Woodman explores the context of her ceramic objects by creating a setting for them within her artwork.

Woodman's ceramic forms are typically vessel based; as she said, 'the vase is the archetypal ceramic object ... the vase is also a symbol for a woman. Metaphorically it's a container; it has that connection for everyone.' She took inspiration from a wide range of cultural sources, such as Chinese Tang dynasty pottery (618–907), Islamic art and ancient Greek and Etruscan pottery. However, here, the strongest connection is to the paintings of Post-Impressionist artist Pierre Bonnard (1867–1947), in particular his depictions of domestic interiors and furniture. The warm, evocative hues of Woodman's colour palette are a reference to the early renaissance painter Fra Angelico (1395–1455), whom she greatly admired.

The scale of *The Summer House* is true to life and immediately absorbs the viewer into its realm. Energetic brush and cloth marks swirl and oscillate across the canvas and reflect the lively shapes and surface decoration of Woodman's spirited ceramics.

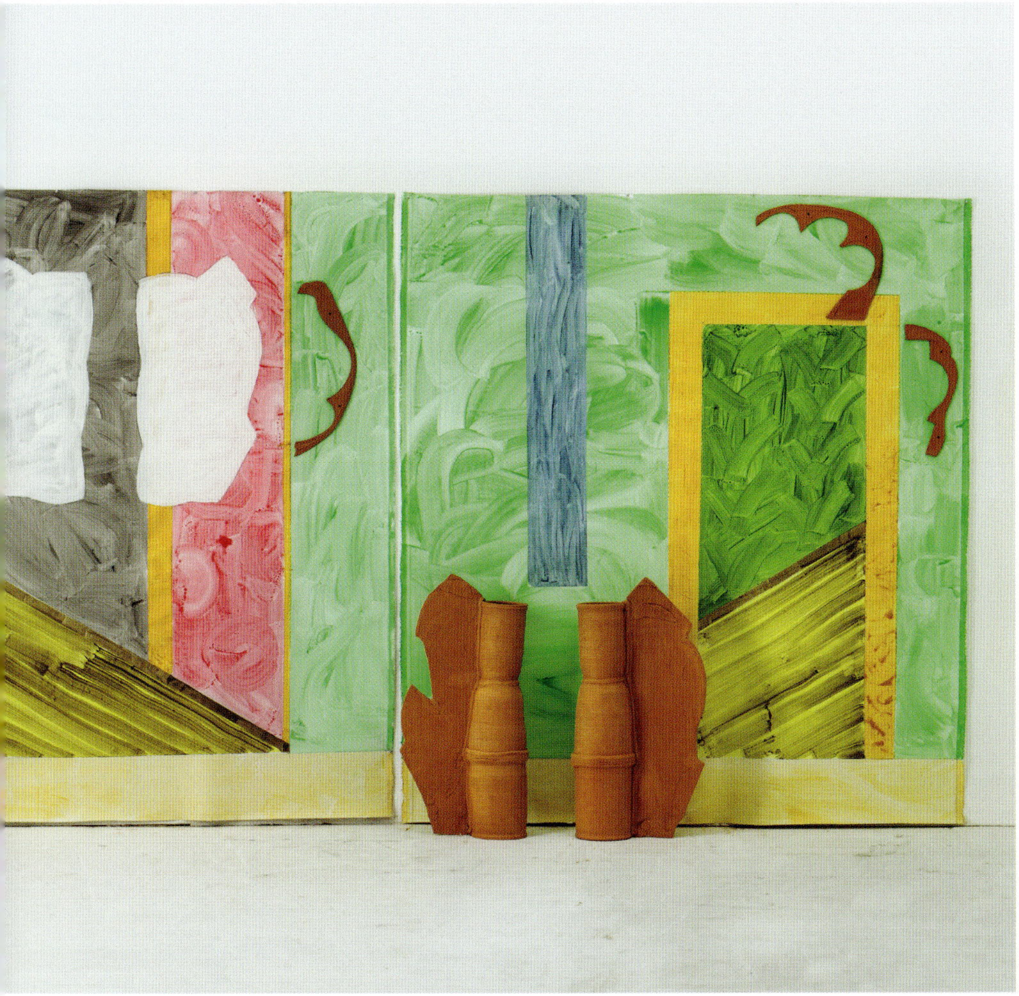

Betty Woodman (American, 1930–2018) started pottery classes at the age of sixteen. She enjoyed using clay and went on to study at the School for American Craftsmen at Alfred University in New York (1948–50). She started out as as a production potter in the 1950s and progressed to site-specific murals, large floor pieces and multimedia installations. She is known for her vases and her signature series, *Pillow Pitchers* (1975–2007), which features vessels based on Cretan pitchers painted with colourful slips and glazes. Woodman has received many prestigious accolades, including; three honorary doctorates and the Brooklyn Museum Modernism Award for Lifetime Achievement in 2008. In 2006, the Metropolitan Museum of Art in New York held a retrospective show, the first ever for a living female ceramicist.

See also
Alison Britton (p.72)
Janice Tchalenko (p.110)
Nicole Cherubini (p.254)

Composition
Woodman linked the painting and the ceramic forms in her installation in a number of subtle ways, such as the floor-standing vases that appear to contain floral blooms and the table laid with jugs and plates. Another interesting aspect of this installation is her use of blank silhouettes in the painting that echo the shapes of the physical ceramics. This creates a playful juxtaposition between the 2D and 3D subjects.

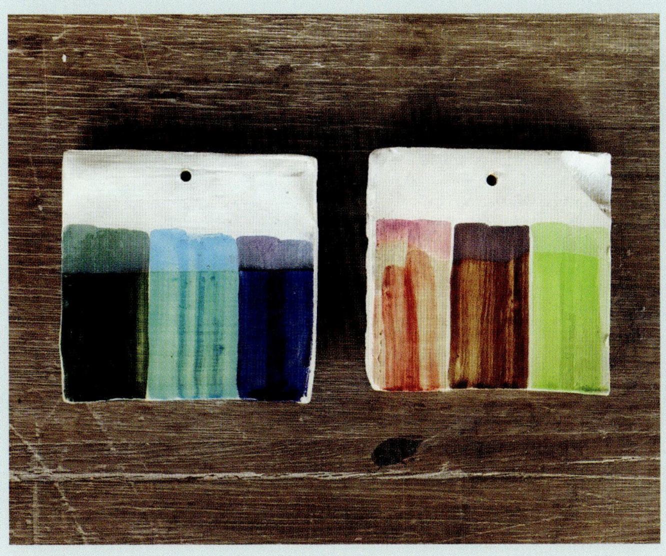

Technical
Woodman made all her ceramic components exclusively on the pottery wheel. The cheerful colour palette seen in T*he Summer House* is very characteristic of her style. Bright, sunny colours like these can be replicated with transparent, low-fired earthenware glazes combined with 6% commercial stains/ pigments, as illustrated on the tiles. You can emulate the painterly qualities by applying the glaze thinly with a soft brush.

Nicole Cherubini

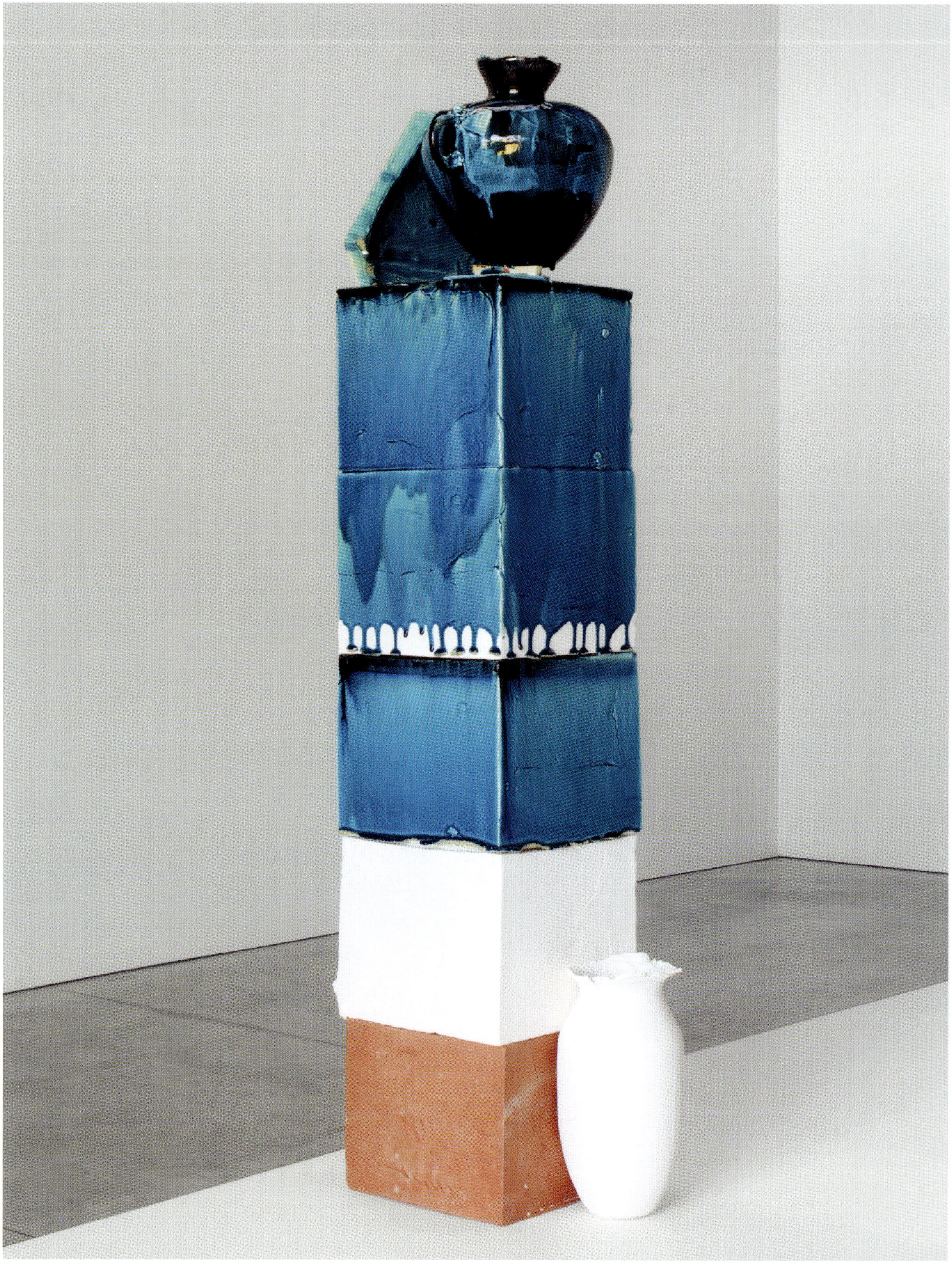

Stella 2016
Earthenware, terracotta, glaze, magic sculpt, pc-11, ink, kiln furniture
174 × 45.7 × 50.8 cm (68½ × 18 × 20 in.)

Sculptor and visual artist Nicole Cherubini creates lavish abstract works that challenge the conventions of high art through the use of clay. There is a familiarity within her forms, with the artist referencing classical vessel and vase shapes to forge a link with historical utilitarian uses of clay. This piece consists of a series of five stacked ceramic boxes on which a decorated vessel – backed by a hexagonal plate – proudly sits. The top tiers of the boxes are liberally coated in an intensely rich turquoise glaze, which cascades and drips down the sculpture's planes. Cherubini's bold choice of glaze colour references an earlier interest in Mexican and Turkish ceramics and Persian artefacts, prompting an appreciation for decadent and extravagant use of materials that can be felt throughout her works.

An intriguing aspect of this sculptural piece is the division between the glazed and the unglazed areas. The vessel at the top is grand and opulent, whereas the unglazed vase at the base is left exposed and bare. At first, this leads the viewer to think that perhaps there is a hierarchy between the two, but actually the intention is to convey the message that what resides beneath the façade is the same material, and in fact no hierarchy exists. Interestingly, there is a deliberate roughness to the finishing; the glazed vessel is still adhered to its kiln furniture, placed upon a shard of ceramic. Edges of rims and surfaces are irregular and appear unrefined. From the humble terracotta at the base to the glossy vessel at the top, *Stella* prompts dialogue about the status of clay in the sculptural world.

Nicole Cherubini (American, born 1970) studied ceramics at the Rhode Island School of Design, the New York University Institute of Fine Arts and the Skowhegan School of Painting and Sculpture in Maine. Her work encompasses both her love of minimalism and decoration, and a desire to reference ceramic history. She creates works that exist between the two-dimensional and the three-dimensional – between painting and sculpture. Her pieces incorporate ceramic objects that may have been cast, thrown or hand formed, as well as other elements, such as photographs, drawings or wooden constructions. Her work has won various accolades, including the Louis Comfort Tiffany Foundation Award in 2007.

See also
Jun Kaneko (p.92)
Bente Skjøttgaard (p.108)
Betty Woodman (p.252)

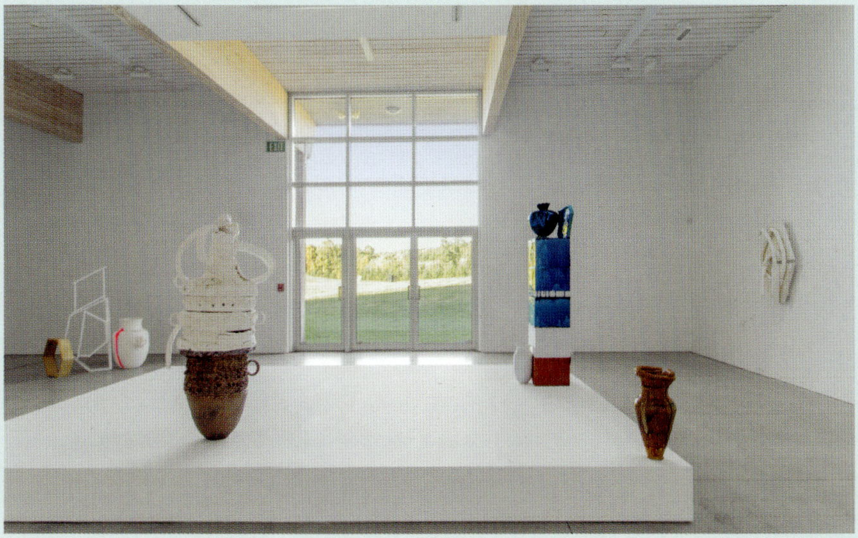

Composition
When Cherubini's piece *Stella* was originally exhibited it was shown within the context of other works, as illustrated here. Each piece was integral to the overall conceptual interpretation. Through interaction of colour, material and position, each piece has an inherent part in the exhibition as a whole. When planning a grouping or exhibition, think of the dialogue that can be created between your pieces. What are you trying to convey by grouping your works? How do the items relate to one another? What stories can be created by positioning the works together?

Phoebe Cummings

Antediluvian Swag 2016
Raw clay, wood, wire
Approx. 180 × 100 × 40 cm (70⅞ × 39⅜ × 15¾ in.)

Phoebe Cummings creates temporary sculptures and environments from raw, unfired clay that challenge the preconceived notion of traditional craft practices. Through her intricate compositions, she explores themes surrounding the passage of time, nature, landscape and the endless possibilities of clay as a material. There are strong references to historical ceramics and decorative arts traditions; in particular, the exuberant style of 18th-century baroque and rococo design is reflected in her floral clay blooms. Unlike most artists, Cummings works largely without a permanent studio and develops her work through residencies or by using the gallery space as a temporary workshop. Often the work is built directly on site and only lasts for the duration of the exhibition.

Housed outdoors at the New Arts Centre's Summer House, Wiltshire, this elaborate and highly detailed garland sculpture by Cummings is a blurring of fact and fiction. Cummings took the structure of familiar plants and petal shapes and blended them into something 'botanically possible but fantastically imagined'. The transient nature of the work and its temporary existence gives the work a performative element – the clay dries, cracks and disintegrates over time. A photograph or a memory may be all that remains of the piece, grounding its existence. Free from the restraints of firing and kilns in general, Phoebe Cummings builds her raw clay pieces around armatures made from chicken wire, singular lengths of wire and wood. This allows her to create huge, complex structures that defy typical ceramic conventions.

Phoebe Cummings (British, born 1981) studied three-dimensional crafts at the University of Brighton before completing a master's degree in ceramics and glass at the Royal College of Art, London, in 2005. She has undertaken a number of artist residencies in the UK, USA and Greenland, including six months as ceramics artist in residence at the Victoria and Albert Museum, London, in 2010. Cummings was the winner of the British Ceramics Biennial Award in 2011, and in 2015 her work was acquired for various permanent collections in the UK. She was the inaugural winner of the Woman's Hour Craft Prize in 2017 and was shortlisted for the Arts Foundation Awards in 2018. In 2019, she was awarded an Honorary Doctorate from the University of Brighton and is Research Associate at the Ceramics Research Centre, University of Westminster.

See also
Rita Gudiño (p.182)
Claire Curneen (p.196)
Hitomi Hosono (p.238)

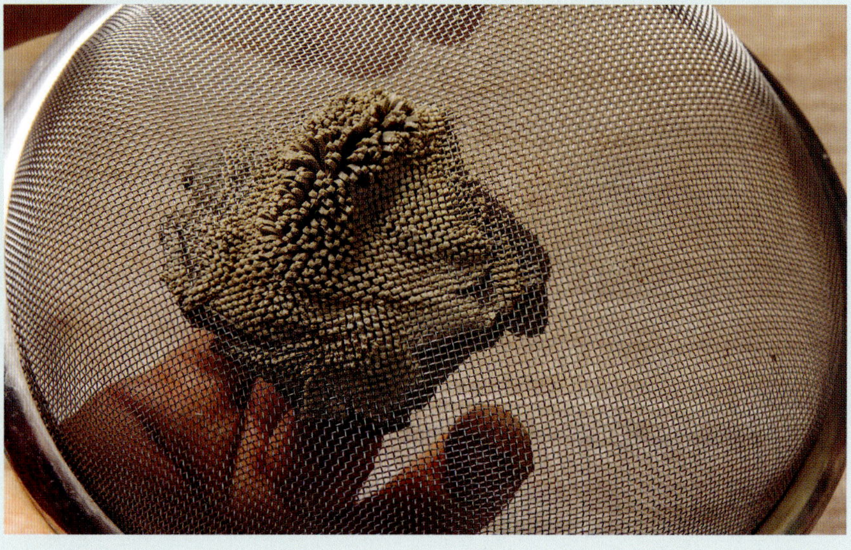

Process
Cummings forms her floral shapes by using hand-modelling techniques. She smears wads of clay between the palm of her hand and fingers to create individual leaves and petals that she later assembles into a three-dimensional form. The clay picks up the subtle imprint of her skin, mimicking organic textures. She also presses clay into low-relief sprig moulds to produce more complex shapes and multiple repetitions. Pushing clay through a sieve (see left) will result in a convincing moss or grass-like texture, which could be used to create lifelike organic pieces.

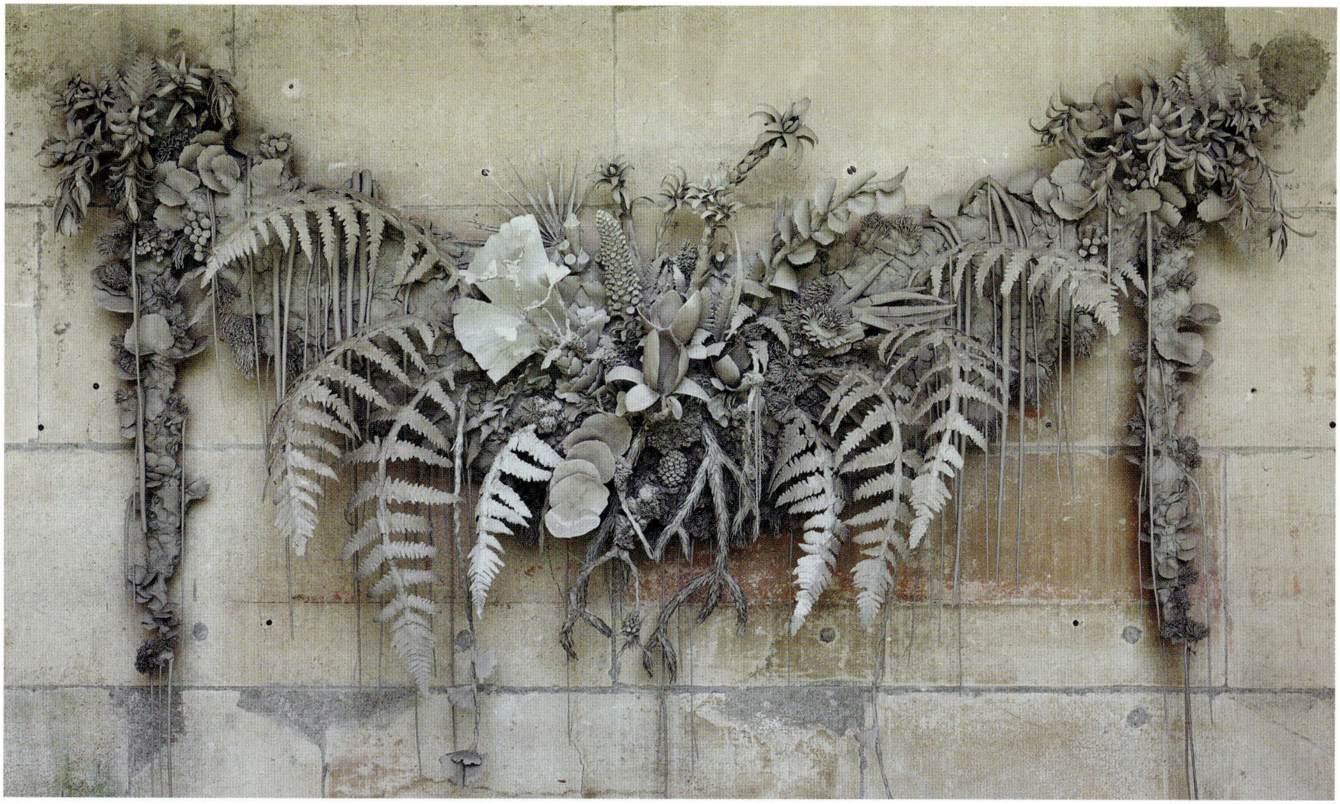

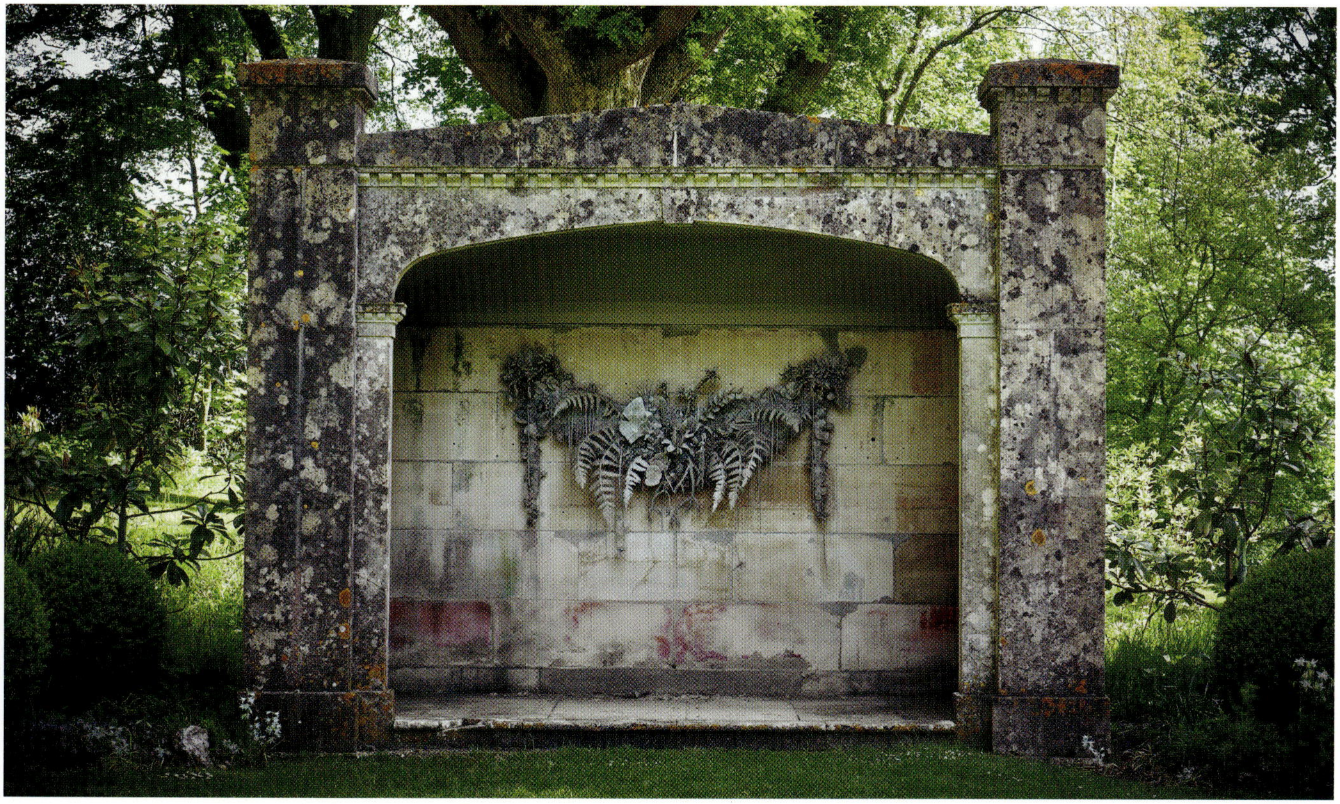

Torbjørn Kvasbø

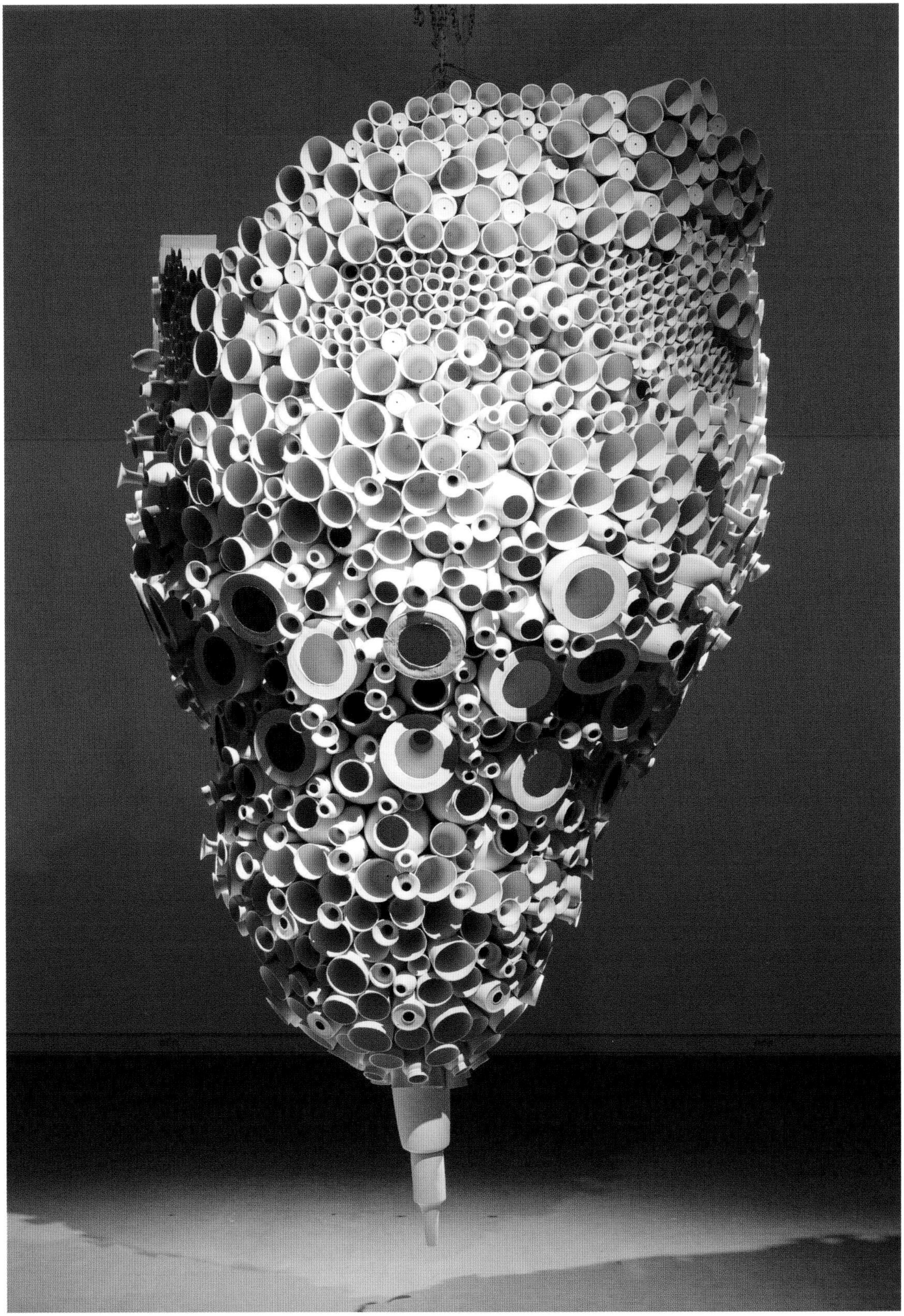

Vaseklase ('Cluster of Vases') 2017
Porcelain, slip cast
Height: 450 cm (177 in.); Diameter: 250 cm (98⅖ in.)

This installation of a mass of suspended pottery forms by Torbjørn Kvasbø hangs magnificently in the exhibition space like a colossal, abandoned wasp's nest. It was made as a tribute to the 150-year history of Norwegian ceramic manufacturing and industrial product design. The project originated at a workshop held at the Porsgrunds Porcelain Factory in 2009, at a point when it was closing down to outsource its production elsewhere. This was the first time Kvasbø had worked with porcelain and the slip-casting process. Kvasbø chose historic moulds from the factory's archive, giving him the opportunity to recontextualize objects from Norwegian design icons such as Nora Gulbrandsen (1894–1974), Eystein Sandnes (1927–2006) and Grete Rønning (born 1937). That first Cluster of Vases consisted of 250 objects – some of the last to be made at the factory – and was purchased by The National Museum in Oslo, Norway, in 2010.

The installation featured here is the second version of Kvasbø's original piece and was made in 2017. Kvasbø worked in collaboration with Porsgrunds Porcelain Factory, the gallery Kunsthall Grenland and the Porcelain Biennale in Porsgrunn. The installation was on a much larger scale than before and consisted of 2,000 individual pieces. All of the vases were deliberately left rough and unpolished to emphasize the making process. Kvasbø's intention was to address the origins of the individual vase shape in relation to Norwegian industrial and cultural heritage, referencing the factory's unique history and influential designers who have contributed to its legacy.

Torbjørn Kvasbø (Norwegian, born 1953) lives and works in Venabygd, Norway. With a career spanning more than forty years, he is considered a leading figure in contemporary ceramic art. Kvasbø trained at the Bergen School of Applied Arts from 1975 to 1978. His background is deeply rooted in the Leach/Hamada tradition ,but combines the physical, organic qualities of abstract expressionism. From 1996 to 2000, Kvasbø was the professor and head of the ceramics department at the University of Gothenburg, Sweden. And subsequently, professor and head of the ceramic and glass department at Konstfack in Stockholm from 2000 to 2008. Kvasbø won the Grand Prize at the Gyeonggi International Ceramic Biennale in Korea in 2017. In 2018, he was elected president of the International Academy of Ceramics.

See also
Shōji Hamada (p.140)
Adam Frew (p.164)
Paolo Polloniato (p.262)

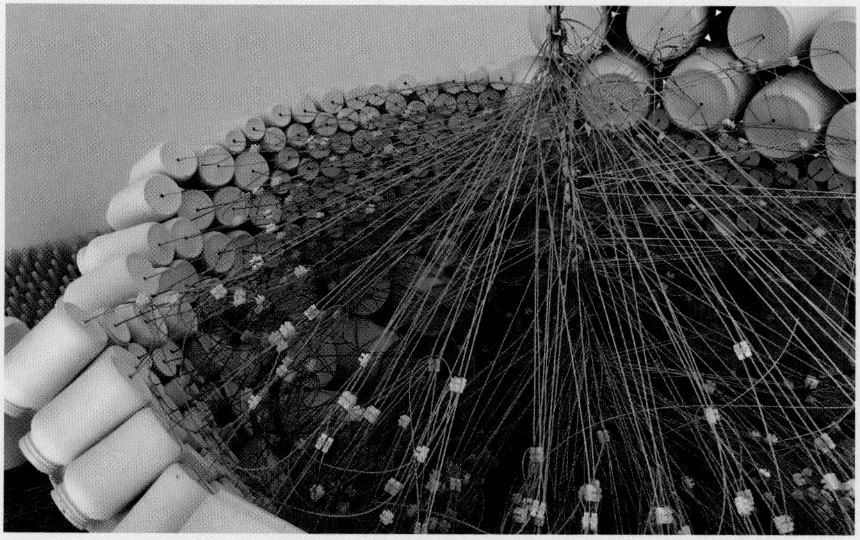

Technical
To secure the installation in its location, Kvasbø threaded a steel wire through a small hole in the bottom of each vase. This was fixed to a strong central chain hanging from the ceiling. Kvasbø carefully placed more components on top of one another, playing with gravity, form and movement. The installation constantly evolves and changes each time it is displayed, depending on the size and parameters of the exhibition space. Using an internal frame or wire can lift your work from the flat plane and allow for another viewing aspect. It also allows you to construct pieces beyond the restrictions of the kiln and create works on a much larger scale.

Bouke de Vries

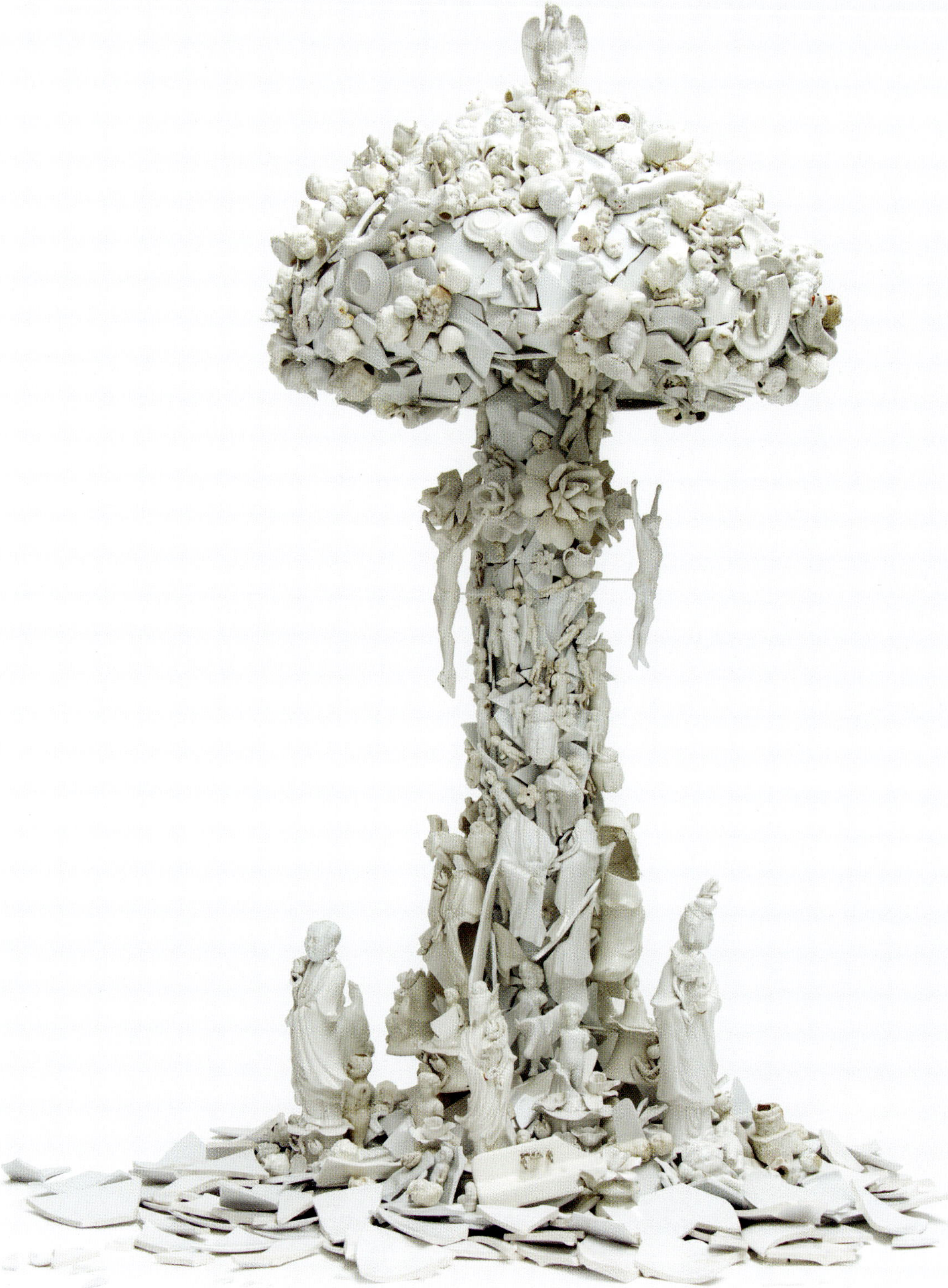

Cloud 2 2018
Porcelain, metal and acrylic
Height: 60 cm (23⅔ in.)

Bouke de Vries draws upon skills as a restorer to bring new narratives to broken and damaged ceramics. This extravagant work, *Cloud 2*, is the grand centrepiece from an 8-metre (26-foot) table installation entitled *War & Pieces*. De Vries took inspiration from the decadent European banquets of the 17th and 18th centuries that were traditionally held on the eve of a significant battle. Through his fragmented tableaux, De Vries portrays an epic scene of fighting and destruction raging across the landscape of the table.

The idea for the installation derived from the artist's research into elaborate table centrepieces from the period. These were typically made from sugar, a prized commodity, which represented wealth and status. De Vries has playfully orchestrated the narrative of a momentous war that has erupted between sugar, porcelain and plastic – the modern material threating them all. There are undertones of humour and satire as the myriad figures fight with knives and forks and bludgeon each other with serving utensils.

As the battle rages across the table, the climax to the scene is *Cloud 2*, a huge nuclear mushroom cloud that has blown everything to smithereens. Shards of broken crockery and figurines are swept up by its great plume. Within the structure there are numerous portrayals of the crucified Christ as well as Guan Yin, the ancient Chinese *bodhisattva* of mercy. A sorrowful angel perched at the top of the cloud weeps as she surveys the death and destruction. The piece is an evocative sight, something that De Vries appreciates is rather disturbing but, at the same time, hauntingly beautiful.

Bouke de Vries (Dutch, born 1960) studied at the Design Academy Eindhoven and Central St Martin's in London; he now works and lives in London. After working with fashion designers John Galliano (born 1960), Stephen Jones (born 1957) and Zandra Rhodes (born 1940), he changed career and studied ceramic conservation and restoration at West Dean College of Arts and Conservation in West Sussex. De Vries employs the skills he acquired as a restorer in his artwork, adopting the *kintsugi* technique – traditionally used in Japan to repair ceramics with lacquer and gold – which leaves a gold seam where the cracks were. He uses *kintsugi* to add new meaning to found objects such as broken figurines, beach shards and archaeological finds.

See also

Matt Davis (p.78)
Michelle Erickson (p.212)
Linda Sormin (p.264)

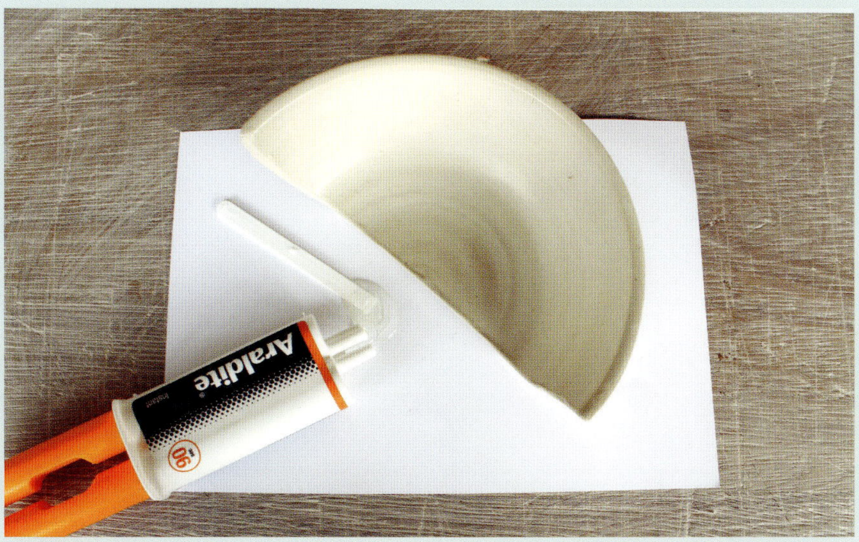

Technical
De Vries employs advanced assembly and ceramics restoration techniques to create his fascinating works. He sourced broken fragments of German Hummel porcelain figurines and crockery from internet auction sites and skilfully arranged the components to create a new narrative. The cloud piece is constructed in two parts (cloud and base), which are assembled on site. With no kilns or firing schedules involved, a piece like this can be built around an internal frame or armature. At a very basic level, you could secure components with a strong epoxy resin or wire bracing hidden from view.

Paolo Polloniato

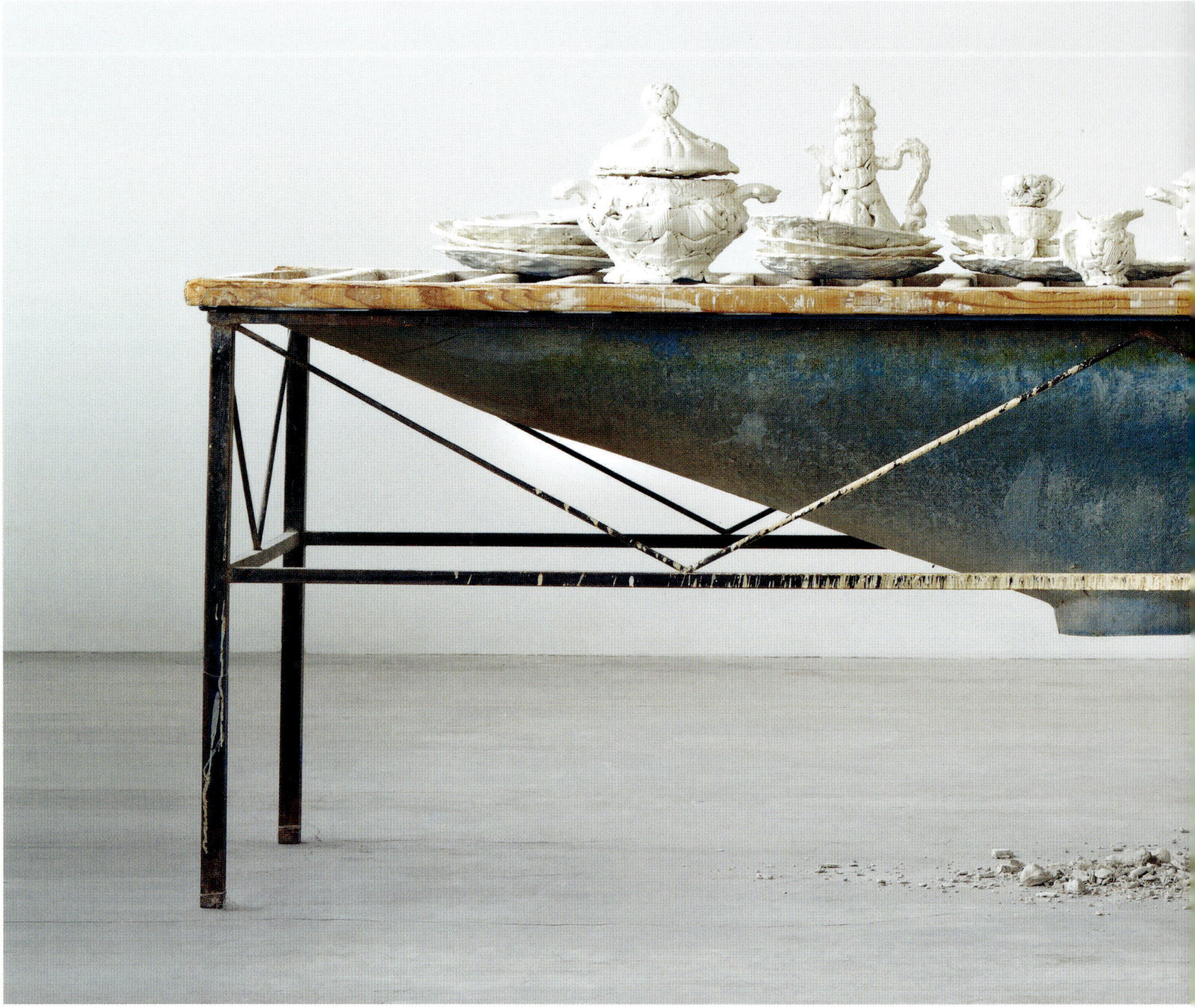

Pieniarendere 2018
White earthenware, wood and iron
300 × 100 × 100 cm (118 × 39⅓ × 39⅓ in.)

Paolo Polloniato was born in Nove, Italy, a small town renowned as an important district for industrious ceramic production in Europe since the 19th century, and is still based in the town. In recent years, the region as a whole has suffered economic decline and many factories have ceased production. Polloniato created Pieniarendere as a tribute to his home town and to act as a comment on the loss of skill and traditions associated with the ceramics industry.

For this piece Polloniato used moulds he found abandoned in empty factories as well as moulds from his family's business. He deliberately chose the moulds of an 18th-century service – comprising elaborate dining vessels and tureens made in Nove – that originally would have adorned the table of rich and noble clientele. Polloniato's intention was to revise the subsequent casts from the moulds into conceptual objects. He achieved this by pressing the moulds with fragments of clay joined together to create a patchy effect symbolic of scars, reflecting the dwindling of the town. The pieces were bisque fired to 1000°C (1832°F) and left unglazed.

The composition of *Pieniarendere* references the famous painting by Leonardo da Vinci (1452–1519), *The Last Supper*, with a redundant slip-casting bench standing in for the table and the disorderly tableware items representing the figures. The slats on the bench (designed to allow slip to drain from the moulds in ceramic production) force the pieces to tilt and teeter, implying they could fall in. Underneath the bench, in the centre, lies a pile of raw ceramic dust, about which Polloniato says: 'The glorious past is dead. The indelible ruins of this glorious past remain'.

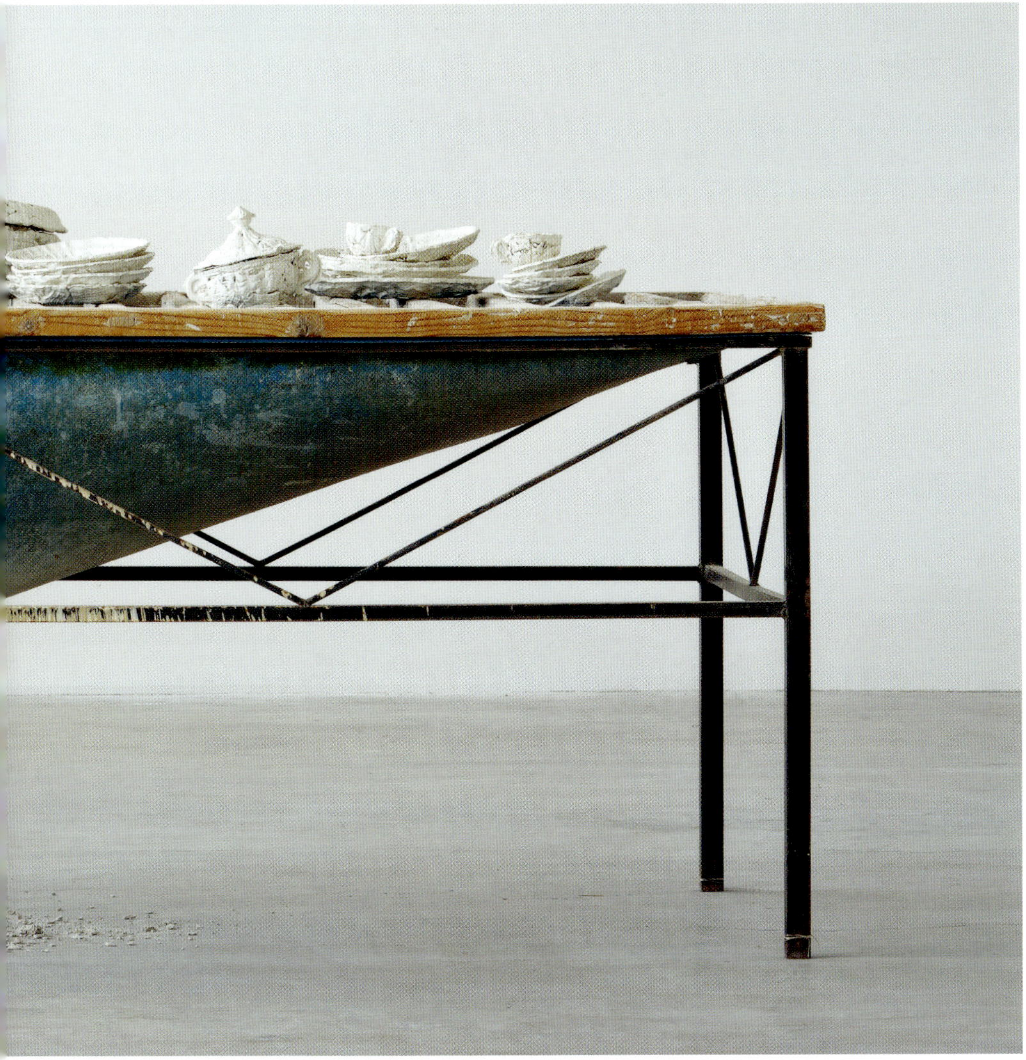

Paolo Polloniato (Italian, born 1979) was born in Nove near Venice to a family of master ceramicists and maiólica decorators that had been working for the Manifattura Antinibon, now Barettoni, since the mid-19th century. Polloniato studied at the Fine Arts Academy in Venice and then started making ceramics. He moved to Paris and Brussels for a few years, returning to Nove in 2013 to open a workshop. He employs traditional techniques to express contemporary concepts. He looks for old moulds belonging to different periods and styles and uses them to make raw clay models. He also uses new moulds to create modern pieces.

See also

Vicky Lindo (p.240)

Torbjørn Kvasbø (p.258)

Bouke de Vries (p.260)

Subject Matter

Drawing upon life experiences can be a powerful theme to explore in clay. Polloniato calls upon his family history and heritage in this installation. Each installation carries significance to the region of Nove and the impact that the loss of the ceramic industry has had on his personal experiences and that of others. Reflect on your own sentimental or nostalgic objects and how to capture your response in your art.

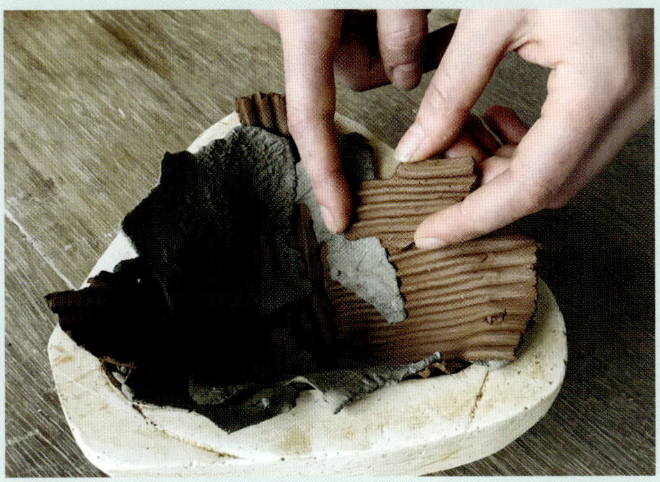

Composition

Consider how you can reinterpret a disused mould and fashion something new from it. Like Polloniato, you could press scraps of clay in random sections, leaving gaps or overlays. Try colouring the clay with stain or oxide or using contrasting clay bodies, such as red clay with white clay. This could be another simple but effective way to add visual interest to your piece.

Linda Sormin

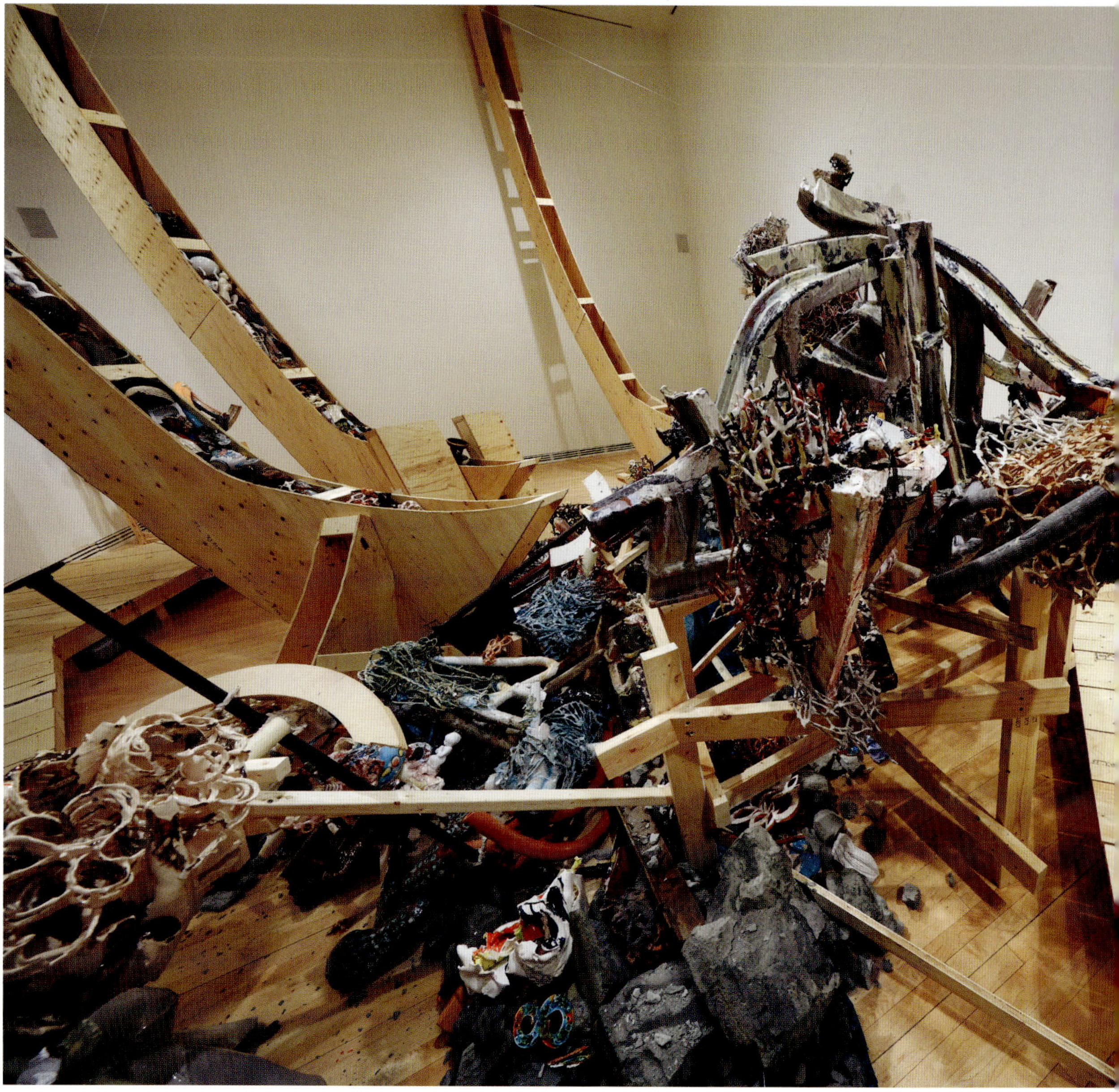

See also

Sterling Ruby (p.218), **Bouke de Vries** (p.260)

Linda Sormin (Thai, born 1971) was born in Bangkok and emigrated to Canada with her family at the age of five. During the 1990s she spent four years working in community development, disaster relief and humanitarian aid in Thailand and Laos. She studied English Literature at Andrews University in Ontario before studying ceramics at Sheridan College in Michigan and at New York State College of Ceramics at Alfred University. She creates ceramic objects and mixed-media installations that explore themes of transition, fragility, survival and migration. Sometimes her work includes contributions of damaged or discarded pieces of ceramics. She has also encouraged community participation when creating some of her installations.

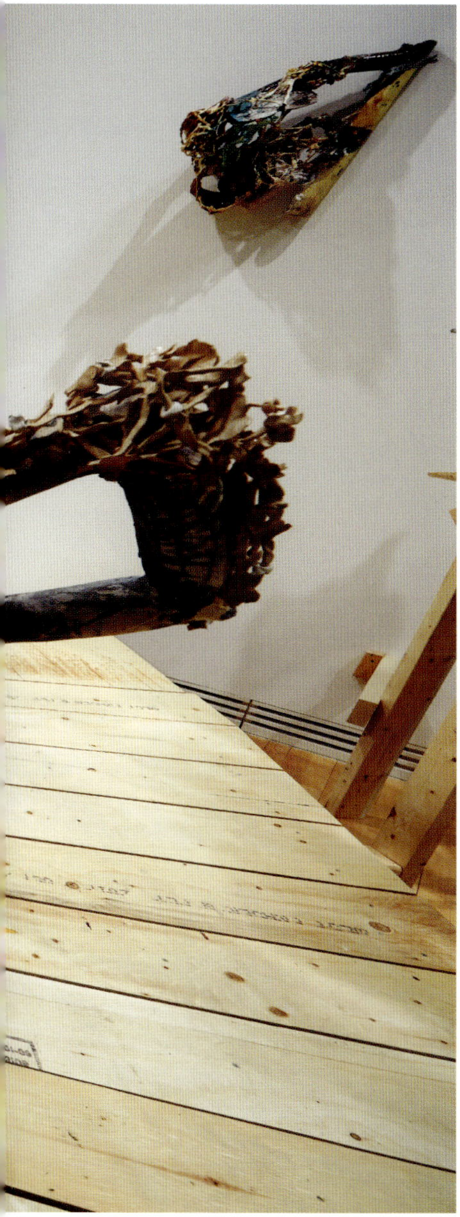

Fierce Passengers 2018
Ceramic, wood, mixed media
Dimensions variable

Transition, fragility, migration and upheaval are themes that artist Linda Sormin explores through sculpture and site-responsive installations. In 2018 – following a two-week residency – Sormin installed her immersive work, *Fierce Passengers*, at Carleton University Art Gallery (CUAG) in Ottawa. Prior to setting up, Sormin invited members of the public to loan or donate objects to be included in the installation that represented personal feelings of loss, longing or sentiment during times of change and uncertainty. Sormin, an immigrant herself, explains, 'I was thinking about how culture carries us, like "Fierce Passengers", through times of transition. What stories might be told, through objects, of the lives of people who have once owned them?'

The ambitious project consisted of more than one hundred different items and occupied the expanse of a double-height gallery space. The installation is full of energy and is extremely gestural. Huge curved wooden struts, resembling a giant ribcage, formed the foundation for the structure. Sormin's intention was to partially recreate the hull of a boat and imply that this is a dry dock of sorts, where ships are built and repaired. Placed within the structure, a series of intermingling wooden frames, sourced objects and richly decorated ceramic sculptures are precariously positioned and bring visual complexity.

A wooden boardwalk winds and snakes though the unruly chaos of the installation, leading the viewer to encounter different angles and perspectives at every turn. Sormin enjoys the movement and interaction this gives to the piece and, like the migrant experience, it evokes feelings of trepidation and nervousness when faced with the unknown.

Material
An interesting aspect of this installation is Sormin's inclusion of raw Leda clay, a glacio-marine substance that lies beneath parts of the Ottawa region and turns to liquid when under pressure or agitated (such as in earthquakes). This quality of instability and movement resonates strongly with Sormin's themes of change and migration.

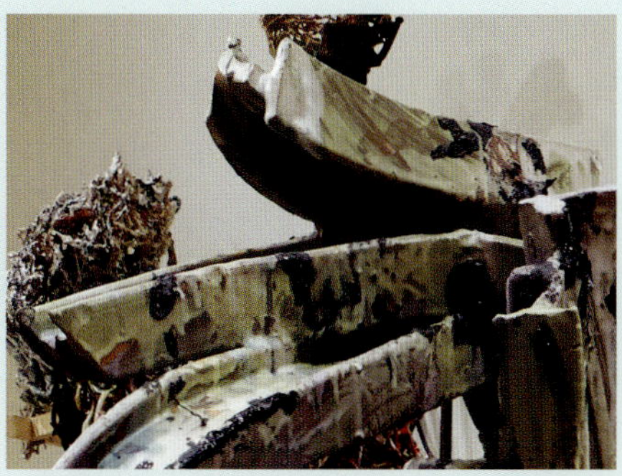

Technical
Sormin created the ceramic components for this installation using various techniques, including throwing, hand building, extrusion and moulding. Often, she will repeatedly fire pieces, turning them on their side, adding more glaze and more components until it appears to collapse under its own weight.

Barnaby Barford

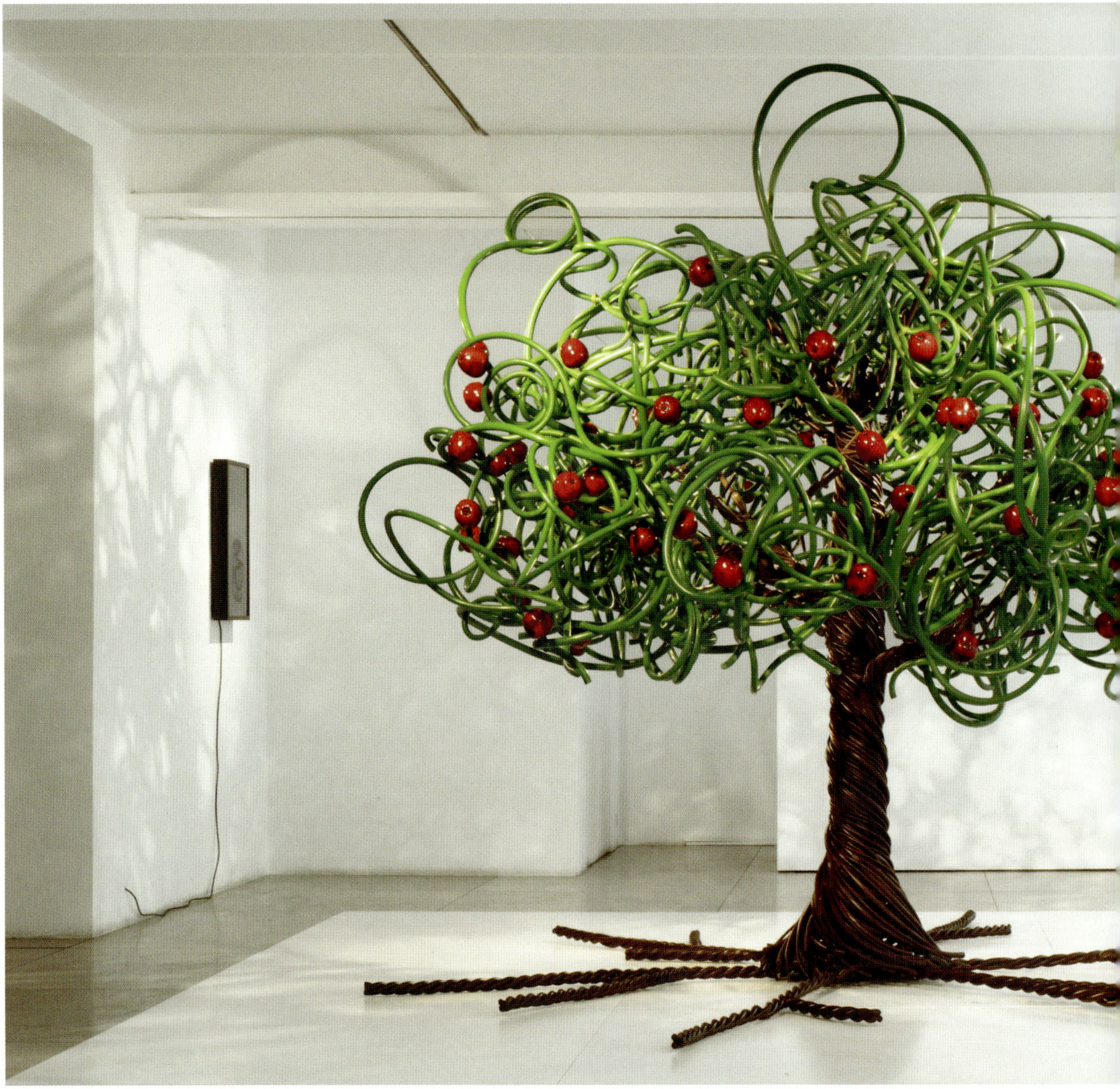

See also

Matt Davis (p.78), **Tana West** (p.270)

Barnaby Barford (British, born 1977) studied three-dimensional design at the University of Plymouth, UK. After he graduated he went to the ISIA Higher Institute for Artistic Industries in Faenza, Italy. Upon his return to the UK, he completed a master's degree in ceramics and glass at the Royal College of Art in London. He creates ceramics using mass-production processes and is known for his monumental sculptures composed of thousands of individual ceramic pieces. He often uses the apple as a motif to explore questions about capitalism, anxiety and consumerism. He has won various awards, including Wallpaper* Young Designer of the Year in 2005 and the prestigious President's Medal at the International Competition of Ceramic Art held by the Museo Internazionale delle Ceramiche in Faenza.

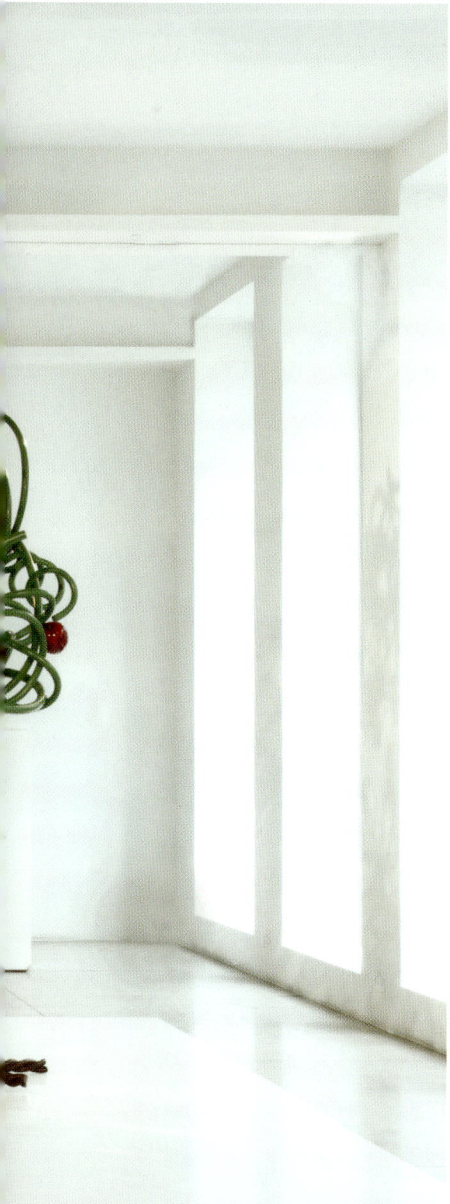

The Apple Tree 2019

Tree: Painted mild steel, PU pipe. 80 Apples: Oil paint on bone china

300 × 300 × 300 cm (118 × 118 × 118 in.)

The Apple Tree comments on modern consumerism and society's incessant need for more – regardless of the detrimental impact to us as individuals, the community and the planet. As Barnaby Barford says, 'In Western culture, we're never satisfied with what we have, no matter how much we begin with ... We're in constant competition with our unachievable, anxiety-inducing appetites.' Using the familiar icon of the apple, Barford explores how far the symbol projects through history, from religious connotations with the Garden of Eden and Adam and Eve to Cézanne, Isaac Newton, William Tell, Snow White and Steve Jobs. 'The apple has been used as a symbol of poison, love, beauty and immortality', says Barford.

Here, among the gnarled steel branches and scribbled loops of green hosing, the apple tree is heavily laden with eighty luscious, ripe apples. The apples themselves are made from bone china and Barford painted them with glossy red oil paint to give an alluring, seductive effect. Emblazoned on each fruit is a single emotive word – for example, status, love, outrage, money, sex, power, glory, freedom, empathy, truth – all words associated with our modern obsession with excess and materialism. The viewer is invited to purchase an apple and, by choosing one from the tree, to confront their own fears and desires. Barford engineered the design of the apples in such a way that the stem makes a satisfying 'snap' when the viewer selects their apple from the tree. Once picked, it cannot be reattached to the tree. Recalling the Garden of Eden when Eve succumbs to temptation, it is this moment, Barford states, that 're-enacts the downfall of mankind'. *The Apple Tree* serves as a poignant reminder of our skewed morals and troubling expectations.

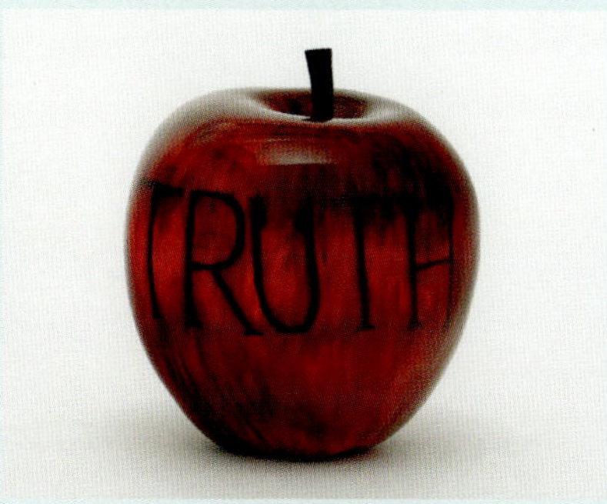

Material

The apples for this installation were slip-cast using bone china, a strong, lightweight material that offers a pure white colour when fired. Bone china is also an apt choice for the themes explored by Barford because of its reputation as a status material throughout centuries of ceramic history. Barford made the apples slightly larger than life and coated them with rich, glossy oil paints to suggest an exaggerated, fairytale version of the fruit. These subtle visual and material choices bring cohesion to the underlying concept. Mixed media may be an area you would like to explore in your own work, especially if you aim to work on a larger scale. If this is the direction you wish to take, consider the relevance for your choices. How can a specific material add or help underpin your core message?

Honor Freeman

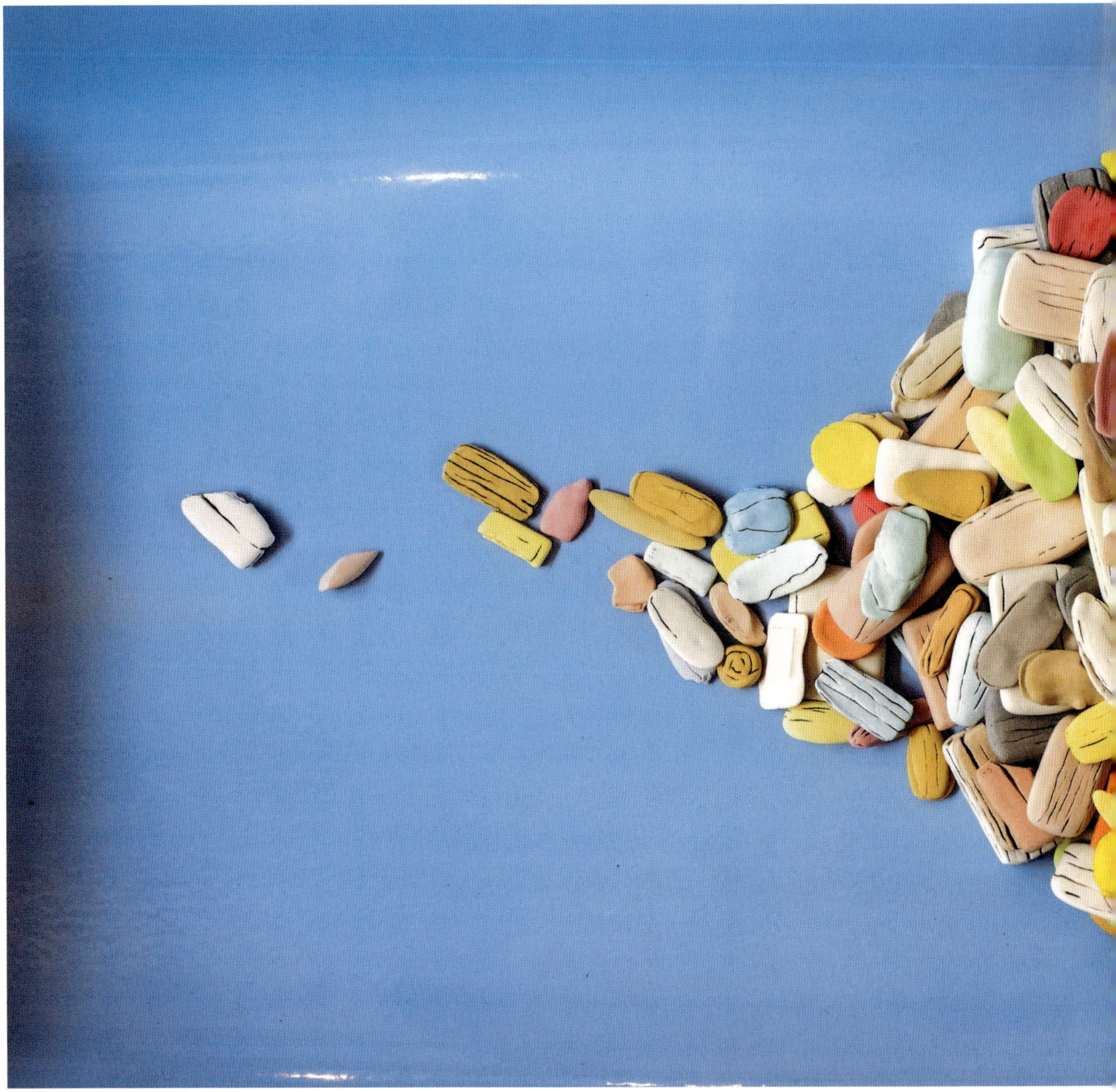

See also

Judy McKenzie (p.118), **Marilyn Levine** (p.204)

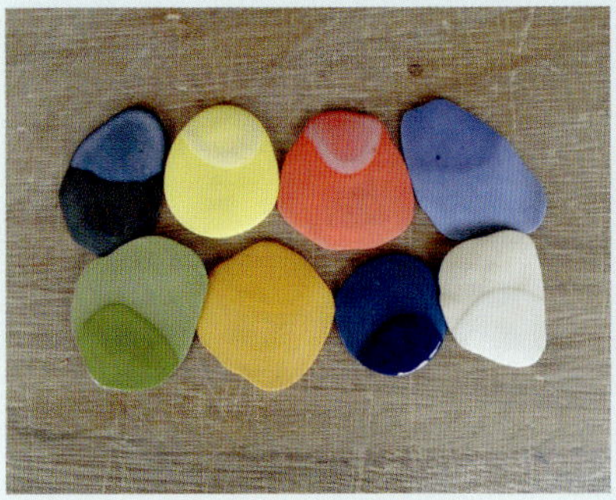

Honor Freeman (Australian, born 1978) is based in Adelaide, Australia, and studied at the South Australian School of Art, University of South Australia, from 1998 to 2001. Following graduation, Freeman held a design associate position and later a tenant residency in the ceramics studio at Jam Factory Craft & Design in Adelaide from 2002 to 2003. She undertook international residencies at Guldagergaard, Denmark's International Ceramic Museum in 2004 and in the US at Indiana University's School of Art and Design in 2007. Freeman has been exhibiting since 2000, with significant solo shows: *Ghost Objects*, Art Gallery of South Australia, (2019) and *Ordinary Alchemy*, Sabbia Gallery, New South Wales (2017). Examples of Freeman's work are held in numerous private and public collections.

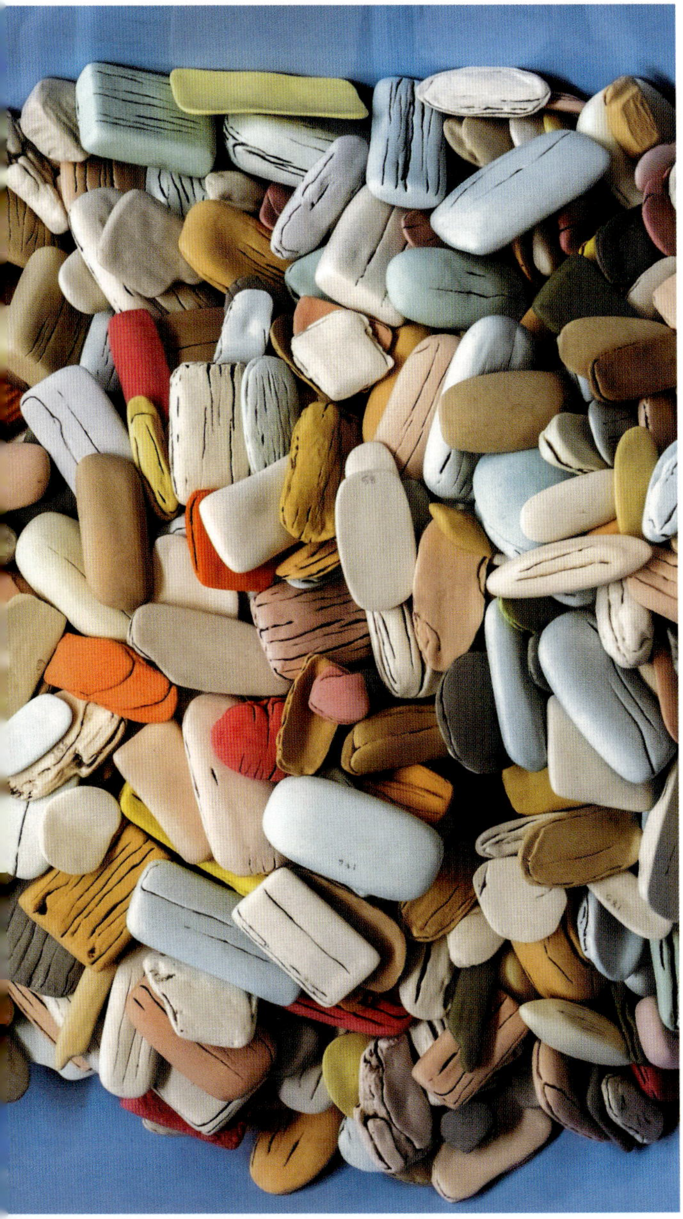

Dissolving Ballast 2019
Slipcast porcelain and bathtub
Dimensions variable

With an interest in mundane and unnoticed objects, Honor Freeman commemorates the ordinariness of life and the rhythms and rituals of day-to-day routines. Her practice often focuses on overlooked domestic and utilitarian items, such as lidded Tupperware containers, tatty kitchen sponges, crumpled handkerchiefs, folded towels and light switches. Through her lifelike ceramic creations, Freeman seeks a correlation between the human interaction and gestures involved when engaging with these familiar items, and the process of making that informs the work. Harnessing the mimetic qualities inherent in clay, Freeman uses the slip-casting method to preserve and measure the passage of time. As Freeman explains, 'I especially love the personal narratives and memories we all have that are associated with familiar objects, and how the transformation from their current form into porcelain can transport us through time'.

This piece was made for the Australian Ceramics Triennale in 2019. Freeman used the familiarity of a pale blue enamelled bathtub – a nostalgic colour evocative of past decades – to display her material deceptions and play with ideas of memory and association. Heaped within the tub at one end, an array of dry and shrivelled soap-ends made from ceramic resembles a mound of tossed pebbles. Within the composition, a few of the smaller soap pieces disconnect from the group and trail towards the plug hole end of the bath – suggesting a metaphor for life and death as they ebb away. Freeman enjoys the still-life element of her work that comes from the slip-cast process. As she explains, 'The casts are a memory of the original, like a tangible whisper or echo of that object, eternally preserved but subtly changed'.

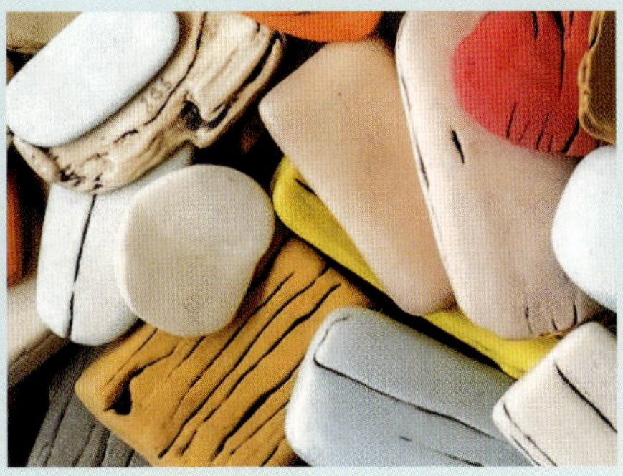

Surface

Freeman created her realistic collection of desiccated soaps by taking a cast of slivers and remains of existing soap pieces, which she collected or was given. She coloured the porcelain slip with a body stain to produce light pastel shades reminiscent of soapy colours. You can colour your own casting slip body by adding 7–10% stain or 3–5% oxide (mixed to a paste with water) to 130ml of porcelain/white casting slip and sieved through a 100 mesh. The extra 30 ml roughly accommodates for the water content in the casting slip. Freeman also considered the feel of the soaps by sanding them smooth, completing the overall visual and tactile effect. This is an important aspect when creating realistic works – the feel and touch of the item should be convincing, too.

Tana West

See also
Jun Kaneko (p.92)
Richard Slee (p.216)
Barnaby Barford (p.266)

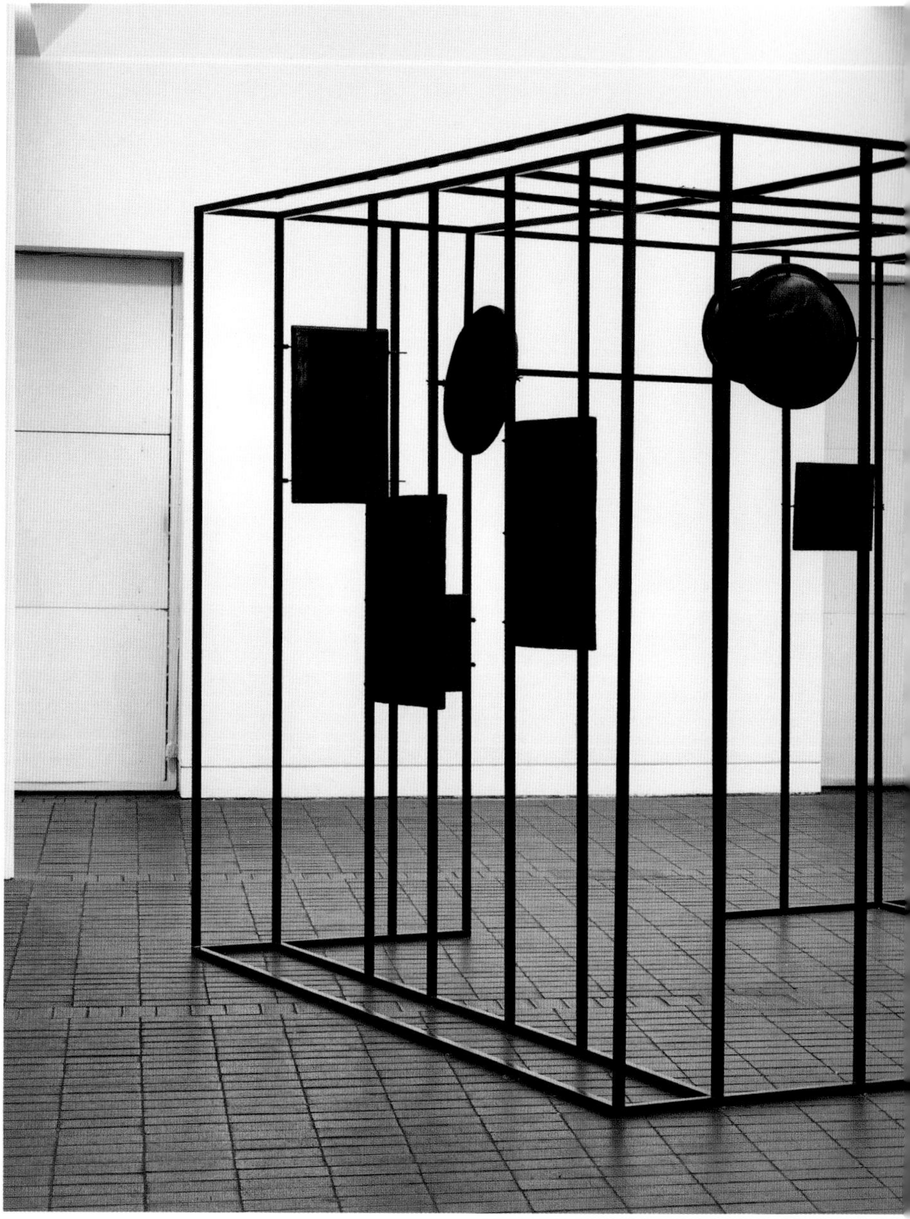

Tana West (British, born 1981) works predominantly with ceramic processes and uses the language of ceramic materials and object making to connect with social, political and historical contexts. Born in Bristol and now based in London, West studied sculpture at Central St Martins in 2003 and completed her master's degree in ceramics and glass at the Royal College of Art in 2014. Her work frequently involves siste-specific and collaborative approaches. In 2017, West won the AWARD at the British Ceramics Biennial for her *(UN)WOVEN* installation project, which was made with the help of an online community from all over Europe, who sent the artist clay-like soil in a variety of ad hoc receptacles. In 2019, West was selected for the prestigious Jerwood Makers Open, for which the *Through a Glass Darkly* installation was commissioned.

Process
West created the mirrors using press-moulding and slip-casting methods. She deliberately used two different processes in order to produce distinct distortions within the clay surface. The slip-cast method produced thin and smooth surfaces, compared to the press-moulded mirrors, which were thicker and had greater variation between each one.

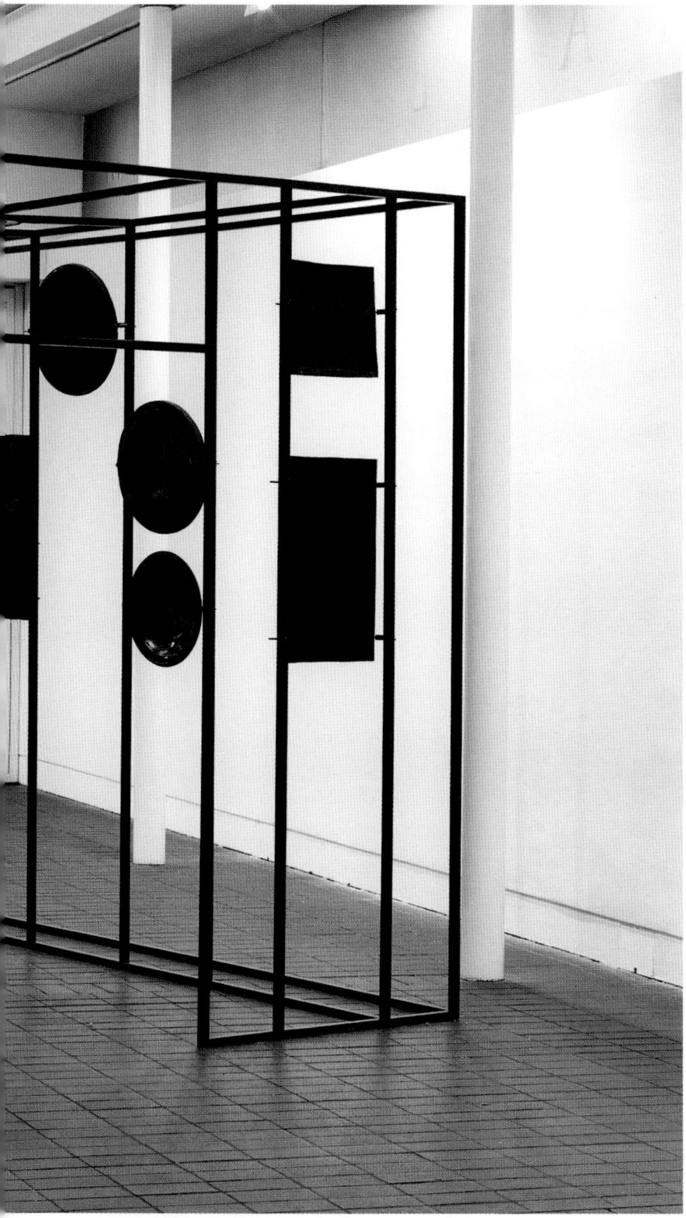

Through a Glass Darkly 2019
Black glazed stoneware mirrors
250 × 300 × 300 cm (98⅜ × 118 × 118 in.)

The thought-provoking work of Tana West explores the themes around recent, highly charged political events and the rise of 'fake news'. West is interested in the role of persuasive news feeds and journalists' language, and how this has led the public discourse to become increasingly divisive. Her 2019 installation *Through a Glass Darkly* confronts these contemporary concerns through the materiality of ceramics.

Positioned within the white space of the Jerwood Gallery in south London, a large steel frame resembling a funfair's hall of mirrors offers an intriguing place of refuge and the viewer is invited to walk inside. Hanging at varying heights within the structure are an assortment of concave and convex 'mirrors', some round, others square or rectangular in shape. Glazed with several different black glazes, offering varying degrees of reflectiveness, the mirrored surfaces display a distorted image of the viewer, prompting them to contemplate their own views and beliefs. West pushes the distortions further by using the serendipity of the glazing and firing processes – side effects such as oil-spot dappling and indents – to produce subtle flattening and fragmentation of the reflection.

With references to security mirrors and the watchful eye of surveillance cameras, this installation suggests a safe space to retreat to; once inside and faced with multiple reflections of ourselves, however, it becomes more cell-like and oppressive, leading us to question the imperfect vision of reality we might hold.

Surface
As seen in this close-up of one of West's tiles, she cleverly exploits the reflective quality of the glaze to absorb the viewer's gaze and underpin her concept. When experimenting with glazes, you can disrupt the finish by pouring one glaze over another, keeping drips and using the liquidity of the glaze to flow into textures and enhance the form.

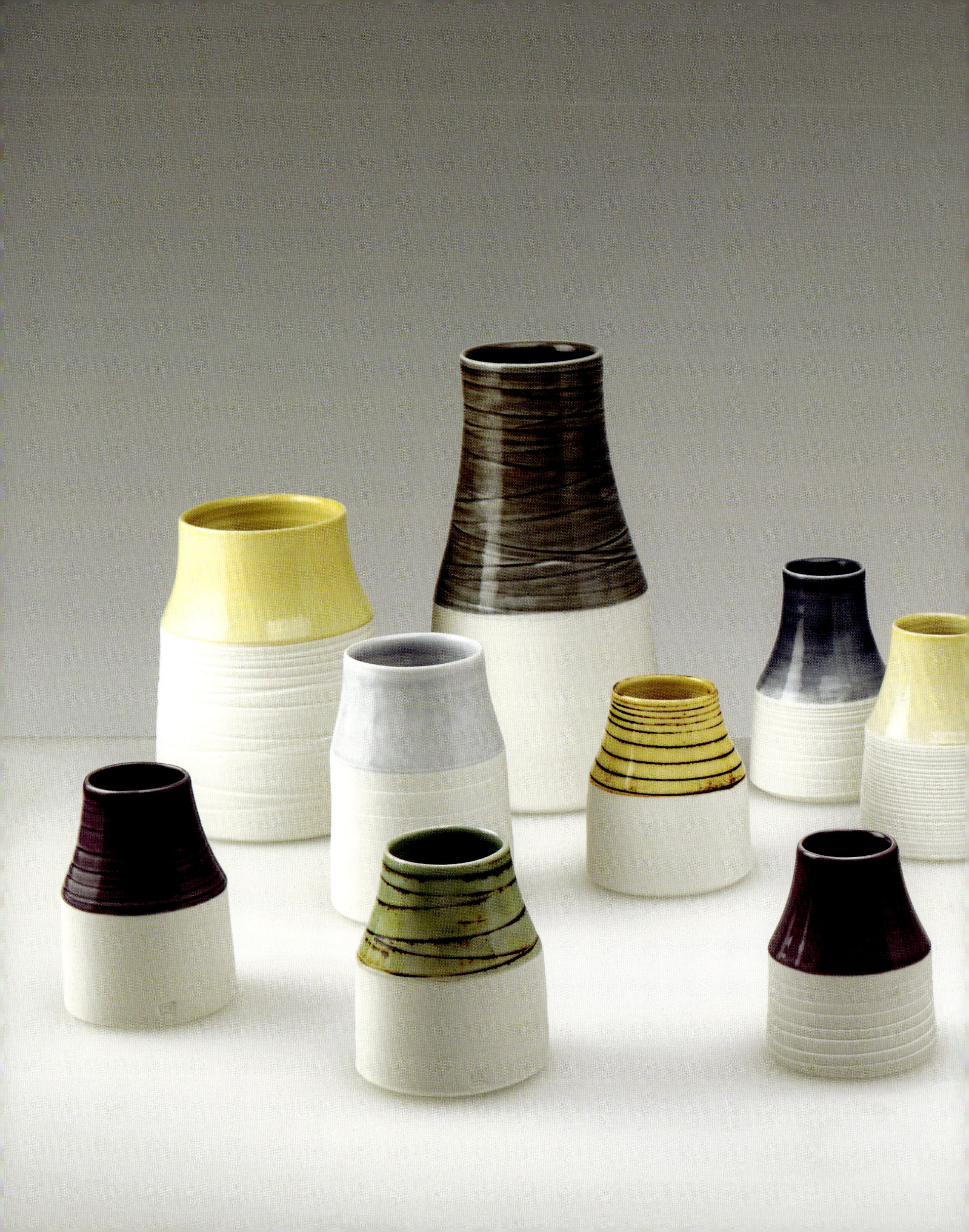

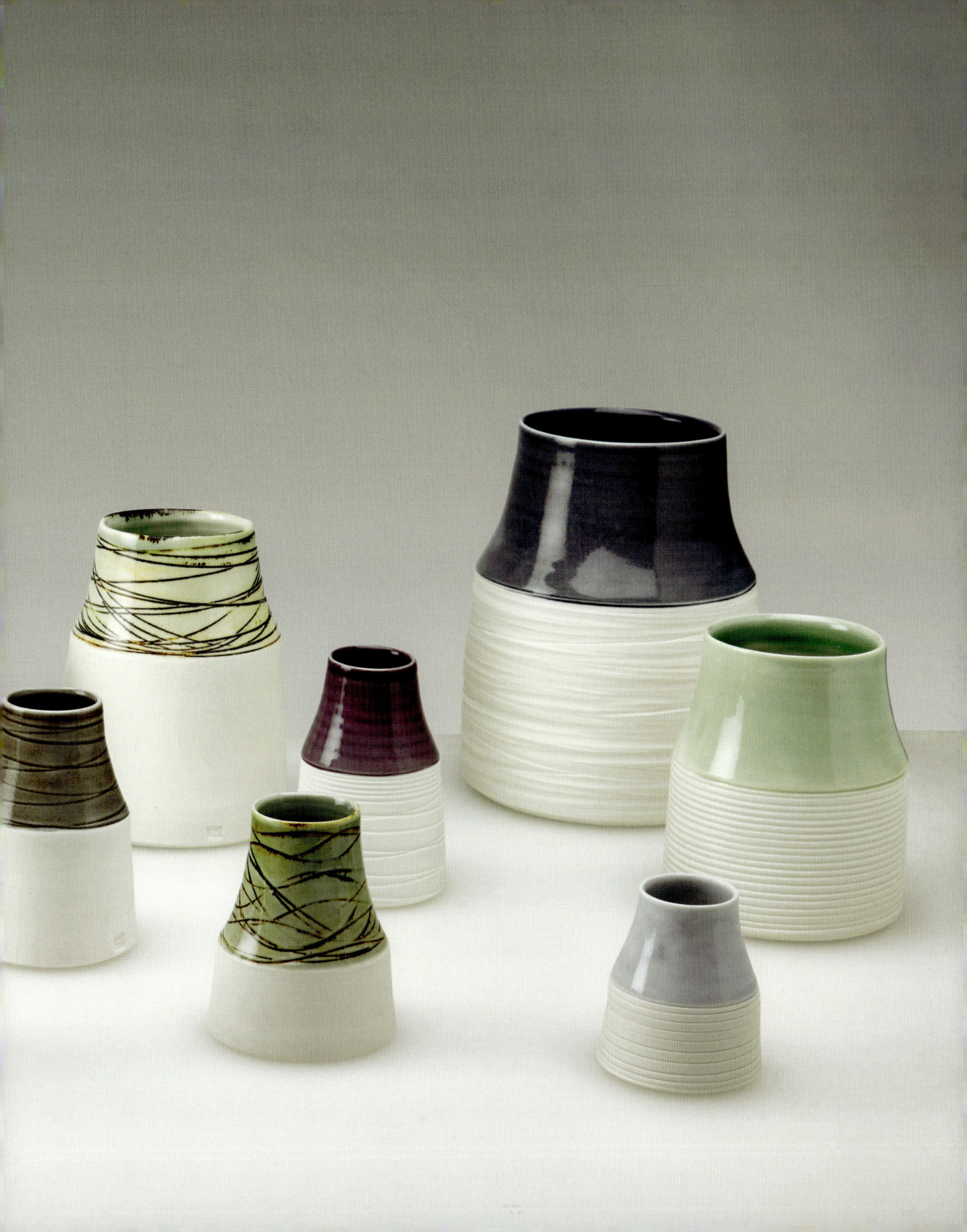

Mixing a glaze recipe

This section will require further reading, but in brief, a glaze base recipe is typically (although not always) formulated to add up to 100%. Additions are included separately. Here is an example:

Stoneware transparent base glaze 1280°C (2340°F/cone 10)

	%
Cornwall stone	70
Whiting	20
China clay	10

The number can be translated into grams - for example, 70g Cornwall stone. and weighed out accordingly. You can multiply the recipe to generate larger amounts so x10 = 700g Cornwall stone. Weigh each material out accurately into a bowl to complete the recipe. Add water - this is difficult to quantify because some materials are thirstier than others. This relies on your judgement but a rule of thumb is 1 litre of water to 1000g of dry weight. When everything is combined, process the glaze twice through a fine mesh sieve (100–120 grade for earthenware, 60–80 grade for stoneware). The consistency of the glaze is very important, as it can be the difference between your glaze being successful or not. A good tip to remember:

Earthenware: consistency of milk.
Stoneware: consistency of cream.

On the following pages are some useful recipes that emulate the glazes of artists featured in this book. Refer to the oxide chart on page 28 for guidance with additions that you can add to the base recipe to create specific colours. US equivalents are listed in (). For a cone conversion chart, see p.276.

Slip decoration

Earthenware slip: 1080°C (1976°F/cones 04–03)

	%
AT ball clay (kentucky ball clay)	70
China clay (kaolin)	30
Zirconium silicate	10

Notes: Add water, sieve 100 mesh, apply to leather-hard clay

Stoneware slip 1200–1280°C (2192–2336°F/cones 5–9)

	%
Hyplas 71 (Tennessee ball clay)	75
Flint (silica)	16
Zirconium silicate	5
Bentonite	4
+ Oxide of your choice	3–6
Or Stain	5–10

Notes: Add water, sieve 100 mesh, apply to leather-hard clay.

Glazes: Earthenware

Transparent shiny: 1080–1120°C (1976–2048°F/ cones 04–02)

	%
Lead bisilicate (ferro 3498)	70
Cornish stone (Cornwall stone)	20
China clay (kaolin)	5
Zinc oxide	5
Additions +	
Honey Glaze: Red iron oxide	3
Green Glaze: Copper oxide	1
Tin Glaze: Tin oxide	8–10

Notes: Excellent clear glaze for over colour slips and underglaze.

Transparent Alkaline: 1020–1080°C (1868–1976°F/cone 06)

	%
High alkaline rrit (Ferro 3110)	70
Cornish stone (cornwall stone)	25
AT ball clay (Kentucky ball clay)	5
Additions +	
Turquoise: Copper oxide	2
Plum: Manganese dioxide	2.5
Royal Blue: Cobalt oxide	1

Notes: High gloss, crackle surface.

Matt white: 1080-1100°C (1976–2012°F/cones 04–03)

	%
Lead bisilicate (ferro 3498)	42
Standard borax frit (ferro 3134)	30
Zinc oxide	18
China clay (kaolin)	5
Tin oxide	5

Notes: Smooth matt white, good all-rounder. Add oxides or stains for pastel shades.

Textured Barium matt: 1080°C (1976°F/cones 04–03)

	%
Nepheline syenite	78
Barium carbonate	12
Lithium carbonate	8
Bentonite	2
Additions +	
Turquoise: Copper Oxide	6
Acid yellow: Chrome	0.75
Dark purple: Cobalt carbonate	0.5
Mottled turquoise: Copper oxide + Vanadium pent oxide	1.5 + 3 (respectively)

Notes: semi-matt, mottled texture. Not suitable for domesticware interiors.

Glazes: Stoneware

Transparent shiny 1260–1280°C (2300–2336°F/cones 8–10); oxidized or reduction

	%
Potash feldspar (custer)	40
Whiting	20
Flint (silica)	30
China clay	10

Notes: Good shine; add oxides or stain of your choice to produce colour glaze.

Smooth dolomite: 1250°C (2282°F/cone 7); oxidized

(see Lucie Rie, p.54)

	%
Potash feldspar	64
Dolomite	13
Whiting	13
Kaolin/china clay	10

Notes: Smooth semi-matt white; soak for 10–15 minutes at top temperature

Crater/lava: 1260–1280°C (2300–2336°F/cones 8–9); oxidized or reduction

(see Morten Løbner Espersen, p.126)

	%
Nepheline syenite	60
Barium carbonate	20
Titanium dioxide	10
Flint (silica)	10
Silicon carbide	3
Bentonite	2
Additions +	
Creamy White: Iron oxide	2
Green: Copper carbonate	3
Blue: Cobalt oxide	0.5

Notes: Apply quite thickly for bigger craters in glaze.

Crystalline: 1240°C (2264°F/cone 6); oxidized

(see Kate Malone, p.116)

	%
Custer (Potash) Feldspar	52
Fluorspar	8
Flint (silica)	9
Zinc oxide	24
China clay	7
+ Oxide of your choice	0.5–3

Notes: Best on porcelain, white clay bodies. Will produce silver grey crystals without oxides. Add Copper 2% or Rutile 8% for green-fawn colours.

Iridescent blue Chun-type: 1260°C, (2300°F/cone 8); oxidized or reduction

	%
Nepheline syenite	55
Whiting	15
China clay	15
Talc	15
Rutile	8
Cobalt carbonate	0.5

Notes: Can run if applied too thickly. Do not soak longer than 10 minutes.

Blue/green Celadon: 1280°C (2336°F/cones 9–10); reduction

(see Gwyn Hanssen Pigott, p.70)

	%
Potash feldspar	35
Flint	25
Whiting	15
China clay	15
Talc	10
Red iron oxide	0.75

Notes: Suitable for porcelain and white stoneware.

Tenmuko: 1280°C (2336°F/cones 9–10); reduction

(see Bernard Leach, p.136; Shōji Hamada, p.140)

	%
Cornish stone	85
Whiting	15
China clay	10
Quartz	20
Red iron oxide	10

Notes: Rich brown, breaks light brown on edges.

Copper red: 1260–1300°C (2300–2372°F/cones 8–10); reduction

(see Thomas Bohle, p.112)

	%
Potash feldspar (custer)	51
Flint (silica)	29
Calcium borate frit	7
Dolomite	9
Whiting	2
Zinc oxide	2
Tin oxide	3
Copper oxide	1

Notes: apply quite thickly to bisque ware. Suitable for porcelain and white stoneware.

Feature surfaces

Runny material: 1260–1300°C (2300–2372°F/cones 8–10); oxidized or reduction

(see Brian Rochefort panel, p.128)

	%
Nepheline syenite	90
Borax frit	10

Notes: Mix with water to a thick paste and apply in blobs.

Dry crackle: 1260–1300°C (2300–2372°F/cones 8–10); oxidized or reduction

(see Takuro Kuwata panel, p.124)

	%
Nepheline syenite	50
Zinc oxide	50

Notes: Mix with water, apply thickly – minimum 6mm.

US–UK material equivalents

US Material	UK Equivalent
Ferro 3110, Pemco P-25	High alkaline frit
Ferro 3249	Low expansion frit
Ferro 3498, O Hommel 14, Frit 28, Pemco Pb-700	Lead bisilicate
Ferro 210701	Lead sesquisilicate
Ferro 3134, Pemco-54, Gerstley Borate	Standard borax frit
Ferro 3124, Ferro 3195, Colemanite	Calcium borate frit
Kaolin (EPK), Georgia China Clay, Tile 6 Kaolin	China clay (kaolin)
Cornwall stone, Carolina stone, Kona A-3, Pyrophyllite	Cornish stone
Custer feldspar, G-200, K-200, Bell	Potash feldspar
Kona F-4, Spruce Pine, NC 4, Minspar 200, Unispar 50	Soda feldspar
Silica	Flint, Quartz
Alberta slip	Fremington red clay
Kentucky ball clay	AT ball clay
Tennessee ball clay	Hyplas 71 ball clay

Crayons – make your own pencils

Apply to earthenware or stoneware.

	%
White ball clay	50
Feldspar	25
Flint (silica)	25
Bentonite	3
Colourant of your choice	10–15

Notes: Mix ingredients with a little water and form a thick clay paste. Roll into thin coils, dry and fire to 800°C/1472°F (soft) to 950°C/1742°F (hard).

Orton pyrometric cone chart

Pyrometric cones are made from a blend of ceramic materials that are designed to melt at specific temperature points. Their purpose is to measure the heat work during a firing and are useful for determining when a firing is complete, if the temperature was inconsistent in different areas of the kiln or if a problem occurred. The cone has a number stamped on it to correspond to a specific temperature point, but it is important to consider the rate of your firing - the amount of degrees per hour the kiln temperature climbs – as this will determine the final bending position of the cone, as listed here:

Cone no.	60°C/ hour	108°F/ hour	150°C/ hour	270°F/ hour
09	917	1683	928	1702
08	942	1728	954	1749
07	973	1783	985	1805
06	995	1823	1011	1852
05	1030	1886	1046	1915
04	1060	1940	1070	1958
03	1086	1987	1101	2014
02	1101	2014	1120	2048
01	1117	2043	1137	2079
1	1136	2077	1154	2109
2	1142	2088	1162	2124
3	1152	2106	1168	2134
4	1160	2120	1181	2158
5	1184	2163	1205	2201
6	1220	2228	1241	2266
7	1237	2259	1255	2291
8	1247	2277	1269	2316
9	1257	2295	1278	2332
10	1282	2340	1303	2377
11	1293	2359	1312	2394
12	1304	2379	1324	2415

Further reading

Adamson, Glenn
Thinking Through Craft
Berg Publishers, 2007

Adamson, Glenn
The Craft Reader
Berg Publishers, 2009

Adamson, Glenn, Droth, Martina, et al.
Things of Beauty Growing: British Studio Pottery
Yale University Press, 2017

Birks, Tony
Hans Coper
Stenlake Publishing, 2013

Bloomfield, Linda
Contemporary Tableware
Bloomsbury, 2013

Bloomfield, Linda
Special Effect Glazes
Herbert Press, 2020

Britt, John
The Complete Guide to Mid-Range Glazes
Lark Books, 2015

Clark, Garth
American Ceramics: 1876 to the Present
Abbeville Press Inc., 1988

Clark, Garth & Courtney, Cathy
Richard Slee
Lund Humphries, 2003

Clark, Garth & Del Vecchio, Mark
Shifting Paradigms in Contemporary Ceramics: The Garth Clark and Mark Del Vecchio Collection
Yale University Press, 2012

Clark, Garth & Hecht, Eugene
George E. Ohr: The Greatest Art Potter on Earth
Skira Rizzoli, 2013

Cooper, Emmanuel
Ten Thousand Years of Pottery
The British Museum Press, 2002

Cooper, Emmanuel
Contemporary Ceramics
Thames & Hudson, 2009

Cooper, Emmanuel
Lucie Rie: Modernist Potter
Yale University Press, 2012

Cooper, Emmanuel
The Potter's Book of Glaze Recipes
Herbert Press, 2018

Daly, Greg
Developing Glazes
Herbert Press, 2018

Davis MacNaughton, Mary, Levin, Elaine & McClain, Mac
Paul Soldner: A Retrospective, exhibition catalogue
Lang Gallery, Scripps College in association with University of Washington Press, 1991

De Waal, Edmund
Bernard Leach (St Ives Artists series)
Tate Publishing, 1999

De Waal, Edmund
The Pot Book
Phaidon, 2011

Doody, Kate & Taylor, Brian
Ceramic Glazes: The Complete Handbook
Thames & Hudson, 2014

Drake, Cathryn
Betty Woodman: Theatres
Museu Nacional do Azulejo, Italy, 2005

Droste, Magdalena
Bauhaus
Bauhaus-Archiv Museum für Gestaltung, 1993

Hamada, Shoji, Kikuchi, Yukom & Wilcox, Timothy
Shoji Hamada: Master Potter
Lund Humphries/Ditchling Museum, 1998

Hamer, Frank & Hamer, Janet
The Potter's Dictionary
A&C Black, 2004

Hanaor, Ziggy
Breaking the Mould: New Approaches to Ceramics
Black Dog Publishing, 2007

Hooson, Duncan & Quinn, Anthony
The Workshop Guide to Ceramics
Thames & Hudson, 2012

Klein, Jacky
Grayson Perry
Thames & Hudson, 2009

Lilley, Clare
Vitamin C: Clay and Ceramic in Contemporary Art
Phaidon, 2017

Morris, Tom
New Wave Clay
Frame Publishers, 2018

Peterson, Susan
Shoji Hamada: A Potter's Way & Work
A&C Black, 2004

Taylor, Louisa
The Ceramics Bible
Chronicle Books, 2011

Vincentelli, Moira
Women and Ceramics: Gendered Vessels
Manchester University Press, 2000

Wardell, Sasha
Slipcasting
A&C Black, 1997

Whiting, David
Modern British Potters and Their Studios
A&C Black, 2009

Online Sources

ceramicartsnetwork.org
cfileonline.org
studiopottery.co.uk

Abstract art
A style of art that does not attempt to represent an accurate depiction of a visual reality, but instead uses shapes, colours, forms and gestural marks to achieve its effect.

Abstract expressionism
A post-World War II art movement that applied new forms of abstract art. Originating in America, the movement can be defined by abstract gestural mark making and the impression of spontaneity.

Agateware
The combination of two or more coloured clays arranged or laminated into a pattern to emulate agate stone.

Airbrush
Small gun device operated by compressed air. It is used for spraying liquids such as glazes and colours, for coverage or decorative effect.

Anagama kiln
An anagama kiln is a wood-fired climbing kiln with a long chamber typically built up a slope or hillside. The design enables a strong draw of air to be pulled through the kiln which increases temperature and deposits ash over the wares. The silica content in the ash reacts with the silica present in the clay body and creates distinctive flashing and glazed areas.

Art Nouveau
A style of decorative art prominent in western Europe and America at the end of the 19th century, characterized by flowing curves and linear designs based on forms of nature.

Arts and Crafts movement
A design movement of the mid-late 19th century, initiated by William Morris, which rejected mass industrialization in favour of a return to simpler and better models for living and production. The aim was to bring art and design to a wider audience.

Ash
Ash derives from natural sources, the most common being wood, paper or straw. Ash is a natural source of silica and flux, and in combination with alumina, such as china clay, it will produce a basic stoneware glaze with a firing range from cone 6 to 14. It is not a consistent material, i.e. it will vary from batch to batch, but this can be part of its appeal for using in a glaze.

Banding wheel
See Whirler

Base
A core set of ingredients mixed together to create a foundation to carry different glazes and colours.

Bauhaus
A revolutionary German art school operational from 1919 to 1933 that combined crafts with the fine arts. The modernist philosophy of the school placed emphasis on 'form follows function' and had a profound influence on architecture, furniture, graphics/typography, art and industrial design.

Bisque-/biscuit-firing
The first firing of ceramicware – typically at a low temperature of 1000°C (1830°F). The purpose is to drive the water content off the clay to render it permanent and strong enough to accept glaze before its final firing.

Bisque-/biscuitware
Unglazed ware that has been fired once. It provides a point whereby the ceramic is durable to receive a glaze before being fired a second time to melt the glaze and fuse it to the body.

Bone china
Developed in the UK around the mid-18th century. bone china is a type of porcelain. The key ingredient consistis of bone ash derived from cattle bone. Typically, a high fired slip casting clay body, pure white in colour and translucent. Bisque fired to approx. 1200°C (2192°F) and followed by a low temperature glaze, 1080°C (1976°F).

Bow harp
A 'C'-shaped frame with adjustable metal wire, used to draw through a block of clay to make uniform sized slabs of clay for hand-building.

Brush-on glaze
A type of thick glaze with added binder (gum arabic) that can be applied to bisqueware with a brush, without effecting the quality of the melt. Brush-on glazes are usually commercially prepared and bought from a pottery supplier.

Burning out
Using the temperature of the kiln to burn away from organic sources or combustible material. Can be used creatively to introduce texture or injunction with resist techniques.

Burnishing
The act of compressing the leather-hard clay surface or slip layer with the back of a spoon or pebble, in a circular motion to create a waxy sheen. The technique is often used in conjunction with smoke-firing because the compressed clay surface traps the smoke more effectively, producing a stronger colour.

CAD
Computer Aided Design. The use of computer software to support the creation, analysis and modification of two-dimensional or three-dimensional designs.

Cast/casting
Forming clay objects by pouring liquid slip into a porous mould. A cast can also refer to the impression or relief taken from a moulded object.

Celadon
A light green-grey-blue stoneware and porcelain glaze. The colour derives from the addition of low quantities of red iron oxide in a base recipe, typically fired in a reduction atmosphere.

Ceramic
Any type of clay form that has undergone physical changes as a result of being fired in a kiln.

Ceramic blanket/fibre/paper
Refractory ceramic material with high temperature-resistant properties. Used to insulate kilns or aid support when firing wares.

China Paints
See enamels

Chun
A traditional high-fire glaze, originating in China. It is characterized by vibrant iridescent blue and purple colours.

Clay
A naturally occurring material taken from the ground composed of fine materials that have derived from weathered granite and feldspathic rocks. Different clay bodies will vary in maturing temperature, strength and colour when fired.

Collaring
The technique of narrowing the neck of bottle forms, specifically in relation to throwing.

Crawling
The beading or pulling of glaze into globules, exposing the clay body underneath. It is a technical fault caused by grease or dust on the ceramicwares prior to glaze firing but can also be used for decorative effect.

Crazing
A series of fine cracks in the surface of a glaze caused by greater contraction of a glaze than the clay body. Typically, a technical fault but used for decorative effect in Raku technique.

Dadaism
Early 20th century art movement, originating in Zürich, Switzerland during the World War I, in negative reaction to the horrors of war. Dada is often nonsensical and satirical in nature.

Decals
Imagery or pictures printed on to ceramic transfer paper. Decals are usually applied to a fired glazed surface, and then refired at a very low temperature. It is another name for a transfer.

Decorating slip
This is essentially liquid clay. It is a mixture of clay and water coloured with metal oxides or pigments. It is applied when the clay is at the leather-hard stage and can be used like paint to create expressive and visually interesting surfaces.

Deflocculant
A soluble alkali, commonly sodium silicate or soda ash added to slip, which causes the clay particles to repel each other and remain in suspension, thereby requiring less water but still fluid enough to be poured.

Dipping
Applying a glaze or slip to ceramicware by submerging or part-submerging the object into a liquid.

Earthenware
Low fired ceramics/pottery that has not been fired to the point of vitrification. Therefore the body remains porous but can be made impervious to water through being covered in glaze.

Enamels
Low temperature colours containing fluxes, typically applied to a fired glazed surface and refired. Also known as on-glaze or china paints.

Engobe
A white or coloured vitreous slip containing flux, which renders it somewhere between a glaze and slip. It is applied to biscuitware (rather than leather-hard clay) before firing.

Extruder
A tool used to compress clay through a die to form continuous lengths of clay in various shapes. Used to make coils, handles, test tiles, tubes and more.

Expansion
The reversible swelling of clay or glaze during heating. Also known as thermal expansion.

Fat oil
A medium used to blend with enamel pigment so it can be applied to a surface.

Fettle/fettling
Cleaning up seam lines on greenware with a knife or sponge prior to firing.

Firing range
This refers to the different temperatures that ceramicwares can be fired at, such as clay, slip, bisque or glaze etc.

Flange
See gallery

Flashing
The visual effect created on a clay or glaze surface when in contact with a direct flame.

Flocking
The application of thousands of nylon fibres, which are electrostatically charged and applied to an earthed adhesive. The fibres are vertically attracted into the adhesive, therefore giving a fabric-like finish to the object.

Flux
The function of a flux is to lower the melting point of the main glass formers in glazes, clay bodies and other ceramic materials. Fluxes also influence colour, strength and durability of a glaze.

Frit
The mixture of silica and fluxes that have been fused at high temperature to make a glass that is ground down into a fine powder. Frits are used in glazes to supply an insoluble form of toxic oxides, such as lead or boron, that would be too harmful to use in their raw state.

Foot
The base of a ceramic object on which it sits.

Funk
An American art movement that developed in the San Francisco bay area of California in the mid-1950s. It was a progression of abstract expressionism, and sought to bring figuration back as the subject matter. Funk was inspired by popular culture and Dadaism, and was often rebellious and provocative in content.

Gallery
A rim created on the inside or outside of a vessel to locate a lid securely. The gallery can also be formed on a lid instead of the container part. Also referred to as a flange.

Glaze
A thin layer of glass that fuses to the surface of a ceramic piece during firing.

The purpose is to provide a suitable surface that is both hygienic and decorative.

Greenware
Raw, unfired, clayware.

Grog
Coarse, ground refractory material added to a clay body to provide strength and 'tooth'. Grog can aid drying, and reduce the overall shrinkage, minimalizing the risk of cracking and warping.

Hand building
Building forms or structures in clay by hand. Typical methods include coiling, pinching and slab building.

Heat work
The amount of heat a piece of ceramic has been subjected to during a firing, represented in terms of time and temperature. Heat work is measured by pyrometric cones placed inside the kiln.

Jigger/jolley
Mostly an industrial process, a jigger/jolley machine presses forms using a spinning mould. A plastic or metal template is fixed to a pivoted arm, which is then pressed down on to plastic clay to shape the form. Jiggering refers to profiling the exterior of a piece – specifically plates. Jollying refers to shaping internal profiles such as cups and bowls. Jiggering/jollying provides the opportunity to create a different external profile to the internal one – for example, jolleying a square cup with a cylindrical inside.

Kairagi
A type of Shinoware, originating from the Momoyama period (1583–1615) in Japan. This is a method of intentional glaze shrinkage characterized by a thick glaze that crawls and repels, exposing the clay body underneath.

Kiln
Piece of equipment or built chamber used to fire ceramicwares. Kilns can be fuelled by electric, gas, oil or wood.

Kintsugi
Japanese art of repair. A method of restoring cracks and broken fragments with golden joinery, emphasizing the repair. Traditionally, the method involves repairing the piece with tree-sap lacquer and gold dust, but modern techniques can emulate the aesthetic with epoxy resin putty and gold dust.

Kneading
A method of mixing the clay to create a smooth homogenous mix. The purpose is to evenly distribute the particles of the clay and prepare it for use. Essential for throwing technique, and for reducing the risk of cracking and warping of the clay.

Lathe
A machine used to carve plaster models and shapes. The lathe rotates the material in a horizontal axis against a tool that shapes it.

Leather-hard
Clay that has hardened but still retains some flexibility. It can withhold its shape and still be joined.

Majolica
Decorated tin glaze earthenware, with applied colourful decoration on top of the raw glaze, originating from the Mediterranean around the 15th century.

Matt
A soft, non-reflective surface.

Maturing point
The temperature at which the clay and glaze become hard and durable.

Mingei
Translated as 'Folk Arts' or 'Arts of the People' – a movement that developed in the late 1920s to 1930s in Japan, led by philosopher Sōetsu Yanagi (1889–1961). Its key principles evolved from the Arts and Crafts movement in Europe and included: the craftsman remaining anonymous; objects being produced by hand; pieces being affordable and available to the masses, functional and representing the regions where they were made.

Modernism
A global movement in society and culture, originating from the early 20th century, that sought a new alignment with the experience and values of modern life. The underlying principles that define the movement: a rejection of history and conservative values (such as realistic depiction of subjects); innovation and experimentation with form, tendency for abstraction; and emphasis on materials, techniques and processes.

Molochite
A high temperature calcined kaolin with low iron content. Fine grade molochite is used to raise the maturing temperatures of glazes, reduce shrinkage in engobes and increase resistance to thermal shock. Coarse grade molochite is typically added to a clay body for strength and texture.

Mould
Moulds are used in the production of ceramics as a means of supporting and forming clay. A mould is typically made from plaster, and clay can be pressed or poured as a liquid to create a cast. Moulds can be a simple one-piece drop-out or made from multiple parts.

Nerikomi (or neriage)
The ancient Japanese technique of layering, cutting and reforming different colours of clay to create intricately patterned sheets.

Opaque
When the glaze colour is not transparent, it hides the colour of the surface it is covering.

Oxide
The chemical combination of oxygen with another component such as metal (e.g. copper oxide).

Oxidization
Firing where a sufficient oxygen supply is present throughout – for example, as in an electric kiln.

Perspective
The representation of three-dimensional objects on a two-dimensional surface to give the illusion of height, width, depth and space.

Plaster (or plaster of paris)
A semi-hydrated calcium sulphate, derived from gypsum. It goes through a manufacturing process which renders it

in state of permanent thirst. When water is added, a chemical reaction occurs, which sets it as a solid. Plaster is used for the production of ceramic moulding because of its absorbent properties to draw moisture from the clay.

Plaster bat
A plaster bat is typically a block of plaster used for reclaiming clay by absorbing moisture out of the material, enabling it to be reused. Kneading on a plaster bat will also help to firm clay which is too soft to use.

Plastic clay
Soft, malleable clay that can be shaped and sculpted freely.

Porcelain
A hard, white translucent clay body, made from a high content of kaolin, china stone and quartz.

Pouring
A method of applying glaze or slip to ceramicware by tipping liquid over the piece.

Prop
A refractory pillar or piece of kiln furniture used to support shelves during firing. A prop can also be a clay support which bears the weight of a piece as it dries, to help maintain a specific position.

Pulling
A method of making a handle from a lump of clay using the hands and shape of the fingers to pull the clay downwards to create a length. This can then be attached to the main body of the piece to form a handle.

Pyrometric cones
Slim pyramids of ceramic material which are designed to soften and bend at specific temperature points in correlation to time, to gauge the heat-work during the firing.

Raku
A rapid-firing technique in which pots are placed in a kiln chamber and fired to 1000°C. The pots are removed red-hot and left to cool. In western Raku, the pots are transferred to a pit to smoulder in combustible material such as sawdust or hay to create a heavy reduction atmosphere. After a period of time, the pots are plunged into a bucket of water to produce attractive crackle effects.

Rapid prototyping
See Three-dimensional (3D) printing

Reclaim
The process of recycling and reusing clay. The cycle involves slaking dry clay pieces into a bucket of water, then putting the clay on a plaster bat to remove excess water before kneading it into fresh useable clay again.

Reduction
The process of reducing the amount of oxygen present in the kiln chamber during a firing to cause a chemical change to occur in oxides present in clay and glazes. This results in unique colours and surfaces.

Refractory
Ceramic materials that are resistant to high temperatures.

Resists
The application of a decorative medium such as wax, latex or paper to a ceramic object to repel slip or glaze. Can be used for lively effect, or as a way to keep areas free of glaze to speed up the cleaning process.

Saggar
A box or lidded container made from fire clay or coarse clay used to protect glazed wares from flames and gases of a fuel-burning kiln. A saggar can also be used as a chamber to smoke-fire individual pieces in a kiln.

Salt firing
A process whereby parcels of salt (sodium chloride) is added to the chamber of a kiln at top temperature (cones 9–14) in a reduction atmosphere. The salt volatizes and reacts with the silica present in the clay body and slips, causing a distinctive orange peel effect.

Sang-de-Boeuf
A deep red reduction glaze produced by the addition of copper oxide. *Sang-de-boeuf* translates as 'oxblood'.

Seam lines
Raised lines on moulded (slip or pressed) or hand-built forms where two or more sections have been joined.

Semi-matt
Part shiny, part matt surface.

Sgraffito
An Italian word for 'scratch back'. The method involves simply drawing through layers of slip to reveal the clay body underneath, creating a striking contrast.

Shino
Traditional Japanese glaze, characterized by high iron content which creates black to red colours. Shinos with high feldspar content can be used to create desirable crawling and textural effects when applied thickly.

Slab building
Constructing a ceramic form using slabs/sheets of clay.

Sieving
The process of removing impurities or lumps by putting glaze, slip or clay through a metal mesh of variable grades.

Slab roller
A type of press consisting of a flat bed and a rotating roller, which is used to make flat sheets of clay in various heights and widths. The machine is manually operated by a turn wheel, which moves the roller across the bed and thus flattens the clay.

Slip
Liquid clay. Slip can be used for joining and decorative purposes, or made into a casting slip with the addition of deflocculant.

Slip casting
Clay is held in suspension as a liquid, which enables it to be poured into a plaster mould. The water content is absorbed by the plaster, leaving behind a unified skin of clay in the shape of the original model.

Slipware
Traditional lead-glazed earthenware pottery decorated with slips before firing.

Soak
Holding the temperature in the kiln at a specific point to even the distribution of heat and bring glazes and the clay body to a point of maturity.

Soft soap
A resist applied to plaster to render it non-porous and prevent sticking of two plaster surfaces. It is applied to the plaster model with a brush, and the excess is wiped away with a natural sponge. Apply three coats, allowing to dry between each application. Plaster can then be poured on top of the model to create the mould.

Sprigging
A technique for decorating pottery forms with low relief moulded details. They are typically thin press-moulded shapes that are applied to greenware or bisque.

Stains
A type of frit, whereby metal oxides and ceramic materials are combined through a refractory process to produce reliable, consistent colours that can be added to a clay body or glaze. Stains are very good for achieving vibrant colours such as yellows, blues and reds.

Stilts
Small triangular or rectangle shapes of refractory material, often with metal or wire spurs that lift the piece away from the kiln shelf, allowing for a complete coating of glaze. Particularly useful as a way to seal earthenware where the body remains porous.

Stoneware
Vitrified clay body fired above 1200°C, (2192°F).

Studio pottery
Small batches or runs of unique pottery that is made by a single artisan or group. Studio potters can be referred to as ceramicists, ceramist, ceramic artists, maker or as an artist who uses clay.

Surrealism
Influential art movement that began in the early 1920s and is known for strange, dreamy imagery that explored the workings of the mind.

T material
Heavily-grogged white clay body.

Tableware
Refers to functional ceramic items intended for use.

Tea ceremony
A Japanese cultural activity steeped in tradition, involving the ceremonial preparation and presentation of matcha, powdered green tea. The practice is rooted in Zen Buddhism and elevates hospitality into an art form.

Tenmoku
A stoneware glaze heavily coloured by iron oxide. Typical colours range from black through to rust browns.

Test tile
A sample of a trial glaze made to examine specific qualities and desirable traits that could be used in application. A test tile should always relate to your work – for example, if you are making thrown work then cut up a thrown beaker into tiles (from the clay body you are using); if slip-casting, cast a series of small pots or button shapes. The tile should give you as much information as possible, such as the melt of the glaze, its thickness, and the way it flows over lines and details.

Thermal shock
The sudden expansion or contraction of clay or glaze as a result of extreme temperature change (hot to cold) that can cause it to break.

Three-dimensional (3D) printing
Three-dimensional modelling process using CAD software and sophisticated machinery to print physical objects (prototypes or models).

Transfers
See Decals

Transparent
Clear base glaze or material that is free of colour or opacity.

Trimming/turning
The shaping of clay at leather-hard stage to refine the profile and add decorative details such as a foot ring.

Undercut
An area (or design fault) on a model that prevents its release from a mould.

Underfired
Clay or glaze that has not reached temperature during the firing and therefore the material has not melted or matured sufficiently.

Vanishing point
The point on the horizon line at which receding parallel lines viewed in perspective appear to converge. As the subject moves further away, it appears smaller and closer together, until it forms a single point.

Vitrification
The fusion of material or body during the firing process around 1200°C (2192°F), rendering it non-porous and impervious to water.

Wabi-sabi
A Japanese philosophy exploring the relationship between imperfection, beauty and the acceptance of transience.

Wedging
See kneading

Whirler
A type of flatbed lathe used for making plaster models and drop out moulds. A whirler is also another name for a banding wheel.

Wood firing
Firing ceramicwares in a kiln, using wood as a source of fuel. Ash from the wood deposits on the wares, reacting with the silica in the clay body and slips to produce beautiful, random effects.

Wooden bat
A wooden disc that is attached to the pottery wheel-head to aid production, by enabling the user to remove a piece without disrupting a form.

Index

Q

R

S

Picture credits

Key: t = top; l = left; r = right; b = bottom

Introduction:

All images are courtesy Louisa Taylor, with thanks to Simon Punter for some of the photography, except the following:

6 © Anne Mette Hjortshøj. Photo: Kasper Agergaard Kristensen; 8 Artokoloro / Alamy Stock Photo; 9 Metropolitan Museum of Art, New York; 10 Metropolitan Museum of Art, New York; 11 © Estate of the artist. Photo: Robert and Lisa Sainsbury Collection / Bridgeman Images; 12–13 © Nicole Cherubini. Photo: Carlos Jiménez Cahua; 14 © Gabriele Koch. Photo Stephen Brayne; 15 Metropolitan Museum of Art, New York; 16–17 Ben Boswell; 18 Kasper Agergaard Kristensen; 20 © Louisa Taylor. Photo: Matthew Booth; 34 Potclays.co.uk / Shimpo International; 35 l © Anne Mette Hjortshøj; 36 Mint Images/ Science Photo Library; 43 Mint Images/Science Photo Library; 44 Bill Brookes.

Main artworks:

52 © Estate of the artist. Photo: Bridgeman Images; 54 © Estate of the artist. Photo: Photo © Bonhams, London, UK/Bridgeman Images; 56 © Estate of the artist. Photo: Princeton University Art Museum/Art Resource NY/Scala, Florence; 58 © Estate of the Artist. Photo: Bridgeman Images; 61 © Elizabeth Fritsch. Photo: Fitzwilliam Museum, University of Cambridge, UK/Bridgeman Images; 63 © Magdalene Odundo. Photo: Museum purchase funded by Helena Woolworth McCann and the Winfield Foundation, by exchange/Bridgeman Images; 64–65 © Gabriele Koch. Photo © The Fitzwilliam Museum, Cambridge; 66–67 © Thea Burger, Executor of Ruth Duckworth Estate. Photo taken by James Prinz Photography; 69 © Estate of the artist. Photo: The Leatrice S. and Melvin B. Eagle Collection, gift of Leatrice and Melvin Eagle./Bridgeman Images; 70–71 © Estate of the artist. Photo: Victoria and Albert Museum, London; 73 © Alison Britton. Image © Philip Sayer, courtesy of Marsden Woo Gallery, London; 74 © Elisabeth Kley. Photographer: Joe DeNardo; 76–77 © Monika Patuszynska. Photos by Olga Grabiwoda; 78 © Matt Davis. Photo: James Oaten; 80 © Sara Flynn, Kyoto Gallery. Photo: Glenn Norwood; 86–87 Photo © Photo Josse/Bridgeman Images; 89 Metropolitan Museum of Art, New York; 90–91 The Leatrice S. and Melvin B. Eagle Collection, museum purchase funded by the Caroline Wiess Law Accessions Endowment Fund/ Bridgeman Images; 92–93 © Jun Kaneko, Courtesy of Jun Kaneko Studio; 94 © Grayson Perry, Courtesy the artist and Victoria Miro; 96–97 © Bodil Manz. Photo: Houston Museum of Fine Arts/Garth Clark and Mark Del Vecchio Collection, Bridgeman Images; 98 © Estate of the artist. Photo: Victoria and Albert Museum, London; 101 © 2010 Robert Dawson Aesthetic Sabotage. Photographer credit: Tino Tedaldi; 103 © Aneta Regel. Photo: Sylvain Deleu; 104–05 © Hideaki Miyamura; 106–07 © Malene Hartman Rasmussen. Image copyright Sylvain Deleu; 108 © Bente Skjøttgaard. Photo: Ole Akhøj; 110 © Estate of the artist. Image copyright Matthew Booth; 113 © Thomas Bohle. Photo: Frigesch Lampelmayer; 114 © Wouter Dam. Img_2804.CR2. Blue Wall Sculpture, made in 2018; 117 © Kate Malone. Image courtesy of Adrian Sassoon, London; 119 Nerikomi plaque: © Judy McKenzie 2018/Photography: Ester Segarra; 120–21 © Nick Weddell. Photo by artist; 122–23 © Pippin Drysdale. Photo by Robert Frith/Acorn Photo; 125 Courtesy of Alison Jacques Gallery, London © Takuro Kuwata. Photo: Keizo Kioku; 126 © Morten Løbner Espersen. Photo: Ole Akhøj, courtesy Pierre Marie Giraud, Bruxelles; 129 © Brian Rochefort. Photo by Marten Elder; 134–35 © Estate of the artist. Photo: Neue Galerie New York/Art Resource/Scala, Florence; 137 © The Bernard Leach Family. All rights reserved, DACS 2020. Photo: Victoria and Albert Museum, London; 138–39 © Estate of the artist. Photo: Gift of Miss Ima Hogg/Bridgeman Images; 141 © Estate of the artist. Photo: DeAgostini Picture Library/Scala, Florence; 143 © Walter Keeler. Image courtesy of Adrian Sassoon, London; 144–45 © Piet Stockmans. Photo from Studio Pieter Stockmans; 146 © Anne Mette Hjortshøj. Photo: Kasper Agergaard Kristensen; 148–49 © Kiho Kang. Photographer: Karina Hagemann; 150–51 © Stuart Carey. Image courtesy of Contemporary Applied Arts © Sophie Mutevelian; 152–53 © Ikuko Iwamoto; 154–55 © Sun Kim. Photo: Michael Harvey; 156–57 © Jill Shaddock; 158–59 © Takeshi Yasuda; 160–61 © Kirsten Coelho Deliberation 2019. Photography Grany Hancock; 162 © Doug Fitch. Photo: Shannon Tofts; 164–65 © Adam Frew; 170 Metropolitan Museum of Art, New York; 172 © Succession Picasso/DACS, London 2020. Photo: De Agostini Picture Library/G. Nimatallah/Bridgeman Images; 174–75 © Artists' Legacy Foundation/VAGA at ARS, NY and DACS, London 2020. Photo: Bridgeman Images; 177 © Estate of Robert Arneson/ VAGA at ARS, NY and DACS, London 2020. Photo: Museum of Fine Arts, Houston/The Leatrice S. and Melvin B. Eagle Collection, gift of Leatrice and Melvin Eagle./Bridgeman Images; 179 © Mo Jupp. Photo: Oxford Ceramics Gallery; 180 © Daphne Corregan. Photography © François Fernandez; 182 © Rita Gudiño. LUAL Kiln Art - Firing as Art & Metaphor of Birthing. Images courtesy Tony Fitzsimmons/Craig Kirkwood; 185 © Catrin Howell. Photo: Stephen Brayne; 186 © Sergei Isupov. John Polak Photography. Courtesy Ferrin Contemporary, North Adams, MA ; 189 © Tip Toland. Photographer: Ann Welch; 190 © Ramesh Mario Nithiyendran. Image courtesy of the artist and Sullivan + Strumpf, Sydney/Singapore; 192 © Kim Simonsson. Image courtesy of Jefunne Gimpel; 194–95 © Shary Boyle. Photo: Private collection, courtesy of the artist; 196 © Claire Curneen. Photo: Sylvain Deleu; 199 © Carolein Smit. Photographer: Winnifred Limburg; 204–05 © Estate of Marilyn Levine. Photo: Museum of Fine Arts, Houston/The Leatrice S. and Melvin B. Eagle Collection, museum purchase funded by the Caroline Wiess Law Accessions Endowment Fund/Bridgeman Images; 206–07 © Paul E. & Virginia I .Soldner Family Partnership LLLP. Digital Image: Museum Associates/LACMA/Art Resource NY/Scala, Florence; 209 © Ron Nagle. Photo: Garth Clark and Mark Del Vecchio Collection, gift of Garth Clark and Mark Del Vecchio/Bridgeman Images; 210–11 © Ken Price Estate. Photo: The Leatrice S. and Melvin B. Eagle Collection, gift of Leatrice and Melvin Eagle./Bridgeman Images; 213 © Michelle Erickson, collection of Seattle Art Museum. Photographer: Gavin Ashworth; 214–15 © Rafa Pérez. Photo: Carlos Hermosilla; 216–17 © Richard Slee. Image courtesy Hales Gallery, London, New York; 219 © Sterling Ruby. Photo by Robert Wedemeyer. Courtesy Sterling Ruby Studio; 221 © Astrid Dahl; 223 © Gitte Jungersen. Photographer: Alf Georg Dannevig; 225 © Lawson Oyekan. Photo © Philip Sayer, courtesy of Marsden Woo Gallery; 227 © Matt Wedel. Courtesy of the artist. Photographer: Jeff McLane; 228–229 © Bertozzi and Casoni. Property Private Collection. Photo by Bernardo Ricci; 231 © Annie Turner. Photography: Michael Harvey; 233 © Anne Marie Laureys. Photograph by Peter Claeys; 235 © Jongjin Park; 236–37 © Halima Cassell. Photo: Sophie Mutevelian; 238–39 © Hitomi Hosono. Images courtesy of Adrian Sassoon, London; 241 © Vicky Lindo and Bill Brookes ; 247 t, b © Clare Twomey. Photo: Peter Macdiarmid/Getty Images; 249 © Jessica Stoller, courtesy of the artist; 250–51 © Edmund de Waal. Courtesy the artist and Gagosian. Photo: Mike Bruce; 252–53 Copyright and courtesy Estate of Betty Woodman/Charles Woodman. Photo: Bruno Brucchi; 254 © Nicole Cherubini. Photo: Carlos Jiménez Cahua; 257 t, b © Phoebe Cummings. Photo: Sylvain Deleu; 258 © Torbjørn Kvasbø. Photo: Morten Løberg. ; 260 © Bouke De Vries; 262–63 © Paolo Polloniato. Photo image by Alberto Parise; 264–65 © Linda Sormin. Photographer: Clarence Sormin; 266–67 © Barnaby Barford. Photographer: Jonathan Webb; 268–69 Photo by Chris Crerar, courtesy of Sabbia Gallery and the Australian Ceramics Association; 270–71 © Tana West. Originally created for Jerwood Makers Open 2019, supported by Jerwood Charitable Foundation/Photographer: Anna Arce 2019.

Technique panels:

All images are courtesy Louisa Taylor, with thanks to Simon Punter for some of the photography, except the following:

60 Matt Cockrem; 62 Ben Boswell; 71 Matt Cockrem; 72 Ben Boswell; 79 © Matt Davis; 111 Ben Boswell; 112 © Thomas Bohle; 116 Ben Boswell; 124 Kayleigh Peters; 127 Angharad Williams; 134 l, r Matt Cockrem; 139 Buyenlarge/Getty Images; 147 l, r Kasper Agergaard Kristensen; 153 Ikuko Iwamoto; 163 l, r Ben Boswell; 165 Sydney Taylor-Smith ; 176 Sydney Taylor-Smith ; 182 l Photo by Craig Kirkwood; 182 r Photo by Tony Fitzsimmons; 188 Sydney Taylor-Smith ; 196 l Photo by Sylvain Deleu ; 224 l, r Ben Boswell; 230 Annie Turner; 234 Jongjin Park; 237 Ben Boswell; 240 Bill Brookes; 246 © Clare Twomey. Photo: Clare Twomey Studio; 248 © Jessica Stoller, courtesy of the artist; 250 Ben Boswell; 255 © Nicole Cherubini. Photo: Carlos Jiménez Cahua; 259 © Torbjørn Kvasbø. Photo: Marita Eri Mo; 267 © Barnaby Barford. Photographer: Sylvain Deleu; 268 Anna Stoodley.